Making Precious Things Plain

Volume 4

Church History Study Guide, Pt. 1

(2nd Edition)

1805—1832

Randal S. Chase

Church History Study Guide, Pt 1.
Making Precious Things Plain, Vol. 4:
1805—1832
(2nd Edition)

Send inquiries to:
Plain and Precious Publishing
3378 E. Sweetwater Springs Drive
Washington, UT 84780

Send e-mail: info@makingpreciousthingsplain.com

For more copies visit www.makingpreciousthingsplain.com

For a listing of all Plain and Precious Publishing products, visit
www.makingpreciousthingsplain.com
or call 435-251-8520.

Printed in the United States of America

978-1-937901-04-2

Cover Image: "Young Joseph," © Walter Rane, All rights reserved. (Used by Permission)

Making Precious Things Plain

Volume 4

Church History Study Guide, Pt. 1

1805—1832

Table of Contents

Acknowledgments

This book is dedicated to Church members everywhere who hunger and thirst for an understanding of the scriptures. It has been my privilege to teach literally thousands of such souls in gospel classes, as well as in CES Institute and Adult Education classes, over the years. They have all inspired me with their dedication to reading, pondering, and feasting upon the word of God. I have learned much from them in the process.

I acknowledge the help and encouragement of my sweet wife Deborah, who has assisted me in all of my endeavors to teach and to write concerning the gospel of Jesus Christ. I acknowledge the encouragement of many friends and students to write these study guides, the patient and meticulous assistance of my editor and son, Michael Chase, who has assisted in this work, and other Church scholars who have provided solid counsel about its form and substance, and who have offered invaluable insights on many topics.

And I acknowledge other knowledgeable and wise gospel scholars and teachers who have written similar study guides in the past, and which I have quoted time and time again in this volume:

Church History in the Fulness of Times [Church Educational System manual, 1993] is an invaluable tool for all students of the Doctrine and Covenants and Church History, and many of the cultural and other ideas presented herein were first obtained from this manual.

Robert L. Millet and Kent Jackson edited *Studies in Scripture, Vol. 1: The Doctrine and Covenants* [1989]. This volume contains chapters from a wide variety of gospel scholars, and was a constant inspiration to me in preparing my lessons on the Doctrine and Covenants and Church History. I love their in-depth discussions of the historical events and doctrines, which were scholarly enough to be reliable but written in a refreshing and accessible way that gospel students at all levels can understand.

Elder Joseph Fielding Smith wrote the classic 4–volume *Church History and Modern Revelation* [1946–1949], which provides many valuable insights into the early Church's doctrine and history. He also wrote the 5–volume *Answers to Gospel Questions* [1957–1966], and the 3–volume *Doctrines of Salvation*, edited by Elder Bruce R. McConkie [1954–1956]. All of these have been of great interest and help to me throughout the years.

Daniel H. Ludlow wrote two volumes of A *Companion to Your Study of the Doctrine and Covenants* [1978], as part of a series of such companions to our study of all the scriptures. These perhaps come closer to the spirit of what this book is all about—making the history and revelations plain to those who just need a little help with their gospel studies. I have had some of Brother Ludlow's family in my classes, and I cherish a personally-signed copy of his Selected Writings book that he provided to me a few years ago.

Most, if not all, of the above-named volumes are now out of print. I am hoping that the portions of them that I have quoted in this volume will continue to spread their insights for years to come.

Foreword

The Prophet Joseph Smith said: "Generations yet unborn will dwell with peculiar delight upon the scenes that we have passed through, the privations that we have endured … in laying the foundation of a work that brought about the glory and blessing which they will realize."[1]

I have reflected on this prophecy many times as I have studied and taught Church History and the Doctrine and Covenants. Every aspect of it has been fulfilled. As a people, we do take particular delight in the heroic deeds of ancestors and Church founders. We read about and travel to visit the scenes that they passed through in New England, New York, Ohio, Missouri, Illinois, and along the pioneer trail west to Utah. We marvel at their faithfulness through great persecution and difficulty. We honor them for laying the foundation of the greatest dispensation in the earth's history—the last dispensation of the fulness of times. And we reap the benefits— the "glory and blessing" of their sacrifice—as we gather together in congregations all around the world and receive covenants and teachings that they transmitted to us.

I believe we are obligated to act upon the favorable circumstances of our birth. We must do more than acknowledge the sacrifice of earlier Saints. We must study faithfully the revelations they received and understand fully the circumstances under which they were given. For this reason, in this study guide we study Church History and the Doctrine and Covenants together, not as separate topics. And then, of course, we must then act upon that knowledge and understanding to carry forward and pass on to future generations the rich legacy we have inherited.

The Doctrine and Covenants Is Both History and Revelation

The question might be asked, "Is the Doctrine and Covenants history or revelation?" History is the record made by men of past events. Revelation is the knowledge given to man from God. Given these definitions, the major portion of the Doctrine and Covenants is revelation. But some portions of the Doctrine and Covenants are history.

The study of the Doctrine and Covenants is a good example of how history and revelation can complement and aid in the understanding of each other. Many of the revelations found in the Doctrine and Covenants are better understood when they are placed in their historical setting. For example, many of the early converts to the Church had previously been baptized in other churches. Many churches did not believe that authority was necessary for ordinances to be acceptable. Many of the churches taught that baptism was only the outward sign of an inward change, and often a baptism in one church was accepted as valid when a person joined another. It is thus not difficult to see why some converts would object to being re-baptized. When seen in that historical setting, Doctrine and Covenants 22 becomes much more significant.

On the other hand, in some instances historical events are better understood in the light of revelation. In the winter of 1833 and 1834, for example, the Saints experienced terrible hardships in Missouri. They had been driven from Jackson County, the place previously designated as the location for the city of Zion (D&C 57:1–3). Crops had been burned, houses plundered, and lives threatened. Some historians attempting to explain why the Mormons encountered so much adversity in Missouri have suggested such causes as the slavery question, Mormon exclusiveness, the doctrine of Zion, and so on. But the Lord explained the persecutions in a revelation:

> "*Verily I say unto you, concerning your brethren who have been afflicted, and persecuted, and cast out from the land of their inheritance—*
>
> "*I, the Lord, have suffered the affliction to come upon them, wherewith they have been afflicted, in consequence of their transgressions; . . .*
>
> "*Behold, I say unto you, there were jarrings, and contentions, and envyings, and strifes, and lustful and covetous desires among them; therefore by these things they polluted their inheritances*" (D&C 101:1, 2, 6).

Thus we can see that the proper study of the Doctrine and Covenants includes the study of both history and revelation. Because a relatively short time has passed since the revelations in the Doctrine and Covenants were received and because the early Saints were conscious of the importance of keeping records, we know much more about the historical settings of these revelations than we do about those of most other scriptures. This knowledge affords us the opportunity to use historical and biographical information to help us better understand the revelations.

How to Use This Book

To facilitate learning, students and teachers may use this study guide in a variety of ways. I have suggested two below, in no particular order of preference. Choose the method that works best for you, but whatever method you choose, complete the assigned scripture reading for each week's lesson before you go to class.

Option 1. Prayerfully read the scriptures associated with the current lesson first, and then read the chapter in this book that corresponds to those scriptures.

Option 2. Carefully and prayerfully read the scriptures associated with the current lesson, using this study guide as a reference to help you understand the context and consequences of the scriptures while you are reading them. To do this, you would keep this book open and use it as a guide and commentary alongside your scriptures.

This study guide comments on most, but not all, of the scriptures in related sections of the Doctrine and Covenants. Rather than a verse-by-verse analysis, I have provided a summary restatement of events, divided into scripture blocks with attached explanations and quotes. An example of how these scripture blocks and comments are organized is shown below:

● **JS-History 1:33 Moroni's prophecies concerning Joseph Smith himself.** The angel called Joseph Smith by name and said "he was a messenger sent from the presence of God to me, and that his name was Moroni; that God had a work for me to do; and that my name should be had for good and evil among all nations, kindreds, and tongues, or that it should be both good and evil spoken of among all people."

Elder Neal A. Maxwell said:

> "Throughout the expanse of human history, no prophet has been scrutinized in such a sustained way, on as wide a scale, or for so long a period of time as Joseph Smith, Jr. The communication capacity of this age and the global impact of his work have so ensured. Young Joseph was told that his name would be 'both good and evil spoken of' throughout the world. Except from a divine source, how audacious a statement! Yet his contemporary religious leaders, then much better known than Joseph, have faded into the footnotes of history, while the work of Joseph Smith grows constantly and globally."[2]

Some Chapters Are Thematic, Not Chronological

While the order of presentation of these chapters on the Doctrine and Covenants and Church History is roughly chronological, it is not strictly so. There are a number of "topical" chapters that combine events and revelations from multiple periods of time, such as the sections in the Doctrine and Covenants on the Savior, the Sabbath Day, and temples. Whenever this occurs, I have sought to explain all of the relevant historical settings that contributed to that topic so that the reader might clearly understand all of the circumstances from which these revelations emerged.

In every chapter, I have provided the historical setting for the revelations discussed. I have also freely included other scriptural references that provide additional light on the topic. In the end, understanding the doctrine is more important than the history, though I believe it is possible to understand both, and it is better if we do.

Note to Teachers

For the convenience of readers, the chapters in this study guide are organized around the lesson topics for the Church's Gospel Doctrine classes. However, teachers should remember that this study guide is not intended to become a substitute for the official lesson manuals of the Church. Your lessons should follow precisely the organization found in your lesson manual, and should be centered on the assigned scriptures for each lesson. Teachers should read their lesson manuals first and take note of the main doctrinal points that are listed there. After doing this, teachers may use this book as a way of enhancing their own personal understanding of the events and scriptures covered in a particular lesson, just as any other gospel scholar might do. But you should never use this book as a guide to teaching your lessons.

Notes:

1. *History of the Church*, 4:609–610.
2. In Conference Report, October 1983; or *Ensign*, November 1983, 54.

CHAPTER I

Preface to the Final Dispensation

(D&C Introduction, D&C 1)
[1805–1820]

৪০১ৎ

INTRODUCTION

The Dispensation of the Fulness of Times

The Bible Dictionary defines a dispensation as "a period of time in which the Lord has at least one authorized servant on the earth who bears the holy priesthood and the keys, and who has a divine commission to dispense the gospel to the inhabitants of the earth. When this occurs, the gospel is revealed anew, so that people of that dispensation do not have to depend basically on past dispensations for knowledge of the plan of salvation."[1]

"AN OBSCURE BOY," ©JOSEPH BRICKEY, USED BY PERMISSION

There have been many gospel dispensations since the Garden of Eden. Those generally identified as dispensational prophets—those charged with initiating the dispensation and receiving the revealed word of God for their people—are Adam, Enoch, Noah, Abraham, Moses, Jesus Christ, and the Prophet Joseph Smith. These are the prophets who presided over the seven gospel dispensations that have occurred since Adam.

But there were also other dispensations. The Bible dictionary identifies dispensations of the gospel "among the Nephites, the Jaredites, and the Lost Tribes of Israel. Melchizedek could also be included, as well as John the Baptist, since they truly held the priesthood and taught the word of the Lord to the people and were unique in their time. There are many other prophets who have had the priesthood and a knowledge of the gospel. Perhaps if more were revealed to us, we would learn that they too should be spoken of as having a dispensation. These could include, among others, Abel, Esaias, Gad, Jeremy, Elihu, Caleb, Jethro, Zenock, and Zenos.[2]

● **D&C 112:30–32 The dispensation of the fulness of times.** The priesthood and the keys of presidency were revealed to the First Presidency and the Twelve Apostles "for the last days and for the last time, in the which is the dispensation of the fulness of times" (v. 30). These revealed doctrines and powers were connected to "all those who have received a dispensation at any time from the beginning of the creation (v. 31). The priesthood keys they received had "come down from the fathers" by "being sent down from heaven unto you."

This final dispensation over which Joseph Smith presides is the "dispensation of the fulness of times" in which the Lord will "gather together in one all things in Christ, both which are in heaven, and which are on earth" (Eph. 1:10). This means that it is a dispensation of restoration and of fulfillment of all the doctrines and purposes of all previous dispensations since the world began. And it also contains things that have not been revealed previously (D&C 121:26–32; 124:41).

"For it is necessary in the ushering in of the dispensation of the fulness of times ... that a whole and complete and perfect union, and welding together of dispensations, and keys, and powers, and glories should take place, and be revealed from the days of Adam even to the present time" (D&C 128:18).

● **D&C 76:8–10 This final dispensation will receive the "wonders of eternity" and "things of many generations" (v.** 8). The people who live in this time will possess great wisdom and understanding—greater than the supposed knowledge of the worldly wise and learned (v. 9). Both by the Spirit and by direct revelation, the Lord will "make known unto them the secrets of my will—yea, even those things which eye has not seen, nor ear heard, nor yet entered into the heart of man" (v. 10).

● **D&C 124:40–41 The reason why the Lord commanded the Saints to build a temple at Nauvoo.** It was in that temple that He intended to "reveal mine ordinances ... unto my people" (v. 40). This included some things that had not existed in previous dispensations—things that had been "kept hid from before the foundation of the world" and only pertained to "the dispensation of the fulness of times" (v. 41).

NAUVOO TEMPLE ©RANDAL S. CHASE, 2002

The Prophet Joseph Smith said that in this, the dispensation of the fullness of times, everything that has been revealed in all former dispensations will again be brought to light, along with "other things that have not been before revealed."[3] This includes *all* of the principles, powers, blessings, and keys of *all* previous dispensations

The Prophet spoke of how "prophets, priests and kings ... have looked forward with joyful anticipation to the day in which we live," writing and singing and prophesying of our day. But they were not privileged to experience it firsthand as we do. "We are the favored people that God has made choice of to bring about the Latter-day glory; it is left for us to see, participate in and help to roll forward the Latter-day glory, 'the dispensation of the fulness of times.'"[4]

Elder B. H. Roberts described the dispensation of the fullness of times as being like an ocean into which the "mighty streams" of previous dispensations flow, "putting us in touch with them, [and] putting them in touch with us." He continued by observing that "God has had but one great purpose in view from the beginning, and that has been the salvation of His children. And now has come the final day, the final dispensation, when truth and light and righteousness must flood the earth."[5]

Elder Bruce R. McConkie said: "We live in the dispensation of the fulness of times. That is to say, we live in the dispensation of the fulness of dispensations. We have received all of the 'keys, and powers, and glories,' possessed by them of old. Angelic ministrants have come from those Biblical dispensations which had distinctive keys and powers—'all declaring their dispensation, their rights, their keys, their honors, their majesty and glory, and the power of their priesthood' (D&C 128:18–21)."[6] Thus, in the dispensation of the fulness of times, the Lord will "gather together in one all things in Christ, both which are in heaven, and which are on earth" (Eph. 1:10, emphasis added).

● **Daniel 2:44–45 Unlike previous dispensations, this final dispensation will never fail (v.** 44). It will "break in pieces and consume all [worldly] kingdoms, and it shall stand for ever" (v. 44). Daniel compared it to a "stone … cut out of the mountain without hands" that will roll forward, gaining size and momentum as it goes, until it utterly destroys all earthly kingdoms and replaces them (v. 45).

President Joseph Fielding Smith said: "We may meet with opposition, but that opposition shall fail in its endeavor to destroy the work of God. … It is not again to be removed, destroyed, or given to other people, and in His own way and time He is going to break down all other systems, that His kingdom may prevail and that He may come and reign as Lord of lords and King of kings upon the face of the whole earth."[7]

● **D&C 65:2 The Kingdom of God will fill the entire earth.** We can see the Church rolling forth as prophesied anciently. Its destiny is to roll forth until it has reached the "ends of the earth" and "filled the whole earth."

The Prophet Joseph Smith said: "No unhallowed hand can stop the work from progressing; persecutions may rage, mobs may combine, armies may assemble, calumny may defame, but the truth of God will go forth boldly, nobly, and independent, till it has penetrated every continent, visited every clime, swept every country, and sounded in every ear, till the purposes of God shall be accomplished, and the Great Jehovah shall say the work is done."[8]

This makes our dispensation different from any of the previous ones:

— This dispensation will not end in apostasy.

— The Church will continue to grow until it fills the earth and the way is prepared for the Lord's Second Coming.

— There are special blessings and responsibilities of living in this dispensation.

Elder Marion G. Romney said:

> Naturally, believing Christians, even those who have a mature faith in the gospel, are concerned and disturbed by the lowering clouds on the horizon. But they need not be surprised or frantic about their portent, for, as has already been said, at the very beginning of this last dispensation … [despite] the tribulations and calamity that He foresaw … and that we now see coming upon us, there would be a people who, through acceptance and obedience to the gospel, would be able to recognize and resist the powers of evil, build up the promised Zion, and prepare to meet the Christ and be with Him in the blessed millennium. And we know further that it is possible for every one of us, who will, to have a place among those people. It is this assurance and this expectation that gives us understanding of the Lord's admonition, "be not troubled."[9]

PREPARING FOR THE SECOND COMING OF CHRIST

Another important difference of this final dispensation is that it will end with the second and final appearance of the Lord Jesus Christ. This makes preparing for the Second Coming of Christ a primary task for all of us. Indeed, early in the history of the Church several members were given identical instruction by the Lord—to "seek to bring forth and establish the cause of Zion":

"THE LIVING CHRIST." ©JOSEPH BRICKEY; USED BY PERMISSION

— D&C 6:6   Joseph Smith &
                       Oliver Cowdery

— D&C 11:6   Hyrum Smith

— D&C 12:6   Joseph Knight

— D&C 39:13   James Covill

This challenge has not been rescinded, and it applies to all of us, not just to the people who received these original revelations. The Lord said when He gave these revelations, "What I say unto one I say unto all" (D&C 61:18, 36; 82:5; 92:1; 93:49). Thus, in the Church today, we are under the same charge to labor to bring forth Zion. Our efforts should be devoted to seeing that great cause brought to pass.

President Harold B. Lee said: "We have some tight places to go before the Lord is through with this Church and the world in this dispensation, which is the last dispensation, which shall usher in the coming of the Lord. The gospel was restored to prepare a people ready to receive Him."[10]

Elder Lee also said:

> Now, I have asked myself, this being the time to prepare for the millennial reign, how shall we set about to prepare a people to receive the coming of the Lord? As I have thought seriously about that matter, I have reached two or three sure conclusions in my own thinking. This preparation demands first that a people, to receive the coming of the Lord, must be taught the personality and the nature of God and His Son, Jesus Christ …

> To my thinking, another requisite of that preparation to receive the Lord at the beginning of His millennial reign demands that the people be taught to accept the divinity of the mission of Jesus as the Savior of the world…

> [There is] still another requirement, as I see it, for a people to be prepared to receive the Savior's coming. We must be cleansed and purified and sanctified to be made worthy to receive and abide that holy presence…

> And now, finally, there is still one more thing that is necessary, to my thinking, before that preparation is made for the millennial reign. We must accept the divine mission of the Prophet Joseph Smith as the instrumentality through which the restoration of the gospel and the organization of the Church of Jesus Christ was accomplished.[11]

We are not here on earth at this time by accident. We have been sent by God to help build His kingdom in this last dispensation. President Ezra Taft Benson said: "There has never been more expected of the faithful in such a short period of time as there is of us."[12]

Despite the shortness of available time to accomplish it all, we must not feel overwhelmed. Choosing to characterize it positively, President Gordon B. Hinckley called our day "a season of a thousand opportunities. It is ours to grasp and move forward. What a wonderful time it is for each of us to do his or her small part in moving the work of the Lord on to its magnificent destiny."[13]

THE IMPORTANCE OF THE DOCTRINE AND COVENANTS

The Doctrine and Covenants Is the Capstone of Our Religion

NAUVOO TEMPLE SPIRE. ©RANDALS CHASE, 2002

The Book of Mormon is often referred to as the keystone of our religion. This is the central stone in an arch that holds the entire structure together. Remove it, and the arch collapses.

In a similar metaphor, President Ezra Taft Benson called the Doctrine and Covenants the "capstone" of our religion. To under- stand this, we can look at the capstone of the Salt Lake Temple, which is the upper half of the ball upon which the statue of angel Moroni stands. It was placed there on 6 April 1892, signifying the completion of the building. Thus, while "the Book of Mormon brings men to Christ … , the Doctrine and Covenants brings men to Christ's kingdom, even The Church of Jesus Christ of Latter-day Angel Moroni on the Saints… The Book of Mormon is the 'keystone' of our religion, and the Doctrine and Covenants is the

Angel Moroni on the Nauvoo Temple capstone

capstone, with continuing latter-day revelation. The Lord has placed His stamp of approval on both the keystone and the capstone."[14]

The Doctrine and Covenants Addresses the Needs of Our Day

● **D&C Introduction, 3rd Paragraph The Doctrine and Covenants differs from all other books of scripture** in that it is "not a translation of an ancient document, but is of modern origin and was given of God through His chosen prophets for the restoration of His holy work and the establishment of the kingdom of God on the earth in these days... **The work that is initiated [therein] is preparatory to His Second Coming, in fulfillment of and in concert with the words of all the holy prophets since the world began."[15]**

President Joseph F. Smith said the Doctrine and Covenants "contains some of the most glorious principles ever revealed to the world, some that have been revealed in greater fulness than they were ever revealed before to the world."[16] This makes the Doctrine and Covenants especially helpful and meaningful to us.

President Joseph Fielding Smith said: "In my judgment there is no book on earth ... with all due respect to the Book of Mormon, and the Bible, and the Pearl of Great Price, which we say are our standards in doctrine. The book of Doctrine and Covenants to us stands in a peculiar position above them all... [It] contains the word of God to those who dwell here now... More precious than gold, the Prophet says we should treasure it more than the riches of the whole earth. I wonder if we do? If we value it, understand it, and know what it contains, we will value it more than wealth; it is worth more to us than the riches of the earth."[17]

● **D&C 1:1–4 The Doctrine and Covenants is revelation for our own day.** One creed of the modern Christian world states that the Bible contains "the whole counsel of God," and another says, "Holy Scripture containeth all things necessary to salvation."[18] Such creeds were refuted by the Prophet Joseph Smith: "We are differently situated from any other people that ever existed upon this earth. Consequently those former revelations cannot be suited to our condition, because they were given to other people who were before us..."[19] The Doctrine and Covenants is given for the Latter-day Saints and the latter days in which they live.

The Doctrine and Covenants Contains Both History and Revelation

● **D&C Introduction, 6th Paragraph The Doctrine and Covenants is tightly connected to Church history.** We cannot fully understand one without understanding the other. "These sacred revelations were received in answer to prayer, in times of need, and came out of real-life situations involving real people. The Prophet and his associates sought for divine guidance, and these revelations certify that they received it. In the revelations one sees the restoration and unfolding of the gospel of Jesus Christ and the ushering in of the dispensation of the fulness of times. The westward movement of the Church from New York and Pennsylvania, to Ohio, to Missouri, to Illinois, and finally to the Great Basin of western America, and the mighty struggles of the Saints in attempting to build Zion on the earth in modern times, are also shown forth in these revelations."[20]

History is a man-made record of past events. Revelation is knowledge given to man from God. The Doctrine and Covenants contains both. Most of it is revelation, but some parts of it are history. To understand fully the doctrine contained in a revelation, we need to know the circumstances under which it was given—what the Prophet was seeking to understand, etc.

The Saints were driven out of Missouri

True to His pattern of waiting until His servants ask for wisdom, the Lord did not simply pour out revelation without a context. The Prophet Joseph Smith would ponder on something he had translated or read in the scriptures, would then take it to the Lord for clarification, and the Lord would then give him a revelation on the matter. Indeed, most of the revelations in the Doctrine and Covenants were received in this manner, as answers to prayers. Therefore, a proper study of the Doctrine and Covenants must include a study of both history and revelation.

The Doctrine and Covenants Is Not and Never Will Be Completed

● **Not all the revelations given to Joseph Smith are included in the Doctrine and Covenants.** The Prophet received many revelations which were not included in the Doctrine and Covenants for a variety of reasons:

— Some of these revelations he was specifically commanded not to include.
— For some, he was commanded to include only portions of the revelation (D&C 76:114–19).
— Some other revelations were not published because it was unnecessary at that particular time.
— Sometimes the revelation was so personal to the individual that the principles therein did not have general application.
— Each of the revelations selected for the Doctrine and Covenants was placed there because the Prophet believed it had some value to the Church in regard to its teachings.

● **Articles of Faith 1:9 The Doctrine and Covenants is a "living" document.**
Revelation did not cease when the Prophet Joseph Smith was martyred. The keys of the kingdom were passed on through the Quorum of the Twelve Apostles, and they are still held today by our living prophet. And with the transfer of those keys to each succeeding prophet came the right to revelation. Because we have living prophets and because we believe that God "will yet reveal many great and important things pertaining to the Kingdom of God," new revelations have been added over time and will yet be added in the future.

President Spencer W. Kimball said: "There are those who would assume that with the printing and binding of these sacred records, that would be the 'end of the prophets.' But again we testify to the world that revelation continues and that the vaults and files of the Church contain these revelations which come month to month and day to day."[21]

Editions of the Doctrine and Covenants

Because it is a living document, the Doctrine and Covenants has expanded and changed over the years. The following chronology lists the various developments in its publication.

The Book of Commandments

1. 1831   Book of Commandments: Decision in November to publish the revelations.

2. 1833   Book of Commandments: Published in Missouri by W. W. Phelps; most of the copies were destroyed by a mob.

3. 1835   Doctrine and Covenants: Revelations first published under this title, with 102 sections and the Lectures on Faith.

4. 1844   Doctrine and Covenants: 111 sections and Lectures on Faith.

5. 1876   Doctrine and Covenants: 136 sections and Lectures on Faith.

6. 1921   Doctrine and Covenants: Headings and footnotes by Elder James E. Talmage added; Lectures on Faith removed because they were not direct revelations but were notes of theological lessons.

7. 1981   Doctrine and Covenants: Sections 137–138, Official Declaration 2, and updated headings and expanded cross-references added.

The Contents of the Doctrine and Covenants

● **D&C Introduction, 8th Paragraph The Doctrine and Covenants contains many different kinds of content that have been accepted as scripture.** Beginning with the phrase "in the revelations" the introduction to the Doctrine and Covenants lists some of the doctrines of the gospel that are explained therein.

Most of the revelations were received as answers to prayers, many of those as a result of the Prophet Joseph Smith's revision of the Bible text, as commanded by the Lord. The doctrines thus introduced produced questions in the Prophet's mind, and he sought answers in prayer. Many of the sections of the Doctrine and Covenants constitute answers to those prayers. The following list is representative of the nature of the contents of the Doctrine and Covenants:

— D&C 1	General revelations
— D&C 7	Translations
— D&C 13	Words spoken by Heavenly Messengers
— D&C 42	Revelations given for the benefit of the priesthood
— D&C 122	Revelations given specifically to Joseph Smith
— D&C 25	Revelations given to other individuals
— D&C 76	Visions
— D&C 87	Prophetic predictions
— D&C 89	Prophetic counsel for living in a wicked world
— D&C 86	Explanations of passages in other standard works
— D&C 109	Words spoken in prayers
— D&C 128	Inspiration sent through letters
— D&C 102	Minutes of special Church meetings
— D&C 134	Official declarations
— D&C 135	Historical narratives

The Doctrine and Covenants Explains the Covenants of Eternal Life

Covenants are part of the doctrine of the kingdom. A gospel covenant is a solemn agreement between us and God in which we promise to do some things and refrain from doing others, [and] God promises certain blessings.

I have contemplated why it is that God does everything by covenant. If the two parties are God and we as individuals, who does the covenant protect? Does it benefit God if I keep my covenants? No. It pleases Him, because He loves me as His child. But He is no more and no less God, whatever I do. The benefits of the covenant all seem to be mine.

What are those benefits? Does it instill any greater confidence that God will keep His word? No. He always keeps His word. The question is, will I keep my word? And if I do, then what can I count on? I can know for certain that He will grant me the associated blessing. So in that sense, I can obligate Him to bless me by simply keeping my part of the covenant. If He says, as He does in D&C 84:33–38, that "all that [the] Father hath" will be given to me if I receive, honor, and magnify my priesthood, then I can expect exaltation if I do my part. Period.

● **D&C 82:10 We can bind the Lord.** "I, the Lord, am bound when ye do what I say; but when ye do not what I say, ye have no promise."

● **D&C 132:5 All blessings are conditional.** Those who desire a blessing from God must "abide the law which was appointed for that blessing, and the conditions thereof," which were determined long before we came here, in the premortal life.

● **D&C 130:20–21 All blessings are predicated on obedience to laws.** We know that there are laws "irrevocably decreed in heaven before the foundations of this world, upon which all blessings are predicated" (v. 20). So, if we desire "any blessing from God," it can be obtained only "by obedience to that law upon which it is predicated" (v. 21).

Happily, God does not expect perfection in this life to qualify for exaltation. Read any one of His covenants, and you will nowhere find a requirement to be perfect in mortality. He knows that is not possible. He made the earth that way in order to provide real choices between good and evil and to allow us to learn "by our own experience" to discern between them. Along the way, it is certain that we will make mistakes. That's why we need a Savior and that's why He provided one. In the economy of covenants, I do very little, simple things, and He blesses me with enormous and incomprehensible blessings. And I can have absolute confidence that I will succeed, so long as I do my humble little part. That is the glorious blessing of doing all things by covenant.

● **D&C 54:3–6 The violation of our covenants is a very serious sin.**
While perfection is not required in this life, if we want to receive eternal blessings, it is necessary to repent of all our sins whenever we commit them, and "become truly humble before [Him] and contrite" (v. 3). Otherwise, the Lord says, "the covenant which they made unto me has been broken, [and] has become void and of none effect" (v. 4).

We would be better off dead than to remain on this earth in an unrepentant state (v. 5), as witnessed by the Lord's taking those who are "past feeling" and utterly unwilling to change into the spirit world where they may have a better chance to reform their behaviors (e.g., the people of Noah's day, the Jaredites, and the Nephites). But for those who humble themselves and recognize their need to repent and call upon the Savior for help, the promise is that "they shall obtain mercy" (v. 6) and obtain every promised blessing of their covenants.

● **D&C 66:2 The "new and everlasting covenant" is the gospel of Jesus Christ.** We might think that any one of our covenants—baptismal, sacramental, temple, or marriage— could qualify as the "new and everlasting covenant." They are all related to it, but they are only a part. The term actually refers to the entire gospel of Jesus Christ with all of its associated teachings and covenants.

Elder Bruce R. McConkie said:

> God's covenant of salvation is the fulness of the gospel. … When men accept the gospel, they thereby agree or covenant to keep the commandments of God, and He promises or covenants to give them salvation in His kingdom.

> The gospel is the everlasting covenant because it is ordained by Him who is Everlasting and also because it is everlastingly the same. In all past ages salvation was gained by adherence to its terms and conditions, and that same compliance will bring the same reward in all future ages. Each time this everlasting covenant is revealed it is new to those of that dispensation. Hence the gospel is the new and everlasting covenant.

> All covenants between God and man are part of the new and everlasting covenant.[22]

We are blessed to live in a time when the "everlasting covenant, even the fulness of [the] gospel, [has been] sent forth unto the children of men, that they might have life and be made partakers of the glories [of God]" (v. 2). In what other age of the world would we rather live? President John

Taylor said our day is "pregnant with greater events than any other period that we know of, or in any other dispensation that has existed upon the earth."[23] And Elder Wilford Woodruff said: "There never was a generation of the inhabitants of the earth in any age of the world who had greater events awaiting them than the present… An age fraught with greater interest to the children of men than the one in which we live never dawned since the creation of the world."[24]

The Prophet Joseph Smith said to the Saints who laid the foundation of this dispensation:

> The blessings of the Most High will rest upon our tabernacles, and our name will be handed down to future ages; our children will rise up and call us blessed; and generations yet unborn will dwell with peculiar delight upon the scenes that we have passed through, the privations that we have endured; the untiring zeal that we have manifested; the all but insurmountable difficulties that we have overcome in laying the foundation of a work that brought about the glory and blessing which they will realize; a work that God and angels have contemplated with delight for generations past; that fired the souls of the ancient patriarchs and prophets; a work that is destined to bring about the destruction of the powers of dark- ness, the renovation of the earth, the glory of God, and the salvation of the human family.[25]

We have seen the fulfillment of this prophecy in our own day and time. Millions of Saints around the world remember and sing praises continually to the Prophet Joseph Smith and to our pioneer ancestors who sacrificed all they had—even their own lives— for the establishment of the Church and dispensation of the fulness of times.

- **D&C 45:9 The Lord established His Church on the earth so that the fulness of the gospel could be proclaimed to the entire world.** The gospel message and its associated covenants are a "light" to the Gentiles in a darkening world. They provide a "standard for my people," providing guiding principles and warnings to Latter-day Saints. And they provide a warning message of the nearness of Christ's Second Coming "to prepare the way before me." God is not sneaking up on His children, hoping to catch them asleep and destroy them. He is making every effort to save them before the inevitable destructions come that will follow the wickedness we see all around us.

THE LORD'S PREFACE TO THE DOCTRINE AND COVENANTS

The Historical Context of D&C 1

The Prophet Joseph Smith said when the Church was not yet two years old "there was a great anxiety to obtain the word of the Lord upon every subject that in any way concerned our salvation."[26] It was in answer to those desires that the Lord provided the many revelations that came like an overflowing surge through the Prophet Joseph Smith to them.

When the Saints reached Kirtland, there was a desire to publish the revelations so that missionaries and members could study them and refer to them. With the Lord's permission, this was done. And when the Book of Commandments was ready for publication, the Lord Himself provided both the preface (D&C 1) and the appendix (D&C 133) for it.

● **D&C 1: Heading The circumstances under which the preface was given.** Note that this section was given by direct revelation through the Prophet Joseph Smith, during a special conference of the Church, held at Hiram, Ohio, November 1, 1831.[27]

The Johnson Home in Hiram, Ohio

Usually, the author of a book writes the preface to introduce his material and tell readers what they can gain from reading it. Although D&C 1 appears first in the book, it was actually given to the Prophet Joseph Smith after many of the other revelations had already been received. We will revisit this situation later, when we are studying what happened at that period of time in Church History. But for now, suffice it to say that this initial section is the Lord's introduction to His book of latter-day revelations. We are hearing His voice through its verses.

At this conference, which was held in the home of John Johnson at Hiram, Ohio, they decided to print 10,000 copies of the Book of Commandments—the predecessor to our current Doctrine and Covenants. During the two-day conference "a number of the brethren arose and said that they were willing to testify to the world that they knew that [the Book of Commandments] were of the Lord."[28]

During the afternoon of that conference, on 1 November 1831, the Prophet received what is now D&C 1. D&C 133—referred to as the Lord's appendix—was also given at that same time. Originally, it was inserted at the end of the Doctrine and Covenants as an appendix, but was later assigned a section number. We are focusing in this chapter only on D&C 1.

The Teachings of D&C 1

● **D&C 1:6 The Lord calls D&C 1 His preface.** This makes it the only book in the world with a preface written by the Lord Himself.

● **D&C 1:1–2 The voice of the Lord is unto all men.** The Lord declares that His "eyes are upon all men" and He expects them to listen wherever they may be on the earth (v.1). He invites them to "listen together," an interesting idea that was quite impossible in the days when this section was given, but which happens now daily through satellite technology. Indeed, when the Lord's prophet speaks today from the pulpit in the Conference Center, the entire world can receive His message "together." The Lord declares that nobody is immune to His warnings, and that all men will eventually see, hear, and consider in their hearts what He has to say (v. 2).

— D&C 63:58 God will not be mocked. He declares that "this is a day of warning, and not a day of many words. For I, the Lord, am not to be mocked in the last days."

— D&C 63:54 The warning voice will polarize the world (see also 1 Nephi 14:7). I remember sitting in a stake conference meeting with my father when I was a young teenager. Our Cottonwood Stake President was President James E. Faust. Our visiting authority was Elder N. Eldon Tanner, who also happened to live within our ward boundaries. He spoke of the division between the "wheat" and the "tares" in the latter days. The thought that was most profoundly impressed on my mind was that if we thought that the world was evil at that time, we should wait until we saw the children of those we considered to be evil, and their children's children. He said that the level of evil would increase with every generation. The idea has remained with me ever since as I've watched the world spiral down into wickedness and perversion.

President Spencer W. Kimball reiterated this thought when he said that as righteousness increases, so will evil.[29] And Heber C. Kimball said the Saints will hardly escape the judgments that will be poured out upon the wicked, but "will be put to tests that will try the integrity of the best of them."[30]

President Ezra Taft Benson prophesied: "We may expect to see the righteousness of the Saints and the progress of the kingdom of God continue unabated, but it will not be without opposition. The council of the Twelve proclaimed in 1845: 'As this work progresses in its onward course, and becomes more and more an object of political and religious interest … no king, ruler, or subject, no community or individual, will stand neutral. All will … be influenced by one spirit or the other; and will take sides either for or against the kingdom of God.'"[31]

— D&C 38:30 "If ye are prepared ye shall not fear." How should we respond to the increasing confusion and wickedness of the world? The Lord offers comforting counsel: "I tell you these things because of your prayers; wherefore, treasure up [this] wisdom in your bosoms … if ye are prepared ye shall not fear."

President Benson continued his 1978 prophecy with these words:

> It is easy to despair when we see about us the moorings of society slipping. We must remember, however, that the Lord sent His Saints into the world "to be a light unto the world, and to be the saviors of men" (D&C 103:9). This is a time when "Zion must arise and put on her beautiful garments" (D&C 82:14). The contrast between the Church and the world will be increasingly marked in the future, which contrast, we hope, will cause the Church to be more attractive to those in the world who desire to live according to God's plan for us, His children.

> The Church will always stand for that which is honest, virtuous, true and praiseworthy. Such a pronounced stand for righteousness constitutes a repudiation against every evil and all false philosophies. The First Presidency and the Twelve are not oblivious to false philosophies and evils and will continue to warn the world and the Saints as the Lord directs.[32]

— D&C 45:39–57 If we heed the voice of the prophets we have hope for protection, while those who do not will suffer the judgments to come. As this scripture makes plain, the Doctrine and Covenants was given to all of God's children, not just the Church. Elder Joseph Fielding Smith taught nearly a century ago that it belongs "to all the world, to the Catholics, to the

Presbyterians, to the Methodists, to the infidel, to the non-believer. It is [their] book if [they] will accept it... The Lord has given it unto the world for their salvation." And thus, the entire world—ourselves included—will be judged by the teachings and covenants that it contains. And "if we fail to comprehend these things, if we will not search, if we will not study, if we will not take hold on the things which the Lord has revealed unto us, then His condemnation shall rest upon us, and we shall be removed from His presence and from His kingdom."[33]

● **D&C 1:3 Wickedness will be laid bare, producing "much sorrow."** Those who rebel will eventually be "pierced with much sorrow" and their iniquities, once done in the dark, "shall be spoken upon the housetops" (an interesting figure of speech in a day of rooftop antennas capturing all kinds of media). By this process "their secret acts shall be revealed" (v. 3). One needs only to watch an hour of prime time television programming and news to see every kind of abomination and perversion laid bare before them.

● **D&C 1:4–7 The voice of warning is given to all people.** The Lord intends to take His message of warning to the world "by the mouths of [His] disciples, whom [He has] chosen in these last days" (v. 4). And they shall go forth and none shall stay them, for … the Lord [has] commanded them" (v. 5). The Lord addresses Himself to all the "inhabitants of the earth" and makes it plain that He has given authority to His servants to publish these revelations and commandments (v. 6). His warning is clear.

"Wherefore, fear and tremble, O ye people, for what I the Lord have decreed in them shall be fulfilled" (v. 7).

President Ezra Taft Benson warned:

> If this voice is not heeded, the angels of destruction will increasingly go forth, and the chastening hand of Almighty God will be felt upon the nations, as decreed, until a full end thereof will be the result. Wars, devastation, and untold suffering will be your lot except you turn unto the Lord in humble repentance. Destruction, even more terrible and farreaching than attended the last great war, will come with certainty unless rulers and people alike repent and cease their evil and godless ways: God will not be mocked. He will not permit the sins of sexual immorality, secret murderous combinations, the killing of the unborn, and disregard for all His holy commandments and the messages of His servants to go unheeded without grievous punishment for such wickedness: The nations of the world cannot endure in sin.
>
> The way of escape is clear. The immutable laws of God remain steadfastly in the heavens above. When men and nations refuse to abide by them, the penalty must follow. They will be wasted away. Sin demands punishment. When the voice of warning goes forth it is always attended by testimony. In the declaration issued by the Apostles of the Lord Jesus Christ in 1845, this is the testimony which was borne, and we who are the Apostles today renew it as our witness.[34]

● **D&C 1:8–9, 11 The Lord's words are available to all people, through His earthly servants, so that "all that will hear may hear" (v. 11).** The Lord's messengers who bear His warning message to the world have the power to seal things both on earth and in heaven (v. 8). This sealing power, held by the Apostles and prophets, gives them authority to identify the "unbelieving and rebellious" and "to seal them up unto the day when the wrath of God shall be poured out upon the wicked without measure" (vv. 8–9).

Whatever their faults as mortal men, the Lord sustains the Apostles and prophets as His mouthpieces on earth, and we would all do well to give heed to them. I was once asked by a friend who felt critical of one of our prophets who had a reputation for being firm and uncompromising in his views, what I thought of him. "He holds the keys, doesn't he?" I asked. "Well, yes," my friend retorted, but …" And before he could finish, I interjected, "That's all I need to know about him. If he holds the keys, God will never allow him to lead me astray. I choose to honor and to follow him."

This does not make me a mindless person. As we all should do, I pray for my own witness of the correctness of things that are said by our prophets. But while we wait for our answers, and unless the Lord tells us otherwise in answer to our prayers, we should sustain those whom the Lord has called. I learned very early on in my life, when I was called as a young bishop at the age of 27, that the Lord calls ordinary men to hold keys and direct His work. It's easy to see their faults. My ward members certainly saw mine. But the Lord does not expect perfection of His ordained servants, and neither should we. He has chosen them, and He will correct them in His own way if they need it. We have no prerogative to do so. And when we do criticize, we incur our Father's displeasure and His Spirit withdraws from us.[35]

The Prophet Joseph Smith said: "All the enemies upon the face of the earth may roar and exert all their power to bring about my death, but they can accomplish nothing, unless some who are among us and enjoy our society, have been with us in our councils, participated in our confidence, taken us by the hand, called us brother, saluted us with a kiss, join with our enemies, turn our virtues into faults, and, by falsehood and deceit, stir up their wrath and indignation against us, and bring their united vengeance upon our heads."[36]

The Prophet also said: "I will give you one of the keys of the mysteries of the Kingdom. It is an eternal principle, that has existed with God from all eternity: That man who rises up to condemn others, finding fault with the Church, saying that they are out of the way, while he himself is righteous, then know assuredly, that that man is in the high road to apostasy; and if he does not repent, will apostatize, as God lives."[37]

● **D&C 1:11 The Lord's "voice" will be available to all people, through His earthly servants.**
The Lord says His "voice … is unto the ends of the earth, that all that will hear may hear." President Spencer W. Kimball said: "We have established new missions covering almost all of the free world, and we are turning our attention more diligently now to one day sharing the gospel with our Father's children behind the so-called iron and bamboo curtains. We have need to prepare for that day. The urgency of that preparation weighs heavily upon us. That day may come with more swiftness than we realize."[38] We have already seen this prophecy fulfilled. The gospel has penetrated the iron curtain into eastern Europe and Russia, and we have a temple inside the bamboo curtain at Hong Kong.

Yet, many political barriers still exist. Concerning these, President Spencer W. Kimball said: "Somehow, brethren, I feel that when we have done all in our power that the Lord will find a way to open doors: That is my faith. Is any thing too hard for the Lord?… I believe the Lord can do anything He sets His mind to do. But I can see no good reason why the Lord would open doors that we are not prepared to enter. Why should He break down the Iron Curtain or the

Bamboo Curtain or any other curtain if we are still unprepared to enter? I believe we have men who could help the Apostles to open these doors—statesmen, able and trustworthy—but, when we are ready for them."[39]

I have heard it said that if we took all of the missionaries we currently have in the field and put them in just one city, Beijing, China, it would take three years for those missionaries to knock on every door. Truly, the work is vast and the laborers are few. But the Lord will find a way for His "voice" to penetrate into places where missionaries cannot go. Today, with the Internet and satellite technology, the voice of the prophets can literally be heard everywhere around the earth, and in most places the video images as well. We have the capacity to "sound in every ear" our message, and the finishing of the work may be closer than we think.

● **D&C 1:10, 12–14 "They who will not hear … shall be cut off."** The message is to "prepare ye for that which is to come, for the Lord is nigh" (v. 12). In that day when the Lord comes again to the earth, He will "recompense unto every man according to his work" and "according to the measure which he has measured to his fellow man" (v. 10). The Lord declares Himself to be angry with the wicked, that His "sword is bathed in heaven" and that "it shall fall upon the inhabitants of the earth" (v. 13), specifically upon those "who will not hear the voice of the Lord, neither the voice of his servants, neither give heed to the words of the prophets and Apostles," and all of these "shall be cut off from among the people" (v. 14).

The members and missionaries of the Church are commanded to warn the world, including our "neighbors" (D&C 88:81), of the desolation and destruction that will soon be poured out without measure upon the wicked and ungodly. "This is a day of warning, and not a day of many words," the Lord says, "for I, the Lord, am not to be mocked in the last days" (D&C 63:58). If men refuse the warning, said Elder Melvin J. Ballard, "they cannot blame the Lord if calamities, judgments and destructions come upon them. The Lord cannot avert it, it must take its course, and yet our Father in His kindness and mercy has offered the way and the means of escape" In Conference Report, October 1923, 30–31).

● **D&C 1:15–16 The world has become proud and idolatrous.** The Lord's complaints against the world are numerous.

— They "have strayed from mine ordinances."
— They "have broken mine everlasting covenant."
— They seek not the Lord to establish His righteousness.
— Every man "walketh in his own way"—not in the ways of the Lord.
— Every man behaves like "the image of his own god … in the likeness of the world."
— Every man's substance (possessions) is his idol.
— The religions of the world have changed the Lord's ordinances and broken His covenants

As we look around us today, we see the literal fulfillment of these complaints, growing worse with the passing of each generation. The Churches of the world have changed the Lord's sacred and simple ordinances into lavish shows of pomp and circumstance. They break the standards and covenants of the gospel of Jesus Christ. They accept for doctrines the philosophies of men—going their own way in order to look more like the world and be accepted by the worldly. They worship material possessions (gods) of their own making—which in the Lord's eyes is idolatry. And all of these things will "wax ... old" and "perish in Babylon" (the world), "which shall fall" (v. 16). Satan has great power over such men to "lead them captive at his will, even as many as [will] not hearken" to the voice of the Lord (Moses 4:4).

While some of this idolatry is individual, there is also a great conspiracy of evil in the world, led by Satan and his followers. President Ezra Taft Benson said this conspiracy is "manifest through governments; through false educational, political, economic, religious, and social philosophies; through secret societies and organizations; and through myriads of other forms. His power and influence are so great that, if possible, he would deceive the very elect. As the Second Coming of the Lord approaches, Satan's work will intensify through numerous insidious deceptions."[40]

● **D&C 1:17–18 "Knowing the calamity which should come upon ... the earth," the Lord initiated the final dispensation by calling "upon [His] servant Joseph Smith, Jun.,** and spake unto him from heaven, and gave him commandments" (v. 17). All of this was done in anticipation of the great destructions that will precede the Lord's Second Coming, "that it might be fulfilled, which was written by the prophets" (v. 18). The Doctrine and Covenants and other prophetic writings contain descriptions of these calamities and judgments that the prophets have predicted for the days immediately before the Lord's Second Coming. The list is long and disturbing.

— "Wonders in the heavens and in the earth, blood, and fire, and pillars of smoke" (Joel 2:30).
— Darkening of the sun, the moon turning to blood [great pollution], and stars falling from heaven [asteroids] (D&C 29:14; 34:9; 45:42; 88:87; 133:49).
— Lightning, thunder, and earthquakes wreaking havoc (D&C 43:25; 45:33; 87:6; 88:89–90).
— The sea heaving itself beyond its bounds [tsunamis] (D&C 88:90).
— Very destructive whirlwinds [tornadoes] (D&C 112:24).
— Overflowing rain, great hailstones, fires and brimstone (Ezek. 38:22).
— A sore affliction, pestilence, the sword, vengeance, and a devouring fire (D&C 97:25–28).
— Famines, pestilence, and earthquakes (Matt. 24:7).
— A desolating scourge or sickness (D&C 5:19; 45:31).
— A plague that will consume eyes, tongue, mouth, feet, and flesh (Zech. 14:12).
— Flies and maggots eating the flesh, a great hailstorm to destroy the crops, flesh falling from the bones, eyes falling from their sockets, beasts of the forest devouring people (D&C 29:16–20).
— Wars upon the face of the earth (D&C 45:26, 63; 63:33; 87).
— Withdrawal of the Spirit from the earth, bands of Gadianton robbers infesting every nation, immorality, murder, and crime increasing, with every man's hand against his brother.[41]
— Desolations (D&C 29:8; 35:11; 45:19; 84:114, 117; 88:85; 112:24).
— The "abomination that maketh desolate" (at Jerusalem) (Dan. 11:31).

— The fire of the Lord's jealousy (Zeph. 3:8).
— Destruction of the great and abominable church (D&C 29:21; 88:94).

We have witnessed the fulfillment of many of these things, but many more are yet to come. Truly, the voice of warning taken forth to the world by our missionaries is important to both the temporal and spiritual salvation of God's children upon this earth.

● **D&C 1:19 God uses servants who are "the weak things of the world" to accomplish His work.** These simple servants will "break down the mighty and strong ones, that man should not counsel his fellow man, neither trust in the arm of flesh." From the very beginning of this dispensation God has followed this pattern, beginning with the calling of a simple and uneducated but faithful boy—Joseph Smith—as the prophet of the restoration.

Elder Spencer W. Kimball said: "I would not say that those leaders whom the Lord chooses are necessarily the most brilliant, nor the most highly trained, but they are chosen, and when chosen of the Lord they are His recognized authority, and the people who stay close to them have safety."[42]

● **D&C 1:20–28 The purposes for the revelations in the Doctrine and Covenants.** Warning the world of great calamities to come is not the only purpose of the revelations in the Doctrine and Covenants. Others include:

— v. 20   "That every man might speak in the name of … the Lord … the Savior of the world"
— v. 21   "That faith also might increase"
— v. 22   "That mine everlasting covenant might be established"
— v. 23   "That the fulness of my gospel might be proclaimed"
— v. 24   To help the Lord's servants "come to understanding"
— v. 25   "And inasmuch as they erred it might be made known"
— v. 26   "And inasmuch as they sought wisdom they might be instructed"
— v. 27   "And inasmuch as they sinned they might be chastened, that they might repent"
— v. 28   "And inasmuch as they were humble they might be made strong, and blessed from on high, and receive knowledge from time to time"

● **D&C 1:29–30 The only true and living church upon the face of the whole earth.** The Lord gave power to Joseph Smith to "receive … the record of the Nephites," and to "translate through the mercy of God, by the power of God, the Book of Mormon" (v. 29). This was essential to demonstrating the heavenly source of his work—a tangible proof that God's hand is in it and that Joseph Smith was indeed His chosen servant. Furthermore, the Lord gave Joseph Smith and his associates "power to lay the foundation of this church, and to bring it forth out of obscurity and out of darkness, the only true and living church upon the face of the whole earth, with which I, the Lord, am well pleased," though the Lord hastens to add that He is "speaking unto the Church collectively and not individually" (v. 30).

Elder Boyd K. Packer said: "The position that The Church of Jesus Christ of Latter-day Saints is the only true Church upon the face of the earth is fundamental… Now to those who think us uncharitable, we say that it was not devised by us; it was declared by Him [in D&C 1:30]… Now this is not to say that the Churches, all of them, are without some truth. They have some truth—some of them very much of it. They have a form of godliness. Often the clergy and adherents are not without dedication, and many of them practice remarkably well the virtues of Christianity. They are, nonetheless, incomplete. By His declaration, 'they teach for doctrines the commandments of men, having a form of godliness, but they deny the power thereof' (JS–History 1:19)."[43]

I once expanded on this theme by saying in a Gospel Doctrine class that "there is no salvation or exaltation outside The Church of Jesus Christ of Latter-day Saints." This so incensed one new convert in the room that he immediately stormed out of the room, slamming the door behind him. After class had finished, I skipped my priesthood meetings to go and find this brother. We spoke at length about his wonderful mother, a devoted Christian of another faith. He was certain that "Jesus would save her" as readily as He would save a Mormon. He was surprised to find that I agreed with him—but only if, when she finally heard the gospel message in its fulness she accepted it with all her heart and lived it to the best of her ability. That would include being baptized by one having the authority to do so, and the acceptance of every other covenant and ordinance that the Lord requires of those who would be saved and exalted. In other words, they must respond to the message of, and join, the Lord's church—the only true and living Church upon the face of the earth.

- **D&C 1:31–33 God cannot look upon sin with any degree of allowance (v. 31)**, but He will forgive anyone and everyone who repents and thereafter keeps His commandments (v. 32). He does not wish to punish or destroy anyone, and in fact rarely does so. "It is by the wicked that the wicked are punished" (Mormon 4:5)—they do it to themselves. Slowly but surely, "he that repents not, from him shall be taken even the light which he has received" (v. 33) until he is left both temporally and spiritually desolate. The Lord warns that His "Spirit shall not always strive with man" (v. 33), and when that Spirit is withdrawn, destruction is not far behind.

- **D&C 1:34–36 Peace shall be taken from the earth.**
As a natural consequence of the withdrawal of the Lord's Spirit, the time was rapidly coming In 1831) when "peace shall be taken from the earth, and the devil shall have power over his own dominion" (v. 35). He will reign with blood and horror upon the earth, at a level and with a vengeance that has never been seen before in the history of the world. Increasingly, nations spend their wealth to develop weapons of human destruction. This is surely inspired by Satan. Elder Melvin J. Ballard noted how nations use these weapons to "swoop … down upon … poor helpless women and children, drop [their] deadly bombs and assassinate … them." He calls this "the work of the devil," and declares flatly that "he is ruling in the midst of them."[44]

At the same time that the Lord is "com[ing] down in judgment upon … the world" (v. 36). He is maintaining "power over his Saints, and shall reign in their midst" (v. 36). And He is "willing to make these things known unto all flesh; for I am no respecter of persons, and will that all men shall know" (v. 34). Again, He does not wish to punish; He would rather save. But all must know that "the day speedily cometh; the hour is not yet, but is nigh at hand" (v. 34) when all these things will occur as a consequence of wickedness.

The Prophet Joseph Smith wrote in a letter to N. E. Seaton on January 4, 1833: "The Lord declared to His servants, some eighteen months [ago], that He was then withdrawing His Spirit from the earth; and we can see that such is the fact, for not only the Churches are dwindling away, but there are no conversions, or but very few: and this is not all, the governments of the earth are thrown into confusion and division; and DESTRUCTION, to the eye of the spiritual beholder, seems to be written by the finger of an invisible hand, in large capitals, upon almost every thing we behold."[45]

If this was true in 1833, it is even more true today. President Joseph Fielding Smith declared in 1956: "I declare to you that [peace] has been taken from the earth; and I say now—no, I don't say it, the Lord says it—'it shall not return until the Lord comes'… There will be no peace in this land or any other land, but there will be plague, trial, and suffering from this time forth until Christ comes. The only escape is by repentance on the part of the people, and they will not repent."[46]

- **D&C 1:37 "Search these commandments."** The commandment to "search" the Doctrine and Covenants is significant. It is the same language our Lord used with regard to the prophecies of Isaiah when speaking to the Nephites (3 Nephi 20:11; 23:1). We must do more than read them; we must "search" them, feast upon them, and seek to understand.

Elder Howard W. Hunter said: "To understand requires more than casual reading or perusal—there must be concentrated study… Not only should we study each day, but there should be a regular time set aside when we can concentrate without interference.

… The important thing is to allow nothing else to ever interfere with our study … There are some who read to a schedule of a number of pages or a set number of chapters each day or week… It is better to have a set amount of time to give scriptural study each day than to have a set amount of chapters to read. Sometimes we find that the study of a single verse will occupy the whole time"[47]

If we fail to do so, our ignorance will not save us. We will stand condemned before God and subject to the consequences. If we do search the scriptures we will know the will of the Lord and grow in our faith, knowledge, and wisdom (Alma 12:9; D&C 76:1–10).

The Prophet Joseph Smith said: "Search the scriptures—search the revelations which we publish, and ask your Heavenly Father, in the name of His Son Jesus Christ, to manifest the truth unto you, and if you do it with an eye single to His glory nothing doubting, He will answer you by the power of His Holy Spirit. You will then know for yourselves and not for another. You will not then be dependent on man for the knowledge of God; nor will there be any room for speculation."[48]

- **D&C 1:37, 39 They "shall all be fulfilled."** The Lord calls the revelations in the Doctrine and Covenants "true and faithful," and He declares that "the prophecies and promises which are in them shall all be fulfilled" (v. 37). "What I the Lord have spoken, I have spoken, and I excuse not myself; and though the heavens and the earth pass away, my word shall not pass away, but shall all be fulfilled" (v. 38). "For behold, and lo, the Lord is God, and the Spirit beareth record, and the record is true, and the truth abideth forever and ever" (v. 39).

- **D&C 1:38 "Whether by mine own voice or by the voice of my servants, it is the same."** We are as much obligated to follow the counsel of an inspired servant of the Lord as we are to obey the Lord Himself. And the Spirit-given prophecies which are uttered by such a servant will be as literally fulfilled as if the Lord had spoken them Himself.

Elder Ezra Taft Benson said: "Here then is the key—look to the prophets for the words of God, that will show us how to prepare for the calamities which are to come... The Lord warned those who will reject the inspired words of His representatives, in these words: "... and the day cometh that they who will not hear the voice of the Lord, neither the voice of His servants, neither give heed to the words of the prophets and Apostles, shall be cut off from among the people (D&C 1:14)."[49]

Notes:

1. "Dispensations," *LDS Bible Dictionary*, 657.
2. See JST Gen. 14:25–40; 1 Ne. 19:10–12; Alma 13:14–19; 33:3–17; D&C 84:6–16; *History of the Church*, 3:386–389; 4:208–209. "*Dispensations," LDS Bible Dictionary*, 657.
3. *Teachings of the Prophet Joseph Smith*, sel. Joseph Fielding Smith [1976], 193.
4. *Teachings of the Prophet Joseph Smith*, 231.
5. In Conference Report, October 1904, 73.
6. "This Final Glorious Gospel Dispensation," *Ensign*, April 1980, 22.
7. *Doctrines of Salvation*, comp. Bruce R. McConkie, 3 vols. [1954–1956], 1:241.
8. *History of the Church*, 4:540.
9. In Conference Report, October 1966, 53–54.
10. In Conference Report, October 1970, 152.
11. In Conference Report, October 1956, 61–62.
12. Quoted by Elder Marvin J. Ashton, in Conference Report, October 1989, 48; or *Ensign*, November 1989, 36.
13. In Conference Report, October 1997, 90–91; or *Ensign*, November 1997, 67.
14. In Conference Report, April 1987, 105; or *Ensign*, May 1987, 83.
15. *Explanatory Introduction of the Doctrine and Covenants* [1981], paragraph 3.
16. *Gospel Doctrine*, 5th ed. [1939], 45.
17. *Doctrines of Salvation*, 3:198–199.
18. Milton V. Backman, *American Religions and the Rise of Mormonism* [1970], 449.
19. "Kirtland council Minute Book," Archives of The Church of Jesus Christ of Latter-day Saints, Salt Lake City, 43–44.
20. Doctrine and Covenants, Preface, Introduction, 6.
21. In Conference Report, April 1977, 115; or *Ensign*, May 1977, 78.
22. *Mormon Doctrine*, 2nd ed. [1966], 529–530.

23. Quoted in Daniel H. Ludlow, ed., *Latter-day Prophets Speak: Selections from the Sermons and Writings of Church Presidents* [1948], 166.

24. In *Journal of Discourses*, 18:110–111.

25. *Teachings of the Prophet Joseph Smith*, 232.

26. *History of the Church*, 1:207.

27. *History of the Church*, 1:221–224.

28. Far West Record: *Minutes of The Church of Jesus Christ of Latter-day Saints*, 1830–1844, 27.

29. *Church News*, 30 June 1979, 5.

30. As cited by President Ezra Taft Benson, in Conference Report, April 1978, 46; or *Ensign*, May 1978, 32.

31. In James R. Clark, comp., *Messages of the First Presidency of The Church of Jesus Christ of Latter-day Saints*, 5 vols., [1965–70], 1:257.

32. "May the Kingdom of God Go Forth," in Conference Report, April 1978, 46; or *Ensign*, May 1978, 33.

33. In Conference Report, October 1919, 146.

34. In Conference Report, October 1975, 48; or Ensign, November 1975, 34.

35. See Gospel Truth: *Discourses and Writings of President George Q. Cannon*, selected, arranged, and edited by Jerreld L. Newquist [1987], 217.

36. *History of the Church*, 6:152.

37. *Teachings of the Prophet Joseph Smith*, 156–157.

38. In Conference Report, April 1979, 3; or *Ensign*, May 1979, 4.

39. "When the World Will Be Converted," *Ensign*, October 1974, 7.

40. "May the Kingdom of God Go Forth," in Conference Report, April 1978, 47; or *Ensign*, May 1978, 33.

41. Smith, DS 3:29, 34; McConkie, in Conference Report, April 1979, 131–132; or *Ensign*, May 1979, 92–94.

42. In Conference Report, April 1951, 104.

43. In Ludlow, *A Companion to Your Study of the Doctrine and Covenants*, 2 vols. [1978], 1:50.

44. In Conference Report, October 1938, 105–106.

45. *History of the Church*, 1:314.

46. *Doctrines of Salvation*, 3:43.

47. *Ensign*, November 1979, 64.

48. *Teachings of the Prophet Joseph Smith*, 11–12.

49. In Conference Report, October 1973, 89; or *Ensign*, January 1974, 69.

The Doctrine and Covenants Testifies of Jesus Christ

(D&C 6; 19; 29; 38; 43; 45; 50; 76; 93; 133; 136)
[Topical Chapter]

৩০৫৪

INTRODUCTION

The Savior and His Atonement Are Central to the Doctrine and Covenants

● **D&C Introduction, 8th Paragraph The Doctrine and Covenants' witness of Jesus Christ.** As with the other standard works, the primary purpose of the Doctrine and Covenants is to witness of Jesus Christ. "The testimony that is given of Jesus Christ—His divinity, His majesty, His perfection, His love, and His redeeming power—makes this book of great value to the human family and of more worth than the riches of the whole earth."[1]

"THE LIVING CHRIST" ©JOSEPH BRICKEY, USED BY PERMISSION

● **D&C 50:41–44 "Fear not, little children ... I am in your midst."** The Savior here uses terms of tender endearment, calling us "little children" and assuring us that "you are mine, and I have overcome the world, and you are of them that my Father hath given me; and none of them that my Father hath given me shall be lost" (vv. 41–42). This is indeed comforting since, as Paul said: "If God be for us, who can be against us?" (Romans 8:31).

Just as the Savior and our Father are one in purpose and love, so too are we, as a people, one with the Savior (v. 43). He will not leave us alone or unprotected. He assures us that "I am in your midst, and I am the good shepherd, and the stone of Israel. He that buildeth upon this rock shall never fall" (v. 44). What's more, we have the assurance that "the day cometh that you shall hear my voice and see me, and know that I am" (v. 45).

For most of us, this will occur after death as we are welcomed with that most sought- after greeting: "Well done, thou good and faithful servant" (Matthew 25:21, 23). But for some, this will occur while they yet dwell upon this earth when their calling and election is made sure. Elder Bruce R. McConkie said: "We have the power—and it is our privilege—so to live, that becoming pure in heart, we shall see the face of God while we yet dwell as mortals in a world of sin and sorrow. This is the crowning blessing of mortality. It is offered by that God who is no respecter of persons to all the faithful in His kingdom."[2]

● **D&C 76:22–24 The Savior appears many times in the Doctrine and Covenants to instruct and bless His servants.** This is perhaps one of the most thrilling appearances. Joseph Smith and Sidney Rigdon had just seen the marvelous vision of the three kingdoms of glory, which included the sight of both the Father and Son sitting upon their thrones.

"And now, after the many testimonies which have been given of him, this is the testimony, last of all, which we give of him: That he lives! For we saw him, even on the right hand of God; and we heard the voice bearing record that He is the Only Begotten of the Father—That by him, and through him, and of him, the worlds are and were created, and the inhabitants thereof are begotten sons and daughters unto God."

This eyewitness account, and others contained in the Doctrine and Covenants, are at the very heart of the book's purpose. Elder Boyd K. Packer said: "[The Atonement of Jesus Christ] is the very root of Christian doctrine. You may know much about the gospel as it branches out from there, but if you only know the branches and those branches do not touch that root, if they have been cut free from that truth, there will be no life nor substance nor redemption in them."[3]

THE ATONEMENT OF JESUS CHRIST

The Doctrine and Covenants contains many revelations that can increase our understanding of the Atonement of Jesus Christ. These revelations give us a sense of the depth of the Savior's suffering and the magnitude of the love that He and Heavenly Father have for us. They also explain in some detail the principles behind the need for an atonement, a resurrection, and our individual repentance.

"THE ATONEMENT: C. BLOCH

The Atonement

● **D&C 19:16–20 The essence and scope of the Atonement.** The Savior here states the essence of the Atonement: "For behold, I, God, have suffered these things for all, that they might not suffer if they would repent; But if they would not repent they must suffer even as I; Which suffering caused myself, even God, the greatest of all, to tremble because of pain, and to bleed at every pore, and to suffer both body and spirit—and would that I might not drink the bitter cup, and shrink" (vv. 16–18). There are several doctrinal concepts here that we should not pass over lightly.

— *"I, God."* Jesus Christ was a God before He came to dwell on earth. He was a God when He suffered in Gethsemane. And He remains a God to this day (D&C 38:1–8).

— *"Suffered … for all."* Though not all men will take advantage of His suffering, and thus some of it will have been wasted, nevertheless, He suffered for the sins of all of God's children, on this and every other earth in all ages of time, as well as for the earth itself and all of its creatures.

Elder Bruce R. McConkie said: "Our Lord's jurisdiction and power extend far beyond the limits of this one small earth on which we dwell. He is, under the Father, the Creator of worlds without number (Moses 1:33). And through the power of His atonement the inhabitants of these worlds, the revelation says, 'are begotten sons and daughters unto God' (D&C 76:24), which means that the atonement of Christ, being literally and truly infinite, applies to an infinite number of earths."[4]

President Marion G. Romney taught that Christ is the Creator and Redeemer of the whole universe, and other than His mortal ministry accomplished on this earth, His role as Savior to other worlds and their inhabitants is the same as it is to this earth and its inhabitants.[5]

President Joseph Fielding Smith said: "Every mortal soul should be exceedingly grateful to the Redeemer of this world for the manifestation of His great love for each of us which is made manifest in His extreme suffering, which brings to us the resurrection of the dead—not only the resurrection of mankind, but of the earth itself and every creature that has dwelt or will dwell upon it in this mortal state."[6]

— *"Not suffer if they would repent."* If we fully and completely repent of our sins, we will not suffer for them. Christ has already done that.

— *"If not they must suffer even as I."* Rejecting the Savior means rejecting the gift of His Atonement. The depth of His suffering should teach us something about the price that must be paid for sin. That price is deeper and more difficult than we can even imagine. It caused Him, "even … the greatest all" to tremble because of pain.

As mortal beings, we cannot comprehend the severe mental and physical suffering that our Lord had to endure. This revelation sheds some light on the matter. It was so severe that blood came from every pore of His body and He cried out in agony to the Father for relief. But we cannot comprehend it. It is known only to Himself.[7]

As for our own suffering if we do not repent, we should not imagine that, if we did pay for our own sins, that we would thereafter be saved. Such is not the case. Bruce C. Hafen said: "Suppose some of us do not repent and, as a result, personally satisfy the law of justice by suffering in payment of our own transgressions. Would that place us in the same position with respect to our salvation and exaltation as those whose payment is made by Christ through operation of the law of mercy? If it would, why not lead a sinful life, accept the punishment for it, and still achieve salvation by our own responsibility? These questions lead us to explore the difference between repenting of our sins and paying for them."[8]

The Savior gives all the credit for His Atonement to the Father, stating clearly that He did it for the glory of the Father, not His own (v. 19), and for the redemption of all mankind. He did His duty and finished the task He had been given in the premortal world to provide the means of salvation to all of His Father's children. Having thus "purchased" us with His own blood, we have become subject to Him and dependent upon Him for our individual salvation. Therefore, He commands us "to repent, lest I humble you with my almighty power; and ... lest you suffer these punishments of which I have spoken" (v. 20).

● **D&C 18:10–11 Every soul is precious to the Savior.** He suffered for all souls, and therefore "the worth of souls is great in the sight of God" (v. 10). If His desire was to punish and destroy us, the best way to have accomplished that would have been not to atone for us. That would have condemned us to an eternity of suffering and an eternal loss of opportunity. But that was not His desire. His desire was (and remains) to save us. He wants us to succeed. He has done everything in His power to help us do so. He is not harsh and angry. He is good and merciful and willing to forgive. "For, behold, the Lord your Redeemer suffered death in the flesh [and] the pain of all men, that all men might repent and come unto him" (v. 11).

The Resurrection

● **D&C 88:14–16 Through His resurrection, the Lord provided a way for the spirit and body to be reunited and inseparably connected.** This was part of the redemption the Savior provided to us (v. 14). He explains that our entire "soul" consists of both our body and our spirit (v. 15), and that when we are resurrected our soul is thus redeemed (v. 16). Had this not been done, our spirits would have been condemned to an eternity without a body and our bodies would have disintegrated into dust, never to rise again (2 Nephi 9:7).

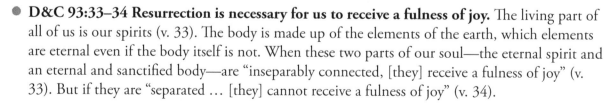

● **D&C 88:17–18 Resurrection is necessary in order to "sanctify" our bodies, cleansing them from "all unrighteousness"** (v. 18), which is not possible while they are in a mortal state. Thus, death and resurrection are actually a blessing, making it possible for us to inherit "celestial glory" (v. 18). And all of this is made possible "through him that quickeneth all things," which means the Creator of all life on earth—the Lord Jesus Christ (v. 17).

● **D&C 93:33–34 Resurrection is necessary for us to receive a fulness of joy.** The living part of all of us is our spirits (v. 33). The body is made up of the elements of the earth, which elements are eternal even if the body itself is not. When these two parts of our soul—the eternal spirit and an eternal and sanctified body—are "inseparably connected, [they] receive a fulness of joy" (v. 33). But if they are "separated ... [they] cannot receive a fulness of joy" (v. 34).

President Joseph F. Smith said: "We are begotten in the similitude of Christ Himself. We dwelt with the Father and with the Son in the beginning, as the sons and daughters of God; and at the time appointed, we came to this earth to take upon ourselves tabernacles, that we might become conformed to the likeness and image of Jesus Christ and become like Him; that we might have a tabernacle, that we might pass through death as He has passed through death, that we might rise again from the dead as He has risen from the dead."[9]

Why was this necessary in order to obtain a fulness of joy? Because, as President Joseph F. Smith further explained, "only resurrected and glorified beings can become parents of spirit offspring. Only such exalted souls have reached maturity in the appointed course of eternal life; and the spirits born to them in the eternal worlds will pass in due sequence through the several stages or estates by which the glorified parents have attained exaltation."[10]

— **Alma 11:42, 44** The resurrection is universal. Amulek taught that "all shall be raised from this temporal death … both old and young, both bond and free, both male and female, both the wicked and the righteous" (vv. 42, 44). Elder Bruce R. McConkie said: "Nothing is more absolutely universal than the resurrection. Every living being will be resurrected."[11]

B. PICART 1728

— **Alma 11:43** The resurrection is literal. Amulek also taught that "the spirit and the body shall be reunited again in its perfect form; both limb and joint shall be restored to its proper frame, even as we now are at this time" (v. 43). We are not talking about some spiritual awakening alone, but the actual physical rising of the dead from their graves, never to die again.

The Prophet Joseph Smith described what he saw in vision about the resurrection:

Would you think it strange that I relate what I have seen in vision in relation [to] this interesting theme… So plain was the vision I actually saw men before they had ascended from the tomb as though they were getting up slowly. They take each other by the hand … [exclaiming] my father and my son, my Mother and my daughter, my brother and my sister… Where is my father, my mother, my sister? They are by my side. I embrace them and they me… By the vision of the Almighty I have seen it… God has revealed His Son from the heavens and the doctrine of the resurrection also. We have a knowledge that those we bury here God [will] bring them up again, clothed upon and quickened by the spirit of the Great God.[12]

— **Alma 11:44** The resurrection is perfect. " … there shall not so much as a hair of their heads be lost; but every thing shall be restored to its perfect frame." We might ask, what does it mean to be raised to our "perfect frame?" Well for one thing, it means that we will be raised as perfectly whole physical beings with no deformities.

President Joseph Fielding Smith said: "There is no reason for any person to be concerned as to the appearance of individuals in the resurrection. Death is a purifying process as far as the body is concerned. We have reason to believe that the appearance of old age will disappear and the body will be restored with the full vigor of manhood and womanhood. Children will arise as children, for there is no growth in the grave. Children will continue to grow until they reach the full stature of their spirits. Anything contrary to this would be inconsistent. When our bodies are restored, they will appear to be in the full vigor of manhood and womanhood, for the condition of physical weakness will all be left behind in the grave."[13]

President Joseph F. Smith, speaking at the funeral of Sister Rachel Grant, the mother of President Heber J. Grant, promised: "Deformity will be removed; defects will be eliminated, and men and women shall attain to the perfection of their spirits, to the perfection that God designed in the beginning. It is His purpose that men and women, His children, born to become heirs of God, and joint heirs with Jesus Christ, shall be made perfect, physically as well as spiritually, through obedience to the law by which He has provided the means that perfection shall come to all His children…"[14]

Also, our "perfect frames" will not be identical. My genetic code is different than yours, and we will continue to have our own identity. I will rise as me, and you will rise as you, in every particular—but in a perfected and exalted state. Thus, He will return our bodies to us, not as they were—full of weaknesses, deformities, and pain—but strong and vigorous and beautiful. When we see men and women in the resurrection, Elder Melvin J. Ballard said, "we shall see them in the very bloom of their glorious manhood and womanhood … glorified, immortalized, celestialized, fitted to dwell in the presence of God."[15]

— **Alma 11:44** The resurrection precedes the judgment. All of God's children "in the body … shall be brought and be arraigned before the bar of Christ the Son, and God the Father, and the Holy Spirit … [and] judged according to their works, whether they be good or whether they be evil."

● **D&C 76:62–70 Those who come forth in the first resurrection inherit eternal life.**

They will enjoy a number of privileges because of their repentance and righteousness:

— They will dwell in the presence of God and His Christ forever and ever (v. 62).

— They will come with Christ when He descends in the clouds of heaven to reign on the earth over His people (v. 63).

— They will rise on the morning of the first resurrection (v. 64) with all the "just" (v. 65).

— They will dwell in Mount Zion (the New Jerusalem), the city of the living God (v. 66).

— They will enjoy the company of innumerable angels, of the people of Enoch, and of the Savior (the "Firstborn") (v. 67).

— Their names are "written in heaven" (in the Lamb's Book of Life), which contains the names of all those who will be exalted in the Celestial kingdom (v. 68).

— They are described as "just men, made perfect through Jesus." Note that while they are good, they are made perfect only through the atonement of Christ (v. 69).

— Their bodies will be celestial, radiating a glory like unto the brightness of the sun—the same glory that is possessed by God the Father, the highest of all (v. 70).

Repentance

● **D&C 18:11–12 The opportunity to repent was made possible by the Savior's suffering.** "For, behold, the Lord your Redeemer suffered death in the flesh; [and] suffered the pain of all men, that all men might [be able to] repent and come unto him" (v. 11). Likewise, "he hath risen again from the dead, that he might bring all men unto him, on conditions of repentance" (v. 12).

"THE MAN BORN BLIND," C. BLOCH

I fear that we may take too much for granted the opportunity to start over when we make mistakes. We would consider it "unfair" if our human weaknesses made it impossible for us to be saved because we all have them. But the truth is—God the Father cannot accept any degree of unrighteousness in His celestial realm. And were it not possible to repent and be forgiven, *none* of us would be savable. Praise be to the Savior, who, through His own suffering, made this possible for us.

● **D&C 58:42 When the Lord forgives, He also forgets.** He declares flatly here that "he who has repented of his sins, the same is forgiven, and I, the Lord, remember them no more." We do not need to worry about lingering guilt. God, the greatest of all, expunges our mistakes from His memory forever when we repent.

● **D&C 19:21–22 Repentance is the most important thing we can teach.** In fact, the Lord commands that we "preach naught [nothing] but repentance" (v. 21). If we attempt to teach the deeper doctrines of the atonement to those who are not aware of its basics, it will overwhelm them, "for they cannot bear meat now, but milk they must receive … lest they perish" (v. 22).

● **D&C 19:23 The atonement should bring us peace of mind.** "Learn of me," the Lord invites, "and listen to my words; walk in the meekness of my Spirit, and you shall have peace in me" (v. 23). Knowing that we can and will be completely forgiven of our repented sins makes God's plan truly a "plan of happiness." Were it not for this assurance, there could be no meaning to life and no true happiness in either this world or the next.

● **D&C 19:24 The plan of salvation came from the Father.** "I am Jesus Christ; I came by the will of the Father, and I do His will." We hear sometimes in the Church about some supposed contest in the premortal council between Christ and Satan, wherein each presented a plan and the Father chose the one proposed by Christ. This is one of what Elder Bruce R. McConkie called "heresies" in the Church:

> The plan of salvation is the gospel of the Father. The plan of salvation originated with the Father; He is the author and finisher of our faith in the final sense; He ordained the laws by obedience to which both we and Christ can become like Him. The Father did not ask for volunteers to propose a plan whereby man might be saved. What He did was ask whom He should send to be the Redeemer in the plan He devised. Christ and Lucifer both volunteered and the Lord chose His Firstborn and rejected the amendatory offer of the son of the morning. Thus Paul spoke of "the gospel of God, …

concerning his Son Jesus Christ our Lord, which was made of the seed of David, according to the flesh" (Romans 1:1–3). It is the Father's gospel, it became the gospel of the Son by adoption, and we call it after Christ's name because His atoning sacrifice put all of its terms and conditions into operation.[16]

● **D&C 34:3 Through the atonement, we are "children" of a loving Savior.** This may be confusing to some. God the Eternal Father is the father of our spirits, and we are, therefore, "children of God." How can we also be children of the Savior? We are His "children" in a number of ways. Our physical bodies belong to Him because they are made of the elements He created, and He is therefore the "father" of our bodies. In addition, this scripture says that, out of His pure love and mercy for us, "he gave His own life, that as many as would believe might become the sons of God." So in that sense, He has also purchased our entire souls with His atonement and resurrection. "Wherefore," He says, "you are my son." This does not change the fact that both we and the Savior are spiritual children of God the Father (John 20:17). It is meant to suggest that both our physical and our eternal life are made possible by the work performed by the Savior.

President Joseph Fielding Smith explained:

> What is a father? One who begets or gives life. What did our Savior do? He begot us, or gave us life from death, as clearly set forth by Jacob, the brother of Nephi. If it had not been for the death of our Savior, Jesus Christ, the spirit and body would never have been united again… If there had been no redemption from death our spirits would have been taken captive by Satan and we would have become subject to Satan's will forever. What did our Savior do? He begot us in that sense. He became a father to us because He gave us immortality or eternal life through His death and sacrifice upon the cross. I think we have a perfect right to speak of Him as Father.[17]

Christ Knows Our Sins, Needs, and Sorrows Perfectly

During His life and culminating in the Atonement, the Savior gained perfect empathy for us in all our sorrows, pains, and afflictions.

● **D&C 122:8 The Savior "descended below" all things in His life and atonement.** The Prophet Joseph Smith received several revelations while he was a prisoner in the jail at Liberty, Missouri. In answer to the Prophet's heartfelt pleadings ("O God, where art thou?") in D&C 121:1–7, the Lord answered him with encouragement and admonition. In the first seven verses of D&C 122, the Lord speaks of the Prophet Joseph's trials. Then in verse 8 the Lord speaks of Himself: "The Son of Man hath descended below them all. Art thou greater than he?" This is a reference not only to the trials and sufferings of His own mortal life, but more especially to His suffering in Gethsemane. That was His greatest trial and the one that required the help of a comforting angel to endure. By

taking upon Himself the weight of all of God's children's sorrow, pain, sin, and disappointment, He truly descended below all things.

- **D&C 62:1 Christ knows how to help us.** He "knoweth the weakness of man and how to succor them who are tempted." The word "succor" means to help. Because the Savior has experienced all our sorrows, pains, and afflictions for us, He understands perfectly how we feel and knows how to help us. Knowing this should increase our confidence in His love and mercy when we are suffering or sorrowing. Indeed, there is nobody else who can possibly know exactly what we are feeling at such times—except Him who has suffered those very pains and sorrows for us. He truly understands.

  — **Alma 7:11–12** Christ knows our weaknesses, sins, and sorrows because He has experienced them. In His own life, He suffered His own "pains and afflictions and temptations of every kind; and this that the word might be fulfilled which saith he will take upon him the pains and the sicknesses of his people" (v. 11). But that is not all. Through His suffering in Gethsemane, He also took upon Him our infirmities, "that his bowels may be filled with mercy, according to the flesh, that he may know according to the flesh how to succor his people according to their infirmities" (v. 12, emphasis added).

  Elder Neal A. Maxwell said: "Can we, even in the depths of disease, tell Him anything at all about suffering? In ways we cannot comprehend, our sicknesses and infirmities were borne by Him even before these were borne by us. The very weight of our combined sins caused Him to descend below all. We have never been, nor will we be, in depths such as He has known. Thus His atonement made His empathy and His capacity to succor us perfect, for which we can be everlastingly grateful as He tutors us in our trials."[18]

- **D&C 133:53 He carries us through our sorrows.** Even those of old, in the days of Enoch and Abraham and Moses, could turn to Him for help. "In all their afflictions he was afflicted. And the angel of his presence saved them; and in his love, and in his pity, he redeemed them, and bore them, and carried them all the days of old." President James E. Faust said concerning His willingness to carry our burdens: "Some injuries are so hurtful and deep that they cannot be healed without help from a higher power and hope for perfect justice and restitution in the next life. Since the Savior has suffered anything and everything that we could ever feel or experience (Alma 7:11), He can help the weak to become stronger. He has personally experienced all of it. He understands our pain and will walk with us even in our darkest hours… The evil influence of Satan would destroy any hope we have in overcoming our mistakes. He would have us feel that we are lost and that there is no hope. In contrast, Jesus reaches down to us to lift us up."[19]

THE SAVIOR'S ROLES AND ATTRIBUTES

The Prophet Joseph Smith said: "[To have faith in God, we must have] a correct idea of His character, perfections, and attributes" (Joseph Smith, comp., Lectures on Faith [1938], 3:4). The Doctrine and Covenants describes the Savior's attributes in some detail, giving us a better idea of His character. Indeed, we may learn more about the Savior's character and attributes from the Doctrine and Covenants than from any other source.

- **D&C 6:20 He will encircle us in the arms of His love.** This promise, given to those who are "faithful and diligent in keeping the commandments of God" will be literally fulfilled for each of them individually. Consider the witness of two modern Apostles who have had this experience.

President George F. Richards said: "More than 40 years ago I had a dream which I am sure was from the Lord. In this dream I was in the presence of my Savior as He stood in mid-air. He spoke no word to me, but my love for Him was such that I have not words to explain. I know no mortal man can love the Lord as I experienced that love for the Savior unless God reveals it to him. I would have remained in His presence, but there was a power drawing me away from Him. As a result of that dream, I had this feeling that no matter what might be required at my hands, what the Gospel might entail me, I would do what I should be asked to do even to the laying down of my life… If only I can be with my Savior and have that same sense of love that I had in that dream, it will be the goal of my existence, the desire of my life."[20]

Elder Melvin J. Ballard said: "I cannot begin this night to tell you what that means—to enjoy the blessings and privileges of dwelling in Christ's presence forever and ever. I know how the soul is thrilled; I know the feeling that comes by being in His presence for but a moment. I would give all that I am, all that I hope to be, to have the joy of His presence, to dwell in His love and His affection and to be in favor with the Master of all things forever and ever."[21]

- **D&C 6:21 He is the light that shines in the darkness.** This world is full of darkness, and the worldly do not comprehend the light that emanates from the Savior. Though He was the Son of God who came unto His own people, "[His] own received [Him] not." He compares Himself to a "light which shineth in darkness, and the darkness comprehendeth it not."

- **D&C 6:32–33 He acknowledges and appreciates and will reward all of our efforts to serve Him.** Wherever "two or three are gathered together in my name," He says, "there will I be in the midst of them" (v. 32). He encourages us to "do good," knowing that "whatsoever ye sow, that shall ye also reap; therefore, if ye sow good ye shall also reap good for your reward" (v. 33).

Shortly after his ordination as our new president and prophet, President Gordon B. Hinckley said: "No calling in this church is small or of little consequence. All of us in the pursuit of our duty touch the lives of others… You have as great an opportunity for satisfaction in the performance of your duty as I do in mine. The progress of this work will be determined by our joint efforts. Whatever your calling, it is as fraught with the same kind of opportunity to accomplish good as is mine. What is really important is that this is the work of the Master. Our work is to go about doing good as did He."[22]

D&C 6:34–36 He offers us protection, assurance, comfort, and consolation in these troubled times. Again we hear sweet terms of endearment as He says, "… fear not, little flock; do good; let earth and hell combine against you, for if ye are built upon my rock, they cannot prevail" (v. 34). We can take great courage in this prophecy as we see the forces of evil gathering all around us to destroy everything that is good and to reign with blood and horror upon the earth. It is clear from this prophecy, and many others like it, that God will overrule them. The ultimate triumph of God's work is assured (1 Nephi 22:27).

When I read this scripture and others like it, I am reminded of a high priests meeting I attended recently wherein my brethren were speaking ominously of the rise of radical terrorists and their plans to destroy us. I said: "Brethren, those men are doomed. No matter how powerful they may think they are, God is more powerful still, and the prophecies are clear. The work of God will triumph and all such forces of evil will be utterly destroyed." While developments can and will be troubling, Elder Ezra Taft Benson said he hoped "that we will keep ever burning in our hearts the spirit of this great work which we represent. If we do so, we'll have no anxiety; we'll have no fear; we'll not worry about the future because the Lord has given us the assurance that if we live righteously, if we keep His commandments, if we humble ourselves before Him, all will be well… Though times become perilous, even though we be surrounded by temptation and sin, even though there be a feeling of insecurity, even though men's hearts may fail them and anxiety fill their souls, if we only trust in God and keep His commandments we need have no fear."[23]

Though He knows our weakness He says with compassion, "I do not condemn you; go your ways and sin no more; perform with soberness the work which I have commanded you. Look unto me in every thought; doubt not, fear not" (vv. 35–36). "All that the Latter-day Saints have to do is to be quiet, careful and wise before the Lord, watch the signs of the times, and be true and faithful; and when [we] get through [we] will understand many things [we] do not today."[24]

D&C 6:37 He reminds us that He has atoned for our sins and we will be saved.
Lest we should forget, He reminds us of the "wounds which pierced my side, and also the prints of the nails in my hands and feet"—those five special tokens of His sacrifice—and promises that if we will "be faithful, [and] keep my commandments … [we] shall inherit the kingdom of heaven." I love these assurances. They offer all the assurance we need that our efforts, though imperfect, will be sufficient to save us through His merciful atonement.

D&C 19:1 His names reveal His divinity. The names of our Savior are numerous and highly symbolic. Donald W. Parry, Jay A. Parry, and Tina M. Peterson identified 94 different names given to the Savior in the book of Isaiah alone.[25] And John W. Welch identified 33 names for Christ in the Book of Mormon.[26]

In this verse, the Savior uses several of His names to impress upon us His ability to accomplish His purposes and to destroy the works of Satan.

— *I AM:* The name Jehovah means "I Am," the "Self- Existent One," or "The Eternal." It is written in our Old Testament as "Lord" in capital letters. The reason for this was that, according to ancient Jewish practice, the name Jehovah or I Am was not to be spoken for fear of incurring divine wrath.

— *Alpha and Omega:* These are the first and last letters of the Greek alphabet, used widely at the time of Christ. This figure of speech would be the equivalent of the modern English expression "from A to Z." The meaning of the title Alpha and Omega is that "in Him all things are encompassed."

— *Christ the Lord:* Paul uses the Old Testament, mainly the Psalms, to show that Jesus was and is our Lord—meaning our God and King. He is the firstborn Son of the Father, and His royal birthright makes Him preeminent among all the children of God and second only to the Father Himself.

— *Redeemer of the world:* No person can go back into the presence of God except through the power of Christ's atonement, which makes it all possible. That is why He is called the Redeemer: He intercedes for all of us through His atoning act.

● **D&C 19:2–3 He has subdued all things.** Because He accomplished and finished the atonement—"the will of Him whose I am, even the Father, concerning me"—He has now "subdue[d] all things unto myself" (v. 2). There is no force on earth or in the wide expanse of the universe that is not now subject to Him, and He has "retain[ed] all power, even to the destroying of Satan and his works at the end of the world" (v. 3). The outcome is certain, and we need not fear.

● **D&C 19:3 He will judge all men.** On "the last great day of judgment" He will judge "every man according to his works and the deeds which he hath done." We should find great comfort in this, since (as mentioned earlier in this chapter) He and He alone knows us perfectly and can judge our motives and our circumstances accordingly. Having literally "walked in our shoes" by bearing our burdens, our temptations, our sorrows, our sicknesses, as well as our sins, His assessment will be perfectly just. You and I will not be judged by our neighbors or by those who inappropriately take judgment unto themselves. We will be judged by the one Perfect Judge— and Him alone.

● **D&C 29:1 His mercy has atoned for our sins.** His motives are pure. He willingly suffered for our sakes, with pure charity and a desire to save us. He is the great I AM, but He is also our personal Redeemer.

● **D&C 29:2 He will gather His people and protect them.** Loving them as a mother hen loves her little chicks, He will "gather his people"—those who will "hearken to my voice and humble themselves before me, and call upon me in mighty prayer"—under His "wings" of mercy and protection as the world cycles rapidly down into destruction.

● **D&C 38:1–2 He knows all things.** With the perfect omniscience of a God, He "looked upon the wide expanse of eternity, and all the seraphic hosts of heaven, before the world was made" (v. 1), and He knew "all things" in advance because "all things are present before mine eyes" (v. 2).

- **D&C 38:3 He is the Creator of the world.** He "spake, and the world was made" through the power of His faith and the obedience which all the elements show unto Him (Helaman 12:7–17). His was the intelligence and driving force behind the creation, "and all things came by [Him]." Elder Joseph Fielding Smith said: "The dust of the earth is obedient... Everything in the universe obeys the law given unto it... Everywhere you look you find law and order, the elements obeying the law given to them, true to their calling."27

- **D&C 43:34 He is the Savior of the world.** He invites us to "treasure these things up in your hearts, and let the solemnities of eternity rest upon your minds." In other words, keep an eternal perspective on things, knowing that all eternity is in the control of our God, and He has done all that is necessary to save us if we will do our part.

- **D&C 45:3–5 He is our Advocate with the Father.** This is a wonderfully personal description of how the Savior will save us. He describes the scene when we will be found standing next to Him before the Father, ready for judgment. He assures us that He will be there "pleading your cause before him" (v. 3). He will remind the Father that He—the Savior—suffered and died despite the fact that He was sinless and deserved no such punishment. He will remind the Father of His own spilled blood and death, which was done "that thyself [God the Father] might be glorified" (v. 4). And then He will say on our behalf, "Wherefore, Father, spare these my brethren that believe on my name, that they may come unto me and have everlasting life" (v. 5). In other words, He will plead our case at the judgment and we will be reconciled unto the Father because He has met the demands of justice on our behalf. We will, no doubt, fall to our knees in gratitude for His advocacy on that day.

There are a number of places in the Doctrine and Covenants where the Lord describes Himself as our advocate—D&C 29:5; D&C 45:3–5; D&C 62:1; and D&C 110:4—and each of them adds a different dimension to this important role He plays in our lives.

- **D&C 50:44 He is the Good Shepherd.** To fully appreciate what a "good shepherd" does, and therefore to understand our relationship with the Lord, we turn to this description provided by Joseph Fielding McConkie:

> By day or night a good shepherd would always be found with his sheep. With the rising of the sun in the morning, if his sheep were sharing a communal fold he would call them forth, each shepherd in turn doing so by name (John 10:3–4)... In the lands of the Bible, today as anciently, the shepherd will be found leading his sheep rather than driving them (John 10:4). It is his duty to protect the flock from wild animals (1 Sam. 17:34–35) and robbers (John 10:1). While they graze he will call them from time

to time to assure them that he is near. While the sheep hear his voice they continue grazing, but should they instead hear the voice of another they become startled and begin to scatter. Should a sheep stray, the shepherd will search until it is found (Luke 15:4). As the sun begins to set, the good shepherd will lead his sheep to a place of shelter and protection, either a fold or a natural enclosure, where he will assure himself that none have been lost (Jeremiah 33:13).[28]

● **D&C 50:44 He is the Stone of Israel—the foundation upon which we should build.** This figure of speech is referring to the Chief Cornerstone of the Kingdom—Christ—who provides a solid anchor to all who dwell in that kingdom. "He that buildeth upon this rock shall never fall." The image of a stone, symbolizing a stabilizing anchor, is used repeatedly throughout the scriptures. The central symbol in all such metaphors is the Savior, whom Paul identified as "the chief corner stone" of God's Kingdom (Eph. 2:20). The Psalmist declared: "I will praise thee: for thou hast heard me, and art become my salvation. The stone which the builders refused is become the head stone of the corner" (Ps. 118:21–22; compare Matt. 21:42; Mark 12:10; Luke 20:17; Acts 4:11; 1 Pet. 2:7).

● **D&C 76:5 He is merciful and gracious to those who fear Him.** The word "fear" here does not mean to "be afraid." To fear God is to feel reverence and awe for Him and to obey His commandments.[29]

● **D&C 76:5 He delights to honor those who serve Him in righteousness and truth to the end.** His joy comes from seeing us do well.

● **D&C 93:2 He is the source of the light of Christ.** The Savior identifies Himself as

"the true light that lighteth every man that cometh into the world." This "light of Christ" is given to every person who comes into this world, and is their guiding influence for good, long before they become subject to the Holy Spirit and whether or not they know anything at all about God or His plan of salvation. It is the evidence of a loving God who does not leave His children alone in this world. If they will give heed to it, it will lead them away from evil and protect them.

— **Moroni 7:13**, 16–19 The light of Christ is sometimes referred to as our conscience, because it "inviteth and enticeth to do good continually" (v. 13). It is "given to every man, that he may know good from evil" (v. 16). By this means, every man has the power to distinguish between good and evil, and is left without excuse if he chooses evil (vv. 16–17) or if he rejects that which is good (vv. 18–19).

— The light of Christ should not be confused with the Holy Ghost. The light of Christ is not a person. It is an influence that comes from God and prepares a person to receive the Holy Ghost. It is an influence for good in the lives of all people (John 1:9; D&C 84:46–47). As people learn more about the gospel, their consciences become more sensitive (Moro. 7:12–19). People who hearken to the light of Christ are led to the gospel of Jesus Christ (D&C 84:46–48)."[30]

— **D&C 88:12–13 The light of Christ does much more than provide a conscience.** This little-understood power, which emanates from the Savior Himself, accomplishes a number of incredible things that are described in this scripture. We will discuss them in greater detail in a later chapter that includes this revelation (D&C 88).

- It "proceed[s] forth from the presence of God."

- It "fill[s] the immensity of space."

- It is "the light which is in all things."

- It "giveth life to all things."

- It is "the law by which all things are governed."

- It is "the power of God who sitteth upon his throne."

● **D&C 93:5–19 John the Beloved's list of the Savior's roles.** This set of scriptures cannot be found in the Bible but was written by the Beloved Disciple at some point in his ministry. In this revelation, it is given to the Prophet Joseph Smith by the Savior.

— He "was in the beginning, before the world was" (v. 7).
— His role was to be the "the Word, even the messenger of salvation" (v. 8).
— He is the light and the Redeemer of the world (v. 9).
— He is the Spirit of truth (v. 9).
— He came into the world, because the world was made by Him (v. 9).
— He is the source of life (v. 9).
— He is the source of light (v. 9).
— The worlds were made by Him (v. 10).
— All men were made by Him (v. 10).
— All things were made by Him, and through Him, and of Him (v. 10).
— He is the Only Begotten of the Father (in the flesh) (v. 11).
— He is full of grace (v. 11).
— He is full of truth, even the Spirit of truth (v. 11).
— He came and dwelt in the flesh, and dwelt among us (v. 11).
— He received not of the fulness at the first (v. 12).
— He received grace for grace, and continued until He received a fulness (vv. 12–13).
— He was called the Son of God (v. 14).
— The heavens were opened, and the Holy Ghost descended upon Him in the form of a dove, and sat upon Him (v. 15).
— There came a voice out of heaven saying: This is my beloved Son (v. 15).
— He eventually received a fulness of the glory of the Father (v. 16).
— He received all power, both in heaven and on earth (v. 17).
— The glory of the Father was with Him, for He dwelt in Him (v. 17).

The Lord promises that "if you are faithful you shall receive the fulness of the record of John" (v. 18). But He gave us this partial list "that you may understand and know how to worship, and know what you worship, that you may come unto the Father in my name, and in due time receive of his fulness" (v. 19).

THE SAVIOR'S SECOND COMING

We will devote an entire chapter to this topic later, but for now we can consider the attributes of our Lord when He descends in great power at the Second Coming. It will be a day of great contrasts—a day of fear and destruction for the wicked, and a day of rejoicing and peace for the righteous.

- **D&C 133:42–45 His loving-kindness and goodness to those whom He has redeemed.** At the Second Coming, His "adversaries and all nations shall tremble" because of the "terrible things" they will experience (vv. 42–43). The very mountains will "flow down at [His] presence" (v. 44). Yet despite the terribleness of that day for the wicked, it will be a day of great rejoicing for "him who rejoiceth and worketh righteousness, who remembereth thee in thy ways" (v. 44). The blessings He has prepared for the righteous are so great and unimaginable that men have never heard nor seen anything like them (v. 45).

- **D&C 133:46–49 His glory at the Second Coming will be brighter than the sun.** When He descends from heaven with His "dyed garments … clothed in his glorious apparel, traveling in the greatness of his strength" (v. 46), He will be "red in his apparel, and his garments like him that treadeth in the wine-vat" (v. 48). "And so great shall be the glory of his presence that the sun shall hide his face in shame, and the moon shall withhold its light, and the stars shall be hurled from their places" (v. 49).

- **D&C 133:50–51 He will administer vengeance upon the wicked.** He will declare, "I have trodden the wine-press alone, and have brought judgment upon all people" (v. 50). As for the wicked, He will declare, "I have trampled them in my fury, and I did tread upon them in mine anger, and their blood have I sprinkled upon my garments, and stained all my raiment; for this was the day of vengeance which was in my heart" (v. 51).

- **D&C 133:52 The righteous will receive His loving kindness.** On that great day of the Lord's coming, the righteous "shall mention the loving kindness of their Lord, and all that he has bestowed upon them according to his goodness … forever and ever."

Elder Joseph Fielding Smith said: "Isaiah has pictured this great day when the Lord shall come with His garments, or apparel, red and glorious, to take vengeance on the ungodly (Isa. 64:1–6). This will be a day of mourning to the wicked, but a day of gladness to all who have kept His commandments. Do not let anyone think that this is merely figurative language, it is literal, and as surely as we live that day of wrath will come when the cup of iniquity is full. We have received a great many warnings. The great day of the Millennium will come in; the wicked will be consumed and peace and righteousness will dwell upon all the face of the earth for one thousand years."[31]

- **D&C 136:22 He will deliver and protect the righteous with great power.** This is the same God "who led the children of Israel out of the land of Egypt" with miracles and great power, "and my arm is stretched out [again] in the last days, to save my people Israel." As we observe the great destruction of the wicked around the world, we can stand in holy places, where we will be blessed with the wisdom and warnings we need to abide the day.

CONCLUSION

The purpose of this chapter was to summarize some of the many revelations to be found in the Doctrine and Covenants that testify of the mission and attributes of the Lord Jesus Christ. This modern book of scripture is yet another "testament" of Jesus Christ. Indeed, every revelation found in the Doctrine and Covenants came from Him and bears the unmistakable impress of His voice and character.

- **D&C 18:34–36 The Doctrine and Covenants contains the words of Christ.** Bearing witness of the divine source of these revelations, the Lord declared, "These words are not of men nor of man, but of me; wherefore, you shall testify they are of me and not of man; For it is my voice which speaketh them unto you; for they are given by my Spirit unto you, and by my power you can read them one to another; and save it were by my power you could not have them; Wherefore, you can testify that you have heard my voice, and know my words."

- **D&C 19:23 The words of Christ bring us peace.** "Learn of me," He invites, "and listen to my words; walk in the meekness of my Spirit, and you shall have peace in me."

- **D&C 59:23 "Peace in this world, and eternal life in the world to come" is the promised reward of listening to His words and repenting of our sins.** How thankful we should be that we have this rich source of His words—the Doctrine and Covenants—to guide us in our quest to obtain those promised blessings.

Notes:

1. Explanatory Introduction, The Doctrine and Covenants [1981], paragraph 8.
2. In Conference Report, October 1977, 52; or *Ensign*, November 1977, 34.
3. In Conference Report, April 1977, 80; or *Ensign*, May 1977, 56.
4. *Mormon Doctrine,* 2nd ed. [1966], 65.
5. As quoted in Robert G. Mouritsen, "I Have a Question," *Ensign*, April 1976, 32.
6. *Answers to Gospel Questions,* comp. Joseph Fielding Smith Jr., 5 vols. [1957–1966], 5:93.
7. See *Answers to Gospel Questions*, 5:15.
8. *The Broken Heart: Applying the Atonement to Life's Experiences* [1989], 148.
9. *Gospel Doctrine,* 5th ed. [1939], 428–429.

10. *Improvement Era*, Vol. 19, 942; or Gospel Doctrine, 69–70.

11. *Mormon Doctrine*, 638.

12. In Scott H. Faulring (ed.), *The Diaries and Journals of Joseph Smith: An American Prophet's Record* [1989], 366–367.

13. *Answers to Gospel Questions*, 4:185.

14. As quoted in *Answers to Gospel Questions*, 4:187–188.

15. Bryant S. Hinckley, *Sermons and Missionary Services of Elder Melvin J. Ballard* [1949], 186.

16. "Our Relationship with the Lord," in *Brigham Young University Devotional and Fireside Speeches* (March 2, 1982).

17. *Answers to Gospel Questions*, 4:177–179.

18. *Ensign*, November 1981, 8.

19. "The Atonement: Our Greatest Hope," *Ensign*, November 2001, 20.

20. In Conference Report, October 1946, 139; or *Ensign*, May 1974, 119.

21. *Sermons and Missionary Services of Elder Melvin J. Ballard*, 245.

22. "This Is the Work of the Master," *Ensign*, May 1995, 71; or Teachings of Gordon B. Hinckley [1997], 65–66.

23. In Conference Report, October 1950, 145–146.

24. Wilford Woodruff, *Millennial Star*, 24 November 1890, 740.

25. Understanding Isaiah [1998], 595–596.

26. "Ten Testimonies of Jesus Christ from the Book of Mormon," in *Doctrines of the Book of Mormon: The 1991 Sperry Symposium*, ed. Bruce A. Van Orden and Brent L. Top [1992], 223–242.

27. In Conference Report, April 1929, 54–55.

28. "Special Witnesses of the Birth of Christ," in *Sydney B. Sperry Symposium*, (1987), 179–193.

29. "Fear," LDS Bible Dictionary, 672.

30. "Light of Christ," LDS Bible Dictionary, 725.

31. *Church History and Modern Revelation*, 4 vols. [1946–1949], 1:191–192.

New England & New York Period

[1820–1831]

☙◎❧

The Smith Family in New England

All but one of Joseph Smith Sr. And Lucy Mack Smith's eleven children were born in New England. They buried their firstborn son (unnamed) and another son, Ephraim, in unknown cemeteries. That left eight children in the family by the time they moved to western New York in the last months of 1816—Alvin (18), Hyrum (16), Sophronia (13), Joseph (10), Samuel (8), William (5), Catharine (4), and Don Carlos (8 months). Lucy, the mother, was 40 years old at the time.

Life was not easy for the Smith family. They moved eight different times in the first nineteen years of marriage in New England, though none of those moves was for more than forty miles at a time.

All are around or near the upper Connecticut River or one of its tributaries—the towns of Tunbridge, Randolph, Royalton, Sharon, and Norwich in the state of Vermont, and the town of Lebanon in New Hampshire (See the map immediately following this introduction). The Prophet Joseph Smith was born on December 23, 1805, in Sharon, Vermont.

Joseph Smith birthplace monument at Sharon, Vermont

The Smiths were a close-knit and hard-working family. Their love and devotion were essential to their survival, and their parents taught them to trust and depend on each other. The legendary stories of Joseph in 1813 (age 8), with his brother Hyrum sitting by his side and applying pressure to his badly diseased leg, and his later wanting to be held by his father during leg surgery, reveal the deep level of love that they shared. This theme repeated itself throughout their lives.

At each new location in New England, the Smiths worked hard and sought stability, but each time their circumstances left them struggling for temporal security. The Lord was not going to prosper them in New England; He needed them elsewhere, in Western New York where the Nephite record lay buried in the Hill Cumorah.

Their final year in New England, 1816, was arguably the worst. The family had already experienced three crop failures when, in 1816, summertime arrived but summer didn't, snowing right on through June, July, and August. This "year without a summer" was not unique to New England. It actually happened in many parts of the world in 1816 as a result of the eruption of Mount Tambora in the East Indies, which produced massive dust and ash clouds that blocked sunlight and darkened the Earth.

With their crops once again wiped out, and with no other way to survive in their native New England, the Smiths decided to move to Western New York, where land was plentiful and crops were good for those willing to work hard. As did many others in New England at the time, they packed up their wagon and headed west.

The Restoration Accelerates in New York

Once the Smith family had relocated in Manchester (Palmyra), New York, the restoration timeline accelerated. The events that occurred there will be discussed in more detail as part of the chapters for this period of time, and a detailed summary appears at the end of this (and every) section introduction. Since our course of study includes both Church History and the Doctrine and Covenants, historical summaries are provided for each chapter. The associated revelations and the years during which they occurred are also summarized at the beginning of each chapter. But I have provided a quick summary of the revelations contained in Section I of this manual to illustrate the accelerated pace of the Lord's work once Joseph and his family were in place in Western New York.

Year	Month	Revelations (D&C #)	Place
1823	September	2	Manchester, New York
1828	July	3	Harmony, PA
1828	Summer	10	Harmony, PA
1829	February	4	Harmony, PA
1829	March	5	Harmony, PA
1829	April	6, 7, 8	Harmony, PA
1829	May	11, 12, 13	Harmony, PA
1829	June	14, 15, 16, 17, 18	Fayette, NY
1830	March	19	Manchester, NY
1830	April	20, 21	Fayette, NY
1830	April	22, 23	Manchester, NY
1830	July	24, 25, 26	Harmony, PA.
1830	August	27	Harmony, PA.
1830	September	28, 29, 30, 31	Fayette, NY
1830	October	32, 33	Fayette, NY
1830	November	34	Fayette, NY
1830	December	35, 36, 37	Fayette, NY
1831	January	38, 39, 40	Fayette, NY

One item of particular interest stands out in the summaries provided with each section introduction—the extraordinary youth of the Prophet Joseph Smith during all of these events. As a young boy, and later as a very young man, he experienced profoundly spiritual events and was called upon to show great wisdom and judgment. The influence of the Lord in his life is obvious when one considers his extraordinary youth and inexperience.

Map of Early Church History Sites in New England, New York, and Pennsylvania

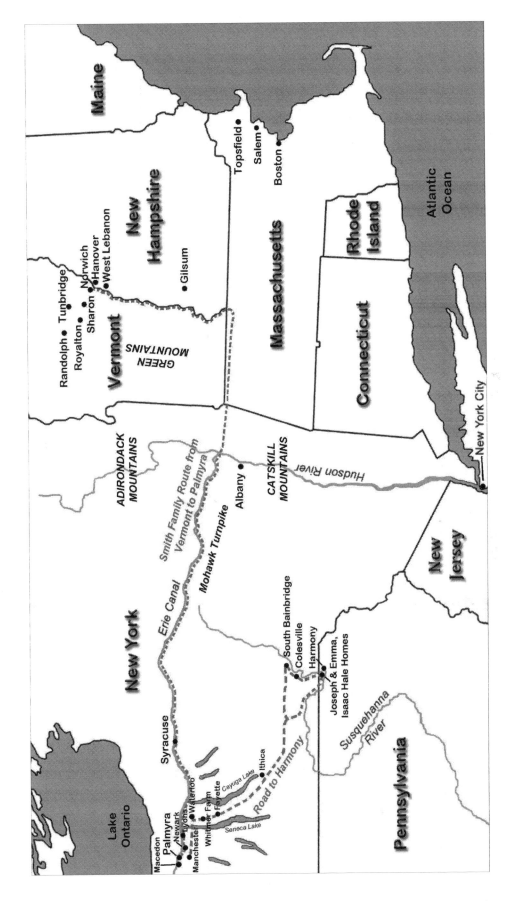

©RANDAL S. CHASE, 2006-0709

Church History Chronology
New England & New York Period

PLACE:	DATE:	EVENT:	AGE OF THE PROPHET
		Smith Family Events Prior to the Restoration:	
Tunbridge, VT	1796 Jan	Joseph's parents are married and start a farm in Tunbridge, Vermont	
Randolph, VT	1802	Joseph's parents sell their farm and open a store in Randolph	
	1805	Joseph's parents lose everything due to a dishonest partner	
Sharon, VT	**1805 Dec 23**	**Joseph Smith is born** and is named after his father, fulfilling ancient prophecy	
Tunbridge, VT	1807 Mar	Joseph's family moves back to Tunbridge, Vermont.	1
South Royalton, VT	1808-1810	Joseph's family moves to South Royalton, Vermont.	2
West Lebanon, NH	1812 May	Joseph's family moves again—to West Lebanon (near the only surgeon who could save his leg).	6
	1813	Joseph contracts typhus fever, nearly loses his leg, has surgery without anesthetic.	8
Salem, Mass	1814	Joseph stays with his uncle Jesse Smith while recovering from his operation	
Norwich, VT	1815 May	Joseph's family moves to Norwich, Vermont, and rents a farm.	9
	1816 June	Tambora volcano erupts on Sumbawa—ash circles the Earth	
	Fall	"Year without a summer" results—snow falls in summer—resulting in a third crop failure.	10
		Joseph Smith Sr. leaves the family to search for better living conditions in western New York	
Palmyra, NY	1817 Jan	Smiths move to Main Street in Palmyra, New York.	11
	1818	Revival fever sweeps the eastern U.S.; Joseph begins searching scriptures for answers.	12
	1819 Apr	The Smiths obtain their own farm in Manchester township, south of Palmyra.	13
		Events of the Restoration:	
	1820 **Spring**	**The First Vision occurs—the Father and Son appear to Joseph.**	14
	1823 Sep 21-22	The Angel Moroni visits Joseph 3 times in one night and again the next morning (see D&C 2).	17
	Nov	Joseph's oldest brother Alvin dies suddenly	
	1824 Sep 22	Joseph meets the Angel Moroni at the Hill Cumorah.	18
	1825 Sep 22	Joseph meets the Angel Moroni at the Hill Cumorah.	19
Harmony, PA	Sep	Joseph & his father accept gold digging job in Harmony, PA	
		Joseph meets Emma Hale, daughter of the man in whose home they boarded	

Church History Chronology — New England & New York Period (Cont'd.)

PLACE:	DATE:		EVENT:	REVELATION RECEIVED	AGE OF THE PROPHET
Palmyra, NY	1826	Jan	Joseph's parents lose their farm again, move back into their log cabin home		20
		Mar	Joseph's first harassing lawsuit in South Bainbridge, NY—for being a "disorderly person"		
		Sep 22	Joseph meets the Angel Moroni at the Hill Cumorah		
So. Bainbridge, NY Palmyra, NY	1827	Jan 18	Joseph and Emma elope and are married by Esq. Tarble at Mr. Stowell's home		21
			Joseph and Emma move north, live with the Smiths in Palmyra		
		Sep 22	Joseph receives the Book of Mormon plates from the Angel Moroni at the Hill Cumorah		
Harmony, PA			Persecution makes translation impossible in Palmyra		22
		Dec 27	Joseph & Emma move back to Harmony; Joseph begins copying BOM characters		
	1828	Jan	Book of Mormon translation begins (first 116 pages) with Emma as scribe as time permits		
New York City, NY		Feb 28	Martin Harris takes a sample of the writing on the plates to Professor Anthon		
Harmony, PA		Apr 12	Book of Mormon translation begins again with Martin Harris as the scribe		
		June	Martin Harris loses the 116 pages after begging Joseph to let him show them to his family		
		June 15	Joseph and Emma's first child, whom they named Alvin, is born and dies the same day		
		July	Joseph receives a revelation condemning him for his careless loss of the 116 pages	D&C 3	
			The Angel Moroni takes the plates away from Joseph until he fully repents	D&C 10	
		Summer	Due to the secret plans of conspirators, Joseph is not to re-translate the 116 pages		
		Sep	The plates are returned and re-translation begins but is painfully slow		
	1829	Feb	Joseph's family comes to Harmony for a visit		23
		Mar	Martin Harris visits Harmony, seeking forgiveness	D&C 4	
		Apr 7	Oliver Cowdery arrives in answer to Joseph's prayer for an able scribe	D&C 5	
			Book of Mormon translation begins again, with Oliver Cowdery as scribe	D&C 6–9	
		May	Hyrum Smith & Joseph Knight are given personal direction through revelation	D&C 11–12	
		May 15	Aaronic Priesthood received from John the Baptist	D&C 13	
			Book of Mormon Translated—65 days		
			The first baptisms occur as Joseph and Oliver baptize each other		
		May-June	Melchizedek Priesthood received from Peter, James & John near Colesville, NY		
Fayette, NY		June	Persecution forces Joseph & Emma to move to Fayette; David Whitmer retrieves them	D&C 14–16	
			Book of Mormon translation completed (after only 65 days)	D&C 17–18	
			Three Witnesses see the Angel Moroni and the plates		
Palmyra, NY		June 11	Book of Mormon printing begins; Thomas B. Marsh arrives in Palmyra; baptized 1 year later		
		Sep			
		Oct 8	Joseph & Oliver Cowdery purchase a King James Bible/Apocrypha for use with JST		
Fayette, NY	1830	Mar 26	Book of Mormon printing is finished; Martin Harris mortgages his farm to pay for printing	D&C 19	24
		Apr 6	The Church is organized; revelations received on Church organization and government	D&C 20–21	
			All who wish to be members—Joseph, Oliver, Joseph's parents, Martin Harris, etc.—are baptized		
			Revelation received on the need for authorized baptism; 5 separate callings received also	D&C 22–23	
			Joseph and Emma quietly return to Harmony, PA		
Fayette, NY		June 1	The 1st conference of the Church is held in Fayette		
			First ordained missionary sent (Samuel H. Smith); B.Young & H.C. Kimball join @ Mendon, NY		
Harmony, PA		June	JST: Joseph records the vision of Moses (became Moses 1 in the Pearl of Great Price)	Moses 1	

Church History Chronology — New England & New York Period (Cont'd.)

PLACE:	DATE:	EVENT:	REVELATION RECEIVED	AGE OF THE PROPHET
Colesville, NY	**1830** June 28	Emma Smith is baptized along with many of the Colesville Saints amid severe persecutions.		24
	July	Revelation given to Oliver Cowdery; he is to receive doctrine from Joseph, not give it to him.	D&C 24	
		Revelation given to Emma Smith; she is to sustain Joseph, collect hymns, beware of pride.	D&C 25	
		Revelation given concerning the law of common consent (sustaining by members).	D&C 26	
	Aug	Persecution becomes intense; more converts baptized; two revelations about the sacrament.	D&C 27	
		Joseph and Emma leave Harmony for the last time, leaving all earthly possessions behind		
		Emma is pregnant again—this time with twins; they travel over hot, dusty, bumpy roads		
Fayette, NY	Sep 1	The 2nd conference of the Church is held in Fayette; Parley P. Pratt is baptized		
	3	Thomas B. Marsh baptized by David Whitmer and ordained an elder by Oliver Cowdery		
		A revelation to Oliver about Hiram Page; only the prophet receives revelation for the Church.	D&C 28	
		A revelation of important doctrines: 2nd Coming, pre-existence, the fall, and the atonement.	D&C 29	
		Missionaries (including Oliver Cowdery) are sent west to teach the Lamanites.	D&C 30–31	
	19	Orson Pratt is taught and baptized by his brother Parley		
	Oct	Additional missionaries are called to the work.	D&C 32–33	
	21	JST completed up to Genesis 5:28 (manuscript bears this date)	JST Gen. 2–5	
Kirtland, OH		In Kirtland, Ohio, the missionaries convert Sidney Rigdon and his congregation		
Fayette, NY	Nov 4	Orson Pratt visits the Prophet in Fayette and receives a revelation through the Prophet.	D&C 34	
		Severe winter sets in with 4 feet of snow and freezing rain		
	Dec 10	Sidney Rigdon and Edward Partridge arrive in New York and meet the Prophet for the first time		
		Revelation to Sidney Rigdon; He is called to act as scribe for Joseph Smith on the JST (v. 20).	D&C 35	
		Revelation to Edward Partridge.	D&C 36	
		The Saints are commanded to gather to Kirtland, Ohio.	D&C 37	
		JST: "Prophecy of Enoch" received (History of the Church, 1:131–133).	Moses 7; JST Gen. 7	25
Kirtland, OH	**1831** Jan 1	At the 3rd conference of the Church, revelations given on gathering & forsaking the world.	D&C 38–40	
		The revelation to move to Kirtland is announced.		
		Joseph & Emma travel to Kirtland in bitter cold weather over immense drifts of snow in a sleigh.		
		Emma is now at least 6 months pregnant with her twins.		
Jackson County, MO		The missionaries to the Lamanites arrive in Missouri.		

CHAPTER 3

Joseph Smith's First Vision

(Joseph Smith–History 1–25)
[1820]

ജ∞യ

INTRODUCTION

The Messiah Ben Joseph

The disciples in Jesus' day knew all about the coming "prophet of the Restoration"— known as the Messiah ben Joseph—that would gather Israel together prior to the coming of the Messiah to reign on earth. This great prophet, a descendant of the tribe of Joseph, was especially important to the Samaritans (partly descended from Joseph), and a sore subject for the Jews, who despised the Samaritans as unworthy "half-breeds."

"YOUNG JOSEPH." ©WALTER RANE, USED BY PERMISSION

- **John 1:19–21 Jewish leaders asked John the Baptist, "Art thou that prophet?"** Troubled by his rising popularity, mighty preaching, and baptisms, the leaders of the Jews sent priests to ask John the Baptist, "Who art thou?" (v. 19). There had been many who had pretended to be the Messiah over the years, but John made it clear, "I am not the Christ" (v. 20). Well then, who? "Art thou Elias?"—meaning Elijah, who they knew would come prior to the advent of the Messiah. John said: "I am not." There was only one other possibility if he was not the Christ and not Elijah. They asked, "Art thou that prophet?"—meaning the prophet descended from Joseph who would also come before the Messiah. And John said again, "No" (v. 21).

- **The important role of the Messiah ben Joseph.** W. Cleon Skousen said: "From the most ancient times, Jewish tradition has proclaimed that a great servant of God from the House of Joseph would come in the latter days to prepare the way for the coming of Shilo, the Great Messiah. In fact, so profound was the respect of the rabbis for this 'Joseph' that they began calling him 'Messiah ben Joseph' and called their [coming Savior] 'Messiah ben David.' Literally translated, these appellations mean, 'The anointed One, son of Joseph,' and 'The anointed One, son of David.' A comprehensive study of this mysterious 'Messiah ben Joseph' was made by

Dr. Joseph Klausner, Professor Emeritus of Hebrew literature and Jewish history at the Hebrew University in Jerusalem1 … [who] put down the basic attributes which Jewish tradition variously ascribed to him."[2]

Skousen summarizes the characteristics listed by Dr. Klausner as the following:

● He will rise up shortly before the coming of the Messiah ben David (p. 486).

● He will be a descendant of Joseph through Ephraim (p. 487).

● His mission will commence at about the time Elijah comes (Malachi 4:5–6) (p. 498).

● In preparing the world for the coming of the Messiah ben David, the Messiah ben Joseph will enter into a great contest with the anti-Christ forces (p. 496).

● As part of the contest with the anti-Christ, Messiah ben Joseph will be killed (p. 496).

Dr. Klausner's list of the Samaritan version of the Messiah ben Joseph tradition includes:

● He would be a descendant of Joseph through Ephraim (a "son of Ephraim") (p. 484).

● They called him Teal, meaning "a restorer," "he who returns," or, according to others, "he who causes to return" (p. 484).

● He would call the people to repentance and bring back better days for Israel.

● He "will restore everywhere the true Law to its former validity and convert all peoples, especially the Jews, to the Samaritan [Ephraimite] religion" (p. 484).

The Greatness of the Prophet Joseph Smith

President Brigham Young said: "It was decreed in the counsels of eternity, long before the foundations of the earth were laid, that he, Joseph Smith, should be the man, in the last dispensation of this world, to bring forth the word of God to the people, and receive the fulness of the keys and power of the priesthood of the Son of God. The Lord had His eyes upon him, and upon his father, and upon his father's father, and upon their progenitors clear back to Abraham, and from Abraham to the flood, from the flood to Enoch, and from Enoch to Adam. He has watched that family and that blood as it has circulated from its fountain to the birth of that man. He was fore-ordained in eternity to preside over this last dispensation."[3]

● **D&C 5:7–10 The Lord declared that this dispensation would have His words through Joseph Smith.** The Lord said that many would not believe Joseph's words, just as they had not believed Him when He was on earth (v. 7). This was true, He said, even "if it were possible that you should show them all these things which I have committed unto you" (v. 7). But because of their unbelief He would not permit Joseph to show them everything that he had been shown; these would be made known only unto "future generations" (vv. 8–9). In the meantime, the Lord said: " … this generation shall have my word through you" (v. 10).

As a dispensational prophet called to restore knowledge of all previous dispensations to the earth, the Prophet Joseph Smith knew much more than he was able to tell us. He said at the Nauvoo funeral of Lorenzo D. Barnes in April 1843: "It is my meditation all the day, and more than my meat and drink, to know how I shall make the Saints of God [to] comprehend the visions that roll like an overflowing surge before my mind. O how I wo[u]ld delight to bring before you things which you never thought of, but poverty and the cares of the world prevent. But I am glad I have the privilege of communicating to you some things which, if grasped closely, will be a help to you when … the clouds [are] gather[ing] … and the storms are ready to burst upon you like peals of thunder."[4]

The Prophet later lamented, in a sermon he preached in the east grove at Nauvoo on April 7, 1844, that he could not tell us all that he knew. "Would to God, brethren, I could tell you who I am! Would to God I could tell you what I know! But you would call it blasphemy, and there are men upon this stand who would want to take my life… If the Church knew all the commandments, one-half they would reject through prejudice and ignorance… When God offers a blessing or knowledge to a man, and he refuses to receive it, he will be damned."[5]

● **D&C 135:3 President John Taylor's assessment of Joseph Smith's mission is well-known.** He wrote it following the assassination of Joseph and Hyrum Smith on June 27, 1844, and it was later placed in our Doctrine and Covenants as section 135.

> Joseph Smith, the Prophet and Seer of the Lord, has done more, save Jesus only, for the salvation of men in this world, than any other man that ever lived in it. In the short space of twenty years, he has brought forth the Book of Mormon, which he translated by the gift and power of God, and has been the means of publishing it on two continents; has sent the fulness of the everlasting gospel, which it contained, to the four quarters of the earth; has brought forth the revelations and commandments which compose this book of Doctrine and Covenants, and many other wise documents and instructions for the benefit of the children of men; gathered many thousands of the Latter-day Saints, founded a great city, and left a fame and name that cannot be slain. He lived great, and he died great in the eyes of God and his people; and like most of the Lord's anointed in ancient times, has sealed his mission and his works with his own blood; and so has his brother Hyrum. In life they were not divided, and in death they were not separated! [v. 3]

In this chapter we see how the hand of God was active upon the earth as He prepared it for the restoration of His gospel and Church through the Prophet Joseph Smith.

THE APOSTASY AND RENAISSANCE

The Great Apostasy

After Jesus Christ was crucified, His Apostles presided over the Church. But soon persecution, divisions, and apostasy increased, and within a few decades, there was a falling away from the Church, as the Apostles had prophesied.

- **Acts 20:28–30 Peter said "the flock" (Church) would not be spared from apostasy.** He counseled Church leaders to "take heed" and to "feed the church of God" (v. 28), because "after my [Peter's] departing shall grievous wolves enter in among you, not sparing the flock" (v. 29). And even among Church leaders themselves "shall men arise, speaking perverse things, to draw away disciples after them" (v. 30).

Paul warned of a coming apostasy

- **2 Thessalonians 2:1–3 Paul said the Second Coming of Christ would not occur until after a "falling away" first.** There were already in his day false doctrines circulating that the Second Coming was at hand (vv. 1–2). He admonished Church members to not be deceived "by spirit, nor by word, nor by letter as from us" that the Paul warned of a coming apostasy Second Coming was at hand (v. 2). Note the reference to false letters being sent to congregations in the name of Paul. He said: "Let no man deceive you by any means: for that day shall not come, except there come a falling away first" (v. 3).

- **2 Timothy 4:3–4 Paul said the Church would "not endure sound doctrine."** He warned Timothy that congregations of the Church would "heap to themselves teachers, having itching ears" (a figure of speech meaning teachers willing to teach whatever they wanted to hear). "And they shall turn away their ears from the truth, and shall be turned unto fables" (v. 4).

A recent book, *The Inevitable Apostasy and the Promised Restoration*, by Tad R. Callister,6 provides a comprehensive explanation of the great apostasy—in my opinion the best since Elder James E. Talmage's *The Great Apostasy*,[7] and a good deal easier to read. Observations by Church leaders of the time are among the many hundreds of evidences cited by Callister that the predictions of the Apostles were literally fulfilled. He also cites dozens of modern non-Mormon scholars who verify the reality and effects of the great apostasy. I recommend this excellent book to anyone who wishes to understand what happened to the original Church of Jesus Christ.

One scholar observed that both before and after the death of the Apostles "the heresies … came in, like locusts, to devour the harvests of the Gospel."[8]

Persecution from the Romans, perversion from sexual rites adopted from the pagans, and the silent, slow, but deadly influx of Greek philosophy all took their toll. Will Durrant observed that "Christianity did not destroy paganism; it adopted it. The Greek mind, dying, came to ... life in the theology and liturgy of the Church... The Greek mysteries passed down into the impressive mystery of the Mass... Christianity was the last great creation of the ancient pagan world."[9] And William Manchester noted that "Christianity was in turn infiltrated, and to a considerable extent subverted, by the paganism it was supposed to destroy."[10]

Greek philosophy overtook the Church

As a result of these forces, the great Apostasy occurred. President Spencer W. Kimball observed: "... when the light of that century went out, the darkness was impenetrable, the heavens were sealed, and the 'dark ages' moved in. The thickness of this spiritual darkness was not unlike that physical darkness in Nephite history when 'neither candles, neither torches; neither could there be fire kindled with their fine and exceedingly dry wood' (3 Nephi 8:21). The spiritual vapor of darkness was impenetrable, and centuries were to pass with hardly the dim uncertain light of a candle to break its austere darkness."[11] And so the world entered that long night of apostasy, the Dark Ages. "The Church, no longer sanctioned by God, exercised an oppressive tyranny on the minds of men and shackled them with chains of false traditions. Truth was turned to superstition, joy to despair, and worship to ritual."[12]

And Elder Bruce R. McConkie said: "When the gospel sun went down almost two millennia ago, when the priesthood was taken away and a dreary dusk descended in the congregations that once had known light, when light and truth no longer shone forth from heaven, and when those on earth no longer were taught and directed by Apostles and prophets, then spiritual darkness reigned. Darkness covered the earth and gross darkness the minds of the people (Isaiah 60:2). The dark ages had their beginning, and the light of heaven no longer dwelt in the hearts of those who professed to worship Him."[13]

There were many consequences of the great Apostasy:

— There was no priesthood authority on the earth.
— There were no Apostles or prophets on the earth.
— Essential knowledge about the nature of God was lost.
— The doctrines of the gospel were corrupted.
— Sacred ordinances, such as baptism, were changed.
— The original Church became divided into discordant groups.
— The darkness of the Apostasy lasted many centuries.

- **D&C 1:15–16 The Lord's evaluation of the apostasy.** "For they have strayed from mine ordinances, and have broken mine everlasting covenant; They seek not the Lord to establish his righteousness, but every man walketh in his own way, and after the image of his own god … in the likeness of the world, and whose substance is that of an idol, which waxeth old and shall perish in Babylon … "

- **Mormon 1:13–14 Mormon described the effects of the apostasy upon the Nephites.** "But wickedness did prevail upon the face of the whole land, insomuch that the Lord did take away his beloved disciples, and the work of miracles and of healing did cease because of the iniquity of the people. And there were no gifts from the Lord, and the Holy Ghost did not come upon any, because of their wickedness and unbelief."

- **JS–History 1:8–9 The confusion among sects was profound in 1820.** The Prophet Joseph Smith observ- ed that their infighting was so intense "that it was impossible for a person young as I was, and so unac- quainted with men and things, to come to any certain conclusion who was right and who was wrong" (v. 8). He said that the Presbyterians, Baptists, and Method- ists used "all the powers of both reason and sophistry" to prove each other wrong and themselves correct (v. 9).

Early 1800s Methodist circuit-rider

- **JS–History 1:19, 21 None of the Christian sects were acceptable to the Lord.** The boy prophet had gone into the grove to determine which religious party was correct and was surprised when "I was answered that I must join none of them, for they were all wrong" (v. 19). The Lord called their man-made creeds "an abomination in his sight" and the ministers who professed them "corrupt," a term that suggests self-serving. "They draw near to me with their lips, but their hearts are far from me," the Lord said. "They teach for doctrines the command- ments of men, having a form of godliness, but they deny the power thereof" (v. 19).

This assessment was reinforced for the Prophet a few days after the vision. "I happened to be in company with one of the Methodist preachers, who was very active in the before mentioned religious excitement; and, conversing with him on the subject of religion, I took occasion to give him an account of the vision which I had had" (v. 21). Imagine the Prophet's surprise when his trusted minister "treated my communication not only lightly, but with great contempt, saying it was all of the devil, that there were no such things as visions or revelations in these days; that all such things had ceased with the Apostles, and that there would never be any more of them" (v. 21).

Preparing the Way for the Restoration

The darkness of the Apostasy lasted many centuries. However, God foresaw the Apostasy and planned for the Restoration. Beginning in the 14th century, the Lord inspired the social, educational, religious, economic, and governmental conditions under which He could more easily restore the gospel through Joseph Smith.[14]

- The Renaissance was a rebirth of learning, particularly in literature, art, and science. Inventions such as the printing press emerged. This was no chance occurrence, but rather "a development predetermined in the Mind of God to illumine the benighted minds of men in preparation for the restoration of the gospel of Jesus Christ, which was appointed to be accomplished some centuries later."[15]

- The Reformation began when John Wycliffe, Martin Luther, and John Calvin challenged the practices and teachings of existing churches, believing they had strayed from the teachings of Christ. Through their protests, they created a religious climate in which men could inquire freely concerning doctrine and truth and God could restore His priesthood authority.

- Discovery of the Americas: America—the land promised to the posterity of Joseph in Egypt—was colonized by religious people and eventually became an independent nation.

— 1 Nephi 13:12 Columbus was led by the Spirit to the Americas. Nephi saw in vision "a man among the Gentiles, who was separated from the seed of my brethren [the Americas] by the many waters; and I beheld the Spirit of God, that it came down and wrought upon the man; and he went forth upon the many waters, even unto the seed of my brethren, who were in the promised land."

Christopher Columbus

Columbus himself said: "Who can doubt that this fire was not merely mine, but also the Holy Spirit who encouraged me with a radiance of marvelous illumination from His sacred Scriptures, ... urging me to press forward?... With a hand that could be felt, the Lord opened my mind to the fact that it would be possible ... and He opened my will to desire to accomplish that project ... The Lord purposed that there should be something miraculous in this matter of the voyage to the Indies."[16]

Columbus saw his voyages as a fulfillment of a divine plan for his life—and for the soon-to-come Second Coming of Christ. As he put it in 1500: "God made me the messenger of the new heaven and the new earth of which He spoke in the Apocalypse of St. John [Rev. 21:1] after having spoken of it through the mouth of Isaiah; and He showed me the spot where to find it." Columbus also cited various scriptures that he believed validated his mission: John 10:16—"And other sheep I have, which are not of this fold: them I also must bring, and they shall hear my voice; and there shall be one fold, and one shepherd." And Isaiah 60:9—"For, the islands wait for me, and the ships of the sea in the beginning: that I may bring thy sons from afar, their silver and their gold with them, to the name of the Lord thy God."[17]

— **1 Nephi 13:13–16 The Pilgrims and others found and were prospered in the Americas.** Nephi said: "I beheld the Spirit of God, that it wrought upon other Gentiles; and they went forth out of captivity, upon the many waters" (v. 13). Eventually there were "multitudes of the Gentiles upon the land of promise; and I beheld the wrath of God, that it was upon the seed of my brethren; and they were scattered before the Gentiles and were smitten" (v. 14). These Gentiles "did prosper and obtain the land for their inheritance. ... They were white, and exceedingly fair and beautiful. ... [They] did humble themselves before the Lord; and the power of the Lord was with them" (vv. 15–16).

"Certain dissenters among the Puritans, Roger Williams chief among them, argued that there ought to be a clear distinction between church and state and that no particular religion ought to be imposed upon the citizens. He also taught that all churches had fallen away from the true apostolic succession. Williams was banished from Massachusetts in 1635, and within a few years, he and others with similar ideas succeeded in obtaining a charter to establish the colony of Rhode Island, which allowed total toleration of all religions."[18]

● <u>Independence of the United States of America:</u> The land had to be independent of all other nations in order to protect its inhabitants against the tyranny of false creeds and oppressive kings of that time.

— **1 Nephi 13:17–19 The Gentiles upon the land were protected against all other nations who sought to destroy them.** The Lord protected these Gentiles when "their mother Gentiles were gathered together upon the waters, and upon the land also, to battle against them... The power of God was with them, and ... the wrath of God was upon all those that were gathered together against them to battle" so that "the Gentiles that had gone out of captivity were delivered by the power of God out of the hands of all other nations" (vv. 17–19).

● <u>The Constitution of the United States</u> was established, guaranteeing the religious freedom that would be necessary for the Restoration. The Prophet Joseph Smith said: " ... the Constitution of the United States is a glorious standard; it is founded in the wisdom of God. It is a heavenly banner; it is to all those who are privileged with the sweets of liberty, like the cooling shades and refreshing waters of a great rock in a thirsty and weary land."[19]

— **D&C 101:77–80 The founders of the nation were inspired of God.** The Lord declared that "the laws and constitution of the people, which I have suffered to be established ... should be maintained for the rights and protection of all flesh, according to just and holy principles; That every man may act in doctrine and principle ... according to the moral agency which I have given unto him, that every man may be accountable for his own sins in the day of judgment" (vv. 77–78).

The Lord said: " ... it is not right that any man should be in bondage one to another. And for this purpose have I established the Constitution of this land, by the hands of wise men whom I raised up unto this very purpose, and redeemed the land by the shedding of blood" (vv. 79–80). Thus, "God inspired the earlier explorers and colonizers of America and the framers of the Constitution of the United States to develop a land and governing principles to which the gospel could be restored."[20]

The founders of the United States were inspired

In a day when some denigrate or minimize the principles of the Constitution and deny heavenly influence in its framing, it is well to remember how the founding of the United States fits into God's overall plan to save His children. As the cradle for the Restoration, the protector of the Church's assets, leaders, and missionaries, and the blessed land promised to the posterity of Joseph and Ephraim, it is the most blessed place on earth, and regardless of our individual nationalities we should have special reverence for its role.

THE SMITHS IN NEW ENGLAND

Joseph Smith's Noble Ancestry

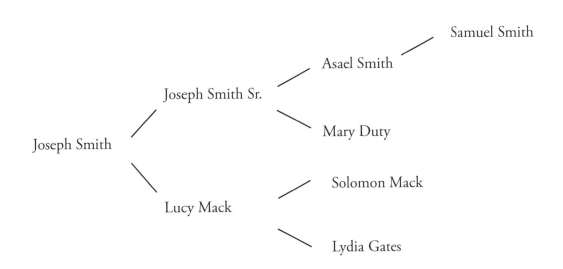

Joseph Smith's Grandparents

● **Samuel Smith (Great-Grandfather).**

— A highly religious man; all his children were baptized
— Active in public worship
— Member of the Congregationalist Church
— Those who knew him said he was …
  • "A man of integrity and uprightness"
  • "A strenuous advocate for the doctrine of Christ"

● **Asael Smith and Mary Duty (Paternal Grandparents).**

— Hard working, but the depression of the 1780s took away their family farm.
— Religious, but believed in Universalism (everyone will be saved).
— Made many family Bible notations, showing that he read, believed, and honored it.
— Disliked evangelical preaching and rejected the organized churches of his day.
— Was a strong advocate of truth and of free and equal religious liberty.
— Believed God guided the Revolutionary War and the Constitution.
— Was a gifted writer, and wrote words of counsel to his children.
— 1/5 of his will contains exhortations on how to be saved through Christ.
— Prophesied of the restoration through someone in his posterity:

"It has been borne in upon my soul that one of my descendants will promulgate a work to revolutionize the world of religious faith."

— Lived to see it. The summer after the organization of the Church, his son Joseph Sr. and grandson Don Carlos gave him a Book of Mormon which he diligently read.
— Was convinced that the work of his grandson, Joseph Smith, was of divine origin.
— Was not baptized, due to his weakened physical condition; died shortly after this visit
— His wife, Mary Duty Smith, later moved to Kirtland, where she died in 1836, firm in the faith.

● **Solomon Mack and Lydia Gates (Maternal Grandparents).**

— Solomon Mack was born in Lyme, Connecticut, September 26, 1735.
— Was indentured at age 4 due to his father's debts.
— Was treated cruelly by his master, who was his only male model.
— Sought worldly wealth most of his life, just as his master did.
— Enlisted at age 21 in the service of his country and fought in the Revolutionary War.
— Was converted at age 75 and repented strongly of his sins.
— Married a young school teacher, Lydia Gates, who home educated all her children.
— She was a woman of "piety, gentleness, and reflection."
— She also regularly called her children together to pray, both morning and evening.
— She urged them to love each other, and also to love Him who made them.
— She raised a very close-knit family.

Joseph Smith's Parents

● **Joseph Smith's parents, Joseph Sr.** and Lucy Mack Smith, also greatly influenced his life.

— Both were deeply devoted to God.
— Both were devoted parents, teaching their children the principles of faith and righteousness.
— Both had profound religious experiences.
— Both searched actively for religious truth.
  • Feeling none resembled the Church of Christ, Joseph Sr. didn't join any church.
  • Lucy felt it was her duty to be baptized and joined the Presbyterian Church.
  • When the gospel was restored, both recognized the truth and embraced it.

● **Joseph Smith Sr.**

— Was a hard working man, but poor throughout his life.
— Was humble, simple, and unpretentious.
— Was cheerful and possessed a keen sense of humor.
— Had great faith, but (like his father) was uneasy about religions and clergy of his day.
— Believed the churches were corrupt and was skeptical of their authority.
— Had several dreams about receiving the blessings of the true gospel of Christ.
— Was a devoted father and exemplified great loyalty to Joseph throughout his life.
— Wept (and immediately believed) when he heard Joseph's story of his vision.
— When Moroni appeared to Joseph, counseled his son to "be obedient to the vision."
— Wept again when the plates were delivered by Moroni to his son.
— Was one of the eight witnesses to the Book of Mormon.
— Was one of the first members baptized into the Church on April 6, 1830.
— With his son, Don Carlos, completed a mission that same year to New York.
— Held the office of a high priest in the Church and was the Church's first Patriarch.
— Loved the Kirtland Temple.

● **Lucy Mack Smith**

— Was a kind, wise, sympathetic, and understanding wife and mother.
— Was reared by God-fearing parents and taught to "walk uprightly before the Lord."
— Yearned to find God, but (like her husband) distrusted ministers.
— Often worshiped on her own, reading the Bible and meditating, and taught her children to do the same.
— Believed in prayer and taught her children to pray.
— Once, while critically ill as a young mother, made a covenant with God that she would serve Him completely if He would let her live to

care for her family. Soon afterward she heard a voice comfort her, and she made a remarkable recovery.

— Was a woman of great faith and courage. Despite the many adversities in the Church, she never wavered or lost faith in God.

— Saw her husband and each of her sons, except William, laid to rest.

— Her dying husband paid this tribute to her: "Mother, do you not know, that you are the mother of as great a family as ever lived upon the earth?"

Joseph Smith's Childhood

Adversity during his childhood prepared Joseph Smith Jr. for future challenges. His family repeatedly experienced crop failures and the dishonesty of others—moving 8 times in Joseph's first 8 years. When Joseph was about 8 years old, his entire family suffered from typhoid fever. Joseph recovered from his fever after two weeks but suffered complications that eventually required four surgeries. The final and most serious complication involved a swelling and infection in the tibia of his left leg, a condition that today would be called osteomyelitis.

"OBSCURE BOY" ©JOSEPH BRICKEY. USED BY PERMISSION

Joseph's mother Lucy recorded the story in her history: "His leg soon began to swell and he continued to suffer the greatest agony for the space of two weeks longer… Hyrum sat beside him, almost day and night for some considerable length of time, holding the affected part of his leg in his hands and pressing it between them, so that his afflicted brother might be enabled to endure the pain… At the end of three weeks, we thought it advisable to send again for the surgeon. When he came he made an incision of eight inches, on the front side of the leg, between the knee and ankle. This relieved the pain in a great measure, and the patient was quite comfortable until the wound began to heal, when the pain became as violent as ever."[21]

Dr. Nathan Smith, president of the New Hampshire Medical Society and head of Dartmouth Medical School, was the world's foremost authority on what was then known as necrosis, or bone death. As it turned out, the Smiths were, at that time, living in the very town where this man and this school were located—a blessing from God to preserve the

life and limb of His prophet. Dr. Smith had pioneered a new treatment that involved removing dead bone by drilling, chipping, and breaking away the diseased area. But he and his colleagues considered the boy's leg to be incurable because of the advanced state of the disease and believed that amputation was the only thing that could save his life. However, when both Lucy and the boy Joseph insisted, they agreed to try the new procedure instead.

Lucy Mack Smith said:

> The principal surgeon, after a moment's conversation, ordered cords to be brought to bind Joseph fast to a bedstead; but to this Joseph objected. The doctor, however, insisted that he must be confined, upon which Joseph said very decidedly, "No, doctor, I will not be bound, for I can bear the operation

much better if I have my liberty… I will tell you what I will do—I will have my father sit on the bed and hold me in his arms, and then I will do whatever is necessary in order to have the bone taken out." [Joseph then asked his mother to leave the room, assuring her that] "The Lord will help me, and I shall get through with it."

To this request I consented, and getting a number of folded sheets and laying them under his leg, I retired, going several hundred yards from the house, in order to be out of hearing. The surgeons commenced operating by boring into the bone of his leg, first on one side of the bone where it was affected, then on the other side, after which they broke it off with a pair of forceps or pincers. They thus took away large pieces of the bone. When they broke off the first piece, Joseph screamed out so loudly, that I could not forbear running to him. On my entering the room, he cried out, "Oh, mother, go back, go back; I do not want you to come in—I will try to tough it out, if you will go away."

When the third piece was taken away, I burst into the room again—and oh, my God! What a spectacle for a mother's eye! The wound torn open, the blood still gushing from it, and the bed literally covered with blood. Joseph was pale as a corpse, and large drops of sweat were rolling down his face, whilst upon every feature was depicted the utmost agony! I was immediately forced from the room, and detained until the operation was completed; but when the act was accomplished, Joseph put upon a clean bed, the room cleared of every appearance of blood, and the instruments which were used in the operation removed, I was permitted again to enter.[2]

The surgeons successfully saved Joseph's leg and life. He eventually became strong and healthy again, though he had to use crutches for three years and limped slightly the rest of his life. This inspiring story reveals much about the Smith family: Hyrum's tenderness, sympathy, and untiring support for his brother; Lucy's love and deep concern for her son; Joseph's love for and faith in his father and his compassion for his mother; and both the family's and Joseph's faith in the Lord. The Smiths were always a close-knit and hard- working family. Their love and devotion were essential to their survival, and their parents taught them to trust and depend on each other. This pattern repeated itself throughout their lives.

God Moves the Smiths to Western New York

The entire family emerged from that year of sickness with gratitude to God for preserving them. But it left the Smith family financially broken, so in 1813, they moved to Norwich, Vermont, hoping to start all over again by farming a hillside there. Life was never easy for the Smith family. They moved eight different times in the first nineteen years. At each new location, the Smiths worked hard and sought stability, but each time their circumstances left them struggling for temporal security. The Lord was not going to prosper them in New England; He needed them elsewhere, in Western New York where the Nephite record lay buried in the Hill Cumorah.

Smith home in Norwich, Vermont

Their final year in New England, 1816, was arguably the worst. The family had moved to Norwich, Vermont, to try one last time. They had already experienced three crop failures, for a variety of reasons but not for lack of effort. Then in 1816 summertime arrived but summer didn't, snowing right on through June, July, and August. This "year without a summer" was not unique to New England. It actually happened in many parts of the world as a result of the April 10, 1815 eruption of Mount Tambora in the East Indies— the largest eruption in recorded history—which sent 25 cubic miles of dust and ash into the air, blocking sunlight and darkening the Earth. This produced worldwide crop failures and mass starvation.

June was the coldest month ever experienced in New England and as far south as South Carolina. There were four killing frosts between June and August, destroying nearly all fruit and many crops. Snow fell 10 inches in Vermont, and July also began with snow and ice. On the 4th of July, ice was a quarter-inch thick throughout New England. The farmers in New England, including Vermont, began a mass exodus toward the western reserves in New York, Penn- sylvania, and Ohio, where newspapers reported there was good farmland available and crops were plentiful.

Smith farm, western New York near Palmyra

With no other way to survive in their native New England, the Smiths also decided to move, in their case to Western New York. Joseph Smith Sr. went first and purchased land near Palmyra, then sent instructions for Lucy to pack up their belong- ings in a wagon. He hired Caleb Howard to drive the team, though he proved to be cruel and dis honest and Lucy had to finish the trip without his help.

THE FIRST VISION

The Religious Atmosphere in Western New York

● **JS–History 1:1–2 The Prophet Joseph wrote his history to put false reports to rest concerning himself and the Church.** The events recorded in Joseph Smith–History in the Pearl of Great Price were written and dictated by the Prophet Joseph Smith in 1838, nearly 18 years after the first vision occurred, and 8 years after the organization of the Church (v. 2). He was concerned about "many reports which have been put in circulation by evil-disposed and designing persons, in relation to the rise and progress of the Church of Jesus Christ of Latter-day Saints, all of which have been designed by the authors thereof to militate against its character as a Church and its progress in the world" (v. 1). He wanted to "write this history, to disabuse the public mind, and put all inquirers after truth in possession of the facts, as they have transpired, in relation both to myself and the Church, so far as I have such facts in my possession" (v. 1).

JS–History 1:5–6 About two years after the Smiths arrived in West- ern New York, there arose a great religious excitement, with many churches contending for converts. The contest for converts became so "hot" that the area became referred to as "the burned-over district." There was no place in the United States more exercised over the subject of religion. Joseph said it "created no small stir and division amongst the people" as the Methodists, Baptists, and Presbyterians vied for converts (v. 5).

Typical revivalist camp meeting in the early 1800s

While in the beginning these "Christian" sects expressed love for any person who would accept Christ through whatever denomination he chose, it devolved into a contest of words as "great confusion and bad feeling ensued— priest contending against priest, and convert against convert; so that all their good feelings one for another, if they ever had any, were entirely lost in a strife of words and a contest about opinions" (v. 6).

JS–History 1:7–8 The Smiths became divided over religion. They had always been close as a family, relying on each other for support with every need. But now, in the midst of all this confusion, they became divided over religion. Joseph reported, "I was at this time in my fifteenth year. My father's family was proselyted to the Presbyterian faith, and four of them joined that church, namely, my mother, Lucy; my brothers Hyrum and Samuel Harrison; and my sister Sophronia" (v. 7). Joseph himself "became somewhat partial to the Methodist sect, and I felt some desire to be united with them" but could not "come to any certain conclusion who was right and who was wrong" (v. 8).

We see here the two main motivations for the Prophet Joseph Smith taking this matter to the Lord in prayer: (1) The troublesome division that had emerged in his family over religion, and (2) Joseph's uncertainty about who was right and who was wrong among the Christian sects. Both of these things were powerful and important enough to take him into the grove.

JS–History 1:8 The religious character of the Prophet emerged in his youth. From this story we also see two important characteristics of the boy prophet: (1) he was given to serious reflections, and (2) he had deep inner convictions about the importance of religion. He said: "During this time of great excitement my mind was called up to serious reflection and great uneasiness" and "though my feelings were deep and often poignant, still I kept myself aloof from all these parties, though I attended their several meetings as often as occasion would permit."

- **JS–History 1:9–10 He wanted to know who was right, and how he could know it.** As we might expect from a young teenage boy, "My mind at times was greatly excited, the cry and tumult were so great and incessant" (v. 9). In the midst of this war of words and opinions, he wondered, "What is to be done? Who of all these parties are right; or, are they all wrong together? If any one of them be right, which is it, and how shall I know it?" (v. 10).

- **JS–History 1:11–13 Joseph turned to the scriptures for answers—searching and pondering them.** As his mother had taught him, by both precept and example, Joseph turned to the scriptures for answers. And as he did this, he came upon James 1:5: "If any of you lack wisdom, let him ask of God, that giveth to all men liberally, and upbraideth not; and it shall be given him" (v. 11). The Spirit descended upon him as he read these words. "Never did any passage of scripture come with more power to the heart of man than this did at this time to mine. It seemed to enter with great force into every feeling of my heart" (v. 12). He could not get it out of his mind. He "reflected on it again and again, knowing that if any person needed wisdom from God, I did; for how to act I did not know" (v. 12).

Relying solely on the scriptures for an answer was not possible because "the teachers of ... the different sects understood the same passages of scripture so differently as to destroy all confidence in settling the question by an appeal to the Bible" (v. 12). Eventually, he concluded that he would never know which church to join unless he did "as James directs, that is, ask of God" and he determined to do exactly that (v. 13).

A Vision in the Sacred Grove

- **JS–History 1:14 Joseph's prayer on this morning was different from other prayers he had offered—it was his first vocal prayer.** He "retired to the woods to make the attempt... It was the first time in my life that I had made such an attempt, for amidst all my anxieties I had never as yet made the attempt to pray vocally."

Joseph said that "It was on the morning of a beautiful, clear day, early in the spring of eighteen hundred and twenty" (v. 14). This raises an interesting question as to what day it might have been. Spring begins officially on March 21st, so it would presumably have been after that date, but very early on in the season. I have, for years, favored the date of April 6th, since that date has so many significant events associated with it in the history of the earth. What better day could there be for the light of the restoration to dawn upon the earth?

Meridian Magazine published an article by Dr. John Pratt which stated that evidence from the Enoch calendar implied that by far the most likely date for the First Vision was Sunday, March 26, 1820.[23] That was certainly fascinating, based on ancient calendar systems and their predictions for world history. But then, two months later,

"YOUNG JOSEPH." ©WALTER RANE. USED BY PERMISSION

another researcher looked at weather reports of the time to try to locate a day that was "beautiful" and "clear" as opposed to overcast or rainy. And he came up with precisely the same date.

John C. Lefgren concluded:

> Combining all of this evidence, there were three days of early spring on which the weather qualified as being possible for the First Vision [that is, clear and beautiful]. On the first two of them the Smith family would almost certainly have been totally occupied in producing maple sugar. On the third of those days, there would have been no more work to do in producing maple sugar, and it would have been a day of rest. That day coincided with Sunday, the weekly Sabbath. Thus it is one day which is indicated as being far more likely than any other for the First Vision. It must have been on the morning of Sunday, March 26, 1820, that Joseph Smith reached out to God and the glorious response changed the course of history. The brief statement that the marvelous event occurred 'on the morning of a beautiful, clear day, early in the spring' of 1820 was enough to pinpoint the very day it occurred.[24]

Whatever day it was, it was certainly the most important date in the history of the world since the birth, death, and resurrection of our Lord nearly two thousand years earlier. As Elder Parley P. Pratt said in his well-known hymn "The Morning Breaks,"[25] this was "The dawning of a brighter day, majestic, ris[ing] on the world."

● **JS–History 1:15–17 Satan was determined to keep Joseph from praying.** Joseph reported, "After I had retired to the place where I had previously designed to go, having looked around me, and finding myself alone, I kneeled down and began to offer up the desires of my heart to God. I had scarcely done so, when immediately I was seized upon by some power which entirely overcame me, and had such an astonishing influence over me as to bind my tongue so that I could not speak. Thick darkness gathered around me, and it seemed to me for a time as if I were doomed to sudden destruction" (v. 15).

I have personally observed Satan's power to bind the tongues of people. On one occasion my young niece came to stay with my wife and me, and in the middle of the night was overcome by some force that also rendered her helpless and unable to speak. After casting this evil influence from her by means of the priesthood, her faculties were restored and we rejoiced in the power of God to deliver us from such attacks of the evil one.

Joseph Smith said that "the power of this enemy which had seized upon [him]" caused him to "sink into despair" and nearly abandon himself to destruction—"not to an imaginary ruin, but to the power of some actual being from the unseen world, who had such marvelous power as I had never before felt in any being" (v. 16).

● **JS–History 1:16–17 Truths revealed by the First Vision.** Joseph's description of what happened next is both simple and profound. "Exerting all my powers to call upon God to deliver me out of the power of this enemy which had seized upon me ...—just at this moment of great alarm, I saw a pillar of light exactly over my head, above the brightness of the sun, which descended gradually until it fell upon me" (v. 16). The appearance of this light dispelled all darkness and immediately banished Satan from the scene (v. 17).

"When the light rested upon me I saw two Personages, whose brightness and glory defy all description, standing above me in the air. One of them spake unto me, calling me by name and said, pointing to the other—'This is My Beloved Son. Hear Him!'" (v. 17).

The dawn of the restoration had arrived, and in that moment, millennia of darkness and confusion were dispelled as a number of important truths were manifest:

— Satan and his power are real.
— Satan works to thwart God's plans.
— The Lord's power is greater than Satan's.
— The heavens are open to those with faith.
— God hears and answers prayer.
— Revelation has not ceased.
— God lives.
— The Father and Son are separate beings.
— The Father and Son are beings of glory.
— The Father wants us to listen to His Son, the Savior.

President Gordon B. Hinckley said: " I submit that in the few minutes that Joseph Smith was with the Father and the Son, he learned more of the nature of God the Eternal Father and the risen Lord than all the learned minds in all their discussions through all centuries of time."[26] And President David O. McKay said: [The First Vision] "answers all the [questions] regarding God and His divine personality... His relation to His children is clear. His interest in humanity through authority delegated to man is apparent. The future of the work is assured. These and other glorious truths are clarified by that glorious first vision."[27]

The entirety of our claim to be the true and Restored Church rests upon the validity of this simple story of the First Vision. If Joseph Smith talked with God the Father and His Beloved Son, then he is God's prophet and all else that he taught us is true. And if not, then our Church is no different than any other sect of Christendom, acting without direct authority from heaven. I know by the witness of the Holy Ghost that Joseph's story is true. He saw what he said he saw. And this is, indeed, the Church of the Living Christ restored to the earth in these latter days.

● **JS–History 1:18–19 Joseph was told that he was to join none of the churches of his day.** It had never occurred to Joseph that they could all be wrong (v. 18), and when he inquired of the "Personages who stood above me in the light, which of all the sects was right ... and which I should join ... I was answered that I must join none of them" (vv. 18–19). The Lord told him "all their creeds were an abomination," their teachers were "corrupt," and "their hearts are far from me," and also that "they teach for doctrines the commandments of men, having a form of godliness, but they deny the power thereof" (v. 19).

We should not think that the Lord was speaking of all individuals within these churches, many of whom are genuinely sincere in their desire to serve God and to follow Jesus Christ. Elder

James E. Talmage said: "When we say that the Lord is not pleased with those churches, we do not mean that He is not pleased with the members thereof... The church as such may be wholly corrupt because of the false claims that are being made for it, and yet within that church as members there may be people who are doing their best."[28]

● **JS–History 1:20 "... and many other things did he say unto me, which I cannot write at this time."** This is a fascinating statement, which naturally leaves us wondering what else the Lord told the Prophet during this vision. We do get glimpses into those other subjects from other writings and interviews where the Prophet gave additional details about the First Vision:

— He saw many angels.[29]
— The two Personages exactly resembled each other.[30]
— He was told the fullness of the Gospel would, at some future time, be made known to him.[31]
— His sins were forgiven him.[32]
— He was filled with unspeakable joy that remained with him for several days.[33]

● **JS–History 1:20 The vision weakened Joseph physically.** Man in his natural state is not able to endure the presence of God; his body must be "quickened" first (D&C 67:11–12). Hyrum L. Andrus explained: "The divine medium by which Moses beheld [his] great vision is designated as both the glory of God and the Spirit of God. Again, Moses bore record that his natural eyes could not have beheld God, for without being transfigured he would 'have withered and died in his presence.' 'But,' he declared of God, 'his glory was upon me; and I beheld his face, for I was transfigured before him.' (Moses 1:11). The transfiguring agent was identified as the glory of God."[34]

Joseph Smith tells us that "When I came to myself again, I found myself lying on my back, looking up into heaven. When the light had departed, I had no strength; but soon recovering in some degree, I went home."

● **JS–History 1:20 He told his mother first.** After arriving at his home, Joseph leaned up against the fireplace, obviously affected by what he had just witnessed. When his mother inquired as to what was wrong, he said: "Never mind, all is well... I have learned for myself that Presbyterianism is not true." This was the faith selected by his mother from among the competing parties, and Joseph wished her to know it was not correct. It is probable that he went on to say that none of the Christian creeds were correct.

WAITING FOR FURTHER INSTRUCTION

Negative Responses to the First Vision

The Prophet Joseph Smith tells us in verse 20 of Joseph Smith–History, "It seems as though the adversary was aware, at a very early period of my life, that I was destined to prove a disturber and an annoyer of his kingdom; else why should the powers of darkness combine against me? Why the opposition and persecution that arose against me, almost in my infancy?" It is an excellent question and the answer should be obvious. The first vision had just dispelled millennia of spiritual darkness and was destined to produce the last and best dispensation in the history of the earth. There would not be any lasting peace in the boy prophet's life from that time forward. His was a life of constant strife against the forces of evil and ignorance. Satan tried everything he could to stop him.

- **JS–History 1:21 Joseph's Methodist minister treated his vision with contempt.** It is well to remember that Joseph had been somewhat partial to the Methodist sect before his first vision. It would be natural for him to take the matter to the leader of that group and to expect encouragement. Instead, Joseph was "greatly surprised at his behavior; he treated my communication not only lightly, but with great contempt, saying it was all of the devil, that there were no such things as visions or revelations in these days; that all such things had ceased with the Apostles, and that there would never be any more of them" (v. 21).

*Reverend George Lane
(1784-1859)*

  This was the orthodox Christian creed: God does not speak to man anymore; the scriptures are sufficient without further revelation. This un-Biblical claim that revelation has ceased grew out of the creeds of apostate Christian churchmen in the fourth and fifth century who reasoned that since God had not spoken to them then He would evidently not speak to anyone again. It never occurred to them that they might not qualify for the revelations of heaven due to apostate creeds and adoption of pagan rituals.

- **JS–History 1:22–23 The warring Christian sects were united in their opposition to the young prophet's claims.** Joseph found that his relating of the vision to others "excited a great deal of prejudice against me among professors of religion, and was the cause of great persecution, which continued to increase" (v. 22). He was amazed that a young and obscure farm boy "of no consequence in the world" would attract the attention and vitriolic attacks of "men of high standing" who would "excite the public mind against me, and create a bitter persecution" (v. 22). There he was, "an obscure boy, of a little over fourteen years of age, and one, too, who was doomed to the necessity of obtaining a scanty maintenance by his daily labor" being attacked by the "great ones of the most popular sects of the day" in a "spirit of the most bitter persecution and reviling" (v. 23). It caused him great sorrow.

- **JS–History 1:24–25 Joseph Smith's testimony of the truth of his first vision.** Joseph's unwavering affirmation of his vision throughout his life is one of the most compelling evidences of its truth. Given the magnitude of what he faced over the next 24 years of his life, we could expect a fraudulent man to give up his scheme and admit his deception. But that never happened because "it was … a fact that I had beheld a vision" (v. 24). Like Paul standing before King Agrippa, Joseph was accused of being dishonest, crazy, or both, and like Paul he was ridiculed and reviled for his claims of seeing a vision and hearing a voice.

The Prophet Joseph Smith said:

> "All this did not destroy the reality of [Paul's] vision. He had seen a vision, he knew he had, and all the persecution under heaven could not make it otherwise; and though they should persecute him unto death, yet he knew, and would know to his latest breath, that he had both seen a light and heard a voice speaking unto him, and all the world could not make him think or believe otherwise" (v. 24).

"So it was with me. I had actually seen a light, and in the midst of that light I saw two Personages, and they did in reality speak to me; and though I was hated and persecuted for saying that I had seen a vision, yet it was true" (v. 25).

He was baffled by their persecution of him for telling the truth.

"I have actually seen a vision; and who am I that I can withstand God, or why does the world think to make me deny what I have actually seen? For I had seen a vision; I knew it, and I knew that God knew it, and I could not deny it, neither dared I do it … [because] by so doing I would offend God, and come under condemnation" (v. 25).

I remember well the first time I read these verses in earnest, while serving my mission. As the scripture in James had penetrated the Prophet Joseph's being, I can truthfully say that these words of the Prophet penetrated mine. The Spirit bore witness to me then, and does to this day, that he was telling the truth. The story is simply true. And all the disbelief and persecution and opposition in the world will never make it otherwise.

Notes:

1. *The Messianic Idea in Israel* [1955].
2. "The Last Days of Joseph and His Remarkable Prophecies Concerning the Future," *The Third Thousand Years* [1964], 156–158.
3. *Discourses of Brigham Young*, sel. John A. Widtsoe [1941], 108.
4. *History of the Church*, 5:362.
5. Quoted in Orson F. Whitney, Life of Heber C. Kimball [1945], 322–323; or *Teachings of the Prophet Joseph Smith*, sel. Joseph Fielding Smith [1976], 112, 322.
6. *The Inevitable Apostasy and the Promised Restoration* [2006].
7. *The Great Apostasy* [1953].
8. *The Ante-Nicene Fathers*, 10 volumes, Alexander Roberts and James Donaldson, eds. [1885; reprinted 1980–1985], 1:309.
9. *The Story of Civilization, Part III: Caesar and Christ* [1944], 595.
10. *A World Lit Only by Fire* [1993], 11.
11. *The Teachings of Spencer W. Kimball*, edited by Edward L. Kimball [1982], 424.
12. *The Teachings of President Ezra Taft Benson* [1988], 85.
13. In Conference Report, April 1978, 17; or *Ensign*, May 1978, 12.
14. *See Mormon Doctrine*, 2nd ed. [1966], 717.
15. James E. Talmage, *Jesus the Christ*, 3rd ed. [1916], 749.
16. In Kevin A. Miller, "Why Did Columbus Sail," in Christian History, Issue 35 [Vol. XI, No 3].
17. "Why Did Columbus Sail," in *Christian History, Issue 35*.
18. *Church History in the Fulness of Times* [Church Educational System Manual, 1993], 10.
19. *Teachings of the Prophet Joseph Smith*, 147.
20. M. Russell Ballard, in Conference Report, October 1994, 85; or *Ensign*, November 1994, 66.

21. Lucy Mack Smith, *History of Joseph Smith*, 55.

22. *History of Joseph Smith*, 56–58.

23. John Pratt, "Enoch Calendar: Another Witness of the Restoration," *Meridian Magazine* [5 Aug. 2002].

24. "Oh, How Lovely Was the Morning: Sun., 26 Mar. 1820?" *Meridian Magazine* (2002).

25. *Hymns*, no. 1.

26. *Church News*, 24 October 1998, 6.

27. *Gospel Ideals* [1954], 85.

28. In Conference Report, October 1928, 120.

29. Dean C. Jessee, "The Early Accounts of Joseph Smith's First Vision," *BYU Studies,* 9 (Spring, 1969), 275–294.

30. *History of the Church*, 4:536.

31. *History of the Church*, 4:536.

32. 1831–32 history in "Kirtland Letter Book" [manuscript at Church Historian's Library], 1829–1835, 1–6.

33. "History of the Church" [manuscript at Church Historian's Library], A-1, 120–22.

34. *Doctrinal Commentary on the Pearl of Great Price* [1967], 53–54.

CHAPTER 4

The Coming Forth of the Book of Mormon

(Joseph Smith-History 26–68; D&C 2–5; 10; 17) [1820–1830]

෪ඏ

INTRODUCTION

The Book of Mormon and the Restoration

President Ezra Taft Benson noted that "a … powerful testimony to the importance of the Book of Mormon is to note where the Lord placed its coming forth in the timetable of the unfolding Restoration."[1] When we consider all of the key events and line them up chronologically, the only thing that preceded the Book of Mormon was the First Vision. All else—the restoration of the priesthood, the organization of the Church, and key doctrines such as the three degrees of glory, celestial marriage, and work for the dead— came after it. This tells us something about how essential the Lord viewed the Book of Mormon to be in the process of the Restoration.

The Book of Mormon and Our Own Spirituality

The Prophet Joseph Smith said to the Twelve Apostles on 28 November 1841: "I told the brethren that the Book of Mormon was the most correct of any book on earth, and the keystone of our religion, and a man would get nearer to God: by abiding by its precepts, than by any other book."[2] If this is so, then we can benefit more spiritually from reading and teaching the Book of Mormon than by any other means. So are we using it as we should?

President Ezra Taft Benson said, "No."

> We have not been using the Book of Mormon as we should. Our homes are not as strong unless we are using it to bring our children to Christ… Our Church classes are not as spirit-filled unless we hold it up as a standard… Reading the Book of Mormon is one of the greatest persuaders to get men on missions. We need more missionaries. But, we also need better-prepared missionaries coming out of the wards and branches and homes where they know and love the Book of Mormon… We are to get a testimony of it, we are to teach from it, we are to hold it up as a standard and "hiss it forth." Have we been doing this? Not as we should, nor as we must…
>
> Do eternal consequences rest upon our response to this book? Yes, either to our blessing or our

condemnation. Every Latter-day Saint should make the study of this book a lifetime pursuit. Otherwise he is placing his soul in jeopardy and neglecting that which could give spiritual and intellectual unity to his whole life. There is a difference between a convert who is built on the rock of Christ through the Book of Mormon and stays hold of that iron rod, and one who is not.[3]

PREPARING TO RECEIVE THE PLATES

After Three Years, Joseph Seeks to Know His Status

● **JS–History 1:26–27 For three years Joseph waited for further instructions.** After his first vision, Joseph was clear on the status of the sectarian world—"that it was not my duty to join with any of them" (v. 26). He also knew for sure that he could turn to God and get answers. He continued to suffer ridicule and abuse from many people (v. 27), but his family members supported him believingly. He resolved to "continue as I was until further directed" (v. 26). As it turned out, that would mean waiting for three years.

● **JS–History 1:28 Joseph was in many ways a typical teenage boy, living a normal life.** It had been three years—a long period of time for a teenage boy—and in all that time he had heard nothing more from the Lord. He began to worry about his spiritual standing. "During the space of time which intervened between the time I had the vision and the year eighteen hundred and twenty-three—having been for- bidden to join any of the religious sects of the day, and being of very tender years, and persecuted by those who ought to have been my friends

Joseph was a typical but hard-working teen

… I was left to all kinds of temptations; and, mingling with all kinds of society, I frequently fell into many foolish errors, and displayed the weakness of youth, and the foibles of human nature; which, I am sorry to say, led me into diverse temptations, offensive in the sight of God" (v. 28).

The Prophet assures us: "In making this confession, no one need suppose me guilty of any great or malignant sins. A disposition to commit such was never in my nature. But I was guilty of levity, and sometimes associated with jovial company, etc., not consistent with that character which ought to be maintained by one who was called of God as I had been. But this will not seem very strange to any one who recollects my youth, and is acquainted with my native cheery temperament" (v. 28). Imagine that!—a teenage boy acting foolishly, pulling tricks on people, and hanging out with the wrong crowd at times. He was, after all, a youngster, and one who loved life and loved to laugh.

● **JS–History 1:29 On September 21, 1823, Joseph sought to know his status with the Lord.**

It having been three years, and feeling "condemned for my weakness and imperfec- tions," the Prophet lay in bed on the evening of September 21, 1823, and offered prayer to his God. He desired "forgiveness of all my sins and follies" and also asked for "a manifestation to me, that I might know of my state and standing before him." He says he had "full confidence in obtaining a divine manifestation, as I previously had one."

Cabin where the Smiths lived at the time

In his diary, the Prophet Joseph Smith said of that evening: "When I was about 17 years old I had another visitation … in the night … after I had retired to bed. I had not been asleep, but was meditating upon my past life and experience. I was very conscious that I had not kept the commandments and I repented heartily for all my sins and transgressions, and humbled myself before Him whose eyes are on all things"[4]

The Appearance of the Angel Moroni

Later, in Nauvoo, the Prophet Joseph Smith added other details of the vision: "On the evening of the 21st of September, AD 1823, while I was praying unto God … light like that of day, only of a far purer and more glorious appearance, and brightness burst into the room, indeed the first sight was as though the house was filled with consuming fire; the appearance produced a shock that affected the whole body; in a moment a personage stood before me surrounded with a glory yet greater than that with which I was already surrounded."[5]

● **JS–History 1:30–32 The Angel Moroni appeared in Joseph's bedroom in answer to his prayer.** In his history contained in the Pearl of Great Price, Joseph said, "I discovered a light appearing in my room, which continued to increase until the room was lighter than at noonday, when immediately a personage appeared at my bedside, standing in the air, for his feet did not touch the floor" (v. 30).

Upstairs room where Moroni appeared

The Prophet described the angel's appearance. "He had on a loose robe of most exquisite whiteness. It was a whiteness beyond anything earthly I had ever seen; nor do I believe that any earthly thing could be made to appear so exceedingly white and brilliant. His hands were naked, and his arms also, a little above the wrist; so, also, were his feet naked, as were his legs, a little above the ankles. His head and neck were also bare. I could discover that he had no other clothing on but this robe, as it was open, so that I could see into his bosom" (v. 31). He was beholding a resurrected person, so this vision gives us some idea of how resurrected persons look when they appear.

The angel's robe was not the only thing that was "exceedingly white, but his whole person was glorious beyond description, and his countenance truly like lightning. The room was exceedingly light, but not so very bright as immediately around his person. When I first looked upon him, I was afraid; but the fear soon left me" (v. 32).

Joseph's siblings slept through the vision

Keep in mind that Joseph was not alone in this bedroom. Several siblings lay sleeping beside him. But they were not awakened by either the light or the voice of this angel. It would seemthat only Joseph could see and hear him. The others slept blissfully throughout the vision.

Oliver Cowdery said: "The stature of this personage was a little above the common size of men in this age; his garment was perfectly white, and had the appearance of being without seam… [The angel identified himself as Moroni], a messenger sent by commandment of the Lord, to deliver a special message, and to witness to him [Joseph] that his sins were forgiven, and that his prayers were heard."[6]

● **JS–History 1:33 Moroni's prophecies concerning Joseph Smith himself.** The angel called Joseph Smith by name and said "he was a messenger sent from the presence of God to me, and that his name was Moroni; that God had a work for me to do; and that my name should be had for good and evil among all nations, kindreds, and tongues, or that it should be both good and evil spoken of among all people."

Elder Neal A. Maxwell said: " Throughout the expanse of human history, no prophet has been scrutinized in such a sustained way, on as wide a scale, or for so long a period of time as Joseph Smith Jr. The communication capacity of this age and the global impact of his work have so ensured. Young Joseph was told that his name would be 'both good and evil spoken of' throughout the world. Except from a divine source, how audacious a statement! Yet his contemporary religious leaders, then much better known than Joseph, have faded into the footnotes of history, while the work of Joseph Smith grows constantly and globally."[7]

● **JS–History 1:34, 42 Moroni told Joseph about the Nephite plates containing an account of the inhabitants of ancient America and the Savior's ministry among them.** He said the book was deposited nearby and was "written upon gold plates, giving an account of the former inhabitants of this continent, and the source from whence they sprang. He also said that the fulness of the everlasting Gospel was contained in it, as delivered by the Savior to the ancient inhabitants" (v. 34). Moroni told Joseph that "the time that they should be obtained was not yet fulfilled" but that when he did receive them, along with the breastplate and Urim and Thummim, he was not to show any of these things to anyone (v. 42). A vision then opened before Joseph's mind so that he "could see the place where the plates were deposited, and that so clearly and distinctly that I knew the place again when I visited it" (v. 42).

● **JS–History 1:35 Moroni also told Joseph about the Urim and Thummim.** He described them as "two stones in silver bows—and these stones, fastened to a breastplate, constituted what is called the Urim and Thummim—deposited with the plates; and the possession and use of these stones were what constituted 'seers' in ancient or former times; and that God had prepared them for the purpose of translating the book."

Moroni Departs and Reappears—Three Times

● **JS–History 1:43 The angel's departure.** Joseph said: "I saw the light in the room begin to gather immediately around the person of him who had been speaking to me, and it continued to do so until the room was again left dark, except just around him; when, instantly I saw, as it were, a conduit open right up into heaven, and he ascended till he entirely disappeared, and the room was left as it had been before this heavenly light had made its appearance." The angel ascended, as it were, through a pneumatic tube of light. I have often imagined these columns of light to be the same as those that ancient prophets called "pillars of fire." It would be a wondrous thing to behold.

● **JS–History 1:44–45 The second appearance of the angel—speaking of judgments coming upon the earth.** We can imagine the Prophet laying there, "musing on the singularity of the scene, and marveling greatly at what had been told to me by this extraordinary messenger" (v. 44). While he did so, "my room was again beginning to get lighted, and in an instant, as it were, the same heavenly messenger was again by my bedside" (v. 44). Joseph said that the angel rehearsed again what he had said before "without the least variation," then told him about great judgments which were coming upon the earth "in this generation"—great desolations by famine, sword, and pestilence. And then, "he again ascended as he had done before" (v. 45).

● **JS–History 1:46–47 The third appearance of the angel—warning Joseph not to view the plates as having monetary value.** By this time, Joseph said: "so deep were the impressions made on my mind, that sleep had fled from my eyes, and I lay overwhelmed in astonishment at what I had both seen and heard" (v. 46). But we can imagine his great "surprise when again I beheld the same messenger at my bedside, and heard him rehearse or repeat over again to me the same things as before" (v. 46). This time, the angel "added a caution to me, telling me that Satan would try to tempt me (in consequence of the indigent circumstances of my father's family), to get the plates for the purpose of getting rich" (v. 46). He counseled the young prophet concerning motives—that he should have no others than the building of Christ's kingdom. If he allowed any other consideration to enter his heart, he could not obtain the plates. The angel then ascended into heaven again as he had done before, leaving Joseph to "ponder on the strangeness of what I had just experienced; when almost immediately … the cock crowed, and I found that day was approaching, so that our interviews must have occupied the whole of that night" (v. 47).

● **JS–History 1:48–50 The fourth appearance of the angel—instructing Joseph to tell his father what he had seen and heard.** Joseph had been up all night and was exhausted. He tried to work on the farm with his father, as usual, but was not able. His father told him to go home. He started to do so, "but, in attempt- ing to cross the fence out of the field where we were, my strength entirely failed me, and I fell helpless on the ground, and for a time was quite unconscious of anything" (v. 48).

The field and fence near Joseph's home

When he came to, he heard a voice calling him by name. "I looked up, and beheld the same messenger standing over my head, surrounded by light as before. He then again related unto me all that he had related to me the previous night, and commanded me to go to my father and tell him of the vision and commandments which I had received" (v. 49). Joseph did this, returning to the field and "rehears[ing] the whole matter" to his father, who assured him that "it was of God, and told me to go and do as commanded by the messenger" (v. 50).

From the very beginning, Joseph Smith Sr. believed in and sustained the prophetic calling of his son. Soon after D&C 4 was given to him in answer to his desire to know what the Lord would have him do, he became one of the eight witnesses to the Book of Mormon. He became the first Patriarch to the Church December 18, 1833, and an assistant counselor in the First Presidency in 1837, in which calling he served faithfully until his death in 1840.[8]

E. Cecil McGavin noted: "Joseph Smith Sr. was filled with the testimony of the truth, and was always anxious to share it with others. He was almost sixty when he made the tedious journey … to carry the gospel to his father and mother, his sisters and brothers. Soon after his return [home], he was imprisoned for a small debt of fourteen dollars, rather than deny the divinity of the Book of Mormon and be forgiven the debt! He was cast into a cell with a condemned murderer and left for four days without food. Later he was transferred to the prison workyard where he preached the gospel and converted two persons whom he later baptized. He was in prison a full month before his family was able to obtain his release."[9]

Moroni's Message Clarified Old Testament Prophecies

In explaining the restoration of the gospel during these visions, the angel Moroni quoted or summarized at least five Old Testament prophecies, indicating that they would soon be fulfilled. In 1842, Joseph Smith explained Moroni's message to John Wentworth, a newspaper editor: "This messenger proclaimed himself to be an angel of God, sent to bring the joyful tidings that the covenant which God made with ancient Israel was at hand to be fulfilled, that the preparatory work for the Second Coming of the Messiah was speedily to commence; that the time was at hand for the gospel, in all its fulness to be preached in power, unto all nations that a people might be prepared for the millennial reign."[10] Moroni accomplished these things by quoting the following scriptures.

- **JS–History 1:36 Moroni quoted Malachi 3:1–3.** These verses about the preparation for the Second Coming of the Lord, say "the Lord, whom ye seek, shall suddenly come to his temple, even the messenger of the covenant, whom ye delight in" (Malachi 3:1). We know from modern revelation that this "messenger of the covenant" is the Lord Himself. We are told that when the Lord comes again He will be like "a refiner's fire, and like fullers' soap: And He shall sit as a refiner and purifier of silver" (Malachi 3:2–3). In other words, He will purge all wickedness from the earth. The scripture also makes mention of the sons of Levi making offerings again at the temple of the Lord (Malachi 3:3). We should note the heavy emphasis on the temple in these predictions. The restoration has barely begun, and already Joseph is learning of the importance of the temple to the Lord's work.

- **JS–History 1:36–37 Moroni quoted Malachi 4:1.** Joseph said he quoted Malachi 4 "with a little variation from the way it reads in our Bibles." Instead of quoting Malachi 4:1 as it reads in the Bible, he said: "For behold, the day cometh that shall burn as an oven, and all the proud, yea, and all that do wickedly *shall burn as stubble*; for *they that come shall burn them*, saith the Lord of Hosts, that it shall leave them neither root nor branch" (v. 37, emphasis added to highlight changed words). This prophetic language has multiple meanings. It can refer to the utter destruction of the wicked at the Second Coming. But it also has symbolic meaning concerning eternal families—that those who choose to do wickedly will not be eternally connected to their ancestors or descendants, but will live singly and without eternal family relationships forever.

- **JS–History 1:38–39 Moroni quoted Malachi 4:5–6.** Moroni quoted these two verses differently also. He said "Behold, I will *reveal unto you the Priesthood, by the hand of* Elijah the prophet, before the coming of the great and dreadful day of the Lord. And he *shall plant in the hearts of the children the promises made to the fathers*, and *the hearts of the children shall turn to their fathers. If it were not so, the whole earth would be utterly wasted at his coming.*"

Here, at the very beginning of the restoration, we have Moroni emphasizing the importance of genealogical and temple work, and stating that without it the entire history of the world and plan of salvation would have been a "waste." It will be 13 years before the keys of this work will be restored (1836), yet the groundwork is already being laid. As if to emphasize its importance, this one scripture appears in all four of our standard works—the one described above in the Pearl of Great Price and three more as follows.

— **D&C 2** This version of Malachi's words, as quoted by Moroni, appears in the Doctrine and Covenants. It clarifies that Elijah will restore the priesthood and that the "children" will be made aware of "promises" made to "the fathers." What are these promises? Certainly they include the promises made to Adam, Enoch, Abraham, Moses, and others about the work that would be done in the latter days to save their temporal and spiritual posterity. But I believe also that these "promises" are the ones we made personally to our ancestors before we came here. They agreed to come during times of spiritual darkness to carry forward the race and set the stage for the restoration. We agreed, as those who would be blessed to enjoy all priesthood keys and temples, that we would do their work for them so that they can enjoy similar blessings to us in eternity.

— **Malachi 4:5–6 and 3 Nephi 25:5–6.** These versions of Malachi's words, which read identically, say that if we fail to turn our hearts toward our fathers that the Lord will "come and smite the earth with a curse" (v. 6). What is that curse? Evidently it is that the earth and its entire history would have been a "waste" without this genealogical and temple work—as explained in D&C 2 and in JS-History 1:36–37. How important is temple work, then? And why is this instruction repeated so many times throughout the scriptures? Again, early in the young Prophet's life, he is already being taught temple principles and being prepared to be a restorer of these blessings to the earth.

- **JS–History 1:40 Moroni quoted Isaiah 11.** He said that the prophecies contained in this chapter were "about to be fulfilled." It is interesting to note that in D&C 113, we find the Prophet Joseph Smith explaining the scripture to others, perhaps based on what Moroni told him in this vision. Several of these verses refer to a latter-day prophet who will restore Israel and hold the keys of the priesthood. These refer specifically to the Prophet Joseph himself.

- **JS–History 1:40 Moroni quoted Acts 3:22–23.** He quoted this scripture without any modification, explaining that the prophet referred to in Acts "was Christ; but the day had not yet come when 'they who would not hear his voice should be cut off from among the people,' but soon would come."

- **JS–History 1:41 Moroni quoted Joel 2:28–32.** This scripture, about revelation in the latter days and also some of the destructions that will precede the Second Coming of the Lord, he said also "was not yet fulfilled, but was soon to be."

- **JS–History 1:41 Moroni quoted other scriptures.** He told the Prophet Joseph Smith that "the fulness of the Gentiles was soon to come in" and "quoted many other passages of scripture, and offered many explanations which cannot be mentioned here."

A PERIOD OF PREPARATION

When Joseph Smith was first shown the gold plates at the tender age of 17, he was not yet prepared to receive and translate them. But the Lord prepared Joseph to receive and translate the plates over the next four years. There were a number of things that Joseph had to learn before he could receive the plates:

— The need to be strictly obedient to the Lord's commandments
— The sacredness of the ancient record
— The power of Satan, who would attempt to destroy both Joseph and the record
— The future destiny of the work to which Joseph had been called

Instruction at the Hill Cumorah

● **JS–History 1:50–52** <u>First Visit to Cumorah:</u>
After his father had told him to be obedient
to the instructions of the angel, Joseph went
to the place where Moroni had told him the
plates were deposited. Because he had seen
it clearly in vision, "[he] knew the place
the instant that [he] arrived there" (v. 50).
He describes the Hill Cumorah, which was
nearby "the village of Manchester, Ontario
county, New York" [where he lived], as being
"a hill of consider- able size, and the most
elevated of any in the neighborhood" (v. 51).

The Hill Cumorah as it appeared in 1907

The plates lay hidden "On the west side of
this hill, not far from the top, under a stone
of considerable size … deposited in a stone
box. This stone was thick and rounding in
the middle on the upper side, and thinner
towards the edges, so that the middle part of
it was visible above the ground, but the edge all around was covered with earth" (v. 51). Today, in
approximately that location, a large statue of Moroni now graces the Hill Cumorah in New York.

Using a lever, the Prophet lifted up the edge of the stone covering the box, and looking in he saw,
"the plates, the Urim and Thummim, and the breastplate." The box in which they lay was formed
by "laying stones together in some kind of cement. In the bottom of the box were laid two stones
crossways of the box, and on these stones lay the plates and the other things with them" (v. 52).

● **JS–History 1:53** <u>Learning to be Obedient:</u> The angel had warned Joseph that he would be
tempted to seek the gold plates for worldly gain (v. 46). Unfortunately, when he beheld this
block of golden plates, he allowed himself to marvel and wonder at their monetary worth.
Because of this, when he "made an attempt to take them out, [he] was forbidden by the
messenger." Lucy Mack Smith said: "The angel told him … that the time had not yet come for
the plates to be brought forth to the world; that he could not take them from the place wherein
they were deposited until he had learned to keep the commandments of God—not only till he
was willing but able to do it."[11] Moroni said he could not have them until "four years from that
time" (v. 53). This was greatly disappointing to Joseph, but he learned important lessons about
righteous motivation and obedience.

<u>A Vision of Christ and Satan:</u> During that first visit to Cumorah, though he could not obtain
the plates, the Lord gave Joseph Smith a vision of His glory followed by a vision of the Prince of
Darkness so that Joseph would be able to recognize the difference between the two powers, and
to resist temptation.[12]

A Warning of Persecution to Come: According to Oliver Cowdery, Moroni told the Prophet during that first visit, "When it is known that the Lord has shown you these things, the workers of iniquity will seek your overthrow: they will circulate falsehoods to destroy your reputation, and also will seek to take your life."[13]

● **JS–History 1:53–54** <u>Annual Visits to Cumorah.</u> Moroni told Joseph Smith to return to the place where the plates were deposited "precisely in one year from that time, and that he would there meet with me, and that I should continue to do so until the time should come for obtain- ing the plates" (v. 53). This he did every year on the 21st of September for four years, 1824– 1827. Each time he went he found Moroni there and "received instruction and intelli- gence from him … respecting what the Lord was going to do, and how and in what manner his kingdom was to be conducted in the last days" (v. 54).

Angel Moroni statue near the spot where the angel met Joseph each year

He also learned much about the Nephites and Lamanites whose history the record contained. Lucy Mack Smith said that the family would gather together every evening for the purpose of listening to Joseph's descriptions of their ancient culture—their dress, mode of traveling, animals, cities, buildings, mode of warfare, and religious worship. "This he would do with as much ease … as if he had spent his whole life among them… I presume our family presented an aspect as singular as any that ever lived upon the face of the earth—all seated in a circle, father, mother, sons and daughters, and giving the most profound attention to a boy, eighteen years of age, who had never read the Bible through in his life… The sweetest union and happiness pervaded our house, and tranquility reigned in our midst" (History of Joseph Smith, 82–83).

Important Family Events While Waiting for the Plates

● **JS–History 1:55–56 The Prophet's brother Alvin Smith dies.** The Smiths were not wealthy and had to work hard on their farm and in day jobs around the area to support themselves (v. 55). As the eldest brother, Alvin was an important key to their earning power. He had also labored hard to build a nice frame home for his parents so they wouldn't have to live in the original log cabin anymore. But during that first year after Joseph's first visit to the Hill Cumorah, his brother Alvin died on November, 15, 1823, leaving the family in financial difficulty (v. 56).

Alvin Smith grave stone in Palmyra

Lucy Mack Smith said "Alvin was taken very sick" and treatment by several different physicians did not help. After a few days of sickness, he called his family to his side and bid them farewell. He charged Hyrum (the next oldest) to take care of his parents and finish the frame house that Alvin had begun for them. To Joseph he said, "'I want you to be a good boy, and do everything that lies in your power to obtain the Record. Be faithful in receiving instruction, and in keeping every commandment that is given you. Your brother Alvin must leave you; but remember the example which he has set for you; and set the same example for the children that are younger than yourself, and always be kind to father and mother." "Alvin was a youth of singular goodness of disposition—kind and amiable, so that lamentation and mourning filled the whole neighborhood in which he resided [when he died]."[14]

- **JS–History 1:56–58 Joseph meets and marries Emma Hale.** In answer to the family's financial crisis, "In the month of October 1825, [Joseph] hired with an old gentleman by the name of Josiah Stoal, who lived in Chenango county, State of New York. He had heard something of a silver mine having been opened by the Spaniards in Harmony, Susquehanna county, State of Pennsylvania" (v. 56). While employed by Mr. Stoal, Joseph boarded with the Hale family in Harmony, Pennsylvania, and there, for the first time, "I … saw my wife (his daughter), Emma Hale" (v. 57).

Emma Hale Smith

DEGUARROTYPE OF PAINTING BY MAUDSLEY, 1842

Because of Joseph's continuing testimony of his first vision, persecution followed him wherever he went, including to Harmony, Pennsylvania. Emma's parents "were very much opposed to our being married. I was, therefore, under the necessity of taking her elsewhere; so we went and were married at the house of Squire Tarbill, in South Bainbridge, Chenango county, New York (v. 58). They were married on January 18, 1827, while Joseph was still employed by Mr. Stoal (v. 57). Though they had to elope in order to get married, no one need suppose that Joseph "stole" Emma Hale from her father or did anything inappropriate or illegal. Both Emma and Joseph were of legal age and could make their decisions about marriage without consent. Nevertheless, Isaac Hale resented it and never forgave Joseph for it. There was no way they could make a home in Harmony.

TRANSLATION OF THE RECORD BEGINS

Joseph Receives the Plates

- **The Angel Moroni told the Prophet in 1823 that great persecution would come.** "When it is known that the Lord has shown you these things, the workers of iniquity will seek your overthrow: they will circulate falsehoods to destroy your reputation, and also will seek to take your life."[15]

- **JS–History 1:58–59 Joseph finally received the Book of Mormon plates on September 22, 1827.** Joseph and Emma moved back to Joseph's parents home near Palmyra, where he farmed with his father that spring and summer season (v. 58). The year was 1827, and this was the year in which Moroni had told Joseph he could obtain the plates. Thus, "On the twenty-second day of September, one thousand eight hun dred and twenty-seven, having gone as usual at the end of another year to

Joseph finally received the plates in 1827

the place where they were deposited, the same heavenly messenger delivered them up to me" (v. 59). Emma rode to the hill with Joseph, in a borrowed carriage, in the middle of the night, and waited patiently in the dark while Joseph met with Moroni and received the plates.

The Angel Moroni warned again as he delivered the plates to Joseph, as he had during their first visit at the Hill Cumorah in 1823: "You are but a man, therefore you will have to be watchful and faithful to your trust, or you will be overpowered by wicked men; for they will lay every plan and scheme that is possible to get it away from you, and if you do not take heed continually, they will succeed."[16]

- **JS–History 1:60–61 Joseph soon learned that Moroni's prophecies would be literally fulfilled.** Leaving the Hill Cumorah, Joseph temporarily hid the plates in an old log. Later, while transferring them to his home, he was attacked several times. This quickly taught Joseph why Moroni had given him the warning concerning the safety of the plates.

Translating Begins in Harmony, Pennsylvania

After Joseph had received the plates, the harassment and persecution in Palmyra became very severe, forcing Joseph and Emma to move to Harmony, Pennsylvania, the home of his in-laws, the Hales. Some of the anger that existed at the time of their marriage had subsided, and the Hales consented to have them return.

Martin Harris, a prominent resident of Palmyra, was one of the first to believe in Joseph Smith's work. He gave Joseph fifty dollars to assist him in moving to Harmony, Pennsylvania. It was there in the temporary peace of Harmony that the translation began.

The home where Joseph and Emma lived in Harmony Pennsylvania, and where the Book of Mormon translation began (No longer standing)

Persecution soon arose in Harmony. Isaac Hale heard that Joseph had the plates with him and demanded to see them. When Joseph refused his demand, he refused to let them stay. Joseph purchased a modest home and farm, nearby across the road, which bordered on the back of the property with the Susquehanna River. Joseph worked on his farm to support his family and translation work was very slow. He learned how to use the Urim and Thummim to translate and managed to copy and translate a few characters. It was there, in that home, that Emma acted as Joseph's first scribe, but because of his and her many duties very little was able to be translated. She became pregnant with their first child during that time.

In 1879, Emma bore solemn witness of the plates and their miraculous translation:

> I know Mormonism to be the truth; and believe the Church to have been established by divine direction. I have complete faith in it. In writing for your father I frequently wrote day after day, often sitting at the table close by him, he sitting … and dictating hour after hour with nothing between us… He had neither manuscript or book to read from … If he had anything of the kind he could not have concealed it from me …

> Joseph Smith could neither write nor dictate a coherent and well-worded letter; let alone dictating a book like the Book of Mormon. And, though I was an active participant in the scenes that transpired, and was present during the translation of the plates, and had cognizance of things as they transpired, it is marvelous to me, "a marvel and a wonder," as much as to anyone else …

> My belief is that the Book of Mormon is of divine authenticity—I have not the slightest doubt of it. I am satisfied that no man could have dictated the writing of the manuscripts unless he was inspired; for, when acting as his scribe, your father would dictate to me hour after hour; and when returning after meals, or after interruptions, he would at once begin where he had left off, without either seeing the manuscript or having any portion of it read to him. This was a usual thing for him to do. It would have been improbable that a learned man could do this, and, for one so ignorant and unlearned as he was, it was simply impossible.

> The plates often lay on the table without any attempt at concealment, wrapped in a small linen table cloth, which I had given him to fold them in. I once felt of the plates, as they thus lay on the table, tracing their outline and shape. They seemed to be pliable like thick paper, and would rustle with a metallic sound when the edges were moved by the thumb.[17]

Martin Harris and the Anthon Transcript

Sometime between December 1827 and February 1828, Martin Harris received a vision affirming the divinity of Joseph's work. Martin had received much criticism from his wife, family, and neighbors for his support of Joseph Smith. He desired scientific "proof" of Joseph's work to convince them—a weakness that persisted in his life.

In February 1828, he traveled to Harmony to obtain a copy of the ancient characters and their translation. He took them east to show them to a "learned man" who could verify their authenticity and accuracy. Eventually, he actually showed them to two learned men.

Martin Harris

● **JS–History 1:62–65 The first learned man, Professor Charles Anthon, unwittingly fulfilled an ancient prophecy made by Isaiah.** He recognized the characters as being of ancient origin, and claimed he could translate them, though he certainly could not—the world was years from the time when the Rosetta stone provided a way to translate ancient Egyptian characters. Probably for his own academic career's sake he sought to obtain the record, and when Martin Harris told him he could not have it because the record was "sealed," he made his famous and prophecy-fulfilling statement, "I cannot read a sealed book" (Isaiah 29:11; 2 Nephi 27:15–18) and promptly tore up the certificate of authenticity he had given to Martin.

Martin then took the characters to a second learned man, Professor Samuel Mitchell, who also verified their authenticity as ancient characters.

HARD LESSONS ABOUT STRICT OBEDIENCE

The Lost Manuscript

Martin's assistance, both financially and as a scribe were very valuable to Joseph Smith. Convinced of the authenticity of the Book of Mormon plates after his visit with learned men, Martin prepared to come to Harmony to help with translating. His wife insisted on coming with him, but she stirred up so much prejudice toward Joseph that Martin had to take her home before the work could begin.

For the next two months—April 12 to June 14, 1828—Martin was Joseph's scribe as he translated 116 pages. Those pages were 13 x 17 inches in size, the equivalent of 300 pages of 8 ½ x 11 inch paper. Their work covered the writings and events of the prophet Lehi on the large plates of Mormon.

Martin's great weakness was pride. He was convinced that if he could show his family their work, they would believe him. He asked the Prophet for permission from the Lord for him to show his family the manuscript. At Martin's insistence, Joseph asked twice, and both times the answer was "no." Unsatisfied with the answer he insisted that Joseph ask again.

Joseph was afraid of offending Martin Harris, who had befriended him and supported him with both his money and his time. Joseph was young and had very few friends—especially friends with Martin Harris' reputation. He was worried about offending his prominent friend and about losing his valuable support. He foolishly pestered the Lord a third time and was told he could do it, though it wasn't wise.

Martin made a solemn covenant that he would show them only to certain people—his wife, her sister, his mother and father, and his brother—and would write to Joseph regularly. Martin then hurried off to Palmyra, where he violated his covenant by showing them to others. Some scholars assert (based on D&C 3:12–13 and 10:6–7) that it was Martin who wanted to "test" the Lord (not just others)—that he wanted to see if Joseph would translate the record precisely the same a second time. If he could, then it would constitute scientific proof for his wife and family. Seeking such proof would indeed constitute "trusting in his own judgment" rather than trusting in God. But whether or not this is true, we know for certain from revelation (D&C 10:8–13) that after the transcript fell into other hands, those who possessed it wanted to change it so that Joseph's new translation would not match it and would show him to be a fraud.

Tragedy struck Joseph's young family during this time. The following day, Emma prematurely delivered their first child—who died the same day. They named the child Alvin—after Joseph's beloved deceased older brother. The grave of this firstborn child still lies today in the cemetery not too far east of the site of Joseph and Emma's home. Emma nearly died herself from complications of the childbirth. Joseph sat up with her night after night until she was out of danger and began to mend.

Moroni Withdraws the Record

Meanwhile, Martin Harris had not written to Joseph as promised. Emma eventually convinced him to go to Palmyra to investigate what had happened. When he got there, he discovered, to his horror, that the manuscript had been lost. Joseph fell into deep anguish and self-condemnation for allowing the record out of his possession.

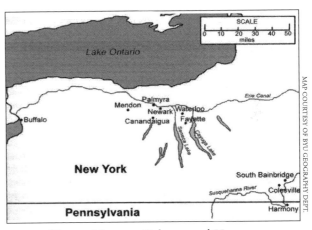

The road between Palmyra and Harmony

Joseph's mother tried to console him, assuring him that "the Lord would forgive him, after a short season of humiliation and repentance." The entire family was full of grief, but Joseph in particular because "he better understood the consequences of disobedience. And he continued pacing back and forth, meantime weeping and grieving, until about sunset, when, by persuasion, he took a little nourishment. The next morning, he set out for home. We parted with heavy hearts, for it now appeared that all which we had so fondly anticipated, and which had been the source of so much secret gratification, had in a moment fled, and fled forever."[18]

Joseph returned to Harmony in July of 1828, and went to the Lord in prayerful sorrow. Moroni appeared, demanded the Urim and Thummim and condemned him for his serious offense. He offered some hope, however, with a promise: "If you are very humble and penitent, it may be you will receive them [the Urim and Thummim] again; if so, it will be on the 22nd of next September."[19]

The Purposes of God Cannot Be Frustrated

A few days later, in July 1828, Moroni appeared again to Joseph and gave him the Urim and Thummim long enough for him to receive a revelation from the Lord—which is now recorded as D&C 3. This revelation is a thorough scolding of the Prophet for his foolishness and a warning that if he did not learn to be obedient he might lose his sacred calling. I believe it to be one of the evidences of the truth of Joseph's testimony, because an egotistical fraud would never have published such a stern condemnation of himself and his weaknesses.

- **D&C 3:1–3 The Lord reminded Joseph that the works of God cannot be frustrated (v. 1).** God knows the end from the beginning because "his course is one eternal round" (v. 2). This means that all things, past, present, and future are continually before Him. As Elder Neal A. Maxwell said: "What we mortals encounter as the unforeseen, God has already seen."[20] We cannot comprehend how this is done because all things in this mortal life have a beginning and an end. But we may rest assured that God knows and comprehends everything, and "it is not the work of God that is frustrated, but the work of men" (v. 3). This should give us absolute confidence in His promises to us.

- **D&C 3:4 The Lord will not permit His prophet to lead us astray.** While scolding the Prophet Joseph Smith, the Lord said: "although a man may have many revelations, and have power to do many mighty works, yet if he boasts in his own strength, and sets at naught the counsels of God, and follows after the dictates of his own will and carnal desires, he must fall and incur the vengeance of a just God upon him." The Lord makes a very important assurance in this verse—that if His chosen prophet should stray from the truth and attempt to lead the people of God astray, He will not permit it. He will remove such a prophet before this can destroy His work. We can, therefore, have absolute confidence that we will never go astray so long as we follow the Lord's Prophet.

  Elder L. Tom Perry said: "I pray that all the members of the Church will recognize that there is safety when we follow the prophet and strictly heed his voice."[21] Elder J. Reuben Clark Jr. said: "You will never make a mistake by following the instructions and the counsel of him who stands at the head as God's mouthpiece on earth."[22] President Ezra Taft Benson said: "Keep your eye on the Prophet, for the Lord will never permit His Prophet to lead this Church astray. Let us live close to the Spirit, so we can test all counsel."[23] And President Joseph Fielding Smith said: "I think there is one thing which we should have exceedingly clear in our minds. Neither the President of the Church, nor the First Presidency, nor the united voice of the First Presidency and the Twelve will ever lead the Saints astray or send forth counsel to the world that is contrary to the mind and will of the Lord."[24]

- **D&C 3:5–8 The Lord chastened Joseph for fearing man (Martin's opinion of him) more than God.** The Lord had entrusted Joseph with the plates and other sacred things and given him strict commandments concerning them (v. 5). This refers in part to Joseph Smith's first interview with Moroni and the cautions and promises made to him at that time (JS-History 1:33–54, 59). And yet, because of his youth and inexperience he had too often "transgressed the commandments and the laws of God" (v. 6). Because of the "persuasions of men" he had "feared man more than God" (vv. 6–7). Because of this, Joseph had "set at naught the counsels of God, and despise[d] his words" (v. 7). If he had been more faithful and trusting in the Lord "he would have extended his arm and supported you against all the fiery darts of the adversary; and he would have been with you in every time of trouble" (v. 8). Like all of us, Joseph needed to learn to trust the Lord and His promises, no matter how difficult the situation.

- **D&C 3:9–11 Joseph will fall unless he learns to be obedient.** The Lord said: "Behold, thou art Joseph, and thou wast chosen to do the work of the Lord, but because of transgression, if thou art not aware thou wilt fall" (v. 9). He reminded Joseph that He is merciful and that if he would repent "thou art still chosen, and art again called to the work" (v. 10). But if not, "thou shalt be delivered up and become as other men, and have no more gift" (v. 11).

The Prophet took this counsel to heart. He said to the Saints in Kirtland, "I declare unto you the warning which the Lord has commanded me to declare unto this generation, remembering that the eyes of my Maker are upon me, and that to Him I am accountable for every word I say."[25] And he counseled the Saints at Nauvoo that "Whatever God requires is right, no matter what it is, although we may not see the reason thereof till long after the events transpire."[26]

DEGUEROTYPE OF MAUDSLEY PAINTING, 1842

● **D&C 3:12–15 The wickedness of Martin Harris and of Joseph.** When Joseph Smith gave to Martin Harris the 116 pages of transcript "which God had given thee sight and power to translate, thou deliveredst up that which was sacred into the hands of a wicked man" (v. 12). Martin had "set at naught the counsels of God, and ... broken the most sacred promises which were made before God, and ... depended upon his own judgment and boasted in his own wisdom" (v. 13). Evidently, Martin had willfully ignored his promises to God and to Joseph and showed the manuscript to more than just his immediate family in a boastful manner. And as wicked as that was, Joseph also shared in the blame for persisting in his requests to let Martin take the manuscript. For that reason, and because he had "suffered the counsel of thy director [Moroni as well as the Lord] to be trampled upon from the beginning" (v. 15), Joseph had "lost thy privileges for a season" (v. 14).

● **D&C 3:16–20 The Lord's work will go forward, with or without Joseph Smith.** His promises to the seed of Lehi—that "the knowledge of a Savior [would come unto them] ... through the testimony of their fathers" will all be fulfilled (vv. 16–18). It was for this purpose that "these plates [were] preserved, which contain these records—that the promises of the Lord might be fulfilled, which he made to his people" (v. 19). Unlike men, the Lord will not violate His covenant promises. He had promised "that the Lamanites might come to the knowledge of their fathers, and that they might know the promises of the Lord, and that they may believe the gospel and rely upon the merits of Jesus Christ, and be glorified through faith in his name, and that through their repentance they might be saved" (v. 20), and He will fulfill those promises one way or the other.

At the close of this revelation, Moroni then took back the Urim and Thummim—and the plates—leaving Joseph to think about what he had done for the next two months.

The Designs of Evil Men

The sections of the Doctrine and Covenants are not inserted chronologically. If we look at the headings for D&C 3, D&C 4, and D&C 10, we note the following:

— D&C 3 was given in July 1828.
— D&C 10 was given in September of 1828, though this fact was missed in versions of the Doctrine and Covenants prior to 1921.
— D&C 4, a revelation to Joseph Smith Sr., came after D&C 10 in February 1829.
— D&C 5–9 were all given in March and April of 1829.

We can conclude, therefore, that the next revelation Joseph Smith received after the scolding he received in D&C 3 was the revelation contained in D&C 10.

- **D&C 10:1–3 The plates and his prophetic calling are restored to Joseph Smith.** This revelation was given in September 1828 after what must have been a long and difficult summer for Joseph and Emma. The Lord reminded Joseph that "because you delivered up those writings which you had power given unto you to translate by the means of the Urim and Thummim, into the hands of a wicked man, you have lost them" (v. 1). "And you also lost your gift at the same time, and your mind became darkened" (v. 2). But now, these gifts were "restored unto you again; therefore see that you are faithful and continue on unto the finishing of the remainder of the work of translation as you have begun" (v. 3).

- **D&C 10:4–5 Advice on how to fulfill our callings.** It would have been tempting for Joseph to work overtime now to make up for lost time. It had been one year since he received the plates at the Hill Cumorah, and at this point he had nothing to show for it. All of his work was stolen and lost. But the Lord gave him wise counsel on how to proceed:

  — Be diligent—keeping at it until the assignment is finished (v. 4), but …
  — Do all things with reason—don't overdo things or go beyond your strength (v. 4).
  — Pray always, recognizing that we need the Lord's help to succeed (v. 5).

  Joseph was not to "make up for lost time," but proceed with wisdom and order. Joseph heeded this advice and did not return immediately to translating. He farmed his land and provided for his family for a while.

- **D&C 10:6–9 How the 116-page manuscript was lost.** In the Lord's eyes, "enemies," including Martin Harris—"the man in whom you have trusted" (v. 6) had sought to destroy the Lord's work. Martin's wickedness consisted of "tak[ing] away the things wherewith you have been entrusted" and seeking "to destroy your gift" (v. 7). And once they were in Martin's hands, other "wicked men have taken them from you" (v. 8). The net effect was that Joseph had "delivered … up … that which was sacred, unto wickedness" (v. 9).

- **D&C 10:10–14 God revealed the conspiracy of Joseph's enemies to try to destroy him.** "Satan hath put it into their hearts to alter the words which you have caused to be written, or which you have translated, which have gone out of your hands" (v. 10).

  Because of these alterations, they now "read contrary from that which you translated and caused to be written" (v. 11). This Satan-inspired conspiracy sought to trap Joseph by comparing their altered manuscript with whatever he re- translated, and then saying that "they have caught you in the words which you have pretended to translate" (v. 13). But God will not permit this conspiracy to succeed (v. 14). He had planned for this eventuality more than 2,000 years earlier in the days of the prophet Nephi by having him keep a second record of events on the smaller plates of Nephi.

  — **1 Nephi 9:2–6 and Words of Mormon 6–7 The Lord had told Nephi more than 2,000 years earlier to keep two parallel records**—a secular history on the "large plates," and the religious or spiritual history on the "small plates." Neither Nephi nor Mormon (who felt compelled to include the small plates with his own record) knew why, but they believed that God had a purpose. The Lord was preparing, more than 2,000 years earlier, for the events that were now transpiring in Joseph Smith's day.

Mormon included the small plates with his record

- **D&C 10:15–21 Testing God is evil.** Evil men try to "tempt" (test) God—set up tests to see if He will respond as they wish. Martin Harris was guilty of this—always seeking to have external verification of the truth of things by means of Martin's choosing (as when he took a copy of the characters to Professor Anthon). As mentioned earlier, it could even have been Martin Harris himself who "put it into their hearts to get thee to tempt the Lord thy God, in asking to translate it over again" (v. 15). Whether or not this is true, we know that those who obtained the transcript through him said: "if God has given him power to translate … he will also give him power again" (v. 16). And the author of all these thoughts was Satan (v. 14).

They conspired, "if he translates again [and] bringeth forth the same words, behold, we have the same with us, and we have altered them; Therefore they will not agree, and we will say that he has lied in his words, and that he has no gift, and that he has no power" (vv. 17–18). By this process, they sought to "destroy him, and also the work" that they might not be embarrassed if Joseph happened to retranslate the record precisely as before, and they could therefore ensure themselves the "glory of the world" (v. 19) by "proving" Joseph a false prophet with their altered manuscript. Notice that they had absolutely no interest in discovering the truth. They were only interested in destroying Joseph and his work because "Satan has great hold upon their hearts [and] stirreth them up to iniquity against that which is good" (v. 20). The Lord said: "their hearts are corrupt, and full of wickedness and abominations; and they love darkness rather than light, because their deeds are evil" (v. 21). It did not even occur to them to ask of God if Joseph's work were true (v. 21); they wanted only to destroy it.

Proving God is appropriate. While God considers "testing" Him to be evil, He actually invites us to "prove" Him (as He does with the principle of tithing; Malachi 3:10). The difference is that "proving" Him involves keeping His commandments and reaping the rewards of doing so, while "testing" Him is a negative experiment whereby the faithless challenge God to demonstrate His power to convince them of things they will not otherwise believe. This is the same spirit that demands, "Show me a sign, and then I will believe," as Korihor demanded in the Book of Mormon (Alma 30).

- **D&C 10:12, 20–36, 63 An explanation of how temptation affects the wicked.** Satan has a "cunning plan" to destroy God's work (v. 12). He stirs up the wicked to iniquity against the righteous (v. 20). Nevertheless, temptation is not force, and those who are thus "stirred up" cannot blame the devil for their actions. They have their agency and the Lord "will require this at their hands" (v. 23). Satan inspires the wicked to anger against God's work (v. 24). He is the father of all lies, deception, and "flattery" (vv. 25–36)—the notion that evil deeds are somehow justified because they are more "reasonable" or even "superior" to the ways of the righteous. Indeed, it seems that there is nobody more self-righteous than an unrighteous man who is seeking to justify his behavior. Through this means, Satan sought to overpower and contradict Joseph's testimony of his work (v. 33), using Martin Harris as his tool for doing so. Even among the righteous, Satan encourages contention over doctrine and religion (v. 63), thus darkening the minds of men and driving the Spirit from them.

President Joseph F. Smith said: "By every possible means he seeks to darken the minds of men and then offers them falsehood and deception in the guise of truth. Satan is a skillful imitator, and as genuine gospel truth is given the world in ever-increasing abundance, so he spreads the counterfeit coin of false doctrine. Beware of his spurious currency, it will purchase for you nothing but disappointment, misery and spiritual death. The 'father of lies' he has been called, and [so] adept has he become through the ages of practice in his nefarious work, that were it possible he would deceive the very elect."[27]

President Spencer W. Kimball said: [Satan] "will use his logic to confuse and his rationalizations to destroy. He will shade meanings, open doors an inch at a time, and lead from purest white through all the shades of gray to the darkest black."[28]

- **D&C 10:40, 44–45 The Lord instructed the Prophet not to retranslate the first 116 pages** of manuscript, but to translate Nephi's second set of records instead. These small plates of Nephi contained "things which, in my wisdom, I would bring to the knowledge of the people" that would suit the Lord's purposes equally well (v. 40). As a matter of fact, "there are many things engraven upon the plates of Nephi which do throw greater views upon my gospel" than what Joseph had previously translated (v. 45). That is because these small plates contained a more sacred or spiritual record as opposed to the more temporal historical record to be found on the large plates (Jacob 1:2–4).

- **D&C 10:41–43 Joseph was to translate the small plates of Nephi instead.** Joseph Smith was commanded to "translate the engravings which are on the [small] plates of Nephi, down even till you come to the reign of king Benjamin," which apparently corresponded to the Book of Lehi that he had previously translated from the large plates (v. 41). Thus, instead of re-translating the record of Lehi, he was to translate "the record of Nephi; and thus I will confound those who have altered my words" (v. 42). By this means, "I will show unto them that my wisdom is greater than the cunning of the devil" (v. 43). Of course, this would not be done right away. Oliver Cowdery didn't arrive to assist with the translation until April 1829, nearly seven months later.

The sequence of translation for the Book of Mormon. When Joseph Smith originally began translating with Martin Harris in 1828, he evidently started with the Book of Lehi from Mormon's abridgment of the large plates of Nephi (heading to D&C 10). There is some indication from the historical record that when Joseph and Oliver began their translation activities one year later in April 1829, they translated the remainder of the large plates (from Mosiah to Moroni) first, then translated the small plates from 1 Nephi to Words of Mormon to replace the lost 116 pages. Thus, by the time these replacement pages from the small plates were translated (June 1829), it had been nearly a year since the original 116 pages had been lost (July 1828).

One of the evidences of this is the fact that five weeks after they started, 15 May 1829, they were on 3 Nephi and the Savior's sermon on baptism to the Nephites. Not until arriving at the Whitmer residence in Fayette did Joseph translate the small plates of Nephi, which contain 1 Nephi through the Words of Mormon. We draw this conclusion from the fact that in the original manuscript of the Book of Mormon, John Whitmer's work as a scribe in Fayette, New York, only dealt with material from the small plates.

<u>Alma quoting Nephi is evidence of the authenticity of the translated record.</u> Given that the large plates were finished before the small plates were translated, we have an amazing proof of the Book of Mormon's authenticity in Alma 36. As Alma recounted the story of his conversion, the joy he experienced, and his desire to be with God, he compared himself to Lehi: "Yea, methought I saw, even as our father Lehi saw, God sitting upon his throne, surrounded with numberless concourses of angels, in the attitude of singing and praising their God" (Alma 36:22). These words are quoted verbatim from 1 Nephi 1:8, which at the time had not yet been translated. Alma was translated before 1 Nephi. That Alma could quote directly from Lehi makes sense, since

The Sequence of Translation

The Large Plates
~~The Book of Lehi~~
Mosiah
Alma
Helaman
3 Nephi
4 Nephi
Mormon
Ether
Moroni

▽

The Small Plates
1 Nephi
2 Nephi
Jacob
Enos
Jarom
Omni
Words of Mormon

Alma had charge of the small plates of Nephi (Alma 37:23) and thus would have been aware of the precise language used by Nephi in the sacred record. But for Joseph Smith to manufacture a quote from a record he had not yet translated is next to impossible. The truth is, the record is authentic.

- **D&C 10:53–56 The Lord will save truly converted members of His Church; only the wicked need fear.** The Lord declares of our dispensation, "If this generation harden not their hearts, I will establish my church among them" (v. 53). And those who belong to His Church "need not fear, for such shall inherit the kingdom of heaven" (v. 55). "But it is they who do not fear me, neither keep my commandments but build up churches unto themselves to get gain, … that do wickedly and build up the kingdom of the devil … it is they that I will disturb, and cause to tremble and shake to the center" (v. 56).

- **D&C 10:57–58, 69–70 The Lord Himself gives the revelations in the Book of Mormon.** We are reading the words of "Jesus Christ, the Son of God … the light which shineth in darkness, and the darkness comprehendeth it not" (vv. 57–58). He is "the life and light of the world, your Redeemer, your Lord and your God" (v. 70). He assures us that those who are "of my church, and endureth of my church to the end, him will I establish upon my rock, and the gates of hell shall not prevail against them" (v. 69).

Some Purposes of the Book of Mormon

- **D&C 10:59–68 The Lord lists several reasons for the coming forth of the Book of Mormon.** He is the same who said "Other sheep have I which are not of this fold" to His disciples in Jerusalem, and they "understood me not" (v. 59). The Book of Mormon is the record of His dealings with those other sheep, and it demonstrates a number of important things.

— It shows that the Lord has other "sheep" and that they are of Israel (v. 60).

— It shows the marvelous works the Book of Mormon peoples did in His name (v. 61).

— It will bring to light true doctrine (v. 62).

— It will help stop the contention over doctrine that characterizes Christianity (v. 63).

— It foretells the gathering of Israel to the true Church in the last days (v. 65).

— It helps establish the doctrine of Christ (vv. 67–68).

TRANSLATION BEGINS AGAIN

Important Developments While Translating

A number of important events and revelations occurred during the time Joseph lived in Harmony, Pennsylvania, from March to June of 1829. Most of these will be discussed in later chapters, but are listed here to place them in their historical context.

- **D&C 4** <u>Joseph's father visits him in Harmony</u>. Worried about their son, Joseph's parents came to visit him in February of 1829. Knowing prophetically that they were coming, Joseph went out to meet them. Joseph's father wanted to know what he could do to help his son. Joseph inquired of the Lord and received this revelation. The Lord told Joseph's father that a great and marvelous work was beginning, and those who desire to work for this cause must serve God with all their hearts, might, mind and strength (v. 2). If we desire to serve God in this manner, we are "called to the work" (v. 3).

- **D&C 5** <u>A revelation to Martin Harris</u> (March 1829). Martin Harris came again to Harmony, Pennsylvania, seeking the Lord's forgiveness. Though he had humbly repented of his foolishness in losing the manuscript, Martin Harris still seemed troubled by a desire to have direct evidence of the existence of the plates. In this revelation, the Lord told Martin that he could receive his desires only by being faithful and humble but that, if he did so, he would be called as one of the three special witnesses who would see the plates. We will discuss that promise in more detail later in this chapter.

- **JS–History 1:66–67** <u>Oliver Cowdery arrives to act as Joseph's scribe</u> (April 5, 1829). Time was moving quickly and the work of translation was painfully slow. Joseph needed another scribe, and sought earnestly for the Lord to send him someone to help with the translation. Meanwhile, Oliver Cowdery arrived at the Smith farm near Palmyra and took up residence there while he taught school in that area. Hearing of Joseph's visions and seeking his own witness concerning them, he was convinced of the truth of the work, and headed south toward Harmony to meet the Prophet Joseph Smith for himself and see if he could assist. He arrived on April 5, 1829 and began two days later to function as Joseph's scribe.

- **D&C 6–9** <u>Revelations to Oliver Cowdery</u> (April 1829). These revelations contain much important information about the Apostle John and about the process of revelation. They are discussed in chapters 5 and 6.

D&C 11–12 <u>Revelations to Hyrum Smith and Joseph Knight</u> (May 1829). These two faithful men paid separate visits to Joseph in Harmony, Pennsylvania during May 1829, and they received revelations concerning what they could do to assist in the work.

- **JS–History 1:68–73; D&C 13** <u>The Aaronic and Melchizedek priesthoods restored</u> (May 1829). On May 15th Joseph and Oliver received the Aaronic priesthood on the banks of the Susquehanna River behind Joseph's home. Sometime during the next few weeks they received the Melchizedek priesthood also, while fleeing persecution.

- <u>First converts and gifts of the Spirit</u> (May/June 1829). During this important period some converts were made, particularly near Colesville, New York, where Joseph Knight and his family resided. Gifts of the Spirit began to be manifested among these converts—healings, tongues, and more—which will be discussed later on as part of Chapter 15.

- <u>JS–History 1:74–75 Increased persecution</u> (May/June 1829). As the first new converts came into the Church, opposition also increased. Joseph and Oliver visited Colesville, New York, and eventually had to flee for their lives back toward Harmony, Pennsylvania. It was during that hurried retreat through the wilderness along the Susquehanna River that they were met by Peter, James and John, and received the Melchizedek priesthood. Because of the circumstances, the precise date of the event was not recorded at the time, but we will discuss this in more detail in chapter 8.

- <u>The move to Fayette, New York to complete the translation</u> (June 1829). The work of translation moved on at a rapid pace. They had labored with little cessation on the translation of the Book of Mormon throughout April, and had completed nearly 2/3 of the Book of Mormon translation by June of 1829. However, increasing persecution in Harmony, Pennsylvania made it impossible for Joseph and Oliver to finish the translation there. They wrote to David Whitmer to ask if he and Joseph could live with the Whitmer family in Fayette, New York, while they completed their work. The Whitmers were friends of Oliver Cowdery, and he had stopped there on his way to Harmony and told them Joseph's story. David consented and came to Harmony, Pennsylvania to get Joseph, Emma, and Oliver.

Lucy Mack Smith said:

> The letter was written and delivered, and was shown by Mr. Whitmer to his father, mother, brothers, and sisters, and their advice was asked … His father reminded him that he had as much wheat sown upon the ground as he could harrow in two days … [and] a quantity of plaster of paris to spread, which must be done immediately; consequently, he could not go, unless he could get a witness from God that it was absolutely necessary. This suggestion pleased David, and he asked the Lord for a testimony concerning his going for Joseph, and was told by the voice of the Spirit to go as soon as his wheat was harrowed in.
>
> The next morning, David went to the field, and found that he had two heavy days' work before him. He … said to himself that, if he should be enabled, by any means, to do this work sooner than the same had ever been done on the farm before, he would receive it as an evidence, that it was the will of God, that he should do all in his power to assist Joseph Smith in the work in which he was engaged. He then fastened his horses to the harrow … [and] drove around the whole of it, continuing … till noon, when, on stopping for dinner, he looked around, and discovered to his surprise, that he had harrowed in full half the wheat. After dinner he went on as before, and by evening he finished the whole two days' work.[29]

That was the first miracle. There was another one to come. David's father sensed that God's hand was in this development and advised him to go immediately to Harmony as soon as his "plaster of paris" [fertilizer] was sown. Lucy Mack Smith continued:

> The next morning, David … went out to sow the plaster, which he had left, two days previous, in heaps near his sister's house, but, on coming to the place, he discovered that it was gone! He then ran to his sister, and inquired of her if she knew what had become of it. Being surprised she said: "Why do you ask me? Was it not all sown yesterday?" "Not to my knowledge," answered David.
>
> "I am astonished at that," replied his sister, "for the children came to me in the forenoon, and begged of me to go out and see the men sow plaster in the field, saying that they never saw anybody sow plaster so fast in their lives. I accordingly went, and saw three men at work in the field, as the children said, but, supposing that you had hired some help, on account of your hurry, I went immediately into the house, and gave the subject no further attention."[30]

David and his entire family were profoundly impressed, and David immediately set out on the 135-mile journey to Pennsylvania, making it there in two days. This was the first time that David Whitmer and Joseph Smith had met. They loaded up the Smiths and Oliver Cowdery and returned back to Fayette, New York.

The Miracle of Translation

There in the peaceful environment of the Whitmer farm, Joseph and Oliver completed the translation of the Book of Mormon. The dates of their beginning in Harmony, Pennsylvania, and of their finishing in Fayette, New York are a matter of public record. All told, they accomplished their work of translating about 500 printed pages in about 65 working days. That amounts to about 10 pages per working day.

Oliver Cowdery said: "These were days never to be forgotten—to sit under the sound of a voice dictated by the inspiration of heaven, awakened the utmost gratitude of this bosom! Day after day I continued, uninterrupted, to write from his mouth, as he translated with the Urim and Thummim, or as the Nephites would have said, 'Interpreters,' the history or record called 'The Book of Mormon.'"[31]

Oliver also said: "I wrote with my own pen, the entire Book of Mormon (save a few pages) as it fell from the lips of the Prophet Joseph Smith, as he translated it by the gift and power of God, by means of the Urim and Thummim, or, as it is called by the book, 'holy interpreters'… The book is true. Sidney Rigdon did not write it; Mr. Spaulding did not write it; I wrote it myself as it fell from the lips of the Prophet."[32]

THE BOOK OF MORMON IS PUBLISHED

The Time Line of its Printing

To protect the sacred manuscript, Oliver was instructed to make a copy of the entire thing to take to the printers. He began making this copy (called the "printers manuscript") on July 10, 1829. On August 18, 1829, a contract was made with the Grandin Print Shop in Palmyra, New York to print 5,000 copies. Grandin at first refused to participate but miraculously changed his mind. Martin Harris mortgaged his farm to guarantee the $3,000 needed for the job. His wife considered this the "last straw" and divorced him. The time line thereafter was as follows. — 24 Aug 1829   The first 24 pages of the manuscript were delivered; typesetting began.

Grandin Print Shop in Palmyra, New York

— 26 Mar 1830   The first copies of the Book of Mormon were completed 6 months later.

— 6 Apr 1830   Just 11 days later, the Church was organized at Fayette, New York.

The Miracle of the Printing of the Book of Mormon

In May 2003, Gordon L. Weight published a booklet titled Miracle on Palmyra's Main Street: An "Old-Time" Printer's Perspective on Printing the Original Copies of the Book of Mormon.[33] In this interesting summary he relates several miracles that surrounded the actual printing of the Book of Mormon at the Grandin Press. Following is a brief summary of his findings.

● **New Type:** In the contract, Joseph stipulated that the printing must be done with "new type"— printing press characters that had not previously been used. To obtain new type Grandin would have had to order it from Germany or China, causing a substantial delay. Joseph then gave Grandin sufficient new type to do the job—96 to 128 sets of fonts. Where did he get this type?

It was not available anywhere at the time.

- **Typesetting:** Each printed sheet—called a signature—contained 16 pages of the book, which when folded and cut would produce the finished product. Each letter of an entire 16–page signature had to be hand-set. There was a total of 570 printed pages, each requiring 2 hours to set. That means that typesetting alone would require 1,140 hours (4 ½ months at 60 hours per week). Once a signature was printed, the type had to be "redistributed"—removed and cleaned before it could be used for a new signature (570 hours or 2 ½ months). Therefore, typesetting activities alone would have required 7 months of labor.

- **Printing:** A 16–page signature contained 8 pages on each side of the paper. To complete 5,000 books, 5,000 impressions of each signature had to be made. At 1 ½ minutes per sheet (100 sheets per hour) it would have taken 25 hours (3 days) per page, and each signature would have required a minimum of 6 days to do both sides. Therefore, it would have required 222 days for the actual printing of the pages (8 ½ months at 10 hours per work day). Remember that because of the need to remove type, clean it, and reset it before you could move on to the next page, that while printing was going on, no typesetting could be done, nor could they print while typesetting. Therefore, when added together, typesetting (4 ½ months), redistribution of type (2 ½ months) and printing (8 ½ months), under the best of circumstances would have required a minimum of 15 ½ months to complete. And yet, somehow, the work was completed in a little more than 6 months. It was truly a miracle, and Brother Weight offers a number of interesting suggestions as to how the Lord made it possible. I highly recommend this little booklet to anybody who wishes more information on this interesting topic.

WITNESSES OF THE BOOK OF MORMON

As mentioned earlier in this chapter, Martin Harris repented of his foolishness in losing the manuscript of the first 116 pages, but he still seemed troubled by a desire to have direct evidence of the existence of the plates. In March 1829, he went to Harmony, Pennsylvania, to seek the Lord's forgiveness but also to see if he could be one of the witnesses mentioned by the Lord in the Book of Mormon. In answer to this request, the Lord gave Joseph Smith the revelation contained in D&C 5, which told Martin that he could receive his desires by being faithful and humble.

- **D&C 5:11–18 Three witnesses will testify of the Book of Mormon.** The Lord had intended from the beginning to obtain "the testimony of three of my servants, whom I shall call and ordain, unto whom I will show these things, and they shall go forth with my words that are given through you [the Book of Mormon]" (v. 11). These witnesses "shall know of a surety that these things are true, for from heaven will I declare it unto them. I will give them power that they may behold and view these things as they are; And to none else will I grant this power, to receive this same testimony among this generation" (vv. 12–14). But Martin Harris must "wait yet a little while, for ye are not yet ordained" (v. 17).

The Lord declared that, having sent forth the testimony of these witnesses with the Book of Mormon, "whosoever believeth on my words, them will I visit with the manifestation of my Spirit; and they shall be born of me, even of water and of the Spirit" (v. 16). "And their testimony shall also go forth unto the condemnation of this generation if they harden their hearts against them" (v. 18).

- **D&C 5:21–22 A warning and a promise to Joseph Smith.** Joseph had succumbed to the persuasions of Martin Harris before, and the Lord here warns him that he must "repent and walk more uprightly before me, and to yield to the persuasions of men no more" (v. 21). If he will "be firm in keeping the commandments wherewith I have commanded you … behold I grant unto you eternal life, even if you should be slain" (v. 22). This is an interesting premonition of things that were yet to come in his life.

- **D&C 5:23–29, 32 Martin Harris may be one of the witnesses if he will repent.** The Lord then turned His attention to Martin Harris, "the man that desires the witness" (v. 23). "Behold, I say unto him, he exalts himself and does not humble himself sufficiently before me; but if he will bow down before me, and humble himself in mighty prayer and faith, in the sincerity of his heart, then will I grant unto him a view of the things which he desires to see" (v. 24). He may then testify to the world that "I know of a surety that they are true, for I have seen them, for they have been shown unto me by the power of God and not of man" (v. 25). But he is not to say any more than that (a weakness in his prideful character) (v. 26). And if he ever denies his testimony he will be condemned (v. 27).

With his past history of pestering the Lord through Joseph for inappropriate things, the Lord warns, "except he humble himself and acknowledge unto me the things that he has done which are wrong, and covenant with me that he will keep my commandments, and exercise faith in me, behold, I say unto him, he shall have no such views, for I will grant unto him no views of the things of which I have spoken" (v. 28). If he fails to thus qualify himself, Joseph is to inform him that he can do no more for the Lord and should not "trouble me any more concerning this matter" (v. 29). The Lord also predicts that "if my servant Martin Harris humbleth not himself and receive a witness from my hand, that he will fall into transgression" (v. 32).

- **D&C 5:30–35 Joseph is to wait awhile before resuming translation.** "I say unto thee Joseph, when thou hast translated a few more pages thou shalt stop for a season, even until I command thee again; then thou mayest translate again" (v. 30). He warns Joseph that he has enemies "lying in wait to destroy thee" (v. 32). "And there are many that lie in wait to destroy thee from off the face of the earth; and for this cause, that thy days may be prolonged, I have given unto thee these commandments" (v. 33). Therefore, Joseph was to "Stop, and stand still until I command thee, and I will provide means whereby thou mayest accomplish the thing which I have commanded thee. And if thou art faithful in keeping my commandments, thou shalt be lifted up at the last day" (vv. 34–35).

Three Witnesses Are Shown the Plates by Moroni

Three months later, in June 1829, at about the time that the Book of Mormon translation was completed in Fayette, New York, Joseph Smith received D&C 17, which designates those who will be His three witnesses of the Book of Mormon. They are the three who had the most to do with the coming forth of the book: Martin Harris (who paid for its printing), Oliver Cowdery (who acted as scribe for most of it), and David Whitmer (whose family had provided safe shelter while the work was completed).

- **D&C 17:1–5 They were commanded to bear witness of what they would see.** This would include "a view of the plates, and also of the breastplate, the sword of Laban, the Urim and Thummim … and the miraculous directors [Liahona] which were given to Lehi while in the wilderness" (v. 1). It is interesting to note that the Urim and Thummim that Joseph Smith used and that were shown to the three witnesses were the ones "given to the brother of Jared upon the mount, when he talked with the Lord face to face" (v. 1), making them very ancient—nearly 4,000 years old.

David Whitmer

These three witnesses would receive this witness only "by your faith … even by that faith which was had by the prophets of old" (v. 2). It was that same kind of faith that had allowed Joseph Smith to receive them (v. 5). And thereafter these witnesses will be required to "testify of them, by the power of God" (v. 3), that "you have seen them, even as my servant Joseph Smith, Jun., has seen them" (v. 5). "And this you shall do that my servant Joseph Smith, Jun., may not be destroyed, that I may bring about my righteous purposes unto the children of men in this work" (v. 4).

Oliver Cowdery

Elder Bruce R. McConkie said: "Whenever the Lord has established a dispensation by revealing His gospel and by conferring priesthood and keys upon men, He has acted in accordance with the law of witnesses which He himself ordained. This law is: 'In the mouth of two or three witnesses shall every word be established.'… Never does one man stand alone in establishing a new dispensation of revealed truth, or in carrying the burden of such a message and warning to the world. In every dispensation, from Adam to the present, two or more witnesses have always joined their testimonies, thus leaving their hearers without excuse in the day of judgment should the testimony be rejected."[34]

- **D&C 17:8 "For my grace is sufficient for you."** These three men were promised that if they would do all that they were instructed in this revelation, the Lord's grace was sufficient to ensure their salvation. In hindsight, this promise is interesting, given their eventual disaffection with Joseph Smith personally and with the Church in general. Like all of us, they displayed weakness in their faith and their characters, but they never

Martin Harris

did deny their witness of this great event. It is hopeful to note that the Lord's saving grace is sufficient to save them so long as they do not deny their witness of this heavenly manifestation.

The Eight Witnesses

In addition to the Three Witnesses, eight others were shown the gold plates with the Lord's permission. These individuals were not shown the plates by an angel (the power of God) but by Joseph Smith. And they saw and handled only the plates, not the other items seen by the Three Witnesses. They were individuals who had assisted Joseph in important ways as he translated the work:

— Joseph Smith Sr.

— Hyrum Smith

— Samuel H. Smith

— Hiram Page

— Christian Whitmer

— Jacob Whitmer

— Peter Whitmer Jr.

— John Whitmer

Other Witnesses

During June 1829, while Joseph and Oliver were busy finishing the translation at the Whitmer's farm in Fayette, Mary Whitmer labored faithfully to take care of their every need, without complaint and despite much persecution from her neighbors and friends. As a reward for her faithfulness, the Angel Moroni appeared to her in broad daylight and showed her the plates.[35]

Others knew of the existence of the plates without actually seeing them. We do not know for sure how many had opportunity to lift the plates while they were being moved from place to place to keep them hidden from Joseph Smith's enemies. But we do know that Joseph's parents, Lucy and Joseph Sr., felt them through a pillow case, during this time, as did a man by the name of Joshua McCune.[36]

Always Faithful to Their Witness

We have the printed witness of both the three witnesses and the eight witnesses in the front of every Book of Mormon. These are their official pronouncements that stand as sentinels of truth against those who would deny the divine origin of the book. It is also interesting to read their unofficial reaffirmations given toward the end of their lives. All of the Three Witnesses and three of the Eight Witnesses later left the Church. Only a few returned, but none ever denied his testimony.

During the period when he was excommunicated from the Church, Oliver Cowdery said: "I have never denied my testimony, which is attached to the front page of the Book of Mormon, and I declare to you here that these eyes saw the angel, and these ears of mine heard the voice of the angel, and he told us his name was Moroni; that the book was true, and contained the fullness of the gospel, and we were also told that if we ever denied what we had heard and seen that there would be no forgiveness for us, neither in this world nor in the world to come." (1848) "I wrote, with my own pen, the entire Book of Mormon (save a few pages) as it fell from the lips of the Prophet Joseph Smith, as he translated it by the gift and power of God, by the means of the Urim and Thummim, or, as it is called by that book 'Holy Interpreters.' I beheld with my eyes, and handled with my hands, the gold plates from which it was transcribed. I also saw with my eyes and handled with my hands the 'Holy Interpreters.' That book is true... I wrote it myself as it fell from the lips of the Prophet."[37]

Martin Harris said in 1875: "I had the privilege of being with the Prophet Joseph Smith, and with these eyes of men, (pointing to his eyes) I saw the angel of the Lord, and I saw the plates and the Urim and Thummim and the sword of Laban, and with these ears (pointing to his ears), I heard the voice of the angel, and with these hands (holding out his hands), I handled the plates containing the record of the Book of Mormon, and I assisted the Prophet in the translation thereof. I bear witness that this testimony is true."[38]

David Whitmer said in 1878: "He (the angel) stood before us. Our testimony, as recorded in the Book of Mormon, is strictly and absolutely true … " (1886) "As sure as the sun shines and I live, just so sure did the angel appear unto me and Joseph Smith and I heard his voice and did see the angel standing before us."[39]

David Whitmer said one year later (1887), in the last year of his life: "It is recorded in the American Encyclopaedia [sic] and the Encyclopaedia Britannica [sic], that I, David Whitmer, have denied my testimony as one of the three witnesses to the divinity of the Book of Mormon, and that the other two witnesses, Oliver Cowdery and Martin Harris, denied their testimony to that book. I will say once more to all mankind, that I have never at any time denied that testimony or any part thereof. I also testify to the world, that neither Oliver Cowdery nor Martin Harris ever at any time denied their testimony. They both died reaffirming the truth of the divine authenticity of the Book of Mormon."[40]

Notes:

1. In Conference Report, October 1986, 3; or *Ensign*, November 1986, 4.

2. *History of the Church*, 4:461.

3. In Conference Report, April 1975, 96–97; or Ensign, *May* 1975, 65.

4. *Joseph Smith Diary*, [9 November 1835], Church Archives.

5. *Times and Seasons*, 1 Mar. 1842, 707.

6. *Latter-day Saints' Messenger and Advocate*, Feb. 1835, 79.

7. In Conference Report, October 1983; or *Ensign*, November 1983, 54.

8. Hyrum M. Smith and Janne M. Sjodahl, *Doctrine and Covenants Commentary* [1978], 23; and Andrew Jenson, *Latter-day Saint Biographical Encyclopedia: A Compilation of Biographical Sketches of Prominent Men and Women in the Church of Jesus Christ of Latter-day Saints*, 4 vols. [1901–1936], 1:181–182.

9. *The Family of Joseph Smith*, [1965], 68; see also Lucy Mack Smith, *History of Joseph Smith*, ed. Preston Nibley [1958], 172–173, 179–186.

10. *History of the Church*, 4:536–537.

11. *History of Joseph Smith*, 81.

12. B. H. Roberts, *A Comprehensive History of the Church*, 1:78–80.

13. *Latter-day Saints' Messenger and Advocate*, October 1835, 199.

14. *History of Joseph Smith*, 86–88.

15. Oliver Cowdery, *Latter-day Saints' Messenger and Advocate*, October 1835, 199.

16. *History of Joseph Smith*, 110.

17. Joseph Smith III, "Last Testimony of Sister Emma," *Saints' Advocate*, 2 (October 1879), 51.

18. *History of Joseph Smith*, 129.

19. *History of Joseph Smith*, 134.

20. *Ensign*, November 1987, 31.

21. *Living with Enthusiasm* [1996], 124.

22. In Conference Report, October 1945, 166.

23. In Conference Report, October 1966, 123.

24. "Eternal Keys and the Right to Preside," *Ensign*, July 1972, 88.

25. Letter to N.E. Seaton, Esq., Kirtland, January 4th, 1833, in James R. Clark, comp., *Messages of the First Presidency of The Church of Jesus Christ of Latter-day Saints*, 6 vols. [1965–75], 1:5.

26. *Teachings of the Prophet Joseph Smith*, sel. Joseph Fielding Smith [1976], 256.

27. "Witchcraft," *Juvenile Instructor*, Sept. 1902.

28. *The Teachings of Spencer W. Kimball*, [1982], 151–152; see also Moroni 7:17.

29. *History of Joseph Smith*, 147–148.

30. *History of Joseph Smith*, 148–149.

31. *Messenger and Advocate*, 1 (October 1834), 14–16.

32. Quoted in Joseph Fielding Smith, *The Restoration of All Things*, [1945], 114.

33. *Miracle on Palmyra's Main Street: An "Old-Time" Printer's Perspective on Printing the Original Copies of the Book of Mormon* [2003], available at 4649 S. 345 East, Murray, UT 84107, 801–262–9290.

34. *Mormon Doctrine*, 436.

35. *A Comprehensive History of the Church*, 1:125–127.

36. Brenton G. Yorgason, *Little Known Evidences of the Book of Mormon* [2003], 19.

37. Ludlow, *A Companion to Your Study of the Book of Mormon* [1976], 27, 35–36.

38. *A Companion to Your Study of the Book of Mormon*, 38.

39. *A Companion to Your Study of the Book of Mormon*, 37.

40. *Address to All Believers in Christ* [1887], 8; as quoted in *A Comprehensive History of the Church*, 1:145.

CHAPTER 5

Oliver Cowdery and the Spirit of Revelation

(D&C 6, 8–9) [1828–1829]

෨෦෨

INTRODUCTION

Oliver Cowdery Arrives

As we learned in our previous chapter, Martin Harris lost the first 116 pages of the Book of Mormon transcript in June of 1828. This transgression created a new problem—the lack of a scribe. The Prophet was told in late summer of 1828 when the plates were returned to him by Moroni not to labor more than he had the strength and means provided (D&C 10:4). As a result, Joseph apparently did little translating from June 14, 1828 until April 7, 1829, after Oliver Cowdery arrived.

In the winter of 1828 Oliver Cowdery taught school near the home of Joseph Smith Sr. near Palmyra, New York. It was the custom of the day for teachers to board in the homes of their pupils, and since the Smiths had children in Oliver's school, he came to stay with them. While there he heard stories about the Book of Mormon plates and asked Father Smith to tell him the details. After some hesitation, Father Smith finally consented, and Oliver became one of the few in whom the family confided the story.

Lucy Mack Smith said that Oliver was highly impressed with what he heard, and after meditating upon it had it "impressed upon his mind, that he should yet have the privilege of writing for Joseph." He decided to visit Joseph in Harmony, Pennsylvania in the spring after school was finished, by riding down with Samuel Smith who was already planning to go there. "I have made it a subject of prayer," he said, "and I firmly believe that it is the will of the Lord that I should go. If there is a work for me to do in this thing, I am determined to attend to it."[1]

The following April, Samuel Smith took Oliver Cowdery to Harmony, Pennsylvania, to visit Joseph. They arrived on April 5, 1829. Lucy Mack Smith said: "Joseph had been so hurried with his secular affairs that he could not proceed with his spiritual concerns so fast as was necessary for the speedy completion of the work; there was also another disadvantage under which he labored, his wife had so much of her time taken up with the care of her house, that she could write for him but a small portion of the time. On account of these embarrassments, Joseph called upon the Lord, three days prior to the arrival of Samuel and Oliver, to send him a scribe, according to the promise of the angel; and he was informed that the same should be forthcoming in a few days. Accordingly, when Mr. Cowdery told him the business that he had come upon, Joseph was not at all surprised."[2] Two days later, on April 7, 1829, Joseph began in earnest the translation of the Book of Mormon, with Oliver Cowdery acting as scribe.

Joseph's home in Harmony, Pennsylvania

PRINCIPLES OF REVELATION

Oliver Cowdery as Scribe

It was customary in those early days of the restoration for believers to ask Joseph Smith for a revelation concerning themselves. They were anxious to know the Lord's will for them, much like we do today with our patriarchal blessings. And often, the same counsel was given to more than one person. Missionary work, in particular, was a consistent theme of these early revelations.

Later in the month of April, Joseph received a revelation for his new scribe (D&C 6). In this revelation Oliver Cowdery was given a further testimony of the divinity of the work.

● **D&C 6:1–9 Similar counsel to Oliver Cowdery and others.** We see here the first example of similar counsel to more than one person.

    — Verses 1–9 are identical to   D&C 11:1–9—a revelation given to Hyrum Smith.

    — Verses 1–5 are identical to   D&C 12:1–5—a revelation given to Joseph Knight Sr.

               and   D&C 14:1–5—a revelation given to David Whitmer.

The message in these verses is of universal importance to all Saints—indeed, the Lord has said: "What I say unto one I say unto all" (D&C 61:18, 36; 82:5; 92:1; 93:49).

● **D&C 6:1–5 Those who desire to serve will be called to the work.** The restoration is "a great and marvelous work" (v. 1), and the Lord's words are "quick and powerful" (v. 2). "Quick" in biblical language does not mean "swift" but rather means something "living, alive."[3] Thus, to be quickened by the Spirit means to be given spiritual life. The "field" (world) is characterized as "white already to harvest" (v. 3), which means that there are souls ready and waiting to hear the life-giving words of the Lord. Those who desire to "thrust in his sickle and reap" will be "called of God" in answer to their prayers (vv. 3–5).

- **D&C 6:6–7 The establishment of Zion is the grand purpose of the restoration** (vv. 6–7). The charge "to bring forth and establish the cause of Zion" is also our work—to build up the kingdom of God and to preach the gospel to all the world. We make solemn, sacred covenants to do this. And it was also required of Oliver and others who came to the Prophet's aid in those early days.

- **D&C 6:8–13 Oliver Cowdery's sacred gift was to know the "mysteries" and to be able to expound them to others.** Whatever Oliver desired of the Lord "so it shall be unto you; and if you desire, you shall be the means of doing much good in this generation" (v. 8). As with so many others, Oliver was to "say nothing but repentance unto this generation; keep [the Lord's] commandments, and assist to bring forth [His] work, according to [His] commandments," with the promise that if he would do so he would be blessed (v. 9). Oliver also learned that he had a special gift and calling which was "sacred and cometh from above" (v. 10). This gift was to "know mysteries which are great and marvelous," and if he would exercise it properly "thou mayest find out mysteries, that thou mayest bring many to the knowledge of the truth, yea, convince them of the error of their ways" (v. 11).

Oliver was a participant in many of the most sublime revelations of this dispensation: the restoration of the Aaronic and Melchizedek priesthoods, the visitations of Moses, Noah (Elias), and Elijah to restore the keys of the priesthood, and the appearance of the Savior Himself in the Kirtland Temple. He saw the angel Moroni as one of the three witnesses to the Book of Mormon, and he was present on multiple occasions when the Prophet Joseph Smith received revelation from on high. He was the "second elder" of the Church, and held all the keys of this dispensation along with Joseph. He was a gifted writer and teacher, and taught and baptized many souls who believed on his words. In every way possible, his life was a fulfillment of this promise made to him in 1829.

The Lord cautioned him not to make his gift known "unto any save it be those who are of thy faith" and to "trifle not with sacred things" (v. 12). In other words, he was not to brag or be prideful concerning his gifts, and was not to take them lightly. And he was promised that if he would "do good … and hold out faithful to the end, thou shalt be saved in the kingdom of God, which is the greatest of all the gifts of God; for there is no gift greater than the gift of salvation" (v. 13). This was a promise of exaltation for Oliver Cowdery.

- **D&C 6:14–16, 22–24 Oliver had already received a personal witness of the truthfulness of this work.** Through this revelation, the Lord was speaking of things that nobody knew except Oliver himself. He said: "thou hast inquired of me, and behold, as often as thou hast inquired thou hast received instruction of my Spirit. If it had not been so, thou wouldst not have come to the place where thou art at this time" (v. 14), meaning to Harmony, Pennsylvania. The Lord continued, "thou hast inquired of me and I did enlighten thy mind; and now I tell thee these things that thou mayest know that thou hast been enlightened by the Spirit of truth" (v. 15). He reminds Oliver "that there is none else save God that knowest thy thoughts and the intents of thy heart" (v. 16).

This scripture indicates that our thoughts and the intents of our hearts are private. Elder Bruce R. McConkie said: "Men's thoughts are secret and cannot be pried into by other men, or for that matter by devils."[4]

If he needed a further witness that God was speaking to him, he was invited to "cast your mind upon the night that you cried unto me in your heart, that you might know concerning the truth of these things" (v. 22). This was a reference to the prayer Oliver had offered in the privacy of his bedroom while staying with the Smiths in Palmyra before he had even met the Prophet Joseph Smith. "Did I not speak peace to your mind concerning the matter?" the Lord asks. "What greater witness can you have than from God?" (v. 23). And now again, he was receiving a witness "for if I have told you things which no man knoweth have you not received a witness?" (v. 24).

The Smith home in Manchester, New York

The Prophet Joseph Smith said that after he had received this revelation [D&C 6], Oliver told him that, one night while staying with the Smiths in New York, he knelt in prayer to ask the Lord if these things were true. The Lord manifested to him that they were true. He had not mentioned this experience to anyone, "so that after this revelation was given, he knew that the work was true, because no being living knew of the thing alluded to in the revelation, but God and himself."[5]

● **D&C 6:17–21 The Lord's personal counsel to Oliver Cowdery.** He had been given this revelation (D&C 6) "as a witness unto thee—that the words or the work which thou hast been writing are true" (v. 17). He was counseled to diligently "stand by my servant Joseph ... in whatsoever difficult circumstances he may be for the word's sake" (v. 18). As Joseph's counselor, he was to "admonish him in his faults, and also receive admonition of him" (v. 19). He was to "be patient; be sober; be temperate; have patience, faith, hope and charity" (v. 19). He was to "treasure up these words in thy heart" and "be faithful and diligent in keeping the commandments of God, and I will encircle thee in the arms of my love" (v. 20). And lest he forget from whom he had received this counsel the Lord testifies to him that he is "Jesus Christ, the Son of God ... the same that came unto mine own, and mine own received me not. I am the light which shineth in darkness, and the darkness comprehendeth it not" (v. 21).

● **D&C 6:25–28 Oliver's other gift if he desired it—to translate ancient records.** Oliver wanted to be able to translate the ancient record just as Joseph was doing. The Lord said he would grant him "if you desire of me, to translate, even as my servant Joseph" (v. 25). But he seemed to be referencing scriptures other than the Book of Mormon because he said: "there are records which contain much of my gospel, which have been kept back because of the wickedness of the people" (v. 26). If Oliver manifested "good desires—a desire to lay up treasures for yourself in heaven—then shall you assist in bringing to light, with your gift, those parts of my scriptures which have been hidden because of iniquity" (v. 27). Both Oliver Cowdery and Joseph Smith now had "the keys of this gift, which shall bring to light this ministry; and in the mouth of two or three witnesses shall every word be established" (v. 28).

- **D&C 6:29–31 "They can do no more to you than to me."** Oliver was warned that people might reject his teachings, and "if they reject my words, and this part of my gospel and ministry, blessed are ye, for they can do no more unto you than unto me" (v. 29). This was a reference to the fact that the Lord's enemies had put Him to death. Even if Oliver's enemies "do unto you even as they have done unto me, blessed are ye, for you shall dwell with me in glory" (v. 30). However, "if they reject not my words … blessed are they, and then shall ye have joy in the fruit of your labors" (v. 31). Oliver never was a martyr for the cause of Christ, but he might have been. President Joseph Fielding Smith said that if Oliver Cowdery had remained true, and had been faithful to his testimony and his calling as the "second Elder" and Assistant President of the Church, he would have been the one that went to Carthage with the Prophet Joseph Smith rather than his brother Hyrum.[6]

- **D&C 6:32–37 Oliver is instructed to look unto Christ and do good continually.** Though the infant Church was not yet officially organized and the believers were few, the Lord reassured Oliver that "where two or three are gathered together in my name, as touching one thing, behold, there will I be in the midst of them—even so am I in the midst of you" (v. 32). The Lord's reassurances here were very personal and affectionate. "Fear not to do good, my sons, for whatsoever ye sow, that shall ye also reap; therefore, if ye sow good ye shall also reap good for your reward" (v. 33). Also, "fear not, little flock; do good; let earth and hell combine against you, for if ye are built upon my rock, they cannot prevail" (v. 34). Although believers at that point were probably less than a dozen, the eventual destiny of their work was global, and no enemy would ever be allowed to destroy them or their work.

The Prophet Joseph Smith prophesied while at Nauvoo, "The Standard of Truth has been erected; no unhallowed hand can stop the work from progressing; persecutions may rage, mobs may combine, armies may assemble, calumny may defame, but the truth of God will go forth boldly, nobly, and independent, till it has penetrated every continent, visited every clime, swept every country, and sounded in every ear, till the purposes of God shall be accomplished, and the Great Jehovah shall say the work is done."[7] He also asked, "Brethren, shall we not go on in so great a cause? Go forward and not backward. Courage, brethren; and on, on to the victory! Let your hearts rejoice, and be exceedingly glad" (D&C 128:22).

In this earlier time, when their efforts must have seemed somewhat obscure, the Lord reassured them that He did not condemn them for their weaknesses, and they should "go your ways and sin no more; perform with soberness the work which I have commanded you" (v. 35). They should be neither faithless nor fearful. "Look unto me in every thought; doubt not, fear not" (v. 36). The Lord had suffered all things for them as evidenced by "the wounds which pierced my side, and also the prints of the nails in my hands and feet," so if they would "be faithful [and] keep my commandments" they could be assured that they would eventually "inherit the kingdom of heaven" (v. 37).

The Spirit of Revelation Is Explained to Oliver

The Lord had told Oliver previously that he was to continue as scribe until the translation of the Book of Mormon was completed, that there were other ancient records to come forth, and that he might have the privilege of translating these at some future day if he would remain faithful (D&C 6:25–28). The Book of Mormon says that there are many such records, and at some time, when the people are prepared by faith to receive them, they will also be translated and published. But Oliver was "exceedingly anxious" to participate <u>now</u> in the translation of the plates of Mormon. Joseph inquired of the Lord concerning these things and received two revelations: D&C 8–9.[8]

● **D&C 8:1, 11 Oliver may receive knowledge con- cerning the engravings through faith and the Spirit.** He could receive "knowledge of whatsoever things you shall ask in faith, with an honest heart, believing that you shall receive" (v. 1). This makes faith an absolute require- ment for gaining "knowledge concerning the engravings of old records … , which contain … my scripture … spoken by the manifestation of my Spirit" (v. 1). Since these (and all) scriptures are given through the Spirit to prophets, it requires the Spirit to accurately translate those scriptures into another language. Thus, the Spirit is also an absolute requirement to do this work. The Lord invites Oliver to "Ask that you may know the mysteries of God, and that you may translate and receive knowledge from all those ancient records which have been hid up, that are sacred; and according to your faith shall it be done unto you" (v. 11).

● **D&C 8:2–5 The spirit of revelation comes by the power of the Holy Ghost.** Presuming that a person has sufficient faith and the Spirit to help them, what is the process by which revelations come? These verses provide the answer. The Lord says, "I will tell you in your mind and in your heart, by the Holy Ghost, which shall come upon you and which shall dwell in your heart" (v. 2). Thus, revelation is not purely intellectual and not purely emotional. We receive knowledge in our minds through the Spirit, and at the same time we receive a witness in our hearts that the idea that has come to us is from God.

The Prophet Joseph Smith described the way that ideas come into our minds from the Spirit: "A person may profit by noticing the first intimation of the spirit of revelation; for instance, when you feel pure intelligence flowing into you, it may give you sudden strokes of ideas, so that by noticing it, you may find it fulfilled the same day or soon; i.e., those things that were presented unto your minds by the Spirit of God, will come to pass; and thus by learning the Spirit of God and understanding it, you may grow into the principle of revelation until you become perfect in Christ Jesus."[9]

Elder Boyd K. Packer said: "I have come to know that inspiration comes more as a feeling than as a sound… The Lord has a way of pouring pure intelligence into our minds to prompt us, to guide us, to teach us, to warn us. You can know the things you need to know instantly! Learn to receive inspiration."[10] Elder Packer cautioned, however, that "all inspiration does not come from God (D&C 46:7). The evil one has the power to tap into those channels of revelation and send conflicting signals which can mislead and confuse us. There are promptings from evil sources which are so carefully counterfeited as to deceive even the very elect (Matt. 24:24). Nevertheless, we can learn to discern these spirits."[11]

This is one of the great challenges we all face—learning to distinguish between promptings from the Spirit and those feelings that are counterfeits: our own enthusiasm, emotional rushes, and false ideas planted in our minds by Satan. It is only by experience that we can come to discern consistently the spirit of revelation. As the Prophet Joseph Smith said: "By learning the Spirit of God and understanding it, you may grow into the principle of revelation."[12]

To Oliver Cowdery the Lord said: "Now, behold, this is the spirit of revelation; behold, this is the spirit by which Moses brought the children of Israel through the Red Sea on dry ground. Therefore this is thy gift; apply unto it" (vv. 3–4). Note this call to action, not merely waiting for the Lord to do it for him. If he (and we) will do this, "blessed art thou, for it shall deliver you out of the hands of your enemies" (v. 4).

● **D&C 8:6–9 Oliver Cowdery and the Gift of Aaron.** In addition to the gift of translation, Oliver was given "the gift of Aaron" which "has told you many things" (v. 6). This gift can only be bestowed through the power of God (v. 7), and it requires absolute faith (v. 8). The Lord promises Oliver, "you shall hold it in your hands, and do marvelous works; and no power shall be able to take it away out of your hands, for it is the work of God" (v. 8). Furthermore, "whatsoever you shall ask me to tell you by that means, that will I grant unto you, and you shall have knowledge concerning it" (v. 9).

Elder Joseph Fielding Smith said: "Like Aaron with his rod in his hand going before Moses as a spokesman, so Oliver Cowdery was to go before Joseph Smith. Whatever he should ask the Lord by power of this gift should be granted if asked in faith and in wisdom. Oliver was blessed with the great honor of holding the keys of this dispensation with Joseph Smith, and, like Aaron, did become a spokesman on numerous occasions. It was Oliver who delivered the first public discourse in this dispensation."[13]

● **D&C 8:10–12 The power of faith.** Oliver Cowdery was educated and eager, but he was a novice with spiritual things. The Lord counsels him to "remember that without faith you can do nothing; therefore ask in faith" (v. 10). Also, he was not to take lightly his gifts or the process by which they would be manifest. "Trifle not with these things; do not ask for that which you ought not" (v. 10), as Martin Harris had done. Instead, he was to ask for the gifts he had already been promised, "that you may know the mysteries of God, and that you may translate and receive knowledge from all those ancient records which have been hid up, that are sacred" and if he does this "according to your faith shall it be done unto you" (v. 11). The Lord assures him that these promises are from Him, and that it is He who guided Oliver Cowdery toward this work (v. 12).

President J. Reuben Clark Jr. said: "As I think about faith, this principle of power, I am obliged to believe that it is an intelligent force. Of what kind, I do not know. But it is superior to and overrules all other forces of which we know… You brethren, we brethren, have had this great power given unto us, this power of faith. What are we doing about it? Can you, can we, do the mighty things that the Savior did? Yes. They have been done by the members of the Church who had the faith and the righteousness so to do. Think of what is within your power if you but live the Gospel, if you but live so that you may invoke the power which is within you."[14]

Oliver Was Unable to Translate

Oliver Cowdery proceeded to attempt to translate the Book of Mormon; however, Oliver's faith was insufficient to receive the essential inspiration to accomplish the task. He was bitterly disappointed and sought to know why he could not translate. In the revelation he received through Joseph (D&C 9), the Lord instructed him to be content to serve for the time being as scribe.[15] Elder Joseph Fielding Smith speculated that Oliver's motive was curiosity, "and the Lord taught him his place by showing him that translating was not the easy thing he had thought it to be."[16] In this revelation (D&C 9), the Lord says that Oliver's failure came because he did not "continue as [he] commenced" (v. 5). Elder Smith concludes that, when Oliver found the task to be more difficult than he had anticipated, his faith deserted him.

● **D&C 9:1–4 Oliver's primary calling was to write while Joseph Smith translated.** Oliver learned through this experience that his place was to act as scribe for Joseph Smith, who was the one called and appointed by the Lord to do the translating. Future events suggest that Oliver Cowdery may have desired to be equal with the Prophet and was not fully satisfied to sit and act as his scribe. But after his failure to translate, he was more willing to accept the will of the Lord. The Lord commanded Oliver to "commence again to write for my servant, Joseph Smith … until you have finished this record, which I have entrusted unto him" (v. 1). If he would faithfully do this, the Lord had "other records" that Oliver might "assist to translate" (v. 2). He gently advises Oliver to "be patient, my son, for it is wisdom in me, and it is not expedient that you should translate at this present time" (v. 3). The work he was called to do was to "write for my servant Joseph" (v. 4).

● **D&C 9:6 How to react when things don't turn out as we expect.** Oliver was advised by the Lord to "not murmur, my son, for it is wisdom in me that I have dealt with you after this manner" (v. 6). The Lord has higher purposes in the events of our lives, and we often do not fully understand or appreciate them until much later. One of the Lord's purposes in this case was to teach Oliver (and the rest of us) how to discern the spirit of revelation. This could not be done if he had easily and without effort received the gift of translation. Yet, the Lord had to encourage him to make the effort before he could teach him the lesson. And there were other more personal reasons in Oliver's life for his having to learn this important lesson.

This scripture has great meaning to me because I, too, have sometimes felt angry, disappointed, or confused when things didn't turn out as I thought they would. The first of these was when I was called on my mission and received my setting-apart blessing from Elder Harman G. Rector. I was told that I would be called to leadership positions "even to being called to be an assistant to the President." I served faithfully and honorably and worked hard throughout my mission, and I served as a District Leader in two different districts. But I never was called to be an Assistant to the President. I was called in my final months to be a "teaching assistant," traveling around the mission and helping the elders to improve their teaching. But I did not consider that to be the fulfillment of my blessing, and I was disappointed and worried that some how I had failed. It took a few years of maturing spiritually after my mission for me to realize that I was putting a capital "A" on Assistant, and the Lord had intended only for me to "assist" (with a small "a") the mission president in the important work of improving missionary teaching.

The author as a missionary

● **D&C 9:5, 7 Oliver took the process too lightly, with insufficient effort.** There were a number of reasons for Oliver's failure. One was "because that you did not continue as you commenced, when you began to translate" (v. 5). This suggests that he started out all right, using his faith and the spirit of revelation to translate the first few lines. But then, perhaps taking it too lightly, he began to assume that it would get easier and stopped applying himself as he had before, that the Lord withdrew the privilege from him (v. 5). The Lord said to him, "Behold, you have not understood; you have supposed that I would give it unto you, when you took no thought save it was to ask me" (v. 7).

This principle could occupy an entire chapter by itself. The Lord never does for us what we can do for ourselves. If He did, He would be denying us the opportunity to learn and to grow from our own experience, which is the fundamental purpose of life. This "let God do it" attitude is very popular among Christian sectarians who imagine a God who takes control of every detail of every life, and we are supposed to sit back and let God make everything happen. On the flip side of that belief are those who say, "If there were a God, He would never have let this happen." In both cases, they are assuming that God operates as Satan proposed in the beginning—controlling everything without human agency or accountability. It might be less messy, but this is certainly not how God operates. We must make more effort than to simply ask Him. We must think and take action before He can guide us.

● **D&C 9:8–9 How we may discern between right and wrong choices.** The action the Lord expects us to take is to "study it out in your mind" and then "ask me if it be right" (v. 8). This suggests that we must carefully do our homework on a problem, consider the options, and then make a decision. Then, and only then, we can take our decision to the Lord and ask Him if what we have decided is right. The Lord said to His disciples, "If any man will do [God's] will, he shall know of the doctrine, whether it be of God, or whether I speak of myself" (John 7:17, emphasis added). We can only receive a testimony of tithing by paying it. We can only know the Book of Mormon is true after we have read it. We can only know that the course that we are pursuing is correct by choosing it and then asking God if He will bless us in doing so.

When reading the rest of these verses, we should keep in mind what the Lord said in His previous revelation to Oliver Cowdery before he attempted to translate: "I will tell you in *your mind and in your heart,* by the Holy Ghost, which shall come upon you and which shall dwell in your heart" (D&C 8:2, emphasis added). The Lord says in these later verses that "if it is right I will cause that your bosom shall burn within you; therefore, you shall *feel* that it is right" (v. 8, emphasis added). This is the portion of revelation that comes to our heart through the Spirit. "But if it be not right you shall have no such feelings, but you shall have a stupor of thought that shall cause you to forget the thing which is wrong" (v. 9). This is the portion of revelation that comes to our mind, and we will be confused and uncertain and forgetful of things that God does not want us to do. Thus we will receive no confirmation in either our minds or our hearts, and we will know by this that it is wrong.

Elder S. Dilworth Young said: " If I am to receive revelation from the Lord, I must be in harmony with Him by keeping His commandments. Then as needed, according to His wisdom, His word will come into my mind through my thoughts, accompanied by a feeling in the region of my bosom. It is a feeling which cannot be described, but the nearest word we have is 'burn' or 'burning.' Accompanying this always is a feeling of peace, a further witness that what one heard is right. Once one recognizes this burning, this feeling, this peace, one need never be drawn astray in his daily life or in the guidance he may receive."[17]

However it is given, revelation comes only from the Lord (v. 9), who is the source of all truth and light. Thus, we must be "in tune" with Him before we can discern His will. Any degree of willful unrighteousness will disqualify us from receiving the Spirit and thereby being able to discern the spirit of revelation. But if we are faithful and energetic and righteous, the Lord will pour out His revelations upon us through a variety of circumstances and means.

The Prophet Joseph Smith received revelation in different ways as he matured in his calling. At first, his communications with the heavens were direct—visitations from God, His Son, and angels. Then he used the Urim and Thummim as a medium. Finally, "he learned to bring his spirit into such harmony with divinity that it became, as it were, a Urim and Thummim to him, and God's will was revealed without the intervention of external aids."[18]

● **D&C 9:10–11 Fear blocks faith, and therefore revelation also.** When Oliver Cowdery began, he was full of faith. But as he began to lose his gift, he allowed fear to overcome him. The Lord said to him, "it is not expedient that you should translate now. Behold, it was expedient when you commenced; but you feared, and the time is past, and it is not expedient now."

The Prophet Joseph Smith said: "Doubt and faith do not exist in the same person at the same time; so that persons whose minds are under doubts and fears cannot have unshaken confidence; and where unshaken confidence is not, there faith is weak; and where faith is weak the persons will not be able to contend against all the opposition, tribulations, and afflictions which they will have to encounter in order to be heirs of God, and joint heirs with Christ Jesus; and they will grow weary in their minds, and the adversary will have power over them and destroy them."[19]

● **D&C 9:12–14 If we faithfully perform our callings, God will prosper and protect us.** The Lord holds up Joseph Smith as an example of someone whom He blessed far beyond his capacity in order to perform His work. "For, do you not behold that I have given unto my servant Joseph sufficient strength, whereby it is made up?" (v. 12).

Elder Neal A. Maxwell said:

> We have no hesitancy … in stipulating that Joseph was, by the standards of the world, "not learned." Isaiah foresaw it (Isaiah 29:11–12). Joseph did not have the skilled, formal tutoring [Paul] had at the feet of Gamaliel (Acts 22:3). Emma Smith reportedly said that Joseph, at the time of the translation of the Book of Mormon, could not compose a "well-worded letter let alone dictating a book like the Book of Mormon … [which was] marvelous to me, a marvel and a wonder, as much as to anyone else." This obscure young man apparently paused while translating and dictating to Emma … concerning the "wall of Jerusalem,"—and said, in effect, "Emma, I didn't know there was a wall around Jerusalem."[20]

Neither Joseph nor Oliver were to feel condemned by their weakness—and neither should we. They were to "do this thing which I have commanded you, and you shall prosper"—and so will we (v. 13). He would not let them fail in their sacred task of bringing forth the Book of Mormon, and He will not let us fail in our responsibilities either, so long as we are "faithful, and yield to no temptation" and "stand fast in the work wherewith I have called you," which, if we will do, "a hair of your head shall not be lost, and you shall be lifted up at the last day" (vv. 13–14).

Notes:

1. *History of Joseph Smith*, Lucy Mack Smith, ed. Preston Nibley [1958], 139.

2. *History of Joseph Smith*, 141.

3. "Quick," *LDS Bible Dictionary*, 756.

4. *Mormon Doctrine*, 777; see also 1 Kings 8:39.

5. *History of the Church*, 1:35.

6. *Doctrines of Salvation*, comp. Bruce R. McConkie, 3 vols. [1954–1956], 1:221–222.

7. *History of the Church*, 4:540

8. *History of the Church*, 1:36.

9. *Teachings of the Prophet Joseph Smith*, sel. Joseph Fielding Smith [1976], 151.

10. In Conference Report, October 1979, 28–29; or *Ensign*, November 1979, 20.

11. *Ensign*, November 1989, 14).

12. *History of the Church*, 3:381.

13. *Church History and Modern Revelation*, 1:52.

14. In Conference Report, April 1960, 21.

15. *History of the Church*, 1:36–38.

16. *Church History and Modern Revelation*, 1:50–51.

17. "The Still Small Voice," *Ensign*, May 1976, 23).

18. John A. Widtsoe, *Evidences and Reconciliations*, arr. G. Homer Durham, 3 vols. in 1 [1960], 90.

19. Joseph Smith, comp., *Lectures on Faith* [1985], 126; as published in the *Messenger and Advocate*, [May 1835].

20. In Conference Report, October 1983; or *Ensign*, November 1983, 54.

CHAPTER 6

The Principles of Revelation

(D&C 6; 9; 11; 29; 43; 50; 60–62; 88; 98; 109)
[Topical Chapter]

℞℞℞

In our previous chapter we learned about Oliver Cowdery's experiences with receiving (and not receiving) revelation at the time the Book of Mormon was translated. The subject of personal revelation is of such great importance that we need a second chapter on the topic. This chapter is a topical one—ranging throughout the Doctrine and Covenants to bring together many principles of revelation that are found therein.

"In Your Mind and In Your Heart"

As noted in our previous chapter, the Lord had responded through the Spirit to the prayers of Oliver Cowdery as often as he had inquired through prayer, and it was through that Spirit that Oliver had been led to visit the Prophet Joseph Smith in Harmony, Pennsylvania (D&C 6:14). The Lord describes this inspiration as the "enlightening" of his mind (D&C 6:15).

In a subsequent revelation to Oliver Cowdery, the Lord says, "I will tell you in your mind and in your heart, by the Holy Ghost, which shall come upon you and which shall dwell in your heart" (D&C 8:2). Thus, we learned that revelation is a dual process—receiving thoughts in our minds and a confirming witness in our hearts.

Elder Harold B. Lee said: "Thus the Lord, by revelation, brings [ideas] into our mind as though a voice were speaking. May I bear humble testimony, if I may be pardoned, to that fact? I was once in a situation where I needed help. The Lord knew I needed help and I was on an important mission. I was awakened in the hours of the morning as though someone had wakened me to straighten me out on something that I had planned to do in a contrary course, and there was clearly mapped out before me as I lay there that morning, just as surely as though someone had sat on the edge of my bed and told me what to do. Yes, the voice of the Lord comes into our minds and we are directed thereby."[1]

Elder Boyd K. Packer said: "I have come to know that inspiration comes more as a feeling than as a sound… The Lord has a way of pouring pure intelligence into our minds to prompt us, to guide us, to teach us, to warn us. You can know the things you need to know instantly! Learn to receive inspiration" (in Conference Report, October 1979, 28–29; or Ensign, November 1979, 20). Elder Packer later added that, "These delicate, refined spiritual communications are not seen with our eyes nor heard with our ears. And even though it is described as a voice, it is a voice that one feels more than one hears."[2]

Of all of these, Elder Marion G. Romney said: "The type of revelation most common is that which comes into our minds and feelings and induces us to do what is right."[3]

Men, Women, and Children Receive Revelation

The Old Testament Joel prophesied of the last days, "I will pour out my spirit upon all flesh; and your sons and your daughters shall prophesy, your old men shall dream dreams, your young men shall see visions" (Joel 2:28). In the book of Acts in the New Testament, after quoting Joel's prophesy, Luke adds the promise that "on my servants and on my handmaidens I will pour out in those days of my Spirit; and they shall prophesy" (Acts 2:18).

Elder Bruce R. McConkie said: "Revelations are not reserved for a limited few or for those called to positions of importance in the Church. It is not position in the Church that confers spiritual gifts. It is not being a bishop, a stake president, or an Apostle that makes revelation and salvation available. These are high and holy callings which open the door to the privilege of great service among men. But it is not a call to a special office that opens the windows of revelation to a truth seeker. Rather, it is personal righteousness; it is keeping the commandments; it is seeking the Lord while He may be found. God is no respecter of persons. He will give revelation to me and to you on the same terms and conditions."[4]

Elder McConkie later observed: "It is the privilege and the right of every member of the Church to receive revelation and to enjoy the gifts of the Spirit. When we are confirmed members of the Church, we receive the gift of the Holy Ghost, which is the right to the constant companionship of that member of the Godhead, based on faithfulness. The actual enjoyment of this gift depends upon personal worthiness… Religion comes from God by revelation and deals with spiritual things; and unless and until a man has received revelation, he has not received religion, and he is not on the path leading to salvation in our Father's kingdom."[5]

This promise is not restricted to adults. Children, in the purity of their innocence, are often vessels of revelation that adults may be too occupied or faithless to receive. They dream dreams, they see spiritual beings, and they feel the Spirit when it falls upon them.

I have a niece who has struggled with conception despite many interventions from medical experts and much prayer. She was finally able to have one child, a beautiful little girl who is now about three years old. Since that time they have had no success in conceiving again. Then, a short time ago, while their daughter was staying with her grandparents (my brother and sister-in-law), she had a dream while taking a nap. When her grandmother asked her if she had sweet dreams, she responded, "Yes, I saw my brother and sister." We have all learned to take seriously the dreams of this little girl. And within a few weeks her mother conceived again, apparently with two fertilized eggs now attached to her womb. Can you blame us if we are expecting a boy and a girl?

Levels or Degrees of Revelation

Revelation comes to us in variety of ways and in various levels of intensity. The following list is adapted from the Encyclopedia of Mormonism.[6]

Degree:		Type:	Definition:	Example/Reference:
Highest	1.	**Theophanies**	Seeing God face to face	First Vision JSH 1:15–20
	2.	**Testimony of Christ (2nd Comforter)**	A direct revelatory witness of Jesus Christ (Calling & Election Made Sure)	Peter's Testimony Matt. 16:13–17
	3.	**Angelic Visitations**	Angels physically appearing	Angel Moroni's visits JSH 1:30–32
	4.	**Revelation thru the Urim & Thummim**	Open communication through use of the seer stones	Books of Mormon/Moses were given in this manner
	5.	**Open Visions**	Looking into heaven, or seeing other dispensations	Vision of Celestial kingdom D&C 76
	6.	**Hearing God's Voice**	Physically hearing His voice	His witness to the Nephites 3 Nephi 11:3–5
	7.	**Dreams**	While sleeping, as metaphors of a principle or needed action	Lehi's Vision 1 Nephi 8:2–32
	8.	**Gifts of the Spirit**	Receiving and using the gifts of the Holy Ghost	Prophecy, Healing, Tongues, Testimony, etc. D&C 46
	9.	**Burning in the Bosom**	Given as a confirmation of the truth/correctness of things	Our initial testimonies D&C 9:8
	10.	**Still, Small Voice**	Whisperings of the Spirit	As Elijah described it 1 Kings 19:11–12
Lowest	11.	**Light of Christ**	Basic knowledge of right/wrong given to all persons at birth	Our conscience Alma 12:31–32 D&C 84:46–48

I remember very well the first time I experienced the Spirit as a child. I was in a Sacrament meeting in Nephi, Utah, on a summer night (there were no air conditioned chapels in those days). My father was in the bishopric and sitting on the stand. My mother and I were seated on hard wooden benches as the young men prepared to pass the sacrament. We were singing a hymn, and I had my head laid in my mother's lap, listening to her sing. I was overcome with a feeling of warmth and peace, very pleasing to my young soul. I knew that I was in the right place and that my Heavenly Father wanted me there. It was strong enough that I have never forgotten it. I did not know then, but have come to understand since, that I was receiving a witness from the Holy Spirit.

Speaking of revelation to children, Janette Hales Beckham said:

> A few weeks ago our four-year-old grandson, Michael, reported to his parents, "When I pray, my heart feels like a roasted marshmallow."… My daughter Karen [also] shared her experience. She said, "When I was just a little girl, I started reading the Book of Mormon for the first time. After many days of reading, I came one night to 1 Nephi 3:7… I felt strongly impressed … but the deep impression was really more of a feeling. I had seen my parents mark verses in their scriptures with red pencils. So I got up and searched through the house until I found a red pencil, and with a great sense of solemnity and importance, I marked that verse in my own Book of Mormon." Karen continued, "Over the years as I read the scriptures, that experience was repeated time and time again… In time I came to recognize that feeling as the Holy Ghost."[7]

How the Holy Ghost Communicates with Us

Precisely how the Holy Ghost communicates to our hearts and minds is a mystery. As a lifelong broadcaster, I prefer to understand it through the metaphor of radio waves, though I am sure that the Lord and His Spirit use higher physics than those that we know about in this world. Still, it is instructive to know how information can move through space unnoticed and yet be perceived by those who are "in tune."

Radio waves carry the information we hear on radio and watch on television. Simply put, radio waves are forms of light. The light we see coming off the ceiling lights in our room are also forms of radio waves—those that our eyes are capable of discerning. But there are many light (radio wave) frequencies we cannot see, and some of these are used by broadcasters. If our eyes were capable of seeing it, the radio waves coming off of broadcasting towers would look like a light glowing brightly and filling up the area surrounding the tower with pulsating, ever-changing light. And this light goes forth from the tower to fill the air with their encoded messages. Hundreds of them are traveling through the room you now occupy, and you are not even aware of them because your eyes are not capable of seeing them nor your ears of hearing them. You need an appropriate receiver that is properly in tune with those frequencies of light.

- **D&C 88:7–13 How the light of Christ and the Holy Spirit inspire us.** In a similar manner to how light can carry the signals of radio and television stations here on earth, the light of Christ and of the Holy Spirit "proceedeth forth from the presence of God to fill the immensity of space" (v. 12). In a way which we do not fully understand, this same light is the source of light for the sun, the moon, and the stars (vv. 7–9). This same light keeps the earth in its proper orbit (v. 10), and enlightens and quickens our personal understanding of things (v. 11). Furthermore, this light "giveth life to all things," "is the law by which all things are governed," and is the very "power of God who sitteth upon his throne" (v. 13). Thus, if our spirits are properly "in tune" we can detect the guiding messages of the light of Christ and of the Holy Spirit, but if we are not in tune then they will go completely undetected by us.

— **Moroni 7:16–18 The light of Christ is given to every person born into the world.** God has not left His children alone in this world to fend for themselves. He granted His light unto each of His children sent to earth (v. 16). This light is sometimes referred to as our conscience because it enables us to "know good from evil" (v. 16). Those things that are good and that persuade us to believe in Christ are "sent forth by the power and gift of Christ; wherefore ye may know with a perfect knowledge it is of God" (v. 16). On the other hand, that which leads us to not believe in or follow Christ, or to deny him, or to refuse to serve God "then ye may know with a perfect knowledge it is of the devil; for after this manner doth the devil work, for he persuadeth no man to do good, no, not one; neither do his angels; neither do they who subject themselves unto him" (v. 17). Thus, each child of God has an innate ability to tell the difference between good and evil, between right and wrong, which makes them fully accountable for their choices, no matter how much or little they may know about the entire plan of salvation. They are required to judge and choose righteously according to the light they've been given.

Eliza R. Snow, author of the hymn "O My Father" and the second General President of the Relief Society, explained:

> We believe that we are the offspring of our Father in heaven, and that we possess in our spiritual organiza- tions the same capabilities, powers and faculties that our Father possesses, although in an infantile state, requiring to pass through a certain course or ordeal by which they will be developed and improved, according to the heed we give to the principles we have received. We believe that God is no respecter of persons, but that He confers blessings upon all His children, in propor- tion to the light they have, or in proportion as they proceed according to the light and knowledge they possess, in the different circumstances of life that may surround them. We believe that the spirit which enlightens the human family proceeds from the presence of the Almighty; that it spreads throughout all space, that it is the light and life of all things, and that every honest heart possesses it in proportion to his virtue, integrity and his desire to know the truth and do good to his fellow men.[8]

● **D&C 85:6 The Holy Ghost whispers in a still, small voice.** Neither the Holy Spirit nor the Lord speaks to us in a loud or demanding voice. Their communications are accomplished through "the still small voice, which whispereth through and pierceth all things," though its effect can be penetrating, sometimes causing "bones to quake while it maketh manifest." This is the same still, small voice that Elijah heard after the loud and convulsive winds, earthquakes, and fires that preceded it (1 Kings 19:12). It is the same still, small voice that often spoke to Laman and Lemuel but they were "past feeling" and could not detect it (1 Nephi 17:45). And it is the same "still, small voice of perfect mildness" that spoke out of the darkness to those who stood around the prison walls that had just collapsed, freeing the prophets Nephi and Lehi in about 30 BC (Helaman 5:30).

Elder Dallin H. Oaks said:

> Some [people] have looked exclusively for the great manifestations that are recorded in the scriptures and have failed to recognize the still, small voice that is given to them… We need to know that the Lord rarely speaks loudly. His messages almost always come in a whisper… Not understanding these principles of revelation, some people postpone acknowledging their testimony until they have experienced a miraculous event. They fail to realize that with most people … gaining a testimony is not an event but a process …
>
> Visions do happen. Voices are heard from beyond the veil. I know this. But these experiences are exceptional… Most of the revelation that comes to leaders and members of the Church comes by the still, small voice or by a feeling rather than by a vision or a voice that speaks specific words we can hear. I testify to the reality of that kind of revelation, which I have come to know as a familiar, even daily, experience to guide me in the work of the Lord.[9]

It is vitally important that we understand these principles of how the Holy Ghost communicates, because there are dangers of expecting divine communication to come in more dramatic or spectacular ways. Particularly the spiritually immature are prone to seek some kind of sign in answer to their prayers rather than listening carefully to the promptings of the Spirit and paying attention to the tender confirmations that come to their hearts.

- **D&C 6:15 The Holy Ghost enlightens our minds.** As noted in our previous chapter, the Prophet Joseph Smith said revelation may come as "sudden strokes of ideas" that flow into our minds as "pure intelligence" (Teachings of the Prophet Joseph Smith, sel. Joseph Fielding Smith [1976], 151). This is the method by which he received inspiration on the subject of baptism for the dead, which; he said "seems to occupy my mind, and press itself upon my feelings the strongest" even while he was in hiding from the pursuit of his enemies (D&C 128:1). As was true in Liberty Jail, the Prophet was able to discern heavenly communication even under the most trying of circumstances. He was a remarkable servant of God and the greatest revelator of this (and possibly any) dispensation.

- **D&C 6:22–23 The Holy Ghost brings peace to our minds.** While Oliver Cowdery stayed in the home of Joseph Smith's parents for a time before meeting the Prophet, he prayed for and received a peaceful assurance that Joseph's calling and work were divine. This feeling of peace, rather than some kind of divine "burning in the bosom" is often the kind of confirmation that comes when we take a problem to the Lord through prayer. Instead of fear and the doubt that so often consume us as we wrestle with our spiritual and temporal problems, the Spirit conveys a sense of peace—the assurance that all will be well.

We experienced this recently when we received a panicked phone call from my daughter in another state. She was in a state of absolute panic, weeping and fearful, because a police officer had just arrived at her home and told her and her children to evacuate immediately to escape 40-foot high flames that were rushing over the nearby hillside toward their home. After we offered our feeble support and advice over the phone, my wife and I retired to the bedroom and knelt in prayer for her and for her family. As we did, we asked for the Lord to protect her from danger and turn back the flames if it be possible. A sense of peace filled our hearts—the sweet peace of the Spirit. No confusion. No fear. Only the peace that comes from Christ through the Holy Spirit through faith and prayer. We did not know everything, nor precisely how the Lord would respond—whether He would protect their home or just them personally. But it did not matter. We knew that all would be well, and that was sufficient to put our hearts at ease.

- **D&C 11:13–14 While enlightening our minds, the Holy Ghost touches our hearts.** How can we know that the ideas we have received are from God and not just our own enthusiasm or the deceptions of Satan? The Lord answers, "I will impart unto you of my Spirit, which shall enlighten your mind" and "which shall fill your soul with joy" (v. 13). Thus, we are not simply asking for ideas, nor are we asking for some manifestation or feeling. We need to know our inspiration comes from the Lord. We receive the idea into our minds, and we feel the peaceful confirmation in our hearts that what we have received is the Lord's will. And "by this shall you know, all things whatsoever you desire of me, which are pertaining unto things of righteousness, in faith believing in me that you shall receive" (v. 14).

- **D&C 9:7–8 The Holy Ghost may cause a burning in the bosom (Luke 24:32).** Although D&C 9 has to do with Oliver Cowdery's attempt to translate the Book of Mormon, the principles also apply to personal revelation. The disciples on the road to Emmaus felt this warm confirmation in their bosoms as they walked unknowingly with the resurrected Lord. It usually confirms the correctness of what is then happening to us or what we are thinking or doing. It is not a "sign" that stands independent of all other considerations. It is the Lord's way of saying, "Yes, my child, proceed with what you are thinking or doing."

Some people struggle with the concept of a "burning in the bosom." Perhaps that's because they expect a dramatic physiological sign. I have encountered numerous young people who, while seeking a testimony, have stumbled over this concept. Elder Boyd K. Packer said: "This burning in the bosom is not purely a physical sensation. It is more like a warm light shining within your being."[10]

Elder Dallin H. Oaks said: "I have met persons who told me they have never had a witness from the Holy Ghost because they have never felt their bosom 'burn within' them. What does a 'burning in the bosom' mean? Does it need to be a feeling of caloric heat, like the burning produced by combustion? If that is the meaning, I have never had a burning in the bosom. Surely, the word 'burning' in this scripture signifies a feeling of comfort and serenity."[11]

- **D&C 98:12 The Holy Ghost usually reveals things "line upon line, precept upon precept" rather than all at once.** We usually receive revelation in accordance with our preparation to receive it. As we become more prepared, more is revealed to us. Thus, the Lord gives gentle promptings, while still requiring us to think, to exercise faith, to work, to struggle at times, and to act. "Seldom does the whole answer to a decisively important matter or complex problem come all at once," said Elder Richard G. Scott. "More often, it comes a piece at a time, without the end in sight."[12]

President Joseph F. Smith said:

> When I as a boy first started out in the ministry, I would frequently go out and ask the Lord to show me some marvelous thing, in order that I might receive a testimony. But the Lord withheld marvels from me, and showed me the truth, line upon line, precept upon precept, here a little and there a little, until He made me to know the truth from the crown of my head to the soles of my feet, and until doubt and fear had been absolutely purged from me. He did not have to send an angel from the heavens to do this, nor did He have to speak with the trump of an archangel. By the whisperings of the still small voice of the Spirit of the living God, He gave to me the testimony I possess. And by this principle and power He will give to all the children of men a knowledge of the truth.[13]

Some Cautions about Personal Revelation

● **D&C 23:6 Feel free to pray over everything in your life.** The Lord invited Joseph Knight (and all of us) to "pray vocally before the world as well as in secret, and in your family, and among your friends, and in all places.'" There is nothing wrong with asking the Lord for the things we desire, whatever they may be. The Psalmist said: "Trust in the LORD, and do good; so shalt thou dwell in the land, and verily thou shalt be fed … and he shall give thee the desires of thine heart" (Psalms 37:3–4). And the Prophet Joseph Smith said: "Seek to know God in your closets; call upon Him in the fields.

Follow the directions of the Book of Mormon, and pray over and for your families, your cattle, your flocks, your herds, your corn, and all things that you possess; ask the blessing of God upon all your labors, and everything that you engage in."[14]

Elder Paul H. Dunn once observed that many people can't believe that a God who created the universe and fathered billions of souls could possibly "care a whit what happens to a single individual with his small concerns." But he bore solemn witness "that God lives, that He cares, and that He knows each one of us individually by name." Observing that somewhere between youth and growing up many of us lose the simple faith of a child, he reminded us that "our frustrations and disappointments may be just pinpricks in the eternal scheme of things, but since they do not seem that way to us, they do not seem that way to the Lord… The Lord is waiting to help you cope today if you will lay your human-size needs at His divine feet."[15]

President Gordon B. Hinckley reminded us that prayer is personal: "It's individual, it's something that no one else gets into, in terms of your speaking with your Father in Heaven in the name of the Lord Jesus Christ. Be prayerful. Ask the Lord to forgive your sins. Ask the Lord for help. Ask the Lord to bless you. Ask the Lord to help you realize your righteous ambitions… Ask the Lord for all of the important things that mean so much to you in your lives. He stands ready to help. Don't ever forget it."[16]

● **D&C 109:44 Pray for the Lord's will to be done and be willing to submit to Him.**

Though we are invited to pray for whatever we desire, the Savior taught us to add to our prayers,

"Thy will be done in earth, as it is in heaven" (Matthew 6:10). And the Prophet Joseph Smith prayed at the dedication of the Kirtland Temple, "Thy word must be fulfilled. Help thy servants to say, with thy grace assisting them: Thy will be done, O Lord, and not ours." That can sometimes be difficult to do when we want something very much.

Bishop H. Burke Peterson told the following story about learning to submit to God's will:

> At a recent stake conference the stake president called a young father, who had just been ordained an elder, from the audience to bear his testimony. The father had been active in the Church as a boy, but during his teenage years had veered somewhat from his childhood pattern. After returning from the military service he married a lovely girl and presently children blessed their home. Without warning an undisclosed illness overcame their little four-year-old daughter. Within a very short time she was on the critical list in the hospital. In desperation and for the first time in many years, the father went to his knees in prayer—asking that her life be spared.

As her condition worsened and he sensed that she would not live, the tone of the father's prayers changed—he no longer asked that her life be spared—but rather for a blessing of understanding—"Let Thy will be done," he said. Soon the child was in a coma, indicating her hours on earth were few. Now, fortified with understanding and trust, the young parents asked for one more favor of the Lord. Would He allow her to awaken once more that they might hold her closely? The little one's eyes opened, her frail arms outstretched to her mother and then to her daddy for a final embrace. When the father laid her on the pillow to sleep till another morning, he knew their prayers had been answered—a kind, understanding Father in Heaven had filled their needs as He knew them to be. His will had been done—they had gained understanding— they were determined now to live that they might live again with her.[17]

Our greatest happiness will come from trusting in the Lord, because He and He alone knows what is coming in our lives. It can be difficult to trust that the best thing will result from doing His will when the immediate, apparent consequences of doing so seem unpleasant or frightening. But if we question everything He asks us to do, or dig in our heels at every unpleasant challenge, we actually make it harder for the Lord to bless us.[18]

Elder Marion G. Romney said: "We need have no fear that our well-being will not be served by such an approach. It is God's work and glory … 'to bring to pass the immortality and eternal life of man.' (Moses 1:39)… The obtaining of eternal life by each individual person, including specifically you and me, is part of the work of God and adds to His glory. His will concerning us and our affairs cannot be other than for our advancement toward immortality and eternal life. Submitting to His will in every instance will be for our own good. And this we must do in faith if we would have peace and happiness in our present state of imperfect living."[19]

● **D&C 28:2, 6–7 We receive revelation only for our own lives, stewardships, and responsibilities.** The early members of the Church, all being converts from orthodox Christian sects, knew little or nothing about the principles of revelation. In particular, some struggled with the question of who can receive revelations for the Church as a whole. The Lord made this crystal clear when He said: "no one shall be appointed to receive commandments and revelations in this church excepting my servant Joseph Smith, Jun., for he receiveth them even as Moses" (v. 2). They were not to "command him who is at thy head, and at the head of the church; For I have given him the keys of the mysteries, and the revelations which are sealed, until I shall appoint unto them another in his stead" (vv. 6–7; see also D&C 43:2–4).

Expanding on this doctrine, the Prophet Joseph Smith said: "It is contrary to the economy of God for any member of the Church, or any one, to receive instruction for those in authority, higher than themselves."[20] This means that we can receive revelation for ourselves and for those over whom we have proper stewardship. But we cannot receive revelation for others, nor for our leaders, nor for the Church.

Only the President of the Church receives revelation to guide the entire Church. Only the bishop receives revelation for the ward. We can each receive revelation to guide our own lives, but when we claim to receive revelation for another person outside our circle of responsibility we are deceived. God's house is a house of order, and it does not work that way.

Consider the all-too-frequent circumstance of one young person telling a potential mate that he has prayed about it and the Lord has told him that the two of them are supposed to be married. This is never appropriate. John H. Groberg said: " I would … caution you that you cannot receive a one-sided revelation from God in regards to an eternal marriage. Only as both parties feel the same way can you have the assurance that it is from the Lord. Those who try to force another's free will into their supposed-revelation mold are doing a great disservice to themselves and to their friends."[21]

This is not to say that we cannot receive revelation concerning others for our own blessing and benefit. But when we do, we should keep all such sacred communications to ourselves. I once had a dream in which I was shown who would be our next stake president. But that was for my own edification, not for the Church. Subsequent events made it important that I had received this witness for myself. But if I had proceeded to tell others what God had entrusted to me for my own benefit, I would have been violating His "economy of revelation."

● **D&C 11:12–14 Be sure that the revelation has come from God.** Sometimes what we think is a revelation may be a projection of our own desires. And sometimes false revelations may come from Satan. Revelations from God will be in accordance with scripture and the counsel of the living prophets. One way to discern this is to "put your trust in that Spirit which leadeth to do good—yea, to do justly, to walk humbly, to judge righteously; and this is my Spirit" (v. 12). Anything that leads to injustice, pride, or unrighteous judgment of others does not come from the Lord. Also, the Spirit of the Lord will always "enlighten your mind" and "fill your soul with joy" (v. 13). That which brings confusion, darkness, or sorrow does not come from the Lord. By these two tests we can know whether "all things whatsoever you desire of me … are pertaining unto things of righteousness," and if so we will receive them through faith (v. 14).

● **D&C 9:8–9 How we may discern between right and wrong choices.** The action the Lord expects us to take is to "study it out in your mind" and then "ask me if it be right" (v. 8). This suggests that we must carefully do our homework on a problem, consider the options, and then make a decision. Then, and only then, we can take our decision to the Lord and ask Him if what we have decided is right. The Lord said to His disciples, "If any man will do [God's] will, he shall know of the doctrine, whether it be of God, or whether I speak of myself" (John 7:17, emphasis added). We can only receive a testimony of tithing by paying it. We can only know the Book of Mormon is true after we have read it. We can only know that the course that we are pursuing is correct by choosing it and then asking God if He will bless us in doing so.

• **D&C 50:23–24 That which does not edify is not of God.** During a time when some were being deceived by those who would shake and quake and roll around, supposedly under the influence of the Spirit, the Lord taught the Saints that "that which doth not edify is not of God, and is darkness" (v. 23). God does not manifest His Spirit through unseemly means, but with dignity and solemnity. "That which is of God is light; and he that receiveth light, and continueth in God, receiveth more light; and that light groweth brighter and brighter until the perfect day" (v. 24).

In addition, the First Presidency said: "When … inspiration conveys something out of harmony with the accepted revelations of the Church or contrary to the decisions of its constituted authorities, Latter-day Saints may know that it is not of God, no matter how plausible it may appear… Anything at discord with that which comes from God through the head of the Church is not to be received as authoritative or reliable."[22]

When Answers Do Not Seem to Come

Elder Boyd K. Packer said:

> Sometimes you may struggle with a problem and not get an answer. What could be wrong? It may be that you are not doing anything wrong. It may be that you have not done the right things long enough. Remember, you cannot force spiritual things. Sometimes we are confused simply because we won't take no for an answer… Put difficult questions in the back of your minds and go about your lives. Ponder and pray quietly and persistently about them. The answer may not come as a lightning bolt. It may come as a little inspiration here and a little there, 'line upon line, precept upon precept' (D&C 98:12). Some answers will come from reading the scriptures, some from hearing speakers. And, occasionally, when it is important, some will come by very direct and powerful inspiration. The promptings will be clear and unmistakable.[23]

Each of these suggestions, and several others, are discussed below.

• **D&C 9:9 Sometimes the answer is "no."** When God wishes us to go a different direction from the one we are anticipating, instead of peace and confirmation we receive negative feelings— confusion, feelings of unrest and uneasiness, or a "stupor of thought." Such confusion and uneasiness never come from the Lord. Their presence is a manifestation of the lack of the Spirit and therefore of the Lord's disapproval of the course we are anticipating.

President James E. Faust said: "Of all that we might do to find solace, prayer is perhaps the most comforting. We are instructed to pray to the Father, in the name of His Son, the Lord Jesus Christ, and by the power of the Holy Ghost. The very act of praying to God is satisfying to the soul, even though God, in His wisdom, may not give what we ask for. President Harold B. Lee taught us that all of our prayers are answered, but sometimes the Lord says no."[24]

● **D&C 88:68; 98:2 Sometimes we must wait for an answer or a blessing.** Revelation will come in the Lord's own time and way. We are instructed to "sanctify [ourselves] that [our] minds become single to God." If we do this, our righteous desires will be granted, but "it shall be in his own time, and in his own way, and according to his own will." We do not always receive revelation at the time or in the way we expect. If we try to force revelation to come when and how we want it, we may be deceived. Elder Dallin H. Oaks said: "Many people do not understand this principle. They believe that when they are ready and when it suits their convenience, they can call upon the Lord and He will immediately respond, even in the precise way they have prescribed. Revelation does not come that way… We cannot force spiritual things."[25]

Elder Richard G. Scott said: "It is a mistake to assume that every prayer we offer will be answered immediately. Some prayers require considerable effort on our part… When we explain a problem and a proposed solution [to our Heavenly Father], sometimes He answers yes, sometimes no. Often He withholds an answer, not for lack of concern, but because He loves us— perfectly. He wants us to apply truths He has given us. For us to grow, we need to trust our ability to make correct decisions. We need to do what  we feel is right. In time, He will answer. He will not fail us."[26]

● **D&C 9:5, 7 Sometimes we must increase efforts to be in tune spiritually so we can receive and recognize the whisperings of the Spirit.** Remember that Oliver Cowdery took the process too lightly, with insufficient effort. He started out all right, using his faith and the spirit of revelation to translate the first few lines. But then, perhaps taking it too lightly, he began to assume that it would get easier and stopped applying himself as he had before, and the Lord withdrew the privilege from him (v. 5), saying, "Behold, you have not understood; you have supposed that I would give it unto you, when you took no thought save it was to ask me" (v. 7).

Elder Joseph B. Wirthlin said: "To soundly plant good seeds in your heart requires prolonged, intense, unremitting pondering. It is a deep, ongoing, regenerating process which refines the soul."[27]

Elder Henry B. Eyring said:

> Just as soil needs preparation for a seed, so does a human heart for the word of God to take root. Before he told the people to plant the seed, Alma told them that their hearts were prepared. They had been persecuted and cast out of their churches. Alma with his love and the circumstances of their

lives, which led them to be humble, had prepared them. They were then ready to hear the word of God. If they chose to plant it in their hearts, the growth in their souls would surely follow, and that would increase their faith... First of all that to plant the seed, ... they have to try it by keeping commandments... That feeling of surrender is not likely to come unless they experience some feeling of being loved and some value in their being meek and lowly of heart.[28]

● **Sometimes we must increase our efforts to study and pray,** recognizing that we may not have done this as long, as faithfully, or as honestly as we should. This kind of understanding requires more than casual reading; it requires concentrated study. Elder Howard W. Hunter suggested a regular time set aside each day when we can concentrate without interference.[29] President Kimball urges us not to get casual in our relationships with God or with His written word: "When it seems that no divine ear is listening and no divine voice is speaking, that I am far, far away. If I immerse myself in the scriptures the distance narrows and the spirituality returns. I find myself loving more intensely those whom I must love with all my heart and mind and strength, and loving them more, I find it easier to abide their counsel."[30]

Scripture study prepares us for prayer

● **Isaiah 59:2 Sometimes we must be more faithful in obeying the commandments.** Revelation comes only from the Lord, who is the source of all truth and light. Thus, we must be "in tune" with Him before we can discern His will. Any degree of willful unrighteousness will disqualify us from receiving the Spirit and thereby being able to discern the spirit of revelation. Elder S. Dilworth Young said: " If I am to receive revelation from the Lord, I must be in harmony with Him by keeping His commandments. Then as needed, according to His wisdom, His word will come..."[31]

● **D&C 9:10–11 Sometimes we let our fears block faith, and therefore revelation also.** When Oliver Cowdery began, he was full of faith. But as he began to lose his gift, he allowed fear to overcome him. The Lord said to him, "it is not expedient that you should translate now. Behold, it was expedient when you commenced; but you feared, and the time is past, and it is not expedient now." President James E. Faust said: "Action is inhibited by fear... You rightly have concerns about measuring up and finding your place in life. You more often recognize your inadequacies rather than your strengths... We can overcome all of our fears, not all at once, but one at a time. As we do so we will grow in confidence."[32]

Elder Marvin J. Ashton said: "God has not given us the spirit of fear, but the power of love and of a sound mind... Satan wants us to feel unequal to our worldly tasks. If we turn to God, He will take us by the hand and lead us through our darkest hours."[33]

● **D&C 88:62, 71 Sometimes we need to set the matter aside temporarily while we ponder and pray.** Flashes of inspiration often come when we least expect them, while our minds are no longer consumed by the matter. The Lord commands us to ponder His sayings in our hearts "for a little season" and call upon Him while He is near (vv. 62, 71). Many of the most profound revelations of this dispensation have resulted from a prophet prayerfully pondering upon the scriptures for a while. These are but a few examples.

— Joseph Smith's first vision (JS-History 1:12).
— Joseph Smith's visions of Moroni in his bedroom (JS-History 1:47).
— The restoration of the priesthood (JS-History 1:68–69).
— Joseph Smith and Sydney Rigdon's vision of kingdoms and Christ (D&C 76:19–24).
— President Joseph F. Smith's vision of the spirit world (D&C 138:1, 11).
— President Spencer W. Kimball's revelation on priesthood (Official Declaration 2).

● **D&C 58:25–28 Sometimes we may be seeking counsel on matters that we should determine for ourselves, using our best judgment based on study and reason.** In these cases the Lord may leave us to decide on our own. The Lord often allows us to make our own decisions in righteousness. The Lord said: "For behold, it is not meet that I should command in all things; for he that is compelled in all things, the same is a slothful and not a wise servant; wherefore he receiveth no reward" (v. 26). We are commanded to be "anxiously engaged in a good cause, and do many things of [our] own free will, and bring to pass much righteousness" (v. 27). We are not helpless, and the Lord does not want us to be totally dependent upon Him for every action. "For the power is in them, wherein they are agents unto themselves. And inasmuch as men do good they shall in nowise lose their reward" (v. 28).

● **D&C 60:5; 61:22 Sometimes the Lord does not mind which choice we make.** Some issues are not of great importance, and we may do as we wish. Other times we may be blessed regardless of which choice we make because they are equally good. When the Lord asked the elders to return speedily to the East from Jackson County, Missouri, He said: "Let there be a craft made, or bought, as seemeth you good, it mattereth not unto me, and take your journey speedily for the place which is called St. Louis" (D&C 60:5). He also didn't care whether they went by water or by land (D&C 61:22), nor whether they went all together or two by two (D&C 62:5). In all these cases the Lord said simply, "it mattereth not unto me." He was more concerned that they "be faithful, and declare glad tidings unto the inhabitants of the earth, or among the congregations of the wicked" as they went (D&C 62:5).

● **D&C 9:6 Sometimes we have already received an answer but have not accepted it because it was not what we had hoped for or expected.** We must not murmur when things don't turn out as we expect. If we insist on what we want and are angry when we don't receive it, we may close off the Spirit's communication with us. To Oliver Cowdery the Lord said: "Do not murmur, my son, for it is wisdom in me that I have dealt with you after this manner" (D&C 9:6). The Lord has higher purposes in the events of our lives, and we often do not fully understand or appreciate them until much later.

● **D&C 88:64–65; 122:7 The Lord will always do what is best for us if we will turn to Him and trust Him.** The Lord promises us "Whatsoever ye ask the Father in my name it shall be given unto you, that is expedient for you" (v. 64). But we must be careful not to ask amiss because if we ask for "anything that is not expedient for you, it shall turn unto your condemnation" (v. 65). To the Prophet Joseph Smith in Liberty Jail the Lord said: "know thou, my son, that all these things shall give thee experience, and shall be for thy good (D&C 122:7). Through this and other experiences of his life, the Prophet Joseph Smith learned that "Whatever God requires is right, no matter what it is, although we may not see the reason thereof till long after the events transpire."[34]

Eliza M. Hickock wrote in her poem "Prayer":

> "And so I pray and calmly wait.
> I know not if the blessing sought
> Will come just in the way I thought,
> But leave my prayers with Him alone,
> Whose ways are wiser than my own—
> Assured that He will grant my quest,
> Or send some answer far more blessed."[35]

Notes:

1. "Divine Revelation," *Brigham Young University Speeches of the Year* [15 October 1952], 6–7.

2. *That All May Be Edified* [1982], 335.

3. *Brigham Young University Speeches of the Year* [10 April 1956], 8.

4. *Improvement Era*, December 1969, 85.

5. In Conference Report, April 1971, 100–101; or *Ensign*, June 1971, 78.

6. Daniel H. Ludlow, ed., 5 vols. [1992], 3:1225.

7. *Ensign*, November 1997, 75.

8. *Biography and Family Record of President Lorenzo Snow* (1884), 332.

9. "Teaching and Learning by the Spirit," *Ensign*, March 1997, 11–12, 14.

10. In Conference Report, October 1994, 77; or *Ensign*, November 1994, 60.

11. *Ensign*, March 1997, 13.

12. In Conference Report, October 1989, 40; or *Ensign*, November 1989, 32.

13. *Gospel Doctrine*, 5th ed. (1939), 7.

14. *Teachings of the Prophet Joseph Smith*, 247.

15. *Ensign*, May 1979, 8–9.

16. *Teachings of Gordon B. Hinckley* [1997], 468.

17. General conference address, October 1973; or *Ensign*, January 1974, 18.

18. See Richard G. Scott, *Ensign*, May 1996, 24–25.

19. In Conference Report, October 1944, 55–56.

20. *Teachings of the Prophet Joseph Smith,* 21.

21. "What Are You Doing Here?" *New Era,* Jan. 1987, 37–38.

22. In James R. Clark, comp., *Messages of the First Presidency of The Church of Jesus Christ of Latter-day Saints,* 6 vols. [1965–75], 4:285.

23. In Conference Report, October 1979, 29–30; or *Ensign,* November 1979, 21.

24. "He Healeth the Broken in Heart," *Ensign,* July 2005, 6–7.

25. *Ensign,* March 1997, 10–11.

26. In Conference Report, October 1989, 38; or *Ensign,* November 1989, 30–31.

27. *Ensign,* May 1982, 24.

28. *Ensign,* November 1995, 38.

29. *Ensign,* November 1979, 64–65.

30. *The Teachings of Spencer W. Kimball* [1982], 135.

31. "The Still Small Voice," *Ensign,* May 1976, 23.

32. *Ensign,* November 1997, 43–44).

33. General conference address, October 1980; or *Ensign,* November 1980, 60.

34. *Teachings of the Prophet Joseph Smith,* 256.

35. *The Best Loved Religious Poems,* ed. James Gilchrist Lawson [1933], 160.

CHAPTER 7

The First Principles and Ordinances of the Gospel

(D&C 8; 11; 14; 18–20; 22; 27; 29; 31; 35; 39; 42; 45; 58; 63; 68; 75; 84; 88)

[Topical Chapter]

~~~

INTRODUCTION

This chapter, like the one before it, is topical—ranging throughout the Doctrine and Covenants to bring together many scriptures on the first principles and ordinances of the gospel. These principles were not all revealed at once, but over time as the infant Church grew. The Church had not even been organized before the Lord began teaching the Prophet Joseph Smith and his associates concerning these principles and ordinances, and He revealed greater and greater light as time went on.

The 4th Article of Faith says, "We believe that the first principles and ordinances of the Gospel are: first, Faith in the Lord Jesus Christ; second, Repentance; third, Baptism by immersion for the remission of sins; fourth, Laying on of hands for the gift of the Holy Ghost." In this chapter we will review each of these and their relationship to the mission of the Lord Jesus Christ.

THE ATONEMENT OF JESUS CHRIST

The Prophet Joseph Smith said: "The fundamental principles of our religion are the testimony of the Apostles and Prophets, concerning Jesus Christ, that He died, was buried, and rose again the third day, and ascended into heaven; and all other things which pertain to our religion are only appendages to it."[1]

We cannot understand the first principles and ordinances of the gospel unless we understand their relationship to Christ and His atonement for all humankind. "Nothing in the entire plan of salvation compares in any way

The Atonement is central to the Gospel

in importance with that most transcendent of all events, the atoning sacrifice of our Lord. It is the most important single thing that has ever occurred in the entire history of created things; it is the rock foundation upon which the gospel and all other things rest... The doctrine of the atonement embraces, sustains, supports, and gives life and force to all other gospel doctrines. It is the foundation upon which all truth rests, and all things grow out of it and come because of it. Indeed, the atonement is the gospel."[2]

The gospel is "all that is required to take us back to [our Father's] eternal presence." This we cannot do without the atonement, "by which all men are raised in immortality, with those who believe and obey ascending also unto eternal life... Thus the gospel is, in effect, the atonement. But the gospel is also all of the laws, principles, doctrines, rites, ordinances, acts, powers, authorities, and keys needed to save and exalt fallen man in the highest heaven hereafter."[3]

● **D&C 19 This revelation was received in March 1830 in Manchester, New York.** Martin Harris was "sorely troubled in spirit," and he came to Joseph Smith seeking assurance regarding his standing before the Lord. He had already been designated as one of the Three Witnesses, and he had seen that vision. So it is not entirely clear why this revelation was needed. But it turned out to be "one of the great revelations given in this dispensation," according to Elder Joseph Fielding Smith.[4] It contains an explanation of the doctrine of the atonement, as it applies to each individual, and also explains the concept of "Eternal Punishment."

● **D&C 19:1 Five symbolic names of the Lord.** In this one verse the Lord calls himself by five names which identify His position as our Savior.

— Alpha and Omega. The first and the last letter of the Greek alphabet, used as symbols of the beginning and the ending. Christ is so called, because He is the Author and the Preserver of all things (see also Hebrews 1:2, 10).

— Christ the Lord. "Christ" means "anointed." Prophets, priests, and kings were anointed, and our Lord unites all these offices in Himself. He is the anointed Lord. The Greek word Christ is the same as the Hebrew Messiah (Mashiac), a title used in John 1:41, and 4:25.

— I am He. This is equivalent to the name "Jehovah" (D&C 18:21).

— The Beginning and the End. He was in the beginning and will remain throughout all eternities. He is endless (see also v. 4).

— The Redeemer of the World. Christ is our Redeemer. He delivers those who turn to Him from the bondage of sin and guilt. He has 'bought' us (1 Corinthians 6:20; 7:23; 2 Peter 2:1). And the world will in due time be delivered from the power of Satan, from sin and all its consequences, such as war, poverty, ignorance, sickness, and even death.

● **D&C 19:2–3 Through His atonement Christ subdued all things.** He did so to accomplish "the will of him whose I am, even the Father, concerning me" and to "subdue all things unto myself" (v. 2). He thus also retained power over all things, including "the destroying of Satan and his works at the end of the world" (v. 3).

D&C 19:3–4 Through His atonement Christ became the judge of us all. At "the last great day of judgment" He will judge "every man according to his works and the deeds which he hath done" (v. 3). This is because He has paid the price for our iniquities and can thus set the terms under which that payment will have effect in our lives. And He makes clear here what those terms shall be: "And surely every man must repent or suffer, for I, God, am endless," meaning He is the eternal judge of all.

● **D&C 19:15, 18–19 The terrible depth of Christ's suffering.** His suffering was beyond our understanding—"how sore you know not, how exquisite you know not, yea, how hard to bear you know not" (v. 15). The Lord says His "suffering caused myself, even God, the greatest of all, to tremble because of pain, and to bleed at every pore, and to suffer both body and spirit—and would that I might not drink the bitter cup, and shrink" (v. 18). The kind of spiritual anguish and physical pain that can cause blood to ooze from every pore is called "hematodrosis." Under extreme distress and pressure the capillaries burst and produce a bloody sweat. W. Jeffrey Marsh believes that "Christ's was the most severe instance of hematodrosis ever experienced."[5] Consider the following explanations of Christ's suffering, offered by two of His Apostles:

Christ's suffering was intense

Elder Joseph Fielding Smith said:

> We cannot comprehend the great suffering that the Lord had to take upon Himself to bring to pass this redemption from death and from sin… We get into the habit of thinking, I suppose, that His great suffering was when He was nailed to the cross by His hands and His feet and was left there to suffer until He died. As excruciating as that pain was, that was not the greatest suffering that He had to undergo, for in some way which I cannot understand, but which I accept on faith, and which you must accept on faith, He carried on His back the burden of the sins of the whole world. It is hard enough for me to carry my own sins. How is it with you? And yet He had to carry the sins of the whole world, as our Savior and the Redeemer of a fallen world, and so great was His suffering before He ever went to the cross, we are informed, that blood oozed from the pores of His body.[6]

Elder James E. Talmage said:

> Christ's agony in the garden is unfathomable by the finite mind, both as to intensity and cause… He struggled and groaned under a burden such as no other being who has lived on earth might even conceive as possible. It was not physical pain, nor mental anguish alone, that caused Him to suffer such torture as to produce an extrusion of blood from every pore; but a spiritual agony of soul such as only God was capable of experiencing. No other man, however great his powers of physical or mental endurance, could have suffered so; for his human organism would have succumbed, and syncope would have produced unconscious-ness and welcome oblivion. In that hour of anguish Christ met and overcame all the horrors that Satan, "the prince of this world" could inflict… In some manner,

actual and terribly real though to man incomprehensible, the Savior took upon Himself the burden of the sins of mankind from Adam to the end of the world.[7]

THE FIRST PRINCIPLES OF THE GOSPEL

Faith in the Lord Jesus Christ

- **D&C 19:23; 88:118 We develop faith gradually over time through concerted effort.** We must nurture our faith constantly by learning about Christ, listening to His words, and living with the same meekness that He showed while on earth (D&C 19:23).

- **D&C 88:118 We nurture our faith by studying "out of the best books."** We are to diligently "teach one another words of wisdom" (the gospel) and to "seek ye out of the best books" those same words of wisdom. Our Gospel Doctrine classes are an example of how we do this. But we are to focus first upon the scriptures, then augment that knowledge with other worthy sources of knowledge. President Rudger Clawson said: "The standard works of the Church [should] come first, and other literature afterwards. Of course, we must keep track of daily events, things that are going on in the world, but when it comes to reading books of interest and value, let us give preference to the Church works because they are more precious than any other books in the world."[8]

- **D&C 88:118 Our learning should be "by study and also by faith."** Gospel learning is not obtained purely "by study" but also "by faith" (D&C 88:118). In other words, it is not purely an intellectual exercise. The Lord wants us to be well educated:

"Learning by study and also by faith"

  — "Seek not for riches but for wisdom" (D&C 6:7; 11:7).
  — Teach one another the doctrine of the kingdom" (D&C 88:77).
  — "Teach one another words of wisdom; yea, "Learning by study and also by faith" seek ye out of the best books words of wisdom; seek learning, even by study and also by faith" (D&C 88:118).
  — "Study and learn, and become acquainted with all good books, and with languages, tongues, and people" (D&C 90:15).
  — "Obtain a knowledge of history, and of countries, and of kingdoms, of laws of God and man" (D&C 93:53).
  — "Let him that is ignorant learn wisdom" (D&C 136:32).

President Brigham Young said: "The religion embraced by the Latter-day Saints, if only slightly understood, prompts them to search diligently after knowledge. There is no other people in existence more eager to see, hear, learn, and understand truth."[9] "One of the greatest blessings that can be bestowed upon the children of men is to have true knowledge concerning themselves, concerning the human family and the designs of Heaven concerning them. It is also a great blessing to have wisdom to use this knowledge in a way to produce the greatest good to ourselves and all men. All the power of earthly wealth cannot give this knowledge and this wisdom."[10]

President Young also said: "It is the duty of the Latter-day Saints, according to the revelations, to give their children the best education that can be procured, both from the books of the world and the revelations of the Lord."[11] But we must study with the goal of strengthening our faith, not merely stimulating our intellect. Elder Dallin H. Oaks said: "We should … seek learning by faith in God, the giver of revelation. I believe that many of the great discoveries and achievements in science and the arts have resulted from a God-given revelation. Seekers who have paid the price in perspiration have been magnified by inspiration."[12]

● **D&C 20:69 We demonstrate our faith by our works** (see also James 2:14–17). The specific works mentioned here are "a godly walk and conversation" and "walking in holiness before the Lord." This means that our deeds (our "walk") and our words must be "agreeable to the holy scriptures—walking in holiness before the Lord." To claim to have faith in Jesus Christ while wilfully violating His commandments is hypocrisy.

Elder Spencer W. Kimball said: "Faith is the power behind good works. The exercising of faith is a willingness to accept without total regular proof and to move forward and perform works. 'Faith without works is dead' (James 2:26), and a dead faith will not lead one to move forward to adjust a life or to serve valiantly. A real faith pushes one forward to constructive and beneficial acts as though he knew in absoluteness."[13]

● **D&C 8:10 Without faith we can accomplish nothing.** We must not attempt to do the Lord's work alone. We are to "ask in faith" for His help. The Lord compared our relationship to Him to a branch of a tree: "Abide in me, and I in you. As the branch cannot bear fruit of itself, except it abide in the vine [trunk]; no more can ye, except ye abide in me. I am the vine, ye are the branches: He that abideth in me, and I in him, the same bringeth forth much fruit: for without me ye can do nothing. If a man abide not in me, he is cast forth as a [dead] branch, and is withered; and men gather them, and cast them into the fire, and they are burned" (John 15:4–6).

● **D&C 8:10 We must not exercise faith lightly nor ask for things that are improper.** The Lord commands, "Trifle not with these things." To trifle is to take lightly, and we are not to take matters of faith lightly. Our prayers, for example, should not be half-hearted. Elder Spencer W. Kimball said: "How much do you pray, my young friends? How often? How earnestly? If you should have errors in your life, have you wrestled before the Lord? Have you found your deep forest full of solitude? How much has your soul hungered? How deeply have your needs impressed your heart? When did you kneel before your Maker in total quiet? For what did you pray—your own soul? How long did you thus plead for recognition—all day long? And when the shadows fell, did you still raise your voice in mighty prayer, or did you liquidate it with some trite word and phrase? As you struggle in the spirit and cry mightily and covenant sincerely, the voice of the Lord God will come into your mind, as it did to that of Enos, ' … thy sins are forgiven thee, and thou shalt be blest' (Enos 1:5)."[14]

The Lord also commands, "do not ask for that which you ought not." This suggests that we need help from the Spirit in offering our prayers. Elder Bruce R. McConkie said: "Perfect prayers are always answered; proper petitions are always granted. The Lord never rejects a prayer uttered by the power of the Spirit, or denies a petition sought in the name of Christ, that accords with the divine will."[15] Elder McConkie also said: "Perfect prayers are those which are inspired, in which the Spirit reveals the words which should be used. (3 Ne. 19:24; D&C 50:29–30)."[16]

● **D&C 35:9 With faith, we can exercise all of the gifts of the Spirit on behalf of others.** Those with faith in Christ can "cast out devils," "heal the sick," "cause the blind to receive their sight," "the deaf to hear," "the dumb to speak," and "the lame to walk." These are some of the most miraculous of gifts, but there are many more. While serving as a young bishop, I became aware that virtually every gift known to man resided in my ward as a body of Saints. No one person had all the gifts, but taken together as a ward, they possessed them all, and when they came together to worship they were able to enjoy all the gifts of the Spirit.

Orson Pratt

Elder Orson Pratt said: "These spiritual gifts are distributed among the members of the Church, according to their faithfulness, circumstances, natural abilities, duties, and callings; that the whole may be properly instructed, confirmed, perfected, and saved."[17] This is as the Lord intended it. We need each other. He gives us our several gifts, commanding us to "always [remember] for what they are given" (D&C 46:8–9)—to bless the lives of others, and not for our own self-aggrandizement.

● **D&C 42:48–51 Even with faith, spiritual gifts must be used in accordance with the Lord's will.** The Lord says, "he that hath faith in me to be healed, and is not appointed unto death, shall be healed" (v. 48). This same requirement to submit ourselves to the will of God applies also to the blind who seek to see, the deaf who seek to hear, and the lame who seek to be healed of their disabilities (vv. 49–51).

K. Douglas Bassett relates the following sacred experience:

> When I held my little son in my arms, knowing that he may be sentenced to life in a defective body, I suffered anguish of soul. We had not prepared ourselves to deal with this... Our pain was founded in a deep concern for the welfare of our son. I felt confident with the Lord's help my son would be healed. I fasted and prayed for the Lord's direction in giving Boyd a blessing. As I laid my hands on his head, everything I desired made me anxious for his body to be made whole. But, even in my overzealous state, I had to admit I could feel no spiritual promptings in blessing him to recover from Cystic Fibrosis...
>
> This caused me more pain than when I had first discovered his illness! I felt personally responsible for Boyd's disease. As I searched for an explanation I read these words of President Brigham Young: "In many instances our anxiety is so great that we do not pause to know the spirit of revelation... We have anxiety instead of faith... He lays his hands upon the sick, but they are not healed. It is in consequence of not being completely molded to the will of God."[18] I had prayed for a miracle and ... in God's own time the miracles came, but not in the way that I had expected. There is a God in Heaven who understands the destiny of each of His children. He also understands the pathway of

challenges each will be confronted with in order to reach their destiny (Acts 17:26; Ether 12:27). Without this insight I could not hope to see the reason for this particular challenge in Boyd's life. As his life unfolded, I grew to understand it better.[19]

● **D&C 63:9–11 Signs cannot produce faith, and they are shown only to the already faithful (v. 9).** This is because "signs come by faith, not by the will of men, nor as they please, but by the will of God" (v. 10). Even Christ Himself could do no miracle on behalf of people unless they had faith (Matthew 13:58; Ether 12:12). He invariably asked them, "Believest thou?" before He healed someone of any malady (Matthew 9:2; 20:30–34; Mark 9:23–26; John 4:50; 9:35; 11:26, 40). Signs and spiritual gifts "come by faith," and "without faith no man pleaseth God" (v. 11). The Lord will show no signs to the unbelieving except those signs that show His "wrath unto their condemnation" (such as the signs of destruction in the last days) (v. 11).

● **D&C 27:15–18 The "shield of faith" will protect us against the "fiery darts of the wicked."** We live in a seriously troubled time, wherein the Lord commands us to "lift up your hearts and rejoice, and gird up your loins [meaning prepare yourself], and take upon you my whole armor, that ye may be able to withstand the evil day." If we do so, "having done all … ye may be able to stand" (v. 15). What kind of preparation is required for times like these? The Lord lists the following.

— Knowing the truth (v. 16).
— Living in righteousness (v. 16).
— Understanding the gospel of peace (v. 16).
— Faith, with which "ye shall be able to quench all the fiery darts of the wicked" (v. 17).
— Having hope for, and the assurance of, salvation (v. 18).
— Possessing the Holy Spirit as a guide (v. 18).
— Receiving all the words of Christ (scriptures and revelations) (v. 18).
— Unity—"being agreed as touching all things" (v. 18).
— Enduring all things in faith until He comes (v. 18).

And if we are thus prepared, He promises us that "ye shall be caught up, that where I am ye shall be also" (v. 18).

Sincere Repentance

● **D&C 19:13–15 "I command you to repent."** He who has paid the price for our sins commands us to change our lives or suffer the consequences. "I command you to repent, and keep the commandments which you have received by the hand of my servant Joseph Smith, Jun., in my name" (v. 13), reminding us that "it is by my almighty power that you have received them" (v. 14). He says the level of His suffering was beyond our understanding—"how sore you know not, how exquisite you know not, yea, how hard to bear you know not" (v. 15).

● **D&C 19:17, 19–20 The intensity of our personal suffering if we do not repent.** The Lord knows firsthand of the magnitude of the suffering that justice demands for sins, and He is trying to spare us that suffering. He "suffered these things for all, that they might not suffer if they would repent; But if they would not repent they must suffer even as I" (v. 17).

The Savior gives all the credit to the Father that "I partook and finished my preparations unto the children of men" (v. 19). And having done so, He says, "I command you again to repent … [and] confess your sins, lest you suffer these punishments of which I have spoken" (v. 20). Martin Harris had recently lost the Spirit and been left to suffer the buffetings of Satan—a state which leaves one lonely, in pain and depression, and in fear of eternal destruction. Th2e Lord here says that those sufferings (which are terrible) are only "the smallest, yea, even in the least degree" of the sufferings that await the wicked (v. 20).

Elder B. H. Roberts suggested that we "let the severity of … Christ's Atonement for man's sin bear witness; for it required all that … Christ gave in suffering and agony of spirit and body, to lay the grounds for man's forgiveness and reconciliation with God. The severity of the Atonement should impress men with the fact that … human actions draw with them tremendous consequences that may not be easily set aside if the actions … are wrong. Moral laws have their penalties as physical laws have their consequences… Violations of moral law are attended by shame and suffering; suffering is the consequence or the penalty of violating divine, moral law; and the penalty must be paid, either by the one sinning or by another who shall suffer vicariously for him."[20]

● **D&C 19:21 Preach nothing but repentance.** In addition to personal repentance, we are commanded to "preach naught but repentance." Martin Harris had a tendency to want to show scientific proofs and to make philosophical arguments. He is expressly forbidden to do so here, and he is commanded to "show not these things unto the world until it is wisdom in me" (v. 21). People do not need scientific arguments. They need to repent.

As Daniel H. Ludlow noted, the heading of D&C 19 indicates that it is "a commandment of God" rather than referring to it only as a "revelation." This revelation contains not only instruction but also a clear commandment to repent, repeated three times: "I command you to repent" (verse 15), "I command you again to repent" (verse 20), and "I command you that you preach naught but repentance" (verse 21). "When the doctrine of repentance is fully understood," Ludlow notes, "then it is seen that repentance is all that ever needs to be taught, for repentance means not only to stop doing those things which are wrong but also to start doing those things which are right."[21]

● **D&C 18:11–13 Christ rejoices when we repent.** As a God without sin, He had the power to take the easy road and avoid all suffering and death. But He voluntarily "suffered death in the flesh" and "the pain of all men" so that we "might repent and come unto him" (v. 11) and be saved. He "hath risen again from the dead" to bring about the resurrection for all of us "that he might bring all men unto him, on conditions of repentance" (v. 12). Would someone who has suffered such colossal pain rejoice in the destruction of those for whom He had suffered so they could be saved? Of course not. He wishes that all of us would repent and take advantage of His gift, "And how great is his joy in the soul that repenteth!" (v. 13).

● **D&C 58:42 When we repent, the Lord forgives and forgets our sins.** Sometimes we hear people say something like, "Well, I can forgive him but I'll never forget." How much more merciful is the Lord's assurance here that "he who has repented of his sins, the same is forgiven, and I, the Lord, remember them no more."

Though we often have a hard time forgiving ourselves and forgetting our wrongdoing, we are assured that the Master of all things absolutely forgives and forgets. I need not torture myself with my prior mistakes. If I have fully repented of them, they have become utterly irrelevant to my salvation. I am judged for what I now am, not for what I once was. Elder Neal A. Maxwell said: "Repentance is a rescuing, not a dour doctrine. It is available to the gross sinner as well as to the already good individual striving for incremental improvement."[22]

● **D&C 58:43 The Lord's definition of repentance.** How, then, can I know that my repentance has been acceptable to Him who so mercifully forgives? This is the answer: "By this ye may know if a man repenteth of his sins—behold, he will confess them and forsake them." This means that to repent, we must both confess and turn away from evil.

When we humbly confess our sins the Lord freely forgives us

Confession. Admitting wrongdoing is the first step toward reformation. If we humbly acknow- ledge our weakness and bad behavior, we are manifesting the kind of godly sorrow that leads to changed behavior. If we attempt to hide our sins, we have not yet reached the point where the Lord can and will forgive us.

Elder Richard G. Scott said: "Do not take comfort in the fact that your transgressions are not known by others. That is like an ostrich with his head buried in the sand. He sees only darkness and feels comfortably hidden. In reality he is ridicu- lously conspicuous. Likewise our every act is seen by our Father in Heaven and His Beloved Son. They know everything about us… I invite each one of you to thoughtfully review your life… Is there a dark corner that needs to be cleaned out? … When it is quiet and you can think clearly, does your conscience tell you to repent?"[23]

In his masterful work, *The Miracle of Forgiveness* [1969], Elder Spencer W. Kimball noted that "many offenders in their shame and pride have satisfied their consciences, temporarily at least, with a few silent prayers to the Lord and rationalized that this was sufficient confession of their sins. 'But l have confessed my sin to my Heavenly Father,' they will insist, 'and that is all that is necessary.' This is not true where a major sin is involved. Then two sets of forgiveness are required to bring peace to the transgressor—one from the proper authorities of the Lord's

Church, and one from the Lord Himself" (p. 179). And for sins that have injured others, Elder Kimball teaches that "he, the aggressor, who gave the offense, regardless of the attitude of the other party, should immediately make amends by confessing to the injured one and doing all in his power to clear up the matter and again establish good feelings between the two parties."[24]

Forsaking the Sin. President Ezra Taft Benson said: "Repentance means more than simply a reformation of behavior... True repentance is based on and flows from faith in the Lord Jesus Christ. There is no other way. True repentance involves a change of heart and not just a change of behavior (Alma 5:13)."[25]

THE FIRST ORDINANCES OF THE CHURCH

The Essential Ordinance of Baptism

- **D&C 18:22 Baptism is a requirement for salvation.** Those who repent are required to be "baptized in my name, which is Jesus Christ, and endure to the end" in order to be saved.

- **D&C 22:1–4 Baptism must be done by someone holding proper authority.** After the Church was organized on April 6, 1830, people were invited to be baptized into it. Most of them were already believers in Christ and many had been baptized in their former churches. Believing the doctrine of modern-day Christendom that any baptism will do, there were "some who had previously been baptized desiring to unite with the Church without re-baptism" (D&C 22, Heading).

Jesus was baptized by immersion
By one holding proper authority

In this revelation, the Lord declares that the covenant they would make upon baptism into His true Church was "a new and an everlasting covenant, even that which was from the beginning" (v. 1). Some have supposed that this is a reference to celestial marriage. Elder Joseph Fielding Smith said: "Each ordinance of the Gospel is a covenant which is new and everlasting. It is new and everlasting because it is divine truth and never grows old. ... This was said of baptism... It is so with all the covenants and obligations in the Gospel which pertain to salvation and exaltation of man."[26] In this particular case, the Lord was referring to baptism.

The Lord reminded these new converts that "although a man should be baptized an hundred times it availeth him nothing" if it is not done by proper priesthood authority, "for you cannot

CHRIST BAPTIZED BY JOHN THE BAPTIST, CARL BLOCH

enter in at the strait gate by the law of Moses, neither by your dead works" (v. 2). Indeed it was precisely "because of your dead works that I have caused this last covenant and this church to be built up unto me, even as in days of old" (v. 3). They were scolded for seeking to "counsel your God" concerning this matter, and He commanded them (and us) to "enter ye in at the gate [of baptism], as I have commanded" (v. 4).

● **D&C 20:37 The qualifications a person must meet to be baptized.** Those who "shall be received by baptism into [the Lord's] church" must …

— Humble themselves before God.
— Desire to be baptized.
— Come forth with broken hearts and contrite spirits.
— Witness before the Church that they have truly repented of all their sins.
— Manifest by their works that they have received of the Spirit of Christ unto the remission of their sins (meaning that they have truly changed their lives).
— Be willing to take upon them the name of Jesus Christ.
— Have a determination to serve the Lord to the end of their lives.

● **D&C 20:72–74 Baptism must be performed with proper authority, by immersion, using an ordinance with set words.** The Lord says that "Baptism is to be administered in the following manner unto all those who repent" (v. 72). The person performing the ordinance must be "called of God and [have] authority from Jesus Christ to baptize" (v. 73). This authorized priesthood holder "shall go down into the water with the person who has presented himself or herself for baptism" (v. 73). The words of this ordinance are prescribed by the Lord and must be followed with exactness to ensure that the covenant is clearly stated and not changed: "Having been commissioned of Jesus Christ, I baptize you in the name of the Father, and of the Son, and of the Holy Ghost. Amen" (v. 73). The priesthood holder is then to "immerse him or her in the water, and come forth again out of the water" (v. 74).

● **D&C 76:51 Baptism by immersion symbolizes the death, burial, and resurrection of Christ.** Those who enter the celestial kingdom are those "who received the testimony of Jesus, and believed on his name and were baptized after the manner of his burial," meaning to be "buried in the water in his name." This is an important part of the symbolism of the baptismal ordinance and shows how inappropriate sprinkling is as a token of Christ's death and resurrection. There are also other symbolic aspects of baptism by immersion:

— **John 3:3–5** It also symbolizes the burial of our old self and our rebirth in Christ.
— **Romans 6:3–4** It also symbolizes a washing—being cleansed from our sins.

● **D&C 20:71; 29:49–50 It is not necessary or appropriate to baptize persons who are not capable of being accountable to God.** In order to "be received into the Church of Christ" a person must be of sufficient age and mental fitness to be "accountab[le] before God, and … capable of repentance" (D&C 20:71).

President Joseph Fielding Smith said: "The Lord has made it known by revelation that children born with retarded minds shall receive blessings just like little children who die in infancy. They are free from sin, because their minds are not capable of a correct understanding of right and wrong... Therefore, The Church of Jesus Christ of Latter-day Saints considers all deficient children with retarded capacity to understand, just the same as little children under the age of accountability. They are redeemed without baptism and will go to the celestial kingdom of God, there, we believe, to have their faculties or other deficiencies restored according to the Father's mercy and justice."[27]

Mormon placed the mentally disturbed and retarded in the same category as little children who are under the age of accountability—they do not require baptism, for the atonement of Jesus Christ takes care of them equally with little children who die before the age of accountability. "For behold that all little children are alive in Christ, and also all they that are without the law. For the power of redemption cometh on all them that have no law; wherefore, he that is not condemned, or he that is under no condemnation, cannot repent; and unto such baptism availeth nothing" (Moroni 8:22).

The Lord reiterated this doctrine in a revelation given to the Prophet Joseph Smith in September 1830, just before the beginning of a Church conference at Fayette, New York, "'And again, I say unto you, that whoso having knowledge, have I not commanded to repent? And he that hath no understanding, it remaineth in me to do according as it is written" (D&C 29:49–50).

● **D&C 29:46–47 Children younger than eight years are blameless before God.** It was decided in the premortal council, before the world was even formed, that "little children are redeemed ... through mine Only Begotten" (v. 46). This is because "they cannot sin, for power is not given unto Satan to tempt little children, until they begin to become accountable before me" (v. 47).

Little children are innocent before God

The Prophet Joseph Smith and his wife Emma lost many infant children to death before they reached the age of accountability. Little wonder, then, that he inquired of the Lord concerning this matter and received reassurance concerning them. The Prophet taught, "Baptism is for remission of sins. Children have no sins. Jesus blessed them and said: 'Do what you have seen me do.' Children are all made alive in Christ, and those of riper years through faith and repentance."[28] He also said: "The doctrine of baptizing children, or sprinkling them, or they must welter in hell, is a doctrine not true, not supported in Holy Writ, and is not consistent with the character of God. All children are redeemed by the blood of Jesus Christ, and the moment that children leave this world, they are taken to the bosom of Abraham."[29]

● **D&C 68:25 Parents are accountable to prepare their children for baptism at eight years of age.** The Lord commands parents to teach children to "understand the doctrine of repentance, faith in Christ the Son of the living God, and of baptism and the gift of the Holy Ghost by the laying on of the hands, when eight years old." And if they fail to do so, "the sin be upon the heads of the parents." Thus, the shallow excuse that "I didn't have my children baptized at eight because they weren't ready to make a decision" is really a confession that the parents have failed to do their duty. If they are not ready, the Lord here declares, it's the parents' fault, not because the child could not have been ready.

President Thomas S. Monson said: "There are those who dismiss these responsibilities, feeling they can be deferred until the child grows up. Not so, the evidence reveals. Prime time for teaching is fleeting... Children learn through gentle direction and persuasive teaching. They search for models to imitate, knowledge to acquire, things to do, and teachers to please. Parents and grandparents fill the role of teacher. So do siblings of the growing child. In this regard, I offer four simple suggestions for your consideration: (1) Teach prayer, (2) Inspire faith, (3) Live truth, and (4) Honor God."[30]

Elder Joseph B. Wirthlin said:

> Every home is a house of learning, either for good or otherwise. Family members may learn to be obedient, honest, industrious, self-reliant, and faithful in living gospel principles, or they may learn something else. Learning the gospel in the homes of Church members should be centered on the scriptures and on the words of latter-day prophets ... Teach your children to pray, to rely on the Lord for guidance, and to express appreciation for their blessings. Children learn from you to distinguish between right and wrong. They learn that lying, cheating, stealing, or coveting possessions of others is wrong. Help them to learn to keep the Sabbath day holy and to pay their tithing. Teach them to learn and obey the commandments of God. Teach your young children to work, and teach them that honest labor develops dignity and self-respect. Help them to find pleasure in work and to feel the satisfaction that comes from a job well done.[31]

Confirmation and the Gift of the Holy Ghost

● **D&C 35:5–6 After baptism by water, Church members must receive the gift of the Holy Ghost through the ordinance of confirmation.** In June of 1830, two months after the Book of Mormon had been published and the Church organized, Sidney Rigdon met the Prophet Joseph Smith for the first time in Fayette, New York. (So much for the theory that Sidney Rigdon wrote the Book of Mormon!) Sidney had joined the Church and performed some baptisms, but had not yet conferred the Holy Ghost upon any of those converts. As part of this revelation, he was given "a commandment, that thou shalt baptize by water, and they shall receive the Holy Ghost by the laying on of the hands, even as the apostles of old" (v. 6). Thus it is clear that baptism alone is not enough for entry into the Church. The Prophet Joseph Smith said: "Baptism by water is but half a baptism, and is good for nothing without ... the baptism of the Holy Ghost."[32]

D&C 33:15 Confirmation bestows the Gift of the Holy Ghost. When Ezra Thayre and Northrop Sweet were sent forth to preach and baptize they were also commanded that "whoso having faith you shall confirm in my church, by the laying on of the hands, and I will bestow the gift of the Holy Ghost upon them." A sincere seeker after truth may receive manifestations of the Holy Ghost to persuade them to repent and be baptized. But the gift of the Holy Ghost is more comprehensive. It includes the right to constant companionship, that we may "always have his Spirit to be with [us]" (D&C 20:77).[33]

The manifestations of the Holy Ghost that a person can receive before baptism can be compared to flashes of lightning that "[blaze] forth in a dark and stormy night," while the Gift of the Holy Ghost that a person receives after baptism is like "the continuing blaze of the sun at noonday, shedding its rays on the path of life and on all that surrounds it."[34] Elder McConkie reminded young children that "the gift of the Holy Ghost … is the right to the constant companionship of this member of the Godhead based on faithfulness. This is the greatest gift possible to receive in mortality. There is nothing any of us need as much as the guiding and preserving care of the Holy Spirit—the Spirit that is given by the prayer of faith to those who love and serve the Lord. I testify that if we love the Lord, keep His commandments, and seek His Spirit, we shall be blessed beyond our fondest hopes."[35]

- **D&C 20:41 This ordinance is also called the "baptism of fire and the Holy Ghost."** Apostles and other holders of the Melchizedek priesthood have the power to "confirm those who are baptized into the church, by the laying on of hands for the baptism of fire and the Holy Ghost, according to the scriptures."

- **D&C 19:28, 38 We obtain the Spirit through faithfulness and prayer.** When we are confirmed, the person officiating invites us to "receive the Holy Ghost." This is really a commandment, not an immediate conferral. We are invited to seek and receive the Holy Spirit in our lives. The question I would ask is, "Have we?" President Joseph Fielding Smith said: "Now I am going to say something that maybe I could not prove, but I believe is true, that we have a great many members of this Church who have never received a manifestation through the Holy Ghost. Why? Because they have not made their lives conform to the truth. And the Holy Ghost will not dwell in unclean tabernacles or disobedient tabernacles. The Holy Ghost will not dwell with that person who is unwilling to obey and keep the commandments of God or who violates those commandments willfully. In such a soul the spirit of the Holy Ghost cannot enter. That great gift comes to us only through humility and faith and obedience. Therefore, a great many members of the Church do not have that guidance."[36]

These two verses explain how we might qualify for this blessing. The Lord commands us to "pray vocally as well as in thy heart; yea, before the world as well as in secret, in public as well as in private" (v. 28). He promises that if we will "pray always" He will "pour out [His] Spirit upon [us]" (v. 38). This is a great and significant blessing, "even more than if [we] should obtain treasures of earth" and the corruptibleness that they bring (v. 38).

- **Some of the functions of the Holy Ghost**

The Holy Ghost performs many essential functions in our lives, and they are taught to us throughout the Doctrine and Covenants.

— **D&C 39:6**	He is the Comforter.
	He shows us all things.
	He is a teacher.
— **D&C 42:17**	He knows all things.
	He is a testifier concerning the Father and of the Son.
— **D&C 100:8**	He bears witness to others of the truth of what we teach.
— **D&C 11:12**	He leads us to do good, walk humbly, and judge righteously.

— **D&C 11:13**	He enlightens our minds.
	He fills our souls with joy.
— **D&C 76:10**	He reveals the Lord's mysteries unto us.
— **D&C 84:33**	He sanctifies us.
	He renews and strengthens our bodies.
— **D&C 31:11**	He inspires concerning where to go, what to do, and what to say.
— **D&C 75:27**	He conveys to us from heaven the answers to our prayers.
— **D&C 84:85**	He refreshes our memories.
	He inspires our words when we are teaching or preaching the gospel.

ENDURING TO THE END

● **D&C 14:7 If we keep the commandments and endure to the end, we <u>will</u> be saved.** Having kept all the first principles and ordinances of the gospel, we are then commanded to "endure to the end." This means that temporary or last-minute repentance is not sufficient to save us, and we must with consistency remember and keep our covenants. If we do, the promise is absolutely sure: "you shall have eternal life, which gift is the greatest of all the gifts of God."

● **D&C 24:8 Enduring to the end requires patience and faith.** By July of 1830, only four months since the organization of the Church, the Prophet Joseph Smith and Oliver Cowdery found themselves in the midst of intense persecution at Harmony, Pennsylvania. When they took the matter to the Lord, seeking relief, they were to "be patient in afflictions, for thou shalt have many; but endure them, for, lo, I am with thee, even unto the end of thy days."

Notes:

1. (Teachings of the Prophet Joseph Smith, sel. Joseph Fielding Smith [1976], 121).

2. (Bruce R. McConkie, Mormon Doctrine, 2nd ed. [1966], 60).

3. (Bruce R. McConkie, A New Witness for the Articles of Faith [1985], 134].

4. (Church History and Modern Revelation, 4 vols. [1946–1949], 1:85).

5. (His Final Hours [2000], 47–48).

6. [in Conference Report, October 1947, 147–148]

7. [Jesus the Christ, 3rd ed. (1916), 613]

8. (in Conference Report, October 1937, 113).

9. (Discourses of President Brigham Young, sel. John A. Widtsoe [1941], 247).

10. (Brigham Young, in Journal of Discourses, 10:209).

11. (in Journal of Discourses, 17:45)

12. (Ensign, May 1989, 29).

13. (The Teachings of Spencer W. Kimball [1982], 71).

14. ("Prayer," Brigham Young University Speeches of the Year, 11 October 1961, 8–9).

15. (A New Witness for the Articles of Faith, 384).

16. (Mormon Doctrine, 586).

17. (Masterful Discourses and Writings of Orson Pratt, comp. N. B. Lundwall [1946], 539–541).

18. (in Journal of Discourses, 12:125).

19. [Kisses at the Window, (1985), 15–16]

20. (The Seventy's Course in Theology [1907–1912], 4:127–129).

21. (A Companion to Your Study of the Doctrine and Covenants, 2 vols. [1978], 1:143).

22. (in Conference Report, October 1991, 40; or Ensign, November 1991, 30).

23. (Ensign, May 1995, 77).

24. The Miracle of Forgiveness [1969](p. 186).

25. (The Teachings of Ezra Taft Benson [1988], 71).

26. (Church History and Modern Revelation, 4:156–157)

27. (Answers to Gospel Questions, comp. Joseph Fielding Smith Jr., 5 vols. [1957–1966], 3:20–21).

28. (Teachings of the Prophet Joseph Smith, 314).

29. (History of the Church, 4:554).

30. ("Teach the Children," Ensign, November 1997, 17).

31. [Ensign, May 1993, 70]

32. (Teachings of the Prophet Joseph Smith, 314).

33. (see Dallin H. Oaks in Conference Report, October 1996, 80; or Ensign, November 1996, 60).

34. (Bruce R. McConkie, A New Witness for the Articles of Faith, 262).

35. (Friend, September 1972, 10).

36. ("We Are Here to Be Tried, Tested, Proved," Brigham Young University Speeches of the Year [25 October 1961], 4–5).

Chapter 8

The Restoration of the Priesthood

(JS-History 69–75; D&C 7; 13; 18; 20; 42; 84; 107; 110; 121; 132)
[1829–1830]

❧❧

PRIESTHOOD PRINCIPLES

Surely, the restoration of the priesthood qualifies as one of the greatest blessings of the restoration. The Church of Jesus Christ of Latter-day Saints rests upon the claim of divine authority. Without divine authority, our worship and ordinances would be in vain.

At the time of Joseph Smith, many Christians realized the necessity of priesthood authority and were looking for a restoration of it. One of these was Eliza R. Snow, who wrote in her history:

Feeling that religion was necessary, I sought for it; but, when I asked, like one of old, "What shall I do to be saved?" and was told that I must have a change of heart and, to obtain it, I must feel myself to be the worst of sinners, and acknowledge the justice of God in consigning me to everlasting torment, the common-sense with which God had endowed me, revolted for I knew I had lived a virtuous and conscientious life, and no consideration could extort from me a confession so absurd. Some told me one thing and some another; but there was no Peter, "endowed from on high."

I heard Alexander Campbell [a prominent minister of that day in the Kirtland area] advocate the literal meaning of the Scriptures—listened to him with deep interest—hoped his new light led to a fulness—was baptized, and soon learned that, as well they might, he and his followers disclaimed all authority, and my baptism was of no consequence.[1]

Eliza R. Snow

In his first vision, Joseph Smith was told by the Lord that "all religious denominations were believing in incorrect doctrines, and that none of them was acknowledged of God as His church and kingdom."[2] Nine years following the first vision, in 1829, the authority to establish a church and perform divinely sanctioned ordinances was restored in the wilderness near Harmony, Pennsylvania.

To fully appreciate what the priesthood is and how it functions, we must understand how three priesthood principles—authority, keys, and power—are related and how they differ.

Priesthood Authority

The priesthood is the authority to act on behalf of God. He gives this commission to worthy male members of the Church so they can preach the gospel, administer the ordinances of salvation, and govern His kingdom on earth. The priesthood is conferred by the laying on of hands of another priesthood holder who has proper authority and keys to do so.

Specific priesthood authority is associated with the office or quorum to which a priesthood holder is *ordained* after having the priesthood conferred upon him. There are several offices in the Aaronic priesthood and several more in the Melchizedek, all of which are defined and explained in the Doctrine and Covenants.

Aaronic Priesthood

Office:	Duties:	Quorum:
Deacon	D&C 20:57–59; 84:111	D&C 107:85
Teacher	D&C 20:53–59; 84:111	D&C 107:86
Priest	D&C 20:46–52	D&C 107:87–88
Bishop		D&C 107:13–17, 68, 71–72, 87–88

Melchizedek Priesthood

Office:	Duties:	Quorum:
Elder	D&C 20:38–45; 42:43–44; 43:15–16; 107:11–12	D&C 107:89; 124:137
High priest	D&C 124:133, 136	D&C 107:10, 12, 17
Patriarch	D&C 124:91–93, 124	
Seventy	D&C 107:25, 34, 38, 97	D&C 107:25–26, 93–96; 124:138–39
Apostle	D&C 27:12–13; 107:23, 33, 35, 39, 58	D&C 107:23–24; 112:30–32; 124:128

The following are an example of how the Lord defines the duties of these various priesthood offices in the revelations. D&C 20 is the revelation given at the time of the organization of the Church in 1830. D&C 107 is the "revelation on priesthood" given at sundry times, mostly in Kirtland, Ohio, between November 1831 and March 28, 1835.

● **D&C 20:38–59 Ways in which priesthood holders act on behalf of God to bless His children.** This includes the specific duties of "elders, priests, teachers, deacons, and members of the church of Christ" (v. 38). After noting that Apostles are elders, the Lord describes the duties of priesthood holders.

The duty of elders:

— Baptize (v. 38).
— Ordain other elders, priests, teachers, and deacons (v. 39).
— Administer bread and wine—the emblems of the flesh and blood of Christ (v. 40).
— Confirm those who are baptized into the Church, by the laying on of hands for the baptism of fire and the Holy Ghost, according to the scriptures (vv. 41, 43).

— Teach, expound, exhort, baptize, and watch over the Church (v. 42).
— Take the lead of all meetings (v. 44).
— Conduct the meetings as they are led by the Holy Ghost, according to the commandments and revelations of God (v. 45).

The duty of priests:

— Preach, teach, expound, exhort (v. 46).
— Baptize (v. 46).
— Administer the sacrament (v. 46).
— Visit the house of each member, and exhort them to pray vocally and in secret and attend to all family duties [home teaching] (v. 47).
— Ordain other priests, teachers, and deacons (v. 48).
— Take the lead of meetings when there is no elder present (v. 49).
— When there is an elder present, he is only to do the things listed above (vv. 50–51).
— In all these duties the priest is to assist the elder if occasion requires (v. 52).

The duty of teachers: (Note the emphasis on home teaching).

— Watch over the Church always, and be with and strengthen them (v. 53).
— See that there is no iniquity in the Church, neither hardness with each other, neither lying, backbiting, nor evil speaking (v. 54).
— See that the Church meet together often, and also see that all the members do their duty (v. 55).
— Take the lead of meetings in the absence of the elder or priest (v. 56).
— Warn, expound, exhort, and teach, and invite all to come unto Christ (v. 59).

The duty of deacons: (May do all that teachers do, if occasion requires).

— Assist teachers in all their duties if occasion requires (v. 57).

Note that the Lord says expressly that "neither teachers nor deacons have authority to baptize, administer the sacrament, or lay on hands [to ordain other Aaronic priesthood holders]" (v. 58). These duties are limited to priests and elders.

- **D&C 107:8–12, 23, 25 Ways in which Melchizedek priesthood holders act on behalf of God.** "The Melchizedek priesthood holds the right of presidency" and has "power and authority over all the offices in the church in all ages of the world, to administer in spiritual things" (v. 8). For this reason, any man called to preside in any way over a regularly organized ward, stake, mission, or the general Church must be ordained to the Melchizedek priesthood. Those who serve on stake high councils are likewise ordained high priests.

The duty of the First Presidency: "The Presidency of the High Priesthood [First Presidency of the Church] have a right to officiate in all the offices in the Church" (v. 9). This also applies to stake presidencies with regard to all Church offices within the stake.

The duty of the Apostles: (Called "the twelve traveling councilors" in this revelation).

— Called to be special witnesses of the name of Christ in all the world—thus differing from other officers in the Church in the duties of their calling (v. 23).

The duty of the Seventy:

— Called to preach the gospel (v. 25).
— Called to be especial witnesses unto the Gentiles and in all the world—thus differing from other officers in the Church in the duties of their calling (v. 25).

The duty of high priests:

— Have a right to officiate in their own standing [e.g., in leadership positions], under the direction of the presidency, in administering spiritual things (v. 10).
— May also perform all duties associated with "the office of an elder, priest ... , teacher, deacon, and member (v. 10).

The duty of elders and high priests:

— An elder has a right to officiate in his stead when the high priest is not present [e.g., as a Branch president] v. 11).
— Both high priests and elders administer in spiritual things, agreeable to the covenants and commandments of the Church (v. 12).
— Both high priests and elders have a right to officiate in all the offices of the Church when there are no higher authorities present (v. 12).

● **D&C 20:60, 65–67 Melchizedek priesthood holders must be publicly sustained in the receipt of their priesthood authority.** Priesthood holders must be ordained to their callings under the inspiration of the Holy Ghost residing in the one who ordains him (v. 60). Prior to this ordination, they must be sustained by a "conference" of the Church as part of the business of that con- ference (vv. 61–62). This is accomplished by a "vote of the church to which they belong" [their ward], or from the [stake] conferences" (v. 63). The Lord expressly commands that "no person is to be ordained to any office in this church, where there is a regularly organized branch of the same, without the vote of that church" (v. 65). In those circumstances where there is no immediately-available "branch of the church that a vote may be called" the ordination may proceed under the authority of the presiding Melchizedek priesthood officers until the next conference can be called (v. 66). But in all cases—whether before or after ordination—every Melchizedek priesthood officer must eventually be sustained by the high council and then by a conference (v. 67).

- **D&C 42:11 Melchizedek priesthood ordinations must be "known to the Church."** No man may "preach my gospel" or "build up my church" unless he has been (1) "ordained by some one who has authority" and (2) "it is known to the church that he has authority and has been regularly ordained by the heads of the church." Thus, it is crystal clear that there are no secret ordinations in the Church as apostate polygamous groups have claimed.

Priesthood Keys

Priesthood keys differ from, and are in addition to, priesthood authority. President Joseph F. Smith said: "*The priesthood in general is the authority given to man to act for God.* Every man ordained to any degree of the priesthood, has this authority delegated to him. But it is necessary that every act performed under this authority shall be done at the proper time and place, in the proper way, and after the proper order. *The power of directing these labors constitutes the keys of the priesthood.* In their fulness, the keys are held by only one person at a time, the prophet and president of the Church. He may delegate any portion of this power to another, in which case that person holds the keys of that particular labor."[3]

From this we can see that priesthood ordination is a general conferral of authority and not a specific assignment. The priesthood is organized and hierarchical, with authorities delegating tasks as appropriate to others. Without that specific authority to act, one may not exercise his priesthood properly. For example, I am an ordained bishop, but I hold no keys to administer in any ward as its bishop at the present time. That would require a conferral of keys from a stake president who presides over that ward. Thus, my priesthood office lies dormant until and unless I am authorized again to act in that office.

- **D&C 13:1 The keys of the Aaronic priesthood.** John the Baptist conferred upon Joseph Smith and Oliver Cowdery "the Priesthood of Aaron," and "the keys of the ministering of angels, and of the gospel of repentance, and of baptism by immersion for the remission of sins." These are specific duties and blessings of the Aaronic priesthood. They will be discussed in detail later in this chapter.

- **D&C 107:18–20 The keys of the Melchizedek priesthood.** The Melchizedek priesthood holds "the keys of all the spiritual blessings of the church," and "to have the privilege of receiving the mysteries of the kingdom of heaven," and "to have the heavens opened unto them." These are the specific duties and blessings of the Melchizedek priesthood. They will also be discussed in detail later in this chapter.

- **D&C 132:7 All priesthood keys reside in the president of the Church.** Some have wandered into apostasy because they did not fully understand or recognize this cardinal principle: One cannot act without proper keys, and those always come from the presiding officer of the Church. At the general Church level, all of the Apostles hold all priesthood keys, but only one of them— the president of the Church—is authorized to exercise all priesthood keys on behalf of the entire Church. "There is never but one on the earth at a time on whom this power and the keys of this priesthood are conferred" (v. 7). And that one man is the Apostle who has held that office the longest—the senior Apostle.

From Liberty Jail, January 16, 1839, Joseph Smith and the First Presidency addressed the following letter of instructions to the Apostles:

> Brothers H.C. Kimball and B. Young:
>
> Joseph Smith, Jun., Sidney Rigdon and Hyrum Smith, prisoners for Jesus' sake, send greeting… Inasmuch as we are in prison, for a little season, if need be, the management of the affairs of the Church devolves on you, that is the Twelve…
>
> It will be necessary for you to get the Twelve together, ordain such as have not been ordained, or at least such of them as you can get, and proceed to regulate the Elders as the Lord may give you wisdom… *Appoint the oldest of those of the Twelve, who were first appointed, to be the president of your quorum.*[4]

Liberty Jail in 1888

In obedience to this instruction, President Brigham Young was sustained by the Apostles as president of their quorum. He stood at that time as the senior member of the quorum since Thomas B. Marsh had apostatized and David W. Patten had been martyred in the battle at Crooked River, Missouri.

Five years later, just prior to his martyrdom in 1844, the Prophet Joseph Smith said: "I know not why; but for some reason I am constrained to hasten my preparations, and to confer upon the Twelve all the ordinances, keys, covenants, endowments, and sealing ordinances of the priesthood, and so set before them a pattern in all things pertaining to the sanctuary and the endowment therein."[5]

Elder George Q. Cannon said:

> [The Church] is governed by men who hold the keys of the Apostleship, who have the right and authority. Any one of them, should an emergency arise, can act as President of the Church, with all the powers, with all the authority, with all the keys, and with every endowment necessary to obtain revelation from God, and to lead and guide this people in the path that leads to the celestial glory; but there is only one man at a time who can hold the keys, who can dictate, who can guide, who can give revelation to the Church. The rest must acquiesce in his action, the rest must be governed by his counsels, the rest must receive his doctrines.
>
> It was so with Joseph. Others held the Apostleship—Oliver received the Apostleship at the same time that Joseph did, but Joseph held the keys, although Oliver held precisely the same authority. There was only one who could exercise it in its fullness and power among the people. So also at Joseph's death, there was only one man who could exercise that authority and hold these keys, and that man was President Brigham Young, the President of the Quorum of the Twelve whom God had singled out, who by extraordinary providence had been brought to the front.[6]

Priesthood Power

Priesthood power is the power that is manifest when a worthy priesthood holder performs his duty. This power is not his own; he by himself possesses no special power—only the authority to call upon "the powers of heaven" as an authorized agent of the Lord Jesus Christ. Priesthood power is the force by which the Lord created and governs the heavens and the earth. It is also the power by which He redeems and exalts His children.

● **D&C 121:36–38 priesthood power does not automatically come with the conferral of priesthood office or keys.** Holding the priesthood and/or keys is not enough to ensure that a priesthood act will be accompanied by heavenly power. Indeed, if one misuses his priesthood without proper authority (keys) or without personal righteousness, the Lord says, "Amen to the priesthood or authority of that man" (v. 37). Such unauthorized persons are "left unto [themselves], to kick against the pricks, to persecute the Saints, and to fight against God" (v. 38). They become apostates.

Furthermore, the Lord clearly distinguishes between "the rights of the priesthood" (ordination) and "the powers of heaven" (priesthood power), which can only be manifest "upon the principles of righteousness" (v. 36). Thus, one may have authority and even hold keys, but all of that will be for naught unless he maintains sufficient worthiness to "connect" with the will of heaven. That the priesthood "may be conferred upon us, it is true; but when we undertake to cover our sins, or to gratify our pride, our vain ambition, or to exercise control or dominion or compulsion upon the souls of the children of men, in any degree of unrighteousness, behold, the heavens withdraw themselves" (v. 37). Thus, unless my priesthood actions are connected with the will of heaven, I have no priesthood power.

THE RESTORATION OF THE AARONIC PRIESTHOOD

The Mission of John the Baptist

In D&C 84:28 we are told that John the Baptist was baptized in his "childhood," and "ordained" by an angel when eight days old.

Joseph Fielding McConkie explains what this means:

> John was baptized "in his childhood," not in his infancy. To "suppose that little children need baptism is the gall of bitterness," "the bonds of iniquity," and denies the atonement of Christ, according to Mormon (Moroni 8:14, 20). From the days of Abraham we find the Lord saying, "Thou mayest know for ever that children are not accountable before me until they are eight years old" (JST Genesis 17:11). John would not have been baptized before he reached that age.

> To say that John was "ordained" when eight days of age is not to suggest that he received the priesthood at that time. The word ordained is frequently used in the Doctrine and Covenants to identify something being designated for a certain purpose without suggesting a conferral of authority. For instance, the Prophet's wife, Emma, was "ordained" to teach and exhort (D&C 25:7), gospel ordinances were "ordained" (D&C 49:15), doctrines were "ordained" (D&C 76:13), beasts and fowls were "ordained" for man's use (D&C 49:19), sons of perdition were "ordained" unto their condemnation (D&C 76:48), and wholesome herbs and grain were "ordained" for the use of man (D&C 89:10, 14)…

We do not know at what age John received the priesthood or who conferred it upon him. We know that it was after he was eight years of age and after he had been baptized and that he could trace his priesthood back to Aaron (D&C 84:26–27). We assume that it was done by his father, Zacharias, the rightful heir of the Aaronic priesthood.[7]

- **D&C 27:7 John the Baptist held the Aaronic priesthood and was an "Elias" sent to prepare the people for the coming of Christ.** He was "the son of Zacharias," one of the high priests at the temple at the time John was born (v. 7). Zacharias was visited by "Elias" (meaning a messenger sent to prepare the way—in this case, Noah), who promised him that "he should have a son, and his name should be John, and he should be filled with the spirit of Elias."

- **D&C 27:8 John the Baptist restored the Aaronic priesthood.** The Lord sent him to Joseph Smith and Oliver Cowdery "to ordain you unto the first [Aaronic] priesthood which you have received, that you might be called and ordained even as Aaron."

John was the forerunner to Christ

John the Baptist was a unique prophet in many ways, and the Lord said, "among those that are born of women there is not a greater prophet than John the Baptist" (Luke 7:28). How is this so, considering the long list of prophets in the Old Testament who performed mighty miracles and gave their lives for their testimony? To our knowledge, John performed no mighty miracles. So what constituted his greatness?

— He prepared the way for Jesus Christ.
— He had the unique privilege of baptizing the Savior.
— He was the last prophet of the Mosaic dispensation.
— He was also the first prophet of the New Testament.
— He was, at that time, was the only legal administrator in the kingdom then on the earth, and "the Jews had to obey his instructions or be damned, by their own law."[8]

Thus it was completely appropriate that he was the one sent to bestow the Aaronic priesthood upon Joseph Smith and Oliver Cowdery, thus beginning the dispensation of the fulness of times. He also, in a way, conferred the keys of being an "Elias" on Joseph Smith when he gave him the Aaronic priesthood.

President Joseph Fielding Smith explained:

Malachi [as does Isaiah] speaks of the Lord sending His messenger to prepare the way before Him, and while that does have reference to the coming of John the Baptist, it is one of those prophecies in the scriptures that has a double fulfilment. It has reference also to the coming of the Prophet Joseph Smith, because that messenger which was to come and prepare the way before Him, was to come in this day…

The Lord declared, through one of His prophets, that before His Second Coming a messenger should be sent to prepare the way and make it straight. You may apply this to John if you will, and it is true. John, the messenger who came to prepare the way before the Lord in the former dispensation, also came in this dispensation as a messenger to Joseph Smith; so it applies, if you wish to apply it so, to John who came as a messenger to prepare the way before the Lord.

But I go farther and maintain that Joseph Smith was the messenger whom the Lord sent to prepare the way before Him. He came, and under direction of holy messengers laid the foundation for the kingdom of God and of this marvelous work and a wonder that the world might be prepared for the coming of the Lord.[9]

Circumstances of the Restoration of the Aaronic Priesthood

● **JS–History 68–72 A question concern- ing the authority to baptize.** The restora- tion of the Aaronic priesthood was the first bestowal of divine authority in this dispen- sation. As with so many other revelations, this one came as a result of questions that arose from reading or translating the scrip- tures. It occurred while Joseph and Oliver were working on the translation of the Book of Mormon, when, on May 15, 1829, they went into the woods on the banks of the Susquehanna River behind Joseph's home to inquire of the Lord through prayer regarding baptism for the remission of sins (vv. 68, 72).

They retired to the woods across the road north of the Smith home in order to pray

In the midst of their prayer, Joseph said: "a messenger from heaven descended in a cloud of light, and having laid his hands upon us, he ordained us" (v. 68). The messenger identified himself as "John, the same that is called John the Baptist in the New Testament" and that he was acting "under the direction of Peter, James and John, who held the keys of the Priesthood of Melchizedek" (v. 72).

Though Joseph used the words "ordained us" to describe the event, that was not literally true. He said it in the general sense of their having received priesthood authority. The actual steps were as follows.

1. *Conferral of the priesthood.* John the Baptist conferred the priesthood upon Joseph Smith and Oliver Cowdery. The precise words he used were, "Upon you my fellow servants, in the name of Messiah, I confer the priesthood of Aaron" (v. 69; emphasis added). It is interesting that John the Baptist referred to the Savior as "Messiah," which an authentic Jew of Jesus' time would do. Christ is a Greek name, while Messiah is Hebrew. At this stage of his spiritual and scriptural

understanding, Joseph Smith could not have known this. It is an evidence of the authenticity of his description of the event.

2. *Baptism.* John the Baptist then instruct- ed them to immediately baptize each other. For this purpose they then crossed the road and went down behind the Smith home to the banks of the Susquehanna River.

The banks of the Susquehanna River behind the Smith home in Harmony, Pennsylvania

Joseph first baptized Oliver Cowdery and then Oliver baptized Joseph (vv. 70–71). Because they now possessed the Aaronic priesthood they could perform this sacred ordinance for each other, by which their sins could be remitted and their covenants with the Lord established. Joseph reports that, "Immediately on our coming up out of the water after we had been baptized, we experienced great and glorious blessings from our Heavenly Father. No sooner had I baptized Oliver Cowdery, than the Holy Ghost fell upon him, and he stood up and prophesied many things which should shortly come to pass. And again, so soon as I had been baptized by him, I also had the spirit of prophecy, when, standing up, I prophesied concerning the rise of this Church, and many other things connected with the Church, and this generation of the children of men. We were filled with the Holy Ghost, and rejoiced in the God of our salvation" (v. 73).

3. *Ordination.* Finally, having been thus baptized, they proceeded to ordain each other to the Aaronic priesthood in the same order as they had been baptized (v. 71). Thus we see that the conferral of priesthood is one thing (v. 69), and ordination to an office within the priesthood is entirely another (v. 71). The office to which they would have been ordained on this occasion would have been a priest, since only priests can exercise all the keys of the Aaronic priesthood, including the ordination of other priests.

This sacred event made the scriptures on prayer and priesthood more clear to Joseph and Oliver. Joseph said: "Our minds being now enlightened, we began to have the scriptures laid open to our understandings, and the true meaning and intention of their more mysterious passages revealed unto us in a manner which we never could attain to previously, nor ever before had thought of" (v. 74).

- **JS–History 1:71, Notes 4–7 Oliver Cowdery's account of receiving the Aaronic priesthood.** During his lifetime, Joseph Smith gave additional important information about the restoration of the priesthood. Oliver Cowdery also wrote about what happened on May 15, 1829, and his account is contained in notes 4–7 to Joseph Smith–History 1:71.

Note 4 is of particular interest because it gives us some idea of where Joseph and Oliver were in the translation of the Book of Mormon at the time they received the priesthood: "After writing the account given of the Savior's ministry to the remnant of the seed of Jacob, upon this continent, it was easy to be seen, as the prophet said it would be, that darkness covered the earth and gross darkness the minds of the people. On reflecting further it was as easy to be seen that amid the great strife and noise concerning religion, none had authority from God to administer the ordinances of the Gospel." From this we can conclude that they were at that time translating from 3 Nephi concerning the Savior's visit among the Nephites and His conferral of priesthood authority upon their leaders so that they might baptize the people. Oliver concludes that he and Joseph "only waited for the commandment to be given 'Arise and be baptized.'"

Note 5 makes it plain that the vision received on the banks of Susquehanna River was an open vision received by two separate persons at the same time. "Where was room for doubt?" Oliver exclaims. "Nowhere; uncertainty had fled, doubt had sunk no more to rise, while fiction and deception had fled forever!" This was a real and tangible open vision, and Oliver was a second witness to all of it.

Note 6 quotes John the Baptist as saying, "Upon you my fellow-servants, in the name of Messiah, I confer this Priesthood and this authority, which shall remain upon earth, that the Sons of Levi may yet offer an offering unto the Lord in righteousness!" This varies slightly from the wording found in D&C 13 but retains all of the essential elements of the blessing.

Note 7 constitutes Oliver's reaction to the vision. "I shall not attempt to paint to you the feelings of this heart, nor the majestic beauty and glory which surrounded us on this occasion; but you will believe me when I say, that earth, nor men, with the eloquence of time, cannot begin to clothe language in as interesting and sublime a manner as this holy personage… The assurance that we were in the presence of an angel, the certainty that we heard the voice of Jesus, and the truth unsullied as it flowed from a pure personage, dictated by the will of God, is to me past description, and I shall ever look upon this expression of the Savior's goodness with wonder and thanksgiving while I am permitted to tarry; and in those mansions where perfection dwells and sin never comes, I hope to adore in that day which shall never cease."[10]

These same feelings can be experienced by anyone who receives the priesthood with full purpose of heart and a desire to receive and keep His covenants. I remember distinctly my bishop and my father making it plain to me that I was about to receive more authority from God than any king of the earth possessed, and it impressed my boyish heart very deeply.

Elder James E. Talmage described his ordination to the Aaronic priesthood in similar terms:

As soon as I had been ordained, a feeling came to me such as I have never been able to fully describe. It seemed scarcely possible, that I, a little boy, could be so honored of God as to be called to the priesthood… I felt strong in the thought that I belonged to the Lord, and that He would assist me in whatever was required of me. The effect of my ordination … entered into all the affairs of my boyish life… When at play on the school grounds, and perhaps tempted to take unfair advantage in the game, when in the midst of a dispute with a playmate, I would remember, and the thought would be as effective as though spoken aloud—"I am a deacon; and it is not right that a deacon should act in this way." On examination days, when it seemed easy for me to copy some other boy's work … , I would say in my mind, "It would be more wicked for me to do that than it is for them, because I am a deacon."[11]

The Authority, Keys, and Powers of the Aaronic Priesthood

● **D&C 13:1 The keys associated with the Aaronic priesthood.** This revelation is taken from JS-History 1:69, and is identical in wording. While conferring the Aaronic priesthood, John the Baptist said that it con- tained "the keys of the ministering of angels, and of the gospel of repentance, and of baptism by immer- sion for the remission of sins." He also promised that this priesthood "shall never be taken again from the earth, until the sons of Levi do offer again an offering unto the Lord in righteousness."

Elder Joseph Fielding Smith said: "We may be sure that the Aaronic Priesthood will never be taken from the earth while mortality endures, for there will always be need for temporal direction and the per- formance of ordinances pertaining to 'the preparatory Gospel'"[12]

John preached and baptized by the authority of he Aaronic Priesthood

The promise that the Aaronic priesthood would remain on the earth "until sons of Levi do offer again an offering unto the Lord in righteousness" should be taken literally. There will be blood sacrifices again, at least for a brief period, at the temple in the New Jerusalem.

President Joseph Fielding Smith reminds us that "the great temple, which is yet to be built in the City Zion, will not be one edifice, but twelve. Some of these temples will be for the lesser priesthood. When these temples are built, it is very likely that provision will be made for some ceremonies and ordinances which may be performed by the Aaronic Priesthood and a place provided where the sons of Levi may offer their offering in righteousness. This will have to be the case because all things are to be restored… The sacrifice of animals will be done to complete the restoration … at the beginning of the millennium … long enough to complete the fulness of the restoration in this dispensation. Afterwards sacrifice will be of some other character."[13]

President Smith's explanation is probably based on statements by the Prophet Joseph Smith, who asked, "Else how can the restitution of all things spoken of by the Holy Prophets be brought to pass. It is not to be understood that the law of Moses will be established again with all its rites and variety of ceremonies; this has never been spoken of by the prophets; but those things which existed prior to Moses' day, namely, sacrifice, will be continued."[14] The Prophet said the continuation of sacrifice was just as necessary as the continuation of every other principle and ordinance which existed prior to the time of Christ, such as repentance, baptism, and faith.

- **D&C 84:26–27 Additional info on Aaronic priesthood keys.** During the "revelation on priesthood" given in September of 1832, the Lord explained that the Aaronic priesthood "holdeth the key of the ministering of angels and the preparatory gospel" (v. 26). This means "the gospel of repentance and of baptism, and the remission of sins, and the law of carnal commandments" (v. 27). It is identical with the priesthood that existed among the children of Israel in Moses' day, "which the Lord in his wrath caused to continue with the house of Aaron among the children of Israel until [the time of] John [the Baptist], whom God raised up, being filled with the Holy Ghost from his mother's womb" (v. 27).

- **D&C 107:13–14, 20 The Aaronic priesthood is an appendage to the Melchizedek priesthood.** The Aaronic priesthood is so named "because it was conferred upon Aaron and his seed, throughout all their generations" (v. 13). It is referred to as "the lesser priesthood … because it is an appendage to the greater, or the Melchizedek Priesthood, and has power [only] in administering outward ordinances" (v. 14). It holds "the keys of the ministering of angels, and to administer in outward ordinances, the letter of the gospel, [and] the baptism of repentance for the remission of sins" (v. 20).

The Keys of the Ministering of Angels

If Aaronic priesthood holders live worthy of their priesthood, they have the right to receive and enjoy the ministering of heavenly beings to guide them, protect them, and bless them. President Wilford Woodruff said: "I had the administration of angels while holding the office of a priest. I had visions and revelations. I traveled thousands of miles. I baptized men, though I could not confirm them because I had not the authority to do it. I speak of these things to show that a man should not be ashamed of any portion of the priesthood."[15]

The ministering of angels can occur through personal appearances but can also be unseen—delivered by a voice or by thoughts or feelings communicated to the mind. Elder Dallin H. Oaks said that "most angelic communications are felt or heard rather than seen."[16]

— **Moroni 7:35–37** Through the restoration of the Aaronic priesthood, the ministering of angels is available to all Church members, not just to priesthood holders. This would make young women equally deserving of such ministrations if they are worthy. Indeed, any baptized member of the Church who worthily partakes of the sacrament may receive the ministering of angels. The priests who bless the sacrament by virtue of their Aaronic priesthood "open the door for all Church members who worthily partake of the sacrament to enjoy the companionship of the Spirit of the Lord and the ministering of angels."[17]

The Lord has promised His authorized servants that He "will go before your face. I will be on your right hand and on your left, and my Spirit shall be in your hearts, and mine angels round about you, to bear you up" (D&C 84:88). In the Book of Mormon we have a record of how angels ministered daily to Nephi, the son of Helaman, while he was in prison (3 Nephi 7:18). While Christ was among the Nephites He called down angels from heaven who surrounded their little ones and ministered unto them (3 Nephi 17:23–24).

Angels have always ministered unto men on behalf of God, and will continue to do so in our own time. Moroni said: "my beloved brethren, have miracles ceased? Behold I say unto you, Nay; neither have angels ceased to minister unto the children of men. For behold, they are subject unto him , to minister according to the word of his command, showing themselves unto them of strong faith and a firm mind in every form of godliness. And the office of their ministry is to call men unto repentance, and to fulfil and to do the work of the covenants of the Father, which he hath made unto the children of men, to prepare the way among the children of men, by declaring the word of Christ unto the chosen vessels of the Lord, that they may bear testimony of him " (Moroni 7:29–31). The privilege of receiving such heavenly messengers on behalf of others is among the keys possessed by Aaronic priesthood holders.

The Keys of Repentance and Baptism

Repentance and baptism are also called the "preparatory gospel" (D&C 13; 84:26–27; 107:20). This is because repentance and baptism help us prepare to receive blessings that are administered through the Melchizedek priesthood, such as the gift of the Holy Ghost and temple ordinances. For example, John the Baptist preached repentance and baptized people in preparing the way for the Savior (Matthew 3:1–6, 11). And Aaronic priesthood holders in our day preach repentance through home teaching, missionary work, testimony bearing, and fellowshipping.

Aaronic priesthood holders participate in the ordinance of baptism under the direction of the bishop, and worthy priests may perform baptisms and serve as witnesses at baptisms.

Aaronic priesthood holders also participate in the process of administering repentance to others by preaching repentance and by officiating in the ordinance of the sacrament. Elder Jeffrey R. Holland calls this "a stunning privilege and sacred trust given at such a remarkably young age!"[18] It is a tremendous compliment that the Lord should have such high confidence in His young men. We are all the beneficiaries when they exercise their Aaronic priesthood to place us under covenant and provide the means by which we may be cleansed from our sins at baptism, and again as we partake of the sacrament weekly. They hold the keys to do so.

The sacrament is administered by the Aaronic Priesthood

THE RESTORATION OF THE MELCHIZEDEK PRIESTHOOD

Some weeks after John the Baptist restored the Aaronic priesthood, Peter, James, and John appeared to Joseph Smith and Oliver Cowdery and conferred upon them the Melchizedek priesthood. And although the exact date for the restoration of the Melchizedek priesthood appears not to have been preserved in current Church records, there is much testimony from both Joseph and Oliver that clearly establishes the reality of these events.

The Mission of John the Revelator

● **John 21:20–23 The Savior's promises to John.** John was "the disciple whom Jesus loved" (v. 20), meaning a special friend to the Lord. Peter asked the Lord concerning His promises to John (v. 21), and His response included the promise that "he [will] tarry till I come" (v. 22). From this statement the saying went "abroad among the brethren, that that disciple should not die" though Jesus did not say expressly to Peter "He shall not die" (v. 23). Still, from this statement questions still persist: Did John die? If not, what is his status? If he did, why did Jesus make the statement?

The issue has been debated for centuries among the various Christian sects. Some scholars say that he indeed died and was buried at Ephesus. Others believe he still walks the earth. A third school of thought states that even though he was buried at Ephesus, he is not really dead but simply sleeps in the grave until the Second Coming of the Savior.[19]

● **D&C 7 Joseph Smith and Oliver Cowdery finally solved the issue through an appeal to the Lord.** During the month of April 1829, at Harmony, Pennsylvania, while they were translating the Book of Mormon, a difference of opinion arose between them about the status of John the Apostle, and they agreed to settle the matter by appealing through the Urim and Thummim.[20]

The result of their inquiry is given in D&C 7, which the heading of that section says "is a translated version of the record made on parchment by John and hidden up by himself."[21] We do not know whether Joseph saw the parchment or if its contents were just revealed to him, but we do know the following things.

● **D&C 7:1–6 John was translated.** John's specific request was "Lord, give unto me power over death, that I may live and bring souls unto thee" (v. 2), and the Lord's promise in return was "because thou desirest this thou shalt tarry until I come in my glory, and shalt prophesy before nations, kindreds, tongues and people" (v. 3). Peter's desire to "speedily come unto [Christ] in [His] kingdom" was a righteous desire, but John's was even greater (vv. 4–5). And to make it possible for John to avoid death for a while, the Lord made him "as flaming fire and a ministering angel" to "minister for those who shall be heirs of salvation who dwell on the earth" (v. 6). In other words, he was translated.

The Prophet Joseph Smith taught concerning John's ministry, "John the Revelator was then among the Ten Tribes of Israel who had been led away by Shalmaneser, king of Assyria, to prepare them for their return from their long dispersion."[22] And Heber C. Kimball said John the Revelator appeared in the Kirtland Temple during its dedication, and "was seen in our midst by the Prophet Joseph, Oliver Cowdery and others."[23]

- **D&C 7:7 The keys of Peter, James, and John's ministry.** The Lord made both James and John counselors to Peter, to minister unto his needs as the head of the Church, and to jointly hold with him "this power [the Melchizedek priesthood] and the keys of this ministry until I come." Elder Joseph Fielding Smith said: "These keys were given at the transfiguration to these three Apostles, and they in turn gave them to Joseph Smith and Oliver Cowdery in this dispensation (D&C 27:12–13; 128:20)."[24]

Circumstances of the Restoration of the Melchizedek Priesthood

Though we do not know precisely when the Melchizedek priesthood was restored, we have a number of scriptures and other historical records that tell us details concerning when, where, and how it occurred.

- **D&C 13:1; JS–History 1:70, 72 It was promised by John the Baptist on May 15, 1829.** When he conferred the Aaronic priesthood upon Joseph Smith and Oliver Cowdery, John the Baptist explained that it "had not the power of laying on hands for the gift of the Holy Ghost, but that this should be conferred on [them later]" (v. 70). He was acting "under the direction of Peter, James and John, who held the keys of the Priesthood of Melchizedek, which Priesthood, he said, would in due time be conferred on us, and that I should be called the first Elder of the Church, and he (Oliver Cowdery) the second" (v. 72).

- **D&C 18:9 It had already been restored by June 1829.** By the time D&C 18 was given—sometime in June 1829—the Melchizedek priesthood had already been restored. Joseph Smith, Oliver Cowdery, and David Whitmer had sought to realize the promise made by John the Baptist at the time of the conferral of the Aaronic priesthood that the Melchizedek priesthood would "in due time" be conferred upon Joseph Smith and Oliver Cowdery (JS-History 1:72), and Joseph Smith wrote that section 18 was given to "illustrate the nature of our calling to this Priesthood, as well as that of others who were yet to be sought after."[25] The Lord says in D&C 18:9: "I speak unto you, even as unto Paul mine apostle, for you are called even with that same calling with which he was called," which means they were already Apostles by the time this revelation was given.

- **It had probably been restored by 14 June 1829.** Oliver Cowdery wrote a letter from Fayette, New York, to the Prophet's brother, Hyrum Smith, who was then residing at his family's home near Palmyra in Manchester Township, New York. This letter is significant because it contains words identical to D&C 18:10, 14, 21, and 25. This suggests that the revelation (which refers to Joseph and Oliver as "Apostles") had already been received by this date—thus narrowing the window of possible dates to sometime between May 15 and June 14, 1829.[26]

- **D&C 27:12–13 It was conferred upon Joseph and Oliver by Peter, James, and John.** They were ordained Apostles and special witnesses of Christ (v. 12), and were given the keys of the kingdom for this final dispensation (vv. 12–13).

- **D&C 128:20 It was conferred somewhere in the wilderness between Harmony, Pennsylvania and Collesville, New York.** This detail is corroborated by the testimony of two individuals who heard the Prophet Joseph Smith describe the circumstances and location of the event.

- **It occurred 16–17 miles north of Harmony, Pennsylvania, while fleeing their enemies.** Elder Erastus Snow said: "They were being pursued by their enemies and they had to travel all night, and in the dawn of the coming day when they were weary and worn who should appear to them but Peter, James and John, for the purpose of conferring upon them the Apostleship, the keys of which they themselves had held while upon the earth, which had been bestowed upon them by the Savior."[27]

This is consistent with the account of Addison Everett, who said, "It was night and they traveled through brush and water and mud, fell over logs, etc., until Oliver was exhausted. Then Joseph helped him along through the mud and water, almost carrying him. They traveled all night, and just at the break of day Oliver gave out entirely and exclaimed, 'Oh, Lord! Brother Joseph, how long have we got to endure this thing?'

"They sat down on a log to rest, and Joseph said that at that very time Peter, James and John came to them and ordained them to the Apostleship.

"They had sixteen or seventeen miles to go to get back to Mr. Hale's, his father-in-law's, but Oliver did not complain any more of fatigue."[28]

- **JS–History 1:74 It was restored during times of great persecution.** The Prophet Joseph Smith said that they were "forced to keep secret the circumstances of having received the Priesthood and our having been baptized, owing to a spirit of persecution which had already manifested itself in the neighborhood" (v. 74). The fact that the restoration of the Melchizedek priesthood occurred while they were fleeing for their lives underscores the difficult circumstances. It probably also explains why they didn't have the time or presence of mind to sit down and write about the event, as they had done when the Aaronic priesthood was restored under more peaceful circumstances.

- **It probably occurred before 1 June 1829.** President Brigham Young said: "Joseph Smith, Oliver Cowdery, and David Whitmer were the first Apostles of this dispensation." (in *Journal of Discourses*, 6:320). Yet we know that David Whitmer was not present when Peter, James and John appeared to Joseph and Oliver in the wilderness near Harmony, Pennsylvania. David did not even know the Prophet well until he helped them move away from Harmony to his home in Fayette, New York "in the beginning of the month of June" (*History of the Church*, 1:48–49).

David Whitmer himself said that he had received his ordination from the Prophet Joseph during the month of June 1829.[29]

This ordination would have had to have occurred after June 1, 1829, because Joseph, Emma, Oliver and David Whitmer traveled to the home of Peter Whitmer Sr. in time for their translation activities to resume on June 1. David Whitmer said: "The translation at my father's farm, Fayette Township, Seneca County, New York occupied about one month, that is from June 1, to July 1, 1829."[30]

- **It probably occurred before 29 May 1829.** Since it took three days to travel from Harmony, Pennsylvania to Fayette, New York, and since translation activities started again on June 1, 1829, it follows that they must have left Harmony not later than May 29, 1829. And since the restoration of the Melchizedek priesthood occurred while they still resided at Harmony, we can reasonably conclude that it must have occurred before they left for Fayette.

- Thus, we can reasonably conclude that the Melchizedek priesthood was restored sometime between May 15 and May 29, 1829.

The Authority, Keys, and Powers of the Melchizedek Priesthood

The Melchizedek priesthood is the greater priesthood. It possesses all the authority, knowledge, and covenants necessary for the exaltation of God's children. The specific keys of this priesthood are described primarily in D&C 84 and D&C 107.

- **D&C 84:19 The authority to administer the gospel of Jesus Christ.** The Melchizedek priesthood includes the authority to administer the gospel of Jesus Christ—to govern the Church, preach the gospel, and administer the ordinances of salvation. Holders of the Melchizedek priesthood preside over the Church and its meetings. One cannot serve in a ward bishopric, a stake presidency, a high council, or in any priesthood capacity as a general authority without first being ordained a high priest in the Melchizedek priesthood.

- **D&C 107:8–12 The right of presidency in spiritual things.** The right of presidency is the right to preside in the Church. The President of the Church is the only person on earth who may use (or authorize another person to use) the keys of the priesthood for governing the entire Church. He authorizes other priesthood leaders to hold the keys that are necessary for presiding in their callings: Temple presidents, mission presidents, stake presidents, bishops, district presidents, branch presidents, and quorum presidents.

"High priests after the order of the Melchizedek priesthood have a right to officiate in their own standing, under the direction of the presidency, in administering spiritual things" (v. 10). They also can officiate "in the office of an elder, priest … , teacher, deacon, and member" (v. 10). In other words, they can perform any duty of any priesthood office or of the members under their supervision. Elders, who also hold the Melchizedek priesthood, may likewise preside "when the high priest is not present" (v.¹1). Both high priests and elders preside only when "there are no higher authorities present" (v. 12).

President Harold B. Lee said: "What is priesthood? Well, we've had the definition—it's the power of the Lord given to man to act for Him in things pertaining to salvation. But I have a different definition that to me seems more accurate. Priesthood is the power by which the power of the Almighty works through man. The priesthood is the center, the core, the power by which all the activities of the Church are to be directed."[31]

- **D&C 107:18–19 The keys of all the spiritual blessings of the Church.** The spiritual blessings that come to us through the Melchizedek priesthood ordinances include among others: the blessing and naming of children, bestowing the Gift of the Holy Ghost, administering to the sick, patriarchal blessings, blessings of comfort and counsel, and all the ordinances of the holy temple. A few of these are described in D&C 84 and 107.

— **D&C 84:19–21 Access to temple ordinances and the knowledge of the mysteries of the kingdom.** Generally speaking, the "mysteries of the kingdom" refer to those principles that are taught in holy temples. And "in the ordinances thereof, the power of godliness is manifest" (v. 20). In other words, the principles by which godhood is achieved are revealed in the sacred ordinances of the House of God, "and without the ordinances thereof, and the authority of the priesthood, the power of godliness is not manifest unto men in the flesh" (v. 21). Thus, for a man to receive the temple ordinances he must first have obtained this higher priesthood and shown himself to be a worthy bearer of it. Likewise, to receive all the ordinances of the temple, a woman must be connected to a worthy priesthood holder.

Temple blessings belong to the Melchizedek Priesthood

— **D&C 107:19 The right to have the heavens opened and receive revelation.** The right to commune with heavenly beings. Also, the opportunity to see, commune with, and enjoy the presence of God the Father and His Son, Jesus Christ.

— **D&C 84:19, 22 The ability to see God and stand in His presence.** Receiving and honoring the Melchizedek priesthood is a prerequisite to the ability to "see the face of God" (obtain exaltation). And without this priesthood and the sealing ordinances associated with it, one cannot obtain a celestial glory (D&C 131:2–3). If we desire to see our Father's face again, to stand in His presence, and to live there eternally, we must obtain the ordinances of the Melchizedek priesthood and honor the covenants associated with them.

● **D&C 110:11 The keys of missionary work.** These are the keys of the gathering of Israel that were bestowed upon the Prophet Joseph Smith and his successors by the appearance of Moses in the Kirtland Temple on April 3, 1836. He conferred "the keys of the gathering of Israel from the four parts of the earth, and the leading of the ten tribes from the land of the north."

● **D&C 110:12 The keys to perfection of the Saints.** These are the keys of the "gospel of Abraham" that were bestowed upon the Prophet Joseph Smith and his successors by the appearance of Elias (Noah) in the Kirtland Temple on April 3, 1836. He promised that through these keys "in us and our seed all generations after us should be blessed."

● **D&C 110:13–16 The keys of genealogical and temple work.** These keys were bestowed upon the Prophet Joseph Smith and his successors by the appearance of Elijah in the Kirtland Temple on April 3, 1836. He announced that "the time has fully come, which was spoken of by the mouth of Malachi—testifying that he [Elijah] should be sent, before the great and dreadful day of the Lord come—To turn the hearts of the fathers to the children, and the children to the fathers, lest the whole earth be smitten with a curse" (v. 15). And he said that because "the keys of this dispensation are committed into your hands … by this ye may know that the great and dreadful day of the Lord is near, even at the doors" (v. 16).

THE BLESSINGS OF THE PRIESTHOOD

President Joseph Fielding Smith said: "This matter of holding the priesthood is not a light or a small thing. We are dealing with the Lord's power and authority, which He has given to us by the opening of the heavens in this day so that every blessing might again be available to us, as they were when man was first placed upon the earth."[32]

President Spencer W. Kimball said of the restoration of the Melchizedek priesthood: "It is an event of supreme importance to man in this dispensation, for the priesthood is the power and authority of God delegated to man on earth to act in all things pertaining to the salvation of men. It is the means whereby the Lord acts through men to save souls. Without this priesthood power, men are lost. Only through this power does man 'hold the keys of all the spiritual blessings of the Church,' enabling him to receive 'the mysteries of the kingdom of heaven, to have the heavens opened' unto him (D&C 107:18–19), enabling him to enter the new and everlasting covenant of marriage and to have his wife and children bound to him in an everlasting tie, enabling him to become a patriarch to his posterity forever, and enabling him to receive a fulness of the blessings of the Lord."[33]

Notes:

1. *"Sketch of My Life,"* manuscript at Bancroft Library, University of California.

2. *Times and Seasons,* 1 March 1842.

3. Gospel Doctrine, 5th ed. [1939], 136; emphasis added.

4. In Elder Orson F. Whitney, *Life of Heber C. Kimball* (1945), 237-239; emphasis added.

5. *Millennial Star 5* [March 1845]:151.

6. In *Journal of Discourses,* 19:234.

7. *Witnesses of the Birth of Christ* (1998) 47–48.

8. *Teachings of the Prophet Joseph Smith*, sel. Joseph Fielding Smith [1976], 275–276.

9. *Doctrines of Salvation*, comp. Bruce R. McConkie, 3 vols. (1954–1956), 1:193–195.

10. *Messenger and Advocate*, 1 [October 1834], 14–16.

11. *Incidents from the Lives of Our Church Leaders* (Deacons Instruction Manual, 1914), 135–136.

12. *Church History and Modern Revelation*, 4 vols. [1946–1949], 1:62.

13. *Doctrines of Salvation*, 3:93–94.

14. *Teachings of the Prophet Joseph Smith*, 173.

15. *The Discourses of Wilford Woodruff*, sel. G. Homer Durham [1946], 298.

16. In Conference Report, October 1998, 51; or *Ensign*, November 1998, 39.

17. Dallin H. Oaks, in Conference Report, October 1998, 51; or *Ensign*, November 1998, 39.

18. In Conference Report, October 1995, 89; or *Ensign*, November 1995, 68.

19. Sidney B. Sperry, *Doctrine and Covenants Compendium* [1960], 66–67.

20. *History of the Church*, 1:35–36.

21. *History of the Church*, 1:35–36.

22. *History of the Church*, 1:176.

23. In Elder Orson F. Whitney, *Life of Heber C. Kimball*, 92.

24. *Church History and Modern Revelation*, 1:49.

25. *History of the Church*, 1:61–62).

26. Letter of Oliver Cowdery to Hyrum Smith, 14 June 1829, Fayette, New York, Church Archives.

27. In *Journal of Discourses*, 23:183.

28. Letter of Addison Everett to Oliver B. Huntington, February 17, *1881, Young Women's Journal, II* (November, 1890), 76–77.

29. Larry C. Porter, "The Priesthood Restored," in Robert L. Millet and Kent Jackson, eds., *Studies in Scripture, Vol. 2: The Pearl of Great Price* [1985], 397.

30. *Kansas City Daily Journal*, 5 June 1881.

31. *The Teachings of President Harold B. Lee*, Clyde J. Williams, ed. [1996], 482.

32. In Conference Report, October 1971, 108; or *Ensign*, December 1971, 98.

33. *Ensign*, June 1975, 3.

CHAPTER 9

The Church of Jesus Christ Is Organized

(D&C 19–24; 26–28) [1830]

INTRODUCTION

In the one year from April 1829 to April 1830, many important events transpired which have been discussed in previous chapters.

— The receipt and translation of the plates in less than 65 days.
— The publication of 5,000 copies of the Book of Mormon.
— The receipt of dozens of revelations, giving instruction to individuals and the Church.
— The receipt of much important doctrine on the Savior's mission and atonement.
— A detailed explanation of the first principles and ordinances of the gospel.
— The receipt of the Aaronic and Melchizedek priesthoods.
— The establishment of Church government and the duties of its officers.

All of these important developments were accomplished through the still-young (25 years old) Prophet Joseph Smith.

Of all of these impressive accomplish- ments, none is of greater import than the establishment of the Church of Jesus Christ again on the earth. Through the Church, the keys of the kingdom have been passed down through the years, ensuring an unbroken chain of authority to administer the Lord's affairs upon the earth. Through the Church, the temporal and spiritual needs of God's children are constantly addressed. And through the Church, the earthly Kingdom of God continues to spread around the world, preparing the nations for the return of their rightful King—the Lord Jesus Christ. This

The Whitmer home in Fayette, New York

©RANDAL S. CHASE 2006-0709

Church, which is the Church of the Living Christ in these latter days, was established again upon the earth on a designated day—April 6, 1830—in a humble cabin in Fayette, New York. This chapter explores the events and the implications of that important day.

There are three sections of the Doctrine and Covenants associated with the Church's organization. All were given at the home of Peter Whitmer Sr., in Fayette, New York.

— D&C 20	April	1830	The Constitution of the Church.
— D&C 21	April 6,	1830	Given at organizational meeting.
— D&C 22	April	1830	Given shortly thereafter.

D&C 20 and 22 were accepted by the members of the Church at the time as the "Articles and Covenants of the Church." This made them the first officially canonized scriptures in the Church.

THE CONSTITUTION OF THE CHURCH

(D&C 20)

D&C 20 was given by revelation through the Prophet Joseph Smith, but the revelation was not given all at once. Portions of it were received and written sometime in 1829, and it was not completed until after April 6, 1830.

The Prophet Joseph Smith stated that after he and Oliver Cowdery received the priesthood they continued to receive instructions from the Lord and they waited for the fulfilment of the promise made by John the Baptist concerning the organization of the Church. In the meantime they received several revelations concerning their duties, including the revelations now recorded in D&C 20. These revelations not only gave them much information about how the Church should operate, but also designated the precise day upon which the Church was to be organized.[1]

D&C 20 was first presented to the Church membership for a sustaining vote on June 9, 1830 at the first conference of the Church in Fayette, New York. It is known as the "Revelation on Church Organization and Government"[2] and served as a kind of constitution for the restored Church. It became the standard against which proper conduct and procedure in the Church have been measured ever since that day. Its contents can be broken down into discreet topical sections as follows.

Summarizing the Restoration

● **D&C 20:1–12** The first twelve verses of this revelation teach us much about the Church of Christ and its establishment in the latter days, the authority under which this was done, and the purpose of the Book of Mormon in proving the veracity of the restoration.

— **The name of the Church.** This revelation begins by announcing "the rise of *the Church of Christ* in these last days" (v. 1; emphasis added). The name of the new church as stated in this revelation was "The Church of Christ," but it was later changed to "The Church of Jesus Christ of Latter-day Saints" (D&C 115:4–5). At various times, the Church was also called "The Church of Jesus Christ," "The Church of God," and by a conference of Elders held at Kirtland in May 1834, "The Church of the Latter-day Saints."[3]

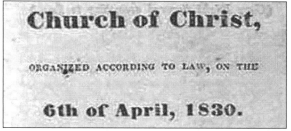

The name of the Church in 1830 (from the Book of Commandments)

The Savior said to the Nephites: "How be it my church save it be called in my name? For if a church be called in Moses' name then it be Moses' church; or if it be called in the name of a man then it be the church of a man; but if it be called in my name then it is my church, if it so be that they are built upon my gospel (3 Ne. 27:8)." This establishes a two-fold The name of the Church in 1836 (on the Kirtland Temple) test for whether a church can claim to be Christ's Church: it must bear His name and it must be built upon His gospel.

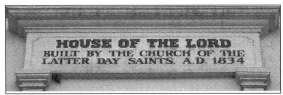

The name of the Church in 1832 (on the Kirtland Temple)

We continue to this day to refer to the Church by various names. But President Joseph Fielding Smith said: "There is no valid reason why Latter-day Saints should speak of themselves as 'Mormons' or of the Church as the 'Mormon Church'... The term Latter-day Saints is added to the name merely to distinguish us from the former-day Saints... While there can be no

The name of the Church in 1842 (Joseph Smith's office door in Nauvoo)

disgrace nor condemnation in being called 'Mormons,' and the ... 'Mormon Church,' the fact remains, and this we should all emphasize, that we belong to The Church of Jesus Christ of Latter-day Saints, the name the Lord has given by which we are to be known and called."[4]

President Boyd K. Packer agrees: "Others refer to us as Mormons. I do not mind if they use that title. However, sometimes we are prone ourselves to say 'Mormon Church.' I do not think it best for us to do so... Every prayer we offer is in His name. Every ordinance performed is in His name. Every baptism, confirmation, blessing, ordination, every sermon, every testimony is concluded with the invocation of His sacred name. It is in His name that we heal the sick and perform other miracles of which we do not, cannot, speak. In the sacrament we take upon ourselves the name of Christ. We covenant to remember Him and keep His commandments. He is present in all that we believe."[5]

— **The Savior's birth date.** D&C 20 declares that it had been 1,830 years "since the coming of our Lord and Savior Jesus Christ in the flesh" and stipulates that the Church was to be organized on April 6th (v. 1).

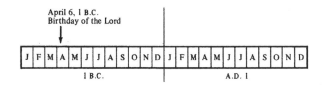

April 6, 1 B.C.
Birthday of the Lord

| J | F | M | A | M | J | J | A | S | O | N | D | J | F | M | A | M | J | J | A | S | O | N | D |

1 B.C.   A.D. 1

The significance of April 6th: We might wonder why the Lord specified this specific date for the restoration of the Church. The reason lies particularly in its significance in the life of the Savior. We know from D&C 20:1 that the Lord was born on this date. We can also deduce that He was resurrected on the same date, based on the following logic:

The Passover occurred on the Jewish date of 15 Nissan, which would mean 14 days after the spring equinox (March 21st + 14 days = April 4th). Based on the assumption that He was crucified on Passover Friday, and the following day was the Jewish Sabbath and nothing could be done with His body until early the following morning, we can deduce that He was resurrected on the morning of April 6th.

Other important and symbolic events have also occurred on this date. The same Passover calculations described above would lead us to conclude that April 6th was the date on which the children of Israel were set free from bondage and departed Egypt.

Also, in the history of the United States, we note that George Washington was inaugurated on April 6th, becoming the first President of the United States, and thereby beginning officially our three-branch system of government. So, in a sense, our nation officially began under Constitutional law on April 6th.

The similarity of significant dates. Consider the following three dates in history:

— **Christ**: The date He was born, and the date on which He was resurrected.
— **Moses**: The date on which the children of Israel were set free from Egypt.
— **Elijah**: The date on which Elijah restored sealing keys at Kirtland, Ohio.

Scientific evidence exists that these three days in history were astrologically similar—with the positions of the sun, moon, and stars precisely the same.[6] This is surely not a coincidence since the Lord does all things perfectly and teaches us through the symbolism and similarity of such events.

— **The legal establishment of the Church.** Like all other churches, the Church had to be "regularly organized and established agreeable to the laws of our country" (v. 1). Under the laws of the state of New York at the time, six individuals had to act as charter members for the organizing process. The six who fulfilled this requirement were Joseph Smith, Oliver Cowdery, Hyrum Smith, David Whitmer, Samuel H. Smith, and Peter Whitmer Jr. But these six were not the only people present. There were more than 30 men, women, and children in attendance.

— **By the will and commandment of God.** The Church was established "by the will and commandments of God … which commandments were given to … Joseph Smith … and … Oliver Cowdery" (vv. 1–3).

— **By authority of the keys of the Melchizedek priesthood.** "Joseph Smith … was called of God, and ordained an apostle of Jesus Christ, to be the first elder of this church; And … Oliver Cowdery … was also called of God, an apostle of Jesus Christ, to be the second elder of this church" (vv. 2–3). The Church of Jesus Christ is built upon the foundation of apostles and prophets, holding the necessary Melchizedek priesthood keys to preside and to administer spiritual blessings to the people (D&C 107:18). And "according to the grace of our Lord and Savior Jesus Christ, to whom be all glory, both now and forever" those keys had previously been given to both Joseph and Oliver (v. 4).

— **The weakness of the Prophet Joseph Smith.** It is remarkable that this criticism of the prophet's weakness should be included in the Church's founding document. But the Lord wants us to realize that despite the fact that "after it was truly manifested unto this first elder that he had received a remission of his sins, he was entangled again in the vanities of the world" (v. 5). Yet, our merciful God forgave him, and "after repenting, and humbling himself sincerely, through faith, God ministered unto him by an holy angel, whose countenance was as lightning, and whose garments were pure and white above all other whiteness; And gave unto him commandments which inspired him" (vv. 6–7).

— **The power by which the Book of Mormon was translated.** Though by himself he was weak (like the rest of us), the Lord gave Joseph Smith "power from on high, by the means which were before prepared, to translate the Book of Mormon" (v. 8). These "means" were the Urim and Thummim and the spiritual gift of translation by which he achieved his miraculous work.

— **The contents of the Book of Mormon.** It "contains a record of a fallen people, and the fulness of the gospel of Jesus Christ to the Gentiles and to the Jews also" (v. 9). Its contents were "given by inspiration" to the prophets whose writings are found within its pages (v. 10). It was subsequently (in our day) "confirmed to others by the ministering of angels" and "declared unto the world" by those who thus received them (v. 10).

— **What the Book of Mormon proves.** The very existence of this sacred record proves to the world "that the holy scriptures are true, and that God does inspire men and call them to his holy work in this age and generation, as well as in generations of old; Thereby showing that he is the same God yesterday, today, and forever" (vv. 11–12).

The Plan of Salvation and the Atonement

● **D&C 20:17–25 Chapter 2 summarized the many scriptures in the Doctrine and Covenants that teach us concerning salvation and the atonement of Jesus Christ.** We will not re-summarize all of those teachings here, except to say that "by these things" (the restoration, the Church, and the Book of Mormon) "we know that there is a God in heaven, who is infinite and eternal, from everlasting to everlasting the same unchangeable God, the framer of heaven and earth, and all things which are in them; And that he created man, male and female, after his own image and in his own likeness" (vv. 17–18).

Under the plan of salvation, God "gave unto [His children] commandments that they should love and serve him, the only living and true God, and that he should be the only being whom they should worship" (v. 19). But through "the transgression of these holy laws man became sensual and devilish, and became fallen man" (v. 20). Therefore, in order to redeem them from this fallen state, "the Almighty God gave his Only Begotten Son, as it is written in those scriptures which have been given of him" (v. 21).

"CASTING OUT SATAN," CARL BLOCH

Jesus rejected Satan's temptations

In order to fulfill His mission, and out of pure charity for each of us, Christ "suffered temptations but gave no heed unto them" (v. 22), "was crucified, died, and rose again the third day" (v. 23), and "ascended into heaven, to sit down on the right hand of the Father, to reign with almighty power according to the will of the Father" (v. 24). Thus becoming the Savior, He has de- clared that "as many as would believe and be baptized in his holy name, and endure in faith to the end, should be saved" (v. 25).

● **D&C 20:30–31 Justification and sanctification.** These verses distinguish between the principles of justification and sanctification, both of which came "through the grace of our Lord and Savior Jesus Christ" and are "just and true" (emphasis added). To properly understand this teaching we must define what each of these terms mean.

— **Justification** means "to be declared righteous," and also "to be put back into the right relationship with a person." Therefore, in a spiritual sense, it means "being reconciled to God the Father." Elder Bruce R. McConkie said: "Reconciliation is the process of ransoming man from his state of sin and spiritual darkness and of restoring him to a state of harmony and unity with Deity."[7]

Justification can come only through the atoning sacrifice of the Savior. It does not come by faith alone nor by obedience or works. It comes solely through the atonement of Christ, which, after we have done all we can do, declares us "perfect" enough to return to our Father in Heaven. Without such justification, none of us would be returning there.

Elder Bruce R. McConkie said: "As with all other doctrines of salvation, justification is available because of the atoning sacrifice of Christ, but it becomes operative in the life of an individual only on conditions of personal righteousness. As Paul taught, men are not justified by the works of the Mosaic law alone any more than men are saved by those works alone. The grace of God, manifest through the infinite and eternal atonement wrought by His Son, makes justification a living reality for those who seek righteousness. (Isa. 53:11; Mosiah 14:11)."[8]

— **Sanctification** is the actual process of cleansing, which, when it has been done, results in justification. Sanctification is possible because of the atonement of Christ. But sanctification is achieved through the cleansing power of the Holy Ghost. Because righteousness is a requirement for the presence of the Spirit, sanctification comes only to "those who love and serve God with all their mights, minds, and strength" (v. 31).

Elder Bruce R. McConkie said:

To be sanctified is to become clean, pure, and spotless; to be free from the blood and sins of the world; to become a new creature of the Holy Ghost, one whose body has been renewed by the rebirth of the Spirit. Sanctification is a state of saintliness, a state attained only by conformity to the laws and ordinances of the gospel. The plan of salvation is the system and means provided whereby men may sanctify their souls and thereby become worthy of a celestial inheritance… Those who attain this state of cleanliness and perfection are able, as occasion may require, to see God and view the things of His kingdom (D&C 84:23; 88:68; Ether 4:7). The Three Nephites "were sanctified in the flesh, that they were holy, and that the powers of the earth could not hold them" (3 Ne. 28:39).[9]

— **Grace** is charity—the pure love of Christ which caused Him to so graciously intervene on our behalf. By ourselves, we do not and cannot qualify for exaltation in the presence of our perfect Father in Heaven. We need a friend, a mediator, who can pay the price of our weaknesses and sins to satisfy the demands of justice, and then intervene on our behalf with the Father to permit us entrance into the celestial kingdom. This He willingly did in obedience to the Father's wishes and because He loves us and wants us to be with Him. That is the grace of Christ.

Salvation does not come because of our works. Neither the law of Moses nor the works associated with the full gospel can produce salvation. We sometimes think we are earning our salvation through our good works, but this is not so. "Salvation comes through Christ's atonement, through the ransom He paid, the propitiation He made; without this no good works on the part of men could redeem them from temporal death, which redemption is resurrection, or redeem them from spiritual death, which redemption is eternal life."[10]

We do our good works because we love the Lord ("If ye love me, keep my commandments." John 14:15). We do good works to demonstrate our faith in the Lord ("I will [show] my faith by my works." James 2:18). And we do good works to become a candidate for exaltation ("He that doeth the will of my Father which is in heaven … shall enter into the kingdom of heaven." Matthew 7:21). But "after all we can do" (2 Nephi 25:23), it is still insufficient to save us. A thousand good deeds cannot erase the consequences of a single sin. For that we are utterly dependent upon the Savior. It is His grace that makes our sanctification possible.

— **Just** means sufficient—in this case sufficient to satisfy the demands of justice. The principles of justification and sanctification through the grace of Christ are therefore just.

— **True** is a testimony of the truth of the principles here taught. The Lord is verifying their correctness and sufficiency to save us all.

FUNDAMENTAL ORDINANCES OF THE CHURCH

Instructions Concerning Baptism

● **D&C 20:37 Qualifications for baptism.** We must remember that every member of the Church in those days (including the Prophet Joseph Smith) were converts to the Church. All had need of baptism into the Church, and needed to understand the qualifications for receiving the ordinance and also the covenants they would be making in the process.

— Humble themselves before God.
— Have a desire to be baptized.

— Come forth with broken hearts and contrite spirits.

— Witness before the Church that they have truly repented of all their sins.

— Be willing to take upon them the name of Jesus Christ.

— Have a determination to serve Him to the end.

— Manifest by their works (behavior) that they have received of the Spirit of Christ.

● **D&C 20:72–74 The ordinance of baptism.**
Baptism must be performed by someone "who is called of God and has authority from Jesus Christ to baptize" (v. 73). The proper mode of baptism is to "go down into the water with the person who has presented himself or herself for baptism" and offer a precise covenant prayer (v. 73):

> [Calling him or her by name]: "Having been commissioned of Jesus Christ, I baptize you in the name of the Father, and of the Son, and of the Holy Ghost. Amen."

Qumran baptismal font from the time of Christ (built to allow total immersion)

When this has been done, the officiator is required to "immerse him or her in the water, and come forth again out of the water" (v. 74).

● **D&C 20:68–69 The duties of members after baptism.** According to these verses, after baptism "the elders or priests are to have a sufficient time to expound all things concerning the church of Christ to their understanding, previous to their partaking of the sacrament and being confirmed by the laying on of the hands of the elders, so that all things may be done in order" (v. 68). Specifically, verse 69 stipulates that newly baptized members, before confirmation, should:

— "Manifest before the church, and ... the elders ... a godly walk and conversation."

— Demonstrate that they are worthy of confirmation.

— Demonstrate that they have shown "works and faith agreeable to the holy scriptures—walking in holiness before the Lord."

This is not often the case in our present day, when newly baptized members are often confirmed members of the Church immediately after baptism. The brethren have, in recent times, expressed concern about immediate confirmations of adult converts, since the scriptures are clear that newly-baptized members must show evidence of their faith before they are confirmed and the Gift of the Holy Ghost is bestowed upon them.

● **D&C 20:71 Children are to be baptized at the age of accountability.** The Lord commands that no one should be "received into the Church of Christ" through baptism "unless he has arrived unto the years of accountability before God, and is capable of repentance." The Lord later clarified that "the years of accountability" means "when eight years old" (D&C 68:25–27). And we know from the Book of Mormon that the same principle applies to those who are "without law" because they are incapable mentally or emotionally of knowing right from wrong. All of these are "alive in Christ" without baptism (Moroni 8:22).

Other Essential Ordinances

● **D&C 20:70 The blessing of young children.** This ordinance is not just a tradition. The Lord requires it of "every member of the church of Christ having children." We are commanded to "bring them unto the elders before the church," who are to "lay their hands upon them in the name of Jesus Christ, and bless them in his name." We normally do this shortly after their birth, but it can actually be done anytime that is deemed appropriate by the presiding officer and consistent with Church instructions. I have seen young children of converts blessed well into their second year of life.

● **D&C 20:75–77 The ordinance of the sacrament.** Because of our need to renew our covenants regularly, we are told that it is "expedient that the church meet together often to partake of bread and wine in the remembrance of the Lord Jesus" (v. 75). This sacred ordinance is to be administered by "the elder or priest" who shall "kneel with the church and call upon the Father in solemn prayer" (v. 76). As is the case with baptism, the precise words of this ordinance are then given by the Lord in verses 77 and 79.

Managing Church Membership

● **D&C 20:80 Transgressors are to be dealt with as the scriptures direct.** This scripture requires Church leaders to keep the Church pure by disciplining those who violate their covenants. More particulars are given on this matter in D&C 64 and D&C 102, and will be discussed in a later chapter. Suffice it to say here that "any member of the church of Christ transgressing, or being overtaken in a fault, shall be dealt with as the scriptures direct." Such actions are taken "that God may be glorified—not because ye forgive not, having not compassion, but that … ye may not offend him who is your lawgiver" (D&C 64:12–13).

● **D&C 20:81–84 Church memberships are to be tracked carefully.** The membership records of new members are to be recorded and maintained by those in authority (v. 81). In those early days, they were distributed by hand at church conferences (v. 82). This is quite primitive by the standards of today's computer and Internet standards. Still, the principle remains the same—to keep the numbers and names of the members in such a way that they will not be forgotten or lost (Mosiah 6:1; Moroni 6:4).

Church clerks are also to keep track of those who "have been expelled from the church, so that their names may be blotted out of the general church record of names" (v. 83). And if any members moved from one area to another, they took with them "a letter certifying that they are regular members and in good standing" (v. 84)—an early version of the membership records that are transferred today from one Church unit to another whenever a member moves.

THE CHURCH IS ORGANIZED

(D&C 21)

D&C 21 was given through the Prophet Joseph Smith, on the occasion of the organization of the Church, on Tuesday, April 6, 1830. It came in response to prayer in the Whitmer home, where a number of people had gathered to organize the Church as commanded in D&C 20.[11]

Six men, who had previously been bap- tized, participated in the official incorporation of the Church as required by New York law. By unanimous vote all those persons present on this occasion (estimated to be at least 30) sustained the proposal to organize the Church according to the commandments of God received in D&C 20. They also voted to accept and sustain Joseph Smith Jr. and Oliver Cowdery as the presiding officers of the Church.

Room in the Whitmer home in Fayette New York, where the Church was organized on April 6, 1830

By the laying on of hands, Joseph Smith, then ordained Oliver Cowdery an elder of the Church, followed by Oliver similarly ordaining Joseph. When the Church was organized, there were no wards or stakes, no seventies, high priests, or bishops. There were no quorums. There was not as yet a First Presidency, nor general authorities. The only executive or presiding officers were the First and Second Elders of the Church—Joseph Smith and Oliver Cowdery.

The sacrament was then administered and passed among the members. Joseph and Oliver then laid hands upon the participants individually "for the bestowal of the Holy Ghost and for the confirmation of each as a member of the Church" (D&C 21:Heading).

At the conclusion of these activities, the Prophet Joseph Smith said: "The Holy Ghost was poured out upon us to a very great degree—some prophesied, whilst we all praised the Lord, and rejoiced exceedingly. Whilst yet together, I received the following commandment [D&C 21]."[12]

- **D&C 21:1 Joseph Smith was called to be a seer, translator, prophet, Apostle, and elder.** On this, the first official meeting of the Church, the Lord commands again, "there shall be a record kept among you" (v. 1), thus emphasizing the public nature of the Church's meetings and ordinations. In the record of this first meeting, they were to note that Joseph Smith was sustained as "a seer, a translator, a prophet, an apostle of Jesus Christ, [and] an elder of the church" (v. 1). This pattern has been repeated for the prophets and Apostles at every Church conference since that day.

● **D&C 21:2–3 The Church of the living Christ.** The Lord testified to the people that Joseph Smith was "inspired of the Holy Ghost to lay the foundation [of the Church], and to build it up unto the most holy faith" (v. 2). This is the Lord's Church—the Church of the Living Christ—and not a man-made institution. This knowledge sustains us in the midst of a troubled world, knowing as we do that the Lord is leading us by the hand through His ordained servants. And it all began "in the year of [our] Lord eighteen hundred and thirty, in the fourth month, and on the sixth day of the month which is called April" (v. 3).

● **D&C 21:4–9 The Prophet's words will guide the cause of Zion.** Members of the Church are commanded to "give heed unto all [the Prophet's] words and commandments which he shall give unto you as he receiveth them, walking in all holiness before me; For his word ye shall receive, as if from mine own mouth, in all patience and faith" (vv. 4–5). If we will do this, "the gates of hell shall not prevail against you; yea, and the Lord God will disperse the powers of darkness from before you, and cause the heavens to shake for your good, and his name's glory" (v. 6).

President Harold B. Lee said:

> We have some tight places to go before the Lord is through with this Church and the world in this dispensation, which is the last dispensation, which shall usher in the coming of the Lord… Now the only safety we have as members of this Church is to do exactly what the Lord said to the Church in that day when the Church was organized. We must learn to give heed to the words and commandments that the Lord shall give through His prophet, "as he receiveth them, walking in all holiness before me … as if from my own mouth, in all patience and faith" (D&C 21:4–5).
>
> There will be some things that take patience and faith. You may not like what comes from the authority of the Church. It may contradict your political views. It may contradict your social views. It may interfere with some of your social life. But if you listen to these things, as if from the mouth of the Lord Himself, with patience and faith, the promise is that "the gates of hell shall not prevail against you; yea, and the Lord God will disperse the powers of darkness from before you, and cause the heavens to shake for your good, and his name's glory" (D&C 21:6)… Your safety and ours depends upon whether or not we follow the ones whom the Lord has placed to preside over His Church. He knows whom He wants to preside over this Church, and He will make no mistake… Let's keep our eye on the President of the Church.[13]

Other principles apply, such as unity. Our prophet is not a dictator; he seeks the counsel of his counselors as presidents at all levels of the priesthood do. And the First Presidency, when they speak unitedly as a presidency, speak "what the Lord would say if He were here in person" (Marion G. Romney, in Conference Report, April 1945, 90). President Ezra Taft Benson said: "The prophet and the presidency—the living prophet and the First Presidency—follow them and be blessed—reject them and suffer."[14]

For major doctrinal pronouncements, our prophet seeks the counsel and sustaining of his counselors and of the Twelve Apostles. Such was the case for the revelation on priesthood that President Spencer W. Kimball announced to the world in 1978. Regarding such major revelations, President Kimball said: "Man never needs to stand alone… The Lord definitely calls prophets today and reveals His secrets unto them as He did yesterday, He does today, and will do tomorrow."[15] He later counseled, "Let us hearken to those we sustain as prophets and seers, as well as the other brethren, as if our eternal life depended upon it, because it does!"[16]

The Lord promises that He will inspire the Prophet "to move the cause of Zion in mighty power for good, and his diligence I know, and his prayers I have heard" (v. 7). Thus, as the prophets take their concerns to the Lord, they can know that He will bless them with "the manifestations of my blessings upon his works" (v. 8).

Again and again we have seen this promise kept, as the prophets have taken their concerns to the Lord in prayer over the Church's safety, its financial security, its growth and need for additional leadership, the need for the priesthood to be given to worthy men of all races, and the safety and protection of its families—and much more— and the Lord has revealed the answer. We sing, "We thank thee, O God, for a prophet to guide us in these latter days," knowing we are not alone, and that Christ is at the head. Thus it was on April 6, 1830, and thus it has been ever since.

The Lord promises to "bless all those who labor in my vineyard with a mighty blessing" if they will "believe on [the Prophet's] words, which are given him through me by the Comforter" (v. 9). The prophets possess the "spirit of prophecy," which John defined as the "testimony of Jesus" (Revelation 19:10). They know him, and that He "was crucified by sinful men for the sins of the world, yea, for the remission of sins unto the contrite heart" (v. 9).

● **D&C 21:10–12 The Prophet is to be ordained by the other living Apostles.** The Lord commanded that Joseph Smith should be ordained to his position as the Lord's prophet "by you, Oliver Cowdery mine apostle; this being an ordinance unto you" (vv. 10–11). Thus was established another pattern that has persisted in the Church ever since that first conference on April 6, 1830—namely, that the Apostles ordain the prophets. And after that ordinance, those who have ordained him "are an elder under his hand, he being the first unto you" (v. 11).

Oliver's calling is to be "an elder unto this church of Christ, bearing my name—And the first preacher of this church unto the church, and before the world, yea, before the Gentiles; yea, and … to the Jews" (v. 12). But Joseph was to be sustained as the head of the Church.

AUTHORITATIVE BAPTISM IS REQUIRED

(D&C 22)

D&C 22 was given in April 1830, a few days after the organization of the Church, in response to some who had been previously baptized in other churches and who didn't think re-baptism was required.[17] Some of these new converts had come from churches which believed in baptism by immersion. For this reason, they fully accepted this mode of baptism when it was given to the Church. They were not so accepting on the question of divine authority. Other churches accepted one another's baptisms as authoritative, so when they desired to come into the Church, they wondered why it was necessary for them to be baptized again.

- **D&C 22:1 Baptism is a "new and everlasting" covenant that was established for God's children from the very beginning of the earth.** The ordinance replaced all old forms that resembled it, which the Lord had "caused to be done away in this thing" (v. 1). Isaiah had prophesied concerning our days that the earth would be "defiled under the inhabitants thereof; because they have transgressed the laws, changed the ordinance, [and] broken the everlasting covenant" (Isaiah 24:5). Paul said that such churches would have "a form of godliness, but deny … the power thereof" (2 Timothy 3:5), and the Lord verified that this had occurred when He appeared to Joseph in the first vision (JS–History 1:19). Baptism was not new. It had been required "from the beginning" of the earth, but in this final dispensation it constituted "a new and an everlasting covenant" unto the Church (v. 1).

- **D&C 22:2–4 Authoritative baptism is required.** The Lord's words here are very clear. "Wherefore, although a man should be baptized an hundred times it availeth him nothing, for you cannot enter in at the strait gate by the law of Moses, neither by your dead works" (v. 2). Why were their previous baptisms "dead" to the Lord? Because they were not done by proper and necessary authority—the very power that the apostate churches reject as unnecessary. "For it is because of your dead works that I have caused this last covenant and this church to be built up unto me, even as in days of old," said the Lord (v. 3). They were therefore commanded to "enter ye in at the gate, as I have commanded, and seek not to counsel your God" (v. 4).

ADDITIONAL DOCTRINAL INSTRUCTIONS

During the months that followed the organization of the Church, a number of important events and revelations transpired. Some of these will be discussed in later chapters.

— June 1830	The first conference of the Church was held in Fayette, New York.
— June 1830	The first ordained missionary was sent out to preach—Samuel H. Smith; As a result, the Youngs and Kimballs were eventually converted at Mendon, New York.
— June 1830	Sidney Rigdon came to New York and the revision of the Bible began.
— June 18, 1830	Many Colesville Saints and Emma are baptized amid severe persecution.
— July (early) 1830	The Book of Moses was received by revelation as Joseph saw and recorded the visions of Moses

The Law of Common Consent

(D&C 26)

D&C 26 was one of three revelations the Prophet received shortly after his return to Harmony, Pennsylvania, from Colesville, New York, in July 1830. It was given to Joseph Smith, Oliver Cowdery, and John Whitmer.[18] John Whitmer was at the time living with Joseph and Emma and assisting in collating and arranging the revelations that had been given to that point. They had temporarily returned to the Prophet's home in Harmony, Pennsylvania, to escape intense persecution in New York, particularly at Colesville.

● **D&C 26:1 They were instructed to study the scriptures and to preach.** While thus unable to travel much, the Lord commanded them to "let your time be devoted to the studying of the scriptures, and to preaching, and to confirming the church at Colesville, and to performing your labors on the land, such as is required … " Later, they would be required to "go to the west [Fayette, New York] to hold the next conference; and then it shall be made known what you shall do."

● **D&C 26:2 All things in the Church must be public (not secret) and subject to common consent.** The Lord very pointedly commands that "all things shall be done by common consent in the church, by much prayer and faith … " This requirement to do all things publicly and with the consent of the members would prevent deviation from the doctrines and principles of the gospel. But this does not mean that the Church is a demo- cracy. We do not "vote" when we sustain an action. By raising our right hands, we are, in fact, making a covenant to support those who have been appointed. We may choose not to sustain—that is our prerogative and our agency—but we are not electing Church officers by so doing.

Hyrum M. Smith and Janne M. Sjodahl said: "In the Church of Christ where the government is that of the King of Heaven, neither autocracy nor democracy obtains, but government in Common Consent. That is to say, the initiative in all that pertains to the government of the Church rests with the Head of the Church, even the Lord Jesus Christ, and He exercises this sovereign function through His authorized servants, upon whom He has bestowed the Holy Priesthood: but it is the privilege of the people to accept, or reject, His laws and ordinances, for God has given every individual free agency. Obedience must be voluntary. The government of the Church has been called a theocracy. It is the form of government that will be general during the Millennium."[19]

The Emblems of the Sacrament

(D&C 27)

D&C 27 was received by the Prophet in August and Sep- tember of 1830 at Harmony, Pennsylvania. In early August, Newel Knight and his wife visited the Smiths in Harmony, Pennsylvania. Neither Sister Knight nor Emma Smith had yet been confirmed, so they decided to do this, and partake of the sacrament, before the Knights returned to their home in New York. Joseph went to obtain some wine for use in the sacra- ment. He says he "had gone only

a short distance when I was met by a heavenly messenger, and received the following revelation [D&C 27], the first four paragraphs of which were written at this time, and the remainder in the September following."[20] In obedience to the revelation they prepared wine of their own making and held their meeting.

In D&C 27, the Lord commands "that you shall not pur- chase wine neither strong drink of your enemies; Wherefore, you shall partake of none except it is made anew among you; yea, in this my Father's kingdom which shall be built up on the earth" (vv. 3–4). This should not be interpreted to mean that we can never use wine for the sacrament. Rather, it says we are not to purchase wine from our enemies and are to use only "new wine of our own make," meaning essentially grape juice.

Hyrum M. Smith and Janne M. Sjodahl explain that "No fewer than thirteen Hebrew and Greek terms are rendered in our Bible by the word 'wine.' There is the pure grape juice, and a kind of grape syrup, the thickness of which made it necessary to mingle water with it previously to drinking (Prov. 9:2, 5). There was a wine made strong and inebriating by the addition of drugs, such as myrrh, mandragora, and opiates (Prov. 23:30; Isa. 5:22). Of the pure wine which was diluted with water or milk, Wisdom invites her friends to drink freely (Prov. 9:2, 5). There was also 'wine on the lees,' which is supposed to have been 'preserves' or 'jellies' (Isa. 25:6). The 'pure wine' is not an intoxicating, but a harmless liquid."[21]

- **D&C 27:1–4 The emblems of the sacrament.** We have become accustomed to the use of bread and water for the sacrament emblems, and we may think that they are the only appropriate tokens we may use. But the Lord said to the Prophet Joseph Smith, "it mattereth not what ye shall eat or what ye shall drink when ye partake of the sacrament if it so be that ye do it with an eye single to my glory" (v. 2). The tokens are not the point; the things for which they stand are the point. Because the emblems of the sacrament are symbolic rather than mystically connected to the physical body and blood of the Lord, any food or liquid may, with permission of priesthood leaders, be used as the emblems by which we remember Him.

  Not fully understanding this, many Christians believe in transubstantiation—that the wafer they eat in remembrance of Christ is literally the body of Christ. Ordinances are symbolic and are intended to be interpreted symbolically, not *literally*. In baptism, in the sacrament, in the temple, and in every other ordinance, we are to focus on the mighty realities for which the symbols stand, not on the symbols themselves.

- **Why the Lord uses symbols to teach us.** *The Life and Teachings of Christ and His Apostles*[22] explains why the Lord frequently uses symbolic language and imagery to teach His children the truths of the gospel—wheat and tares, mustard seeds, candlesticks, olive trees, trumpets, winepresses, the eye, the ear, the heart, baptism, the sacrament, and many more things that symbolize eternal truths.

— Symbolic images and stories convey truth and reality with greater impact than is possible with abstract concepts or words.

— Symbolic images and stories convey different levels of spiritual truth to different levels of spiritual maturity. For example, baptism can be understood as the very obvious symbolism of cleansing, the washing away of sin. But as one ponders its meaning further, deeper spiritual significance becomes evident—the concept of the death and burial of the old sinful man, and the concept of the womb, water, blood, and birth, wherein the new spiritual man is reborn.

— Symbolic images protect the ignorant from damnation until they have an opportunity to obtain the spiritual maturity needed for understanding.

— Symbolic images help us to remember. Images, examples, and stories drawn from the experiences of our everyday lives remind us of gospel principles every time we encounter them. We are thus regularly reminded of them.

— Symbolic images have universal appeal—they are not limited to one person or group of persons in their meaning or application. Every person can be inspired by them in some way.

— Symbolic images and stories impress us with their simplicity and beauty. Some of the most beautiful stories of all time are those that have symbolic meaning—the Good Samaritan, the Ten Virgins, the Golden Rule, etc.

— Symbolic images and stories stimulate us to search and ponder their meanings. This produces the "pondering" necessary for spiritual enlightenment and revelation.

Elder Bruce R. McConkie said:

> To crystallize in our minds the eternal verities which we must accept and believe to be saved, to dramatize their true meaning and import with an impact never to be forgotten, to center our attention on these saving truths, again and again and again, the Lord uses similitudes. Abstract principles may easily be forgotten or their deep meaning overlooked, but visual performances and actual experiences are registered on the mind in such a way as never to be lost…

> He uses ordinances, rites, acts, and performances; He uses similarities, resemblances, and similitudes so that whatever is done will remind all who are aware of it of a greater and more important reality. He uses similes; He uses parables; He uses allegories. If two things have the same semblance or form, if they are like each other in appearance, if they correspond in qualities, it may suit His purposes to compare them…

If we had sufficient insight, we would see in every gospel ordinance, in every rite that is part of revealed religion, in every performance commanded of God, in all things Deity gives His people, something that typifies the eternal ministry of the Eternal Christ.[23]

Elder McConkie's last statement above is important to our understanding of symbolic ordinances. Every emblem or token used in every ordinance has something to do with Jesus Christ. This includes, but is not limited to, those used for baptism, the sacrament, and temple ordinances.

Speaking of temple ordinances, Elder John A. Widt- soe said:

> The holy endowment is deeply symbolic. "Going through the temple" is not a very good phrase; for temple worship implies a great effort of mind and concentration if we are to understand the mighty symbols that pass in review before us. Everything must be arranged to attune our hearts, our minds, and our souls to the work…

No man or woman can come out of the temple endowed as he should be, unless he has seen, beyond the symbol, the mighty realities for which the symbols stand... To the man or woman who goes through the temple, with open eyes, heeding the symbols and the covenants, and making a steady, continuous effort to understand the full meaning, God speaks His word, and revelations come.

The endowment is so richly symbolic that only a fool would attempt to describe it; it is so packed full of revelations to those who exercise their strength to seek and see, that no human words can explain or make clear the possibilities that reside in the temple service. The endowment, which was given by revelation, can best be understood by revelation; and to those who seek most vigorously, with pure hearts, will the revelation be greatest.[24]

In the case of the sacrament, we partake of the emblems in remembrance of Christ's "body which was laid down for you, and my blood which was shed for the remission of your sins" (v. 2). Those are the mighty and saving principles of the sacrament.

Revelation and Instruction from Ancient Prophets

● **D&C 27:5–14 Christ lists those whom He sent to instruct Joseph Smith.** While speaking of those with whom He will "drink of the fruit of the vine with you on the earth," the Lord mentions a number of ancient prophets whom He had sent by this time and would in the future send to instruct Joseph in his latter-day calling.

Those who had already been sent included Moroni, who brought the Book of Mormon and also "the keys of the record of the stick of Ephraim" (v. 5). Also, "John [the Baptist] the son of Zacharias, which Zacharias he (Elias [Noah]) visited and gave promise that he should have a son, and his name should be John, and he should be filled with the spirit of Elias" (v. 7), and whom the Lord had sent to Joseph and Oliver to "ordain you unto the first priesthood which you have received ... even as Aaron" (v. 8). And also "Peter, and James, and John, whom I have sent unto you, by whom I have ordained you and confirmed you to be apostles, and especial witnesses of my name, and bear the keys

of your ministry … the keys of my kingdom, and a dispensation of the gospel for the last times; and for the fulness of times, in the which I will gather together in one all things, both which are in heaven, and which are on earth" (vv. 12–13).

Those who would yet come included "Elias [Noah], to whom I have committed the keys of bringing to pass the restoration of all things spoken by the mouth of all the holy prophets since the world began, concerning the last days" (v. 6). Also "Elijah, unto whom I have committed the keys of the power of turning the hearts of the fathers to the children, and the hearts of the children to the fathers, that the whole earth may not be smitten with a curse" (v. 9).

Also "Joseph and Jacob, and Isaac, and Abraham, your fathers, by whom the promises remain" (v. 10). And also "Michael, or Adam, the father of all, the prince of all, the ancient of days" (v. 11).

The list of heavenly visitors to the Prophet Joseph Smith goes well beyond this short list. During his lifetime he was visited by virtually every major Biblical and Book of Mormon prophet, and many others, who instructed him in his great calling. The following is a list of 59 known visitors that are documented in Church scripture and historical documents.

# Personage(s):	Reference(s): *
1. God the Father	JS–History 1:17; HC 1:5; D&C 76:20
2. Jesus Christ	JS–History 1:17; HC 1:5–6; D&C 76:20–24; 110:2–10
3. Moroni	JS–History 1:30–49; JD 17:374
4. Elijah	D&C 110:13–16; JD 23:48
5. John the Baptist	D&C 13; HC 1:39–40
6–8. Peter, James and John	D&C 27:12; 128:20; HC 1:40–42; JD 18:326
9. Adam (Michael)	D&C 107:53–57; 128:21; 137:5; HC 3:388; JD 18:326; JD 21:94; JD 23:48; JD 9:41
10. Noah (Gabriel)	D&C 128:21; JD 21:94: JD 23:48
# Personage(s):	Reference(s): *
11. Raphael	D&C 128:21
12. Moses	D&C 110:11; JD 23:48; JD 21:65
13. Elias	D&C 110:12; 27:6; JD 23:48
14. Joseph, son of Jacob	D&C 27:10
15. Abraham	D&C 27:10; 137:5; JD 21:94; JD 23:48
16. Isaac	D&C 27:10; JD 21:94
17. Jacob	D&C 27:10; JD 21:94
18. Enoch	JD 21:65
19–27. Twelve Jewish Apostles,	JD 21:94 besides Peter, James, John
28–39. Twelve Nephite Apostles,	JD 21:94 including 3 Nephites
40. Nephi	JD 13:47; JD 21:161
41. Seth	D&C 107:53–57; HC 3:388; JD 21:94
42. Methuselah	D&C 107:53–57; HC 3:388; JD 18:325

# Personage(s):	Reference(s): *
43. Enos	D&C 107:53–57; HC 3:388; JD 18:325
44. Mahalaleel	D&C 107:53–57; HC 3:388; JD 18:325
45. Jared (Bible)	D&C 107:53–57; HC 3:388
46. Lamech	JD 18:325
47. Abel	JD 18:325; HC 3:388
48. Cainan	D&C 107:53–57; HC 3:388
49. Zelph the Lamanite	Times and Seasons, 6:788
50. Alvin Smith (deceased brother)	HC 2:380
51. Mormon	JD 17:374
52. Paul	*Teachings of the Prophet Joseph Smith*, 180
53. Eve	*Oliver B. Huntington Diary, Part 2*, 244, BYU Library
54. Alma	JD 13:47
55. Unnamed Angel	D&C 27 (concerning wine in sacrament); HC 1:106
56. Unnamed Angel	Accepted dedication of the Kirtland Temple (JD 11:10).
57. Unnamed Angel	Visited Joseph Smith 3 times and commanded him to practice polygamy—Eliza R. Snow, *Biography and Family Records of President Lorenzo Snow*, 69
58. "I saw many angels"	Warren Cowdery's account of Joseph's 1st Vision, 159
59. Satan, as an angel of light	D&C 128:20; JD 3:229–230 (and many of his associates)

* (JD = Journal of Discourses; HC = History of the Church).

The Prophet Joseph listed many of these prophets in his rejoicing concerning the cause of Zion in the latter days found in D&C 128:18–20, including the following observation concerning the necessity of these visits: "Neither can they nor we be made perfect without those who have died in the gospel also; for it is necessary in the ushering in of the dispensation of the fulness of times, which dispensation is now beginning to usher in, that a whole and complete and perfect union, and welding together of dispensations, and keys, and powers, and glories should take place, and be revealed from the days of Adam even to the present time" (D&C 128:18).

President John Taylor said:

> Why was it that all these people should be associated with all these dispensations, and all could communicate with Joseph Smith? Because he stood at the head of the dispensation of the fullness of times, which comprehends all the various dispensations that have existed upon the earth …
>
> The Gods in the eternal worlds and the Priesthood that officiated in time and eternity had declared that it was time for the issuing forth of all these things, [and] they all combined together to impart to him the keys of their several missions, that he might be fully competent, through the intelligence and aid afforded him through these several parties, to introduce the Gospel in all its fullness, namely, the dispensation of the fullness of times, when says the Apostle Paul, "He might gather all things in Christ, both which are in heaven and which are in earth, even in him."

Consequently he stood in that position, and hence his familiarity with all these various dispensations and the men who administered in them. If you were to ask Joseph what sort of a looking man Adam was, he would tell you at once; he would tell you his size and appearance and all about him. You might have asked him what sort of men Peter, James, and John were, and he could have told you. Why? Because he had seen them.[25]

Putting on the Whole Armor of God

● **D&C 27:15–18 The "shield of faith" will protect us against the "fiery darts of the wicked."** We live in a seriously troubled time, wherein the Lord commands us to "lift up your hearts and rejoice, and gird up your loins [meaning prepare yourself], and take upon you my whole armor, that ye may be able to withstand the evil day." If we do so, "having done all … ye may be able to stand" (v. 15). What kind of preparation is required for times like these? The Lord lists the following.

— Knowing the truth (v. 16).
— Living in righteousness (v. 16).
— Understanding the gospel of peace (v. 16).
— Faith, with which "ye shall be able to quench all the fiery darts of the wicked" (v. 17).
— Having hope for, and the assurance of, salvation (v. 18).
— Possessing the Holy Spirit as a guide (v. 18).
— Receiving all the words of Christ (scriptures and revelations) (v. 18).
— Unity—"being agreed as touching all things" (v. 18).
— Enduring all things in faith until He comes (v. 18).

And if we are thus prepared, He promises us that "ye shall be caught up, that where I am ye shall be also" (v. 18).

LEARNING TO FOLLOW THE PROPHET

Joseph had returned to Harmony, Pennsylvania for a while, but persecution was getting worse, and he reported an incident of divine protection during this period. He was visiting Colesville, New York, at the latter end of August 1830, in company with John and David Whitmer, and Hyrum Smith. Knowing that such a trip was dangerous, they had prayed for the Lord's protection—specifically that He would "blind the eyes of our enemies, so that they would not know us, and that we might on this occasion return unmolested." This petition was literally fulfilled when, just a short distance from the Knight home in Colesville, they came upon some men working on a public road. Among them were "several of our most bitter enemies." Joseph said that "they looked earnest at us, but not knowing us, we passed on without interruption."[26]

Leaving Harmony, Pennsylvania for the Last Time

Eventually, Joseph could no longer depend on the protection of his father-in-law, Isaac Hale, against the rising threat of persecution; he therefore accepted the invitation of Peter Whitmer Sr. to come and live with him again in Fayette, New York, where they had resided during the completion of the Book of Mormon and the establishment of the Church. Newel Knight took his wagon from Colesville to Harmony to move the family. They arrived at Fayette during the last week of August, 1830 "amidst the congratulations of our brethren and friends." But all was not well.

During this period, and just months after the organization of the Church, Joseph received a letter from Oliver Cowdery which gave him both "sorrow and uneasiness." Oliver claimed that he had discovered an error in one of the commandments, D&C 20:37, which says "And truly manifest by their works that they have received of the Spirit of Christ unto a remission of their sins." Oliver claimed that this was "erroneous," and added: "I command you in the name of God to erase those words, that no priestcraft be amongst us!" Once again, Oliver was attempting to show that he was as inspired as Joseph, and assumed he had the authority to correct the Church's prophet. Joseph asked him "by what authority he took upon him to command me to alter or erase, to add to or diminish from, a revelation or commandment from Almighty God."[27]

Grave of Isaac Hall in Harmony, PA

Leaving Harmony was a day of great sorrow for Emma. This was the last time she would ever see her childhood home or her parents in this life, and they had to leave most of their earthly possessions behind. They also left behind the grave of their firstborn child. Emma was pregnant again—this time with twins—and she had to endure the three-day ride to Fayette, New York over hot, dusty, bumpy roads.

A Rebellion Rising at Fayette, New York

The Prophet Joseph Smith arrived in Fayette only to find that the rebellion of Hiram Page, Oliver Cowdery, and others was still underway. The Prophet wrote, "I found the family in general of his [Oliver Cowdery's] opinion concerning the words [he had disputed previously in his letter to Joseph], and it was not without both labor and perseverance that I could prevail with any of them to reason calmly on the subject. However, Christian Whitmer at length became convinced that the sentence was reasonable, and according to Scripture; and finally, with his assistance, I succeeded in bringing, not only the Whitmer family, but also Oliver Cowdery to acknowledge that they had been in error, and that the sentence in dispute was in accordance with the rest of the commandment."[28]

Shortly thereafter, the Prophet learned about Hiram Page's claims to receiving certain revelations by means of a seer stone. Newel Knight described the circumstances in his journal:

[Hiram Page] had managed to get up some discussions of feeling among the brethren by giving revelations concerning the government of the Church and other matters, which he claimed to have received through the medium of a stone he possessed… Even Oliver Cowdery and the Whitmer family had given heed to them… Joseph was perplexed and scarcely knew how to meet this new exigency. That night I occupied the same room that he did and the greater part of the night was spent in prayer and supplication. After much labor with these brethren they were convinced of their error, and confessed the same, renouncing [Page's] revelations as not being of God.[29]

Hiram Page was 30 years old, having been born in Vermont in 1800. He joined the Church five days after its organization and was baptized by Oliver Cowdery in Seneca Lake. He was one of the Eight Witnesses of the Book of Mormon. Apparently, soon after his baptism, he obtained from an unknown source a stone by means of which he claimed to receive revelations. They were inconsistent with some principles of the Gospel and the revelations received by Joseph Smith. Among other things he claimed to have received a revelation through his stone concerning the place where the City of Zion would be built.

E. Cecil McGavin said: "The Page 'peepstone' … has been preserved as a souvenir in the Archives of the Reorganized Church. The writer was permitted to examine it. It is a flat stone about seven inches long, four wide and one quarter inch in thickness. It is dark gray in color with waves of brown and purple across the surface. A small hole has been drilled through one end of it as if a string had been threaded through it. It is simply impressive enough to make a good paper weight, yet it became a tool through which the adversary attempted to stir up strife and create a schism in the Church."[30]

Keep in mind that the Church was very new and that every member was a convert with little experience in the ways of the Lord. They were like little children, full of enthusiasm and spirit, but seriously lacking in experience—like any new convert. They did not fully comprehend that there was only one person who could receive revelations for the Church. This particular group was convinced that Hiram Page or Oliver Cowdery could receive revelation just as well as Joseph Smith, and this suited the ego of both of them. Oliver Cowdery and the members of the Whitmer family were deceived by the claims of Hiram Page, and Oliver Cowdery scolded the Prophet for not accepting the "revelations" that Hiram Page had given.

The "Economy of Revelation"

(D&C 28)

D&C 28 was received and recorded in the midst of all the above-described confusion, at Fayette, New York, September 1830. Just prior to an appointed conference, the Prophet inquired earnestly of the Lord concerning the matter, and this revelation followed. It was directed to Oliver Cowdery.[31]

- **D&C 28:1–7 Joseph Smith held the keys, and only he received revelations for the Church.** Reiterating what He had said in a prior revelation on the day the Church was organized (D&C 21:10–12), the Lord defines Oliver Cowdery's role as follows: "thou shalt be heard by the church in all things whatsoever thou shalt teach them by the Comforter, concerning the revelations and commandments which I have given" (v. 1). But "no one shall be appointed to receive commandments and revelations in this church excepting my servant Joseph Smith, Jun., for he receiveth them even as Moses" (v. 2). Oliver is commanded to be "obedient unto the things which I shall give unto him" (v. 3).

The Lord said that Oliver, as an Apostle, could "declare faithfully the commandments and the revelations, with power and authority unto the church. And if thou art led at any time by the Comforter to speak or teach, or at all times by the way of commandment unto the church, thou mayest do it. But thou shalt not write by way of commandment, but by wisdom" (vv. 3–5). This is an apt description of the role of Apostles in the Church even to this day. They speak by revelation and wisdom, but they do not speak for the entire Church.

Oliver Cowdery

Oliver would struggle with this principle throughout his life, feeling himself equal to Joseph rather than subject to his direction. But he is explicitly commanded in this revelation not to "command him who is at thy head, and at the head of the church; For I have given him the keys of the mysteries, and the revelations which are sealed, until I shall appoint unto them another in his stead" (vv. 6–7). Thus, only the prophet who sits at the head of the Church can receive revelation for the whole Church.

The Prophet Joseph Smith said: "I will inform you that it is contrary to the economy of God for any member of the Church, or anyone, to receive instructions for those in authority, higher than themselves; therefore, you will see the impropriety of giving heed to them; but if any person have a vision or a visitation from a heavenly messenger, it must be for his own benefit and instruction, for the fundamental principles, government, and doctrine of the Church are vested in the keys of the kingdom."[32]

● **D&C 28:8–9, 14–16 Oliver Cowdery was called to preach to the Lamanites.** This mission call would have eternal consequences for the Church, as will be seen in later chapters. Oliver is called to "go unto the Lamanites and preach my gospel unto them" (v. 8), which meant to go west toward the wilderness beyond New York, through Ohio and on to Missouri, and take the gospel message to the descendants of the Book of Mormon peoples. If they receive and accept his message, Oliver "shalt cause my church to be established among them" (v. 8). As part of this mission, Oliver "shalt have revelations, but write them not by way of commandment" (v. 8).

Referring back to the false doctrine taught by Hiram Page, the Lord says, "it is not revealed, and no man knoweth where the city Zion shall be built, but it shall be given hereafter. [But] Behold, I say unto you that it shall be on the borders by the Lamanites" (v. 9). The Church would later learn that it would be in Missouri, the area to which Oliver was now called to go.

Oliver was to "settle all these things [the false teachings of Hiram Page], according to the covenants of the church, before thou shalt take thy journey among the Lamanites" (v. 14). And after he departed, it would be "given thee from the time thou shalt go, until the time thou shalt return, what thou shalt do" (v. 15). But in general, he must "open thy mouth at all times, declaring my gospel with the sound of rejoicing" (v. 16).

- **D&C 28:10 They were to convene a conference at which Joseph would preside.** Oliver was not to leave on his mission "until after the conference" that was coming up in September 1830, "and my servant Joseph shall be appointed to preside." And with regard to preaching at that conference, "what he saith to thee thou shalt tell" and nothing more (v. 10).

- **D&C 28:11 Oliver was to correct Hiram Page privately.** Oliver is further instructed to "take thy brother, Hiram Page, between him and thee alone, and tell him that those things which he hath written from that stone are not of me and that Satan deceiveth him" (v. 11). This is consistent with the Lord's later instruction to the Church that whenever we are offended we are to discuss the matter privately with the offender (D&C 42:88). It is generally contrary to the Lord's will that we criticize any individual publicly because that seldom leads to anything but hard feelings. It is interesting that Oliver is the one called to do the correcting, because he had himself been deceived by Hiram Page in this matter. Perhaps in this manner, the Lord allowed Oliver to show his obedience and loyalty while helping his friend.

- **D&C 28:12–16 Satan deceived Hiram Page and gave him false revelations.** Being new to the Church, none of its members were experienced in such matters. The Lord was trying to teach them the correct order of things. With regard to Hiram Page, the Lord said: "these things have not been appointed unto him, neither shall anything be appointed unto any of this church contrary to the church covenants. For all things must be done in order, and by common consent in the church, by the prayer of faith" (vv. 12–13). This is how revelation is to be given to the Church—through proper authority, in a public way with common consent, and consistent with the teachings and covenants of the Church.

The Second Conference of the Church

The second conference of the Church was convened on 26 September 1830, at Fayette, New York. The Prophet Joseph Smith said: "The subject of the stone previously mentioned was discussed, and after considerable investigation, Brother Page, as well as the whole Church who were present, renounced the said stone, and all things connected therewith, much to our mutual satisfaction and happiness."[33]

Elder Joseph Fielding Smith said: "… the Prophet persuaded Oliver Cowdery that these things were wrong, and later the whole membership renounced the revelation given through this stone, but this did not come until the Lord had given to the Church the revelation known as section twenty-eight."[34]

The Spirit of the Lord was strongly felt at the conference and another important revelation was received, D&C 29 on the Second Coming of Christ, our premortal existence, the Fall, and the Atonement. And at the conclusion of the conference, the missionaries to the Lamanites, including Oliver Cowdery, were sent west to teach them the gospel (D&C 30–31).

Notes:

1. *History of the Church*, 1:64.

2. *History of the Church*, 1:64–70.

3. *History of the Church*, 2:62–63.

4. *Answers to Gospel Questions*, comp. Joseph Fielding Smith Jr., 5 vols. [1957–1966], 4:175.

5. "The Peaceable Followers of Christ," *Ensign*, April 1998, 64.

6. John Pratt, "Dating the First Easter: Restoration of Priesthood Keys on April 3, 1836, Part 1," *Ensign*, June 1985, 59–68.

7. *Doctrinal New Testament Commentary*, 3 vols. [1966–1973], 2:422–423.

8. *Mormon Doctrine,* 2nd ed. [1966], 408.

9. *Mormon Doctrine*, 675–676.

10. *Doctrinal New Testament Commentary*, 2:231.

11. *History of the Church*, 1:74–79.

12. *History of the Church*, 1:78–79.

13. In Conference Report, October 1970, 152–53; or *Improvement Era*, December 1970, 126–127.

14. "Fourteen Fundamentals in Following the Prophet," *1980 Devotional Speeches of the Year*, 29.

15. In Conference Report, April 1977, 115; or *Ensign*, May 1977, 78.

16. In Conference Report, April 1978, 117; or *Ensign*, May 1978, 77.

17. *History of the Church*, 1:79–80.

18. *History of the Church*, 1:104.

19. *Doctrine and Covenants Commentary*, ed. [1972], 131–132.

20. *History of the Church*, 1:106–108.

21. *Doctrine and Covenants Commentary*, 572.

22. *Church Educational System manual*, 1979, 443–446.

23. *The Promised Messiah: The First Coming of Christ* (1978), 377–378.

24. "Temple Worship," *The Utah Genealogical and Historical Magazine*, April 1921, 60, 62–64.

25. In *Journal of Discourses*, 18:326.

26. *History of the Church*, 1:108–109.

27. *History of the Church*, 1:105.

28. *History of the Church*, 1:105.

2

9. Lyndon W. Cook, *The Revelations of the Prophet Joseph Smith: A Historical and Biographical Commentary of the Doctrine and Covenants* (1985), 39–40; also Church Archives, Salt Lake City, Utah.

30. *The Historical Background of the Doctrine and Covenants* [1949], 93.

31. *History of the Church*, 1:109–111.

32. *History of the Church*, 1:338.

33. *History of the Church*, 1:115.

34. *Church History and Modern Revelation*, 4 vols. [1946–1949], 1:125.

CHAPTER 10

Revelation to Individuals, Pt. 1: Women's Roles, Pride, and Joy

(D&C 23; 25; 29; 38; 61; 68; 78; 90; 98; 136)
[Topical Chapter]

෧෨෬

INTRODUCTION

During this time in Church History, the Book of Moses was received by revelation, and the New Translation of the Bible began. We will end this chapter with a brief review of these two vital developments.

But first, we will begin this chapter with three important topics, also given by revelation to individuals at this time, that are of great relevance to Saints in every dispensation: the role of women in the kingdom, the curse of pride, and being of good cheer in the midst of sorrow.

"What I Say unto One, I Say unto All"

Elder Jay E. Jensen tells about a time when he was serving as a mission president and found himself frustrated and discouraged at the end of a district conference by the many problems that confronted him. As he was traveling home, he was turning the pages of his scriptures, looking for comfort and direction, when he stopped at the third section of the Doctrine and Covenants and likened what he was reading unto himself.

The Book of Moses was not translated from ancient documents. It was received by direct revelation.

Elder Jensen said: "When I read a verse, I often insert my name in it. I did so with verse 5 and found the help I needed to remove my gloomy feelings: 'Behold, you [Jay Jensen] have been entrusted with these things, but how strict were your commandments; and remember also the promises which were made to you [Jay Jensen]' (D&C 3:5). The words 'remember also the promises' struck me with unusual power… During those four days I had focused on nothing but problems. I had not stopped to consider one single promise."[1]

While that particular revelation, and all the revelations discussed in this chapter, were given to specific individuals, their messages are of universal importance to all Saints— indeed, the Lord has said: "What I say unto one I say unto all" (D&C 61:18, 36; 82:5; 92:1; 93:49). This reinforces the universality of the messages and give us permission to "insert ourselves" into the scriptures, just as Jay Jensen did. Nephi counseled that we should "liken all scriptures unto us, that it might be for our profit and learning" (1 Nephi 19:23; emphasis added). In keeping with that counsel we will consider the messages in this chapter as the Lord's counsel to all of us.

THE ROLE OF WOMEN IN THE KINGDOM

Instructions to Emma Hale Smith
(D&C 25)

When this revelation was given (July 1830), it had been just over three years since the Prophet Joseph Smith and Emma Hale were married. Joseph was 25 years of age and Emma 26. In July of 1830, possibly near her birthday, the Lord gave Emma this revelation through her husband. It is the only revelation in the Doctrine and Covenants that is directed by name to a woman. It is a tender moment in which the blessings of the Almighty were pronounced upon "an elect lady." It also places a sacred commission upon her to teach and lead her sisters in the Church, and in so doing it establishes a pattern for all righteous women to follow.

Emma Hale Smith was the daughter of Isaac and Elizabeth Lewis Hale, and was born July 10, 1804. She married the Prophet in 1827, during the time when he was waiting to receive the Book of Mormon plates and was being taught by the Angel Moroni. She believed the Prophet's testimony, but her parents did not. She was baptized by Oliver Cowdery in June 1830. She endured mobbings and persecution throughout her life, sharing them with her husband. Thus, the calling and counsel given to Emma Smith in this revelation were important, and every promise was fulfilled.[2]

DAGUERROTYPE OF PAINTING BY MAUDSLEY, 1842, NAUVOO

Emma Hale Smith

- **D&C 25:16 This revelation is applicable "unto all," not just to Emma Smith.** Therefore the qualities of an elect lady are of value to all women, for "verily, verily, I say unto you, that this is my voice unto all" (v. 16). Thus, this revelation can be thought of as the Lord's explanation of the role of women throughout the Church.

The Need for Personal Righteousness

● **D&C 25:2 She was to guard her virtue.** The Lord expects His daughters (and His sons) to be "faithful and walk in the paths of virtue before me" (v. 2). The Lord "delight[s] in the chastity of women" (Jacob 2:28) because they are the vessels of life and the guardians of virtue. That society where the daughters of God have become haughty and un-virtuous is not far from becoming "ripened in iniquity." Emma was counseled to maintain her personal righteousness, with the promise that, if she would, the Lord would "preserve thy life, and thou shalt receive an inheritance in Zion" (v. 2).

● **D&C 25:4 She was not to murmur.** Apparently, Emma felt bad about the fact that she had never been permitted to see the plates. Other men and women (Mary Whitmer) had been given this privilege, but not her. The Lord counsels her in this verse to "murmur not because of the things which thou hast not seen, for they are withheld from thee and from the world, which is wisdom in me in a time to come."

Elder Joseph Fielding Smith said: "Emma Smith was human, possessing many of the characteristics which are found in most of us. Being the wife of the man whom the Almighty had blessed, she felt, as most women would have felt under like circumstances, that she was entitled to some special favors. It was difficult for her to understand why she could not view the plates, the Urim and Thummim, and other sacred things, which view had been given to special witnesses. At times this human thought caused her to murmur and ask the question of the Prophet why she was denied this privilege."[3]

● **D&C 25:10 She was to lay aside the things of this world.** The Lord asked her to "lay aside the things of this world, and seek for the things of a better." This counsel had special meaning to her. Throughout her life she never enjoyed a home of her own until they reached Nauvoo. They were forever dependent upon the goodness of friends and of the Saints to see that they had shelter, food, and privacy. No doubt, this lack of a "nest" of her own was a great trial to her. But through all that she suffered while Joseph was alive, she continued faithful and hearkened to the counsel given here.

● **D&C 25:14 She was to beware of pride.** "Continue in the spirit of meekness, and beware of pride," the Lord counsels. Emma's complaints manifested pride, which is defined by President Ezra Taft Benson as when "we are tempted daily to elevate ourselves above others and diminish them (Helaman 6:17; D&C 58:41)."[4] In Emma's case, pride was manifested in her feeling that she, as the wife of the prophet, should be able to see the plates. We do not know for sure, but it would seem likely that there were times when Emma was also bothered by the secondary role she was continually asked to take. She made all the same sacrifices as Joseph, faced all the same trials, and often shared in the labor necessary to organize and bring forward the Church and kingdom. But her contributions were not always appreciated, and that problem remains today, though many are finally recognizing and celebrating her extraordinary life.

● **D&C 25:15 She was to keep the commandments.** Like every other child of God, she was required to "keep my commandments continually." Only by that means can we obtain a "crown of righteousness." We cannot choose to sin and then expect the Lord to overlook it. We must do all in our power to keep the commandments, "And except thou do this, where I am you cannot come."

Emma's Responsibilities to Her Husband and Family

- **D&C 25:5 She was to be a comfort to her husband.** This duty was to be considered an "office of [her] calling" as a woman (v. 5). She was to comfort him "in his afflictions, with consoling words, in the spirit of meekness." This is the duty of every man and woman to his or her spouse.

The Prophet Joseph Smith said, [Wives should treat their husbands] "with mildness and affection. When a man is borne down with trouble, when he is perplexed with care and difficulty, if he can meet a smile instead of an argument or a murmur—if he can meet with mildness, it will calm down his soul and soothe his feelings."[5]

He also taught that, "It is the duty of a husband to love, cherish, and nourish his wife, and cleave unto her and none else; he ought to honor her as himself, and he ought to regard her feelings with tenderness."[6]

As a woman, Emma was blessed with that special nurturing gift that all women possess, and she was counseled to use it to comfort her prophet-husband.

Elder Boyd K. Packer observed:

> The whole physical universe is organized in order that man and woman might fulfill the full measure of their creation. It is a perfect system where delicate balances and counterbalances govern the physical, the emotional, and the spiritual in mankind... The separate natures of man and woman were designed by the Father of us all to fulfill the purposes of the gospel plan. Never can two of the same gender fulfill the commandment to multiply and replenish the earth... Only a woman can bestow upon man that supernal title of father. She in turn becomes a mother. Can anyone dispute that her part is different from and more demanding than his? ... Men and women have complementary, not competing, responsibilities. There is difference but not inequality. Intelligence and talent favor both of them. But in the woman's part, she is not just equal to man; she is superior! She can do that which he can never do; not in all eternity can he do it. There are complementing rewards which are hers and hers alone.[7]

- **D&C 25:6 She was to travel with him as his companion.** Even today, when our prophets and Apostles travel, we often see them take their wives with them. The consolation that comes from the companionship of our spouses cannot be replaced by any other comfort. So, whenever it was possible, Emma was commanded to "go with him at the time of his going."

● **D&C 25:6 She was to assist him in his work.** She was to be his temporary scribe whenever "there is no one to be a scribe for him." Emma was a literate lady, with skills equal to those of any of the most educated of Joseph's associates—Oliver Cowdery, John Whitmer, and others. The Lord expected her to use those talents in support of Joseph's work so that he could send Oliver Cowdery "whithersoever I will" from time to time.

● **D&C 25:14 She was to delight in her husband.** Her focus was to be on her husband. She should "delight" in his accomplishments—the "glory which shall come upon him"—and not allow herself to become resentful or prideful. "Let thy soul delight in thy husband, and the glory which shall come upon him" (v. 14). This is not to say that Emma's only purpose in life was to celebrate her husband's greatness. This revelation is full of instruction as to what other things she could do to bless the kingdom—teaching, preaching, counseling, compiling hymns, etc. But in all of this she was to remember that her primary duty was to her family, as is the case with both men and women.

President David O. McKay said: "Aptly it has been said that, 'Often a woman shapes the career of husband, or brother, or son.' A man succeeds and reaps the honors of public applause, when in truth a quiet little woman has made it all possible—has by her tact and encouragement held him to his best, has had faith in him when his own faith has languished, has cheered him with the unfailing assurance 'you can, you must, you will.'"[8]

Emma's Responsibilities in the Church

● **D&C 25:7 She was set apart to lead the sisters.** She was to be "ordained," that is, set apart, by Joseph to (1) expound scripture, and (2) exhort the Church as inspired by the Spirit. This applied particularly to her duties in the Relief Society, but also to her role in the community and among all her fellow members.

● **D&C 25:8 She was to devote herself to writing and learning.** This not only permitted her to further develop her intellectual and writing skills, but it blessed the lives of her family and the Church. Sometimes she was the only person available to serve as scribe to the Prophet. And her letters, hymns, and other writings remain among the most cherished we have in the Church today. This assignment was also part of her Church calling, because the Lord instructed that Joseph was to "lay his hands upon thee, and thou shalt receive the Holy Ghost" in support of this work.

● **D&C 25:11–12 She was to assemble a book of hymns.** The Lord recognized her talent and

spiritual sensitivity when He gave her the privilege of making "a selection of sacred hymns, as it shall be given thee, which is pleasing unto me, to be had in my church" (v. 11). This assignment could have been given to a number of other men or women who were equally talented in music. But the Lord wanted Emma to do it.

Emma was well suited for this calling to assemble hymns since she had a very fine singing voice. Emma worked on the hymn book prior to its publication in Kirtland in 1835. It was not published until then due to the destruction of the printing press in 1832. It contained a preface written by W. W. Phelps and 90 hymns. At least 42 of the hymns had appeared earlier in Church periodicals. Only the words were printed; no music was included. She selected some popular hymns of the day and new hymns by Latter-day Saints. Of the total, 34 were authored by Mormons: 26 by W. W. Phelps, 3 by Parley Pratt, 1 by Thomas B. Marsh and Parley Pratt, and 1 each by Eliza R. Snow, Edward Partridge, Philo Dibble, and William C. Gregg.

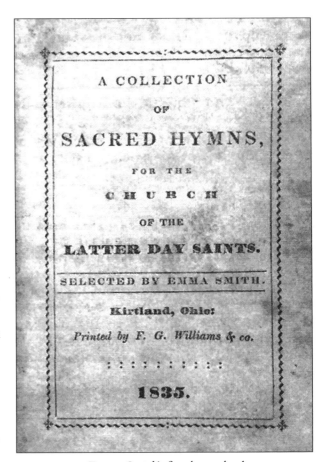

Emma Smith's first hymn book

The Lord loves music. He sang hymns with His disciples, including on the night when He went into Gethsemane to suffer beyond measure (Matthew 26:30; Mark 14:26). "For my soul delighteth in the song of the heart," He affirms in this revelation to Emma, "yea, the song of the righteous is a prayer unto me, and it shall be answered with a blessing upon their heads" (v. 12).

The Lord loves it when we sing and wants us to do so in just about every Church meeting we convene. I never start a gospel lesson without first playing sacred music, because it invites the Holy Spirit like nothing else can ever do. Some say, "Oh, but I can't sing. It's embarrassing when you can't carry a tune." I believe that it doesn't matter. Don't we all smile and feel good when our little ones get up on special days and sing to us in our sacrament meetings? Many of them can't sing, either. But we find it adorable, and our hearts are touched. It's not about the musicality. It's about the sweet spirit of children singing praises to their God, their Lord, and their families. That, my brothers and sisters, is how the Lord views us when we sing. We are His precious children, and He wants to hear us sing. And when we do, He promises to listen and answer the words of the hymns with blessings upon our heads, just as if they had been a personal prayer.

The First Presidency has said: "Inspirational music is an essential part of our church meetings. The hymns invite the Spirit of the Lord, create a feeling of reverence, unify us as members, and provide a way for us to offer praises to the Lord. Some of the greatest sermons are preached by the singing of hymns. Hymns move us to repentance and good works, build testimony and faith, comfort the weary, console the mourning, and inspire us to endure to the end."[9]

Elder Dallin H. Oaks said: "I stopped at a … ward meetinghouse and slipped unnoticed into the overflow area just as the congregation was beginning to sing… As we sang, … I glanced around at members of the congregation and was stunned to observe that about a third of them were not singing. How could this be? … What are we saying, what are we thinking, when we fail to join in singing in our worship services? I believe some of us … are getting neglectful in our worship, including the singing of hymns."[10]

Emma Smith Was an "Elect Lady"

● **D&C 25:3 She was an "elect lady" with a purpose and calling in the kingdom.** Emma was raised up by the Lord to be the earthly and eternal companion of His restoration prophet. She was no ordinary woman. At this moment of blessing, the Lord forgave Emma of her sins and called her "an elect lady, whom I have called" (v. 3). Every woman in the Church has gifts that can bless the lives of those around them. If they use these gifts in their callings, and if they make and keep the necessary sacred covenants, they too can become "elect" and worthy of "an inheritance in Zion" (v. 2).

Elder Bruce R. McConkie said: "An elect lady is a female member of the Church who has already received, or who through obedience is qualified to receive, the fulness of gospel blessings. This includes temple endowments, celestial marriage, and the fulness of the sealing power. She is one who has been elected or chosen by faithfulness as a daughter of God in this life, an heir of God, a member of His household. Her position is comparable to that of the elders who magnify their callings in the priesthood and thereby receive all that the Father hath (D&C 84:38)."[11]

Elder Boyd K. Packer reminds us, "[The gospel ordinances are] bestowed impartially upon man and woman alike… And the highest ordinances in the House of the Lord [are received] together and equally or not at all!"[12] Thus, an elect man like Joseph Smith needs an elect lady like Emma in order to be exalted.

"Oh," some will say, "but she did not remain faithful to the end!" I believe that she did. Yes, she struggled with polygamy. So did my own great-great-grandmother, but I do not love her less when I consider all the sacrifices she made for this work. While others like Oliver Cowdery, Martin Harris, David Whitmer, and many more apostatized when the trials became too much for them, Emma Smith fulfilled all her duties toward her husband and the Church with humility and distinction throughout her married life. She accepted her role with humility and faith, asking nothing special of anyone and constantly administering to the needs of others both inside and outside of her home.

These characteristics continued even after the death of Joseph. After she married Lewis Bidamon, he eventually became unfaithful to her. He fathered a child with a young woman in the city and then abandoned both Emma and the new mother and child. When Emma became aware of the circumstance, she adopted the young child and raised it to maturity. She also hired the mother as her servant so that she could live under the same roof as her baby. Such was the charity of Emma Smith, even when she herself was in pain.

Lucy Mack Smith said: "I have never seen a woman in my life, who would endure every species of fatigue and hardship, from month to month, and from year to year, with that unflinching courage, zeal, and patience, which she has ever done; for I know that which she has had to endure… She has breasted the storms of persecution, and buffeted the rage of men and devils, which would have borne down almost any other woman."[13]

"Oh," some continue to argue, "but Joseph said he would have to go into hell to rescue Emma." He most decidedly did not say this. Benjamin Johnson recorded in his journal what the prophet actually said, as quoted here by Truman G. Madsen:

"FAMILY VISIT TO LIBERTY JAIL." ©JOSEPH BRICKEY, USED BY PERMISSION

"On a Sunday, a beautiful day … they were sitting in the dining room and in came two of his [Joseph and Emma's] children 'as just from their mother, all so nice, bright and sweet.' Joseph said, 'Benjamin, look at these children. How could I help loving their mother; if necessary, I would go to hell for such a woman.' There is the truth about the legend that has grown up [about Joseph going to hell to get Emma out]. Joseph Smith, so far as the evidence leads, never said (a) 'Emma is going to hell,' or (b) 'I'm going to go to dig her out.' He said, 'I would go to hell for such a woman,' meaning, 'I feel strongly and deeply toward my wife.' The distinction is clear."[14]

Joseph loved Emma and his children

The Lord told Joseph on more than one occasion that whatever he prayed for he would receive, and the examples of this promise being literally fulfilled are too numerous to repeat here. But of particular interest while we are on the subject of Emma and the Prophet's children is the following request the Prophet made during the Kirtland temple dedicatory prayer: "Have mercy, O Lord, upon [my] wife and children, that they may be exalted in thy presence, and preserved by thy fostering hand" (D&C 109:69).

The Prophet Joseph Smith himself made it clear how he felt about her when they were reunited in Illinois after his escape from Liberty Jail: "My beloved Emma … even the wife of my youth, and the choice of my heart. Many were the reverberations of my mind when I contemplated for a moment the many scenes we had been called to pass through, the fatigues and the toils, the sorrows and sufferings, and the joys and consolations, from time to time, which had strewed our paths and crowned our board. Oh what a commingling of thought filled my mind for the moment, again she is here, even in the seventh trouble—undaunted, firm, and unwavering — unchangeable, affectionate Emma!"[15]

Can there be any doubt when reading this that the Prophet Joseph Smith loved Emma? And I wonder, when we criticize Emma, if we do not offend the Prophet deeply. I do not believe we can love the Prophet and hate his sweetheart. The early members in Utah were stung by her decision to stay in Nauvoo, near the grave of her husband and in the only home she had ever possessed. I know full well that other women paid a similar price and went west. Some of them were my own grandmothers. But I will not judge Emma. I love and respect her, and look forward, perhaps someday, to meeting her. She was, and is in my eyes, an elect lady.

THE CURSE OF PRIDE

One of the warnings that the Lord gave to Emma Smith was to "beware of pride" (D&C 25:14). Anybody who has read the Book of Mormon knows how deadly pride can be. The Nephites and the Jaredites engaged in continuous cycles of pride, which always lead to their sorrow and destruction. And in our day and age, it is no different. On the occasion when he was announced as the new president of the Church, when asked what he thought was the greatest problem in the world, President Ezra Taft Benson answered simply, "Pride." He later expanded on this theme with an entire conference address in April 1986 on the topic of pride. Following are some of those teachings, as they explain various revelations in the Doctrine and Covenants on the subject of pride.

- **What Is Pride?** President Ezra Taft Benson said: "Most of us think of pride as self-centeredness, conceit, boastfulness, arrogance, or haughtiness. All of these are elements of the sin, but the heart, or core, is still missing. The central feature of pride is enmity—enmity toward God and enmity toward our fellowmen. Enmity means 'hatred toward, hostility to, or a state of opposition.'"[16]

President Benson also said: "In the scriptures there is no such thing as righteous pride. It is always considered as a sin. We are not speaking of a wholesome view of self-worth, which is best established by a close relationship with God. But we are speaking of pride as the universal sin, as someone has described it. Mormon writes that 'the pride of this nation, or the people of the Nephites, hath proven their destruction' (Moroni 8:27). The Lord says in the Doctrine and Covenants, 'Beware of pride, lest ye become as the Nephites of old' (D&C 38:39). Essentially, pride is a 'my will' rather than 'thy will' approach to life. The opposite of pride is humbleness, meekness, submissiveness, or teachableness (Alma 13:28)."[17]

Specific Revelations on Pride

- **D&C 25:14 To Emma Smith on resentment.** The Lord counseled, "continue in the spirit of meekness, and beware of pride. Let thy soul delight in thy husband, and the glory which shall come upon him." This, at a time when Emma was feeling resentful that she had been passed over when others were allowed to see the plates. President Ezra Taft Benson said: "Pride is the great stumbling block to Zion… Pride is ugly. It says, 'If you succeed, I am a failure.'… Pride is essentially competitive in nature… Once the element of competition has gone, pride has gone."[18] Emma's focus needed to be outward —toward Joseph— and not inward toward herself.

Emma Hale Smith

- **D&C 23:1 To Oliver Cowdery on self-centeredness and jealousy.** The Lord called Oliver "blessed, and … under no condemnation" at that time (April 1830). But He cautioned him, "Beware of pride, lest thou shouldst enter into temptation." Who but God could know at this early time that pride would prove to be the downfall of this chosen "second elder" of the Church? Being second was not always sufficient, and he chaffed at having to recognize Joseph's authority over him. It would become his own great stumbling block, because the Lord has declared that "no one can assist in the work except he shall be humble and full of love, having faith, hope, and charity, being temperate in all things, whatsoever shall be entrusted to his care" (D&C 12:8).

As one of Satan's greatest tools, pride causes us to center so much attention on ourselves that we become insensitive to God and our fellow beings. "Pride does not look up to God and care about what is right. It looks sideways to man and argues who is right. Pride is manifest in the spirit of contention… Pride is characterized by 'What do I want out of life?' rather than by 'What would God have me do with my life?' It is self-will as opposed to God's will. It is the fear of man over the fear of God."[19]

Oliver Cowdery

- **D&C 38:39 To the Saints on coveting their riches.** President Benson identified selfishness as one of the more common faces of pride, resulting in self-conceit, self-pity, worldly self-fulfillment, self-gratification, self-seeking, and contention. At their final conference of the Church in Fayette, New York, in 1831, the Saints were anxious to learn more about the move to Ohio that had been commanded in the revelation now known as D&C 37. For many of them, this was a sore trial, having to sell or abandon their properties and gather to another state. The Lord admonished them, "if ye seek the riches which it is the will of the Father to give unto you, ye shall be the richest of all people, for ye shall have the riches of eternity." But that was not the kind of riches that concerned them. How could they simply pull up stakes, and how would they fare in the new and more remote territory of Ohio? "… the riches of the earth are mine to give," the Lord reminded them, "but beware of pride, lest ye become as the Nephites of old."

There is a clear connection between riches and pride, and the early Saints struggled with them both. There was far too much covetousness and competition among the Saints, both in Kirtland and Missouri—so much so that the Lord eventually denied them their inheritances in Zion.

● **D&C 90:17 To the First Presidency of the Church on high-mindedness.** On the occasion of his selecting and ordaining his counselors in the First Presidency, Joseph Smith received a revelation concerning the expectations of the Saints and their leaders. "Be not ashamed, neither confounded" the Lord advised. They should maintain a healthy degree of self-confidence. "But be admonished in all your high-mindedness and pride, for it bringeth a snare upon your souls." It could be a heady experience to be called into leadership of the kingdom in those days. It still is today. But they were to think of themselves as servants and not as rulers. Both of these once-good men— Sidney Rigdon and Frederick G. Williams—would eventually apostatize because of their pride. Of one brother, the Lord said: "I, the Lord, am not well pleased with him, for he seeketh to excel, and he is not sufficiently meek before me" (D&C 58:41).

Sidney Rigdon

● **D&C 98:19–20 To the Saints in Kirtland on their unwillingness to repent.** The Lord warns in this revelation, given in Kirtland on August 6, 1833, that He was "not well pleased with many who are in the church at Kirtland; For they do not forsake their sins, and their wicked ways, the pride of their hearts, and their covetousness… " This would eventually lead to the great apostasy at Kirtland, where as many as 1/3 of the Saints left the Church after they lost their money when the bank failed. Joseph had been warning for months about the spirit of speculation in land sales, the covetousness among the Saints, and the dishonesty of those who operated the bank. But they would not hearken to "the words of wisdom and eternal life" which the Lord and their Prophet had given them, and they ended up with neither temporal nor spiritual riches.

Frederick G. Williams

President Ezra Taft Benson said: "Pride is essentially competitive in nature. We pit our will against God's … in the spirit of 'my will and not thine be done.'… Our will in competition to God's will allows desires, appetites, and passions to go unbridled (Alma 38:12; 3 Nephi 12:30)… Our enmity toward God takes on many labels, such as rebellion, hard-heartedness, stiff-neckedness, unrepentant, puffed up, easily offended, and sign seekers. The proud wish God would agree with them. They aren't interested in changing their opinions to agree with God's."[20]

Solutions for Pride

President Benson said: "The antidote for pride is humility—meekness, submissiveness (Alma 7:23). It is the broken heart and contrite spirit... We can choose to humble ourselves by loving God, submitting our will to His, and putting Him first in our lives.²1 The following are some of the solutions for pride and the blessings that result from doing them.

- **D&C 1:28 Humility.** Those who choose to be humble are "made strong, and blessed from on high, and receive knowledge from time to time." Elder Bruce R. McConkie said: "As spoken of in the revelations, pride is the opposite of humility. It is inordinate self- esteem arising because of one's position, achievements, or possessions; and it has the effect of centering a person's heart on the things of the world rather than the things of the Spirit (1 John 2:15–17). As humility, which is an attribute of godliness possessed by true Saints, leads to salvation, so pride, which is of the devil, leads to damnation (2 Nephi 28:15). 'God resisteth the proud, but giveth grace unto the humble' (James 4:6; 1 Peter 5:5)."²²

- **D&C 19:23 Obedience.** Those who "Learn of [Him], and listen to [His] words" and then do the things they are commanded "in the meekness of [His] Spirit" will have "peace in [Him]." President Benson said: "The proud are not easily taught. (1 Ne. 15:3, 7–11). They won't change their minds to accept truths, because to do so implies they have been wrong."²³

- **D&C 112:10 Prayer.** Those who pray in humility are promised that "the Lord thy God shall lead thee by the hand, and give thee answer to thy prayers." The Lord counseled us to "watch and pray always lest ye enter into temptation; for Satan desireth to have you, that he may sift you as wheat" (3 Ne. 18:18). Prayer is the method by which we can acknowledge our need for and relationship to our Father in Heaven. He already knows what we need; we are not informing Him, we are asking Him to help us. And when we do this, He has promised us the strength to meet any challenge that may cross our paths.

  President Gordon B. Hinckley said: "Be prayerful. You can't do it alone. You know that. You cannot make it alone and do your best. You need the help of the Lord ... and the marvelous thing is that you have the opportunity to pray, with the expectation that your prayers will be heard and answered ... The marvelous thing about prayer is that it is personal, it's individual, it's something that no one else gets into, in terms of your speaking with your Father in Heaven in the name of the Lord Jesus Christ. Be prayerful. Ask the Lord to forgive your sins. Ask the Lord for help. Ask the Lord to bless you. Ask the Lord to help you realize your righteous ambitions ... Ask the Lord for all of the important things that mean so much to you in your lives. He stands ready to help. Don't ever forget it."²⁴

- **D&C 124:97 The Holy Spirit.** William Law was admonished to be "humble" and "without guile." Those who do this will "receive of my Spirit, even the Comforter, which shall manifest unto him the truth of all things, and shall give him, in the very hour, what he shall say." Elder James E. Faust said: "With faith in the Lord and humility, a priesthood leader may confidently expect divine assistance in his problems... Brethren, we can learn, we can study, we can comprehend the basic things we need to know as members of God's holy priesthood. We can learn the giant truths and teach them with intelligence and understanding to those who come to learn. We can also lean upon the strengths of others whose talents are greater than our own."[25]

"REJOICE, AND BE OF GOOD CHEER"

● **D&C 25:13 Because of "the covenants which thou hast made."** Emma Smith and most of the early Saints had reason to be discouraged at times. They made great sacrifices and sometimes did not obtain all of the blessings they longed for. Their patience and faith were severely tried. Yet, in the midst of such tribulation, the Lord advised her to "lift up thy heart and rejoice." How? He suggests one answer: "cleave unto the covenants which thou has made."

When we think of the early pioneers of this dispensation, we think of a people who were undaunted by the severe hardships they faced. Nothing could stop them; they kept on moving through rain and mud and winter storms, burying their loved ones along the way. My own great-great-grandfather William Draper explained why in his journal. It was their temple covenants which they had received before leaving Nauvoo. They knew who they were. They knew what God had promised them, worlds without end. Whatever hardships might come their way, they were sure of the ultimate triumph of right and of their place in the eternal worlds. They labored hard to finish the temple so that they might make these covenants with their God before leaving to go westward.

By the time the Nauvoo temple was dedicated on May 1, 1846, more than 6,000 men and women had received those covenants. And over the months that followed, President Brigham Young charged them, "Let the fire of the covenant which you made in the House of the Lord, burn in your hearts, like a flame unquenchable."[26] The promises we have secured for ourselves and our posterity through our covenants should give us great and unquenchable joy.

● **D&C 29:5 Because the Lord is with us.** To the Prophet Joseph Smith and others the Lord said: "Lift up your hearts and be glad, for I am in your midst … " The Savior is in our midst more often than we imagine. And even when He is not physically present, He is aware of our personal circumstances and ministers to our needs, because He loves us.

In the first meeting the Prophet Joseph Smith held in Kirtland in 1831, Mary Elizabeth Rollins Lightner reports:

> He stood some moments looking over the congregation as if to pierce each heart, then said: "Do you know who has been in your midst this night?" One of the Smiths said, "An angel of the Lord." Joseph did not answer. Martin Harris was sitting at the prophet's feet on a box. He slid to his knees, clasped his arms around the Prophet's knees and said, "I know, it was our Lord and Savior, Jesus Christ." Joseph put his hand on Martin's head and answered, "Martin, God revealed that to you. Brothers and Sisters, the Savior has been in your midst this night. I want you all to remember it. There is a veil over your eyes, for you could not endure to look upon Him. You must be fed with milk and not strong meat. I want you to remember this as if it were the last thing that escaped my lips."[27]

Mary Elizabeth Rollins Lightner (1818-1913)

- **D&C 29:5 Because of the Atonement.** To the Prophet Joseph Smith and others the Lord also said: "Lift up your hearts and be glad, for I … am your advocate with the Father … " Because of the Atonement we will be saved and enjoy the fruits of exaltation, so long as we remain faithful to the end. What greater cause for joy can there be? Elder Jeffrey R. Holland once called the Atonement "The central fact, the crucial foundation, the chief doctrine, and the greatest expression of divine love in the eternal plan of salvation—truly a 'plan of happiness.'"[28] By means of this free gift, we are freed from physical death and can be free from spiritual death as well. That is the "good news" of the gospel. In the words of Moroni, "By Adam came the fall of man. And because of the fall of man came Jesus Christ, … and because of Jesus Christ came the redemption of man. And because of the redemption of man, … they are brought back into the presence of the Lord" (Mormon 9:12–13).

- **D&C 29:5 Because we are in the Church of Jesus Christ and part of His kingdom.** To the Prophet Joseph Smith and others the Lord said: "Lift up your hearts and be glad," for "it is his [God the Father's] good will to give you the kingdom." I testify to you that this is the Church of the Living Christ, and that we are in it. Where else would we want to be in these troublous days? God has given us His kingdom and all of its attendant blessings and privileges. This should bring us great happiness and peace.

  President Gordon B. Hinckley said: "So undergirded beneath and fitly framed above, this Church stands as the creation of the Almighty. It is a shelter from the storms of life. It is a refuge of peace for those in distress. It is a house of succor for those in need. It is the conservator of eternal truth and the teacher of the divine will. It is the true and living Church of the Master."[29] "May you look upon the Church as your great and good friend, your refuge when the world appears to be closing around you, your hope when things are dark, your pillar of fire by night and your cloud by day as you thread the pathways of your lives."[30]

- **D&C 61:36 Because the Lord has not forsaken us and never will.** He addresses us as "little children" as a term of endearment—He loves us like we love little children. But we are also "little children" in our understanding of things. "Be of good cheer, little children," He says, "for I am in your midst, and I have not forsaken you."

  When we are tempted to think that we have been abandoned in our troubles, we might consider the metaphors the Lord Himself has used to assure us that this is not true. Through Isaiah the Lord asked, "Can a woman forget her sucking child?" Well, it is more likely that she would forget her nursing infant than that the Lord will forget us (Isaiah 49:15). Then He offers an even more profound reminder of why He cannot and will not forget us: "I have graven thee upon the palms of my hands [and] thy walls are continually before me" (Isaiah 49:16). With His atonement and crucifixion, the Lord did indeed carve our sorrows into the palms of His hands. And having experienced those sins, sufferings, sorrows, and disappointments for us even before we had to suffer them, our "walls" (circumstances) are truly always of concern to Him. He is a loving, caring, compassionate friend to all of us.

  Elder Marvin J. Ashton said: "None of us will escape tragedy and suffering. Each of us will probably react differently. However, if we can recall the Lord's promise, 'for I the Lord am with you,' we will be able to face our problems with dignity and courage. We will find the strength to be of good cheer instead of becoming resentful, critical, or defeated. We will be able to meet life's unpleasant happenings with clear vision, strength, and power… What a joy it is to see someone of good cheer, who, when others because of an unpleasant happening or development live in angry silence or vocal disgust, meets the situation with cheerful endurance and good spirits."[31]

- **D&C 68:6 Because we are privileged to be the witnesses of Christ in these last days.** To Orson Hyde, Luke S. Johnson, Lyman E. Johnson, and William E. McLellin the Lord said: "be of good cheer, and do not fear, for I the Lord am with you, and will stand by you; and ye shall bear record of me … " The witness He wishes us to bear is that "I [Jesus Christ] am the Son of the living God, that I was, that I am, and that I am to come." This is the missionary spirit. President Ezra Taft Benson said: "Missionary work provides us the happiest years of our lives. I know whereof I speak. I have tasted the joy of missionary work. There is no work in all the world that can bring an individual greater joy and happiness."[32]

- **D&C 78:18 Because the Lord will lead us along through things we "cannot bear."** The Lord acknowledges that we are weak and that we "cannot bear all things now." That is why a Savior was needed in the Lord's plan—to save God's imperfect children. Yet, despite our weaknesses, we can "be of good cheer, for I will lead you along." Though we may sometimes feel overwhelmed, we can know that "the Lord will bless us with the strength to weather every storm and continue to move forward through every adversity."[33]

Elder Neal A. Maxwell said: "God carefully scales 'all these things,' since we cannot bear all things now. He has told us: 'Behold, ye are little children and ye cannot bear all things now; ye must grow in grace and in the knowledge of the truth' (D&C 50:40)… The thermostat on the furnace of affliction [is not] set too high for us—though clearly we may think so at the time. Our God is a refining God who has been tempering soul- steel for a very long time. He knows when the right edge has been put upon our excellence and also when there is more in us than we have yet given. One day we will praise God for taking us near to our limits—as He did His Only Begotten in Gethsemane and Calvary."[34]

- **D&C 136:29 Because through prayer we can obtain peace and joy.** At Winter Quarters, the
Saints languished under a severe winter. They had already suffered through the rain and mud and deaths of the pioneer trail through Iowa. Now, they hunkered down in tents and cabins while the snow drifts piled up around them. They had every reason to be depressed, and no doubt many of them had turned to the Lord for help. In answer, the Lord gave a revelation to President Brigham Young that said, among other things, "If thou art sorrowful, call on the Lord thy God with supplication, that your souls may be joyful."

Elder Marvin J. Ashton said: "Sometimes we are given crosses so we can be taught to pray. Crosses become lighter and more manageable when we learn to pray and when we learn to patiently wait for the answers to our prayers."[35] And President James E. Faust said: "Of all that we might do to find solace, prayer is perhaps the most comforting. We are instructed to pray to the Father in the name of His Son, the Lord Jesus Christ, by the power of the Holy Ghost. The very act of praying to God is satisfying to the soul, even though God, in His wisdom, may not give what we ask for. President Harold B. Lee taught us that all of our prayers are answered, but sometimes the Lord says no. The Prophet Joseph Smith taught that the 'best way to obtain truth and wisdom' is 'to go to God in prayer.' Prayer is most helpful in the healing process."[36]

NEW SCRIPTURES ARE REVEALED TO BLESS THE SAINTS

During a short period of time after the establishment of the Church, the Prophet Joseph Smith was an instrument in restoring one book of ancient scripture and in editing another. In the summer of 1830, he received the Book of Moses by revelation. And at the same time he began a lifelong assignment to correct the errors in the Bible through careful study and inspired revision. Seventy-seven of the revelations in the Doctrine and Covenants were received during the three-year period when the Prophet was translating the Bible. The experience provided a systematic approach to learning gospel truths, and led the Prophet to ask concerning many things that were subsequently explained through revelation.

A full explanation of these scriptures is not included here. The Book of Moses will be covered in chapter 12 and the New Translation of the Bible in chapter 13. But it is important to note that both of these new revelations began at this period of time.

On 8 October 1829 Joseph Smith and Oliver Cowdery purchased a large pulpit-style edition of the King James Bible (containing the Old and New Testaments and the Apocrypha) from E. B. Grandin in Palmyra, New York for $3.75. It was this Bible which was used in the translation.

The first date recorded in the New Translation was June 1830. The Prophet Joseph Smith said: "Amid all the trials and tribulations we had to wade through, the Lord, who well knew our infantile and delicate situation, vouchsafed for us a supply of strength, and granted us 'line upon line of knowledge—here a little and there a little,' of which the following was a precious morsel."[37] Joseph then recorded "selections from the Book of Moses" (Moses 1), the "words of God, which he spake unto Moses at a time when Moses was caught up into an exceedingly high mountain" (v. 1).

- **D&C 26:1 A commandment to study the scriptures.** This message, given in July 1830, was essentially the beginning of the Prophet's gospel study program. Joseph Smith and Sidney Rigdon continued their study of the book of Genesis for many months, and thereafter were commanded to revise selections in both the Old and New Testaments.

Notes:

1. In Conference Report, October 1992, 112; or *Ensign*, November 1992, 80.

2. *Church History and Modern Revelation*, 4 vols. [1946–1949], 1:117.

3. *Church History and Modern Revelation*, 1:125.

4. In Conference Report, April 1989, 4–5; or Ensign, May 1989, 4–6.

5. *Teachings of the Prophet Joseph Smith*, sel. Joseph Fielding Smith [1976], 228.

6. *Elders' Journal of the Church of Latter-day Saints*, Volume 1, Number 4, vol. 1 (October 1837–August 1838), Far West, Missouri, August, 1838, Whole No. 4, 61.

7. "A Tribute to Women," *Ensign*, July 1989, 73–74.

8. "President David O. McKay, 1873–1970," *Improvement Era*, Feb. 1970, 14.

9. *First Presidency Preface, Hymns*, 1985, ix.

10. *Ensign*, November 1994, 11.

11. *Mormon Doctrine*, 2nd ed. [1966], 217.

12. "A Tribute to Women," 74.

13. Lucy Mack Smith, *History of Joseph Smith*, ed. Preston Nibley [1958], 190–191.

14. *Joseph Smith:* The Prophet, 64–65, citing from The Benjamin F. Johnson Letter to George S. Gibbs, [pamphlet, copied from typescript of original 1903 letter, (1968), 4.

15. *History of the Church*, 5:107.

16. In Conference Report, April 1989, 3; or *Ensign*, May 1989, 4.

17. In Conference Report, April 1986; or *Ensign*, May 1986, 6.

18. "Beware of Pride," in Conference Report, April 1989; or *Ensign*, May 1989, 4–6.

19. Ezra Taft Benson, in Conference Report, April 1986, *Ensign*, May 1986, 6–7.

20. In Conference Report, April 1989, 4; or *Ensign*, May 1989, 4.

21. In Conference Report, April 1989, 6; or *Ensign*, May 1989, 6–7.

22. *Mormon Doctrine*, 593.

23. "Beware of Pride," 6.

24. Colorado Springs Young Adult Meeting, April 14, 1996, in *Teachings of Gordon B. Hinckley* [1997], 468.

25. "These I Will Make My Leaders," *Ensign*, November 1980, 35–36.

26. *Journal History of The Church of Jesus Christ of Latter-day Saints*, Sept. 28, 1846, 5.

27. "The Life and Testimony of Mary Lightner," 55–57, in Jack M. Lyon, Jay A. Parry, and Linda R. Gundry, eds., *Best-Loved Stories of the LDS People*, vol. 2 (1999), 404.

28. *Christ and the New Covenant: The Messianic Message of the Book of Mormon*, [1997], 197.

29. *Ensign*, February 2004, 7.

30. *Ensign*, November 1997, 52.

31. In Conference Report, April 1986, 84–85; or *Ensign*, May 1986, 66.

32. *Come unto Christ*, [1983], 95.

33. Gordon B. Hinckley, "Five Million Members—A Milestone and Not a Summit," *Ensign*, May 1982, 46.

34. *All These Things Shall Give Thee Experience* [1979], 44, 46.

35. *Be of Good Cheer*, [1987], 36.

36. *Finding Light in a Dark World*, [1995], 30–31.

37. *History of the Church*, 1:98.

Revelation to Individuals, Pt. 2: Missionary Work and New Converts

(D&C 4; 11–12; 14–16; 18; 30–36)
[1829–1830]

୨୦୦୯

INTRODUCTION

"What I Say unto One, I Say unto All"

The years 1829–1831 were a time of great persecution for the Church, especially in the Harmony and Colesville areas. It was under these trying conditions that the Saints received many important revelations to individuals regarding missionary work and the duties of new converts. While these revelations were given to specific individuals, their messages are of universal importance to all Saints—indeed, the Lord has said: "What I say unto one I say unto all" (D&C 61:18, 36; 82:5; 92:1; 93:49).

- **D&C 6, 11, 12, 14 Similar counsel.** The Lord gave identical counsel to a number of people, thereby giving even greater emphasis to the universality of His words.

  — D&C 6:1–9 to Oliver Cowdery is identical to   D&C 11:1–9—to Hyrum Smith.
  — D&C 6:1–5 to Oliver Cowdery is identical to   D&C 12:1–5—to Joseph Knight Sr.
                                         and   D&C 14:1–5—to David Whitmer.

A Summary of Individual Revelations

- **Those who wished to assist with the work:**

— D&C 4	given to	Joseph Smith Sr., the Prophet's father	February 1829
— D&C 11	given to	Hyrum Smith, the Prophet's brother	May 1829
— D&C 12	given to	Joseph Knight Sr.	May 1829
— D&C 14–16	given to	David, John, and Peter Whitmer	June 1829
— D&C 18	given to	Oliver Cowdery and David Whitmer	June 1829

- **The first missionaries went forth, including an important mission to the Lamanites:**

  — D&C 30   given to   David, Peter, and John Whitmer   September 1830
  — D&C 32   given to   Parley P. Pratt and Ziba Peterson   October 1830

- **Revelations to new converts:**

  — D&C 31   given to   Thomas B. Marsh   September 1830
  — D&C 33   given to   Ezra Thayre and Northrop Sweet   October 1830
  — D&C 34   given to   Orson Pratt   November 1830
  — D&C 35   given to   Sydney Rigdon   December 1830
  — D&C 36   given to   Edward Partridge   December 1830

INSTRUCTIONS TO INDIVIDUALS WISHING TO ASSIST IN THE WORK

Though it precedes D&C 10 in the Doctrine and Covenants, D&C 4 was actually received later. The sections of the Doctrine and Covenants are not inserted chronologically. If we look at the headings for D&C 3, D&C 4, and D&C 10, we note the following:

— D&C 3 was given in July 1828.
— D&C 10 was given in September of 1828, though this fact was missed in versions of the Doctrine and Covenants prior to 1921.
— D&C 4, the revelation to Joseph Smith Sr., came after D&C 10 in February 1829.
— D&C 5–9 were all given in March and April of 1829.

We can conclude, therefore, that the next revelation Joseph Smith received after the scolding he received in D&C 3 was the revelation contained in D&C 10. Both of them occurred in the summer of 1828. He then took some time off, at the suggestion of the Lord (D&C 10:4), and the next revelation he received was this one to his father in February 1829.

A Revelation to Joseph Smith Sr.

(D&C 4)

After Joseph Smith re-obtained the plates, he did immediately begin translating. In order to support his family, he worked on the small farm he had purchased from Emma's father.

Worried about their son, Joseph's parents came to visit him in February of 1829. Knowing prophetically that they were coming, Joseph went out to meet them. Joseph's father wanted to know what he could do to help his son. Joseph inquired of the Lord and received this revelation (D&C 4). This is the first revelation received by Joseph that was on behalf of another individual. Many more would follow. But it seems appropriate that this should be the first, since Joseph Smith Sr. was the first person to believe the story of the Prophet and encouraged him to be faithful to the instructions of Moroni.

As Hyrum M. Smith and Janne M. Sjodahl put it, "Joseph Smith Sr., this God's nobleman, did not scoff; he was not even impatient. He listened reverently to the wonderful story told by his boy, and then, his mind enlightened by a flash of intelligence from the divine Spirit of truth, he declared that the message was from God, and counseled Joseph to do as the angel had commanded him. Now Joseph Smith Sr., came to Harmony, Pa., where his son Joseph had taken refuge on account of persecution by the mob in the State of New York. He came, undoubtedly, to learn more of the work, to the divinity of which he had already borne testimony. Then the Prophet received this Revelation for his beloved father."[1]

Joseph Smith, Sr.

Soon after this revelation was given, Joseph Smith Sr. became one of the eight witnesses to the Book of Mormon when he was shown the plates by his son Joseph. He was baptized by his son on the day the Church was organized, April 6, 1830. He became the first Patriarch to the Church on December 18, 1833 in Kirtland, Ohio. He became an assistant counselor in the First Presidency in 1837. He died in Nauvoo in 1840 as a result of the exposure he had suffered in Missouri, making him a martyr for the cause of truth.

Even though this revelation was given for the Prophet's father, it is addressed to all people who would serve God. Elder Joseph Fielding Smith pointed out that while "this revelation is very short, only seven verses, … it contains sufficient counsel and instruction for a lifetime of study. No one has yet mastered it." Elder Smith says it is intended for "each member of the Church, especially to all who hold the Priesthood." It succinctly lists the qualification of members of the Church who desire to serve God, yet these instructions are "as broad, as high and as deep as eternity."[2]

● **D&C 4 The revelation to Joseph Smith Sr.** The Lord tells Joseph's father that a great and marvelous work is beginning, and those who desire to work for this cause must serve God with all their hearts, might, mind and strength (v. 2). If we desire to serve God in this manner, we are "called to the work" (v. 3).

At this, the dawn of the restoration, the Lord observed in D&C 4 that "the field" [world] is "white already to harvest" (v. 4). This metaphor of ripened fields of wheat, with their white heads of grain waiting for the harvest, means that thousands of souls are ready around the world for the gospel message.

The Lord then lists the essential attributes and attitudes for those who wish to be engaged in the service of God: "Faith, hope, charity and love, with an eye single to the glory of God" (v. 5). Then, as we serve Him, we must remember and maintain "faith, virtue, knowledge, temperance, patience, brotherly kindness, godliness, charity, humility, [and] diligence" (v. 6). If we serve in this manner, we can "Ask, and ye shall receive; knock, and it shall be opened unto you" (v. 7). The Lord declared that whatever He says to one individual He says unto all (D&C 61:36; 82:5; 92:1; 93:49). Thus, this revelation and all others apply equally to us as they do to the individual to whom Joseph Smith originally gave them.

Elder George Albert Smith gave his interpretation of what he thought the revelation meant: "My understanding is that the most important, mission that I have in this life is: first, to keep the commandments, of God, as they have been taught to me; and next, to teach them to my Father's children who do not understand them… It is not necessary for you to be called to go into the mission field in order to proclaim the truth. Begin on the man who lives next door by inspiring confidence in him, by inspiring love in him for you because of your righteousness, and your missionary work has already begun."[3]

● **D&C 4:1–3 An invitation to participate in the latter-day work.** The "marvelous work" referenced in verse 1 is the restoration of the gospel for the last time. The Lord requires those who serve in His kingdom to serve with all their "heart, might, mind and strength"—meaning with total dedication to the Lord's service—if they wish to "stand blameless before God at the last day" (v. 2). If any are willing to thus serve God, they "are called to the work" (v. 3). The terms the Lord uses here are symbolic and we should consider their meaning.

— Heart   Serving with the deepest feelings of our soul.
— Might   Serving with our entire physical effort.
— Mind   Serving with full mental devotion and with purity of thoughts.
— Strength   Serving with all of our physical and spiritual power.

● **D&C 4:4 He that "harvests" with his might brings salvation to himself.** Using the metaphor of a field of ripened wheat, the Lord says, "behold the field is white already to harvest." He has prepared people to hear and receive the message all around the world, and any missionary who "thrusteth in his sickle with his might, the same layeth up in store that he perisheth not, but bringeth salvation to his soul."

Sheaves of wheat in the field

    — **D&C 6:3; 11:3 We must continue to reap until the end—the Second Coming.** The time available for this harvest is short, "therefore, whoso desireth to reap, let him thrust in his sickle with his might, and reap while the day lasts." The Prophet Joseph Smith frequently taught that we should have the building up of Zion as our greatest goal. He also indicated that there was no time to waste, since "ye shall not have time to have gone over the earth, until these things come." He prophesied that the world will see "cholera, war, fires, and earthquakes; one pestilence after another" and that "the time is soon coming, when no man will have any peace but in Zion and her stakes."[4]

President Marion G. Romney said: "The time is short; a world calamity can be avoided only if enough people can be brought to humble themselves and follow the guidance of the Holy Spirit. The revelations of the Lord are explicit as to what will occur if this fails … (D&C 5:19). Whether or not the world will choose the way of escape does not, however, have any bearing on what we must do. We must do all we can to take the revealed means of escape to them and with all our power entreat them to embrace it."[5]

— **D&C 6:3; 11:3 He that reaps this harvest will receive everlasting salvation.** The promise is that a dedicated missionary will "treasure up for his soul everlasting salvation in the kingdom of God." Elder Bruce R. McConkie taught that our own sins are remitted when we minister for the salvation and blessing of another person.[6] And Elder Spencer W. Kimball said: "Remind the transgressor that every testimony he bears, every prayer he offers, every sermon he preaches, every scripture he reads, every help he gives to stimulate and raise others—all these strengthen him and raise him to higher levels... One can hardly help another to the top of the hill without climbing there himself."[7]

— **D&C 75:5 He will be crowned with honor, glory, immortality, and eternal life.** Continuing the harvesting metaphor, the Lord says His dedicated servants will be "laden with many sheaves [bundles of wheat], and crowned with honor, and glory, and immortality, and eternal life." Missionaries sometimes go out to preach the gospel and then return with doubts about whether they have been the means of converting anyone. But according to this scripture, "if they have been faithful, the harvest is sure. The seed they have sown may sprout and come to maturity years after they have been released."[8]

● **D&C 4:5–7 Qualifications needed to do the work of the Lord.** To qualify for this work, missionaries must possess "faith, hope, charity and love, with an eye single to the glory of God" (v. 4). Then, as they go forth, they are to serve with "faith, virtue, knowledge, temperance, patience, brotherly kindness, godliness, charity, humility, [and] diligence" (v. 6) And if they do, they are promised that they may "Ask, and ye shall receive; knock, and it shall be opened unto you" (v. 7). Though knowledge is essential to missionary success, this list says nothing about college degrees. And although enthusiasm for the work is good, we are advised to proceed with temperance (moderation and balance). This list of qualifications is not at all similar to what the world would prescribe. But it is the Lord's list, and "whom the Lord calls, the Lord qualifies."

Happily, we are all quite different in our personalities and gifts. How boring the world (or even eternity) would be if we were all identical! One might have a superior knowledge of the gospel, another the gift of music, and still another the ability to touch others with a charitable spirit. Working together in harmony, we can bless the world with all our gifts. The important thing is to do our very best in the work to which we have been called. If we do so, the Lord will make use of our gifts in accomplishing His work. President Thomas S. Monson once quoted President Harold B. Lee as saying, "Remember, whom the Lord calls, the Lord qualifies."[9]

According to the Lord's instruction in these various revelations to individuals, the best qualified person to teach the gospel is desirous to work, one who has a testimony of the gospel, and one who is so living as to have the companionship and guidance of the Holy Spirit. It is not a matter of intellectuality or prominence, but of spirituality. The preparation for such messengers stretches back into the premortal world, where they were initially prepared and made covenants to serve. Elder Bruce R. McConkie said that "those so endowed spiritually were foreordained and sent to earth to serve at God's command as His ministers."[10]

Earlier in my life I served on a high council where one of my assignments was to monitor and promote young men's progress from priest to elder. Whenever we came together with the families to ordain these young men to the Melchizedek priesthood, I would ask the young men, "How long have you been preparing for this day?" Usually, the answer was "for a year," or "all my life." These were fine answers, but I liked to take the occasion to inform them that they had been preparing for that day since before they were born—that they were foreordained to hold the Melchizedek priesthood and that on this day they were fulfilling a covenant they made in the premortal world. It never failed to impress them, and that is good because we need to understand the eternal nature of priesthood and of missionary work.

A Revelation to Hyrum Smith

(D&C 11)

Having recently received the Aaronic and Melchizedek priesthood, the Prophet Joseph Smith wrote that their understanding of the scriptures was enhanced. They began to discuss their newfound knowledge with any visitor who came to see them, and this brought them great joy. In May of 1829, the prophet's brother Samuel H. Smith came to visit them, and a few days later his brother Hyrum Smith came seeking instructions from the Lord. Joseph inquired through the Urim and Thummim, and received this revelation [D&C 11].[11]

Hyrum Smith

Hyrum Smith was born on February 9, 1800, the second son (after Alvin) of Joseph Smith Sr., and his wife, Lucy. He was a Presbyterian, but when he heard from his brother Joseph concerning his first vision and the receipt of the Book of Mormon plates, he was convinced of the truth of the restoration. On this occasion, he came to visit his brother Joseph to see how he might assist with the work. Soon after receiving the revelation, he became one of the earliest individuals to be baptized, in June 1829. He also was one of the eight witnesses of the Book of Mormon plates, which were shown to him by his brother Joseph.

Hyrum became Second Counselor in the First Presidency in 1837 where he served until 1841. In 1841 he was called to be Patriarch to the Church (following his father's death). The Lord called him "a prophet, and a seer, and a revelator" (D&C 124:91–96). He was called to act in concert with Joseph, to protect him, and to bear witness of the Book of Mormon and the restoration. This he did admirably despite many persecutions, and eventually sealed his testimony with his blood, along with his brother Joseph, at Carthage Jail in 1844.

- **D&C 11:6, 20 Obedience is important in serving the Lord.** As He would say to virtually every other individual who sought to know the Lord's will during this period, the Lord emphasized to Hyrum that he must "keep my commandments, and seek to bring forth and establish the cause of Zion" (v. 6). But passive obedience would not be sufficient. One must not only avoid sin, but must seek to actively perform every duty that is required—"to keep my commandments ... with all your might, mind and strength" (v. 20).

- **D&C 11:7 Seek not for riches, but for eternal life.** We receive this greatest of all the gifts of

God by listening to and obeying the Spirit, keeping the Lord's commandments, and enduring to the end. "Seek not for riches but for wisdom" the Lord says—wise counsel in a day when the world (like Babylon) seems unalterably focused on the pursuit of wealth and fame. If we separate ourselves from such degenerate values, "the mysteries of God shall be unfolded unto you, and then shall you be made rich. Behold, he that hath eternal life is rich" (v. 7). What could be of greater value in the eternities that stretch out ahead of us? Will momentary pleasure ease the pain of eternal loss? No, the greater prize is eternal life—"which gift is the greatest of all the gifts of God" (D&C 14:7).

President David O. McKay said:

> What seek ye first? What do you cherish as the dominant, the uppermost thought in your mind? What this is will largely determine your destiny. Notwithstanding the complexity of human society, we can encompass all purposes by two great important ones. First, the world of material gain; and, second, the world of happiness consisting of love and the power to do good. If it is your purpose to get worldly gain, you may obtain it. You may win in this world almost anything for which you strive. If you work for wealth, you can get it, but before you make it an end in itself, take a look at those men who have sacrificed all to the accomplishment of this purpose, at those who have desired wealth for the sake of wealth itself. Gold does not corrupt man; it is in the motive of acquiring that gold that corruption occurs.[12]

● **D&C 11:8–9 "Say nothing but repentance" to this generation.** No doctrine or message is more important to the salvation of souls. If we truly desire to serve the Lord, "you shall be the means of doing much good in this generation" (v. 8). The Lord welcomes our contribution to His work. But we must do it in the Lord's own way. "Say nothing but repentance unto this generation," He says, and "keep my commandments," which, if we do, we can "assist to bring forth my work, according to my commandments, and you shall be blessed" (v. 9).

"I think that it is high time," the Prophet Joseph Smith wrote, "for a Christian world to awake out of sleep, and cry mightily to that God, day and night, whose anger we have justly incurred. [The condition of the world should] arouse the faculties, and call forth the energies of every man, woman or child that possesses feelings of sympathy for their fellows, or that is in any degree endeared to the budding cause of our glorious Lord."[13] And the message we should bear, he said, was for inhabitants to turn from their sins before it is too late.

DEGUEROTYPE OF PAINTING BY MAUDLEY, 1842, NAUVOO

● **D&C 11:10 Hyrum had special gifts given him from the Lord.** Most of us seek to understand our gifts and calling when we seek patriarchal blessings. Hyrum was no different. He wanted to know his gifts and how he might use them for the benefit of the restored Church. The Lord replied, "Behold, thou hast a gift, or thou shalt have a gift if thou wilt desire of me in faith, with an honest heart, believing in the power of Jesus Christ." The great gift which he possessed was a tender, sympathetic heart and a merciful spirit. The Lord on a later occasion said: "Blessed is my servant Hyrum Smith; for I, the Lord, love him because of the integrity of his heart, and because he loveth that which is right before me, saith the Lord (D&C 124:15)." We can see this great gift being manifested throughout his life in his tender watch care over his brother, the Prophet Joseph Smith.

● **D&C 11:11–14 We should put our trust in the Spirit when discerning truth.** Hyrum was receiving the word of the Lord through his brother Joseph, "For, behold, it is I that speak; behold, I am the light which shineth in darkness, and by my power I give these words unto thee" (v. 11). As he sought for a witness of the latter-day work, he was counseled to "put your trust in that Spirit which leadeth to do good"—both the Spirit of Christ and the Holy Ghost—which teach us "to do justly, to walk humbly, [and] to judge righteously" (v. 12). The Lord promised to "impart unto you of my Spirit, which shall enlighten your mind, which shall fill your soul with joy" (v. 13). And by that manifestation "shall you know, all things whatsoever you desire of me, which are pertaining unto things of righteousness, in faith believing in me that you shall receive" (v. 14). This is a plain description of what we may expect to experience when we ask in faith for a witness and testimony.

● **D&C 11:15 We must be properly called and ordained to the work.** The Lord says multiple times in the revelations that if we desire to do the work we will be called to it. But "you need not suppose that you are called to preach until you are called." One having authority and proper keys must issue the assignment before we presume to take it upon us. We are always called "to stand as witnesses of God at all times and in all things, and in all places that ye may be in, even until death" (Mosiah 18:9). But before setting forth to do a particular assignment in the Church, we must wait for a specific call from the Lord. This is not some esoteric call that comes from reading the scriptures or through college degrees. The standard is clear: a man must be "called of God, as was Aaron" (Heb. 5:4; D&C 27:8; 132:59). This means that his call must come by revelation and ordination, and with the sustaining vote of Church members.

ADAPTED FROM "MELCHIZEDEK PRIESTHOOD RESTORED" ©LIZ SWINDLE

● **D&C 11:16, 21–22 We must "obtain the word" before attempting to teach or preach it.** Enthusiasm, energy, and spirit are wonderful things. But the Lord wants informed messengers who know the gospel and are prepared to teach it with effectiveness. He said to Hyrum, "Wait a little longer, until you shall have my word, my rock, my church, and my gospel, that you may know of a surety my doctrine" (v. 16). In those early days of the Church there was still much to be revealed and explained. The gospel knowledge possessed by most converts was only partial— that which they brought with them from their various churches and creeds. Many young men and women today are in a similar state, having a general knowledge of the gospel but needing greater understanding.

"Seek not to declare my word," the Lord says, "but first seek to obtain my word, and then shall your tongue be loosed; then, if you desire, you shall have my Spirit and my word, yea, the power of God unto the convincing of men" (v. 21). But for now they were to "hold your peace" and "study my word"—both those scriptures which had already gone forth among the children of men, and also those that were yet to come and those that were "now translating"—"until you have obtained all which I shall grant unto the children of men in this generation" (v. 22).

President Spencer W. Kimball said: "The Lord's teachings have always been to those who have 'eyes to see' and 'ears to hear.'… So I ask all to begin now to study the scriptures in earnest, if you have not already done so. And perhaps the easiest and most effective way to do this is to participate in the [Gospel Doctrine] study program of the Church… Over a period of [four] years the Old Testament, the Pearl of Great Price, the New Testament, the Book of Mormon, and the Doctrine and Covenants are all studied thoroughly."[14]

● **D&C 11:17–20 How to prepare for missionary service.** To obtain a knowledge of all these things, we must read the Book of Mormon, study, and pray, and then "according to your desires, yea, even according to your faith shall it be done unto you" (v. 17). These are the same things that all missionaries must do to prepare themselves before they are called to serve. They are to "keep my commandments; hold your peace; appeal unto my Spirit; … cleave unto me with all your heart, [and] assist in bringing to light those things of which has been spoken" (the translation of the Book of Mormon), and "be patient until you shall accomplish it" (vv. 18–19). Furthermore, those seeking to serve must maintain their worthiness, seeking to "keep my commandments … with all your might, mind and strength" (v. 20). As President Thomas S. Monson has said multiple times, "Preparation precedes power." Missionaries must make themselves like the sons of Mosiah, who had "waxed strong in the knowledge of the truth; for they were men of a sound understanding and had searched the scriptures diligently, that they might know the word of God. But this is not all; they had given themselves to much prayer, and fasting; therefore, they had the spirit of prophecy, and the spirit of revelation, and when they taught, they taught with power and authority of God" (Alma 17:1–3).

A Revelation to Joseph Knight Sr.

(D&C 12)

Joseph Knight, Sr.

During that same month (May 1829), the "old gentleman," as Joseph called him, Joseph Knight Sr. came to visit them in Harmony. Brother Knight had heard about how diligently they were working on the translation of the Book of Mormon, and recognizing they would need material support while doing their translating, he brought food and other provisions for them. Joseph reports that his was not an isolated incident. "He several times brought us supplies, a distance of at least thirty miles, which enabled us to continue the work when otherwise we must have relinquished it for a season." But Joseph Knight was also anxious to know his own duty with regard to the work. Joseph inquired of the Lord for him, and obtained this revelation (D&C 12).[15]

We do not know where Joseph Knight was born, but we know

he married Polly Peck and, at the time of the coming forth of the Book of Mormon, was living in New York not far from the Susquehanna River, in Colesville, Broom County, New York. He lived there for 19 years. His son Newel said of him: "My father owned a farm, a grist mill and carding machine. He was not rich, yet he possessed enough of this world's goods to secure to himself and family, not only the necessaries, but also the comfort of life. His family, consisting of my mother, three sons and four daughters, he reared in a genteel and respectable manner, and gave his children a good common school education. My father was a sober, honest man, generally respected and beloved by his neighbors and acquaintances. He did not belong to any religious sect, but was a believer in the Universalist doctrine."[16]

Joseph Knight Sr., employed Joseph Smith as a young teenager in 1826, to work at his farm and grist mill in Colesville, New York. He noticed and respected the solid character of Joseph Smith, and from that time forth he offered Joseph both material and spiritual support in every circumstance. This included employment, food, paper, and writing tools from time to time while he was translating the Book of Mormon in Harmony, Pennsylvania, which greatly endeared the Prophet to him and allowed the Book of Mormon translation to continue during a very difficult time.

- **D&C 12:1–5 The first five verses of D&C 12 are identical to those found in the revelation to Oliver Cowdery (D&C 6:1–5) and David Whitmer (D&C 14:1–5).** See the commentary on these verses in chapter 5, which discusses the revelation to Oliver Cowdery.

- **D&C 12:6–7 A message for every member of the Church.** The Lord commands us to "keep my commandments, and seek to bring forth and establish the cause of Zion" (v. 6). Then, lest we should miss the point, the Lord says to Joseph Knight Sr., "I speak unto you, and also to all those who have desires to bring forth and establish this work" (v. 7).

- **D&C 12:8 Qualities required of those who serve in the Church.** As he had done previously in the revelation to the Prophet's father (D&C 4), the Lord enumerates qualities needed to do his work. This time, He emphasizes "humility," "being full of love," "having faith, hope, and charity," and "being temperate in all things," in whatever calling "shall be entrusted to [your] care." Apparently, Joseph Knight Sr., took this counsel to heart.

Responding to this revelation, from that time forth Joseph Knight became very active in the Church. He was a prominent member of the Colesville (New York) branch. When that branch moved to Ohio by command from the Lord, he went with them. While in Kirtland, Joseph Knight and the Colesville branch lived the law of consecration until that law was broken by others who had previously owned the land on which they lived. As commanded by the Lord, they moved on to Jackson County, Missouri, with Joseph Knight as the director of the company. He was always loyal, following the Saints to Nauvoo and aligning himself with Brigham Young after the Prophet Joseph was martyred. When the Saints were driven from Nauvoo he started on the westward trek but died while wintering among the Ponca Indians in what is now northern Nebraska.[17]

The Prophet wrote of Joseph Knight Sr., after escaping from Liberty Jail:

> I am now recording in the Book of the Law of the Lord,—of such as have stood by me in every hour of peril, for these fifteen long years past—say, for instance, my aged and beloved brother, Joseph

Knight, Sen., who was among the number of the first to administer to my necessities, while I was laboring in the commencement of the bringing forth of the work of the Lord and of laying the foundation of The Church of Jesus Christ of Latter-day Saints. For fifteen years he has been faithful and true, and even-handed and exemplary, and virtuous and kind, never deviating to the right hand or to the left. Behold he is a righteous man; may God Almighty lengthen out the old man's days; and may his trembling, tortured, and broken body be renewed, and the vigor of health turn upon him, if it be Thy will, consistently, O God; and it shall be said of him, by the sons of Zion, while there is one of them remaining, that this man was a faithful man in Israel, therefore his name shall never be forgotten. There are his sons, Newel Knight and Joseph Knight Jun., whose names I record in the Book of the Law of the Lord with unspeakable delight, for they are my friends.[18]

Revelations to the Whitmers

(D&C 14–16)

During translation of the Book of Mormon at Harmony, Pennsylvania, persecution began to increase. As a result, it became necessary for him to move from his home. He first went to the home of his wife's parents but before long it became necessary to look for shelter elsewhere. Oliver Cowdery wrote to David Whitmer, asking if they might come to Fayette to live and finish the work. David came right away during the first part of June 1829 and moved Joseph, Emma, and Oliver to their home at Fayette. The arrangement included free room and board and the assistance, as needed, of the Whitmer brothers until the translation was completed. The Whitmer family was very anxious to help and friendly to the Prophet, and they, too, wanted to know the Lord's will concern- ing themselves. The Prophet inquired of the Lord and received a revelation for each of the three brothers (D&C 14–16).[19]

A Revelation to David Whitmer

(D&C 14)

David Whitmer was baptized in June 1829, and was one of the Three Witnesses to the Book of Mormon. He was also one of the six original members of the Church on April 6, 1830. He shared in all of the trials of the Saints in New York and the early days of Kirtland. He was appointed president of the high council in Clay County, July 3, 1834, and was a leader of the Church in Missouri. When the Saints relocated to Far West, he was sustained as their president. During the difficult days of Missouri he fell into transgression and was rejected as the presiding officer at a general conference held in Far West, February 5, 1838. Becoming bitter in his opposition, he was excommunicated by the high council at Far West on April 13, 1838. After his excommunication he moved to Richmond, in Ray County, Missouri, where he resided until his death on January 23, 1888. Because of his opposition to the Prophet's leadership of the Church, he was accepted by the citizens of Richmond and of Missouri, and the persecution against him ceased. He was considered to be one of the most respected citizens in Richmond.

David Whitmer

Although he became estranged from Joseph Smith and the Church, he was always true to his testimony. He bore it continually during the years that he was out of the Church. He explained his leaving the Church by saying that Joseph Smith and the Church had departed from correct principles and Joseph was a "fallen prophet." He organized a church of his own and continued to preach the Book of Mormon, but he rejected all revelations through the Prophet that came after the early days of the Church when he was a part of it.

The story of David Whitmer is a very interesting and sad one. Had he given heed to this revelation, he might have remained faithful to the end. He did not return to the Church, but he remained faithful to the testimony to the Book of Mormon until the day of his death.[20]

- **D&C 14:1–5** The first five verses of D&C 14 are identical to those found in the revelation to Oliver Cowdery (D&C 6:1–5) and Joseph Knight Sr. (D&C 12:1–5). See the commentary on these verses in chapter 5, which discusses the revelation to Oliver Cowdery.

- **D&C 14:6–7 The need for obedience and endurance.** The requirements for eternal life are (1) keep the commandments, (2) seek to establish Zion, and (3) endure to the end. As simple as this sounds, it had great import for David Whitmer, who rebelled against the word of the Prophet Joseph on multiple occasions, who selfishly sought his own financial interests in Missouri (rather than the cause of Zion), and who decidedly did not "endure to the end" in the Church. Had he taken this counsel to heart, the story of his life might have ended quite differently.

  With regard to enduring, I once asked a class member for a definition of "long- suffering." She paused for a while, then said with all seriousness, "Long-suffering is a definition of life." We all chuckled at her remark, but it was full of truth. Life is hard and full of trials. In the midst of difficulty, and despite the many things that occur that make no sense to us, we must endure to the end. When something tries my faith, I try to remember this motto: "I will not let the things I do not understand get in the way of the things I know."

- **D&C 14:8 David Whitmer will both see and hear sacred things and become a witness of them.** David desired to be one of the three witnesses that were promised in the Book of Mormon to stand as witnesses (2 Nephi 27:12–14; Ether 5:4). Because of his extraordinary support for the Prophet and his work, the Lord told him, "if you shall ask the Father in my name, in faith believing, you shall receive the Holy Ghost, which giveth utterance, that you may stand as a witness of the things of which you shall both hear and see, and also that you may declare repentance unto this generation." This was an extraordinary privilege—to both see and hear the angel Moroni as he showed David the plates and other sacred items . He never betrayed this trust, to the end of his life, despite his general apostasy over matters of doctrine. In 1878, he said: "He [the angel] stood before us. Our testimony as recorded in the Book of Mormon, is strictly and absolutely true … " And in 1886 he said: "As sure as the sun shines and I live, just so sure did the angel appear unto me and Joseph Smith and I heard his voice and did see the angel standing before us."[21]

A Revelation to John Whitmer

(D&C 15)

John Whitmer was the third son of Peter Whitmer Sr. and was baptized by Oliver Cowdery in Seneca Lake in June 1829, shortly after the Prophet Joseph Smith arrived at the Whitmer home. He served as a secretary to Joseph and went with him on the trip to organize the branch of the Church in Colesville. He was also Church historian and went with Oliver Cowdery to Jackson County, Missouri to direct the publication of the Book of Commandments in 1831. He was one of the Eight Witnesses to the Book of Mormon.

John Whitmer

Despite all these faith-promoting experiences, he did not remain faithful. At a meeting of high priests on April 7, 1837, in Far West, Missouri, he was appointed to a committee that oversaw the sale of town lots in Far West. At a conference seven months later, on November 7, 1837, members did not sustain him as one of the assistant presidents in Missouri, but after he made a humble confession of his faults he was temporarily sustained. Nevertheless, he was finally rejected for persistent unchristian-like conduct, along with his brother David and others in Missouri. The high council excommunicated him at Far West on March 10, 1838. The reason given for this action was that he, David Whitmer, and W. W. Phelps had failed to account properly for $2,000 of Church funds. Following his excommunication, he refused to deliver to the Church the records which he had kept as Church historian. Despite a chastising letter from the Prophet and Sidney Rigdon, he still kept the record. It has never been obtained by the Church, though a copy was made and now resides in the Church Historian's Office in Salt Lake City.

John Whitmer died at home at Far West, Missouri, on July 11, 1878. While he never returned to the Church he, like his brother David, remained true to his testimony of the Book of Mormon plates to the day of his death.[22]

- **D&C 15–16 Identical revelations.** The words of this revelation to John Whitmer (D&C 15) are identical to the revelation given to Peter Whitmer Jr. (D&C 16). Thus, we will comment here only upon those verses that seem most appropriate to the later history of John Whitmer.

- **D&C 15:6 Bringing souls unto the Lord is the most important thing we can do.** Like his brother David, John was an important person in the early Church and was given many significant opportunities and trusts. But in the midst of all that heady attention, he is counseled not to forget the reason for the work—declaring repentance unto the world "that you may bring souls unto me, that you may rest with them in the kingdom of my Father." Even the God of Heaven stays focused on this purpose in the midst of His awesome world-building throughout the universe: "For behold, this is my work and my glory—to bring to pass the immortality and eternal life of man" (Moses 1:39). John and his brother David lost focus on this goal when they attempted to profit from the sale of land in Missouri, thus taking advantage of the many Saints who were endeavoring to gather there. It may have been good business, but it was contrary to the interests and salvation of the people.

A Revelation to Peter Whitmer Jr.

(D&C 16)

Peter Whitmer Jr. was the fifth son of Peter Whitmer Sr. He was baptized by Oliver Cowdery in June 1829, when Peter was less than 20 years old. He was one of the eight witnesses to the Book of Mormon, and one of the original six founders of the Church. In September 1830, he was called, along with Parley P. Pratt, Oliver Cowdery, and Ziba Peterson to preach the gospel to the Lamanites (see D&C 32). He was ordained a high priest by Oliver Cowdery on October 25, 1831. Like his brothers, Peter Whitmer Jr. took an active part in the Church in Jackson and

Whitmer Home in Fayette, New York

Clay Counties in Missouri. He suffered through persecutions and mob drivings in 1833, and made his temporary home in Clay County. But as a result of the hardships he suffered, he took sick and died on a small farm about two miles from Liberty, Missouri, September 22, 1836.

Christian Whitmer. Peter Whitmer Jr. was buried by the side of his brother Christian, who had also been a victim of mobocracy and died about ten months before Peter. Christian Whitmer was also one of the eight witnesses to the Book of Mormon plates. Both Peter and Christian died before the difficulties arose that ensnared their brothers David and John. They remained faithful to both the Church and their testimony of the Book of Mormon plates till their deaths.[23]

- **D&C 16:6 Missionary work is still the most important thing we can do with our lives.** While his brother John eventually lost sight of the purpose of the work in these latter days, Peter Whitmer Jr., and his brother Christian, did not. They remained faithful to the end, and essentially died as martyrs due to the severe persecutions they suffered in Missouri. They literally wore out their lives in service to the cause of Zion. And we have taken covenants to sacrifice whatever is necessary for the same purpose of saving souls today.

Elder David B. Haight said: "The goal of every physically able couple in the Church, just as it is for every 19–year-old young man in the Church, should be to serve a mission. No finer example can be given, no finer testimony can be borne by parents to children or grandchildren, than through missionary service in their mature years."[24]

A Revelation to Oliver Cowdery and David Whitmer

(D&C 18)

By this time both the Aaronic and Melchizedek priesthoods had been conferred on Joseph and Oliver. As yet, however, nobody had been ordained an elder in the Church. On this day in June

1829, they were commanded to ordain themselves elders at the next conference. They had to wait for these ordinations because all such ordinations require the common consent (sustaining) of members at a conference.

● **D&C 18:1–5 Rely upon the scriptures in teaching and preaching.** The Lord reminds Oliver that "I have manifested unto you, by my Spirit in many instances, that the things which you have written are true; wherefore you know that they are true" (v. 2). And, since they are true, he (and we) are counseled to "rely upon the things which are written; For in them are all things written concerning the foundation of my church, my gospel, and my rock" (vv. 3–4). If we do it in this manner, building up the Church and teaching the gospel based upon the scriptures and upon Christ ("my rock"), "the gates of hell shall not prevail against you" (v. 5). We are not to rely on the philosophies of men, nor upon intellectual arguments. We are to teach the scriptures. Period.

Oliver Cowdery

Elder Boyd K. Packer emphasized this point while speaking to Church Educational System instructors in 1977: "And there you have it, your commission, your charter, your objective… You are to teach the scriptures… If your students are acquainted with the revelations, there is no question personal or social or political or occupational that need go unanswered. Therein is contained the fulness of the everlasting gospel. Therein we find principles of truth that will resolve every confusion and every problem and every dilemma that will face the human family or any individual in it."[25]

Everything that we teach in this Church should be based upon the scriptures. When speakers and teachers draw from other sources it is all-too-often a matter of speculation or the philosophies of men. I regret that I have heard plenty of this kind of teaching in sacrament, Sunday school, and priesthood meetings. It is satisfying to the carnal mind, but it is not what the Lord would have us teach. Even when mingled with scripture, the philosophies of men will not save us. Whatever we speak or teach should be measured by the four standard works, regardless of who has written it, a member of the Church or an authority from elsewhere. If it is not consistent with the standard works, it is not true.[26]

Elder Bruce R. McConkie said: "The books, writings, explanations, expositions, views, and theories of even the wisest and greatest men, either in or out of the Church, do not rank with the standard works. Even the writings, teachings, and opinions of the prophets of God are acceptable only to the extent they are in harmony with what God has revealed and what is recorded in the standard works. When the living oracles speak in the name of the Lord or as moved upon by the Holy Ghost, however, their utterances are then binding upon all who hear, and whatever is said will without any exception be found to be in harmony with the standard works. The Lord's house is a house of order, and one truth never contradicts another."[27]

Elder McConkie described the all-too-frequent circumstances of our philosophical preaching:

> We come together in congregations, seeking the guidance of the Holy Spirit, studying the revelations, reading the scriptures, and hearing expressions of doctrine and counsel given by those who are

appointed. These teachings ought to be delivered by the power of the Holy Spirit. They ought to be received by the same power. And if they are, then the speaker and the hearer will be mutually edified, and we will have true and proper worship…

We come into these congregations and sometimes a speaker brings a jug of living water that has in it many gallons. And when he pours it out on the congregation, all the members have brought is a single cup and so that's all they take away. Or maybe they have their hands over the cups, and they don't get anything to speak of. On other occasions we have meetings where the speaker comes and all he brings is a little cup of eternal truth, and the members of the congregation come with a large jug, and all they get in their jugs is the little dribble that came from a man who should have known better and who should have prepared himself and talked from the revelations and spoken by the power of the Holy Spirit. We are obligated in the Church to speak by the power of the Spirit… We are commanded to treasure up the words of light and truth and then give forth the portion that is appropriate and needful on every occasion.[2]8

- **D&C 18:8 Oliver was much more educated than Joseph, and it began to bother him that this unschooled farm boy should be at his head.** Eventually, this problem led to Oliver's separation from the Church for a while. But very early on in the Church's history, in this revelation, the Lord cautioned him about pride: "And now, marvel not that I have called him unto mine own purpose, which purpose is known in me; wherefore, if he shall be diligent in keeping my commandments he shall be blessed unto eternal life … "

- **D&C 18:6 The world is ripening in iniquity.** The Lord here declares that "the world is ripening in iniquity." The statement is significant. In the Book of Mormon, the Lord declared that when a people become ripe in iniquity, He will destroy them (Ether 2:9; 9:20). This is at least partly because in such a society there is no longer any agency for children born into it. They are doomed by the society to become wicked. Rather than permit this, the Lord destroys such wicked nations. This is true no matter what the nationality or religion of the people. The Lord rewards righteousness but destroys any nation whose iniquity is ripe (1 Nephi 17:33–35). Note that in this revelation (D&C 18), the warning is to both the Gentiles and the house of Israel.

The Book of Mormon tells us when iniquity has become "ripe" or "full" in the Lord's eyes.

— When the "voice of the people should choose iniquity" (Alma 10:19).
— When the people "turn aside the just for a thing of naught and revile against that which is good, and say that it is of no worth" (2 Nephi 28:16).
— When the people "reject every word of God" (1 Nephi 17:35).
— When the people "cast out the righteous from among [them], then shall [they] be ripe for destruction" (Helaman 13:14).

Anti-Mormon protesters at a gay rally

Some examples of people who have (or will yet) reach this condition are:

— The people in the days of Noah (Moses 7:32–43).
— The Amorites who inhabited the promised land in Moses' day (1 Nephi 17:33–35).
— The Nephites in the days of Mormon and Moroni (Mormon 2:10–15).
— The world today as we approach the 2nd coming of Christ (D&C 101: 10–11, 2 Nephi 28:16).

The results the world can expect if the people do not change their course are clear:

— In 1831, the angels were waiting to reap down the tares of this wicked world (D&C 38:10–12).
— In 1833, Joseph Smith said that "DESTRUCTION" was written "by the finger of an invisible hand, in large capitals, upon almost everything we behold" and that the Lord will "sweep the wicked of this generation from off the face of the land."[29]
— In 1893, after the dedication of the Salt Lake Temple, President Wilford Woodruff said that the angels spoken of in D&C 38 "had been loosed and sent on their mission."[30]

To avoid the destructions that will naturally follow in a society that has become ripe in iniquity, the Lord says in D&C 18:6 that "it must needs be that the children of men are stirred up unto repentance." Repentance is their only hope and time is running out.

● **D&C 18:10–14 The worth of souls is great, and they need to repent to be saved.** God loves His children and intends to save them all if they will allow Him to do so. "The worth of souls is great in the sight of God" (v. 10)—so great that He allowed His most precious and obedient Son, "the Lord your Redeemer" to suffer "death in the flesh; wherefore he suffered the pain of all men, that all men might repent and come unto him"(v. 11). He also "hath risen again from the dead, that he might bring all men unto him, on conditions of repentance" (v. 12). Thus, the Lord has made provision to save both our spirits and our bodies, and "how great is his joy in the soul that repenteth!" (v. 13). That purpose—the salvation of individual souls—is the reason why we are "called to cry repentance unto this people" (v. 14). God wants to save every one of His children.

Elder Gordon B. Hinckley demonstrated with his actions how important individuals ought to be, when he visited a stake conference in California. We can imagine how excited the members must have been that an Apostle and prophet was coming to visit them. Imagine the preparations! Imagine the anticipation! But in the end he would not be with them in their meetings. He had "something more important to do."

Elder Gordon B. Hinckley said:

> I have a friend… More than forty years ago we were in the mission field together. In the years that followed he went off to war. In his loneliness he picked up careless companions. He married out of the Church. He followed habits which had made him feel he would not be welcomed. He moved from one part of the country to another. His identity was lost.
>
> One Sunday I found myself in a California city for a stake conference. My name and picture had been in the local newspaper. The phone rang at the stake center as the stake president and I entered the building that morning. The call was for me, and the caller identified himself. He wanted to see

me. I excused myself from the meeting I was to have held early that morning and asked the stake president to carry on with it. I had something more important to do.

He came, this friend of mine, timidly and somewhat fearfully. He had been away for a long time. We embraced as brothers long separated. At first the conversation was awkward, but it soon warmed as we discussed together days spent in England many years ago. There were tears in the eyes of this strong man as he spoke of the Church of which he had once been so effective a part, and then told of the long, empty years that had followed. He dwelt upon them as a man speaks of nightmares. When he had described those wasted years, we talked of his returning. He thought it would be difficult, that it would be embarrassing, but he agreed to try.

I had a letter from him not long ago. He said: "I'm back. I'm back, and how wonderful it feels to be home again."[31]

- **D&C 18:15–16 The joy we will experience with those we teach will be great.** Oliver Cowdery needed to understand (and so do we), that in the Lord's economy of salvation, it's not about numbers. Each soul is precious, and "if it so be that you should labor all your days in crying repentance unto this people, and bring, save it be one soul unto me, how great shall be your joy with him in the kingdom of my Father!" (v. 15).

May I introduce to you my "one soul?" I labored in the mission field in England for two years and baptized more than 20 souls during that time. I love them all, though I've lost track of them over the years. But one—one very special one—remained faithful to the end of her days. Her name is Ivy Alice Branch Field, and she was my landlady in a city where I labored as a district leader for a time. Time and space do not permit me to tell you all the kindnesses she did for the missionaries and the motherly attention she gave to me personally.

Ivy Alice Branch Field

My companion and I had literally covered the city, knocking on every door in that small town, with no success. We had a small branch there of people who were already members, but no new investigators. We came home that day and sat down dejectedly in the living room. Sister Field came in and said: "What's wrong, boys?" We told her our sad story about how "nobody would listen to our message." Then she said, rather matter-of-factly, "Well, what is it that you boys teach?" We looked at each other in total surprise. How could we have missed it? The one person in that entire city who had interest in our message lived under the same roof. We taught her the gospel, and she accepted it with all her heart.

That decision changed her life. Some in her family rejected her, and she longed to be among the Saints in America. She spent time in Canada, working in the Calgary Alberta Temple, then eventually came to the United States and lived with my wife and me. She continued on with her temple work and eventually moved into an apartment of her own. She was happy and active. Then, suddenly, she died of a stroke in 1973. We buried her in Holladay, Utah, under a headstone that reads: "Ivy Alice Branch Field—Our English Mum."

I hope to spend eternity with all my friends and to have joy in all those associations. But I fully expect that some of the greatest joy will come from this "one soul" that I met and taught in England in 1969–1970. Our joy will not be about numbers; it will be about individuals.

The Lord concludes this thought with "And now, if your joy will be great with one soul that you have brought unto me into the kingdom of my Father, how great will be your joy if you should bring many souls unto me!" (v. 16).

● **D&C 18:20–21 Contend against no one; speak the truth in soberness.** With his well read and literate background, Oliver Cowdery was capable of arguing with any foe. But that was not the spirit he was to take into the mission field. "Contend against no church," said the Lord, "save it be the church of the devil" (v. 20). Like the Master he was serving, he was to "take upon you the name of Christ, and speak the truth in soberness" (v. 21).

The Prophet Joseph Smith said: "The Elders would go forth, and each must stand for himself … to go in all meekness, in sobriety, and preach Jesus Christ and Him crucified; not to contend with others on account of their faith, or systems of religion, but pursue a steady course. This I delivered by way of commandment; and all who observe it not, will pull down persecution upon their heads, while those who do, shall always be filled with the Holy Ghost; this I pronounced as a prophecy, and sealed with hosanna and amen."[32]

The Prophet also said: "Let the Elders be exceedingly careful about unnecessarily disturbing and harrowing up the feelings of the people. Remember that your business is to preach the Gospel in all humility and meekness, and warn sinners to repent and come to Christ. Avoid contentions and vain disputes with men of corrupt minds, who do not desire to know the truth. Remember that 'it is a day of warning, and not a day of many words.' If they receive not your testimony in one place, flee to another, remembering to cast no reflections, nor throw out any bitter sayings. If you do your duty, it will be just as well with you, as though all men embraced the Gospel."[33]

● **D&C 18:34–36 When we read the Doctrine and Covenants, we are hearing the voice of the Lord.** Anyone who is familiar with words of the Lord in scripture can recognize right away the same voice in the Doctrine and Covenants. When we read these revelations, we are reading the very words of Christ as He dictated them to the Prophet Joseph Smith. The Lord testified concerning the revelations, "These words are not of men nor of man, but of me; wherefore, you shall testify they are of me and not of man" (v. 34). It was the Lord's voice that the Prophet Joseph Smith heard by means of the Spirit, and had it not been for the power he was given to do this we could not have them (v. 35). Therefore, as we read the revelations, we can "testify that you have heard my voice, and know my words" (v. 36).

Elder S. Dilworth Young said: "The thing that impresses me about this is, and I have never thought of it before, when I read a verse in the Doctrine and Covenants I am hearing the voice of the Lord as well as reading His words, if I hear by the Spirit. Now I have heard it said many times by men that they have often asked the Lord for a special testimony and oftentimes haven't had it. They seem to want to hear the voice of the Lord. I confess I have often wanted to hear the voice of the Lord, without knowing that all these years I have been hearing it with deaf ears. This woke me up."[34]

● **D&C 18:9, 37–38 The first Apostles are assigned to select the Twelve.** Oliver Cowdery and David Whitmer, along with Joseph Smith, had by this time received the Melchizedek priesthood—Joseph and Oliver from Peter, James, and John, and David Whitmer from Joseph Smith. They had also received the keys of the Apostleship, for the Lord here says, "I speak unto you, even as unto Paul mine apostle, for you are called even with that same calling with which he was called" (v. 9).

These three Apostles were now assigned to "search out the Twelve" (v. 37). Those whom they select must possess "the desires [qualifications] of which I have spoken; And by their desires and their works you shall know them" (vv. 37–38).

President Brigham Young taught that Joseph Smith, Oliver Cowdery, and David Whitmer were the first Apostles of this dispensation.[35] To these, according to President Heber C. Kimball, Martin Harris was later added.[36] These men were to find and ordain twelve others who would form the Quorum of the Twelve.

The finding of these other Apostles would take considerable time. All members were recent converts, and few of them possessed the doctrinal understanding, the experience, or the visions that would be necessary to fulfill such a high and holy calling. It was not until 1835—six years later—that the Twelve were actually chosen by the Three Witnesses.

MISSIONARIES GO FORTH

Samuel Smith's First Mission

In June 1830, the Prophet Joseph Smith's brother Samuel H. Smith was set apart by the Prophet to embark on a mission to the East. This was the first officially-sanctioned mission- ary journey in the Church, and Samuel H. Smith the first missionary. He took several copies of the Book of Mormon with him and traveled 25 miles the first day. Though he tried along the way to sell copies of the Book of Mormon, he was not successful. This left Samuel very discouraged, and that night he slept under an apple tree. In the morning he visited the home of John Greene, a Methodist minister, who was just leaving on his own preaching

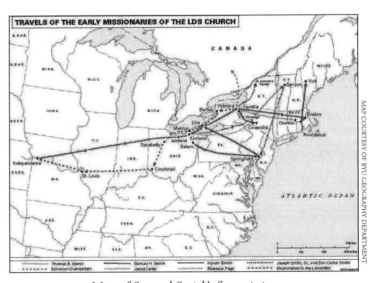

Map of Samuel Smith's first mission

tour and not interested in the book. However, he was friendly toward Samuel and agreed to try to sell subscriptions to purchase copies of the Book of Mormon. Samuel left him a copy of he book and said that he would return in about two weeks.

Samuel returned home from his mission feeling that his work had been fruitless. But the Reverend Greene and his wife read the book he left them, mainly out of curiosity, and were both deeply touched. Reverend Greene gave the book to the Young family, who in turn shared it with the Kimballs. Thus, this supposedly fruitless mission harvested two future apostles and their families, including the man who would lead the Church after the Prophet Joseph Smith's death.[37]

Brigham Young

Heber C. Kimball

What the Missionaries Should Teach

In the many revelations given to those who wished to contribute to the work, one message was predominant: They should teach repentance.

— D&C 11:9	Say nothing but repentance unto this generation.
— D&C 15:6	That which is of most importance is to preach repentance.
— D&C 18:6	Our wicked world needs to be "stirred up" unto repentance.
— D&C 18:10–14	The worth of souls is great, and they need to repent to be saved.

Another common theme was to avoid contention when teaching the gospel:

— D&C 18:20–21	Contend against no one; speak the truth in soberness.
— D&C 38:41	The warning voice should be given in mildness and meekness.

We must overcome fear and feelings of inadequacy and "open our mouths":

— D&C 11:21	Study to "obtain" the word, then the Spirit will make us powerful
— D&C 14:8	If we ask in faith, God will give us the Spirit to help us.
— D&C 19:38	If we pray always, the Lord will pour out His Spirit upon us.

With these instructions as a backdrop, we can turn to the specific instructions the Lord gave to particular missionaries during this period.

Mission Calls for the Whitmers

(D&C 30)

This revelation was received by the Prophet Joseph Smith at Fayette in September 1830. Originally it was published as three revelations in the Book of Commandments, but later the Prophet combined them into one section in the 1835 edition of the Doctrine and Covenants.

- **D&C 30:1–4 David Whitmer is rebuked for listening to Hiram Page and using his influence over other members of the family in favor of the supposed seer-stone.** The Lord said to David, "you have feared man and have not relied on me for strength as you ought" (v. 1). Also, "your mind has been on the things of the earth more than on the things of me, your Maker, and the ministry whereunto you have been called" (v. 2).

So very early on, we have evidence that David Whitmer was exhibiting pride and worldliness, and setting himself at odds with the Prophet Joseph Smith. Specifically with regard to the Hiram Page peepstone incident, the Lord says, "you have not given heed unto my Spirit, and to those who were set over you, but have been persuaded by those whom I have not commanded" (v. 2).

David Whitmer

When we set our hearts on the things of this earth, giving them a higher priority than the things of God, we are left to ourselves to wonder what is wrong. This was the case with David Whitmer (v. 3). Because of this need to ponder and pray, the Lord did not issue a mission call to David, but commanded him to stay at his father's house and give his attention to the work of the kingdom there until further notice (v. 4).

- **D&C 30:5–6 Peter Whitmer is called to accompany Oliver Cowdery on a mission to the Lamanites.** Oliver Cowdery had previously received a call to preach among the Lamanites in the wilderness (D&C 28). Now, Peter Whitmer is called to join him. "I say unto you, Peter, that you shall take your journey with your brother Oliver; for the time has come that it is expedient in me that you shall open your mouth to declare my gospel" (v. 5). As the junior companion in this relationship, he should "give heed unto the words and advice of your brother, which he shall give you" (v. 5). Along the way, he was to expect to be "afflicted in all his afflictions" and constantly "lift … up your heart unto me in prayer and faith, for his and your deliverance; for I have given unto him power to build up my church among the Lamanites" (v. 6).

- **D&C 30:7–8 The unique position of Oliver Cowdery in the Church.** Peter Whitmer Jr., was commanded to give heed to his senior companion, Oliver Cowdery, and to the Lord, as described in this revelation, and if he does he will be "blessed unto eternal life" (v. 8). The Lord explains that nobody in the Church has higher authority than Oliver "concerning church matters, except it is his brother, Joseph Smith, Jun." (v. 7).

Elder Joseph Fielding Smith said:

Oliver Cowdery

> It should be remembered that whenever the Lord revealed priesthood and the keys of priesthood from the heavens, Oliver Cowdery stood with Joseph Smith in the presence of the heavenly messengers, and was a recipient, as well as Joseph Smith, of all this

authority. They held it conjointly, Joseph Smith as the 'first' and Oliver Cowdery as the 'second' Elder of the Church. Thus the law pertaining to witnesses was fully established, for there were two witnesses standing with authority, keys and presidency, at the head of this the greatest of all dispensations. When through transgression Oliver Cowdery lost this wonderful and exalted blessing, Hyrum Smith was chosen by revelation of the Lord to take his place, the Lord calling him in these words: [D&C 124:95–96].[38]

● **D&C 30:9–11 John Whitmer is called to labor among the Saints in Zion.** John Whitmer was very active in the Church as an aid to the Prophet. He assisted in the compilation of the Revelations. He was one of seven high priests appointed to preside in Jackson County. He was Church historian and editor of important Church publications. John was called at this time "to proclaim my gospel, as with the voice of a trump" (v. 9) in the area around Philip Burroughs' home and "wherever you can be heard, until I command you to go from hence" (v. 10).

John Whitmer

In the end, however, John did not remain faithful, and even at this early date the Lord was warning him about the dangers ahead. He should not allow himself to be diverted by worldly concerns or the opinions of others. The Lord said: "your whole labor shall be in Zion, with all your soul, from henceforth" (v. 11). He should boldly open his mouth in defense of the truth, "not fearing what man can do, for I am with you" (v. 11). It was only a few years later when he would apostatize in Missouri because of mob violence, greed, and the persuasions of his equally apostate brother, David.

A Mission Call for Parley P. Pratt and Ziba Peterson

(D&C 32)

On September 26, 1830, a conference of the Church convened at Fayette, New York. During this conference a great interest was manifested towards the Lamanites. Joseph Smith inquired of the Lord and received Doctrine and Covenants 30 and 32, which, among other things, called Peter Whitmer, Parley P. Pratt, and Ziba Peterson to assist Oliver Cowdery in his missionary labors among the Lamanites. Their assignment is generally recognized as the first formal mission call in the history of the Church.

● **D&C 28:8 The call for Oliver Cowdery to teach the Lamanites.** One of the first missionary efforts of this dispensation was this one given to Oliver Cowdery. This call came in September 1830, but had not yet commenced.

● **The arrival and conversion of Parley P.** Pratt. Parley P. Pratt was raised to do hard work and his opportunities for an

Parley P. Pratt

education were limited. He was taught to be moral, and even in his early youth demonstrated a profoundly religious nature. As a teenager he identified himself with the Baptist church. In 1826 he left New York state and settled thirty miles west of Cleveland, Ohio, where he established a fine wilderness home. The next year, 1827, he returned to his boyhood home in Canaan, Columbia county, New York and married Thankful Halsey, on September 9, 1827. The newly married couple returned immediately to their wilderness home.

About eighteen months later Sidney Rigdon, who was connected with Alexander Campbell, Walter Scott and others in an aggressive reform movement, founded the sect of the "Disciples" or "Campbellites" and came into Parley's neighborhood preaching faith, repentance and baptism. Because their doctrine more fully comported with the scriptures than any other Parley had heard, he accepted Sydney Rigdon's teachings, joined the "Disciples," and became a minister in their church. Wanting to take up the ministry as his life's labor, he sold his possessions and started east to visit his relatives in New York.

Along the way, however, he was moved by the Spirit to disembark at Newark, New York, while his wife continued on to her father's home. While in Newark, Parley first heard of and saw the Book of Mormon. Through several sleepless days and nights, he earnestly read it and was convinced of its truthfulness. He hurried off to Palmyra to learn all he could about its origins. At the home of the Smiths, he met with Hyrum, brother of the Prophet, and from him learned the particulars of the Restoration. Then, he and Hyrum Smith went to Fayette, where he met with Oliver Cowdery; and was baptized by him in Seneca Lake about September 1, and was immediately ordained an Elder of the Church.

After these events he continued on to the home of his family in Columbia County, New York, where he baptized his brother Orson, who was then nineteen years old. He returned to Fayette in time to attend the conference, where he met the Prophet Joseph Smith for the first time, and received his appointment to the Lamanite mission.[39]

- **D&C 32:1–2 Parley P.** Pratt is called to the work. As a new and very enthusiastic missionary, Parley P. Pratt is counseled by the Lord to "declare my gospel" and "learn of me" (v. 1). His enthusiasm for the Book of Mormon and for the restoration was profound, but he must "obtain" the word before being fully capable of preaching it with effectiveness. Thus, he received this cautionary advice from the Lord. And in all of this he was to "be meek and lowly of heart" (v. 1), not boastful, argumentative, or overbearing. He was to teach like the Savior taught, not like the boisterous ministers of religion with which he was familiar.

    His specific mission call was to "go with my servants, Oliver Cowdery and Peter Whitmer, Jun., into the wilderness among the Lamanites" (v. 2). This would take him back through his home area near Cleveland (including Kirtland, where Sidney Rigdon lived), and on into the vast plains to the very border of the nation at that time—Independence, Missouri. Along the way he would be instrumental in bringing thousands of souls into the Church.

- **D&C 32:3 The Lord will go with them and protect them.** Ziba Peterson was also called to this mission, and the Lord promises all of them that He Himself "will go with them and be in their midst" and that "nothing shall prevail against them"—comforting words for men about to embark on a mission into largely unknown territory with many dangers.

234 | Church History Study Guide, Pt. 1

- **D&C 32:4–5 Instructions to these (and all) new missionaries.** Missionaries are not free to "wing it" with the gospel. They are to "give heed to that which is written" in the scriptures, and "pretend to no other revelation" (v. 4). And they are instructed to "pray always that I may unfold the same to their understanding" (v. 4). The Lord promises that if they will "give heed unto these words and trifle not, … I will bless them" (v. 5).

The Mission to the Lamanites

According to the summary provided by Robert L. Millet and Kent Jackson,40 the events of this mission were as follows:

The Lamanite missionaries commenced their work with the Catteraugus tribe near Buffalo, New York. Here they were fairly well received, and after leaving copies of the Book of Mormon they continued their journey west.

Near Kirtland, Ohio, they taught the gospel to a minister friend of Parley P. Pratt, Sidney Rigdon, and his congregation. What probably was thought to have been a diversion from the missionaries' major purpose turned out to be a significant accomplishment. Reverend Rigdon had preached the need for a restoration of Christ's primitive church. With such beliefs, Rigdon and many of his congregation accepted the missionaries' message and joined the Church. The missionaries then continued their journey westward toward Missouri.

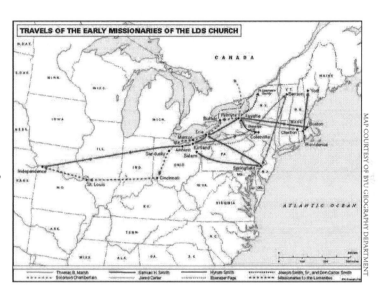

Map of the mission to the Lamanites

Parley wrote in his autobiography that "In the beginning of 1831 we renewed our journey; and, passing through St. Louis and St. Charles, we traveled on foot for three hundred miles through vast prairies and through trackless wilds of snow—no beaten road; houses few and far between; and the bleak northwest wind always blowing in our faces a keenness which would almost take the skin off the face. We traveled for whole days, from morning till night, without a house or fire, wading in snow to the knees at every step, and the cold so intense that the snow did not melt on the south side of the houses, even in the midday sun, for nearly six weeks. We carried on our backs our changes of clothing, several books, and corn bread and raw pork.

Kirtland, Ohio ca. 1907

We often ate our frozen bread and pork by the way, when the bread would be so frozen that we could not bite or penetrate any part of it but the outside crust. After much fatigue and some suffering we all arrived in Independence, in the county of Jackson, on the extreme western frontiers of Missouri, and of the United States."[41]

Upon arriving at Independence, two of the missionaries worked for a time to help finance their mission. The other three continued a short distance to the Delaware Indian lands. The Indians were at first suspicious of the missionaries because they had been exploited by some previous Christian missionaries, but this suspicion was soon lessened by a moving speech by Oliver Cowdery.

Chief Anderson of the Delaware Tribe was very impressed and asked the missionaries to remain during the winter and teach them the Book of Mormon. Success appeared imminent, but it was shattered when other Christian missionaries influenced the Indian agent to evict the Mormon elders from Indian lands. Asked to leave, the disappointed missionaries made their way back to Independence where they stayed, with the exception of Parley P. Pratt. Elder Pratt had been chosen to report the missionaries' labors to Joseph Smith and to visit the Saints they had left behind in Kirtland.

The missionaries who remained in Independence might have wondered what had been accomplished if they considered only their influence among the Lamanites. Often we are called to a work only to find that it takes us in an entirely different direction than we anticipated. If we remember that we are called to serve the Lord then it does not matter in what direction the Lord takes us. The only thing that matters is that we do the work. In this case, the missionaries laid the groundwork for the conversion of thousands of souls who gathered to Kirtland, Ohio, and also for the establishment of Zion in Missouri. They could not have known this when they left, and they probably still did not know it when they returned. But the Lord had used them for important purposes because of their willingness to serve.

REVELATION TO NEW CONVERTS

A Revelation to Thomas B. Marsh

(D&C 31)

Thomas B. Marsh was born in Massachusetts, November 1, 1799. After marrying Elizabeth Godkin in 1820, he went into the grocery business in New York, then worked in a type foundry in Boston. There he joined the Methodist church, but soon withdrew from all sects when he felt that their teachings did not agree with the scriptures. He expected and even predicted the rise of a new church that would contain the truth. He was moved by the Spirit to journey west, and along the way heard of the Book of Mormon. Stopping in Palmyra, he met Martin Harris at the printing office where the Book of Mormon was being printed, and received proof sheets of the first sixteen pages. Convinced of its truth, he met Oliver Cowdery for two days and learned the full story of the coming forth of the Book of Mormon. Returning to his home near Boston, he corresponded with Joseph and Oliver for about a year. Then, hearing that the Church had been organized, he moved to Palmyra in September 1830, and was baptized by David Whitmer. A few days later he was ordained an Elder by Oliver Cowdery.[42]

When the Saints moved to Kirtland, Ohio, Marsh went with them and was eventually called as an Apostle in 1835 and became the first president of that quorum in Church history. But only three years later he became disaffected, and left the Church during a wave of apostasy, according to George A. Smith, when the honor of his wife was questioned in a dispute over milk.

Elder George A. Smith said: "The then President of the Twelve Apostles, the man who should have been the first to do justice and cause reparation to be made for wrong, committed by any member of his family, took that position, and what next? He went before a magistrate and swore that the 'Mormons' were hostile to the State of Missouri. That affidavit brought from the government of Missouri an exterminating order, which drove some 15,000 Saints from their homes and habitations, and some thousands perished through suffering the exposure consequent on this state of affairs."[43]

Marsh became disaffected from the Church at about the same time as persecutions arose against the Saints in Caldwell County, Missouri, in August 1838. After thus turning a traitor to his brethren, Marsh moved away from Far West and lived in Clay County. Later he settled in Richmond, Ray County. He was excommunicated from the Church at a conference held at Quincy, Illinois, on March 17, 1839.[44]

Thomas B. Marsh eventually repented of his apostasy and was re-baptized on July 16, 1857, in Florence, Nebraska. He arrived in Utah in September 1857, and after his return to the Church, was approved by Church leaders and settled in Spanish Fork. He taught school there and was re-ordained an elder in 1859 and a high priest in 1861. He received the endowment and was sealed to Hannah Adams in the Endowment House in 1862. He died in January 1866 and is buried in the Ogden, Utah cemetery.

Thomas B. Marsh gravestone

- **D&C 31:1 "Blessed are you because of your faith."** Thomas B. Marsh was converted to the Church after reading only 16 pages of the Book of Mormon. He soon sold his businesses and moved to Palmyra to be near the Prophet.

- **D&C 31:2, 5–6 The importance of families.** Like many other converts, Thomas B. Marsh's conversion created divisions within his family that distressed him very much. In this blessing, the Lord acknowledges that "you have had many afflictions because of your family; nevertheless, I will bless you and your family, yea, your little ones; and the day cometh that they will believe and know the truth and be one with you in my church" (v. 2). He also had concerns about leaving his family to do missionary work. In this revelation, the Lord promises him that if he will "thrust in your sickle with all your soul" that "your sins are forgiven you" and "your family shall live" (v. 5). Also, he is promised that if he will "go from them only for a little time, and declare my word … I will prepare a place for them" (v. 6).

Having these concerns about his family is not unrighteous, but appropriate. Our families should always be our first concern. But often when we are called to Church responsibilities, we have to find a way to balance those concerns with the need to do the work of the Lord. It is not impossible to do both, and the Lord always blesses our families for the sacrifices made. Thus, Thomas B. Marsh's call was, by extension, a call for his entire family to make a sacrifice, and they are promised significant blessings for doing so.

● **D&C 31:3–4 "The hour of your mission is come" and "your tongue shall be loosed."** How many thousands of missionaries have read this scripture—"lift up your heart and rejoice, for the hour of your mission is come" (v. 3)—and rejoiced along with Thomas B. Marsh! I remember reading this scripture as I departed for England as a missionary in 1968. It is a wonderful moment—full of hope and expectations and joy, but also fear. The missionary wonders, "Will I be able to do this?" and there is the natural fear of speaking to strangers. The Lord addresses that fear here in the case of Thomas B. Marsh. He promises, "your tongue shall be loosed, and you shall declare glad tidings of great joy unto this generation" (v. 3). This was especially true for Thomas B. Marsh, because he became an eloquent speaker. He is instructed to "declare the things which have been revealed to my servant, Joseph Smith, Jun… from this time forth" and to "reap in the field which is white already to be burned" (v. 4).

● **D&C 31:7–8 "They shall be gathered."** Thomas B. Marsh was promised success in his missionary labors. "Yea, I will open the hearts of the people, and they will receive you. And I will establish a church by your hand" (v. 7). But bringing them into the waters of baptism does not end our responsibilities to new converts. The Lord commands, "you shall strengthen them and prepare them against the time when they shall be gathered" (v. 8). This is one of the first indications in the revelations of the coming gathering of the Saints in the latter days. It will be only a few months until they will be asked to gather to Kirtland.

● **D&C 31:9–13 The Lord warns Thomas B.** Marsh concerning his weaknesses. Marsh was given many wonderful promises concerning his missionary efforts. But these promises came with a caution: "Be patient in afflictions, revile not against those that revile. Govern your house in meekness, and be steadfast" (v. 9). There is no better summary of the weaknesses in Marsh's character than this one verse. Had he listened carefully to this counsel he would not have found himself outside the Church within a few years. He lost his patience with the many sufferings that came to the Saints, engaged in accusations against his brethren, allowed his wife's hurt feelings to color his judgment, and did not remain steadfast in the Church as a result.

He was told that he could be "a physician unto the church, but not unto the world, for they will not receive you" (v. 10). This is interesting counsel since he had the power to heal and help the feelings of the Saints as the President of the Quorum of the Twelve Apostles, but he did not. And the world, to whom he turned, never did accept him. They used him as a tool to get to Joseph and his associates. He is commanded to go "whithersoever I will" under the inspiration of the Comforter (v. 11). And then again, some prophetic counsel, which, if he had heeded, would have kept him from apostasy: "Pray always, lest you enter into temptation and lose your reward" (v. 12). And finally, "be faithful unto the end" (v. 13). He is reminded that "these words are not of man nor of men, but of me, even Jesus Christ, your Redeemer, by the will of the Father" (v. 13).

A Revelation to Ezra Thayre and Northrop Sweet

(D&C 33)

This revelation was given in October 1830 at Fayette to Ezra Thayre and Northrop Sweet, who came into the Church at the time the Lamanite missionaries were preaching. They came to Joseph Smith seeking the will of the Lord concerning their role in the Restoration.

Ezra Thayre provided employment for Joseph Smith Sr. in New York and was later baptized by Parley P. Pratt in October of 1830. He was ordained an elder and was among the first to be ordained a high priest at the Church conference in June 1831. He accepted with reluctance a missionary call to accompany Thomas B. Marsh on his journey to Missouri. Later that same month the call was revoked, and he was commanded to repent of pride and selfishness. He was associated with the Colesville Branch while in the Ohio area, into which he had consecrated his money but not his attitude. He was told that unless he repented he would receive his money back and be cut off from the Church. He evidently repented because at a conference held at Amherst, Ohio, January 25, 1832, he was appointed to travel with Thomas B. Marsh. (D&C 75:31). He was a member of Zion's Camp and made the journey with them to Missouri. When they returned, he was chosen to be ordained to the office of Seventy, February 28, 1835.⁴⁵ He was later disaffected from the Church.

Northrop Sweet was also baptized by Parley P. Pratt in October 1830 and was ordained an elder the following June. At first he accepted this revelation but soon left the Church and formed, with others, the "Pure Church of Christ," which quickly dissolved.

● **D&C 33:2–4 The spiritual condition of the world in 1830.** The Lord commands both of these brethren to "open ... your ears and hearken to the voice of the Lord your God" (v. 1). This is prophetic counsel, since eventually their failure to do so would lead them out of the Church. The Lord, who knows them well, says He is "a discerner of the thoughts and intents of the heart" (v. 1). They are called to lift up their voices and preach to "a crooked and perverse generation" (v. 2). The field is "white already to harvest; and it is the eleventh hour, and the last time that I shall call laborers into my vineyard" (v. 3). The Lord's vineyard "has become corrupted every whit; and there is none which doeth good save it be a few; and they err in many instances because of priestcrafts, all having corrupt minds" (v. 4). That was the state of the world in 1830. It is probably even worse today.

● **D&C 33:5–6 The Church was "called forth out of the wilderness."** This is one of several Hebraisms that appear in this revelation, showing the authenticity of its source. Being "called forth out of the wilderness" is a figure of speech that suggests a restoration from apostasy (v. 5). Also, gathering the Lord's elect "from the four quarters of the earth" draws upon language and imagery that means "from all over the earth" (v. 6).

● **D&C 33:8–9 "Open your mouth and it shall be filled."** There was a natural reluctance, because of embarrassment and fear, to publicly preach the gospel. The Lord promises these two that if they will "open [their] mouths ... they shall be filled, and you shall become even as Nephi of old" (v. 8). The Lord also promises that they will enjoy success, being "laden with sheaves upon your backs, for lo, I am with you" (v. 9).

- **D&C 33:10–11 "Make the paths of the Lord straight."** Their message was to be repentance — calling upon the people to "prepare ye the way of the Lord, and make his paths straight; for the kingdom of heaven is at hand" (v. 10). Here we have another Hebrew figure of speech. "Making paths straight" was something done for kings as they traveled. This is, of course, the same message that John the Baptist preached while preparing the way for the coming of the Lord in the meridian of time, including the commandment to be baptized and to receive the Holy Ghost (v. 11).

- **D&C 33:12–14 This is the Lord's gospel, without which men cannot be saved.** The Lord declares that "this is my gospel" and reminds them that humankind "shall have faith in me or they can in nowise be saved" (v. 12). There is no salvation in believing in false gods or religions. Only by knowing and worshiping the true God can we be saved.

  Elder Bruce R. McConkie said: "The issue is not whether men shall worship, but who or what is to be the object of their devotions and how they shall go about paying their devotions to their chosen Most High… There is no salvation in worshiping a false god. It does not matter one particle how sincerely someone may believe that God is a golden calf, or that He is an immaterial, uncreated power that is in all things; the worship of such a being or concept has no saving power. Men may believe with all their souls that images or powers or laws are God, but no amount of devotion to these concepts will ever give the power that leads to immortality and eternal life."[46]

  The Lord declares, "upon this rock [the rock of the gospel of Jesus Christ] I will build my church; yea, upon this rock ye are built, and if ye continue, the gates of hell shall not prevail against you" (v. 13). But we are required to "remember the Church articles and covenants to keep them" (v. 14), which these two men eventually did not.

- **D&C 33:17–18 Living the gospel prepares us to meet the Lord when He comes.** Here we have another Hebraism as the Lord warns them to pray and to have "your lamps trimmed and burning, and oil with you, that you may be ready at the coming of the Bridegroom" (v. 17). This draws upon Jewish wedding customs, where the groom makes a nighttime pilgrimage to the wedding supper with lamps glowing. Guests do not know when the entourage will come, so they must be ready if they wish to participate. They must have a working and glowing lamp with plenty of oil or they cannot be part of the parade. The Bridegroom, of course, is the Lord Jesus Christ and the wedding supper is the Second Coming. He warns, "verily, I say unto you, that I come quickly" (v. 18). Incidentally, oil in Hebrew culture was associated with both prayer and the Holy Spirit, so the invitation to pray is appropriate in this case.

A Revelation to Orson Pratt

(D&C 34)

The Prophet Joseph Smith said: "In the forepart of November, Orson Pratt, a young man nineteen years of age, who had been baptized at the first preaching of his brother, Parley P. Pratt, September 19th (his birthday), about six weeks previous, in Canaan, New York, came to inquire of the Lord what his duty was, and received the following answer: [D&C 34]."[47]

Orson Pratt was born September 19, 1811, in Hartford, New York. He was the younger brother of Parley P. Pratt. When Parley returned to his home with the message of the Gospel, Orson believed him and was baptized. He then traveled 200 miles to see Joseph Smith in Fayette, and on November 4, 1830, received this revelation.

Orson Pratt

On month later, on December 1, 1830, Orson was ordained an elder by the Prophet and went on a mission to Colesville, New York. In the early part of 1831, when the Saints moved to Kirtland, Ohio, he traveled on foot about 300 miles to get there. He filled several short missions to various parts of the Eastern States. He was a member of Zion's Camp and was chosen and ordained an Apostle in 1835. Orson was an accomplished mathematician and one of the clearest and most logical defenders of the Church in those early days. His mathematical ability was a great asset to the Pioneers when they crossed the plains from Winter Quarters to the Salt Lake Valley, as he kept track of the miles between various points. Along with Erastus Snow he entered the Salt Lake Valley on the July 21, 1847, three days before the arrival of the main body of pioneers.[48]

- **D&C 34:1–3 Jesus' love for us.** The Lord lovingly refers to Orson Pratt as "my son," just as He had done anciently with Moses and Abraham. He declares himself to be "the Lord God … even Jesus Christ your Redeemer; the light and the life of the world" (vv. 1–2). He declares that He "so loved the world that he gave his own life, that as many as would believe might become the sons of God" and this is why He can appropriately call Orson Hyde (and each of us) His child.

- **D&C 34:5–10 "Teach my gospel [and] prophesy."** He calls Orson Pratt to "preach my gospel—To lift up your voice as with the sound of a trump, both long and loud, and cry repentance unto a crooked and perverse generation, preparing the way of the Lord for his second coming" (vv. 5–6). He declares that "the time is soon at hand that I shall come in a cloud with power and great glory" (v. 7). That day, He says, will be a "great day" on which "all nations shall tremble" (v. 8). And before that great day comes, "the sun shall be darkened, and the moon be turned into blood; and the stars shall refuse their shining, and some shall fall, and great destructions await the wicked" (v. 9).

Orson Pratt is not only called to "lift up your voice and spare not," but is also told to "prophesy … by the power of the Holy Ghost" (v. 10). This special calling and gift is obvious in all of Orson Pratt's writings, which are full of prophetic insights. Indeed, all of the promises made to Orson Pratt in this revelation were realized. He was heard throughout the world. His ministry was "long"—he was a missionary from 1830 until 1881, a total of 51 years. And he was a member of the Council of the Twelve for 46 years—longer than any other original Apostle appointed in 1835.

A Revelation to Sidney Rigdon

(D&C 35)

The Prophet Joseph Smith said: "In December Sidney Rigdon came to inquire of the Lord, and with him came Edward Partridge; the latter [being] a pattern of piety, and one of the Lord's great men. Shortly after the arrival of these two brethren, thus spake the Lord [D&C 35]."⁴⁹

Sidney Rigdon

Sidney Rigdon was born in Saint Claire, Pennsylvania, on February 19, 1793. He became a Baptist at age 25 and a minister of that faith one year later in 1819, taking charge of a church at Pittsburgh, Pennsylvania. He later became convinced that some of the doctrines of the Baptists were not scriptural, and resigned. While working with his brother-in-law in a tanning business, he became acquainted with Alexander Campbell, the founder of the Church known as the "Disciples" or "Campbellites." Taking up the ministry again, he went to Bainbridge, and later to Mentor, preaching faith, repentance, baptism by immersion for the remission of sins, and righteous living. He was an effective preacher, and had many adherents.

In the Fall of 1830, Parley P. Pratt, Ziba Peterson, Oliver Cowdery, and Peter Whitmer Jr. came to his house in Ohio while on their mission to the Lamanites. Parley P. Pratt, who was also originally from that area and knew him, presented Sidney with a copy of the Book of Mormon and related its story. Sidney Rigdon believed and was baptized (Thus, the folly of the theory that Sidney Rigdon wrote the Book of Mormon!). Many members of Sidney's church in that area were also baptized, thereby establishing a substantial branch of the Church there. Sidney Rigdon and Edward Partridge shortly thereafter went to Fayette to visit the Prophet and seek the will of God concerning them. This revelation was the result of that inquiry.

In the course of his ministry, Sidney Rigdon accompanied the Prophet on missions to Ohio and Missouri, suffered a tar and feathering at Hiram, Ohio, received wonderful manifestations in Kirtland (including the vision of the kingdoms of glory), served as a counselor in the First Presidency, served missions to Canada and the Eastern States, was imprisoned at Liberty Jail with the Prophet, went with the Prophet to Washington on behalf of the persecuted Saints, and assisted in numerous ways in building up the Church.

Unfortunately, he did not endure to the end. When the crucial trial came in Nauvoo, he proved to be untrue and even sought to lead the Saints astray. After the death of the Prophet he sought to become the leader of the Church. He refused to submit to the leadership of the Apostles, which had been sustained by the people, and after continuing his agitation for a while, was excommunicated by the high council in Nauvoo, September 8, 1844. He died outside the Church on July 14, 1876.⁵⁰

● **D&C 35:1–2 The Savior's work is "one eternal round"—eternal, without beginning or end, and the same "today as yesterday, and forever" (v. 1).** He is "Jesus Christ, the Son of God, who was crucified for the sins of the world" so that "as many as will believe on my name … may become the sons of God" (v. 2).

The Prophet Joseph Smith said: "I want to reason more on the spirit of man; for I am dwelling on the body and spirit of man—on the subject of the dead. I take my ring from my finger and liken it unto the mind of man—the immortal part, because it had no beginning. Suppose you cut it in two; then it has a beginning and an end; but join it again, and it continues one eternal round. So with the spirit [intelligence] of man. As the Lord liveth … it had [no] beginning, [and] it will have [no] end."[51]

● **D&C 35:3–6 Sidney Rigdon prepared the way by teaching Biblical truths to his congregation, which the Lord acknowledged, but now he was called to do a "greater work" (v.** 3). He was now "sent forth, even as John, to prepare the way before me, and before Elijah which should come" (v. 4). He had been sent to the earth to do this work, yet "[he] knewest it not" (v. 4). He had indeed baptized people in his old church, "but they received not the Holy Ghost" (v. 5). Now he was called to "baptize by water, and they shall receive the Holy Ghost by the laying on of the hands, even as the apostles of old" (v. 6).

● **D&C 35:5–10 Miracles, signs, and wonders will follow.** The restoration is described as "a great work in the land, even among the Gentiles" in which "their folly and their abominations shall be made manifest in the eyes of all people" (v. 7). He promises "miracles, signs, and wonders, unto all those who believe on my name" (v. 8), including the power to "cast out devils; … heal the sick; … cause the blind to receive their sight, and the deaf to hear, and the dumb to speak, and the lame to walk" (v. 9).

Do these gifts exist in the Church? They certainly do. Miracles have happened in all our lives, I am certain. Sometimes we forget what the Lord has done for us, which must disappoint Him very much. We ought to write these things down in our journals and never forget them, because they are gifts from a loving Father and are intended to strengthen our faith. I have seen family members healed by blessings, seen missionary sons speak with other tongues when their natural ability to do so was not present, and seen prophecies of humble bishops and patriarchs fulfilled in the lives of many. But these things are not done in public and showy ways; they are done with sanctity, dignity, and solemnity.

The Prophet Joseph Smith said:

> We believe in the gift of the Holy Ghost being enjoyed now, as much as it was in the Apostles' days; we believe that it [the gift of the Holy Ghost] is necessary to make and to organize the priesthood, that no man can be called to fill any office in the ministry without it; we also believe in prophecy, in tongues, in visions, and in revelations, in gifts, and in healings; and that these things cannot be enjoyed without the gift of the Holy Ghost. We believe that the holy men of old spake as they were moved by the Holy Ghost, and that holy men in these days speak by the same principle; we believe in its being a comforter and a witness bearer, that it brings things past to our remembrance, leads us into all truth, and shows us of things to come; we believe that 'no man can know that Jesus is the Christ, but by the Holy Ghost.' We believe in it [this gift of the Holy Ghost] in all its fullness, and power, and greatness, and glory; but whilst we do this, we believe in it rationally, consistently, and scripturally, and not according to the wild vagaries, foolish notions and traditions of men.[52]

- **D&C 35:12–15 The poor and meek will receive the gospel.** The Lord does not seek out the mighty and powerful to do His work. They are generally too caught up with themselves to do such work. He says, "there are none that doeth good except those who are ready to receive the fulness of my gospel" (v. 12). And to do this work, "I call upon the weak things of the world, those who are unlearned and despised, to thrash the nations by the power of my Spirit" (v. 13). Though they may appear small and weak, such persons shall posses the power of God, for "their arm shall be my arm, and I will be their shield and their buckler; and I will gird up their loins, and they shall fight manfully for me; and their enemies shall be under their feet; and I will let fall the sword in their behalf, and by the fire of mine indignation will I preserve them" (v. 14). Does it not give us great consolation to know that God will be with and protect His humble messengers? "And the poor and the meek shall have the gospel preached unto them, and they shall be looking forth for the time of my coming, for it is nigh at hand" (v. 15).

- **D&C 35:17–19 Joseph Smith is the Lord's mouthpiece to this generation.** The God of Heaven "sent forth the fulness of my gospel by the hand of my servant Joseph; and in weakness have I blessed him" (v. 17). Though unlearned, he was given "the keys of the mystery of those things which have been sealed, even things which were from the foundation of the world, and the things which shall come from this time until the time of my coming" and he will remain in this honored position forever "if he abide in me, and if not, another will I plant in his stead" (v. 18).

- **D&C 35:19–20 Sidney was to watch over and write for the Prophet Joseph Smith.**

As the Prophet Joseph's companion in the work and his spokesperson, Sidney was to "watch over him that his faith fail not" (v. 19). He was also to "write for him; and the scriptures shall be given, even as they are in mine own bosom, to the salvation of mine own elect" (v. 20). This has reference to Sidney's responsibilities to help Joseph in the new translation of the Bible. Soon after this time, Joseph began that work with Sidney's assistance.

- **D&C 35:23 Sidney was to prove Joseph's words from the scriptures.** When not writing for the Prophet, Sidney was to preach the gospel. The Lord says, "it shall be given unto him to prophesy" but Sidney was to "preach my gospel and call on the holy prophets to prove his words, as they shall be given him." The commandment to "call on the holy prophets to prove his words" meant that Sidney Rigdon was to use his knowledge of the words of the prophets in the scriptures to show that Joseph Smith taught the truth.

A Revelation to Edward Partridge

(D&C 36)

Edward Partridge was born in Pittsfield, Berkshire, Massachu- setts, on August 27, 1793. He was of Scottish descent, his father's ancestors having emigrated from Berwick, Scotland and settled in Hadley, Massachusetts. At the age of sixteen he went to learn the hatter's trade. At age 20 Edward was impressed with need for "universal restoration" and joined the Campbellites. He first heard the gospel in Kirtland, Ohio, from the missionaries to the Lamanites, at the same time as Sidney Rigdon. He obtained a copy of the Book of Mormon and began to investigate.

Shortly thereafter he traveled with Sidney Rigdon to New York, arriving in Fayette in December 1830. On the 11th of December he was baptized by the Prophet Joseph. He was thereafter called upon to "proclaim the gospel with a loud voice" as were all the early converts to the Church. He was called to the bishopric on February 4, 1831, and the Lord declared that he was pure before him. He remained faithful to the restored Church and died in Nauvoo, May 27, 1840, the same year in which Joseph Smith Sr., died.

Edward Partridge received this revelation at the same time that Sidney Rigdon received his, with the Prophet Joseph Smith recording simply, "And the voice of the Lord to Edward Partridge was: [D&C 36]."[53]

Edward Partridge

- **D&C 36:1 Christ is Jehovah.** Christ declares himself to be the "Mighty One of Israel," and "the Lord God." These are names used by Jehovah, the Lord of Hosts of the Old Testament.

- **D&C 36:1–2 Edward Partridge is called to the work and promised the Comforter.** The Lord declares Edward to be "blessed" and forgives him of his sins, then calls him "to preach my gospel as with the voice of a trump" (v. 1). Only recently baptized, he is promised the gift of the Holy Ghost through the laying on of hands of Sidney Rigdon, and is assured that "you shall receive my Spirit, the Holy Ghost, even the Comforter, which shall teach you the peaceable things of the kingdom" (v. 2).

- **D&C 36:6 "Come forth out of the fire, hating even the garments spotted with the flesh."** This figure of speech seems rather odd to us in our day, but was well understood in ancient Israel. To tell people to "come forth out of the fire, hating even the garments spotted with the flesh" is a call to personal purity. Thus, people were to "save [themselves] from this untoward generation" by becoming and remaining pure.

  Elder Bruce R. McConkie said: "To stay the spread of disease in ancient Israel, clothing spotted by contagious diseases was destroyed by burning (Lev. 13:47–59; 15:4–17). And so with sin in the Church, the Saints are to avoid the remotest contact with it; the very garments, as it were, of the sinners are to be burned with fire, meaning that anything which has had contact with the pollutions of the wicked must be shunned. And so also with those yet in the world who are invited to join the kingdom."[54]

- **D&C 36:7 Missionaries must embrace the gospel with "singleness of heart."** To embrace a commandment with "singleness of heart" is to have the heart or feelings concentrated upon the Lord's will without vacillating. If they will do this, they may be "ordained and sent forth, even as I have spoken." Those with less than a complete commitment to do the work of the Lord should not pretend to be His messengers in the mission field.

- **D&C 36:8 "Gird up your loins."** This is another Biblical idiom meaning to prepare for a journey, or for work. The Hebrews wore girdles [sashes] when traveling, and when at work. On such occasions they girt their clothes about them [by tucking them under the sash] to ensure free movement of the limbs.

Notes:

1. Smith and Sjodahl, *Doctrine and Covenants Commentary*, ed. [1972], 23.

2. *Church History and Modern Revelation*, 4 vols. [1946-1949], 1:35.

3. In Conference Report, October 1916, 50-51.

4. *Teachings of the Prophet Joseph Smith*, sel. Joseph Fielding Smith [1976], 160-161.

5. "Guidance of the Holy Spirit," First Presidency Message in *Liahona*, August 1980.

6. *Doctrinal New Testament Commentary*, 3 vols. [1965-1973], 3:279.

7. *The Miracle of Forgiveness* [1969], 205.

8. *Doctrine and Covenants Commentary*, 434.

9. "Who Honors God, God Honors," *Ensign*, November 1995, 50.

10. *Doctrinal New Testament Commentary*, 2:316-317.

11. *History of the Church*, 1:43-45.

12. *Treasures of Life* [1962], 174-175.

13. Letter to N. E. Seaton, Esq., Kirtland, January 4th, 1833, in *History of the Church*, 1:313.

14. *The Teachings of Spencer W. Kimball* [1982], 128.

15. *History of the Church*, 1:47-48.

16. Quoted in *Church History and Modern Revelation*, 1:53-54.

17. *Church History and Modern Revelation*, 1:54.

18. *Millennial Star*, 19:756; *History of the Church*, 5:124-125.

19. *History of the Church*, 1:48-51.

20. *Doctrine and Covenants Commentary* 72; *Church History and Modern Revelation*, 1:63.

21. Ludlow, *A Companion to Your Study of the Book of Mormon* [1976], 37.

22. *Doctrine and Covenants Commentary* 74; *Church History and Modern Revelation*, 1:63-64.

23. *Doctrine and Covenants Commentary* 76; *Church History and Modern Revelation*, 1:64-65.

24. *Ensign*, May 1987, 61.

25. Address to full-time educators in the Church Educational System, October 14, 1977.

26. See "Using the Scriptures in Our Church Assignments," *Improvement Era*, January 1969, 13.

27. *Mormon Doctrine*, 2nd ed. [1966], 765.

28. "The Seven Deadly Heresies," Brigham Young University fireside address, June 1, 1980, in *Devotional Speeches of the Year* (1980).

29. Letter to N.E. Seaton, January 4, 1833, *History of the Church*, 1:314-315.

30. *Millennial Star*, 56:643-644; in *Church History and Modern Revelation*, 2:70.

31. In Conference Report, October 1976; or *Ensign*, November 1976, 97.

32. *History of the Church*, 2:431.

33. *Teachings of the Prophet Joseph Smith*, 43.

34. In Conference Report, April 1963, 74.

35. In *Journal of Discourses*, 6:320.

36. In *Journal of Discourses*, 6:29.

37. Joseph Fielding Smith, *Essentials in Church History*, [1979].

38. "Patriarch Hyrum G. Smith," *Utah Genealogical and Historical Magazine*, April 1932, 51-52.

39. *History of the Church*, 1:119, Footnote.

40. Robert L. Millet and Kent Jackson, eds., *Studies in Scripture, Vol. 1: The Doctrine and Covenants* [1989], 158-159.

41. *Autobiography of Parley P. Pratt*, 5th ed. (1961), 52.

42. *History of the Church*, 1:117, Footnote.

43. In *Journal of Discourses*, 3:284.

44. Andrew Jenson, *Latter-day Saint Biographical Encyclopedia: A Compilation of Biographical Sketches of Prominent Men and Women in the Church of Jesus Christ of Latter-day Saints*, 4 vols. [1901], 1:74.

45. *History of the Church*, 2:185.

46. In Conference Report, October 1971, 167; or *Ensign*, December 1971, 129.

47. *History of the Church*, 1:127-128.

48. *Church History and Modern Revelation*, 1:143-144.

49. *History of the Church*, 1:128.

50. *Doctrine and Covenants Commentary*, 181.

51. *History of the Church*, 6:311.

52. *History of the Church*, 5:27.

53. *History of the Church*, 1:131.

54. *Doctrinal New Testament Commentary*, 3:428.

KIRTLAND AND MISSOURI PERIOD

[1820–1831]

ဆာင္း

The Gathering to Ohio

In every dispensation of the Gospel, the Lord has required His people to gather. And the gathering in the latter-days was to be the greatest of all. The Prophet Joseph Smith said: "All that the prophets … have written, from the days of righteous Abel, down to the last man that has left any testimony on record for our consideration, in speaking of the salvation of Israel in the last days, goes directly to show that it consists in the work of the gathering."[1]

Kirtland, Ohio ca. 1907

The Church was less than a year old when the Lord called upon His Saints in January 1831 to gather to Kirtland, Ohio. The members in New York responded obediently, selling their farms, gathering their belongings, and departing for Ohio. Martin Harris sold his farm and paid the $3,000 due to the printer of the Book of Mormon. Many of the Saints traveled together. The Colesville Saints traveled in one group, while other groups came from Fayette, Waterloo, and other places. Hyrum Smith and his father traveled overland before the ice broke, but the rest waited for the waterways to become passable. Lucy Smith led her children and a group of friends and neighbors by way of Buffalo, New York.

Sarah Studevant Leavitt said:

> I read the Book of Mormon, The Doctrine and Covenants, and all the writings I could get from the Latter-day Saints. It was the book of Doctrine and Covenants that confirmed my faith in the work. I knew that no man, nor set of men, that could make such a book or would dare to try from any wisdom that man possessed. I knew it was the word of God and a revelation from Heaven and received it as such. I sought with my whole heart a knowledge of the truth and obtained a knowledge that never has nor never will leave me. The next thing was to gather with the Saints. I was pondering over in my heart how it was possible for such a journey with what means we could muster. We had a good farm, but could not get much for it, but the voice of the Spirit said: "Come out of Babylon, O my people, that you be not partakers of her plagues." From the time the voice spoke so loud, clear and plain to my understanding, I knew the way would be open for us to gather with the Saints.[2]

Caroline Barnes Crosby said:

> We began to make arrangements to move to Ohio. It really seemed a great undertaking to me, but I had become so homesick that I could not think of staying there (in Massachusetts) another winter. We, therefore, decided on leaving the first of November 1835. When my husband first broke the subject to his father, he seemed very much distressed and used all the persuasion he was master of to induce him to stay, but all in vain; we had set our faces as a flint Zion-ward and were ready to forsake all to gain that part. When he saw that we were determined to go, he did what he could to help us away. We bid farewell to the brethren and sisters who wept freely and mourned our departure, but not as those without hope—for they intended many of them to join us again at some of the gathering places of the Church before many years if it was the Lord's will.[3]

At the time the Saints arrived, Kirtland, Ohio, had a population of about 1,000. The area was generally but not entirely flat, wooded, and with rich farmable soil. Several small streams and rivers flowed through the area. The commercial center was the Gilbert and Whitney General Store, which also contained a post office. Nearby, there was also a gristmill, a few shops, a sawmill, and a hotel.[4]

A Place of Many Revelations

More revelations were received during the Kirtland period than during any other in Church history. This is where the Church was fully organized and where the doctrines of salvation were explained. This is where the first House of the Lord was built, and the initial ordinances thereof began. The Lord had much to reveal to the Saints, and they needed to gather to receive it.

Year	Month	Revelations (D&C #)	Place
1831	February	41, 42, 43, 44	Kirtland, OH
	March	45, 46, 47, 48, 49	Kirtland, OH
	May	50	Kirtland, OH
	May	51	Thompson, OH
	June	52, 53, 54, 55, 56	Kirtland, OH
	July	57	Zion, Jackson County, MO
	August	58, 59, 60	Zion, Jackson County, MO
	August	61, 62	By Missouri River, MO
	August	63	Kirtland, OH
	September	64	Kirtland, OH
	October	65	Hiram, OH
	October	66	Orange, OH
	November	1, 67, 68, 69, 133	Hiram, OH
	November	70	Kirtland, OH
	December	71	Hiram, OH
	December	72	Kirtland, OH
1832	January	73, 74	Hiram, OH
	January	75	Amherst, OH
	February	76	Hiram, OH
	March	77, 78, 79, 80, 81	Hiram, OH

Year	Month	Revelations (D&C #)	Place
	April	82, 83	Jackson County, MO
	April	83	Independence, MO
	August	99	Hiram, OH
	September	84	Kirtland, OH
	November	85	Kirtland, OH
	December	86, 87, 88	Kirtland, OH
1833	February	89	Kirtland, OH
	March	90, 91, 92	Kirtland, OH
	May	93, 94	Kirtland, OH
	June	95, 96	Kirtland, OH
	August	97, 98	Kirtland, OH
	October	100	Perrysburg, NY
	December 101	Kirtland, OH	
1834	February	102, 103	Kirtland, OH
	April	104	Kirtland, OH
	June	105	Fishing River, MO
	November	106	Kirtland, OH
1835	March	107	Kirtland, OH
	August	134	Kirtland, OH
	December	108	Kirtland, OH
1836	January	137	Kirtland, OH
	March	109 Kirtland, OH	
	April	110	Kirtland, OH
	August	111	Salem, MA
1837	July	112	Kirtland, OH

Temples are the Key

Especially in the early days of any dispensation, the Saints must physically gather into one place to receive spiritual blessings. As the Church spreads throughout the world, they can gather in wards and stakes, and have temples built near them where they can receive all of the blessings of the Gospel without having to leave their homelands. The most important of those blessings are the temple blessings.

The Prophet Joseph Smith said: "What was the object of gathering … the people of God in any age of the world? … The main object was to build unto the Lord a house whereby He could reveal unto His people the ordinances of His house and the glories of His kingdom, and teach the people the way of salvation… It is for the same purpose that God gathers together His people in the last days, to build unto the Lord a house to prepare them for the ordinances and endowments, washings and anointings."[5]

Map of Early Church History Sites Between Ohio and Missouri

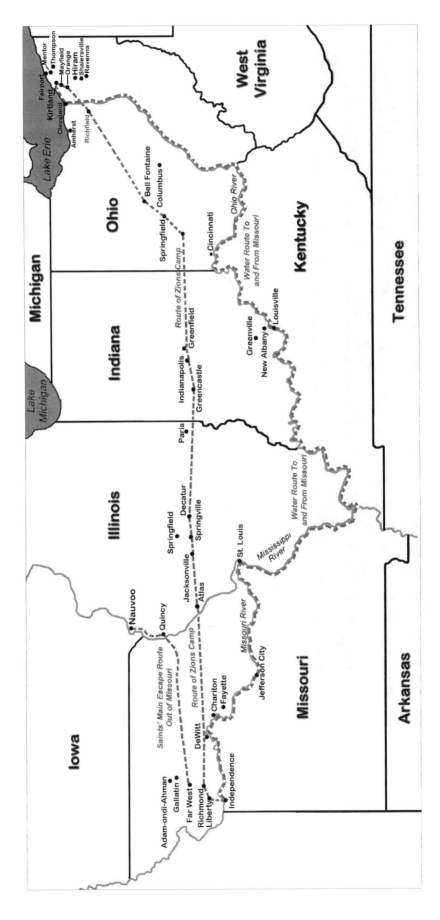

Church History Chronology
Kirtland and Missouri Period

PLACE:	DATE:		EVENT:	REVELATION RECEIVED	AGE OF THE PROPHET
Fayette, NY	**1830**	Sep	Missionaries (including Oliver Cowdery) are called to teach the Lamanites.	D&C 30, 31	24
		Oct 17	The missionaries to the Lamanites depart for their missions from Fayette, NY		
Kirtland, OH		Nov 4	In Kirtland, Ohio, the missionaries convert Sidney Rigdon and his congregation		
Fayette, NY			Sidney Rigdon and others visit the Prophet in New York.	D&C 34	
			Severe winter sets in with 4 feet of snow and freezing rain		
		Dec	Revelations are given to some important new converts—Orson Pratt and Sidney Rigdon.	D&C 35, 36	
			The Saints are commanded to gather to Kirtland, Ohio.	D&C 37	
	1831	Jan 2–5	At the 3rd conference of the Church, revelations given on gathering & forsaking the world.	D&C 38, 39, 40	25
			The revelation to move to Kirtland is announced		
Kirtland, OH			During January the Saints move from New York to Kirtland, Ohio		
			Joseph & Emma travel to Kirtland in bitter cold weather over immense drifts of snow in a sleigh		
			Emma is now at least six months pregnant with her twins		
Jackson County, MO			The missionaries to the Lamanites arrive in Missouri		
Kirtland, OH		Feb	Joseph and Emma arrive in Kirtland; live with Whitneys		
		4	Edward Partridge is called as the first bishop in the Church.	D&C 41	
		9	Joseph receives "The Law," and other revelations.	D&C 42, 43, 44	
			Isaac Morley begins a cabin for Joseph on his land		
		Mar 7	JST: Joseph is commanded to begin a re-translation of the New Testament.	D&C 45	
		8	Many instructions are given by the Lord as the Church grows rapidly.	D&C 46, 47, 48, 49	
			The revelation on eternal marriage is received but not published.	D&C 132	
			Joseph and Emma move into one-room log home of their own		
		Apr 30	Emma gives birth to twins who die within three hours		
		May 9	Joseph and Emma adopt the Murdock twins, whose mother had died in childbirth		
			The Prophet's mother—Lucy Mack Smith—arrives with the Colesville Saints		
			Joseph heals Mrs. Johnson's arm and the Johnson family joins the Church		
			Missionaries are sent to the Shakers		
			False revelations and manifestations cause problems.	D&C 50	
Thompson, OH			The Law of Consecration is introduced to help poor converts.	D&C 51	
Kirtland, OH			Consecration disputes slow the re-translation process		
		June 3	Fourth general conference of the Church is held; first high priests are ordained		

Church History Chronology — Kirtland & Missouri Period (Cont'd).

PLACE:	DATE:	EVENT:	REVELATION RECEIVED	AGE OF THE PROPHET
Kirtland, OH	1831 June 7	Missouri designated as Zion; next conference is to be held there; JST translation paused.	D&C 52	
	19	Consecration problems force Colesville/other members to move on to Missouri.	D&C 53- 56	25
Jackson County, MO	July	Joseph leaves for a visit to Jackson County, MO		
		Joseph and others arrive and hold a conference in Missouri		
Independence, MO	20	Independence, MO designated as the place for the City of Zion.	D&C 57	
Kaw Township, MO	Aug 1	the Colesville Saints arrive in Missouri		
Independence, MO		More revelation on Zion is received.	D&C 58	
	2	The Land of Zion is dedicated for the gathering of the Saints		
	3	The Independence Temple site is dedicated		
	7–8	Further instruction concerning Zion.	D&C 59–60	
	12–13	Further instruction concerning Zion.	D&C 61–62	
Kirtland, OH	27	Joseph and others arrive back in Kirtland.	D&C 63	
	Sep 11	Saints warned against debt; told to repent and forgive.	D&C 64	
Hiram, OH	12	Joseph and Emma move in with the Johnsons at Hiram, OH		
	Oct	JST: Re-translation of the Bible is begun again.	D&C 65	
		Ezra Booth leaves the Church and publishes lies in the press		
Orange, OH	25	The first of many important conferences convenes.	D&C 66	
Hiram, OH	Nov 1	A conference of elders votes to publish the Book of Commandments after settling disputes.	D&C 67–69	
	1,3	The Lord reveals His preface and appendix to the Book of Commandments (D&C).	D&C 1, 133	
Kirtland, OH	12	The Lord calls the Book of Commandments the "foundation of the Church".	D&C 70	
Hiram, OH	Dec 1	JST: Delayed; Joseph and Sidney are commanded to engage Booth's lies in public debate.	D&C 71	
Kirtland, OH	4	Newel K. Whitney is called as bishop in Ohio; duties explained; consecration again commanded.	D&C 72	
Hiram, OH	1832 Jan 3	JST: Re-translation delayed while Joseph and Sidney begin their mission to counter Booth's lies.	D&C 73–74	26
	10	Re-translation of the Bible is begun again.		
Amherst, OH	25	Joseph sustained as President of the high priesthood at a general conference.	D&C 75	
		Missionaries are sent to Canada—first organized missionary effort outside the U.S.		
Hiram, OH	Feb 16	Joseph and Sidney receive a vision of the degrees of glory.	D&C 76	
	Mar	Other revelations on doctrine are received.	D&C 77–81	
	24	Joseph Smith and Sidney Rigdon are mobbed, tarred and feathered		
	29	Joseph and Emma's adopted son, Joseph Murdock, dies from exposure received during mobbing		
Mendon, NY	Apr 30	President Brigham Young is baptized at age 30 in his own mill pond near Mendon, New York		
Jackson County, MO	26	The Prophet makes second visit to Missouri.	D&C 82	
Independence, MO	30	A general council is held in Jackson County, Missouri.	D&C 83	
	June 1	The first Church periodical—Evening & Morning Star—is published in Missouri		
Greenville, IN	June	The Prophet is delayed by an accident in Greenville, IN; arrives back in Kirtland later that month		
Hiram, OH	Aug	A revelation to John Murdock on missionary work is received.	D&C 99	
Kirtland, OH	Sep 22–23	A revelation on priesthood is received.	D&C 84	
	Oct	Joseph and Newell K. Whitney travel to Albany, New York, and Boston to purchase supplies		

Church History Chronology — Kirtland & Missouri Period (Cont'd).

PLACE:	DATE:	EVENT:	REVELATION RECEIVED	AGE OF THE PROPHET
Kirtland, OH	1832 Nov 6	Joseph Smith III is born on the day Joseph returns; he is their first natural-born child to survive		
Kirtland, OH	27	A revelation on the Law of Consecration is received.	D&C 85	26
	Dec 6	Re-translation of the Bible is begun again.	D&C 86	
	25	Joseph speaks his prophecy on the Civil War.	D&C 87	
	26–27	The Olive Leaf revelation, parts 1 & 2, are received.	D&C 88	
Kirtland, OH	1833 Jan 3	The Olive Leaf revelation, part 3, is received.	D&C 88	27
	22–23	The School of the Prophets is organized to teach and train Church missionaries		
	Feb 2	JST: New Testament re-translation is completed (*History of the Church*, 1:324).		
Kirtland, OH	27	The Word of Wisdom revelation is received.	D&C 89	
Kirtland, OH	Mar 8	Revelation concerning the First Presidency and keys of the kingdom is received.	D&C 90	
		JST: Translation of Old Testament nears completion; Lord emphasizes importance of this work		
	9	JST: Revelation on the Apocrypha received; translation not necessary.	D&C 91	
	15	Revelation to Frederick G. Williams of the First Presidency is received.	D&C 92	
	18	The First Presidency is organized and counselors are ordained at a Church conference		
	28	Revelation on priesthood is received.	D&C 107	
	May 6	JST: Lord says hasten this work; various revelations received on families, priesthood, temples.	D&C 93–94	
	June 1, 4	Further instructions on the Kirtland Temple and the Kirtland stake.	D&C 95–96	
	July 2	JST: The first revision of the Bible is "finished"—actually this is only first draft (*History of the Church*, 1:368).		
Independence, MO	20–23	A mob destroys W.W.Phelps' print shop, stopping publication of Book of Commandments		
	23	The Saints sign an agreement to leave Jackson County.		
Kirtland, OH	23	Cornerstone for the Kirtland Temple is laid		
	Aug 2	Revelation on Zion, the pure in heart, the temple in Zion, and God's protection is received.	D&C 97	
	6	Revelation on how the Saints should respond to their enemies & constitutional law.	D&C 98	
	21	First word about persecutions in Zion arrives in Kirtland with Oliver Cowdery's report		
Independence, MO	Aug–Nov	The Saints continue to be persecuted in Missouri		
Kirtland, OH	Oct 5	The Prophet leaves Kirtland to preach the gospel in Canada		
Perrysburg, NY	12	The Prophet worries about his family and the Saints in Missouri.	D&C 100	
Independence, MO	31	The Battle of the Big Blue occurs near Independence as mobs attack the Saints.		
Kirtland, OH	Nov 4	The Prophet returns to Kirtland from is mission to Canada		
Independence, MO	5	The mob disarms the Saints in Missouri and then attacks them		
Independence, MO	7	The Saints are driven out of Jackson County to Clay County, Missouri.		
Kirtland, OH	25	News reaches Kirtland of the expulsion of the Saints from Jackson County		
	Dec 10	The Prophet writes a letter to the Missouri Saints concerning Zion & reasons for their plight		
	16	A revelation about the reasons for the Missouri Saint's difficulties & the redemption of Zion.	D&C 101	
	18	The first Patriarch to the Church—Joseph Smith Sr.—is ordained		
Richland, NY	31	President Wilford Woodruff is baptized at age 26 in an icy stream near Richland, New York		

Church History Chronology — Kirtland & Missouri Period (Cont'd).

PLACE:	DATE:		EVENT:	REVELATION RECEIVED	AGE OF THE PROPHET
Kirtland, OH	1834 Feb	17	Duties of the stake presidency and high council explained; high council is organized.	D&C 102	28
		24	Parley P. Pratt and Lyman Wight return from Missouri.	D&C 103	
		26	The Prophet leaves Kirtland to recruit volunteers for Zions Camp		
Chardon, OH	Apr	1–3	The Prophet attends court in the Hurlburt case		
Lake Erie		12	The Prophet goes fishing on Lake Erie		
Norton, OH		22	Church conference is held in Norton, OH		
Kirtland, OH		23	The united order in Kirtland is temporarily dissolved; JST calls for publication.	D&C 104	
	May	5	Zions Camp is organized and marches west to liberate the Saints in Jackson County		
Clay County, MO	June	19	Zions Camp arrives in Clay County,		
Fishing River, MO		20	Zions Camp stops at Fishing River, Missouri		
		22	Zions Camp is miraculously protected from militia attack by immense storm		
Fishing River, MO		22	Revelation received for Zions Camp to disband; some participants are angry.	D&C 105	
Rush Creek, MO		24	Cholera breaks out among Zions Camp participants; some die		
		25	Zions Camp is disbanded		
Kirtland, OH	Aug	1	Zions Camp arrives back in Kirtland		
	Oct		The Prophet visits the Saints in Ohio		
	Nov		The School of the Elders opens in Kirtland		
		25	A revelation to Warren Cowdery is received.	D&C 106	
	Dec	5	Oliver Cowdery set apart as an Assistant President of the Church		
			A new Church periodical—LDS Messenger & Advocate—begins publication (until 1838).		
Kirtland, OH	1835 Feb	14	The Three Witnesses choose 12 Apostles—mainly from members of Zions Camp.		29
		28	The First Quorum of Seventy is organized		
	Mar	28	The revelation on priesthood is compiled (portions of it from 1831).	D&C 107	
	July	3	Mummies and scrolls purchased from Michael Chandler when he displays them in Kirtland, OH		
			Joseph Smith begins translation of the Book of Abraham from Egyptian papyri		
	Aug	17	A special conference approves the Doctrine and Covenants and publication begins		
			The Declaration on Government is adopted at conference.	D&C 134	
	Oct	8–11	Joseph attends to his father who is ill		
	Nov		Plastering on the Kirtland Temple begins		
			The first hymn book of the Church (compiled by Emma Smith) is published		
	Dec	26	A revelation to Lyman Sherman is received.	D&C 108	
Kirtland, OH	1836 Jan	21	Spiritual manifestations received in Kirtland Temple, including vision of celestial kingdom.	D&C 137	30
			Endowments begin in the Kirtland Temple		
	Feb	15	Joseph and others begin studying Hebrew under Professor Joshua Seixas		
	Mar	27	Dedication of the Kirtland Temple with many spiritual outpourings received.	D&C 109	30
			Two weeks of spiritual joy follow		

Church History Chronology — Kirtland & Missouri Period (Cont'd).

PLACE:	DATE:		EVENT:	REVELATION RECEIVED	AGE OF THE PROPHET
Kirtland, OH	1836	Apr 3	Joseph and Oliver see visions of Christ, Moses, Elias, and Elijah in the Kirtland Temple.	D&C 110	3
			Joseph warns the Saints of coming apostasies and trouble in Kirtland		
Ontario, Canada		May 9	President John Taylor is baptized at age 27 in Black Creek at Georgetown, Ontario, Canada		
Fairport, OH		17	Joseph goes out to meet his grandmother Mary Duty and accompany her to Kirtland		
Clay County, MO		June	The citizens of Clay County ask the Saints to leave the county		
Kirtland, OH		19	President Lorenzo Snow is baptized at age 22 in the Chagrin River, which runs through Kirtland, Ohio		
		20	Frederick G.W. Smith is born—Joseph and Emma's second son to survive after birth		
Kirtland, OH		July 25	The Prophet & others leave Kirtland for the East, seeking money for debts (without success).		
New York, NY		30	The Prophet and his companions visit the part of New York City burned in the 1835 fire		
Salem, MA		Aug 6	The Prophet receives a revelation concerning their failed efforts to obtain money.	D&C 111	
Far West, MO		Sep	Missouri Saints move to Far West and elsewhere—creating Caldwell & Daviess Counties		
Kirtland, OH		Nov 2	Kirtland Safety Society (bank) is organized and established		
Clay County, MO		Dec 26	Caldwell County is created for the Mormons		
Kirtland, OH	1837	Jan 2	Kirtland Safety Society (bank) opened for business.		31
		Apr 6	Solemn assembly held in the Kirtland Temple		
		May	Nationwide financial panic of 1837 hits Ohio; Joseph is denounced by dissenters in Kirtland, OH		
		30	Joseph is acquitted in Grandison Newell case		
		June	Joseph becomes seriously ill for awhile		
		4	Heber C. Kimball is called to take the Gospel to England		
Preston, England		July	The British Mission is opened by members of the 12—first mission outside North America		
Kirtland, OH		23	A revelation to Thomas Marsh regarding the duties of the 12 Apostles is received.	D&C 112	
			The Kirtland Safety Society bank fails and many lose their money and possessions		
		Aug	Much apostasy occurs among both leaders and members in Kirtland		
		Sep 3	"Old Standard" apostates break up a meeting in the Kirtland Temple		
			Three of the Twelve Apostles are rejected at a conference in Kirtland, OH		
Kirtland, OH		7	Joseph leaves Kirtland for a visit to Missouri		
Far West, MO		Nov 7	Church conference held in Far West, MO		
Kirtland, OH		Dec	Joseph returns to Kirtland amidst great dissension in the Church		
Kirtland, OH	1838	Jan 12	Joseph Smith flees from his enemies and heads west to Missouri.		32
		Mar 15	Kirtland Camp (righteous Saints) forms to help exodus from Kirtland to Missouri		
		July 6	Kirtland Camp (righteous Saints) begins exodus from Kirtland to Missouri		
		July-Oct	Righteous Saints flee Kirtland in fear of their lives and migrate west to Missouri		

Notes:

1. *Teachings of the Prophet Joseph Smith*, sel. Joseph Fielding Smith [1976], 83.

2. Autobiography, "History of Sarah Studevant Leavitt," in *Writings of Early Latter-day Saints and their Contemporaries* [1992], 6.

3. Caroline Barnes Crosby reminiscing her departure from Massachusetts for Kirtland in 1835, from her memoirs, microfilm of holograph, LDS Church Archives.

4. *Church History and Modern Revelation*, 4 vols. [1946–1949], 1:160–161.

5. *History of the Church*, 5:423–424.

CHAPTER 12

Gathering to Ohio and Missouri (Zion)

(D&C 37–45; 29)

[1831]

℘℧

INTRODUCTION

The Church at the End of 1830

Toward the end of 1830, Church membership numbered only a few hundred. In the western New York area, about seventy baptized members were frequently in contact with the Prophet as they gathered for meetings. Meanwhile, in Kirtland, Ohio, and nearby communities, over a hundred settlers had been baptized within a month of the arrival of the missionaries to the Lamanites, and this number was rapidly increasing.

Two early converts from Kirtland, Sidney Rigdon and Edward Partridge, traveled to New York to inquire of the Prophet Joseph regarding the Lord's will for them personally. Edward Partridge had not been baptized in Kirtland but was baptized by the Prophet Joseph in Fayette on December 11, 1830.

Joseph Smith commenced an inspired revision of the Bible in June of 1830. In connection with this work, some writings of Moses (the Book of Moses) were revealed, including visions and prophecies of Enoch (Moses 6 and 7) and a short description of the City of Enoch or Zion. (Moses 7:18–19). During the month of December 1830, Joseph Smith received by revelation the remainder of the book of Moses. Chapters 6 and 7 dealt specifically with the establishment of Zion in Enoch's day.

The Book of Moses Received by Revelation

(August 1830)

The Prophet Joseph Smith said: "Amid all the trials and tribulations we had to wade through, the Lord, who well knew our

Sidney Rigdon

Edward Partridge

infantile and delicate situation, vouchsafed for us a supply of strength, and granted us 'line upon line of knowledge—here a little and there a little,' of which the following was a precious morsel."[1] He then recorded the vision of Moses that became chapter 1 of the Book of Moses in the Pearl of Great Price.

The Book of Moses is a priceless book of scripture that may be taken for granted by many members. Joseph Smith had only recently completed the translation of the Book of Mormon from ancient plates. Now he was giving to the world an entire book of ancient writings by the prophet Moses, without benefit of any ancient record. It was given purely by revelation and written down by various scribes. All of this occurred between June and August of 1830.

Robert J. Matthews tells us that the Book of Moses was revealed as part of Joseph Smith's translation of the Bible, but it was not at that time called the Book of Moses. It was revealed in the summer and early fall of 1830, with some portions in November and December 1830 and some in February 1831.

Sidney Rigdon was neither the genius for, nor the recorder for, the early part of the Bible translation, so most of the Book of Moses had already been revealed before Rigdon came among the Saints. There were various scribes for this material, necessitated by the frequent movements of the early brethren, such as Oliver Cowdery's call to Ohio and Missouri, John Whitmer's call to Ohio, and Sidney Rigdon's entry into the Church and his arrival in Fayette, New York. These are all reflected in the changes of handwriting and the dating found on the original manuscripts of Joseph Smith's translation of the Bible.[2]

- **Doctrinal contributions of the Book of Moses.** Robert J. Matthews also listed the many doctrinal contributions of the Book of Moses. Following is a brief summary of his list.

  — The gospel of Jesus Christ, including baptism and other ordinances, was had from the beginning. The early patriarchs, beginning with Adam, worshiped Jesus and taught His gospel to their children and to the rest of mankind (Moses 6:22–23, 48–68). This fact is almost entirely lacking in all other translations of the Bible available today.

  — The Holy Ghost was operative among men from the beginning. The Book of Moses makes it very clear that the Holy Ghost was operative among people who had the gospel from the very beginning of man on this earth (Moses 6:52–68; 8:23–24).

  — There was a symbolic purpose to animal sacrifice. The symbolic nature of animal sacrifice is clearly portrayed in the Book of Moses, wherein it is specified that the sacrifice must be a firstling of the flock and that it was a similitude of the atoning sacrifice of Jesus Christ. This was revealed to Adam (Moses 5:4–9), and he was the first man on this earth to offer animal sacrifice in this manner and for this purpose.

— The "why" and "how" of creation. We learn [from Moses 1] that the events recorded therein were originally experienced by Moses after the time of the "burning bush" but before he had parted the waters of the Red Sea (Moses 1:17, 25–26), and also before he had written the book of Genesis (Moses 1:40–41). It seems to have been given to prepare him for writing Genesis… It was made known to Moses that God had created worlds without number, and that there were many inhabitants thereof. Furthermore, Moses was told that this creation was done by the deliberate action of the Almighty. [In answer to Moses' questions concerning why and how the Lord had done these things, Moses learned that God's work and glory consisted of] building worlds and populating them with people, [all] for the salvation and exaltation of His children.

In answer to the second question as to the HOW of things, Moses was informed that all things were done by the power of the Only Begotten, but that only an account of the creation of this world would be given to Moses. In the subsequent explanation he was told of the six creative periods of the formation of the earth. Thus, the information in the early chapters of Genesis actually seems to have been given to Moses in answer to these two specific questions: "WHY?" and "HOW?"[3]

All these things were important for Moses to understand before he began his ministry for his dispensation. They were equally important for the Prophet Joseph Smith and the Latter-day Saints to know, and were received with great joy in 1830. The Book of Moses is evidence of the marvelous gift of revelation possessed by Joseph. He produced it in a matter of months at a time when the major focus was on the Book of Mormon and just prior to the Saints' move to Kirtland, Ohio.

GATHERING TO KIRTLAND, OHIO

The writings of Enoch concerning Zion, which were contained in the Book of Moses, sparked a great deal of interest among the Saints. They wanted to know when and where Zion would be established in this dispensation. Very soon after the Saints had received the "prophecy of Enoch" (Moses 7), the Lord gave them the revelation now known as D&C 37.[4] Clearly, two things were needed before Zion could be realized: (1) revelation from the Lord giving His laws under the revealed order of Zion, and (2) the preparation and sanctification of the Saints.

● **D&C 37:1–4 The Saints are called to gather at the Ohio.** In this brief revel- ation, the Lord commands the Prophet Joseph Smith to postpone any more work on the new translation of the Bible "until ye shall go to the Ohio" (v. 1). By this, the Lord means Kirtland, Ohio, the hometown of Sidney Rigdon and Edward Partridge. The reasons given for this gathering to Ohio are (1) "because of the enemy," and (2) "for your sakes" (v. 1).

Saints gathered out of New York to Kirtland, Ohio

The "because of the enemy" part of this explanation would have been understandable to all Church members. Certainly, the opposition and persecution in New York had become intolerable, with many mob threats at Colesville and elsewhere, and many vexatious lawsuits against the Prophet for daring to preach anything other than orthodox Christianity.

The "for your sakes" part would have seemed more nebulous because they did not yet understand anything about temples or consecration or, for that matter, any of the higher doctrines and purposes of the Church. For this purpose, they needed to gather together. From the beginning, it was understood that Kirtland was only a temporary gathering place. The place of the City Zion was farther west in Missouri, and eventually the Church would need to gather there. Still, the Lord commanded the entire Church to go to Ohio at this time for purposes that they did not fully understand until later.

The Prophet Joseph Smith said that the main purpose in gathering the Lord's people in any dispensation is "to build unto the Lord a house whereby He could reveal unto His people the ordinances of His house and the glories of His kingdom, and teach the people the way of salvation," since these things can only be taught in a sacred edifice "built for that pur- pose."[5] This was certainly true for the gather- ing to Kirtland.

The Lord told Joseph himself not to go until he had "preached my gospel in those parts" (meaning the branches of the Church in New York), "and have strengthened up the church whithersoever it is found, and more especially in Colesville; for, behold, they pray unto me in much faith" (v. 2).

Early photo of the Kirtland Temple

PHOTO BY ANDERSON, 1907

But the Church as a whole should begin preparations to "assemble together at the Ohio" before the time when Oliver Cowdery would return from his Lamanite mission. (v. 3). The Lord makes it clear that there should be no force in this matter of gathering. "Here is wisdom," He says, "let every man choose for himself until I come" (v. 4). Most of the Saints did gather; a few did not.

- **D&C 38 The commandment to gather was repeated on January 2, 1831.** Joseph and the others immediately began preparing to leave for Ohio, but first they held a conference early in January in Fayette. Because D&C 37 had given the commandment for the Saints to assemble in Ohio, the conference was eager to learn more about the matter, and during the third conference of the Church, the Prophet received D&C 38.[6]

The Lord promised the Saints that after they had gathered to Kirtland, Ohio, He would give them His "law" for the government and blessing of the Church. They had already received much instruction through revelations up to this point, but this would be something more and something special. "The law" is found in D&C 42, which was received shortly after the Church moved to Ohio. The Elders were also promised "an endowment" after they relocated to Ohio, and for this purpose they later learned they would need to build a temple. The calling of bishops in the Church was also foreshadowed in this revelation [vv. 34–38], and it was only a short time later when bishops were ordained.[7]

● **D&C 38:4 The city of Enoch.** The Saints continued to have great interest in the prophecies of Enoch. These were contained in the Book of Moses 6–7, which was only recently received by revelation through the Prophet Joseph Smith. In this new revelation (D&C 38), the Lord refers to himself as "the same which have taken the Zion of Enoch into mine own bosom," thus acknowledging their interest in the topic.

● **D&C 38:5–8 Destruction of the wicked.** Referring to the wicked in all ages of the earth, the Savior says, "the wicked have I kept in chains of darkness until the judgment of the great day, which shall come at the end of the earth" (v. 5). These are those "that will not hear my voice but harden their hearts, and wo, wo, wo, is their doom" (v. 6). Here we have another Hebraism, where the word "wo" is repeated three times. In Hebrew culture, the way that something is given emphasis is to repeat it three times. We would say something like "and great wo" or "great is their wo." As for the righteous, the Lord assures His little Church that "mine eyes are upon you. I am in your midst and ye cannot see me" (v. 7). With His Second Coming, the day would soon come "that ye shall see me, and know that I am; for the veil of darkness shall soon be rent, and he that is not purified shall not abide the day" (v. 8).

● **D&C 38:9–39 Promises to the Saints if they will gather in Ohio.** The commandment to gather in Ohio was a great test of faith for the Saints, and not everyone heeded the call to gather with full devotion. But those who did were privileged to participate in great events related to the restoration of the Lord's Church and kingdom in the latter days. The Lord made the following promises to those who were obedient to the call.

— D&C 38:9, 15   The kingdom is theirs, and blessings heretofore unknown.
— D&C 38:18–20   They will receive an inheritance in a land of promise.
— D&C 38:21–22   The Lord will be their king and lawgiver.
— D&C 38:32; 41:2–3   The Lord will give His law unto the Church.
— D&C 38:32   They will receive an endowment from on high.
— D&C 38:33; 39:15   Missionaries will be sent to all nations.
— D&C 38:39   They will enjoy material prosperity.

● **D&C 38:23–42 Commandments for a Zion people.** Because the city of Enoch became a Zion people, the Saints needed to understand that the same would be required of them as they gathered together in these latter days. Therefore, the Lord includes a number of commandments in this revelation which describe the requirements for being a Zion people.

— D&C 38:24–25   Esteem your brother and sister as yourself.
— D&C 38:27   Be one.
— D&C 38:32   Gather together in one location (Ohio).
— D&C 38:39   Beware of pride and the love of riches.
— D&C 38:40–41   Labor with might to raise the voice of warning (in meekness).
— D&C 38:42   Go out from the wicked and be clean.

Dr. Daniel H. Ludlow said: "In ancient Israel, certain vessels (bowls, urns, vases, and other containers) and utensils were used in religious feasts and ceremonies. The vessels that were to be used in the temple had special significance and were handled only by those who were worthy and authorized and who had properly prepared themselves. In a somewhat similar manner, the Lord has indicated that His Saints should come 'out from among the wicked' (38:42) and leave the worldliness of Babylon so they will be worthy to 'bear the vessels of the Lord' (133:5)."[8]

The Case of James Covill
(D&C 39–40)

James Covill did not become a leader in the Church. In fact, he did not even become a member. He was one of those in New York who did not have the faith to gather to Ohio. The Prophet Joseph Smith said: "Not long after this conference of the 2nd of January closed, there was a man came to me by the name of James Covill, who had been a Baptist minister for about forty years, and covenanted with the Lord that he would obey any commandment that the Lord would give to him through me, as His servant, and I received the following: [D&C 39]."[9]

- **D&C 39:1–4 The faithful have power to become the sons of God.** This is strange doctrine to a Baptist minister like James Covill who has no concept of who God truly is and what man may become. The Lord makes it clear that it is He who is speaking by calling himself by a variety of name-titles: "him who is from all eternity to all eternity, the Great I AM, even Jesus Christ—The light and the life of the world; a light which shineth in darkness and the darkness comprehendeth it not; The same which came in the meridian of time unto mine own, and mine own received me not" (vv. 1–3). And the same, I might add, who would be rejected today by Pharisaic ministers of orthodox Christianity, who would scoff at any man who claimed to be a prophet or even the Lord Himself if He did not teach what they teach to the people. But for those who will listen and receive the word of the Lord, He has given "power to become my sons; and even so will I give unto as many as will receive me, power to become my sons" (v. 4).

- **D&C 39:5–6 To receive the gospel is to receive Christ.** How many times the Lord has offered the invitation: "Come, follow me" (Luke 18:22) or "Come unto me" (Matthew 11:28; 19:14; 25:36; Mark 10:14; Luke 18:16; John 6:45, 65; 7:37). We all yearn to follow Him, but how shall we do it properly? He provides the answer in this revelation to a man who is investigating the Church: "I say unto you, he that receiveth my gospel receiveth me; and he that receiveth not my gospel receiveth not me" (v. 5). And how does one receive the gospel of Jesus Christ? It is through "repentance and baptism by water, and then … the baptism of fire and the Holy Ghost, even the Comforter, which showeth all things, and teacheth the peaceable things of the kingdom" (v. 6).

- **D&C 39:7–14 James Covill failed to keep his covenant to obey.** Prior to receipt of this revelation, Covill had covenanted that he would obey any command that the Lord would give him through the Prophet Joseph Smith (History of the Church, 1:143). Unfortunately, he did not keep that covenant. The Lord said to him in this revelation, "my servant James, I have looked upon thy works and I know thee" (v. 7). The Lord acknowledged that Covill's "heart is now right before me at this time; and, behold, I have bestowed great blessings upon thy head" (v. 8), but He reminds Covill that "thou hast seen great sorrow, for thou hast rejected me many times because of pride and the cares of the world" (v. 9). This is fair warning that James Covill will have to humble himself and be obedient this time.

"But, behold, the days of thy deliverance are come," the Lord says, "if thou wilt hearken to my voice, which saith unto thee: Arise and be baptized, and wash away your sins, calling on my name, and you shall receive my Spirit, and a blessing so great as you never have known" (v. 10). If he will do this, the Lord will use him for a "greater work. Thou shalt preach the fulness of my gospel" (v. 11). Also, "power shall rest upon thee; thou shalt have great faith, and I will be with thee and go before thy face" (v. 12). He received a call to "labor in my vineyard, and to build up my church, and to bring forth Zion, that it may rejoice upon the hills and flourish" (v. 13). These are great promises. Can we imagine such things being said to us in our patriarchal blessings? It should have given James Covill a great desire to serve. But it didn't. He was called to serve in Ohio (v. 14), but rejected the call.

- **D&C 40:1–3 Why James Covill failed to obey the word of the Lord.** In the end, fear of persecution and the cares of the world caused his rejection of the gospel. Apparently, this had been a pattern in his life (D&C 39:7–8). The Lord explained to the Prophet Joseph and to Sidney Rigdon, "the heart of my servant James Covill was right before me, for he covenanted with me that he would obey my word. And he received the word with gladness, but straightway Satan tempted him; and the fear of persecution and the cares of the world caused him to reject the word" (vv. 1–2). This is sometimes the case with potential new converts who receive a witness of the truth of the restored gospel, then fail to respond out of fear or worldliness. When James Covill did this, "he broke my covenant, and it remaineth with me to do with him as seemeth me good" (v. 3).

President Joseph Fielding Smith said: "The Lord will reveal the truth once; then when this testimony has been given, the person should accept the truth and receive the gospel by baptism and the laying on of hands for the gift of the Holy Ghost… Cornelius received a manifestation in strict conformity to the instruction given by Moroni, and had he turned away there would have been no further light or direction for him. The Spirit of the Lord will not argue with men, nor abide in them, except they yield obedience to the Lord's commandments."[10]

Speaking of James Coville, Elder Joseph Fielding Smith also said: "We are led to believe that in this promised blessing, this foolish man was convinced of the truth, for it is clear that the Lord revealed to him things which he and the Lord alone knew to be the truth. However, when he withdrew from the influence of the Spirit of the Lord and had time to consider the fact that he would lose the fellowship of the world, and his place and position among his associates, he failed and rejected the promises and blessings which the Lord offered him."[11]

The Saints Gather to Kirtland

Between January and May 1831, most Church members in New York sold, rented, or left their farms and made the 300–mile journey to Ohio, making great sacrifices to be obedient. Newly baptized converts flowed into Kirtland from New England, the southern States, and Canada. Almost 1,000 Saints had gathered to Kirtland by the time the Temple was built. Thus, the first phase of the gathering in this dispensation was being accomplished.

In the latter part of January, the Prophet Joseph Smith and his wife departed for Kirtland in company with Sidney Rigdon and Edward Partridge. They arrived about the first of February. Once again, just as she had been when they moved from Palmyra to Harmony, Emma was pregnant—this time with twins. One can only imagine the uncomfortableness she experienced as their horse-drawn sleigh bounced over the icy roads toward Ohio. It must have been a blessed relief to finally arrive at their destination.

The village of Kirtland, Ohio

Elder B. H. Roberts described the arrival of the Prophet Joseph Smith in Kirtland:

About the first of February, 1831, a sleigh containing four persons drove through the streets of Kirtland and drew up in front of the store of Gilbert and Whitney. One of the men, a young and stalwart personage, alighted, and springing up the steps walked into the store and to where the junior partner was standing.

"Newel K. Whitney! Thou art the man!" he exclaimed, extending his hand cordially, as if to an old and familiar acquaintance.

"You have the advantage of me," replied the merchant, as he mechan- ically took the proffered hand, "I could not call you by name as you have me."

"I am Joseph the Prophet," said the stranger smiling. "You've prayed me here, now what do you want of me?" The Prophet, it is said, while in the East had seen the Whitneys, in vision, praying for his coming to Kirtland.[12]

Newell K. Whitney's store in Kirtland, Ohio

The Prophet says they were "kindly received and welcomed into the house of Brother Newel K. Whitney. My wife and I lived in the family of Brother Whitney several weeks, and received every kindness and attention which could be expected, and especially from Sister Whitney."[13] Elizabeth Whitney was a kind and gracious hostess, and since Emma was expecting another baby in three months, she was no doubt grateful for the comfort of a nice home.

A LITERAL GATHERING OF ISRAEL

- **10th Article of Faith We believe in a literal gathering of Israel in the latter days.** For most Christians, the "gathering" is merely a metaphor, suggesting that true believers will come unto Christ and be saved. For members of The Church of Jesus Christ of Latter-day Saints, however, the gathering is more than a metaphor. It is a fact. The tenth Article of Faith proclaims: "We believe in the literal gathering of Israel and in the restoration of the Ten Tribes; that Zion (the New Jerusalem) will be built upon the American continent; that Christ will reign personally upon the earth; and, that the earth will be renewed and receive its paradisiacal glory."

  The Prophet Joseph Smith said: "All that the prophets ... have written, from the days of righteous Abel, down to the last man that has left any testimony on record for our consideration, in speaking of the salvation of Israel in the last days, goes directly to show that it consists in the work of the gathering."[14]

- **D&C 29:1–2, 7–8 The Church was commanded to physically gather the elect.** The Lord declared to the Saints very early in this history of the Church (September 1830) that He would "gather his people even as a hen gathereth her chickens under her wings, even as many as will hearken to my voice and humble themselves before me, and call upon me in mighty prayer" (v. 2). He charged the Church with "the gathering of mine elect"—those who will "hear my voice and harden not their hearts" (v. 7). This was a command for a physical gathering—"that they shall be gathered in unto one place upon the face of this land, to prepare their hearts and be prepared in all things against the day when tribulation and desolation are sent forth upon the wicked" (v. 8).

  Elder Bruce R. McConkie said: "This promised gathering of the Lord's chosen people was the hope and prayer of all the prophets of Israel. Of it they spoke, and wrote, and prophesied. Even after the Lord Jesus had completed His earthly ministry, the ancient Apostles asked, 'Lord, wilt thou at this time restore again the kingdom to Israel?' He answered that this glorious eventuality was not for their day; that it was not for them to know 'the times or the seasons, which the Father hath put in his own power' (Acts 1:6–8); and that the gathering of Israel was, thus, to await the great day of restoration. [This gathering] shall continue until the righteous are assembled into the congregations of the Saints in all the nations of the earth."[15]

How Israel is Gathered Today

In the 1800s, a convert was baptized and then "gathered" geographically with the Saints to an appointed place: Kirtland, Ohio; Independence, Far West, Nauvoo, or Salt Lake City. This was primarily because of the small size of the Church and the need for Saints to gather into one place in order to be able to properly strengthen each other and build temples. Today, this is not needed. The Church has stakes and temples all around the world, making it possible for God's children to be nurtured and endowed without having to leave their homelands.

- **D&C 115:6 Gathering into stakes in every nation.** The Lord declared in April 1838 that "the gathering together upon the land of Zion, and upon her stakes, may be for a defense, and for a refuge from the storm, and from wrath when it shall be poured out without mixture upon the whole earth." Thus, we are to understand that the gathering is not just to one place—Zion—but to Zion's stakes around the world.

The Prophet Joseph Smith said as early as April 8, 1844, "I have received instructions from the Lord that from henceforth wherever the Elders of Israel shall build up churches and branches unto the Lord throughout the States, there shall be a stake of Zion. In the great cities, as Boston, New York, etc., there shall be stakes. It is a glorious proclamation."[16]

The British Saints gathered to Nauvoo in the 1840s

Elder Bruce R. McConkie said:

> We are now in a new era of church growth and development. In the early days of this dispensation, in the very nature of things, if the Saints were to survive as a people, they had to assemble together in chosen places. Otherwise, they would have been lost among the masses of men overcome by the world. But now, in large measure, we are past that stage of our history… We are becoming a world church—not an American church, not a British church, not a Mexican church, but a church for all mankind, for the honest and upright in every nation. The place of gathering for the Mexican Saints is in Mexico; the place of gathering for the Guatemalan Saints is in Guatemala; the place of gathering for the Brazilian Saints is in Brazil; and so it goes throughout the length and breadth of the whole earth. Japan is for the Japanese; Korea is for the Koreans; Australia is for the Australians; every nation is the gathering place for its own people.[17]

In April 1973, President Harold B. Lee, the 11th President of the Church, quoted the words of this scripture (D&C 115:6) in general conference, and in doing so, he in effect, announced that the pioneering phase of gathering was now over. The gathering is now to be out of the world into the Church in every nation.[18]

Elder Harold B. Lee said: "The Lord has placed the responsibility for directing the work of gathering in the hands of the leaders of the Church to whom He will reveal His will where and when such gatherings would take place in the future. It would be well—before the frightening events concerning the fulfillment of all God's promises and predictions are upon us, that the Saints in every land prepare themselves and look forward to the instruction that shall come to them from the First Presidency of this Church as to where they shall be gathered and not be disturbed in their feelings until such instruction is given to them as it is revealed by the Lord to the proper authority."[19]

● **D&C 133:14 Gathering out of spiritual Babylon.** The Lord commanded His Saints to "go ye out from among the nations, even from Babylon, from the midst of wickedness, which is spiritual Babylon." Thus, we understand that the gathering is to be spiritual (not merely geographical), leaving the world's wickedness behind and accepting the commitment to live more righteously. This does not negate our belief in a literal gathering of the descendants of Israel. It elaborates on how the gathering is to occur and what the requirements are for a person who wishes to gather with the Saints in these latter days.

THE IMPORTANCE OF ESTABLISHING ZION

The early Saints had read prophecies about the city of Zion, or New Jerusalem, being established in the latter days. They had now gathered to Ohio, preparing themselves to become a Zion people like those who dwelt in the city of Enoch. But there was also the matter of the New Jerusalem, which the scriptures predicted would be built in the latter days.

● **Isaiah 2:2–3 The law will go forth out of Zion.** Isaiah predicted that the Lord's house would be "established in the top of the mountains, and shall be exalted above the hills; and all nations shall flow unto it" (v. 2). Many people would gather there, and the "law" (political kingdom) would be administered from Zion (v. 3), while the "word of the Lord" (Christ) would come "from Jerusalem" (v. 3).

● **3 Nephi 20:21–22 The New Jerusalem will be built "in this land" and the tribes of Israel will gather to it.** The Lord said that He would "establish my people, O house of Israel ... in this land, unto the fulfilling of the covenant which I made with your father Jacob" (vv. 21–22). The place of their gathering "shall be a New Jerusalem" and "the powers of heaven shall be in the midst of this people; yea, even I will be in the midst of you" (v. 22).

● **3 Nephi 21:20–25 The Gentiles will assist Israel in building the New Jeru- salem.** Those gentiles who will "not repent and come unto my Beloved Son, them will I cut off from among my people, O house of Israel" (v. 20), and the Lord will "execute vengeance and fury upon them" (v. 21). But those who "will repent and hearken unto my words, and harden not their hearts, I will establish my church among them, and they shall come in unto the covenant and be numbered among this the remnant of Jacob, unto

The shining city of New Jerusalem

whom I have given this land for their inheritance" (v. 22). "And they shall assist my people, the remnant of Jacob, ... that they may build a city, which shall be called the New Jerusalem" (vv.

23–24). The Lord said "the powers of heaven shall be in the midst of this people," including the Savior Himself (vv. 22, 25; see also 3 Nephi 20:22).

- **3 Nephi 21:24–28 The Gentiles will also assist in gathering Israel.** At the same time, the Gentiles will "assist my people that they may be gathered in, who are scattered upon all the face of the land, in unto the New Jerusalem" (v. 24). And when this is fully come to pass, "then shall the power of heaven come down among them; and I also will be in the midst" (v. 25). The gospel will be preached throughout the world, to "all the dispersed of my people, yea, even the tribes which have been lost, which the Father hath led away out of Jerusalem" (v. 26). In this way, "the Father [will] prepare the way whereby they may come unto me, that they may call on the Father in my name ... [and] be gathered home to the land of their inheritance" (vv. 27–28).

- **Moses 7:61–62 The Book of Mormon and the revelations will sweep the earth with a witness of Jesus Christ.** Eventually, the earth will experience its paradisiacal rest, but before that happens "the heavens shall be darkened, and a veil of darkness shall cover the earth; and the heavens shall shake, and also the earth; and great tribulations shall be among the children of men" (v. 61). Yet, throughout all these difficulties the Lord promises, "my people will I preserve" (v. 61). He will restore His Church by sending down righteousness from heaven (revelations like those in the Doctrine and Covenants) and causing truth to spring out of the earth (the Book of Mormon) (v. 62). All of these will "bear testimony of mine Only Begotten; His resurrection from the dead; yea, and also the resurrection of all men" (v. 62). And both of these—the Book of Mormon and the revelations ("righteousness and truth")— "will I cause to sweep the earth as with a flood" (v. 62).

- **Moses 7:62 There will be a temple in the New Jerusalem.** The Lord will "gather out mine elect from the four quarters of the earth, unto a place which I shall prepare, an Holy City." There, in that Holy City, His people may prepare for the Second Coming, and there in that Holy City will be a "tabernacle" (temple). And the name of the city will be "Zion, a New Jerusalem."

The Prophet Joseph Smith said:

> The building up of Zion is a cause that has interested the people of God in every age; it is the theme upon which prophets, priests, and kings have dwelt with peculiar delight; and they have looked forward with joyful anticipation to the day in w hich we live; and fired with heavenly and joyful anticipations they have sung and written and prophesied of this our day; but they died without the sight; we are the favored people that God has made choice of to bring about the Latter-day glory... [It is] a work that God and angels have contemplated with delight for generations past; that fired the souls of the ancient patriarchs and prophets; a work that is destined to bring about the destruction of the powers of darkness, the renovation of the earth, the glory of God, and the salvation of the human family.[20]

A "Zion People"

The Lord's use of the name "Zion" for the New Jerusalem raises the question as to what Zion means. It is used in a spiritual sense to represent righteous people throughout the scriptures.

- **D&C 97:21 Zion is "the pure in heart."** This definition uses the term Zion to describe those whose hearts are pure and who will rejoice while the wicked mourn. This is what is meant by a "Zion people."

— **Moses 7:18** The Lord's people must be of one heart and mind. This means both spiritually and temporally. They must all dwell "in righteousness" and there must be "no poor among them."

— **D&C 105:5** Only when some Zion people have been established—a pure people capable of living the celestial law—will the Lord come to inherit His people; "otherwise," He says, "I cannot receive her unto myself."

— **Psalm 102:16** When Zion has been established, the Lord will "appear in his glory."

President Spencer W. Kimball said: "What does this mean to us? It means that if the members of the Church do real proselyting in their home wards that the number of converts could grow to astronomical figures and even hasten the time when the Lord will be returning to the earth in His second advent."[21]

Thus, we can see that we are not waiting for the Lord to come—He is waiting for us to be ready for Him to come. The sooner we are prepared to be a Zion people, the sooner He can come to inherit His people and their Holy City, the New Jerusalem.

President Kimball also said: "This day will come; it is our destiny to help bring it about! Doesn't it motivate you to lengthen your stride and quicken your pace as you do your part in the great sanctifying work of the kingdom? It does me. It causes me to rejoice over the many opportunities for service and sacrifice afforded me and my family as we seek to do our part in establishing Zion."[22]

The Location of the "City of Zion"

The Lord's use of the name "Zion" for the New Jerusalem suggests another definition for Zion—a physical location where the City of Zion will be built. Enoch's ancient city was called Zion. Both the old Jerusalem and the New Jerusalem are called Zion. And the American continents are also designated as "the land of Zion."

- **Moses 7:19 The city of Enoch was called Zion, a "City of Holiness."** As a result of Enoch's "preaching in righteousness unto the people of God," they established the very first "City of Holiness, even ZION." This is what we must do again today.

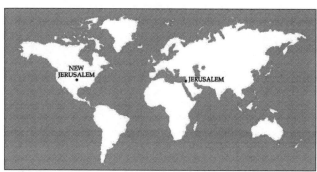

- **2 Samuel 5:6–7 The old Jerusalem was called Zion.** David captured the "city of David," which is Jerusalem, and which is referred to here as "the strong hold of Zion" (see also 1 Kings 8:1).

- **Joseph Smith said: "The whole of America is Zion."** You know there has been great discussion in relation to Zion—where it is, and where the gathering of the dispensation is, and which I am now going to tell you. The prophets have spoken and written upon it; but I will make a proclamation that will cover a broader ground. The whole of America is Zion itself from north to south, and is described by the Prophets, who declare that it is the Zion where the mountain of the Lord should be, and that it should be in the center of the land. When Elders shall take up and examine the old prophecies in the Bible, they will see it."[23]

While all of this is true, there is also to be a specific latter-day city named Zion—the New Jerusalem—that will be built and inhabited by a Zion people. One of the first major problems of this dispensation arose from the desire to know the location where this city of Zion would be built. This is why Hiram Page was using a stone that he claimed gave him powers of seership. Interest was high among the Saints, and the Prophet had been promised that the site of the New Jerusalem would be revealed to him (D&C 42:62).

- **Ether 13:2–8 The New Jerusalem will be built upon the American continent.** The Lord promised the prophet Ether that "a New Jerusalem should be built up upon this land, unto the remnant of the seed of Joseph" (v. 6). From the day when the floods of Noah receded off the land, the Americas became "a choice land above all other lands, a chosen land of the Lord; wherefore the Lord would have that all men should serve him who dwell upon the face thereof" (v. 2). They are also "the place of the New Jerusalem, which should come down out of heaven, and the holy sanctuary of the Lord" (v. 3).

The prophet Ether saw both the old Jerusalem and the New Jerusalem in vision, and saw that they are not the same city. The New Jerusalem, like the old one, will become "a holy city of the Lord; and ... built unto the house of Israel ... upon this land, unto the remnant of the seed of Joseph" (vv. 5–6). This, he said, was symbolic of how Joseph was separated from his brethren and then became the means by which they were saved (v. 7). Likewise, "the remnant of the house of Joseph shall be built upon this land; and it shall be a land of their inheritance; and they shall build up a holy city unto the Lord, like unto the Jerusalem of old; and they shall no more be confounded, until the end come when the earth shall pass away" (v. 8).

- **Ether 13:9–12 Both cities of Jerusalem will be holy and blessed.** Just as eventually there will be "a new heaven and a new earth; and they shall be like unto the old save the old have passed away, and all things have become new" (v. 9), so too will there be a "New Jerusalem; and blessed are they who dwell therein, for it is they whose garments are white through the blood of the Lamb" (v. 10). Those who dwell there will be "numbered among the remnant of the seed of Joseph, who were of the house of Israel" (v. 10).

The inhabitants of the old Jerusalem will also be blessed because "they have been washed in the blood of the Lamb; and they are they who were scattered and gathered in from the four quarters of the earth, and from the north countries, and are partakers of the fulfilling of the covenant which God made with their father, Abraham" (v. 11). All of this is in fulfillment of the prophecy that "they who were first [the Jews] ... shall be last; and ... they who were last [scattered Israel] ... shall be first" (v. 12).

- **D&C 57:2–3 The "City of Zion" will be built in Independence, Jackson County, Missouri.** The Lord said concerning that location, "this is the land of promise, and the place for the city of Zion" (v. 2). Independence, Missouri, is "the center place; and a spot for the temple is lying westward, upon a lot which is not far from the courthouse" (v. 3).

- **D&C 105:32 The kingdom established in the new Zion will be the kingdom of God.** All the kingdoms of the world will be "constrained to acknowledge that the kingdom of Zion is in very deed the kingdom of our God and his Christ," and will therefore be "subject unto her laws."

- **D&C 45:66–67 The New Jerusalem will be a place of refuge for the Saints.** While great destructions descend upon the wicked in the last days, the New Jerusalem will be "a land of peace, a city of refuge, a place of safety for the saints of the Most High God" (v. 66). Furthermore, "the glory of the Lord shall be there, and the terror of the Lord also shall be there, insomuch that the wicked will not come unto it, and it shall be called Zion" (v. 67).

GATHERING TO MISSOURI

The idea of ultimately gathering to a New Jerusalem "on the borders by the Lamanites" had been known to the Saints even before they gathered to Ohio. Those who were paying attention to the revelations knew that Kirtland was a temporary stop along the way. While many of the following events will be discussed in greater detail in later chapters, it is useful at this point to consider the following revelations which started coming while the Saints were still in New York, and continued on for nearly a year in both Kirtland and Missouri.

The water route from Kirtland to Independence

A Chronology of Latter-Day Revelation on the New Jerusalem

- Sep 1830   **The city of Zion will be "on the borders by the Lamanites"** (D&C 28:9)—the precise location to be identified later.

- Sep/Oct 1830   **Four missionaries called to preach to the Lamanites** (D&C 30:5–6; 32:1–3)—the first Church members to actually go to Missouri.

- Feb 1831   **A promise to reveal the location of the New Jerusalem** (D&C 42:62). The Lord will reveal it in His own due time.

- June 1831   Joseph Smith, Sidney Rigdon, and others called to go to Missouri (D&C 52:2–5, 42–43). The Lord will consecrate the land of Missouri as the land of their inheritance.

- June 1831   **The Colesville Saints told to continue on to Missouri** (D&C 54:8). The Colesville Saints had come from Colesville, New York. Despite persecutions and several forced migrations, they tended to remain together for many years, from New York to Ohio and on to Missouri.

- July 1831 **The city of Zion will be in Missouri, with Independence as the center place** (D&C 57:1–3). A temple will also be built in Independence.

- July & Aug 1831 **Saints are to purchase lands and receive inheritances in Missouri** (D&C 57:4–7; D&C 58:52–58), but in an orderly way and not in haste.

  A number of important callings in Missouri are also extended (D&C 57:7–11, 13, 14–16). Edward Partridge is to be a bishop. Sidney Gilbert is to establish a store. W. W. Phelps is to be a printer. And Oliver Cowdery is to edit publications.

- 1 Aug 1831 **Those who were "honored in laying the foundation" of Zion** (D&C 58:7) included members of the Colesville Branch and others who had arrived in Jackson County.

  The establishment of Zion as a city and people will not occur immediately after the Saints arrived in Jackson County (D&C 58:1–7, 44–45). Much hard work lay ahead and Zion will not be redeemed until after "many years." This helped the Saints to remain faithful through the coming difficulties in Missouri and afterward. The Lord's people must be tried in all things to become worthy of Zion (D&C 136:31).

- 2 Aug 1831 **The Prophet and the Colesville Saints laid the first log for a house in Kaw Township**, 12 miles west of Independence, in what is now Kansas City, Missouri. This was ceremoniously done "as a foundation of Zion."

  Sidney Rigdon dedicated the land of Zion as a gathering place for the Saints (D&C 58:57). His prayer included the temple lot, but Joseph Smith dedicated the actual spot for the temple.

- 3 Aug 1831 **The Prophet dedicated the spot for the temple in Zion** a little west of Independence, Missouri.

THE NEW TRANSLATION OF THE BIBLE

Seventy-seven of the revelations in the Doctrine and Covenants were received during the three-year period when the Prophet was translating the Bible. The experience provided a systematic approach to learning gospel truths, and led the Prophet to ask concerning many things that were subsequently explained through revelation. Because this "translation" was occurring largely during this period of time (1831–1832), and because it was related to the receipt of the Book of Moses, which we discussed earlier in this chapter, we will pause to discuss it more fully at the end of this chapter.

Kent Jackson said:

Shortly after the Church was organized, the Prophet Joseph Smith was instructed by the Lord to undertake a careful reading of the Bible to revise and make corrections in accordance with the inspiration he would receive. The result was a work of profound significance for the Church that included the revelation of many important truths and the restoration of many of the "precious things" that Nephi had foreseen would be taken from the Bible (1 Ne. 13:28–29; see also vv. 23–27). The inspired process began in June 1830. Over the next three years, the Prophet made changes, additions, and corrections as were given him by divine inspiration while he filled his calling to provide "a more correct translation." Collectively, these are called the Joseph Smith Translation (JST) or, as Joseph Smith referred to it, the New Translation. These titles are properly used for the text as written on the original manuscript pages. The title Inspired Version (I.V. refers to the edited, printed version, published in book form in Independence, Missouri, by the Community of Christ (formerly the Reorganized Church of Jesus Christ of Latter-day Saints). First published in 1867, the most recent edition [of the I.V.] was published in 1991.[24]

How the New Translation Began

On 8 October 1829 Joseph Smith and Oliver Cowdery purchased a large pulpit-style edition of the King James Bible (containing the Old and New Testaments and the Apocrypha) from E.B. Grandin in Palmyra, New York for $3.⁷5. It was this Bible which was used in the translation.

The first date recorded in the New Transla- tion was June 1830. The Prophet Joseph Smith said: "Amid all the trials and tribulations we had to wade through, the Lord, who well knew our infantile and delicate situation, vouchsafed for us a supply of strength,

The King James Bible used in the Inspired Revision (JST) process

and granted us 'line upon line of knowledge—here a little and there a little,' of which the following was a precious morsel."[25] Joseph then recorded "selections from the Book of Moses" (Moses 1), the "words of God, which he spake unto Moses at a time when Moses was caught up into an exceedingly high mountain" (v.1).

- **D&C 26:1** This message to study the scriptures in July 1830 was essentially the same nine months later when the Prophet was commanded to translate the New Testament. Joseph Smith and Sidney Rigdon continued their study of the book of Genesis for many months.

Purposes of the New Translation Process

- **The New Translation made Joseph a Bible scholar and led to many revelations.** The Prophet Joseph Smith's study of the Bible and his reliance on the Spirit gave him access to a flood of revelation that has benefitted all of us. Smith and Sjodahl said: "There can be no doubt that the close study of the Scriptures, such as that in which the Prophet engaged during these years particularly—for he was always a Bible student—was one of the means by which the Holy Spirit revealed to him the grand and glorious truths concerning the salvation of the children of men, before he sealed his testimony with his blood."[26]

Robert J. Matthews said: "[The Prophet] did not read through the Bible looking for errors, looking for ways to correct it. He studied the scripture for what he could gain. Then when it was inadequate, either because of loss of material or because of faulty translation, by inquiring of the Lord and studying and pondering and thinking about it, he was able to perceive by revelation what the intention of that passage really was" ("Using the Scriptures," in 1981 Brigham Young University Speeches, 123). Through the experience of translating the Bible Joseph Smith was to come into possession of knowledge he did not previously have… The labor was to be its own reward and would result in the spiritual education of the Prophet."[27]

According to Brother Millet, over 50 percent of the revelations in the Doctrine and Covenants were received during the time period associated with the inspired revision of the Bible. He calls the process "a living lesson in the matter of how to receive revelations." The Prophet immersed himself in the scriptures, and as he did, issues, curiosities, and questions surfaced. When he took these to the Lord, further light and knowledge came to the Latter-day Saints in the form of new revelations.[28]

Timeline of the New Translation of the Bible

8 Oct 1829	Joseph Smith and Oliver Cowdery purchase a King James Bible, with the Apocrypha, from E.B. Grandin in Palmyra, to use for the New Translation.
June 1830	Joseph Smith records the vision of Moses that became chapter 1 of the Book of Moses in the Pearl of Great Price.
21 Oct 1830	Joseph has completed up to Genesis 5:28. A manuscript of Genesis produced at that time by Joseph Smith bears this date.
Dec 1830	"Prophecy of Enoch" received (Moses 7; JST Genesis 7). The Prophet Joseph Smith said: "The Lord greatly encouraged and strengthened the faith of His little flock, which had embraced the fulness of the everlasting Gospel, as revealed to them in the Book of Mormon, by giving some more extended information upon the Scriptures, a translation of which had already commenced… To the joy of the little flock … did the Lord reveal the following doings of olden times, from the prophecy of Enoch."[29]
Dec 1830	Sidney Rigdon called to act as scribe for Joseph Smith (D&C 35:20).
7 Mar 1831	Work on the New Testament begins (D&C 45:60–61).

- **D&C 45:60–61** Work on the Old Testament continued until 7 March 1831. On that date Joseph received a revelation in which he was instructed to begin a translation of the New Testament (D&C 45).

- **D&C 52:1–2** An interruption came in June 1831 when Joseph and others were commanded to go to Missouri to dedicate the land of Zion and hold a conference. They returned to Kirtland in late August 1831.

Dec 1831   Another interruption in the work occurred after Oliver Cowdery and John Whitmer went to Missouri to print the Book of Commandments. The reason is explained in D&C 71.

● **D&C 71:1–2, 7–10 On December 1, 1831, the Lord gave the Prophet Joseph Smith and Sidney Rigdon the unusual direction to engage their enemies in public and private debate.** An apostate, Ezra Booth, published some letters against the Church in a nearby newspaper. The work of translation had to be delayed until the uproar caused by the letters had diminished. (D&C 71:1–2, 7–10). Sidney Rigdon called for a public debate with Ezra Booth through the medium of the Ohio Star. Booth failed to appear as scheduled, and Elder Rigdon announced to the assembled congregation that Booth did not defend his accusations because he knew they would not bear investigation. On December 3, Joseph and Sidney started this assigned mission.

● **D&C 73:1–6 A month later, they returned to Hiram, Ohio, and received D&C 73 on January 10, 1832.** The Lord told them to start translating again, saying, "It is expedient to continue the work of translation until it be finished" (v. 4).

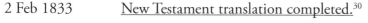
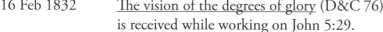
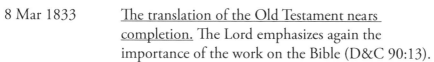
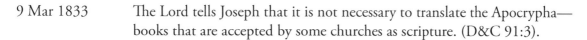

Sidney Rigdon

10 Jan 1832	Joseph and Sidney are commanded to return to the work. The Lord said: "It is expedient to continue the work of translation until it be finished" (D&C 73:4).
16 Feb 1832	The vision of the degrees of glory (D&C 76) is received while working on John 5:29.
2 Feb 1833	New Testament translation completed.[30]
8 Mar 1833	The translation of the Old Testament nears completion. The Lord emphasizes again the importance of the work on the Bible (D&C 90:13).
9 Mar 1833	The Lord tells Joseph that it is not necessary to translate the Apocrypha—books that are accepted by some churches as scripture. (D&C 91:3).
6 May 1833	The Lord tells Joseph Smith to hasten his translation of the scriptures (D&C 93:53).
2 July 1833	Translation of the Bible completed for the time being.[31]
1833–1841	The Lord directs the publication of the New Translation (D&C 94:10; 104:58; 124:89).
27 Jun 1844	Joseph Smith is martyred, having never published the New Translation.

● **The Prophet never finished his New Translation.** He never considered his New Translation to be ready for publication, and he would have made many more corrections had he lived longer. There are, as a result, many parts of the Bible that remain unclear or incorrect and which the Prophet did not have the opportunity to correct the meaning. He revised as far as the Lord permitted him, and it was his intention to do more, but because of persecution this was not able to be accomplished. However, many major errors have been corrected, which has proved to be very helpful to our understanding of the Bible.[32]

How Joseph Smith "Translated" the Bible

Elder Orson Pratt, who had a close association with Joseph Smith and who was very much interested in the New Translation, said on one occasion while reflecting on his life with the Prophet: "I … became intimately acquainted with the Prophet Joseph Smith, and continued intimately acquainted with him until the day of his death. I had the great privilege, when I was in from my missions, of boarding the most of the time at his house… I saw him translating, by inspiration, the Old and New Testaments, and the inspired book of Abraham from Egyptian papyrus."[33]

● **D&C 42:56–57 As part of the process of revising the Bible, the Lord instructed the Prophet to ask questions.** This thoughtful study provided a catalyst for revelation.

● **It was not a typical translation.** To "translate" usually means to change a written work from one language to another, which requires a knowledge of both languages. But when the Prophet Joseph Smith produced his "translation" of the Bible, it was not a typical translation. The Prophet said that what was written down at his dictation "was given unto [him]." His effort was spiritual rather than intellectual, and he was able to transmit not only the literal meaning of the words but the thought in the mind of the original writer.

● **It did not involve changing text from one language to another.** He worked with the English text of the King James Bible. It consisted of adding missing parts, rearranging the order of the words, and adding or deleting words or phrases.

● **These changes were given by revelation.** At one time, in discussing 2 Peter 1, the Prophet said that no man could understand the "secrets … in this chapter … unless by the light of revelation … which unlocks the whole chapter as the things that are written are only hints of things which existed in the prophet's mind."[34] The only way such things can be understood is by that light.

Robert J. Matthews said "The translation was not a simple, mechanical recording of divine dictum, but rather a study-and-thought process accompanied and prompted by revelation from the Lord. That it was a revelatory process is evident from statements by the Prophet and others who were personally acquainted with the work."[35]

The Results

● **3,410 verses in the JST differ from the King James Bible.**

— 25 verses compose the visions of Moses (Moses 1).
— 1,289 changes are in the Old Testament

— 2,096 changes are in the New Testament

● All Old Testament books received revision except Ruth, Ezra, Esther, Lamentations, Haggai, Malachi and The Song of Solomon.

— At the bottom of one of the Old Testament manuscript pages is the following: "The Songs of Solomon are not Inspired Writings." Hence, the Song of Solomon is not contained in the printed edition of the JST.

● All New Testament books received revision except 2 John and 3 John.

● Some of the books which received more revisions than others were as follows:

Old Testament		New Testament	
Genesis	662	Matthew	483
Exodus	66	Mark	349
Psalms	188	Luke	563
Isaiah	178	John	159
		Romans	118
		1 Corinthians	68
		Hebrews	47
		Revelation	75

Robert J. Millet calls our attention to a number of revelations now found in our Doctrine and Covenants that came as a direct result of Joseph Smith's translation of the Bible:

● **Old Testament Scriptures:**

— **D&C 29**
JST Genesis
Doctrinal matters revealed in the early chapters of Genesis—agency, accountability, premortal existence, the Fall of Adam, the revelation of the gospel to Adam and his posterity—received about the same time as the inspired revisions were being made to the early chapters of Genesis.

— **D&C 38:4**
JST Genesis (Enoch)
The Enoch material in the JST of Genesis (November-December of 1830) corresponds to a number of revelations in early 1831 which deal with the establishment of Zion.

— **D&C 42**
Moses 7:18
In February of 1831 the Lord revealed the "Law of the Church." which gives particular details of the law of consecration and stewardship and that there should be "no poor among them."

— **D&C 132**
Revelation on eternal (including plural) marriage. There is evidence it was received as early as 1831, while Joseph translated the Old Testament.

● **New Testament Scriptures:**

— **D&C 46**
1 Cor. 12
An important revelation regarding the gifts of the Spirit which may be tied to Paul's teachings in 1 Corinthians 12.

— **D&C 74**
1 Cor. 7
Paul refers to the holiness of little children (1 Cor. 7:14), but it is not clear what he means or why he associates it with clean or unclean spouses. Joseph Smith clarified the historical context out of which Paul was speaking. The Jews were teaching that uncircumcised children were unclean and that marriage to a non-Jew would render their children unholy as a result. Paul meant that all children (Jewish or Gentile) are holy, "being sanctified through the Atonement of Jesus Christ" and have no need of circumcision (or of baptism until they become accountable).

— **D&C 76**
John 5:29
The "Vision of the Glories" came while prayerfully pondering John.

— **D&C 77**
Valuable insights on the Apocalypse of John the Beloved (Revelation) are given in D&C 77. D&C 77 comments on only 8 of the 22 chapters in Revelation. The New Translation itself clarifies some other chapters of Revelation.

■ D&C 77:1 (Revelation 4:6) The "sea of glass" is the earth in its sanctified and transfigured state. The Prophet Joseph Smith said: "While at dinner, I remarked to my family and friends present, that when the earth was sanctified and became like a sea of glass, it would be one great Urim and Thummim, and the Saints could look in it and see as they are seen."[36] President Brigham Young said: "This Earth will become a celestial body—be like a sea of glass, or like a Urim and Thummim; and when you wish to know anything, you can look in this Earth and see all the eternities of God."[37]

■ D&C 77:2–3 (Revelation 4:7) Beasts have spirits, just as men do, and God loves and saves them all. The Prophet Joseph Smith said: "The grand secret was to show John what there was in heaven. John learned that God glorified Himself by saving all that His hands had made, whether beasts, fowls, fishes or men; and He will glorify Himself with them."[38]

■ D&C 77:4 (Revelation 4:8) The strange imagery of the beasts is symbolic—the eyes representing light and knowledge, the wings representing power and mobility.

■ D&C 77:6–7 This earth has a temporal existence of 7,000 years.

■ D&C 77:12–14 Christ will come in the beginning of the seventh thousand years.

■ D&C 77:8–10 Angels are appointed to restore the gospel and minister on earth, and eventually to destroy it at the command of God.

■ D&C 77:11 (Revelation 7:4) The 144,000 described in Revelation 7:4 will be high priests "ordained out of every nation, kindred, tongue, and people."

Elder Orson Pratt said: "Before the Lord shall come ... there is to be a great work among the nations... The ten tribes will have to come forth and come to this land, to be crowned with glory in the midst of Zion by the hands of the servants of God, even the Children of

Ephraim; and twelve thousand high priests will be elected from each of these ten tribes, as well as from the scattered tribes, and sealed in their foreheads, and will be ordained and receive power to gather out of all nations, kindreds, tongues and people as many as will come unto the general assemblage of the Church of the first-born."[39]

■ D&C 77:15 Two prophets will be raised up to teach the gospel to the Jews, and will be slain in Jerusalem. While they will be raised up "to the Jewish nation" they will not necessarily be from the Jewish nation.

Elder Bruce R. McConkie said: "[These two prophets are] followers of that humble man, Joseph Smith, through whom the Lord of Heaven restored the fulness of His everlasting gospel in this final dispensation of grace. No doubt they will be members of the Council of the Twelve or of the First Presidency of the Church."[40]

| — D&C 84 Hebrews | A number of themes—oath and covenant of the priesthood, the rest of God, etc.—similar to themes found in the book of Hebrews. |
| — D&C 88 D&C 93 | Both sections have language and concepts found in the book of John. |

● **Other Non-Canonical Scriptures:**

| — D&C 91 | A set of instructions regarding the Old Testament Apocrypha. |

● Brother Millet also identifies a number of other revelations in the Doctrine and Covenants that are tied to the work with the Bible directly through instructions found within them.

D&C 25:6; 35:20; 47:1	Information regarding scribes for the JST.
D&C 37:1; 45:60–61; 73:3; 93:53	The interruption and resumption of translation activities
D&C 41:7; 94:10; 104:58; 124:89	Facilities for translating.
D&C 26:1; 42:56–61; 90:13	Related matters found throughout the Doctrine and Covenants.

Notes:

1. *History of the Church*, 1:98.

2. "What is the Book of Moses?" in Robert L. Millet and Kent Jackson, eds., *Studies in Scripture, Vol. 2: The Pearl of Great Price* [1985], 28-30.

3. Adapted from "What is the Book of Moses?" 37-39.

4. *History of the Church*, 1:131-133, 139.

5. *History of the Church*, 5:423.

6. *History of the Church*, 1:140-143.

7. *Church History and Modern Revelation*, 4 vols. [1946-1949], 1:156.

8. *A Companion to Your Study of the Doctrine and Covenants*, 2 vols. [1978], 2:317.

9. *History of the Church*, 1:143-145.

10. *Answers to Gospel Questions*, comp. Joseph Fielding Smith Jr., 5 vols. [1957-1966], 3:29.

11. *Church History and Modern Revelation*, 1:159-160.

12. *History of the Church*, 1:146, Footnote.

13. *History of the Church*, 1:145-146.

14. *Teachings of the Prophet Joseph Smith*, sel. Joseph Fielding Smith [1976], 83.

15. Mexico City Area conference, *Church News*, 2 September 1972, 13.

16. *History of the Church*, 6:319.

17. Mexico City Area conference, 13.

18. Boyd K. Packer, in Conference Report, October 1992, 99; or *Ensign*, November 1992, 71.

19. In Conference Report, April 1948, 55.

20. *History of the Church*, 4:609-610.

21. In Conference Report, October 1976, 4; or *Ensign*, November 1976, 4.

22. "Becoming the Pure in Heart," *Ensign*, May 1978, 80.

23. *History of the Church*, 6:318-319.

24. *The Restored Gospel and the Book of Genesis* [2001], 17-18.

25. *History of the Church*, 1:98.

26. *Doctrine and Covenants Commentary*, [1972], 194.

27. *A Plainer Translation: Joseph Smith's Translation of the Bible, a History and Commentary* [1980], 53.

28. "Joseph Smith's Translation of the Bible and the Doctrine and Covenants," in Robert L. Millet and Kent Jackson, eds., *Studies in Scripture, Vol. 1: The Doctrine and Covenants* [1989], 139.

29. *History of the Church*, 1:131-133.

30. *History of the Church*, 1:324.

31. *History of the Church*, 1:368.

32. See Joseph Fielding Smith, *Doctrines of Salvation*, comp. Bruce R. McConkie, 3 vols. [1954-1956], 3:191.

33. In Ezra C. Dalby, "Joseph Smith, Prophet of God," address delivered 12 December 1926, Salt Lake City, 14; "The Lengthened Shadow of the Hand of God," *Ensign*, May 1987, 54.

34. *History of the Church*, 5:401-402.

35. *A Plainer Translation*, 53.

36. *History of the Church*, 5:279.

37. In *Journal of Discourses*, 8:200.

38. *Teachings of the Prophet Joseph Smith*, 291.

39. In *Journal of Discourses*, 16:325.

40. *Doctrinal New Testament Commentary*, 3 vols. [1965-1973], 3:509.

CHAPTER 13

The Law and Order of the Church

(D&C 41–59; 66–77)
[1831–1832]

ℰℭℛ

INTRODUCTION

I have had the opportunity to serve on a high council in a newly-formed stake. When we began, we literally had no stake officers except for the stake presidency, their clerks and secretaries. They had to build a stake from scratch, largely blindly because they knew very few people in the assembled stake. They were reliant upon the Lord for revelation to know whom to call and what to do. It was inspiring to see how the Lord led them and how the right people ended upon in the right places to bless the lives of the stake members.

Kirtland in 1831–1832 was very much like our new stake. The Church was largely unorganized and everything they did was a new experience. The Saints received many revelations and had to make many adjustments. Every member of the Church was a convert, including Joseph Smith. None of them had ever been part of a fully- functioning Church of Jesus Christ.

At the beginning, most of the officers were not yet called. Many of the doctrines were not yet revealed, and those that were already received were not well understood.Like little children,

The Church operates according to precise procedures of common consent

the members rejoiced in their circumstances but were sometimes overwhelmed with them. Into this vacuum the Lord sent dozens of revelations to establish the true order of the Church.

A Revelation on Church Organization and Doctrine

(D&C 41)

D&C 41 was given through the Prophet Joseph Smith on February 4, 1831, at the Newel K. Whitney home in Kirtland, Ohio.[1] This was the first in a series of revelations on how the Church should be governed.

● **D&C 41:1–3 The elders shall govern the Church by the spirit of revelation.**

Members of the Church were commanded to be obedient, with a promise of "the greatest of all blessings" if they would and the "heaviest of all cursing" if they would not (v. 1). The elders (leaders) of the Church who had already been appointed were to "assemble yourselves together to agree upon my word" (v. 2). And through prayer they would "receive my law, that ye may know how to govern my church and have all things right before me" (v. 3).

● **D&C 41:4–6 True disciples will receive and keep the Lord's law.** The Lord says to His leaders "ye shall see that my law is kept" (v. 4). He who receives and obeys the Lord's laws "the same is [His] disciple" and he who does not "the same is not [His] disciple, and shall be cast out from among you" (v. 5).

The Lord does not want "the things which belong to the children of the kingdom" to be given to the unworthy, like "pearls to be cast before swine" (v. 6). Discipleship is more than membership; it is obedience to the word of the Lord.

President Spencer W. Kimball said: "Defining and describing Zion will not bring it about. That can only be done through consistent and concerted daily effort by every single member of the Church. No matter what the cost in toil or sacrifice, we must 'do it.' That is one of my favorite phrases: 'Do It.'"[2]

The Office of a Bishop

(D&C 41, 51, 58)

In the early months of the Church, the pastoral responsibilities of watching over the members rested mainly upon the Prophet Joseph Smith. At the time of the organization of the Church on April 6, 1830, four new offices were introduced:

— Melchizedek priesthood   Elder
— Aaronic priesthood   Priest, teacher, deacon

As the Saints increased in number and, in the early months of 1831, began to move from New York to Ohio, there was need for additional leadership. Five new offices were added:

— Aaronic priesthood	Bishop	1831, February
— Melchizedek priesthood	High priests	1831, June
	Patriarch	1833, December
	High council	1834, January
	Apostles	1835, February

The Church needed a bishop. The Saints were gathering into Kirtland by the thousands, without jobs or land or homes. In order to deal with this situation, and to prepare His people for a coming Zion society, the Lord would soon introduce the law of consecration and set the bishop at the head of its administration.

- **D&C 41:7–11 Edward Partridge is named as the first Pre- siding Bishop of the Church.** The Lord recognized the need of His leaders to have homes and temporal security. He command- ed that the Saints build a home for Joseph and his family "in which to live and translate" (v. 7). Sidney Rigdon, who already owned a home in Kirtland from the time before he joined the Church, was to "live as seemeth him good, inasmuch as he keepeth my commandments" (v. 8).

Edward Partridge

Edward Partridge, another local resident who had joined the Church, was to be sustained "and ordained a bishop unto the church," to leave his hatter's shop and serve full time in this new capacity (v. 9). The Lord declares his worthiness for this responsibility "because his heart is pure before me, for he is like unto Nathanael of old, in whom there is no guile" (v. 11).

Guile is trickery, a hidden agenda, or a self-serving attitude. A bishop—who administers over temporal things—would need to be guileless. The duties of a bishop are not well known at this point, but he will need to "see to all things … appointed unto him in my laws in the day that I shall give them" (v. 10). In other words, he should fulfill all the duties of his office as and when they are given to him in the future.

- **D&C 72:2, 8 Newel K.** Whitney was ordained a bishop in December 1831. Bishop Partridge had been called to Missouri, where he continued to preside. Another bishop was needed to direct the temporal affairs of the Church in Ohio, so Newel K. Whitney was called as a bishop "in this part of the Lord's vine- yard" (v. 2). Since communication with bishop Partridge in Missouri was difficult, this revelation also provided for the first system of bishop's recommends (called "certificates") (vv. 17– 18).

Newel K. Whitney

At this time, Bishop Partridge sought instructions from the Prophet concerning his duties, and received D&C 51 in response.

- **D&C 51:1–12 He was "to organize this people" that they "may be one."** This included, among other things:

   — Apportioning to the people their property, "every man equal according to his family, according to his circumstances and his wants and needs" (v. 3).
   — Issuing a certificate to each person that would secure to him his stewardship (v. 4).
   — Receive the surplus from the stewardships and store it in a storehouse (v. 5).
   — Administer relief for the poor out of the storehouse (v. 13).

- **D&C 51:15–20 Wherever we live we are to act as if our stay there is permanent, not excusing inactivity or slothfulness because "we won't be there long."** The Saints knew their time in Kirtland would be limited. But the Lord gave them "a privilege of organizing themselves according to my laws" while they were there (v. 15). Kirtland was a consecrated spot "for a little season, until I, the Lord, shall provide for them otherwise, and command them to go hence" (v. 16). In the meantime, they were commanded to "act upon this land as [if they would be there] for years, and this shall turn unto them for their good" (v. 17).

This principle applied also to "Edward Partridge, in other places, in all churches" (v. 18). In other words, it applies to all of us. Wherever we go, and for whatever period of time—short or long—we are to serve and help to build the kingdom as if we are going to live in that area forever. The kingdom does not need drifters; it needs workers. And those who are "a faithful, a just, and a wise steward shall enter into the joy of his Lord, and shall inherit eternal life" (v. 19).

● **D&C 58:17–18 Bishops are also judges in Israel.** While speaking of the mission and calling of Bishop Edward Partridge in Missouri, the Lord said: "And whoso standeth in this mission is appointed to be a judge in Israel" (v. 17). His judgment will be needed in both temporal and spiritual matters. (1) He is a judge, "as it was in ancient days, to divide the lands of the heritage of God unto his children" (v. 17)—a temporal administrator of sacred funds and commodities and of stewardships. And (2) he is "to judge his people by the testimony of the just, and by the assistance of his counselors, according to the laws of the kingdom" (v. 18)—a spiritual judge of the people's standing before the Lord.

Reading and Heeding the Words of the Lord

● **D&C 41:12 The importance of studying and living by the scriptures.** When the Lord speaks, it is not a light matter. We must regard the word of the Lord with the greatest of seriousness and sanctity. "Wherefore, beware how you hold them," the Lord says, "for they are to be answered upon your souls in the day of judgment."

President Harold B. Lee said: "We need to teach our people to find their answers in the scriptures… But the unfortunate thing is that so many of us are not reading the scriptures. We do not know what is in them, … [and] therein is one of our biggest dangers of today."[3]

Elder Carlos E. Asay said: "I fear that many of us rush about from day to day taking for granted the holy scriptures… Little wonder we develop anemic souls and lose our direction in living. How much better it would be if we planned and held sacred fifteen or twenty minutes a day for reading the scriptures. Such interviews with Deity would help us recognize His voice and enable us to receive guidance in all of our affairs."[4]

Elder Spencer W. Kimball said: "I find that when I get casual in my relationships with divinity and when it seems that no divine ear is listening and no divine voice is speaking, that I am far, far away. If I immerse myself in the scriptures the distance narrows and the spirituality returns. I find myself loving more intensely those whom I must love with all my heart and mind and strength, and loving them more, I find it easier to abide their counsel."[5]

THE LAW OF THE CHURCH

(D&C 42)

While the Saints were still in New York, the Lord promised them that after they gathered to Ohio He would give them "my law" (D&C 38:32; 41:2–3). Consequently, twelve elders met on February 9 in prayer, and seven elders met later, on February 23, to inquire of the Lord about the "law" He had promised to give them. Section 42 is the fulfillment of that promise and the answer to those prayers. The Lord said to them as the revelation began, "hearken and hear and obey the law which I shall give unto you" (D&C 42:2).

This revelation was given in two pieces—the first on February 9, 1831 (vv. 1–73) and the second on February 23, 1831 (vv. 74–93), in the Newel K. Whitney home in Kirtland. Because it is comprised of these two distinct, though closely related, revelations, it was originally printed in the Book of Commandments as two chapters: verses 1 through 73 were chapter 44; verses 74 through 93, though not in that order, comprised chapter 47. This latter part, according to Elder Joseph Fielding Smith, was "given for the establishment of the City of Zion—New Jerusalem—which was to be built by the law of consecration and obedience to the fulness of the Gospel."[6]

"Known simply as 'The Law,' or 'The Law of the Church,' section 42 contains instructions relative to the law of consecration and stewardship, the Decalogue [Ten Commandments], and the law of discipline with regard to members who violate Church rules."[7]

"From the beginning of the law's implementation, there were difficulties in living it fully. Although the Prophet wrote to Martin Harris on 22 February 1831 that the Saints had 'received the laws of the kingdom since we came here and the Disciples in these parts have received them gladly,' John Whitmer indicated that there were 'some that would not receive the Law.' Whitmer explained: 'The time has not yet come that the law can be fully established, for the disciples live scattered and are not organized, our numbers are small, and the disciples untaught, consequently they understand not the things of the kingdom.'"[8]

Fundamental Duties of Church Leaders

As the Saints began to gather at Kirtland, Ohio, in 1831, they were entering a large community of Saints on the frontier—the unsettled land in Ohio known then as the Western Reserve. Many settlers who moved to that area left behind the cultural and religious norms of New England for life on the Western frontier, which was often marked by lawlessness and moral laxity. The Lord here established a basic framework of laws to govern His church and to sanctify His people (D&C 41:3–4; 88:34).

● **D&C 42:4–9 A mission call for all the elders.** The elders are called to preach the gospel, baptize, and build up the Church. All of them were called on missions by this revelation, though Joseph and Sidney's mission would be only brief (vv. 4–5). They are to go forth "in the power of my Spirit, preaching my gospel, two by two, in my name, lifting up your voices as with the sound of a trump, declaring my word like unto angels of God" (v. 6). They are to preach repentance, baptize, and "build up my church in every region" (vv. 7–8). Their missions will last until the time comes for the Lord to reveal to them the location of the New Jerusalem, which occurred five months later (D&C 57) in July 1831. (v. 9).

- **D&C 42:11 The necessity of public sustainings and ordin- ations.** Those who are called to the ministry must be publicly called, sustained, and set apart, and teach the gospel found in the scrip- tures. This scripture is crucial to our understanding of who is authorized to receive and hold priesthood keys, since many apostate groups claim secret or private ordinations as the basis of their authority. The requirements are clear: (1) he must be ordained by someone who has authority, (2) it must be known to the Church membership that he has authority, and (3) he must be "regularly ordained" by the heads of the Church. There are no secret ordinations in the Lord's Church.

- **D&C 42:12–13   Teaching from the scriptures, by precept and example.** The source and method of teaching are: (1) they are to "teach the principles of my gospel, which are in the Bible and the Book of Mormon, in the which is the fulness of the gospel" (v. 12); (2) they are to set an example by "observ[ing] the covenants and church articles to do them" (v. 13); and (3) they are to be "directed by the Spirit" in all that they teach (v. 13).

- **D&C 42:14 Teaching with the Spirit.** With regard to teaching by the Spirit, the Lord said that "the Spirit shall be given unto you by the prayer of faith," and then observed with clarity that "if ye receive not the Spirit ye shall not teach."

I do not believe that this is a *commandment* as much as it is a fact. Without the Spirit, teaching is simply not possible. The Spirit is necessary for any person to transmit to any other the thoughts of his mind and the feelings of his heart. Otherwise, there is no way to do it. We may well transmit words, but we will not transmit what is in our minds and hearts, unless we have the Spirit.

The Lord explained it this way: "Therefore, why is it that ye cannot understand and know, that he that receiveth the word by the Spirit of truth receiveth it as it is preached by the Spirit of truth? Wherefore, he that preacheth and he that receiveth, understand one another, and both are edified and rejoice together" (D&C 50:21–22). The Spirit is the Great Communicator— capable of carrying the feelings and thoughts of God to man, or from man to man, with perfect clarity. We either use this means, or we do not truly teach.

The Ten Commandments

● **D&C 42:18–29** The laws revealed here are similar to the Ten Commandments recorded in Exodus 20:2–17. Elder Joseph Fielding Smith emphasized that the Ten Command- ments are part of the laws of God and that they are as binding today as they were in the days of Moses. They were revealed to people in similar situations. Both the Israelites and the Latter-day Saints were God's people arriving at a new location; both were leaving behind an old way of life and seeking to know the will of the Lord forthem under new circumstances.

The Law is given in every dispensation

The Saints Were Commanded To:	The Saints Were Commanded Not To:
Love wife (v. 22)	Kill (vv. 18–19).
Love God: (v. 29)	Steal (v. 20).
Serve him	Lie (v. 21).
Keep His commandments	Lust (v. 23).
Remember the poor (v. 30)	Commit adultery (v. 24).
Make garments plain (v. 40)	Speak evil (v. 27).
Be clean (v. 41)	Do harm to neighbor (v. 27).
	Be proud (v. 40).
	Be idle (v. 42).

● **D&C 100:16** Later, the Lord revealed His intention to "raise up … a pure people." Latter-day Saints, like the ancient Israelites, are a covenant people with the responsibility and the privilege to help establish God's kingdom through obedience to His laws.

Scriptures and Revelation

● **D&C 42:56–60** Scriptures govern the Church and are to be proclaimed to the world. The process for receiving revelation in those days was very simple and clear: "Thou shalt ask, and my scriptures shall be given as I have appointed, and they shall be preserved in safety" (v. 56). But they were to "hold thy peace concerning them, and not teach them until ye have received them in full" (v. 57). This particular section, for example was given in two pieces and was not complete until the second one was received.

Then, once fully received, the Lord's commandments were to be taught "unto all men; for they shall be taught unto all nations, kindreds, tongues and people" (v. 58). Also they were to use these revelations as a "law to govern my church" (v. 59). So, whether used for doctrine or for instruction on how to administer the Church, those that "doeth according to these things shall be saved, and he that doeth them not shall be damned if he so continue" (v. 60).

- **D&C 42:61–62 Revelations are promised to those who ask and are worthy.** Those were astounding times for the infant Church. The Lord declared, "If thou shalt ask, thou shalt receive revelation upon revelation, knowledge upon knowledge, that thou mayest know the mysteries and peaceable things—that which bringeth joy, that which bringeth life eternal" (v. 61). The entire body of the revelations contained in the Doctrine and Covenants is tangible evidence that the Lord kept His word on this matter. But the timetable remained in the Lord's hands. For example, He said: "it shall be revealed unto you in mine own due time where the New Jerusalem shall be built." This principle also applies to our personal prayers. If we ask in faith, the Lord will hear and will answer, but He will answer in His own way and "in [His] own due time," according to what is best for us.

- **D&C 42:63–64 The Saints are to flee to the west to avoid coming dangers.** The Church was to send missionaries "to the east and to the west, to the north and to the south" (v. 63). Those who are converted in the east shall be instructed to "flee to the west, and this in consequence of that which is coming on the earth, and of secret combinations" (v. 64). Why did the Lord move His people westward time after time—fromNew York to Kirtland, to Missouri and Illinois, and finally to the Mountain West? The answer is partly revealed in these two verses. "That which is coming on the earth" included a devastating and bloody Civil War which would take the lives of hundreds of thousands of young men and leave the country reeling in sorrow. The Lord moved the Saints out of the way before that great calamity struck.

Dead Civil War soldiers on the field of Gettysburg

- **D&C 42:65–69 The Saints are blessed to know the mysteries and covenants.** If the Saints will observe and keep the laws of God, "great shall be thy reward; for unto you it is given to know the mysteries of the kingdom, but unto the world it is not given to know them" (v. 65). They are to keep "the laws which ye have received and be faithful" (v. 66). And they will "hereafter receive church covenants, such as shall be sufficient to establish you, both here and in the New Jerusalem" (v. 67). If people lack wisdom, they may ask of God, "and I will give him liberally and upbraid him not" (v. 68). With all these promised blessings, we ought to "lift up your hearts and rejoice, for unto you the kingdom, or in other words, the keys of the church have been given" (v. 69). In the Church we enjoy every blessing, every covenant, every key, and every scripture that God has given to man. We are truly a blessed people.

Marriage Is Ordained of God

● **D&C 42:74–77 The obligations of married partners are to be faithful and pure in their lives.** If a person divorces a spouse "for the cause of fornication," and "they … testify before you in all lowliness of heart that this is the case, ye shall not cast them out from among you" (v. 74). In other words, divorce is justified when a companion violates the marriage vow. But if a person has "left their companions for the sake of adultery, and they themselves are the offenders, and their companions are living, they shall be cast out [excommunicated] from among you" (v. 75). Marriage and family are sacred, and the leaders of the Church are commanded to be "watchful and careful, with all inquiry, that ye receive [allow to remain in the Church] none such among you if they are married" (v. 76). Unmarried persons who commit fornication must also be excommunicated unless they "repent of all their sins" (v. 77).

©RANDAL S. CHASE, 1971-0201

President Harold B. Lee said: "Satan's greatest threat today is to destroy the family, and to make mockery of the law of chastity and the sanctity of the marriage covenant."[9] As a result, for thousands of years marriage has been looked upon as either "sinful" (by the churches) or "unnecessary" (by the free love crowd). Since eternal life may only be achieved through celestial marriage, Satan does all within his power to "forbid" men and women to marry. Celibacy, living together out of wedlock, homosexuality, adultery, abortion, and birth control are but a few of the many methods employed by Satan to pervert men's minds and prevent the creation and continuance of this holy union.

Dealing with Transgressors

● **D&C 42:79, 84–87 Civil courts vs.** Church courts. Some offenders should be tried by civil courts, according to the laws of the land. This includes those who kill, steal or rob, or lie (vv. 79, 84–86). But if a person sins—does "any manner of iniquity"—he or she should be "delivered up unto the law … of God"—meaning dealt with by the Church, possibly even including being tried by a Church disciplinary council.

● **D&C 42:80–83 Conduct of Church disciplinary councils.** Those who need to be tried for their membership must be brought "before two elders of the Church, or more, and every word shall be established against him or her by two witnesses [members] of the Church" (v. 80) We do not rely on the testimony of those outside the Church, and for every fact we need two witnesses—"but if there are more than two witnesses it is better" (v. 80). The process must be orderly. The leaders "shall lay the case before the Church," "according to the law of God," and then those in charge will "lift up their hands against him or her" (vote) to determine their guilt or innocence (v. 81). Where possible, the bishop should be present (v. 82). And all disciplinary councils should be conducted in the same manner (v. 83).

Priesthood disciplinary councils are not courts of retribution; they are courts of love. When people are placed on probation, disfellowshipped or excommunicated from the Church, it is done not to punish but to help them. Elder Theodore M. Burton reminds us that "the word discipline has the same root as the word disciple. A disciple is a student or follower—one who is learning. Church discipline, then, must become a teaching process."[10]

When a person is disciplined by such a council, he should not be publicly embarrassed, thrust out of meetings, or abandoned by leaders and members. This is precisely the time when such persons need increased attention and love, showing them how to begin again, abandon sinful practices, perform righteous deeds, and transform their lives. The goal is to eventually reinstated them into full fellowship in the Church.

Elder John A. Widtsoe said:

> It should always be remembered that the Church exists to save, not to condemn men. Every effort should be made to have contending parties settle their own difficulties, with the aid of ward teachers if necessary; and to induce those who have erred to tread the way of forgiveness and thus make unnecessary the calling together of a church tribunal of justice.

> Should it be necessary to call a person to a church trial, those composing the council must use every endeavor to bring about reconciliation or confession in humility. Excommunication should be the last resort.

> All should be eager to keep those who are in the Church in full fellowship with the community of Saints. We should increase our tenderness and helpfulness toward those who may, because of their errors, be subjected to disfellowshipment or excommunication.[11]

Receiving Revelation for the Church

(D&C 43)

This revelation was given through the Prophet Joseph Smith in February 1831 at Kirtland, Ohio.[12] At the time, certain individuals were claiming to receive revelation, which caused great concern to the Prophet and some of the members. The best-known example was a woman named Hubble who came to Kirtland, claiming to be a prophetess. She succeeded in persuading some members of the Church that her revelations were authentic and valid.

John Whitmer recorded the following about Mrs. Hubble: "She professed to be a prophetess of the Lord, and professed to have many revelations, and knew the Book of Mormon was true, and that she should become a teacher in the Church of Christ. She appeared to be very sanctimonious and deceived some who were not able to detect her in her hypocrisy; others, however, had the spirit of discernment and her follies and abominations were manifest."[13]

Mrs. Hubble was not the first, nor the only, false spirit that arose in the early Church. Elder George A. Smith said: "There was a prevalent spirit all through the early history of this Church, which prompted the Elders to suppose that they knew more than the Prophet. Elders would tell you that the Prophet was going wrong."[14]

On the day the Church was organized, April 6, 1830, the Lord told the Saints how revelation would come to the Church. He said, speaking of the President of the Church, "Him have I inspired to move the cause of Zion in mighty power" (D&C 21:7). This instruction was difficult for some Saints to accept. Many came from religious backgrounds that permitted any member of the congregation to proclaim doctrine for the entire congregation.

Just five months later, in September 1830, the problem affected even such great souls as David Whitmer and Oliver Cowdery when Hiram Page pretended to receive revelation for the Church through his peep stone. In reaction to that incident, the Lord gave revelation that included the following: "I say unto thee, no one shall be appointed to receive commandments and revelations in this church excepting my servant Joseph Smith, Jun., for he receiveth them even as Moses" (D&C 28:2).

Nevertheless, the problem continued in Kirtland, and the resulting confusion caused great sorrow and bewilderment among the members. Joseph Smith took the matter to the Lord and received counsel on how to discern and deal with false teachers and false spirits, and that counsel is contained in D&C 43.

- **D&C 43:1–7 Revelation comes only through proper channels.** The Lord reminded the Saints that they had received the law of the Church "through him whom I have appointed unto you to receive commandments and revelations from my hand" (vv. 1–2). "And this ye shall know assuredly—that there is none other appointed unto you to receive commandments and revelations until he be taken, if he abide in me" (v. 3). That seems crystal clear. It also indicates that after the Prophet's death another will be appointed in his stead to perform the same role as revelator. And even that person—the one who replaces him—will be "appointed unto this gift … through him" (v. 4).

The Lord continues, "And this shall be a law unto you, that ye receive not the teachings of any that shall come before you as revelations or commandments" (v. 5). This, so that "you may not be deceived, that you may know they are not of me" (v. 6). Any such revelator must be "ordained of [God]" and "shall come in at the gate" before he is authorized to "teach those revelations which you have received and shall receive through him" (v. 7).

We recall that in September, 1830, the Lord gave D&C 28 to the Church regarding the receipt of revelation. This was in response to the Hiram Page incident at Fayette, which deceived the Whitmer family and others at the time. Now, 18 months later, it became necessary for the Lord to give further instruction on this matter. This time it was as a result of the activities of a woman, Mrs. Hubble, who tried to give revelation to the Church, and some were willing to follow her.

The Prophet Joseph Smith reports that "she professed to be a prophetess of the Lord, and professed to have many revelations, and knew the Book of Mormon was true, and that she should become a teacher in the Church of Christ. She appeared to be very sanctimonious and deceived some who were not able to detect her in her hypocrisy; others, however, had the spirit of discernment and her follies and abominations were manifest."[15]

People are sometimes very easily deceived. Followers can be found for almost any foolish idea, and cults arise to teach strange and even dangerous doctrines. This revelation (D&C 43) establishes clearly the process by which revelation will be given to the Church, and it still applies today. Only the one man who holds the keys and stands as the Presiding high priest and President of the Church will be the spokesman of the Lord to the members of the Church. Individuals may receive the inspiration and revelation for their own guidance, but not for the Church. Moreover, no member of the Church will profess to receive a revelation for his own guidance that is contradictory of any revelation coming from the President of the Church.[16]

- **D&C 43:15–16 The promise of a heavenly endowment.** Speaking to the leaders of the Church, the Lord said: "Ye are not sent forth to be taught, but to teach the children of men the things which I have put into your hands by the power of my Spirit" (v. 15). They must never be looking to others for revelation, as in the case of Mrs. Hubble. Then, the Lord gives this inspiring and prophetic counsel: (1) "ye are to be taught from on high," (2) ye must "sanctify yourselves," and if we do (3) "ye shall be endowed with power" (v. 16). This has reference to the coming temple endowment under which they will receive marvelous promises and powers through their initiatory ordinances.

The Fourth General Conference

(D&C 44)

In the latter part of February 1831, the Lord directed that the missionaries who had dispersed to various parts of the country were summoned to a general conference at Kirtland. The Conference convened on June 3, 1831. It was the Fourth General conference of the Church, and the first gathering of its kind in Kirtland.[17]

- **D&C 44:1–2 A call for a conference in Kirtland.** Conferences should involve Church leaders and members from everywhere—"the elders of my church should be called together, from the east and from the west, and from the north and from the south, by letter or some other way" (v. 1). And if "they are faithful, and exercise faith in me, I will pour out my Spirit upon them in the day that they assemble themselves together" (v. 2). Every conference is a spiritual feast, with members feeling rejuvenated by the Spirit they felt and the testimonies they heard. This is why the Lord commands us to hold conferences, and the wisdom of that commandment is obvious to those who fully participate in them.

- **D&C 44:3–6 Organizing for a growing Church.** Church leaders were instructed to "go forth into the regions round about, and preach repentance unto the people" (v. 3). And since many will be converted, they were to "organize yourselves according to the laws of man; That your enemies may not have power over you" (vv. 4–5). A growing Church would certainly attract enemies to oppose it, and careful and legal planning would allow them to "be preserved in all things; that you may be enabled to keep my laws; that every bond may be broken wherewith the enemy seeketh to destroy my people" (v. 5). And in all of their activities they must not forget the poor, but "visit the poor and the needy and administer to their relief" (v. 6).

Official Church Records

● **D&C 21:1** Very early in the Church's history—April 6, 1830, the day the Church was organized—the Lord said: "Behold, there shall be a record kept among you." The record was to record that Joseph Smith had been sustained at that meeting as "a seer, a translator, a prophet, an apostle of Jesus Christ, [and] an elder of the church through the will of God the Father, and the grace of your Lord Jesus Christ."

● **D&C 47:1–4** Shortly after the Church was organized, a new Church historian, John Whitmer, was appointed to "write and keep a regular history, and assist … my servant Joseph, in transcribing all things which shall be given you, until he is called to further duties" (v. 1). He could also preach and teach in meetings (v. 2), but his main responsibility was to "keep the church record and history continually" because Oliver Cowdery had been "appointed to another office" (v. 3). Previous to this, Oliver Cowdery had acted as historian and recorder. John Whitmer said he would rather not keep the Church history, but he was promised the assistance of the Holy Ghost in his duties (v. 4) and said, "The will of the Lord be done, and if He desires it, I wish that He would manifest it through Joseph the Seer."[18] In response to that request, D&C 47 was given.[19]

John Whitmer

● **D&C 69:3, 7–8 The historian should record all important things about the Church.** In a later revelation, the historian was given instructions to "continue in writing and making a history of all the important things which he shall observe and know concerning my church" (v. 3) The historian's duties included traveling "many times from place to place, and from church to church, that he may the more easily obtain knowledge" (v. 7). It also involved "preaching and expounding, writing, copying, selecting, and obtaining all things" with regard to Church history (v. 8). The Lord declared that these duties "shall be for the good of the church, and for the rising generations that shall grow up on the land of Zion, to possess it from generation to generation, forever and ever" (v. 8). In other words, it had an important purpose for the Church at that time, and would also bless those in generations to come as they could look back upon the things that happened in those days. We today are the beneficiaries of their efforts to keep an accurate record.

President Wilford Woodruff kept meticulous journals throughout his adult life, and many of the facts of Church history that we possess today came through his journals. President Woodruff said all of the following concerning journals:

> Believing it to be beneficial to review our past life and not only our privilege but duty to keep an accurate account of our proceedings, … it is to this intent that I shall endeavor henceforth to keep a journal of my travels that when required of may give an account of my stewardship.[20]

> I have never spent any of my time more profitably for the benefit of mankind than in my journal writing, for a great portion of the Church history has been compiled from my journals and some of the most glorious gospel sermons, truths, and revelations that were given from God to this people

through the mouth of the Prophets Joseph and Brigham, Heber and the Twelve could not be found upon the earth on record only in my journals and they are compiled in the Church history and transmitted to the Saints of God in all future generations. Does not this pay me for my troubles? It does.[21]

We are living in one of the most important generations that man ever lived on Earth and we should write an account of those important transactions which are taking place before our eyes in fulfillment of the prophecies and the revelations of God. There is a great flood of revelations fulfilling in our day and as they are transpiring before our eyes we want a record made of them. If the power and blessings of God are made manifest … you should make a record of it. Keep an account of the dealing of God with you daily. I have written all the blessings I have received and I would not take gold for them.[22]

Wilford Woodruff (1853)

Recording Personal Spiritual Blessings

(D&C 46)

The Church is not alone in its responsibility to record significant events in its history. We are commanded to also do this with regard to our personal lives and histories. This is so that our own posterity might know and be inspired by our examples. It is also so that we will not forget the blessings we receive.

- **D&C 46:32** The Lord commanded, "ye must give thanks unto God in the Spirit for whatsoever blessing ye are blessed with." The Lord is disturbed when He grants unto us a blessing and we receive it, and then quickly forget it. He refers to this as "consuming upon our lusts" the blessing we have received (James 4:3; D&C 46:9). He wants us to be thankful enough for the blessings received that we will not forget them. And generally, that requires a journal.

- **D&C 59:21** The Lord is not offended when we enjoy our bless**ings.** But He is offended when we fail to acknowledge His hand in the receipt of them. "And in nothing doth man offend God, or against none is his wrath kindled, save those who confess not his hand in all things, and obey not his commandments."

President Spencer W. Kimball said: "What could you do better for your children and your children's children than to record the story of your life, your triumphs over adversity, your re- covery after a fall, your progress when all seemed black, your rejoicing when you had finally achieved?"[23]

This does not mean that we should record only spectacular successes or events. Our private journals should record the way we face up to challenges that beset us. Our personal record can be a source of blessing to ourselves and to others. Do not suppose that your experiences will not be interesting to your posterity. Experiences of work, relations with people, and an awareness of the rightness and wrongness of action will always be relevant.

May I relate a personal experience with my father's journal? When my family moved to St. George, we did so with the distinct impression that the Lord wanted us there, but we did not know precisely why. We accepted a new job there and made the move. But through no fault of our own we found ourselves unemployed within a year. I had always relied on my father for wise advice, so in the midst of my confusion I went to my father's journal and began to read. My father had been dead for nearly 16 years at that point.

I found a place in his journal where he addressed situations like the one I was in. He said that whenever he found himself in a situation where he didn't know what to do in order to solve a problem that he simply went out and found a way to serve others. And in doing so, he said, the answer to his dilemma would always come. I thanked him for his fatherly advice and called the stake president to offer to volunteer in teaching stake CES adult education classes in the area where we lived. He agreed, and assigned a high councilor to assist me.

As it turned out, the high councilor was an official at the local state college, and when he saw that I was capable of teaching well, he recommended me to their administration. From that, I got a good-paying job. Also, his daughter was an editor for a publishing company, and when she visited him and attended my class, she invited me to write these books. And here I am doing so today. Where did these opportunities come from? From serving. And where did the advice to serve come from? From my father's journal, which for me is every bit as much scripture as anything that I read in the standard works.

High Priests and Many Missionaries

(D&C 52)

The month of June 1831 opened on June 3 with a significant and spiritual conference— the first one in Kirtland, wherein the first high priests among the general membership were ordained and 34 elders received mission calls. Missionaries who were already serving in various parts of the country came to attend this conference. A number of powerful events took place at this conference, according to the Prophet Joseph Smith:

— "The Lord displayed His power."
— "The man of sin [Satan] was revealed."
— "The authority of the Melchizedek priesthood was manifested and conferred for the first time upon several of the Elders."
— "It was clearly evident that the Lord gave us power in proportion to the work to be done, and strength according to the race set before us, and grace and help as our needs required."
— "Harmony prevailed."
— "Several were ordained."
— "Faith was strengthened."
— "Humility, so necessary for the blessing of God to follow prayer, characterized the Saints."

D&C 52 was received the day after the conference closed.[24]

With regard to the Melchizedek priesthood, we should not imagine that the Prophet meant this was the first time that priesthood was conferred on anybody. What he meant was that it was at this conference that the office of high priest was conferred upon men in this dispensation. Of course, men had been ordained to be Apostles prior to this conference, and Apostles are also high priests. But the men who were ordained high priests at this conference were the first among the general Church membership to received this ordination.[25]

In D&C 52, the Lord first instructs Joseph Smith and Sidney Rigdon to go to Missouri, where He will reveal the place of inheritance for the Saints in Zion (vv. 3–5). Lyman Wight and John Corrill are also commanded to depart speedily, and John Murdock and Hyrum Smith are to travel there by way of Detroit (vv. 7–8).

● **D&C 52:9–10 General instructions for traveling missionaries.** These traveling missionaries are told how to proceed along the way to Missouri. This direction concerning how to teach applies not only to missionaries, but to all who teach the gospel. They were to teach "none other things than that which the prophets and apostles have written, and that which is taught them by the Comforter through the prayer of faith" (v. 9). They are to travel "two by two," preaching along the way "in every congregation, baptizing by water, and the laying on of the hands by the water's side" (v. 10).

● **D&C 52:14–19 A pattern for discerning the spirits of those they meet.** The Lord gives a "pattern" here to help us discern whether those who claim to speak for God are accepted by Him. The Lord warns that "Satan is abroad in the land, and he goeth forth deceiving the nations" (v. 14). The missionaries are to seek out "he that prayeth, whose spirit is contrite" and who "obey mine ordinances" (v. 15). When a man speaks, if his "spirit is contrite" and his "language is meek and edifieth, the same is of God if he obey mine ordinances" (v. 16). Those who are weak and trembling "shall be made strong, and shall bring forth fruits of praise and wisdom, according to the revelations and truths which I have given you" (v. 17). He that is overcome by his fears "and bringeth not forth fruits … is not of me" (v. 18). By this pattern, the Lord says, "ye shall know the spirits in all cases under the whole heavens" (v. 19). This is a description of the gift of discernment.

Elder Stephen L Richards said:

> The gift of discernment is essential to the leadership of the Church. I never ordain a bishop or set apart a president of a stake without invoking upon him this divine blessing, that he may read the lives and hearts of his people and call forth the best within them. The gift and power of discernment in this world of contention between the forces of good and the power of evil is essential equipment for every son and daughter of God. [This gift] arises largely
>
> out of an acute sensitivity to impressions—spiritual impressions, if you will—to read under the surface as it were, to detect hidden evil, and more importantly to find the good that may be concealed. The highest type of discernment is that which perceives in others and uncovers for them their better natures, the good inherent within them. It's the gift every missionary needs when he takes the gospel to the people of the world. He must make an appraisal of every personality whom he meets. He must be able to discern the hidden spark that may be lighted for truth. The gift of discernment will save him from mistakes and embarrassment, and it will never fail to inspire confidence in the one who is rightly appraised.[26]

A Revelation to Sidney Gilbert

(D&C 53)

In 1817, Newel K. Whitney met Sidney Gilbert in Kirtland, Ohio. Gilbert took a liking to Whitney and, recognizing his abilities, took him into his store as a clerk and gave him some training in bookkeeping. A few years later they formed a partnership in Kirtland called Gilbert and Whitney. When the missionaries to the Lamanites passed through Kirtland on their way to Missouri, they taught these two prosperous men the gospel. Eventually, they both became stalwart members of the Church. They first joined Sidney Rigdon's congregation—the "Disciples"—and were thus prepared for the message of the missionaries when it arrived in Kirtland.[27] In June 1831, Sidney Gilbert asked the Prophet Joseph Smith to inquire of the Lord as to what his calling and appointment should be in the Church. He wished to serve. The result of that inquiry was D&C 53.

● **D&C 53:4 Sidney Gilbert is called to be an agent of the bishop.** This call meant that he was to assist the bishop with business affairs. Only a few months earlier, the bishop had received the weighty responsibility to administer the law of consecration, and he needed a man skilled in accounting and business practices to assist him. This would be similar to what a ward or stake financial clerk does today.

Sidney Gilbert was eventually sent to Missouri to help in the establishment of Zion. The Saints in Missouri were commanded to purchase land for their inheritance. Edward Partridge, as bishop, was charged with dividing the land among the Saints as inheritances. He was assisted in this work by Sidney Gilbert, who acted as his agent. Sidney Gilbert was also instructed to open a store and sell goods "without fraud," for the good of Zion. All of these activities were intended to prepare for the Saints who would soon arrive in that area, where they would be required to keep "the law of the Lord"—consecration.[28]

Unfortunately, Sidney Gilbert got caught up in the rebellious spirit of the leaders in Missouri, led by the stake presidency there—David Whitmer, John Whitmer, and William W. Phelps. The Lord warned them through the Prophet Joseph Smith that unless they remembered what the Lord had taught them in former commandments and "brought forth fruit meet for their Father's kingdom," and to cease from polluting the holy land by their unrighteous attitudes and behavior, "there remaineth a scourge and a judgment to be poured out upon the children of Zion."[29]

Gilbert & Whitney Store Receipt

The Prophet spoke in very emphatic terms at that time about the attitude and bitterness of Sidney Gilbert. He also rebuked William W. Phelps.[30]

Eventually, Sidney Gilbert repented and became one of the most faithful elders in Zion. When the mob attacked the Saints at Independence, he offered his life as a ransom, along with others. He was also a faithful servant in temporal things.[31] Sadly, the Prophet reports that Gilbert said on one occasion, when called to preach the Gospel, that he would "rather die than go forth to preach to the Gentiles." He met an untimely death when Zions Camp came to Missouri and he was one of the 68 members of that camp who were struck with cholera and one of the 14 who died.

ATTITUDE AND OBEDIENCE

The Church received the "Law of the Church" in D&C 42, and they struggled somewhat with its principles—particularly obedience to the authorities of the Church and living the law of consecration. Thus, over the next two or three months, from June to August 1831, the Lord sent forth a number of revelations about how latter-day Saints should conduct their lives. Rather than treat these revelations individually, we will discuss them topically here, since the same themes seem to be found in most or all of them. Those themes are attitude and obedience.

The Importance of Attitude

(D&C 54–59)

The Lord teaches in the Doctrine and Covenants that we must have appropriate attitudes as well as actions, neither being complete without the other.

- **D&C 52:15–16 Pray and speak with a contrite spirit, and with meek and edifying language (vv. 15–16).** A person who does this is acceptable to the Lord "if he obey mine ordinances" (v. 16).

- **D&C 52:40 Remember the poor and the needy, the sick and the afflicted.** This is required if we want our prayers to be answered. Anybody who neglects these things "the same is not my disciple."

- **D&C 53:2 Do not permit worldly concerns to thwart your gospel living.** The Lord who "was crucified for the sins of the world" commands us to "forsake the world."

- **D&C 54:10 Be "patient in tribulation" until the Lord comes again.** The Lord promises us, "behold, I come quickly, and my reward is with me, and they who have sought me early shall find rest to their souls."

- **D&C 55:1 Have an "eye single to the glory of God."** Remission of sins does not come to all who are baptized, only to those having "an eye single to [God's] glory." Such persons, when they are baptized, shall indeed "have a remission of your sins and a reception of the Holy Spirit by the laying on of hands."

- **D&C 55:3 Be contrite.** Those who are contrite, when they are confirmed by the laying on of hands, will receive the Holy Ghost.

- **D&C 56:16 The rich must avoid selfishness.** The Lord says that our riches will "canker [our] souls" if we "will not give your substance to the poor." And in the day of the Lord's "day of visitation, and of judgment, and of indignation" such persons will lament that "the harvest is past, the summer is ended, and my soul is not saved!"

● **D&C 56:17–18 The poor must also avoid selfishness and laziness.** The "love of money" is not just a rich man's disease. Sometimes the poor lust after worldly wealth as much or more than the rich do. "Wo unto you poor men, whose hearts are not broken, whose spirits are not contrite, and whose bellies are not satis- fied," says the Lord, "and whose hands are not stayed from laying hold upon other men's goods, whose eyes are full of greediness, and who will not labor with your own hands!" (v. 17). The poor who are "pure in heart, whose hearts are broken, and whose spirits are contrite" will receive the kingdom of God when it comes "in power and great glory unto their deliverance" and "the fatness of the earth shall be theirs" (v. 18).

● **D&C 58:24–29 Use your agency to do good without waiting to be commanded.** The Lord invited the Saints to "bring their families to this land [Zion], as they shall counsel between themselves and me" (v. 25). They should not wait for the Lord to tell them to do so because "it is not meet that I should command in all things; for he that is compelled in all things, the same is a slothful and not a wise servant; wherefore he receiveth no reward" (v. 26). The Lord expects us to be "anxiously engaged" in good causes and to "do many things of their own free will, and bring to pass much righteousness" (v. 27). All normal children of God over the age of eight are "agents unto themselves. And inasmuch as [they] do good they shall in nowise lose their reward" (v. 28). But if [a man] "doeth not anything until he is commanded, and receiveth a commandment with doubtful heart, and keepeth it with slothfulness, the same is damned" (v. 29).

● **D&C 59:16–21 Be thankful for your blessings and use them wisely.** God is offended when we are unthankful. He has given us "the fulness of the earth"—beasts, fowls, that which climbeth upon the trees and walketh upon the earth, herbs and all the other good things which come of the earth, for food and raiment, and for our houses, barns, orchards, gardens, and vineyards" (vv. 16–17). Every one of these things were created "for the benefit and the use of man, both to please the eye and to gladden the heart" (v. 18). We may use them freely "for food and for raiment, for taste and for smell, to strengthen the body and to enliven the soul" (v. 19). There is no sin in enjoying these things. In fact, "it pleaseth God that he hath given all these things unto man; for unto this end were they made to be used, with judgment, not to excess, neither by extortion" (v. 20). Thus, so long as they are obtained honestly and used with wisdom and prudence, we may use them freely. In none of this do we offend God, except when we "confess not his hand in all things, and obey not his commandments" (v. 21).

The Importance of Obedience

The same revelations which speak of the need for a proper attitude also speak of the need to be obedient. The early Saints were sometimes disobedient—as we are—and needed reminding of the importance of *doing* the will of the Lord, and not just speaking of it. We are reminded by these revelations that the only way to achieve true joy and lasting happiness is by being obedient to all the commandments of God.

Elder George Q. Morris said: "Anything we hope for, anything we desire, anything we should have will come to us through the principle of obedience and by the same token all may be lost by disobedience. How simple the gospel is! The requirement is an obedient heart."[32]

- **D&C 54:1–6 If we do not keep our covenants, they become void and of none effect.** The Colesville Saints had attempted to live the law of consecration in Kirtland, but a disagreement over land forced them to cancel their plan. Since they had covenanted to live the law of consecration in Ohio, the branch members were worried about their standing before the Lord. Branch President Newel Knight thus sought guidance through Joseph Smith, and the Prophet received D&C 54 for them.

  Speaking to Branch President Newel Knight, the Lord tells him to "stand fast in the office whereunto I have appointed you" (v. 2). Since the Saints in Kirtland had broken their covenant of consecration, "even so it has become void and of none effect" (v. 4). If they wish to escape the violence of their enemies, "let them repent of all their sins, and become truly humble before me and contrite" (v. 3). The Lord pronounces a wo upon those "by whom this offense cometh" (v. 5) and a blessing on "they who have kept the covenant and observed the commandment, for they shall obtain mercy" (v. 6).

- **D&C 56:1–3 We must be obedient to obtain salvation.** The Lord's anger "is kindled against the rebellious, and they shall know mine arm and mine indignation, in the day of visitation and of wrath upon the nations" [the Second Coming] (v. 1). Those who refuse to "take up [their] cross and follow me, and keep my commandments, the same shall not be saved" (v. 2). The disobedient "shall be cut off in mine own due time, after I have commanded and the commandment is broken" (v. 3).

- **D&C 56:4–10 When we fail to do our duty, the Lord releases us and calls another.** The Lord can "command and revoke, as it seemeth me good" and can hold the rebellious accountable for their disobedience (v. 4). "Wherefore, I revoke the commandment which was given unto my servants Thomas B. Marsh and Ezra Thayre" to travel together to Missouri. Evidently, Thomas was willing and obedient, but Ezra was not. So the Lord gave "a new commandment unto my servant Thomas, that he shall take up his journey speedily to the land of Missouri, and my servant Selah J. Griffin shall also go with him" (v. 5).

  The Lord said concerning Ezra Thayre that he "must repent of his pride, and of his selfishness, and obey the former commandment which I have given him concerning the place upon which he lives" (v. 8). If he does so, he can still be appointed "to go to the land of Missouri" (v. 9). Otherwise, he will be refunded the money he consecrated to the Church and must "leave the place, and … be cut off out of my church" (v. 10).

  In addition, the Lord revoked the assignment given to "Selah J. Griffin and Newel Knight, in consequence of the stiffneckedness of my people which are in Thompson, and their rebellions"

(v. 6). Newell Knight will lead "as many as will go … , that are contrite before me … to the land which I have appointed [Missouri]" (v. 7).

- **D&C 58:42–43 When we repent, the Lord forgives and forgets our sins.** When a person fully repents, "the same is forgiven, and I, the Lord, remember them no more" (v. 42). And "by this ye may know if a man repenteth of his sins—behold, he will confess them and forsake them" (v. 43).

- **D&C 59:9–14 We must keep the Sabbath Day holy.** In order to stay "unspotted from the world" we must go to church and partake of the sacrament "upon my holy day" (v. 9). On the Sabbath, we are to "rest from [our] labors, and to pay [our] devotions unto the Most High" (v. 10). Now, this does not mean that we shouldn't be striving to serve God "on all days and at all times" (v. 11). That should be done every day of the week. But on the Sabbath we worship God and do "none other thing" (vv. 12–13). Necessary tasks, like the preparation of food, should be done "with singleness of heart" in order that our Sabbath worship "may be perfect" and our "joy may be full" (v. 13). That is the Lord's definition of worship—"fasting and prayer, or in other words, rejoicing and prayer" (v. 14).

A Revelation to William W. Phelps

(D&C 55)

Around the middle of June 1831, while the Prophet was preparing for his journey to Missouri, William W. Phelps and his family arrived in Kirtland. He was born on February 17, 1792, at Hanover, Morris County, NJ. In New York he had edited three newspapers (founding two of them). Over his lifetime, he was "a printer, hymn writer, poet, journalist, newspaper editor, judge, orator, scribe, lawyer, educator, pioneer, explorer, writer of books and pamphlets, topographical engineer, superintendent of schools, surveyor general, weather man, chaplain of the lower house of representatives, and speaker of the house in the legislature" (W. D. Bowen, "*The Versatile W. W. Phelps*," [Master's thesis, Brigham Young University, 1958], l). Though only 30 years old at the time he was first introduced to the Church, he was well educated and had been a potential candidate for lieutenant governor of New York.

William W. Phelps

He read the Book of Mormon, spoke to Sidney Rigdon about it, then made this visit to Kirtland, where he was eventually baptized, and became active in editorial work. He worked for a time as one of the Prophet's scribes, and he assisted Emma Smith in preparing the first hymn book.[33]

William W. Phelps was not yet a member of the Church when he received this revelation in response to his desire to "quit the folly of my ways, and the fancy and fame of this world" and do the will of the Lord.[34] In the revelation, he is called to help in preparing books for children in the

Church. This is the earliest revelation to specifically encourage education and schools in the Church. He was also an accomplished poet and musician, writing the words and arranging the music for a hymn sung at the dedication of the Kirtland Temple—"The Spirit of God Like a Fire Is Burning"— which has been sung at every temple dedication since then.

- **D&C 55:1–3 William W.** Phelps was called and chosen of the Lord. He is commanded to be "baptized by water, which if you do with an eye single to my glory, you shall have a remission of your sins and a reception of the Holy Spirit by the laying on of hands" (v. 1). And then, immediately thereafter he would be "ordained by the hand of my servant Joseph Smith, Jun., to be an elder unto this church, to preach repentance and remission of sins by way of baptism in the name of Jesus Christ, the Son of the living God" (v. 2). Being thus ordained, this new member who had only just received the Gift of the Holy Ghost himself, "on whomsoever you shall lay your hands, if they are contrite before me, you shall have power to give the Holy Spirit" (v. 3).

- **D&C 55:4–6 Phelps was called to print for the Church, both in Kirtland and Missouri.** He was to "assist my servant Oliver Cowdery to do the work of printing, and of selecting and writing books for schools in this church, that little children also may receive instruction" (v. 4).

Thus, the Lord's and the Church's mission to engage in the education of its people was established early on, in June 1831. Phelps was also to "journey with my servants Joseph Smith, Jun., and Sidney Rigdon [to Zion in Missouri], that you may be planted in the land of your inheritance to do this work" (v. 5). Joseph Coe was assigned to go with them (v. 6).

In Missouri, William W. Phelps "founded *The Evening and Morning Star*, a monthly magazine devoted to the interests of the Church, and published by the Church. Its first number appeared at Independence, June

Notice in the first issue, June 1832

1832. The printing office was destroyed by a mob in July 1833, but in the following December another printing office was established at Kirtland, and the publication of the Star was resumed there."[35]

In 1837, William W. Phelps was appointed to act, along with David and John Whitmer, as the presidency of the Church in Zion. But he became disaffected, along with the Whitmers, as a result of the persecutions there and some questionable land transactions for which they were severely reprimanded. Eventually, at a meeting on February 6, 1838, in Far West, Phelps and the other members of the stake presidency were "rejected" (not sustained) by the congregation of Saints in the Carter settlement. Other branches of the Church followed suit. During a court of inquiry held at Richmond, Missouri, in November 1838, Phelps, who had become bitter, was among those who testified against Church leaders. He was finally excommunicated from the Church at a conference held at Quincy, Illinois, March 17, 1839.[36]

Phelps' apostasy affected deeply the personal lives of the Prophet Joseph Smith and his family. Phelps assisted the mobs at Far West in ransacking the homes of the Saints, including the Prophet's home. Joseph's wife Emma and their children had their possessions ransacked and thrown into the street. Emma subsequently had to make her way out of the state of Missouri to protect herself and her children, finally making it to Quincy, Illinois, where most of the Saints had fled for safety.

In 1841, when he came to his senses and realized the gravity of what he had done, Phelps wrote a letter to the Prophet Joseph Smith asking for forgiveness and reinstatement into the Church. The Prophet showed his discipleship by the immediate and frank forgiveness which he granted to Phelps, closing his letter with the words, "Come on dear brother, since the war is past. For friends at first are friends again at last."[37] Phelps was deeply touched, and remained thereafter one of the Prophet's most loyal friends. It was Phelps who wrote the majestic words to "Praise to the Man" when he heard of the prophet's martyrdom, and Emma asked him to read them at the Prophet's funeral.

In 1848, William W. Phelps came to Utah, where he became quite prominent. He helped to write the Constitution of Deseret, and was preceptor in the University. He died in Salt Lake City, March 7, 1872, at 80 years of age.

Revelation to William E. McLellin

(D&C 66)

We do not know for certain when William E. McLellin (sometimes written M'Lellin or Mclellan) was born, but it was in the state of Tennessee, about the year 1806. He first heard the Gospel preached by Elders Samuel H. Smith and Reynolds Cahoon, while those brethren were en route from Kirtland to Independence, Missouri, in the early summer of 1831, just a few months before section 66 was given in October 1831.

William E. McLellin

He closed up his affairs as soon as possible and followed these missionaries to Jackson County. On the way to that place he was baptized and ordained an Elder. During the same summer he made his way to Kirtland, where we find him in attendance at the special conference of October 25, seeking to learn the will of the Lord, through the Prophet, respecting himself.[38]

McLellin accepted the Gospel with faith but also had many weaknesses. He was eventually chosen as one of the original Twelve Apostles of this dispensation and was ordained to that office on February 15, 1835, by Oliver Cowdery, David Whitmer, and Martin Harris. While traveling with that quorum on a mission, he wrote a letter of criticism to the First Presidency and was suspended from fellowship. After confession and repentance he was restored to fellowship and served as the clerk for the Twelve. Then, on Friday, May 11, 1838, he came before a bishop's court in Far West, Missouri, where he said he had no confidence in the presidency of the Church, and as a result he had quit praying and keeping the commandments of the Lord, and had indulged himself in his sinful lusts. He was excommunicated from the Church for unbelief and apostasy.

After his excommunication, McLellin attempted to establish a church of his own, with himself at the head, without success. He took an active part with the mob in Missouri, robbing and driving the Saints. He personally robbed the Prophet's home and took considerable property. He also sought to flog the Prophet while he was a prisoner in chains at Richmond, but backed away when the sheriff insisted he would first remove the chains to ensure a fair fight. He had only a superficial education, but had a good command of language. He later adopted the profession of medicine. He finally died in obscurity at Independence, Jackson county, Missouri, April 24, 1883.[39]

- **D&C 66:1–2 The "new and everlasting covenant" is the gospel of Jesus Christ** (see also D&C 132:4–7). The Lord declares McLellin to be "blessed … for receiving mine everlasting covenant, even the fulness of my gospel, sent forth unto the children of men" (v. 2).

- **D&C 66:3–13 He was pronounced "clean, but not all"**—something that could be said about all of us. The Lord then gives him specific personal counsel: "repent, therefore, of those things which are not pleasing in my sight" which the Lord says He will "show … unto you" (v. 3). In the process, the Lord will also show unto him "my will concerning you" (v. 4), which was to "proclaim my gospel from land to land, and from city to city … in those regions round about where it has not been proclaimed" (v. 5). He is not to remain at Kirtland nor to go to Zion in Missouri. He is to "think not of thy property" but to focus on the things of the Spirit (v. 6). He was called to go to the eastern part of the country, with Samuel H. Smith as his junior companion (vv. 7–8). The Lord promises to make him "strong in every place; and I, the Lord, will go with you" (v. 8). He will also enjoy the gift of healing (v. 9).

In a prophetic bit of counsel, the Lord tells him, "Return not till I, the Lord, shall send you. Be patient in affliction… Seek not to be [en]cumbered. Forsake all unrighteousness. Commit not adultery—a temptation with which thou hast been troubled" (v. 10). If he will follow this counsel and be faithful, he will "magnify thine office, and push many people to Zion with songs of everlasting joy upon their heads" (v. 11). And if he continues faithful to the end, he will receive "a crown of eternal life at the right hand of my Father" (v. 12).

We are left to wonder what might have been if William E. McLellin had listened to the counsel of the Lord in this revelation. In the end, he was conquered by the very weaknesses enumerated here, and became a bitter enemy to the Prophet Joseph Smith and the Church.

THE BOOK OF COMMANDMENTS

The Lord's Preface and Appendix to the Commandments

(D&C 1, 133)

On 1 November 1831, just a few days after sec- tion 66 had been received, a special conference convened to consider publishing the revelations given over a nine-year period up to that time. The compilation was to be entitled the Book of Commandments.

After it was decided to publish the revelations already received, several elders bore testimony that these revelations were true. During those twelve days of meetings, the Prophet received six revelations: D&C 1, 67–70, and 133. In D&C 1, the Lord revealed His preface for His Book of Commandments. This was placed at thefirst of the book, where prefaces belong. We dis- cussed this revelation in detail in Chapter 1.

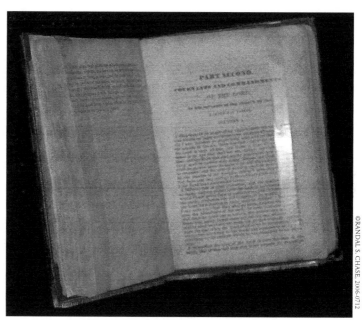

Early copy of the Book of Commandments

D&C 133 was received at the close of the conference and two days after the Preface (D&C 1). It is called "the Appendix" because it was received after the revelation approving the selection of revelations to be published (D&C 67), and has occupied a position near the end of the Doctrine and Covenants in all of its editions, though that placement is out of its chronological order. The tone of D&C 133 is very similar to D&C 1 because it is largely a continuation of the same theme.[40]

A Dispute over the Language of the Revelations

(D&C 67)

At this point in the conference, Joseph Smith asked the brethren if they were willing to place their names upon a witness to the world that these revelations and commandments were of God. Some brethren were hesitant, feeling that the language of the commandments was inadequate and needed to be reworded. They probably thought that they were critiquing the language of the Prophet Joseph Smith, who was admittedly not a master of language at that point in his life. But they were actually criticizing the Lord, whose words they were.

- **D&C 67:6–9 In response, the Lord revealed a challenge to these critics.** The Lord invites them to select out of the Book of Commandments the revelation that they think is the worst among them "and appoint him that is the most wise among you" (v. 6). Then ask that person, or "any among you" to write a revelation "like unto it" (v. 7). If he can, "then ye are justified in saying that ye do not know that they are true; But if ye cannot make one like unto it, ye are under condemnation if ye do not bear record that they are true" (vv. 7–8). He also reminds them that "there is no unrighteousness in them, and that which is righteous cometh down from above, from the Father of lights" (v. 9). If they had been written by an imposter or even a well-intentioned man, they would contain some degree of unrighteousness.

Some of the brethren present felt, because of their superior education, that they could improve in the language of the revelations. They spent considerable time discussing the language of the revelations, as they had been given. The Prophet, through prayer, received a revelation in which the Lord submitted a challenge to these learned men. It appears that this revelation silenced all the critics, except one—William E. McLellin, who was given to some boasting in his own strength, evidently forgetting the word of the Lord given to him about this weakness at his request at the conference of October 25th. McLellin accepted the challenge and attempted to write a better revelation.[41]

The Prophet Joseph Smith said: "After the foregoing was received, William E. M'Lellin, as the wisest man, in his own estimation, having more learning than sense, endeavored to write a commandment like unto one of the least of the Lord's, but failed; it was an awful responsibility to write in the name of the Lord. The Elders and all present that witnessed this vain attempt of a man to imitate the language of Jesus Christ, renewed their faith in the fulness of the Gospel, and in the truth of the commandments and revelations which the Lord had given to the Church through my instrumentality; and the Elders signified a willingness to bear testimony of their truth to all the world."[42]

The effect of William E. McLellin's failure upon the other brethren present was that the brethren renewed their desire to bear witness of the Book of Commandments. They did so, and that testimony is included at the front of the Doctrine and Covenants to this day.

- **Testimony of the Witnesses to the Book of the Lord's Commandments.** Joseph Smith prepared by inspiration the testimony that appears at the beginning of our Doctrine and Covenants:

    The Testimony of the Witnesses to the Book of the Lord's Commandments, which commandments He gave to His Church through Joseph Smith, Jun., who was appointed by the voice of the Church for this purpose:

    We, therefore, feel willing to bear testimony to all the world of mankind, to every creature upon the face of the earth, that the Lord has borne record to our souls, through the Holy Ghost shed forth upon us, that these commandments were given by inspiration of God, and are profitable for all men, and are verily true.

    We give this testimony unto the world, the Lord being our helper; and it is through the grace of God the Father, and His Son, Jesus Christ, that we are permitted to have this privilege of bearing this testimony unto the world, in the which we rejoice exceedingly, praying the Lord always that the children of men may be profited thereby.

The names of the Twelve were:

Thomas B. Marsh	Orson Hyde	William Smith
David W. Patten	Wm. E. McLellin	Orson Pratt
Brigham Young	Parley P. Pratt	John F. Boynton
Heber C. Kimball	Luke S. Johnson	Lyman E. Johnson

The Lord Himself also bore witness of the truth of the revelations when He said: "And now I, the Lord, give unto you a testimony of the truth of these commandments which are lying before you" (D&C 67:4). What greater witness can we have?

Personal Revelation

● **D&C 67:1–4 Sometimes fear prevents faith and, therefore, revelation.** The Lord hears our prayers, knows our hearts and our desires, and His eyes are upon us (vv. 1–2). He controls all things in heaven and earth, and "the riches of eternity are [His] to give" (v. 2). We sometimes hope to receive blessings but fail to do so because of "fears in your hearts" (v. 3), and verily this is the reason that ye did not receive.

The Prophet Joseph Smith said: "Doubt and faith do not exist in the same person at the same time; so that, persons whose minds are under doubts and fears cannot have unshaken confidence; and where unshaken confidence is not, there faith is weak; and where faith is weak the persons will not be able to contend against all the opposition, tribulations, and afflictions which they will have to encounter in order to be heirs of God, and joint heirs with Christ Jesus; and they will grow weary in their minds, and the adversary will have power over them and destroy them."[43]

● **D&C 67:10–14 How it is that men can see God while still in their mortal flesh.** These good men, leaders of the restored Church and witnesses to the revelations, were promised that "inasmuch as you strip yourselves from jealousies and fears, and humble yourselves before me, for ye are not sufficiently humble, the veil shall be rent and you shall see me and know that I am." But they would not accomplish this "with the carnal neither natural mind, but with the spiritual" (v. 10).

The Lord explains that "no man has seen God at any time in the flesh, except quickened by the Spirit of God. Neither can any natural man abide the presence of God, neither after the carnal mind" (vv. 11–12). This is because "God is a Holy Person; no unclean thing can enter into His presence. Therefore, a mortal, sinful man must be quickened by the Spirit (the Holy Ghost) before he can endure the presence of God."[44]

Hyrum L. Andrus said: "No natural man has ever seen God, for such a person cannot bear the presence of Deity. He must first be relatively innocent or be sanctified by the powers of the Spirit, and this through living faith in Christ. He may then, by being enveloped in the powers of the Holy Spirit (or encircled in God's glory) be transfigured and brought into the presence of God. (D&C 67:11; Moses 1:2, 11)."[45]

This change is called "transfiguration," which should not be confused with what happens when one is "translated." Transfiguration is a temporary change, such as happened to the Prophet Joseph Smith at the time of the First Vision. Translation is a semipermanent state that protects the person from sickness, pain, and death until the day of his quick death and resurrection.

The Lord cautions these early brethren that "Ye are not able to abide the presence of God now, neither the ministering of angels; wherefore, continue in patience until ye are perfected. Let not your minds turn back; and when ye are worthy, in mine own due time, ye shall see and know" (vv. 13–14).

On special occasions Church leaders have testified that they have experienced the fulfillment of this promise. "I know that God lives," said President George Q. Cannon. "I know that Jesus lives; for I have seen Him."[46] Elder Melvin J. Ballard also bore a similar witness: "I know, as well as I know that I live and look into your faces, that Jesus Christ lives… For in the visions of the Lord to my soul, I have seen Christ's face, I have heard His voice. I know that He lives."[47]

Before this can happen, certain weaknesses have to be overcome, such as jealousy, fear, and lack of humility. These very weaknesses had been manifested during the criticism of the revelations, so they were obviously not prepared at that time to see the Lord face to face. They also exist today and must be overcome if we are to see God.

The Mind and Will of the Lord

(D&C 68)

As the conference closed, a group of elders—Orson Hyde, Luke Johnson, Lyman E. Johnson and William E. McLellin— came to the Prophet and sought the will of the Lord concerning themselves, and their ministry. This revelation was the result of the Prophet's inquiry in their behalf.

Orson Hyde

● **D&C 68:1 Orson Hyde will proclaim the gospel among many lands and peoples.** He was called "to proclaim the everlasting gospel, by the Spirit of the living God, from people to people, and from land to land, in the congregations of the wicked, in their synagogues, reasoning with and expounding all scriptures unto them."

These prophecies were literally fulfilled. In 1832, Orson Hyde and Samuel H. Smith traveled about 2,000 miles on foot through New York, Massachusetts, Maine, and Rhode Island. In 1835 he was ordained an Apostle. In 1837 he went on a mission to England. In 1840 he fulfilled another prophecy by serving a mission to Jerusalem. Along the way, he crossed the Atlantic Ocean, traveled through England and Germany, visited Constantinople, Cairo, and Alexandria. On October 24, 1841, upon the Mount of Olives, he offered a prayer, dedicating Palestine for the return and gathering of the Jews.[48]

- **D&C 68:2–4 The Lord defines what is "scripture" or the word of the Lord.** Those ordained ministers of Christ who go forth into the world are commanded to "speak as they are moved upon by the Holy Ghost" (vv. 2–3). "And whatsoever they shall speak when moved upon by the Holy Ghost shall be scripture, shall be the will of the Lord, shall be the mind of the Lord, shall be the word of the Lord, shall be the voice of the Lord, and the power of God unto salvation" (v. 4). The Lord reiterated this in D&C 1, which was given at the same time as D&C 68, when He said: "whether by mine own voice or by the voice of my servants, it is the same" (D&C 1:38).

- **D&C 68:13 The principle of continuous revelation.** In verse 13, the Lord identifies the remainder of that revelation as "addition[s] to the covenants and commandments"—that is, to the Book of Commandments. These additions, given even before the Book of Commandments was printed, illustrate the principle of continuous revelation in the Church. The revelations can and will be added to by living prophets.

- **D&C 68:14–24 The qualifications of a Presiding Bishop.** The Lord informs His early Church that "There remain hereafter, in the due time of the Lord, other bishops to be set apart unto the church" who will perform the same duties as the first one did (v. 14). The Lord then enumerates the qualifications of Presiding Bishops. While some of these apply to local ward bishops as well, they are intended specifically for the Presiding Bishop of the whole Church.

  — They shall be high priests who are worthy (v. 15).
  — They shall be appointed by the First Presidency of the Melchizedek priesthood, unless they are literal descendants of Aaron (v. 15).
  — If they are literal descendants of Aaron they have a legal right to the bishopric, if they are the firstborn among the sons of Aaron (vv. 16–18).
  — ust as a high priest of the Melchizedek priesthood has authority to officiate in all the lesser offices he may also officiate in the office of bishop (v. 19).
  — He must be called and set apart and ordained unto this power, under the hands of the First Presidency of the Melchizedek priesthood (v. 19).
  — Even a literal descendant of Aaron must be designated by the First Presidency, and found worthy, and anointed, and ordained under the hands of this Presidency, otherwise they are not legally authorized to officiate in their priesthood (v. 20).
  — Proof that one has the right of this priesthood office, descending from father to son, must be provided. Or, it may be provided by revelation from the Lord through the First Presidency (v. 21).
  — A Presiding Bishop cannot be tried or condemned by any disciplinary council other than the First Presidency of the Church (v. 22). If he is tried and condemned by the First Presidency, he is subject to the same penalties and need for repentance as others, and also may be forgiven (vv. 23–24).

- **D&C 68:25–28 The responsibility of parents to teach and baptize their children.** If parents in the Church have children and they fail to "teach them … to understand the doctrine of repentance, faith in Christ the Son of the living God, and of baptism and the gift of the Holy Ghost by the laying on of the hands, when eight years old, the sin be upon the heads of the parents" (v. 25). What sin? The sin of not preparing a child for baptism by the time they are eight years old.

When a parent says, "I will not have my child baptized until they are old enough to understand what they are doing," they are actually confessing that they have failed, and the sin of that failure will be held to their account. God has declared that eight years of age is the age of accountability, and all the "philosophies of men" to the contrary do not make His commandment of none effect.

The commandment is clear: "their children shall be baptized for the remission of their sins when eight years old, and receive the laying on of the hands" (v. 27). And parents are also accountable to "teach their children to pray, and to walk uprightly before the Lord" (v. 28).

● **D&C 68:29 A commandment to keep the Sabbath day holy.** Whatever the rest of the world may consider to be acceptable on the Sabbath Day, "the inhabitants of Zion shall … observe the Sabbath day to keep it holy."

Elder Spencer W. Kimball said: "The Sabbath is a holy day in which to do worthy and holy things. Abstinence from work and recreation is important but insufficient. The Sabbath calls for constructive thoughts and acts, and if one merely lounges about doing nothing on the Sabbath, he is breaking it. To observe it, one will be on his knees in prayer, preparing lessons, studying the gospel, meditating, visiting the ill and distressed, sleeping, reading wholesome material, and attending all the meetings of that day to which he is expected. [Failure] to do these proper things is a transgression on the omission side."[49]

● **D&C 68:30–32 The need to overcome idleness and greediness.** The inhabitants of Zion must remember and do whatever things they are called to do "in all faithfulness; for the idler shall be had in remembrance before the Lord" (v. 30, meaning "shall not be exalted"). The Lord observes that "there are idlers among [us]; and their children are also growing up in wickedness; they also seek not earnestly the riches of eternity, but their eyes are full of greediness" (v. 31).

We live in a time when people think they are entitled to things without putting forth the necessary effort to earn them. Whether it is a temporal dole of unearned money and substance, or a spiritual dole of unearned salvation and exaltation, the Lord condemns slackers who think they will receive the harvest without effort. This is contrary to the law of the harvest and one of the most destructive weapons available to Satan, who wishes to lull us away into carnal security and lead us away carefully down to hell (2 Nephi 28:21). "These things ought not to be," says the Lord, "and must be done away from among [members of the Church]" (v. 32).

● **D&C 68:33 A command to pray.** Prayer is such a crucial element of salvation that the Lord has continually scolded those who neglect it. The brother of Jared was scolded for *three hours* by the Lord for not remembering his prayers. In our own time, the Lord has said that "he that observeth not his prayers before the Lord in the season thereof, let him be had in remembrance before the judge [bishop] of my people."

President Ezra Taft Benson said: "We must constantly be watchful as well as prayerful to ensure that our thoughts, words, and deeds stay in the 'spiritual safe zone.' Just as the Savior promised protection to the Nephites, His promise is likewise conveyed to us today through the scriptures and living prophets who testify that if we are diligently watchful and prayerful, we will be given the strength to shun any temptation."[50]

Notes:

1. *History of the Church*, 1:146-147.

2. In Conference Report, April 1978, 122; or *Ensign*, May 1978, 81.

3. *Ensign*, Dec. 1972, 3.

4. *Ensign*, November 1978, 53-54.

5. *The Teachings of Spencer W. Kimball*, ed. Edward L. Kimball [1982], 135.

6. *Church History and Modern Revelation*, 4 vols. [1946-1949], 1:168.

7. Lyndon W. Cook, *The Revelations of the Prophet Joseph Smith: A Historical and Biographical Commentary of the Doctrine and Covenants* [1985], 60.

8. *The Revelations of the Prophet Joseph Smith: A Historical and Biographical Commentary of the Doctrine and Covenants*, 60.

9. *Church News*, 19 August 1972, 3.

10. In Conference Report, April 1983, 96-97; or *Ensign*, May 1983, 71.

11. *Program of the Church of Jesus Christ of Latter-day Saints* [1937], 164-165.

12. *History of the Church*, 1:154-156.

13. *History of the Church*, 1:154, Footnote.

14. In *Journal of Discourses*, 11:7.

15. *John Whitmer's History of the Church*, chapter 3; *History of the Church*, 1:154, Footnote.

16. See *Church History and Modern Revelation*, 1:172.

17. Smith and Sjodahl, *Doctrine and Covenants Commentary* [1972], 249.

18. *John Whitmer's History of the Church*, ch. vi.

19. *History of the Church*, 1:166, Footnote.

20. *Diary of President Wilford Woodruff*, 20 January 1872, Church Archives, Introduction to the first volume of his diaries. In Larry C. Porter and Susan Easton Black, eds., *The Prophet Joseph: Essays on the Life and Mission of Joseph Smith* [1988], 1.

21. *Diary of President Wilford Woodruff*, 17 March 1857.

22. *Diary of President Wilford Woodruff*, 6 September 1856.

23. "The Angels May Quote from It," *New Era*, October 1975, 5.

24. *History of the Church*, 1:175-177.

25. *History of the Church*, 1:176, Footnote.

26. In Conference Report, April 1950, 163.

27. *Church History and Modern Revelation*, 1:160-161.

28. *Church History and Modern Revelation*, 1:189.

29. *History of the Church*, 1:291.

30. *Church History and Modern Revelation*, 2:143-144.

31. *Church History and Modern Revelation*, 3:31-32.

32. In Conference Report, April 1953, 112-113.

33. Richard H. Cracroft and Neal E. Lambert, *A Believing People: Literature of the Latter-day Saints* [1979], footnote 1, 255.

34. Walter D. Bowen, "The Versatile W. W. Phelps: Mormon Writer, Educator, and Pioneer" (M.A. thesis, Brigham Young University [1958], 24.

35. *Doctrine and Covenants Commentary*, 317.

36. Andrew Jenson, *Latter-day Saints' Biographical Encyclopedia*, 4 vols. [1901-1936], 3:695.

37. *History of the Church*, 4:164.

38. *History of the Church*, 1:220, Footnote.

39. *Millennial Star*, Vol. 26, 807-809; *Latter-day Saints' Biographical Encyclopedia*, 1:83.

40. *Church History and Modern Revelation*, 2:24, 34.

41. *Church History and Modern Revelation*, 2:18-19.

42. *History of the Church*, 1:226.

43. *Lectures on Faith* as published in the *Messenger and Advocate*, (May 1835), Lecture Sixth, 126.

44. Daniel H. Ludlow, *A Companion to Your Study of the Doctrine and Covenants*, 2 vols. [1978], 1:355.

45. *The Glory of God and Man's Relation to Deity* [1964], 54.

46. *Deseret Weekly*, 6 October 1896.

47. In Conference Report, April 1920, 40.

48. *Doctrine and Covenants Commentary*, 409.

49. *The Miracle of Forgiveness*, 96-97.

50. *The Teachings of Ezra Taft Benson* [1988], 435.

Chapter 14

The Law of Consecration

(D&C 82–83; 104)
[1832]

☙☼☙

A COMMANDMENT TO CONSECRATE

In February 1831, soon after the Saints began to gather in Kirtland, Ohio, the Lord revealed that they should begin to live the law of consecration. He said: "And behold, thou wilt remember the poor, and consecrate of thy properties for their support that which thou hast to impart unto them, with a covenant and a deed which cannot be broken" (D&C 42:30).

This is consistent with what the Lord has done in every dispensation where He has gathered together a group of chosen people. He immediately offers to them the opportunity to become a Zion people He did this with Enoch's people,

Copely farm in Thompson, Ohio, where the Colesville Saints first practiced the law of consecration

and they accepted His offer and were translated. He did it again with Melchizedek's people with the same result—they were translated. He tried it with the children of Israel at Mt. Sinai, but they rejected His offer and brought upon themselves the restrictive society of the Mosaic law. He tried it among the Nephites after His visit to them, and it worked for about 200 years (four generations), then fell apart. Now, here in February 1831, He will try it again with His Latter-day Saints.

Although they are often mentioned together, consecration and sacrifice are not the same thing. They are closely related and involve similar devotion, but they are fundamentally different in their nature and duration.

— To "consecrate" means to set apart or dedicate something to the service of the Lord. In doing so, I do not give anything up—I *share* what I have (and will continue to have) to the kingdom. For example, if I can play the piano and I agree to share that talent with my ward members by accepting a call from my bishop, I am *consecrating* that talent to the service of others. Thus, the law of consecration is an organized way in which individuals consecrate their time, talents, and possessions to the Church to build up the Lord's kingdom and serve others.

— To "sacrifice" means to give something up or give it away as an act of service or devotion. Thus we sacrifice our tithes and offerings, we sacrifice (give away) our sins (Alma 22:18), and we sacrifice (give up) our will to God because we trust in His greater wisdom (Luke 22:42).

The topic of this chapter is consecration and the system the Lord provided for Saints to live together in righteousness while practicing this principle. As in previous dispensations, the early Latter-day Saints had mixed results with this principle, and we still do to this day.

WHY WE CONSECRATE

The Underlying Principles of Consecration

● **D&C 104:13–14 The earth is the Lord's.** A person's willingness to consecrate results from the recognition that the earth and everything in it belongs to the Lord (Psalm 24:1). Persons who do not believe this will not see themselves as "stewards" over the blessings they possess, but as the sole owners of self-made circumstances. To establish a proper mind frame, the Lord declares that "every man [is] accountable, as a steward over earthly blessings, which I have made and prepared for my creatures" (v. 13). Lest we forget, He reminds us that He is the one who "stretched out the heavens, and built the earth, my very handiwork; and all things therein are mine" (v. 14).

Bishop Victor L. Brown said: "[Unless we] feel in total harmony [with the principle that everything we have belongs to the Lord,] it will be difficult, if not impossible, for us to accept the law of consecration. As we prepare to live this law, we will look forward with great anticipation to the day when the call will come. If, on the other hand, we hope it can be delayed so we can have the pleasure of accumulating material things, we are on the wrong path."[1]

● **D&C 104:15–16 The Lord's way is to exalt the poor and humble the rich.** The Lord wants us to be provided for, but He wants it "done in mine own away" (vv. 15–16). And what is that way? It is "that the poor shall be exalted, in that the rich are made low" (v. 16). We should not misunderstand. This is not socialism, nor taxing the rich to provide handouts for the poor. No, the Lord's way provides for personal growth for both the rich and poor as they come together in a covenant bond. The poor must work for what they receive, and every man must contribute his excess to the common good of the whole. That is consecration.

The United Order did this in the early days of the Church. Elder Marion G. Romney said: "The united order exalts the poor and humbles the rich. In the process both are sanctified. The poor, released from the bondage and humiliating limitations of poverty, are enabled as free men to rise to their full potential, both temporally and spiritually. The rich, by consecration and by imparting of their surplus for the benefit of the poor, not by constraint but willingly as an act of free will, evidence that charity for their fellow men characterized by Mormon as 'the pure love of Christ' (Moro. 7.47)."[2]

The Church Welfare Program does this today. Elder Romney also said: "The ... welfare program ... affords an opportunity for its members, while receiving the help they need, to preserve and develop within themselves through self-effort, those pioneer virtues of industry and thrift which are the priceless possessions of every self-respecting person and which are indispensable to man's eternal progression. In this way the Church would conquer idleness and indolence and exalt the poor, saving them from the awful degradation of the temporal, political, and spiritual bondage into which the panaceas of the world, which neglect the development of these fundamental virtues, inevitably lead."[3]

Welfare Square in Salt Lake City

- **D&C 29:34–35 Consecration is a spiritual law, not just a temporal or economic program.** It helps participants prepare for eternal life in a celestial kingdom wherein the inhabitants live the law of consecration. The Lord said: "I say unto you that all things unto me are spiritual, and not at any time have I given unto you a law which was temporal" (v. 34). Although it involves the temporal security of God's people it is not a temporal commandment, "for my commandments are spiritual; they are not natural nor temporal, neither carnal nor sensual" (v. 35).

- **D&C 19:26 We must not "covet" our possessions.** In D&C 19, Martin Harris was commanded not to "covet" his possessions, but to use them freely to print the Book of Mormon. This is an interesting use of the word "covet," since we normally think of it as unrighteous wishing that we possessed the means or circumstances of another. But coveting is not just a sin for the "have nots" of the world; it is also a sin for those who cling to their own possessions at the sacrifice of their spiritual well-being. President Brigham Young said: "I am more afraid of covetousness in our Elders than I am of the hordes of hell… All our enemies … in the world, and all hell with them marshaled against us, could not do us the injury that covetousness in the hearts of this people could do us; for it is idolatry."[4]

President Brigham Young also said:

> When we consider the condition of the Latter-day Saints, and see how many there are who seem to have their eyes fixed upon the things of this world, things that are not lasting, but that perish in the handling, and how anxious they are to obtain them, how do you think I feel about it? We see many of the Elders of Israel desirous of becoming wealthy, and they adopt any course that they think will bring them riches, which to me is as unwise as anything can be—to see men of wisdom, men that seem to have an understanding of the world and of the things of God, searching after minerals throughout these mountains …
>
> These treasures that are in the earth are carefully watched, they can be removed from place to place according to the good pleasure of Him who made them and owns them. He has His messengers at His service, and it is just as easy for an angel to remove the minerals from any part of one of these

mountains to another, as it is for you and me to walk up and down this hall… People do not know it, but I know there is a seal set upon the treasures of earth; men are allowed to go so far and no further. I have known places where there were treasures in abundance; but could men get them? No. You can read in the Book of Mormon of the ancient Nephites holding their treasures, and of their becoming slippery; so that after they had privately hid their money, on going to the place again, lo and behold it was not there, but was somewhere else, but they knew not where. The people do not understand this; I wish they did, for they would then do as I do, pay attention to the legitimate business that God has given them to perform.[5]

- **D&C 64:34 Consecration must be done willingly, not grudgingly nor by force.** Consistent with all spiritual laws, participation in consecration is voluntary, not forced. God insists that every man "should be an agent unto himself" in this matter (D&C 29:35). In the matter of consecration, "the Lord requireth the heart and a willing mind" and only the "willing" and the "obedient" may participate in this celestial program among a Zion people. This demonstrates the folly of thinking that consecration will one day be announced from the pulpit by decree from Church authorities. It is far more likely that the Saints, out of necessity or charity or both, will voluntarily begin to live this way out of the pure desires of their hearts.

Elder Lorenzo Snow said: "In things that pertain to celestial glory there can be no forced operations. We must do according as the Spirit of the Lord operates upon our understandings and feelings. We cannot be crowded into matters, however great might be the blessing attending such procedure. We cannot be forced into living a celestial law; we must do this ourselves, of our own free will… Whatever we do in regard to the principles of the united order, we must do it because we desire to do it. Some of us are practicing in the spirit of the united order, doing more than the law of tithing requires."[6]

TIMELINE OF REVELATIONS ON CONSECRATION

The revelations to Joseph Smith concerning the law of consecration began in February 1831, soon after the Prophet Joseph Smith arrived in Ohio. They continued over the next four and one-half years, as the Lord revealed line-by-line the many principles connected with the law of consecration.

Date	Where Received	Where Recorded	Content
4 Feb. 1831	Kirtland, Ohio	D&C 41:9	Edward Partridge appointed as first bishop
9 Feb. 1831	Kirtland, Ohio	D&C 42:30–34	Law of consecration explained.
Feb. 1831	Kirtland, Ohio	D&C 44:6	Saints to administer to the poor according to law.
7 Mar. 1831	Kirtland, Ohio	D&C 45:64–75	Call to gather Zion: prospect of New Jerusalem.
Mar. 1831	Kirtland, Ohio	D&C 48	Saints who settled in Ohio to save money for inheritance in Zion.
May 1831	Thompson, Ohio	D&C 51:3-15	Bishop Partridge to appoint portions (stewardships) according to family size, circumstances, wants, and needs. Storehouse to be established.
June 1831	Kirtland, Ohio	D&C 56:16–20	Rich and poor commanded to repent.
20 July 1831	Jackson County	D&C 57	Missouri appointed and consecrated as the land of inheritance and center place for Zion.

Date	Where Received	Where Recorded	Content
1 Aug. 1831	Jackson County	D&C 58:1–9, 50–57	Zion to come after much tribulation. Early immigrants honored to lay foundation of Zion. Lands to be purchased in Independence.
Aug. 1831	Kirtland, Ohio	D&C 63:27–31	Saints commanded to purchase lands with money and forbidden to obtain lands by blood.
12 Nov. 1831	Kirtland, Ohio	D&C 70:1–8	Elders appointed stewards over revelations. Surpluses to be consecrated to the Church.
4 Dec. 1831	Kirtland, Ohio	D&C 72	Newel K. Whitney appointed as second bishop of the Church in Kirtland. Further duties of bishop made known.
Mar. 1832	Hiram, Ohio	D&C 78	Saints commanded to establish storehouses in Zion and to further organize so Church would be independent.
26 April 1832	Jackson County	D&C 82:11–12	United order to be established to manage affairs in Zion and Kirtland.
30 April 1832	Independence	D&C 83	Widows and orphans to be provided for by consecration of the Church to storehouses.
27 Nov. 1832	Kirtland, Ohio	D&C 85	To receive an inheritance in Zion a person must be willing to live the law of consecration.
25 June 1833	Kirtland, Ohio	History of the Church 1:364–365	Letter from the Prophet to bishop Edward Partridge on the size of a member's stewardship.
2 Aug. 1833	Kirtland, Ohio	D&C 97:10–21	House (temple) in Zion (Jackson County) commanded. Zion is pure in heart.
6 Aug. 1833	Kirtland, Ohio	D&C 98	Saints commanded to follow the Constitution. Law of war and law of forgiveness given to Saints.
12 Oct. 1833	Perrysburg, NY	D&C 100:13–17	Chastened Zion to be redeemed.
10 Dec. 1833	Kirtland, Ohio	History of the Church 1:453–456	Letter from the Prophet to retain lands: petition to God to return Saints to land of inheritances.
16 Dec. 1833	Kirtland, Ohio	D&C 101	Reasons given for Saints' expulsion from Jackson County. Zion not to be moved out of her place. Saints to rely on constitutional process.
24 Feb. 1834	Kirtland, Ohio	D&C 103	Saints to redeem Zion after tribulation. Zion to be redeemed by power.
23 April 1834	Kirtland, Ohio	D&C 104:47–66	Separation of united order in Kirtland and Zion. Sacred treasury provided for.
22 June 1834	Fishing River, MO	D&C 105	Redemption of Zion postponed until Saints are prepared, endowed, and numerous. United order dissolved until after Zion's redemption.
1 Sept. 1835	Kirtland, Ohio	*History of the Church* 2:254	Prophet's letter to elders of the Church relating his June 1831 vision to go to western Missouri.

CONSECRATION IS NOT SOCIALISM OR COMMUNISM

Some have suggested that the law of consecration and the system of the united order are a religious kind of socialism or communism, a system envisioned by Karl Marx in 1818. Others assert that it developed from one of the other economic philosophies of Joseph Smith's day or from communal experiments within the Church. These assumptions are false. The united order was not a communal system like socialism or communism.

President J. Reuben Clark Jr. called communism "Satan's counterfeit for the united order," and said that those who suggest the united order was akin to socialism or communism "either do not know or have failed to understand or are wilfully misrepresenting."[7]

Karl Marx, Founder of Communism

The Prophet Joseph Smith attended a presentation on socialism in September 1843 at Nauvoo. His response was to declare that he "did not believe the doctrine."[8] He also said: "I preached on the stand about one hour on the 2nd chapter of Acts, designing to show the folly of common stock [holding property in common]. In Nauvoo every one is steward over his own [property]."[9]

Elder Marion G. Romney outlined the differences between the revealed system of the united order and socialistic programs:

1. The cornerstone of the united order is belief in God and acceptance of Him as Lord of the earth and the author of the united order. Socialism, wholly materialistic, is founded in the wisdom of men and not of God. Although all socialists may not be atheists, none of them in theory or practice seek the Lord to establish His righteousness.

2. The united order is implemented by the voluntary free-will actions of men, evidenced by a consecration of all their property to the Church of God… Socialism is implemented by external force, the power of the state …

3. The united order is operated upon the principle of private ownership and individual management. Thus in both implementation and ownership and management of property, the united order preserves to men their God-given agency, while socialism deprives them of it.

4. The united order is non-political. Socialism is political, both in theory and practice. It is thus exposed to, and riddled by, the corruption that plagues and finally destroys all political governments that undertake to abridge man's agency.

5. A righteous people is a prerequisite to the united order. Socialism argues that it as a system will eliminate the evils of the profit motive.[10]

THE PROCESS OF CONSECRATION

To fully appreciate the difference between a welfare state and the law of consecration, we need to examine the process by which consecration is accomplished under the Lord's plan. It can be thought of as a four-step process.

Step #1:
Consecrating Possessions

● **Church members voluntarily consecrate their possessions to the Church by legal deed (D&C 42:30–32).** This is the first step and perhaps the one that requires the most faith. To be effective, and to allow the issuance of stewardships, this had to be done voluntarily (v. 31; D&C 64:34) and with a legal deed of ownership—secure enough that ownership of the properties was sure and "cannot be taken from the Church" (v. 32). The Lord said: "consecrate of thy properties … with a covenant and a deed which cannot be broken" (v. 30). Not everything was thus consecrated—only those things that had real value (e.g., property) or could be used to make a living (e.g., farm animals, tools), plus money and goods that could be used to help the poor.

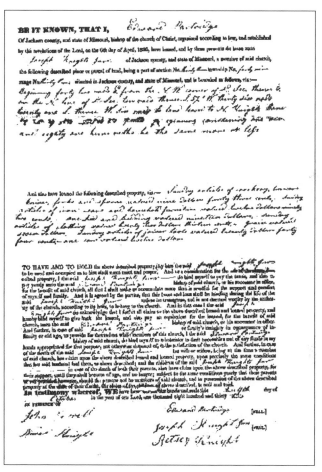

1832 Deed of Consecration to Bishop Partridge

These consecrated properties are "laid before the bishop" (D&C 42:31). The bishop was thus the agent through which consecration was made. Bishops had to be men of uncommon character, a man whose "heart is pure before me … [and] in whom there is no guile" (D&C 41:11).

Step #2:
Receiving a Stewardship

● **In return, the bishop deeds back the man's property, with a covenant of stewardship** (D&C 42:32). The Lord said: "every man shall be made accountable unto me, *a steward over his own property*, or that which he has received by consecration" (v. 32, emphasis added). Why was this done? Why go through the process of deeding my property to the bishop and then having him deed it right back to me? The answer lies in the principle of covenant stewardship. When I receive it back, I do so with a covenant and promise to take care of it and use it for the blessing and benefit of not only my own family but also the entire system within which my stewardship operates.

- **The stewardship property is owned by the recipients (D&C 51:4).** This is private property, not communal property. It is given to them with a deed of ownership so each member will be fully responsible and accountable for managing it. The Lord says, "when [the bishop] shall appoint a man his portion, give unto him a writing that shall secure unto him his portion, that he shall hold it, even this right and this inheritance in the Church."

  Hugh Nibley said: "One is 'a steward over his own property,' namely 'that which he has received by consecration, as much as is sufficient for himself and family' (D&C 42:32). That is 'his own property' to which he has exclusive right, and that is the limit of his stewardship—and it is all consecrated, whether given or received. One does not begin by holding back what he thinks he will need, but by consecrating everything the Lord has given him so far to the Church; then he in return receives back from the bishop by consecration whatever he needs."[11]

- **Stewardships come with a covenant of accountability for their use and management (D&C 104:11–13).** The Lord said: "It is wisdom in me; therefore, a commandment I give unto you, that ye shall organize yourselves and appoint every man his stewardship; That every man may give an account unto me of the stewardship which is appointed unto him. For it is expedient that I, the Lord, should make every man accountable, as a steward over earthly blessings, which I have made and prepared for my creatures." Elder Alexander B. Morrison said: "The scriptures speak repeatedly of the sacred responsibility God places upon His servants to act as faithful agents or stewards. (See, for example, Genesis 26:5; Matthew 20:8; 25:14–29; Luke 16:2; and Titus 1:7). The word of the Lord given through the Prophet Brigham Young seems particularly appropriate for our time: 'Thou shalt be diligent in preserving what thou hast, that thou mayest be a wise steward; for it is the free gift of the Lord thy God, and thou art his steward' (D&C 136:27)."[12]

- **The size of the stewardship depends on the circumstances, wants, and needs of the family (D&C 42:32).** In every case, he was to receive "sufficient for himself and family" (v. 32). This would mean that the size and nature of stewardships would vary according to the size and needs of each individual family. I might receive back exactly what I consecrated. I might receive back more than what I consecrated. I might receive back less. It all depended upon the family's circumstances. The bishop was commanded to "appoint unto this people their portions, every man equal according to his family, according to his circumstances and his wants and needs" (D&C 51:3, emphasis added).

  Notice that the bishop was to take into account the family's righteous "wants" so long as they were "just" and not selfish (D&C 82:17).

- **The bishop and the member decide by mutual consent how much is enough.** This judgment was not up to the bishop alone. He was to make this assessment in concert with the individual, and they had to both agree on how much was enough to satisfy the legitimate needs and wants of the family.

The Prophet Joseph Smith said:

> Therefore, to condescend to particulars, I will tell you that every man must be his own judge how much he should receive and how much he should suffer to remain in the hands of the bishop. I speak of those who consecrate more than they need for the support of themselves and their families.

The Prophet Joseph Smith

> The matter of consecration must be done by the mutual consent of both parties; for to give the bishop power to say how much every man shall have, and he be obliged to comply with the bishop's judgment, is giving to the bishop more power than a king has; and upon the other hand, to let every man say how much he needs, and the bishop be obliged to comply with his judgment, is to throw Zion into confusion, and make a slave of the bishop. The fact is, there must be a balance or equilibrium of power, between the bishop and the people, and thus harmony and good will may be preserved among you.[13]

- **The stewardship also depends on the particular training, skills, and knowledge of the recipient.** The bishop had to take into account the individual's unique circumstances— talents, interests, etc.—recognizing the unique needs and worth of each soul. A blacksmith received what was needed to operate a blacksmith shop. A printer received a print shop. A baker received a bakery.

Hyrum M. Smith and Janne M. Sjodahl noted the individual stewardships that were granted to Church leaders at Kirtland, based on their personal skills and desires (D&C 104:19–46):

> Specific directions are here given for stewardships. Sidney Rigdon is given charge of the tannery (v. 20). He had, at one time, been engaged in the very useful business of a tanner and was competent in this stewardship. Martin Harris, who was a successful farmer, is given charge of a piece of land (v. 24). He was also to manage a publication business, under the direction of the Prophet (v. 26). Oliver Cowdery and Frederick G. Williams are given charge of the printing office (v. 30). John Johnson is to be a real estate agent (v. 36). Newel K. Whitney is assigned to the mercantile establishment (v. 39). Joseph Smith is given charge of the Temple lot (v. 43). He is also to take care of his father (v. 45), for the Lord recognizes the duty of children to provide for their parents, as well as the duty of parents to care for their children.[14]

- **Participants must be righteous in order to participate (D&C 51:4).** If a steward "transgresses and is not accounted worthy by the voice of the church, according to the laws and covenants of the church, to belong to the church" he is no longer eligible to participate. In such cases, the participant is given back the money and property he consecrated and is required to leave the system.

For example, the Lord said concerning Ezra Thayre, "my servant Ezra Thayre must repent of his pride, and of his selfishness, and obey the former commandment which I have given him concerning the place upon which he lives" [the law of consecration] (D&C 56:8). If he did, he would retain his rights and blessings (v. 9). But if he did not, "he shall receive the money which he has paid, and shall leave the place, and shall be cut off out of my church, saith the Lord God of hosts" (v. 10).

Step #3
Managing Stewardships and Contributing Surpluses

- **Stewards must regularly report to the bishop on their stewardships (D&C 72:3–4).** The Lord requires "at the hand of every steward, to render an account of his stewardship, both in time and in eternity" (v. 3). This "return and report" process can be seen throughout the plan of salvation, and is essential to proper stewardship. By this process the Lord can determine "who is faithful and wise" both in this world and when we "inherit the mansions prepared for [us] of my Father" (v. 4).

- **Stewards consecrate any surplus they have generated to the bishop (D&C 42:33).** The Lord said: "if there shall be properties in the hands of the church, or any individuals of it, more than is necessary for their support after this first consecration, … a residue [is] to be consecrated unto the bishop."

- **The bishop places all surplus property and goods into a "bishop's storehouse" (D&C 51:13).** This Presiding Bishop was to "appoint a storehouse unto this church; and let all things both in money and in meat, which are more than is needful for the wants of this people, be kept [there] in the hands of the bishop."

- **The lazy and indolent do not receive a stewardship (D&C 42:42, 53).** The system rewards those willing to work with the means to make their living. It does not provide handouts to the lazy and indolent. "Thou shalt not be idle," the Lord said: "for he that is idle shall not eat the bread nor wear the garments of the laborer (v. 42).

- **Participants pay for whatever they obtain from each other (D&C 42:54).** People were not to borrow from their neighbor but to pay for whatever they received from anyone else (v. 54). In this way, every person's stewardship is productive, with nobody taking advantage of any other person's labor. Each has a profitable enterprise from which they can generate the means to purchase whatever they need from others.

- **New stewards then participate like all other stewards (D&C 42:53, 55).** Those who receive their portion from the bishop's storehouse are to "stand in the place of thy stewardship" and work (v. 53). And again, if this new steward "obtainest more than that which would be for thy support, thou shalt give it into my storehouse, that all things may be done according to that which I have said" (v. 55).

Step #4
Managing Surpluses

- **The surplus is used to provide new stewardships to others (D&C 42:33).** The Lord commanded, "it shall be kept to administer to those who have not, from time to time, that every man who has need may be amply supplied and receive according to his wants." President J. Reuben Clark Jr., said: "Whatever a steward realized from the portion allotted to him over and above that which was necessary in order to keep his family under the standard provided … was turned over by the steward to the bishop, and this amount of surplus, plus the residues …, went into a bishop's storehouse (D&C 51:13) … and the materials of the storehouse were to be used in creating portions … for caring for the poor (D&C 78:3), the widows and orphans (D&C 83:6), and for the elders of the Church engaged in the ministry, who were to pay for what they received if they could, but if not, their faithful labors should answer their debt to the bishop (D&C 72:11 ff)."[15]

Bishops Storehouse in early Salt Lake City

● **The bishop also uses the surplus to care for the poor, to build houses of worship, and for other worthy purposes (D&C 42:34–35).** These purposes are both spiritual and temporal, and are discussed throughout the revelations on consecration. Those purposes are summarized below.

An Example of How Consecration Works

To illustrate this celestial principle and how it might work among a righteous people, let us take an imaginary example of a young man who has recently come of age to receive his own stewardship. He wants to be a dentist, and he has prepared himself for this stewardship by attending dental school, graduating, and obtaining a license to practice. How does he proceed?

Step #1: Consecrating Possessions.

The bishop's storehouse already contains sufficient money and equipment to set this young man up in his dental practice. Perhaps a member whose stewardship is manufacturing has already donated the necessary equipment. Or, if not, then the funds of the storehouse can be used to purchase the equipment from a vendor. Also, because of the consecrations that have been made, land and building materials are available to construct him an office. The young man needs only to go to the bishop and consecrate to the system whatever he possesses of value and express a desire to receive a stewardship.

Step #2: Receiving a Stewardship.

Seeing that he is fully qualified, worthy, and willing to enter into his stewardship with a covenant, the bishop arranges for him to receive his stewardship—everything necessary for him to practice dentistry. He makes a covenant with the bishop to manage and maintain his stewardship to the best of his ability, and to consecrate to the storehouse any surplus he may generate from his practice. He and the bishop agree together as to what his family's needs and wants are, and anything above that will be considered to be "surplus." He receives his property and equipment with a deed, makes his solemn covenant of stewardship, and begins his practice.

Step #3: Managing Stewardships and Contributing Surpluses.

To understand the genius of this system, we should ask ourselves three questions at this point:

— First, how much debt does the young man have? He has none. The land and building and equipment are all paid for. So, too, is his house and his car. All were received as part of his stewardship. So he begins his stewardship debt-free and able to concentrate on managing his practice and spending plenty of time with his family. He is truly free.

— Second, how expensive will his fees need to be in order for him to practice? Not very expensive. People can obtain dental services from him for a reasonable cost that does not have to cover the cost of his equipment or facilities. Nor does he have to generate unreasonable sums of money to satisfy his desired lifestyle. That has already been negotiated and agreed to with his bishop, and his home and cars, etc., are all paid for. The entire community benefits from dental services at a very reasonable price.

— Third, how much excess will he generate from his practice? Quite a bit, since he has no payments to make. After keeping what he and the bishop have agreed he should keep to satisfy his family's needs and wants, he then gives back to the storehouse all of the excess he generates each year. It might be safe to say that at least half of what he generates will be excess, if not more. A large amount of money flows back into the storehouse from this young man every year of his life, providing the means to set others up in their own stewardships.

Step #4: Managing Surpluses.

It should not be difficult to imagine how an entire community would benefit from such a system. Nobody is in debt. Everybody has what they need and want. And this young man's story is multiplied by thousands of people, in all walks of life, who are consecrated stewards. It is not surprising, therefore, that societies that have lived this law have become extremely blessed as a people. They all get rich—together. And they all stay focused on the more important things of life—family, Church, and the welfare of their neighbors. They become, indeed, a celestial people.

THE PURPOSES OF CONSECRATION

The goal of the system is not just "to get rich," but to shape a people into a Zion society where they have "all things common" (Acts 4:32) and there are "no poor among them" (Moses 7:18). Both temporally and spiritually, they are united and unfettered and blessed. Thus, consecration achieves a number of important things for those who live it.

Temporal Reasons for Consecration

● **D&C 42:31 To care for the poor and needy.** When we "impart of [our] substance unto the poor, [we] will do it unto [the Lord]." We become the Lord's heart and hands as we minister to the needs of those who have asked Him for assistance. We become the answer to their prayers. So, in that sense, we are doing it unto (for) the Lord as well as unto the worthy poor themselves.

- **D&C 42:42 To teach us to be industrious and to avo**thousands of "idle poor" who feel entitled to the care of others without regard to their own productivity. This is contrary to the laws of heaven and a manifestation of the "I will do everything for you" promises of Lucifer in the Premortal life. That is not the Lord's way. He commands, "Thou shalt not be idle; for he that is idle shall not eat the bread nor wear the garments of the laborer." The poor must labor for what they receive, both as their way of contributing to the blessings of others, and also for the sake of their own self-dignity.

  The ever-increasing practice of dispensing money and commodities with no expectation of work has produced in our society a love for idleness, a feeling that the world owes them a living. President J. Reuben Clark Jr., an Apostle and respected government official, calls this dole system "a breeding ground for some of the most destructive political doctrines that have ever found any hold ... and I think it may lead us into serious political trouble ... Society owes to no man a life of idleness, no matter what his age. I have never seen one line in Holy Writ that calls for, or even sanctions this. In the past no free society has been able to support great groups in idleness and live free."[16]

- **D&C 51:3, 9 To make us "equal" in earthly opportunities.** Bishop Partridge was charged to "appoint unto this people their portions, every man equal according to his family, according to his circumstances and his wants and needs" (v. 3). The Lord commanded, "let every man ... be alike among this people, and receive alike, that ye may be one, even as I have commanded you" (v. 9). This did not mean identical, but that every steward has all that he needs and desires in righteousness. This revelation makes it plain that "equality" does not mean identical-ness. It means that every man is to be "equal according to his family, according to his circumstances and his wants and needs" (see also D&C 82:17; 78:5–6). This kind of equality will vary as much as each man's circumstances, family, wants, and needs.

  President Brigham Young said:

  > Every man and woman has got to feel that not one farthing of anything in their possession is rightfully theirs, in the strict sense of ownership. When we learn this lesson, where will be my interest and my effort? I do not own anything—it is my Father's. How came I by my possessions? His providence has thrown them into my care; He has appointed me a steward over them, and I am His servant, His steward, His hired man, one with whom He has placed certain property in charge for the time being, that is, pertaining to the things of this world

  > ...

  > Were you to make an equal distribution of property today, one year would not pass before there would be as great an inequality as now. [Then] how could you ever get a people equal with regard to

their possessions? They never can be, no more than they can be in the appearance of their faces. Are we equal? Yes. Wherein? We are equal in the interest of eternal things, in our God, not aside from Him.

We behold Church property, and not one farthing of it is yours or mine. Of the possessions that are called mine, my individual property, not a dollar's worth is mine; and of all that you seem to possess, not a dollar's worth is yours.

Did you ever organize a tree, gold, silver, or any other kind of metal, or any other natural production? No, you have not yet attained to that power, and it will be ages before you do. Who owns all the elements with which we are commanded and permitted to operate? The Lord, and we are stewards over them. It is not for me to take the Lord's property placed under my charge and wantonly distribute it; I must do with it as He tells me. In my stewardship I am not to be guided by the mere whims of human folly, by those who are more ignorant than I am, not by the lesser power, but by the superior and wiser.[17]

- **D&C 82:18 To provide a common pool of resources from which to help people.** Our consecrated money and goods are "cast into the Lord's storehouse, to become the common property of the whole church" (v. 18). Notice that it is what goes into the *storehouse* that becomes common property, and not the *private property* of the people.

Each stewardship is considered private property, and only the residues and surpluses consecrated for the storehouse became the "common property of the whole church." It is referred to as the "common property" because every covenant member of the order had access to it, according to his just "wants" and "needs," including the need to improve his stewardship (D&C 82:17–18). This is not communism but joint-capitalism, which we will explain later in this chapter.

- **D&C 78:5–6 To make it possible to focus on spiritual things.** The Lord wants His Saints to be "equal in the bonds of heavenly things, yea, and earthly things also" (v. 5). "For if ye are not equal in earthly things ye cannot be equal in obtaining heavenly things" (v. 6). For example, people who are unequally yoked with the cares of the world will be unequally able to give their attention to spiritual things.

- **D&C 82:18 To improve our talents for the benefit of all.** While taking a stewardship upon himself and learning to manage it "for the benefit of the church of the living God," "every man may improve upon his talent, [and] … gain other talents, yea, even an hundred fold." In other words, we learn new skills and improve upon existing ones, all to the glory of God and for the benefit of ourselves and everyone around us.

- **D&C 42:35 To purchase lands and build buildings.** The Church needs places of worship and temples and administrative buildings around the world. Thus, the money and goods that are consecrated to the Lord may be used for "purchasing lands for the public benefit of the church, and building houses of worship, and building up of the New Jerusalem which is hereafter to be revealed."

- **D&C 42:70–73 To support full time Church officers and workers.** The Lord instructed that "the elders or high priests who are appointed to assist the bishop as counselors in all things, are to have their families supported out of the property which is consecrated to the bishop" (v. 71).

"Or they are to receive a just remuneration for all their services" (v. 72). And "the bishop, also, shall receive his support, or a just remuneration for all his services in the church" (v. 73). Thus, those who labor full-time in the management of the affairs of the Church are entitled to either be paid for their service or to receive goods from the bishop's storehouse. All consecrated goods and money may be used for this purpose as well as for the poor.

● **D&C 78:14 To help the Church "stand independent above all other creatures."** The traumatic events of those early days of the Church would have been made much worse if the Church and its people had all been financially insolvent. The Lord commanded the Saints to consecrate, "notwithstanding the tribulation which shall descend upon you, that the church may stand independent above all other creatures beneath the celestial world."

Spiritual Reasons for Consecration

● **D&C 42:40 To help us to overcome greed and pride.** The goods provided under this system are not "designer clothes" nor "luxury items" that feed the greed and the ego of the proud. The Lord commands, "thou shalt not be proud in thy heart; let all thy garments be plain, and their beauty the beauty of the work of thine own hands."

President Ezra Taft Benson said: "One of Satan's greatest tools is pride: to cause a man or a woman to center so much attention on self that he or she becomes insensitive to their Creator or fellow beings. It's a cause for discontent, divorce, teenage rebellion, family indebtedness, and most other problems we face. If you would find yourself, learn to deny yourself for the blessing of others. Forget yourself and find someone who needs your service, and you will discover the secret to the happy, fulfilled life."[18]

● **D&C 51:9 To teach us to be honest.** This is a system which requires households to declare their needs and wants to the bishop. There are all kinds of opportunities for greed and selfishness under such a system. The Lord said as He implemented this plan, "And let every man deal honestly."

● **D&C 51:19 To teach us to be accountable, faithful, and wise.** Managing a stewardship which requires us to report the results teaches us to be accountable. Being properly and consistently accountable makes us faithful. And learning to make the proper decisions along the way makes us wise. These are all godlike characteristics which we must obtain if we wish to be exalted. The Lord has promised that faithful and wise stewards will inherit all that the Father has (D&C 78:22).

President Brigham Young said:

> I am decidedly in favor of practical religion—of everyday useful life. And if I today attend to what devolves upon me to do, and then do that which presents itself tomorrow, and so on, when eternity comes I will be prepared to enter on the things of eternity. But I would not be prepared for that sphere of action, unless I could manage the things that are now within my reach. You must all learn to do this …

If you cannot provide for your natural lives, how can you expect to have wisdom to obtain eternal lives? God has given you your existence—your body and spirit, and has blest you with ability, and thereby laid the foundation of all knowledge, wisdom, and understanding, and all glory and eternal lives. If you have not attained ability to provide for your natural wants, and for a wife and a few children, what have you to do with heavenly things?19

- **D&C 70:14 To teach us to be unselfish.** The Lord said: "in your temporal things you shall be equal, and this not grudgingly, otherwise the abundance of the manifestations of the Spirit shall be withheld." Consecration against our will or with a bad attitude will not bless us. We might as well not give the gift because there will be no reward for giving grudgingly. The Prophet Joseph Smith said we must "consecrate to the bishop before [we] can be considered a legal heir to the kingdom of Zion; and this, too, without constraint."20 Thus, our offerings must be voluntary, given from the heart, and with pure charity for those who need it.

- **D&C 82:17 To teach us to be just and fair.** While living this law, "you are to have equal claims on the properties, for the benefit of managing … your stewardships, every man according to his wants and his needs, inasmuch as his wants are just." In other words, we need to learn to be fair and equitable in our requests from the system, not greedy and self-serving.

- **D&C 78:3–4 To provide for the salvation of the Saints.** The Lord intended this practice to be "permanent and everlasting" and to "advance the cause" of Zion (v. 4). Its purpose was to provide for "the salvation of man" and for "the glory of your Father who is in heaven" (v. 4). How does consecration do this? By teaching us how to hold and manage wealth without it destroying us spiritually.

President Brigham Young said:

> "The worst fear that I have about [members of this Church] is that they will get rich in this country, forget God and His people, wax fat, and kick themselves out of the Church and go to hell. This people will stand mobbing, robbing, poverty, and all manner of persecution, and be true. But my greater fear for them is that they cannot stand wealth; and yet they have to be tried with riches, for they will become the richest people on this earth."21

- **D&C 78:7 To learn to live a celestial principle while still on earth.** Consecration is a celestial law—the inhabitants of the celestial world live by this law. Therefore, "if you will that I give unto you a place in the celestial world, you must prepare yourselves by doing the things which I have commanded you and required of you" (to consecrate). "President Brigham Young taught that the dominion God gives human beings is designed to test them, enabling them to show to themselves, to their fellow beings, and to God just how they would act if entrusted with God's power."22

- **D&C 82:19 To keep our "eye single to the glory of God."** Instead of self-interest and self-aggrandizement, consecration encourages "Every man seeking the interest of his neighbor, and doing all things with an eye single to the glory of God." It is charity in action. I become as interested in your happiness and security as in my own, and we both work for our common good.

THE UNITED ORDER

● **D&C 78:3 An organization is needed to manage and administer the law of consecration.** In March 1832, the Lord revealed that there must be an organization to regulate and administer the law of consecration among His people. The system cannot function properly in an informal or chaotic context. The Lord said: "[let] there be an organization of my people, in regulating and establishing the affairs of the storehouse for the poor of my people, both in this place [Kirtland] and in the land of Zion."

● **D&C 92:1–2 The Lord called this organization the "United Order."** In March 1833, the Lord directed that Frederick G. Williams, who had recently been appointed a counselor in the First Presidency, be accepted into the system of consecration at Kirtland. While doing so, the Lord referred to the system as the "united order." He said: "I give unto the united order, organized agreeable to the commandment previously given, a revelation and commandment concerning my servant Frederick G. Williams, that ye shall receive him into the order" (v. 1). At the same time, the Lord said to Frederick G. Williams that "you shall be a lively member in this order; and inasmuch as you are faithful in keeping all former commandments you shall be blessed forever" (v. 2).

● **D&C 104 Further instructions on the united order.** In a subsequent revelation the Lord said the following about the united order and its participants.

— Saints who transgress against the united order shall be cursed (vv. 1–10).
— The Lord provides for His Saints in His own way (vv. 11–16).
— Gospel law governs the care of the poor (vv. 17–18).
— Stewardships and blessings of various brethren are designated (vv. 19–46).
— The united order in Kirtland and the order in Zion are to operate separately (vv. 47–53).
— This sacred treasury of the Lord can be used to print the scriptures (vv. 54–66).
— The united order is to operate on the basis of common consent (vv. 67–77).
— Those in the united order are to pay all their debts, and the Lord will deliver them from financial bondage (vv. 78–86).

THE LAW OF CONSECRATION TODAY

The Law of Consecration Was Revoked

● **D&C 56:4 The Lord both gives and revokes His commandments, as needed.** He warned the Saints in June 1831 that "I, the Lord, command and revoke, as it seemeth me good; and all this to be answered upon the heads of the rebellious."

● **D&C 58:31–33 The Lord's promises are conditioned upon obedience.** The Lord asks a question whether there has ever been a time when He has "promised and have not fulfilled" (v. 31). Of course, the answer is no. The problem is that men are not obedient. "I command and men obey not," He said, and therefore "I revoke and they receive not the blessing" (v. 32).

But then, like selfish children, "they say in their hearts: This is not the work of the Lord, for his promises are not fulfilled" (v. 33). They fail to see the connection between keeping their covenants and receiving the blessings attached to those covenants. This was the case with the Saints who were driven out of the land of Zion. They questioned whether the Lord had kept His promises concerning Zion, without thinking about their own role in its demise.

- **D&C 105:34 The law of consecration was revoked until the time of Zion's future redemption.** The Lord said: "Let those commandments which I have given concerning Zion and her law be executed and fulfilled, after her redemption."

- **D&C 105:2–4 The people in Zion were not living the law of consecra- tion nor keeping the command- ments.** The Lord said: "Behold, I say unto you, were it not for the transgres- sions of my people, speaking concern- ing the church and not individuals, they might have been redeemed even now" (v. 2). But they were not behaving like a Zion people, nor keeping their covenants: (vv. 3–4).

The Saints were driven out of Zion

— They had not learned to be obedient to the things which the Lord required.
- — They were full of all manner of evil.
- — They did not impart of their substance to the poor and afflicted among them.
- — The were not united according to the "union required by the law of the celestial kingdom" [the united order].

- **D&C 105:5–6 The law of consecration is a celestial law.** "Zion cannot be built up unless it is by the principles of the law of the celestial kingdom; otherwise I cannot receive her unto myself" (v. 5). A Zion people must live by celestial laws, and consecration is one of those. Because they did not do so, they "must needs be chastened until they learn obedience, if it must needs be, by the things which they suffer" (v. 6).

Elder Orson Pratt said:

> It is true we are not now required to consecrate all that we have; this law has not been binding upon us since we were driven from the land of Zion. The reason why this law was revoked was because the Lord saw we would all go to destruction in consequence of our former tradition in relation to property if this law had continued to be enforced after we were driven out, hence He revoked it for the time being, as you will find recorded in one of the revelations given June 22nd, 1834, after we were driven from Jackson County [D&C 105]... Here you perceive that, for the salvation of this people and of the nations of the earth among the Gentiles, God saw proper to revoke this commandment and to lay it over for a future period, or until after the redemption of Zion. Zion is

not yet redeemed, and hence we are not under the law of full consecration. But is that any reason why we should not be under some other law differing from the one we were formerly required to practice?23

How We Can Consecrate Today

Though we are do not live the law of consecration as a people, we are nonetheless asked to consecrate as individuals. We have made covenants to do so.

Elder Bruce R. McConkie said: "Now I think it is perfectly clear that the Lord expects far more of us than we sometimes render in response. We are not as other men. We are the Saints of God and have the revelations of heaven. Where much is given much is expected.

We are to put first in our lives the things of His kingdom. We are commanded to live in harmony with the Lord's laws, to keep all His commandments, to sacrifice all things if need be for His name's sake, to conform to the terms and conditions of the law of consecration. We have made covenants so to do—solemn, sacred, holy covenants, pledging ourselves before gods and angels."24

What, then, can we do to live the law of consecration today, in a time when there is no organized process for us to do it as a people? We can do any and all of the following.

- **Make the sacrifices the Lord requires now—our time, talents, and possessions—for the building up of the Kingdom of God upon the earth, and for the establishment of Zion.**
  Elder Bruce R. McConkie explained the difference between the law of consecration and the law of sacrifice: "The law of consecration is that we consecrate our time, our talents, and our money and property to the cause of the Church. Such are to be available to the extent they are needed to further the Lord's interests on earth. The law of sacrifice is that we are willing to sacrifice all that we have for the truth's sake—our character and reputation; our honor and applause; our good name among men; our houses, lands, and families; all things, even our very lives if need be."25

  Elder McConkie also said: "We are not always called upon to live the whole law of consecration and give all of our time, talents, and means to the building up of the Lord's earthly kingdom. Few of us are called upon to sacrifice much of what we posses, and at the moment there is only an occasional martyr in the cause of revealed religion. But what the scriptural account means is that to gain celestial salvation we must be able to live these laws to the full if we are called upon to do so. Implicit in this is the reality that we must in fact live them to the extent we are called upon so to do. How, for instance, can we establish our ability to live the full law of consecration if we do not in fact pay an honest tithing? Or how can we prove our willingness to sacrifice all things, if need be, if we do not make the small sacrifices of time and toil, or of money and means, that we are now asked to make?"26

- **Pay tithing and fast offerings, and give generously in other ways to those in need.** By doing this, we can help care for the poor and carry on the important activities of the Church.

Elder Marion G. Romney said: "We ... should live strictly by the principles of the united order [or law of consecration] insofar as they are embodied in present Church practices, such as fast offering, tithing, and the welfare activities. Through these practices we could as individuals, if we were of a mind to do so, implement in our lives all the basic principles of the united order... What prohibits us from giving as much in fast offerings as we would have given in surpluses under the united order? Nothing but our own limitations."[27] Thus, each of us could, individually, calculate what is "surplus" in our means and give it willingly to the Church in support of any one of its vital programs.

- **Serve willingly in the Church.** The Lord has admonished each person to "learn his duty, and to act in the office in which he is appointed, in all diligence" (D&C 107:99).

  President Ezra Taft Benson said: "Opportunities to lose oneself for the good of others present themselves daily; the mother who serves her children's needs; the father who gives his time for their instruction; parents who give up worldly pleasure for quality home life; children who care for their aged parents; home teaching service; visiting teaching; time for compassionate service; giving comfort to those who need strength; serving with diligence in Church callings; community and public service in the interest of preserving our freedoms; financial donations for tithes, fast offerings, support of missionaries, welfare, building and temple projects. Truly, the day of sacrifice is not past."[28]

- **Serve as a full-time missionary.** We may not often think of missions as a form of consecration, but they certainly are. Elder Robert D. Hales said: " Going on a mission teaches you to live the law of consecration. It may be the only time in your life when you can give to the Lord all your time, talents, and resources. In return, the Lord will bless you with His Spirit to be with you. He will be close to you and strengthen you."[29]

- **Develop Christlike love for others.** "Every man seeking the interest of his neighbor" (D&C 82:19) is the foundation of the law of consecration. President Thomas S. Monson tells numerous stories of the Christlike service his parents gave, of his service as an Aaronic priesthood holder, and as a young ward bishop. This is just one of them:

  > I have many memories of my boyhood. Anticipating Sunday dinner was one of them. Just as we children ... sat anxiously at the table, with the aroma of roast beef filling the room, Mother would say to me, "Tommy, before we eat, take this plate I've prepared down the street to Old Bob and hurry back." I could never understand why we couldn't first eat and later deliver his plate of food. I never questioned aloud but would run down to Bob's house and then wait anxiously as Bob's aged feet brought him eventually to the door. Then I would hand him the plate of food. He would present to me the clean plate from the previous Sunday and offer me a dime as pay for my services. My answer was always the same: "I can't accept the money. My mother would tan my hide." He would then run his wrinkled hand through my blond hair and say, "My boy, you have a wonderful mother. Tell her thank you." ... Sunday dinner always seemed to taste a bit better after I had returned from my errand.[30]

- **Strive to consecrate willingly.** We must willingly consecrate, not do so grudgingly. The revelations tell us that "the Lord requireth the heart and a willing mind; and the willing and obedient shall eat the good of the land of Zion in these last days" (D&C 64:34). Willingness is manifested by our attitude as well as our actions. For example, do we consecrate our time and talents grudgingly?

Elder Neal A. Maxwell said: "We tend to think of consecration only in terms of property and money. But there are so many ways of keeping back part."[31] When we withhold sharing our gifts of music, teaching, or leadership, or when we do so grudgingly, we are not consecrating and we should not expect the blessings of doing so.

Elder Maxwell also said: "The submission of one's will is really the only uniquely personal thing we have to place on God's altar. The many other things we 'give' … are actually the things He has already given or loaned to us. However, when you and I finally submit ourselves, by letting our individual wills be swallowed up in God's will, then we are really giving something to Him! It is the only possession which is truly ours to give!"[32]

SOME CONCLUSIONS ABOUT CONSECRATION

Elder Bruce R. McConkie said:

> We might well ask, "Isn't it enough to keep the commandments? What more is expected of us than to be true and faithful to every trust? Is there more than the law of obedience?" In the case of (the) rich young (man) there was more. He was expected to live the law of consecration, to sacrifice his earthly possessions, for the answer of Jesus was: "If thou wilt be perfect, go and sell that thou hast, and give to the poor, and thou shalt have treasure in heaven: and come and follow me." As you know, the young man went away sorrowful, "for he had great possessions" (Matt. 19:16–22). And we are left to wonder what intimacies he might have shared with the Son of God, what fellowship he might have enjoyed with the Apostles, what revelations and visions he might have received, if he had been able to live the law of a celestial kingdom. As it is, he remains nameless; as it might have been, his name could have been had in honorable remembrance among the Saints forever …
>
> The work of the kingdom must go forward, and the members of the Church are and shall be called upon to bear off its burdens. It is the Lord's work and not man's. He is the one who commands us to preach the gospel in all the world, whatever the cost. It is His voice that decrees the building of temples, whatever the cost. He is the one who tells us to care for the poor among us, whatever the cost, lest their cries come up to His throne as a testimony against those who should have fed the hungry and clothed the naked but who did not. And may I say also—both by way of doctrine and of testimony—that it is His voice which invites us to consecrate of our time, our talents, and our means to carry on His work. It is His voice that calls for service and sacrifice. This is His work. He is at the helm guiding and directing the destiny of His kingdom.[3]3

Notes:

1. "The Law of Consecration," *BYU Devotional Speeches of the Year*, 1976, [1977], 439.

2. In Conference Report, April 1966, 97.

3. In Conference Report, April 1947, 128.

4. In *Journal of Discourses*, 5:353.

5.In *Journal of Discourses*, 19:36-39.

6In *Journal of Discourses*, 19:346.

7.In Conference Report, October 1943, 11.

8.*History of the Church*, 6:33.

9.*History of the Church*, 6:37-38.

10. In Conference Report, April 1966, 97.

11. *Approaching Zion*, edited by Don E. Norton [1989], 170.

12. *Feed My Sheep: Leadership Ideas for Latter-day Shepherds* [1992], 21.

13. *History of the Church*, 1:364.

14. *Doctrine and Covenants Commentary*, [1972[, 673.

15. In Conference Report, October 1942, 56.

16. In Conference Report, April 1938, 106-107.

17. In *Journal of Discourses*, 4:29.

18. In Conference Report, April 1979; or *Ensign*, May 1979, 34.

19. *Discourses of Brigham Young*, John A. Widtsoe, ed. [1954], 11, 13.

20. *History of the Church*, 1:364.

21. Preston Nibley, *President Brigham Young: The Man and His Work*, 4th ed. [1960], 127.

22. "Subduing the Earth," in *Nibley on the Timely and the Timeless*, Truman Madsen, ed. [1978], 90; *Encyclopedia of Mormonism*, 1-4 vols., Daniel H. Ludlow, ed. [1992], 432.

23. In *Journal of Discourses*, 15:358-359.

24. *Sermons and Writings of Bruce R. McConkie* [1998], 384; or *Ensign*, May 1975, 51.

25. In Conference Report, April 1975, 75; or *Ensign*, May 1975, 50.

26. *Sermons and Writings of Bruce R. McConkie*, 382; or *Ensign*, May 1975, 50.

27. In Conference Report, April 1966, 100; or *Improvement Era*, June 1966, 537.

28. In Conference Report, April 1979; or *Ensign*, May 1979, 34.

29. In Conference Report, April 1996, 50; or *Ensign*, May 1996, 36.

30. "The Long Line of the Lonely," *Ensign*, Feb. 1992, 4.

31. In Conference Report, October 1992, 90; or *Ensign*, November 1992, 66. 353

32. In Conference Report, October 1995, 30; or *Ensign*, November 1995, 24.

33. In Conference Report, April 1975, 75-76; or *Ensign*, May 1975, 51-52.

CHAPTER 15

Gifts of the Spirit are Manifested

(D&C 42; 46–50)
[1830–1832]

ॐ

INTRODUCTION

On December 5, 1839, the Prophet Joseph Smith wrote a letter to his brother Hyrum Smith, reporting the state of affairs in Washington, DC. The Prophet had gone to seek the help of the President of the United States in obtaining redress for those who had been driven off their land in Missouri. Among other things, he wrote, "In our interview with the President [Van Buren], he interrogated us wherein we differed in our religion from the other religions of the day. [I] said we differed in mode of baptism, and the gift of the Holy Ghost by the laying on of hands. We considered that all other considerations were contained in the gift of the Holy Ghost, and we deemed it unnecessary to make many words in preaching the Gospel to him. Suffice it to say he has got our testimony."[1]

President Martin Van Buren

Three years earlier, an article published in Kirtland in the *Messenger and Advocate* declared, "It is the gift of the Holy Ghost … which makes the difference, and it is this alone, and the society which has this power are the people of God and those who have not are not."[2] This is consistent with the Savior's declaration that the gifts of the Holy Ghost would "follow them that believe" (Mark 16:17), meaning His true and faithful disciples. Therefore, whenever the true Church of God is upon the earth, these gifts must be present.

They were present in the restored Church from the very beginning. During the organization of the Church the Prophet recorded, "The Holy Ghost was poured out upon us to a very great degree—some prophesied, whilst we all praised the Lord, and rejoiced exceedingly."[3]

Unfortunately, counterfeits of these gifts also appeared almost from the start. For example, Hiram Page's professed revelations threatened to split the Church a few months after its organization. Of that incident, the Prophet Joseph Smith said: "The branch of the Church in this part of the Lord's vineyard … were striving to do the will of God, so far as they knew it, though some strange notions and false spirits had crept in among them. With a little caution and some wisdom, I soon assisted the brethren and sisters to overcome them."[4]

SEEKING THE GIFTS OF THE SPIRIT

(D&C 46)

Concerned by the manifestations of these false spirits, the Prophet sought the Lord's will on the matter and received D&C 46 in response. In this revelation, the Lord sets forth a warning against being deceived and then admonishes the Saints to "seek ye earnestly the best gifts, always remembering for what they are given" (v. 8). This revelation established some guidelines for discerning between true and false spiritual manifestations.

- **D&C 46:7–8 Do not be deceived by evil spirits or doctrines of devils.** The Lord warned, "beware lest ye are deceived" (v. 8), and it is easy to be deceived on the matter of spiritual gifts. We see an evangelist swallow poison and not die. We see a preacher shout, "Be ye healed!" and the person rises and walks. We wonder, "Is this fakery or is it real?" The Lord said: "some are of men, and others of devils" (v. 7), suggesting that some of it is fakery and some of it is done through the power of Lucifer. Either way, it is not of God. God grants His gifts in a dignified manner, with solemnity and holiness, and not as a grand show of supernatural power.

The key here is to seek for these gifts "in all holiness of heart, walking uprightly before me … always remembering for what they are given" (vv. 7–8). And as with all things, to avoid being deceived the Lord says we should pray—"ask of God, who giveth liberally" (v. 7). Also, we should trust the Spirit in these matters—whatever "the Spirit testifies unto you even so I would that ye should do in all holiness of heart." Of course this requires that we are living worthy to have that Spirit with us, "walking uprightly before me, considering the end of your salvation, doing all things with prayer and thanksgiving." And if we do these things, we will not be "seduced by evil spirits, or doctrines of devils, or the commandments of men; for some are of men, and others of devils."

Elder Marion G. Romney said:

> Some of these counterfeits are crude and easily detected, but others closely simulate true manifestations of the Spirit. Consequently, people are confused and deceived by them. Without a key, one cannot distinguish between the genuine and the counterfeit…

> Without attempting an exhaustive discussion of this question, I shall take the liberty to suggest three simple tests which, if applied, will prove of great value in making the distinction.

> First, determine whether the alleged supernatural manifestation is edifying. If it is not, then it is not of God because spiritual gifts are given for the edification of God's people… (1 Cor. 14:26–33)…

> Second—this pertains particularly to purported supernatural healings—find out whether the purported healer follows the divinely established procedure … (Mark 6:5, 12–13, laying on of hands; James 5:14–15, anointing with oil)…

> Third, find out whether the worker of the purported miracle has himself received the gift of the Holy Ghost through the prescribed ordinances. If he has not, then his works, whatever they may be, are not the manifestations of the Holy Spirit…

> Now, righteous men, bearing the holy priesthood of the living God and endowed with the gift of the

Holy Ghost, who are magnifying their callings—and such are the only men upon the earth with the right to receive and exercise the gifts of the spirit—will do so circumspectly and in all humility. They will not spectacularly advertise their divine power nor boast about it. Neither will they display it for money. Of this you may be sure.[5]

● **D&C 46:8 "Seek earnestly" the best gifts.** Generally speaking, we are commanded not to covet. But when it comes to spiritual gifts we are invited to "covet" them "earnestly" (1 Corinthians 12:31). That invitation is repeated in this revelation to the Prophet Joseph Smith, wherein the Lord says it will help us to avoid deception: "beware lest ye are deceived; and that ye may not be deceived seek ye earnestly the best gifts." So, how do we "seek earnestly" these gifts?

Elder Dallin H. Oaks explained how his mother applied the principle of seeking gifts of the Spirit: "Having lost her husband, my widowed mother was incomplete. How she prayed for what she needed to fulfill her responsibility to raise her three small children! She was seeking, she was worthy, and she was blessed! Her prayers were answered in many ways, including the receipt of spiritual gifts. She had many, but the ones that stand out in my memory are the gifts of faith, testimony, and wisdom. She was a mighty woman in Zion."[6]

"Seeking earnestly" may also imply that our desire to obtain these gifts must be sincere and active, not just sitting back and envying another's gift. We must earnestly seek to obtain it through honest effort. Thus, if we observe that someone has the gift of music, we may without sin earnestly covet that gift by seeking to improve our own musical abilities.

Finally, we should "seek earnestly" to know what gifts we personally have been given so that we might magnify and act upon them. There are a number of ways we can learn what our gifts are. These are just a few:

— By the observation of parents and others.
— From our patriarchal blessings and other priesthood blessings.
— By accepting an assignment and discovering our abilities.

● **D&C 46:8–9 Remember the reason for which they were given.** People go astray with regard to spiritual gifts when they fail to remember "for what they are given" (v. 8). They are not given as signs to convince the ungodly—those that seek "for a sign that they may consume it upon their lusts" (v. 9). "They are given for the benefit of those who love me and keep all my commandments, and him that seeketh so to do" (v. 9)—in other words, they are given as rewards to the already faithful. And when the Lord gives a gift, He intends "that all may be benefitted," not just the person who received it. So if I do have the gift of music, I must realize that it was given to me so that I can bless the lives of others with it.

Elder Orson Pratt said: "Each member does not receive all these gifts; but they are distributed through the whole body [of the Church], according to the will and wisdom of the Spirit... Some may have all these gifts bestowed upon them, so as to understand them all, and be prepared to detect any spurious gifts, and to preside over the whole body of the Church, that all may be benefitted. These spiritual gifts are distributed among the members of the Church, according to their faithfulness, circumstances, natural abilities, duties, and callings; that the whole may be properly instructed, confirmed, perfected, and saved."[7]

- **D&C 46:31 Do all things in the name of Christ.** Whatever we may do with our gifts—teach, bless, counsel, entertain, befriend, or any of a hundred other things with the help of the Spirit, "all things must be done in the name of Christ, whatsoever you do in the Spirit." We should always include Christ in our efforts in any way possible. When I think of this, I think of John Canaan, a popular LDS singing artist who accompanied a tour of Church History sites that I led a few years ago. He sang to us at each major stop, helping us to feel the Spirit in those sacred places. And even while in the airport, he used his gift to teach the gospel. When accosted by a somewhat hostile Baptist minister who said we weren't Christian, this good man took out his guitar and sang several songs to him in praise of Christ. The man was deeply touched, and he departed with a different understanding.

- **D&C 46:32 Thank God for the gifts He has given us.** The Lord commanded that "ye must give thanks unto God in the Spirit for whatsoever blessing ye are blessed with." This would include whatever gifts of the Spirit we have received. Thus, if someone says, "My goodness, you certainly are gifted at painting!" a proper response would not be to deny the gift, nor to take full credit for it. Perhaps we could say something like, "Thank you. I love to paint and I've worked hard at it. But whatever gift I may have is a gift given from God, and He is the one we should thank for it. I'm just trying to improve on the talent He gave to me." As Elder Bruce R. McConkie said: "Spiritual gifts come from God. They are the gifts of God; they originate with Him and are special blessings that He bestows upon those who love Him and keep His commandments. Because they come by the power of the Holy Ghost, they are also called the gifts of the Spirit."[8]

- **D&C 46:33 Practice virtue and holiness continually.** This means not only that we must maintain personal virtue and holiness, but also that we should behave in virtuous and holy ways in every circumstance. Standing up and loudly demonstrating a supposed gift of healing or of tongues is unseemly and not what the Lord would do. Most gifts are given privately and with great dignity and holiness.

Elder Dallin H. Oaks said: "Spiritual gifts do not come visibly, automatically, and immediately to all who have received the gift of the Holy Ghost. The Prophet Joseph Smith taught that most such gifts are 'not visible to the natural vision, or understanding of man,' and that it 'require[s] time and circumstances to call these gifts into operation.'"[9]

ABOUT SPIRITUAL GIFTS

Why Spiritual Gifts Are Given

Elder Bruce R. McConkie said: "By the grace of God—following devotion, faith, and obedience on man's part—certain special spiritual blessings called gifts of the Spirit are bestowed upon men. Their receipt is always predicated upon obedience to law, but because they are freely available to all the obedient, they are called gifts. They are signs and miracles reserved for the faithful and for none else… Their purpose is to enlighten, encourage, and edify the faithful so that they will inherit peace in this life and be guided toward eternal life in the world to come. Their presence is proof of the divinity of the Lord's work; where they are not found, there the Church and kingdom of God is not."[10]

Thus, spiritual gifts are not given to convince unbelievers or to show off our supernatural power. They are not given to inflate our vanity or as evidence that we are somehow favored of God. Instead, they are blessings of a loving Heavenly Father to His obedient children, as well as manifestations of power through which God accomplishes His purposes.

To Strengthen and Bless Us Individually

● **D&C 46:9 The Lord said: "they are given for the benefit of those who love me and keep all my commandments, and him that seeketh so to do."** When we are sick, the gift of healing can bring blessed relief. When we need counsel, the gift of wisdom manifested through a loving bishop can help us navigate a problem. The gift of music can lift and bear witness to our souls in a way that few other things can. The gift of teaching can give us understanding of gospel principles. The gift of tongues can help a new missionary master a language. And a hundred other blessings can result from these gifts. Elder Dallin H. Oaks said that gifts of the Spirit "can lead us to God. They can shield us from the power of the adversary. They can compensate for our inadequacies and repair our imperfections."[11]

President Joseph Fielding Smith said: "Now, the Lord will give us gifts. He will quicken our minds. He will give us knowledge that will clear up all difficulties and put us in harmony with the commandments that He has given us; He will give us a knowledge that will be so deeply rooted in our souls that it can never be rooted out, if we will just seek for the light and the truth and the understanding that are promised to us and that we can receive if we will only be true and faithful to every covenant and obligation pertaining to the gospel of Jesus Christ."[12]

To Help Us Serve Others

- **D&C 46:11–12, 26** God gave us our gifts for service, not as a badge of honor. If we do not share our gifts they are of no benefit to anyone, and like the foolish man who buried his one talent we will find ourselves condemned at the last day.

While serving as a bishop I became aware of the fact that every gift of the Spirit was present in our ward through one person or another. Nobody had all of them. But as a group, we did. Thus, by coming together as a ward congregation we were able to bless each other's lives with every spiritual gift. "For all have not every gift given unto them; for there are many gifts, and to every man is given a gift by the Spirit of God. To some is given one, and to some is given another, that all may be profited thereby" (vv. 11–12). "And all these gifts come from God, for the benefit of the children of God" (v. 26).

Elder Orson Pratt said: "Spiritual gifts are distributed among the members of the Church, according to their faithfulness, circumstances, natural abilities, duties, and callings; that the whole may be properly instructed, confirmed, perfected, and saved."[13]

Elder Robert D. Hales said: "The phrase 'that all may be profited thereby' [D&C 46:12] is a very important concept to understand about the gifts of the Spirit. The gifts given to each individual are given not only for the one who receives, but also for those who can benefit when the gift is shared with others."[14]

Who May Receive the Gifts of the Spirit

- **Those who are worthy.** While "all have not every gift given unto them ... to every man is given a gift by the Spirit of God (D&C 46:11, emphasis added). That includes both you and me. Every worthy person who has received the gift of the Holy Ghost has received at least one gift, and usually more. As we discussed earlier, we must "seek earnestly" to know what those gifts are so that we can properly improve on them.

- **Those who have the Gift of the Holy Ghost.** The Prophet Joseph Smith taught that one must first possess the gift of the Holy Ghost before he or she can receive the gifts of that Spirit. He said that the gifts of the Spirit "are obtained through that medium [the Holy Ghost] and ... cannot be enjoyed without the gift of the Holy Ghost... The world in general can know nothing about them."[15]

- **Both men and women and also children.** Receiving the gifts of the Spirit does not require priesthood. Even non-members can receive manifestations of the Spirit temporarily, especially when seeking a witness of the truth of the restored gospel. As discussed in earlier chapters about the receipt of revelation, little children often feel the Spirit in profound ways. And Elder Bruce R. McConkie said in Nauvoo on the occasion of the dedication of the Monument to Women: "Where spiritual things are concerned, as pertaining to all of the gifts of the Spirit, with reference to the receipt of revelation, the gaining of testimonies, and the seeing of visions, in all matters that pertain to godliness and holiness and which are brought to pass as a result of personal righteousness—in all these things men and women stand in a position of absolute equality before the Lord. He is no respecter of persons nor of sexes, and He blesses those men and those women who seek Him and serve Him and keep His commandments."[16]

THE GIFTS OF THE SPIRIT

● **D&C 46:10 We should know what gifts have been given to the Church.** The Lord commands, "I would that ye should always remember, and always retain in your minds what those gifts are, that are given unto the church." These are listed in the scriptures in three of the four standard works: D&C 46, 1 Corinthians 12, and Moroni 10. Following is a chart which compares the gifts listed in these three sources.

Gifts of the Spirit — A Comparative List

1 Corinthians 12:5–11	Moroni 10:9–16	D&C 46:13–25
		To know that Jesus is the Christ
		Believe in Christ by others' word
Differences in administration		Differences in administration
Diversities of operations		Diversities of operations
Word of wisdom	Teach the word of wisdom	Word of wisdom
Word of knowledge	Teach the word of knowledge	ord of knowledge
Faith	Great faith	
Gifts of healing	Gifts of healing	Faith to heal and be healed
Working of miracles	Work mighty miracles	Working of miracles
Prophecy	Prophecy	Prophecy
Discerning of spirits	Behold angels/ministering spirits	Discerning of spirits
Diverse tongues	All kinds of tongues	Speak with tongues
Interpretation of tongues	Interpret languages & tongues	Interpretation of tongues

Because it is the most comprehensive, we will use the list provided in D&C 46 as our guide in discussing the gifts that are listed in the scriptures.

● **D&C 46:13 A personal testimony of Jesus Christ.** Knowing "by the Holy Ghost … that Jesus Christ is the Son of God, and that he was crucified for the sins of the world."

This is a gift available to everyone. The Lord has promised that everyone can know for himself—by the power of the Holy Ghost—of the divinity of the Savior and the truthfulness of the gospel (Moroni 10:4–7). President David O. McKay said: "Inspiration, revelation to the individual soul, is the rock upon

HOFFMAN, 1889

which a testimony should be built, and there is no person living who cannot get it if he will conform to those laws and live a clean life which will permit the Holy Spirit to place that testimony in him."[17]

- **D&C 46:14 Belief in others' testimonies of the Savior.** Believing on the words of those who know Jesus is the Christ is also a gift of the Spirit. Such persons are "given to believe on their words, that they also might have eternal life if they continue faithful."

President Harold B. Lee invited the young people of the Church to "Lean on my testimony until you get your own. Some of you may not have a testimony, and so I have said to other groups like you, if you don't have a testimony today, why don't you cling to mine for a little while? Hold on to our testimonies, the testimonies of your bishops, your stake presidents, until you can develop it. If you can say nothing more today than I believe because my president, or my bishop, believes, I trust him, do this until you can get a testimony for yourselves; but I warn you that won't stay with you unless you continue to cultivate it and live the teachings. You are a temple of God worthy to receive the companionship of the Holy Ghost."[18]

- **D&C 46:15 Differences of Administration.** Having a knowledge of "the differences of administration," according to Elder Bruce R. McConkie, is a gift "used in administering and regulating the Church."[19] As used in the New Testament by Paul, this term meant literally the different divisions or courses of the priests and Levites engaged in the temple service. In this revelation it refers to the different duties and responsibilities of the priesthood in its two divisions, the Melchizedek and Aaronic. To know and understand this is a gift of the Spirit."[20]

This could be manifested in understanding how the various organizations of the Church function, and being able to manage them in effective ways. There are various styles of leadership; not all leaders do things in precisely the same way. But through this gift of the Spirit, they can know what the proper thing to do might be in a given circumstance. This is also a gift given of the Spirit, and good administrators have this gift.

- **D&C 46:16 Diversities of Operations (Discernment of Spiritual Gifts).** "Knowing the diversities of operations means being able to discern whether or not a given form of spiritual manifestation is of the Lord."[21] This gift helps us discern whether a teaching or influence comes from God or from some other source. Presiding authorities who hold keys are given this gift as a part of their responsibilities to regulate the spiritual affairs of the Church. Elder Abraham O. Woodruff said: "If the bishop, who is a common judge in Israel, tells a person to restrain this gift, or any other gift, it is the duty of that person to do it. The bishop has a right to the gift of discernment, whereby he may tell whether these spirits are of God or not."[22]

- **D&C 46:17–18 Word of Wisdom and Knowledge.** "There is a [fundamental] difference between wisdom, knowledge, and the ability to instruct." Wisdom, in gospel terms, means to follow correct principles and to use knowledge properly. Knowledge is an understanding of the principles—"a carefully-stored-up supply of facts, generally slowly acquired. The ability to instruct is the gift to impart of this supply to others. Each is a gift of God".[23]

- **D&C 46:19 Faith to be healed.** It is interesting to note that faith is a gift—something given to us from God which is a prerequisite to receiving another gift: to be healed. Therefore, faith is one gift of the Spirit that we should most earnestly seek for because so much else depends upon it. If we have sufficient faith, the Lord is willing to heal all diseases (Psalm 103:3), so long as we are not appointed to death (D&C 42:48).

This gift was evident very early on in the Church's history. The Lord revealed that when Church members were sick they should call for elders to "pray for and lay their hands upon them" in the name of the Lord (D&C 42:43–52). And some months before section 42 was received, Joseph Smith and Oliver Cowdery had been told that they should heal the sick (D&C 24:13–14). These blessings were among the Saints from the very beginning.

Elder Parley P. Pratt wrote of a woman named Chloe Smith who was so ill that she was near death, but was healed by the Prophet Joseph Smith:

> Under these circumstances, President Smith and myself, with several other Elders, called to see her. She was so low that no one had been allowed for some days previous to speak above a whisper, and even the door of the log dwelling was muffled with cloths to prevent a noise. We kneeled down and prayed vocally all around, each in turn, after which President Smith arose, went to the bedside, took her by the hand, and said unto her with a loud voice, "in the name of Jesus Christ arise and walk!" She immediately arose, was dressed by a woman in attendance, when she walked to a chair before the fire, and was seated and joined in singing a hymn. The house was thronged with people in a few moments, and the young lady arose and shook hands with each as they came in; and from that minute she was restored to health.[24]

● **D&C 46:20 Faith to heal.** This is one of the most well-known of the spiritual gifts because our Lord healed so many persons during His mortal ministry. Walter A. Norton said: "Significantly, Christ Himself laid on hands to heal the sick (Mark 6:5, 13; Luke 13:12–13), and sent His Apostles out doing the same (Mark 6:7–13). In Mark 6:13, however, we learn something that is revealed in no other place in the four Gospels; that the Apostles 'anointed with oil many that were sick, and healed them'… In only one other place in the entire New Testament do we find an explicit reference to the ordinance of anointing the sick with oil. That reference is given in the epistle of the Apostle James (5:14–16)."[25]

The same gift of healing was possessed by Joseph Smith, who used it often to bless the Saints in both Kirtland and Nauvoo. In the spring of 1831 a Methodist preacher named Ezra Booth came with a group of people into Kirtland to investigate the claims of the Prophet and his followers. The party included a well-to-do farmer named John Johnson and his wife, Alice, from Hiram, Ohio. Alice's arm was partially paralyzed from rheumatism, and she could not raise it above her head. As they talked with the Prophet, one of the visitors asked if there was anyone on earth who had the power to cure Alice's lame arm. When the conversation turned to another subject, Joseph went up to Mrs. Johnson, took her by the hand, and with calm assurance said: "Woman, in the name of the Lord Jesus Christ I command thee to be whole." As Joseph went from the room, leaving everyone astonished and speechless, she raised her arm. The next day she hung out her

Luke Johnson

first wash in over six years without any pain. Some members of the Johnson family— including two future apostles: Luke and Lyman—joined the Church as a result of the healing. The miracle also attracted wide acclaim throughout northern Ohio.[26]

Lyman Johnson

- **D&C 46:21 Miracles.** The working of miracles is a gift of the Spirit. While they appear surprising—almost magical—to those who witness them, Elder James E. Talmage said that miracles do not violate natural law, but rather they show the operation of higher laws that we may not yet understand.[27] The Lord declared that "signs come by faith, not by the will of men, nor as they please, but by the will of God" (D&C 63:10). He also said: "I am God, and mine arm is not shortened; and I will show miracles, signs, and wonders, unto all those who believe on my name (D&C 35:8). Thus, only those with faith can receive such miracles. Even the Lord Himself had to inquire whether those He healed believed in Him before He could heal them. As President Kimball is famous for saying, "faith precedes the miracle."

- **D&C 46:22 Prophecy.** Prophecy refers to the right to speak for God—in other words, to be His mouthpiece. It may or may not involve foretelling the future. But in a much broader sense, "the testimony of Jesus is the spirit of prophecy" (Revelation 19:10). And therefore, in a broad sense, every Saint who has a personal witness that Jesus is the Christ is a prophet. If a person has this spirit of prophecy, he or she can better understand the writings of the prophets, such as Isaiah, who wrote by the spirit of prophecy. The fruits of the spirit of prophecy are many: besides being able to understand the writings of the prophets, one who possesses the spirit of prophecy may also have the gifts of discernment, revelation, translation of inspired scripture, and prophecy.

Elder Bruce R. McConkie said: "Prophets are simply members of the true Church who have testimonies of the truth and divinity of the work. They are the Saints of God who have learned by the power of the Holy Ghost that Jesus is the Christ, the Son of the living God... That is, every person who receives revelation so that he knows, independent of any other source, of the divine Sonship of the Savior, has, by definition and in the very nature of things, the spirit of prophecy and is a prophet... Both testimony and prophecy come by the power of the Holy Ghost; and any person who receives the revelation that Jesus is the Lord is a prophet and can, as occasion requires and when guided by the Spirit, 'prophesy of all things.'"[28]

Joseph Smith understood this well and made frequent reference to it in his sermons. On one occasion he explained, "No man can be a minister of Jesus Christ except he has the testimony of Jesus; and this is the spirit of prophecy. Whenever salvation has been administered, it has been by testimony."[29]

Several ancient prophets have connected the spirit of prophecy to the Holy Ghost or the Spirit of God (Alma 5:47), to truth (Alma 5:47; 6:8; 43:2), and to the gifts of the Holy Ghost, including the gift of tongues and the gift of translation (Alma 9:21). Modern prophets view the spirit of prophecy and the Holy Ghost as virtually equivalent. Elder Delbert L. Stapley stated, "The Holy Ghost is the spirit of prophecy."[30] And Elder Wilford Woodruff wrote, "It is the privilege of every man and woman in this kingdom to enjoy the spirit of prophecy, which is the Spirit of God."[31]

- **D&C 46:23, 27 Discernment of Spirits.** The gift of "discerning of spirits" (v. 23) is one of the most important spiritual gifts, and is the main subject of D&C 50 (below). "… the bishop of the church, and … such as God shall appoint and ordain to watch over the church … have it given unto them to discern all those gifts lest there shall be any among you professing and yet be not of God" (v. 27). This is somewhat related to the gift of "discernment of operations" with which one may discern the source of spiritual gifts (above), but this one has specific reference to discerning the "spirit" of an individual rather than the source of a spiritual gift.

Elder Stephen L Richards said:

> The gift of discernment is essential to the leadership of the Church. I never ordain a bishop or set apart a president of a stake without invoking upon him this divine blessing, that he may read the lives and hearts of his people and call forth the best within them. The gift and power of discernment in this world of contention between the forces of good and the power of evil is essential equipment for every son and daughter of God. [This gift] arises largely out of an acute sensitivity to impressions— spiritual impressions, if you will—to read under the surface as it were, to detect hidden evil, and more importantly to find the good that may be concealed. The highest type of discernment is that which perceives in others and uncovers for them their better natures, the good inherent within them. It's the gift every missionary needs when he takes the gospel to the people of the world. He must make an appraisal of every personality whom he meets. He must be able to discern the hidden spark that may be lighted for truth. The gift of discernment will save him from mistakes and embarrassment, and it will never fail to inspire confidence in the one who is rightly appraised.[32]

- **D&C 46:24–25 Tongues and Interpretation of Tongues.** The gift of tongues may take two forms: (1) one may be able to speak a foreign tongue [language] or (2) one may be able to understand or interpret a foreign tongue [language]. Whenever the gift of tongues is manifest in an unknown tongue (e.g., the Adamic language), another who is present will be given the interpretation of tongues so that the listeners may benefit from what is being said. In other words, there must always be some spiritual benefit to the manifestation; it will not be given as a "show" of some kind with no knowledge being imparted.

The Prophet Joseph Smith counseled the Saints to speak in tongues only when an interpreter was present:

> There are only two gifts that could be made visible—the gift of tongues and the gift of prophecy. These are things that are the most talked about, and yet if a person spoke in an unknown tongue, according to Paul's testimony, he would be a barbarian to those present. They would say that it was gibberish; and if he prophesied they would call it nonsense. The gift of tongues is the smallest gift perhaps of the whole, and yet it is one that is the most sought after… The greatest, the best, and the most useful gifts would be known nothing about by an observer… Be not so curious about tongues, do not speak in tongues except there be an interpreter

The Prophet Joseph Smith

present; the ultimate design of tongues is to speak to foreigners, and if persons are very anxious to display their intelligence, let them speak to such in their own tongues.[33]

The Prophet Joseph Smith said several more things about the gift of tongues:

Speak not in the gift of tongues without understanding it, or without interpretation. The devil can speak in tongues; the adversary will come with his work; he can tempt all classes; can speak in English or Dutch. Let no one speak in tongues unless he interpret, except by the consent of the one who is placed to preside; then he may discern or interpret, or another may.[34]

The gift of tongues by the power of the Holy Ghost in the Church, is for the benefit of the servants of God to preach to unbelievers, as on the day of Pentecost. When devout men from every nation shall assemble to hear the things of God, let the Elders preach to them in their own mother tongue, whether it is German, French, Spanish or Irish, or any other, and let those interpret who understand the language spoken, in their own mother tongue, and this is what the Apostle meant in First Corinthians 14:27.[35]

If you have a matter to reveal, let it be in your own tongue; do not indulge too much in the exercise of the gift of tongues, or the devil will take advantage of the innocent and unwary. You may speak in tongues for your own comfort, but I lay this down for a rule, that if anything is taught by the gift of tongues, it is not to be received for doctrine.[36]

Additional Spiritual Gifts

As pointed out by Elder Bruce R. McConkie, spiritual gifts are endless in number and infinite in variety. Those listed in the scriptures and described above are simply illustrations of how the Spirit may manifest itself through those who possess the Gift of the Holy Ghost.[37] Elder Marvin J. Ashton said: "[Some] less-conspicuous gifts [include] the gift of asking; the gift of listening; the gift of hearing and using a still, small voice; … the gift of avoiding contention; the gift of being agreeable; … the gift of seeking that which is righteous; the gift of not passing judgment; the gift of looking to God for guidance; the gift of being a disciple; the gift of caring for others; the gift of being able to ponder; the gift of offering prayer; the gift of bearing a mighty testimony; and the gift of receiving the Holy Ghost."[38]

DISCERNING FALSE SPIRITS

(D&C 50)

Because the early members of the Church were eager to receive the gifts of the Spirit, they were easily caught up in the spiritual excesses that were common in revivalist meetings of that day. The Prophet Joseph Smith said in the spring of 1831, "Many false reports, lies, and foolish stories, were published in the newspapers, and circulated in every direction, to prevent people from investigating the work, or embracing the faith."[39]

John Corrill, an early Ohio convert, was disturbed by the bizarre actions of some people who claimed to see visions: "They conducted themselves in a strange manner, sometimes imitating Indians in their maneuvers, sometimes running out into the fields, getting on stumps of trees and there preaching as though surrounded by a congregation, all the while so completely absorbed in visions as to be apparently insensible to all that was passing around them."⁴⁰

John Whitmer said: "Some had visions and could not tell what they saw, some would fancy to themselves that they had the sword of Laban, and would wield it as expert as a light dragon; some would act like an Indian in the act of scalping; some would slide or scoot on the floor with the rapidity of a serpent, which they termed sailing in the boat to the Lamanites, preaching the gospel. And many other vain and foolish maneuvers that are un-seeming and unprofitable to mention. Thus the devil blinded the eyes of some good and honest disciples. I write these things to show how ignorant and undiscerning children are, and how easy mankind is led astray, notwithstanding the things of God that are written concerning His kingdom."⁴¹

John Whitmer

Elder Parley P. Pratt said: "As I went forth among the different branches, some very strange spiritual operations were manifested, which were disgusting, rather than edifying. Some persons would seem to swoon away, and make unseemly gestures, and be drawn or disfigured in their countenances. Others would fall into ecstasies, and be drawn into contortions, cramp, fits, etc. Others would seem to have visions and revelations, which were not edifying, and which were not congenial to the doctrine and spirit of the gospel. In short, a false and lying spirit seemed to be creeping into the Church… After we had joined in prayer in his translating room, he dictated in our presence the following revelation: [D&C 50]."⁴²

Parley P. Pratt

This unseemly and evil influence of the devil entered into the Church to confuse and deceive the Saints. Such behaviors were prevalent among some religious groups of that day, leading some new members of the Church to think that such disorderly conduct was a manifestation of the Spirit. To correct this evil and to warn the Saints against all false spirits, this revelation (Sec. 50) was given.

Despite this revelation, the problem of false and unseemly manifestations did not go away easily. The Prophet Joseph Smith said that during one period when the authorities of the Church were away, "many false spirits were introduced, many strange visions were seen, and wild, enthusiastic notions were entertained; men ran out of doors under the influence of this spirit, and some of them got upon the stumps of trees and shouted, and all kinds of extravagances were entered into by them; one man pursued a ball that he said he saw flying in the air, until he came to a precipice, when he jumped into the top of a tree, which saved his life; and many ridiculous things were entered into, calculated to bring disgrace upon the Church of God, to cause the Spirit of God to be withdrawn, and to uproot and destroy those glorious principles which had been developed for the salvation of the human family." People who persisted in such behaviors were boldly called to repentance, and if they did not repent they were excommunicated from the Church.[43]

Keys to Avoiding Deception

- **D&C 50:1–3 False spirits seek to confuse and deceive us.** The Lord gave the early Church "words of wisdom" concerning "the spirits which have gone abroad in the earth" (v. 1). He warned, "that there are many spirits which are false spirits, which have gone forth in the earth, deceiving the world. And also Satan hath sought to deceive you, that he might overthrow you" (vv. 2–3).

- **D&C 50:23–24 That which is of God will be edifying, not showy or dramatic.** Unseemly displays like rolling around on the floor or shrieking or shouting "doth not edify [and] is not of God, and is darkness" (v. 23). On the other hand, "That which is of God is light; and he that receiveth light, and continueth in God, receiveth more light; and that light groweth brighter and brighter until the perfect day" (v. 24). Thus, if a gift is of God, it will be edifying and cause us to rejoice. It will lead us to do good, to love and serve God, and to believe in Christ. If a spiritual manifestation does not edify, or if it leads us to sin, it is not of God.

We are not immune to such things today. As a gospel teacher, I encounter regularly people who are ready to follow any theory, philosophy, or strange doctrine, especially if seems secret or mysterious. The hypocrites and deceivers in Joseph Smith's day who persisted in such abominations had to be speedily eliminated from the Church (see *Church History and Modern Revelation*, 1:183–184). And those who persist in such things today frequently find themselves outside of the Church, believing that their strange doctrines are correct and the leading brethren are deceived. This is the spirit upon which polygamist seceders left the Church at the turn of the 19th century.

- **D&C 45:56–57 Take the Holy Spirit as your guide in these matters.** The Lord compared us to the ten virgins in His parable concerning the Second Coming: "For they that are wise and have received the truth, and have taken the Holy Spirit for their guide, and have not been deceived— verily I say unto you, they shall not be hewn down and cast into the fire, but shall abide the day" (v. 57).

- **D&C 52:14–19 A pattern for discerning of spirits.** "Satan is abroad in the land, and he goeth forth deceiving the nations" (v. 14), so we need to carefully discern the spirits of those who claim spiritual gifts. The Lord said: "he that prayeth, whose spirit is contrite, the same is accepted of me if he obey mine ordinances" (v. 15). Also, "He that speaketh, whose spirit is contrite, whose language is meek and edifieth, the same is of God if he obey mine ordinances" (v. 16). True followers of Christ will be meek ("trembleth under my power") and "shall bring forth fruits of praise and wisdom, according to the revelations and truths which I have given you" (v. 17). But "he that is overcome and bringeth not forth fruits, even according to this pattern, is not of me" (v. 18). "Wherefore, by this pattern ye shall know the spirits in all cases under the whole heavens" (v. 19).

Teaching by the Spirit

The Church Handbook of Instructions states: "A person may teach profound truths, and class members may engage in stimulating discussions, but unless the Spirit is present, these things will not be powerfully impressed upon the soul."[44] This fundamental truth about the process of teaching is treated in some detail in this portion of the Doctrine and Covenants.

- **D&C 50:13–14 We are to preach the gospel by the Spirit.** The Lord first asks a simple question: "unto what were ye ordained?" (v. 13), then answers it: "To preach my gospel by the Spirit, even the Comforter which was sent forth to teach the truth" (v. 14). This is a statement which every gospel teacher and missionary should consider with seriousness. We are not called to teach the philosophies of men (including our own), but to teach the gospel from the scriptures "by the Spirit."

- **D&C 50:17–20 Any other method of teaching or learning is not of God.** Any person called and ordained or set apart to teach is to "preach the word of truth by the Comforter, in the Spirit of truth" (v. 17). And if it is done "some other way it is not of God" (v. 18). And in the same way, "he that receiveth the word of truth, doth he receive it by the Spirit of truth or some other way? If it be some other way it is not of God" (vv. 19–20).

- **D&C 42:13 Teachers must be a living example of what they teach.** The Lord says that the teacher "shall observe the covenants and church articles to do them" so that they are a living example of what they teach. Then these same covenants and articles of the Church "shall be their teachings, as they shall be directed by the Spirit" (v. 13).

- **D&C 43:8 Teachers should edify.** The Lord said: "when ye are assembled together ye shall instruct and edify each other." When I think of the word "edify" I think of the concept of "feeding in a satisfying way." The Lord's sheep come into His fold to be taught the peaceful and saving principles of His gospel, and to hear the witness and testimony of others to confirm their own faith. They do not come to hear travelogues, to be entertained, or to be taught the philosophies of men (even if they are mixed with scripture). The subjects of our teaching should be "how to act and direct my church, [and] how to act upon the points of my law and commandments, which I have given." If we do this, we will truly edify.

- **D&C 88:122, 128–131 How to conduct a gospel class.** In organizing the school of the prophets in Kirtland, the Lord gave a number of instructions concerning teachers.

  — <u>Someone appointed to teach</u>—"Appoint among yourselves a teacher" (v. 122).

  — <u>Order in the classroom</u>—"let not all be spokesmen at once; but let one speak at a time and let all listen unto his sayings" (v. 122).

  — <u>Class participation</u>—"when all have spoken ... all may be edified of all." Therefore let every person participate "that every man may have an equal privilege" (v. 122).

  — <u>A designated place to teach</u>—the teacher should "be found standing in his place, in the [place] which shall be prepared for him" (v. 128).

— The teacher should arrive first in the classroom—"he shall be first in the house of God" (v. 129), "behold, this is beautiful, that he may be an example" (v. 130).

— Ensure that everybody can hear the teacher—"in a place that the congregation in the house may hear his words carefully and distinctly, not with loud speech" (v. 129).

— The teacher should pray before teaching—the teacher should "offer himself in prayer upon his knees before God, in token or remembrance of the everlasting covenant" (v. 131).

- **D&C 42:14 How to obtain the Spirit before teaching.** The formula is not complex. The Lord says simply, "the Spirit shall be given unto you by the prayer of faith." President Marion G. Romney said: "If you want to obtain and keep the guidance of the Spirit, you can do so by following this simple four-point program. One, pray. Pray diligently. Pray with each other. Pray in public in the proper places… Learn to talk to the Lord; call upon His name in great faith and confidence. Second, study and learn the gospel. Third, live righteously; repent of your sins by confessing them and forsaking them. Then conform to the teachings of the gospel. Fourth, give service in the Church. If you will do these things, you will get the guidance of the Holy Spirit and you will go through this world successfully, regardless of what the people of the world say or do."[45]

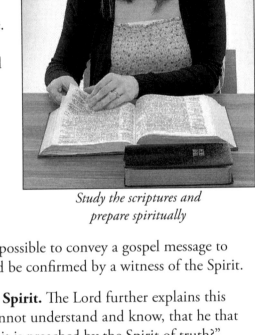

Study the scriptures and prepare spiritually

- **D&C 42:14 "If ye receive not the Spirit ye shall not teach."** This is not so much a commandment ("thou shalt not teach") as it is a principle ("no teaching will take place"). In other words, without the Spirit it is impossible to convey a gospel message to another person in a way that will penetrate his soul and be confirmed by a witness of the Spirit.

- **D&C 50:21–22 Why it is important to teach by the Spirit.** The Lord further explains this principle in section 50. "Therefore, why is it that ye cannot understand and know, that he that receiveth the word by the Spirit of truth receiveth it as it is preached by the Spirit of truth?" (v. 21). As we teach others, our meanings are our own—they spring from our hearts and from our life experiences. Other people will not understand things exactly as I do because they have lived their lives, not mine. But if I am teaching by the Spirit, it is possible to convey an accurate meaning to another person despite our differences of experience. The Spirit knows both the speaker and the hearer intimately and can cause them both to understand the same thing in the same way.

"Wherefore, he that preacheth and he that receiveth, understand one another, and both are edified and rejoice together" (v. 22). Nephi acknowledged this process when he said: "when a man speaketh by the power of the Holy Ghost the power of the Holy Ghost carrieth it unto the hearts of the children of men" (2 Nephi 33:1). And there is absolutely no other way for this to occur.

THE MINISTRY TO THE QUAKERS

(D&C 49)

The Prophet Joseph Smith said: "At about this time [March 1831] came Leman Copley, one of the sect called Shaking Quakers, and embraced the fulness of the everlasting Gospel, apparently honest-hearted, but still retaining the idea that the Shakers were right in some particulars of their faith. In order to have more perfect understanding on the subject, I inquired of the Lord, and received [D&C 49]."[46] After Copley embraced the gospel he was anxious to teach its principles to his former associates. He was, therefore, through this revelation, chosen to accompany Sidney Rigdon and Parley P. Pratt on a mission to them.[47]

"To appreciate fully the teachings received in Section 49 of The Doctrine and Covenants, some knowledge of the origin and beliefs of the "Shakers," whose correct name was "The United Society of Believers in Christ's Second Appearing," is necessary.

Shaking Quaker meeting in 1835

At the beginning of the 18th century (1706), a group of religionists from France went to England and were known there as the French Prophets. James Wardley, a tailor, and his wife Jane, who were seceders from Quakerism came under their influence. In 1747 the Wardleys founded a society in Manchester and began to preach. They declared that Christ was soon to return to reign on the earth, and that He would come in the form of a woman. The society increased in numbers although suffering much from persecution. One of their converts was Ann Lee. She was born February 29, 1736, the daughter of a blacksmith, and was married to a blacksmith at an early age. She gave birth to four children who died in infancy. In 1758 she was converted by Jane Wardley and also began to preach. Among her claimed revelations was one regarding the nature of God described in this manner: "The duality of Deity, God both Father and Mother; one in essence—one God, not two; but God who possesses two natures, the masculine and the feminine, each distinct in function yet one in being, co-equal in Deity." This belief is the basis for the later claim that Ann Lee became the incarnation of the Christ Spirit.

Because of persecution and lack of progress in making converts, Ann Lee and eight of her followers decided to go to America. Arriving there in 1774, they established themselves at Watervliet near Albany, New York. Ann Lee saw two other Shaker communities founded before her death in 1784. The period of greatest growth of this sect was between 1792 and 1835. At one time they numbered nearly 5,000. The sect no longer exists.[48]

Preaching to the Shakers

In early 1831, Parley P. Pratt and others, while on a mission to the Lamanites, stopped at North Union, Ohio, for two nights and one day and worked among the Shakers, leaving seven copies of the Book of Mormon. A few months later, in March 1831, the Lord called Sidney Rigdon, Parley P. Pratt, and Leman Copley on a mission to the Shakers (D&C 49:1).

In May 1831, when these missionaries arrived at the Shaker village, things went well between the missionaries and the Shakers until the conclusion of the evening service on the Sabbath. During that service Elder Rigdon asked for permission to deliver to the Shakers a revelation from Jesus Christ given through Joseph Smith. Granted permission, he read Doctrine and Covenants 49.

● **D&C 49:5–19 Corrects many of the Shaker doctrines:**

— God is both male and female (v. 5).
— Christ is infused in Ann Lee, and in her the Second Coming is fulfilled (vv. 7, 11–12).
— Confession alone brings forgiveness—no outward ordinances are needed (vv. 13–14).
— People can live without sin (v. 8).
— Celibacy is a higher law than marriage (v. 15).
— Pork is forbidden—many Shakers ate no meat at all (vv. 18–19).

"At the conclusion of his reading of the revelation, Elder Rigdon asked the Shakers if they were willing to be baptized for the remission of their sins and receive the laying on of hands for the gift of the Holy Ghost. Ashbel Kitchell, the leader of the group of Shakers, responded: 'The Christ that dictated that, I was well acquainted with, and had been from a boy, that I had been much troubled to get rid of his influence, and I wished to have nothing more to do with him; and as for any gift he had authorized them to exercise among us, I would release them and their Christ from any further burden about us, and take all the responsibility on myself.'"[49]

No converts resulted from the labors of these missionaries. In addition, Leman Copley apostatized from the Church and returned to the Shakers, apparently because he still retained the idea that "the Shakers were right in some particulars of their faith".[50]

Leman Copley's apostasy brought some problems upon the Church, especially for the Colesville Saints, who at that time resided at Thompson, Ohio. Copley had promised to give his large farm of almost 1000 acres to the Church so that the Colesville Saints could live the law of consecration. When Copley apostatized, he reclaimed his land and approximately 100 Saints in Thompson were therefore prevented from keeping their covenant to live the law of consecration. But Leman Copley eventually repented. In 1836 he was re-baptized into the Church.[51]

OTHER TRUTHS IN D&C 49

As part of His correction of Shaker teachings (above), the Lord clarified a number of His doctrines.

- **D&C 49:5–6, 10–14 Nations will bow to the gospel and to Christ.** The Lord declared that "the nations of the earth shall bow to it [the new and everlasting covenant]," either of their own volition or by being brought down, "for that which is now exalted of itself shall be laid low of power" (v. 10). The Father "sent mine Only Begotten Son into the world for the redemption of the world, and have decreed that he that receiveth him shall be saved, and he that receiveth him not shall be damned" (v. 5). After His mortal ministry, the Savior "has taken his power on the right hand of his glory, and now reigneth in the heavens, and will reign till he descends on the earth to put all enemies under his feet" (v. 6).

Until that day, we are commanded to "go among this people, and say unto them … Believe on the name of the Lord Jesus, who was on the earth, and is to come, the beginning and the end; Repent and be baptized in the name of Jesus Christ, according to the holy commandment, for the remission of sins; And whoso doeth this shall receive the gift of the Holy Ghost, by the laying on of the hands of the elders of the church" (vv. 11–14).

- **D&C 49:6–7 The hour and day of the Second Coming is not known to man or the angels.** The Lord assures us that the "time is nigh at hand" (v. 6), "but the hour and the day no man knoweth, neither the angels in heaven, nor shall they know until he comes" (v. 7).

- **D&C 49:8 Characteristics of translated beings.** The Lord calls translated beings "those which I have reserved unto myself" and "holy men that ye know not of." Elder Joseph Fielding Smith said: "'Holy men that ye know not of,' who were without sin, and reserved unto the Lord, are translated persons such as John the Revelator and the Three Nephites, who do not belong to this generation and yet are in the flesh in the earth performing a special ministry until the coming of Jesus Christ."[52]

- **D&C 49:15–17 Marriage is ordained of God for the purpose of having children.** Those who teach that marriage is forbidden for the truly holy "is not ordained of God, for marriage is ordained of God unto man" (v. 15). God has commanded that a man "should have one wife, and they twain shall be one flesh" (v. 16). And the primary purpose of this union is "that the earth might answer the end of its creation … [and] be filled with the measure of man, according to his creation before the world was made" (vv. 16–17).

©RANDAL S. CHASE, 1980–1800

In other words, the number of God's children who will be born into this world was known in the premortal council, and they must all have their opportunity to be born. Elder James E. Talmage said: "The population of the earth is fixed according to the number of spirits appointed to take tabernacles of flesh upon this planet; when these have all come forth in the order and time appointed, then, and not till then, shall the end come."[53]

Elder Harold B. Lee said: "If I were to name the first thing that impresse[d] me always in these fine Latter-day Saint homes, I would say it was a love for and a desire for children. These are homes where the having of children was not delayed because of some social or educational or financial objective, and where the size of the families has not been limited by the practice of birth control."[54]

— D&C 104:17–18 The Myth of Overpopulation: The Lord prepared the earth with sufficient resources for all His children. He did not make a mistake or fail to plan properly. "For the earth is full, and there is enough and to spare; yea, I prepared all things" (v. 17). But isn't there a shortage of oil and of food and of shelter? No. The problem is that God has "given unto the children of men to be agents unto themselves…. [and some have] take[n] of the abundance which I have made, and impart[ed] not his portion, according to the law of my gospel, unto the poor and the needy" (vv. 17–18). Thus, it is the selfishness of men and nations that leaves many of God's children without sufficient to eat or keep them warm. Every such selfish person "shall, with the wicked, lift up his eyes in hell, being in torment" (v. 18).

- **D&C 49:19 Meat is ordained for the use of man,** including "the beasts of the field and the fowls of the air, and that which cometh of the earth." All of these are "ordained for the use of man for food and for raiment, and that he [man] might have in abundance."

- **D&C 49:21 … but is not to be wasted.** The Lord said: "wo be unto man that sheddeth blood or that wasteth flesh and hath no need." Elder Joseph Fielding Smith said: "The killing of animals just for sport is a sin… The Lord pronounced a woe on whosoever wasteth flesh and hath no need and who needlessly shed the blood of His creatures… It is a grievous sin in the sight of God to kill merely for sport. Such a thing shows a weakness in the spiritual character of the individual. We cannot restore life when it is taken, and all creatures have the right to enjoy life and happiness on the earth where the Lord has placed them. Only for food and then sparingly, should flesh be eaten, for all life is from God and is eternal."[55]

- **D&C 49:23 Great changes in the earth before Millennium.** We must watch for "the heavens to be shaken, and the earth to tremble and to reel to and fro as a drunken man, and for the valleys to be exalted, and for the mountains to be made low, and for the rough places to become smooth—and all this when the angel shall sound his trumpet." Anyone who has read the Book of Mormon will see that these are the same destructions that preceded the Lord's first coming to the western hemisphere after His death. In fact, the Book of Mormon events are a symbolic type of that which is to come, as shown in the following comparative chart.[56]

Christs Coming to the Nephites		Second Coming of Christ	
Events in the New World		Events at His Second Coming	
	3 Nephi	D&C	
1. Wicked do not believe He is coming	2:1–3	45:26	People to say "the Lord delayeth His coming"
2. People divide into tribes, not nations	7:2	87:6	Destruction will bring a full end to all nations
3. Followers of Christ united for safety	3:12	45:66,68	Righteous will gather to Zion for safety
4. Wicked who are there become righteous	2:15	45:67,69	No wicked will be there; Only the righteous
5. Faithful remained together & were strong	3:21	45:70	Faithful are strong, seem "terrible" to wicked
6. Gospel preached unto the wicked	5:1–12	133:57–74	Gospel preached unto the wicked
7. Church prospers; Pride enters into it	6:10–16	38:39	Pride will make us "as the Nephites of old"
8. The people begin to "wilfully rebel"	6:17–18	29:9	Wicked will be come "ripe" in iniquity
9. Corrupt judges allow circumvention of law	6:27–30	123:7	Whole earth groans because of corruption
10. Earthquakes change the face of the land	8:8–18	88:90	Thunderings, lightnings, tempests to arise
11. Thick darkness covers the earth for 3 days	8:19–23	87:6	Earthquakes, plagues, storms chasten earth
12. A furious storm begins the destruction	8:5–7	41:42	Vapors of smoke will darken the sun
13. Voice of Christ is heard by everyone	9:1–10:8	133:21–22	Voice of the Lord uttered from Jerusalem
14. Generally, the more righteous are spared	10:12–13	128:24	Only righteous will abide His coming
15. Christ descends from heaven in glory	11:1–11	45:44–46	Christ to come with his holy angels

- **D&C 49:24 The Lamanites will blossom as a rose.** Once an impoverished and scattered remnant, persecuted by the gentiles who came to this land, "before the great day of the Lord shall come, [the descendants of] Jacob shall flourish in the wilderness, and the Lamanites shall blossom as the rose." We are witnessing the rise of the Lamanites in our own time, and this will continue until the Lord returns. Elder Wilford Woodruff said: "Zion is bound to rise and flourish. The Lamanites will blossom as the rose on the mountains... Every word that God has ever said of them will have its fulfillment, and they, by and by, will receive the Gospel. It will be a day of God's power among them, and a nation will be born in a day."[57]

- **D&C 49:25 Zion shall be gathered and flourish and rejoice upon the mountains.** The Lord's people will "flourish upon the hills and rejoice upon the mountains" as they assemble together in "the place which I have appointed."

With regard to the future of the Church and its "flourishing upon the mountains," the Prophet Joseph Smith prophesied during this period:

> I want to say to you before the Lord, that you know no more concerning the destinies of this Church and kingdom than a babe upon its mother's lap. You don't comprehend it ... It is only a little handful of priesthood you see here tonight, but this Church will fill North and South America—it will fill the world ... It will fill the Rocky Mountains. There will be tens of thousands of Latter-day Saints who will be gathered in the Rocky Mountains, and there they will open the door for the establishing of the Gospel among the Lamanites ... This people will go into the Rocky Mountains; they will there build temples to the Most High. They will raise up a posterity there, and the Latter-day Saints who dwell

in these mountains will stand in the flesh until the coming of the Son of Man. The Son of Man will come to them while in the Rocky Mountains.[58]

Notes:

1. *History of the Church*, 4:42.

2. *Latter-day Saints' Messenger and Advocate*, 2 [January 1836], 245.

3. *History of the Church*, 1:78.

4. *History of the Church*, 1:146.

5. In Conference Report, April 1956, 70-72.

6. *Ensign*, September 1986, 72.

7. *Masterful Discourses of Orson Pratt*, N. B. Lundwall, ed. [1962], 539-541.

8. *A New Witness for the Articles of Faith* [1985], 270.

9. *Teachings of the Prophet Joseph Smith*, sel. Joseph Fielding Smith [1976], 244, 246; *Ensign*, September 1986, 69.

10. *Doctrinal New Testament Commentary*, 3 vols. [1965-1973], 2:368.

11. "Spiritual Gifts," *Ensign*, Sept. 1986, 72.

12. *Ensign*, June 1972, 3.

13. *Masterful Discourses and Writings of Orson Pratt*, 541.

14. *Ensign*, February 2002, 12, 14.

15. *Teachings of the Prophet Joseph Smith*, 243-245.

16. *Ensign*, January 1979, 61.

17. "Individual Testimony," *Improvement Era*, September 1963, 733.

18. *The Teachings of Harold B. Lee*, Clyde J. Williams (ed.) [1996], 136.

19. *A New Witness for the Articles of Faith*, 278.

20. Smith and Sjodahl, *Doctrine and Covenants Commentary*, [1978], 274.

21. Richard O. Cowan, *The Doctrine and Covenants, Our Modern Scripture* [1984], 83.

22. In Conference Report, April 1901, 12.

23. *Doctrine and Covenants Commentary*, 274; see also Moroni 10:9-10.

24. *Autobiography of Parley P. Pratt*, edited by his son, Parley P. Pratt (1985), 79-80.

25. *The New Testament and The Latter-day Saints* [1987], 234.

26. *History of the Church*, 1:215-216; *Millennial Star*, 31 December 1864, 834.

27. *The Articles of Faith*, 12th ed. [1924], 220-223.

28. *The Promised Messiah: The First Coming of Christ* [1978], 23-24.

29. *History of the Church*, 3:389-390.

30. In Conference Report, October 1966, 113.

31. In *Journal of Discourses*, 9:324, April 8, 1862.

32. In Conference Report, April 1950, 163.

33. *History of the Church*, 5:30-31.

34. *Teachings of the Prophet Joseph Smith*, 162.

35. *Teachings of the Prophet Joseph Smith*, 195.

36. *Teachings of the Prophet Joseph Smith*, 229.

37. See *A New Witness for the Articles of Faith*, 371.

38. In Conference Report, October 1987, 23; or *Ensign*, November 1987, 20.

39. *History of the Church*, 1:158.

40. Corrill, *Brief History of the Church of Christ of Latter-day Saints (Commonly Called Mormons) Including an Account of the Author for Leaving the Church* [1839], 13.

41. *The Book of John Whitmer*, typescript, Brigham Young University Archives and Manuscripts.

42. *Autobiography of Parley P. Pratt*, 48.

43. *Teachings of the Prophet Joseph Smith*, 213-214.

44. *Church Handbook of Instructions, Book 2: Priesthood and Auxiliary Leaders* [1998], 300.

45. "Guidance of the Holy Spirit," *Ensign*, January 1980, 5.

46. *History of the Church*, 1:167.

47. *Doctrine and Covenants Commentary*, 282.

48. Anne White and Leila S. Taylor, "Shakerism, Its Meaning and Message," *Encyclopedia Americana* [1949], Vol. 24, 642; in Roy W. Doxey, *The Doctrine and Covenants Speaks* (1964), 1:336-337.

49. *Kitchell Journal*, 13); in Robert L. Millet and Kent Jackson, eds., *Studies in Scripture, Vol. 1: The Doctrine and Covenants* [1989], 215.

50. *History of the Church*, 1:167.

51. *History of the Church*, 2:433.

52. *Church History and Modern Revelation*, 4 vols. [1946-1949], 1:192.

53. *The Articles of Faith*, 194.

54. In Conference Report, October 1948, 52.

55. *Church History and Modern Revelation*, 1:193.

56. Adapted From: *Book of Mormon Student Manual, Rel. 121-122*, Church Educational System, 1996.

57. In *Journal of Discourses*, 15:282.

58. Quoted by President Wilford Woodruff, in Conference Report, April 1898, 57.

CHAPTER 16

Keeping the Sabbath Day Holy

(D&C 59) [1831]

ഃരൗദ

INTRODUCTION

D&C 59 was given through the Prophet Joseph Smith on August 7, 1831, in Jackson County, Missouri.[1] The revelation is primarily (1) a tribute to those who were obedient to the commandment to gather to Zion (e.g., Joseph and Polly Knight), (2) a review of the Ten Commandments, and (3) a discussion of the importance and purpose of the Sabbath day.

After being evicted from Leman Copley's farm in Kirtland (when he withdrew from the Church), the Colesville Saints moved on to Jackson County, Missouri. They arrived about two weeks before D&C 59 was received. Polly Knight, wife of Joseph Knight Sr., survived the grueling journey to Zion but passed on August 6 shortly after arriving. She was buried on the date of this revelation. The Prophet Joseph Smith said: "On the 7th, I attended the funeral of Sister Polly Knight, the wife of Joseph Knight, Sen. This was the first death in the Church in this land, and I can say, a worthy member sleeps in Jesus till the resurrection. I also received the following: [D&C 59]."[2]

The Colesville Saints settled in Kaw Township

"Polly Knight's health had been failing for some time, according to a statement made by her son, Newel. She was very ill during her journey from Kirtland to Missouri, 'Yet,' says her son, 'she would not consent to stop traveling; her only, or her greatest desire was to set her feet upon the land of Zion, and to have her body interred in that land. I went on shore and bought lumber to make a coffin in case she should die before we arrived at our place of destination—so fast did she fail. But the Lord gave her the desire of her heart, and she lived to stand upon that land.'"[3]

● **D&C 59:1–2 The Lord's tribute to Polly Knight.** "Behold, blessed, saith the Lord, are they who have come up unto this land with an eye single to my glory, according to my commandments. For those that live shall inherit the earth, and those that die shall rest from all their labors, and their works shall follow them; and they shall receive a crown in the mansions of my Father, which I have prepared for them."

- **D&C 59:3–4 Conditional blessings for those who live in the land of Zion.** Those early Saints who had inheritances "upon the land of Zion, who have obeyed my gospel … shall receive for their reward the good things of the earth, and it shall bring forth in its strength" (v. 3). These are wonderful promises of temporal blessings. But there is more: "they shall also be crowned with blessings from above, yea, and with commandments not a few, and with revelations in their time" if they will be "faithful and diligent before me" (v. 4).

- **D&C 59:5–8 A brief review of basic gospel principles and commandments.** Before beginning His explanation of the Sabbath day, the Lord listed a few of His greatest commandments. "Thou shalt love the Lord thy God with all thy heart, with all thy might, mind, and strength; and in the name of Jesus Christ thou shalt serve him" (v. 5). "Thou shalt love thy neighbor as thyself" (v. 6). "Thou shalt not steal; neither commit adultery, nor kill, nor do anything like unto it" (v. 6). "Thou shalt thank the Lord thy God in all things" (v. 7). "Thou shalt offer a sacrifice unto the Lord thy God in righteousness, even that of a broken heart and a contrite spirit" (v. 8). There is much that we could discuss about these four verses, but that would divert us from the primary topic of the chapter. Some of these principles have already been discussed in earlier chapters, and some will be addressed in later chapters. But in this chapter we will focus on the Sabbath day.

HISTORY OF THE SABBATH DAY

The Lord Established the Sabbath Day

The injunction from God to remember the Sabbath day and to keep it holy has been in force from the very beginning of the earth, at the time of its creation.

- **Genesis 2:1–3 The original Sabbath occurred at the end of the creation.** It took six "days" [creative periods] for the earth's creation to occur. Then, the Lord "rested on the seventh day from all his work which he had made" (v. 2). In memory of the great miracle and blessing of the creation, the Lord "blessed the seventh day, and sanctified it: because that in it he had rested from all his work which God created and made" (v. 3). To observe it was to remember what the Lord had done for us in providing this earth. Thus, until the time of Christ, the seventh day (Saturday) was the Sabbath day for the Lord's people.

- **Moses 3:1–3 Moses' vision of the creation.** This version of the six creative periods includes the Lord's observation, "and all things which I had made were finished, and I, God, saw that they were good" (v. 2).

- **Abraham 5:1–3 Abraham's vision of the creation.** This version of the creation refers to the creative periods as "times" rather than "days," showing that these things were not done in an instant within one of our earthly days. It also reveals that there was more than one God involved in the creation. "And thus we will finish the heavens and the earth, and all the hosts of them.

And the Gods said among themselves: On the seventh time we will end our work, which we have counseled; and we will rest on the seventh time from all our work which we have counseled" (vv. 1–2, emphasis added). And apparently, all of this was carefully planned before it was executed, for "thus were their decisions at the time that they counseled among themselves to form the heavens and the earth" (v. 3).

Keeping the Sabbath Is Commanded in Every Dispensation

In every dispensation, the Lord has reiterated His commandment to keep the Sabbath day holy. The following are just a few of the most well-known examples.

PROVIDENCE LITHOGRAPHIC CO., 1907

- **Exodus 20:8–11 As part of the ten commandments.**

The Lord said on Mt. Sinai concerning the Sabbath:

— Remember the Sabbath day.
— Keep it holy.
— Six days shalt thou labour, and do all thy work.
— The seventh day is the sabbath of the LORD thy God.
— On that day, "thou shalt not do any work, thou, nor thy son, nor thy daughter, thy manservant, nor thy maidservant, nor thy cattle, nor thy stranger that is within thy gates."
— During six "days" the LORD made the heavens, earth, sea, and all that is in them.
— The Lord rested the seventh day.
— Therefore the LORD blessed the Sabbath day, and hallowed it.

- **Exodus 23:10–12 As part of the establishment of a "sabbath year."** Not only was Israel to rest every week on the Sabbath day, but also they were to rest their land every seven years. The Lord said: "six years thou shalt sow thy land, and shalt gather in the fruits thereof: But the seventh year thou shalt let it rest and lie still." They were to use this sabbatical year as an opportunity, "that the poor of thy people may eat: and what they leave the beasts of the field shall eat. In like manner thou shalt deal with thy vineyard, and with thy oliveyard." Then the Lord adds, "Six days thou shalt do thy work, and on the seventh day thou shalt rest: that thine ox and thine ass may rest, and the son of thy handmaid, and the stranger, may be refreshed."

- **Exodus 31:13, 16–17 As a symbolic covenant between Israel and the Lord.** They were to keep the Sabbath as "a sign between me and you throughout your generations; that ye may know that I am the LORD that doth sanctify you" (v. 13). Thus, remembering the Lord and His atonement is the key reason for observing the Sabbath. In every generation, the Sabbath is "a perpetual covenant" (v. 16)—"a sign between me and the children of Israel for ever" that the Lord created all things and rested on the seventh day (v. 17).

- **Exodus 31:14–15 As a capital offense under Israel's civil laws.** This may seem too harsh to us. But the Sabbath was holy to the children of Israel, and also linked to their survival. They were wandering in the wilderness, depending upon the Lord for their food every day (manna). Thus, to forget to honor the Lord was a gross and purposeful sin. It also put the entire camp in jeopardy of losing the Lord's favor and protection. Therefore it was also a crime, and "every one that defileth it shall surely be put to death: for whosoever doeth any work therein, that soul shall be cut off from among his people" (v. 14; see also v. 15 and Exodus 35:2).

- **Leviticus 23:3 As part of the written law of Moses.** Israel was to gather together in "holy convocations" on "the seventh day," which is called "the sabbath of rest." The law stated that "ye shall do no work therein: it is the sabbath of the LORD in all your dwellings."

- **Deuteronomy 5:12–14 When Moses reviewed the law with Israel prior to his departure.** Moses said: "Keep the sabbath day to sanctify it, as the LORD thy God hath commanded thee. Six days thou shalt labour, and do all thy work: But the seventh day is the sabbath of the LORD thy God: in it thou shalt not do any work, thou, nor thy son, nor thy daughter, nor thy manservant, nor thy maidservant, nor thine ox, nor thine ass, nor any of thy cattle, nor thy stranger that is within thy gates; that thy manservant and thy maidservant may rest as well as thou."

- **Jarom 1:5 Keeping the Sabbath prospered the Nephites in 399 BC.** Jarom wrote that the Nephites "waxed strong in the land," at least partly because "They observed to keep the law of Moses and the sabbath day holy unto the Lord. And they profaned not; neither did they blaspheme. And the laws of the land were exceedingly strict."

- **Mosiah 13:16–19, 25–26 Abinadi proclaimed it to the priests of Noah in 148 BC.** He quoted the commandment to them verbatim. Then he asked, "Have ye taught this people that they should observe to do all these things for to keep these commandments? I say unto you, Nay; for if ye had, the Lord would not have caused me to come forth and to prophesy evil concerning this people" (vv. 25–26). They neither taught this commandment to the people, nor did they keep it themselves (Mosiah 12:28–29).

- **Mosiah 18:23 Taught by Alma at the waters of Mormon in 147 BC.** They were all subject to the law of Moses in those days, and Alma taught it to them. As part of this, "he commanded them that they should observe the sabbath day, and keep it holy, and also every day they should give thanks to the Lord their God." There is a clear connection between keeping the Sabbath day and our attitude toward the Lord. If we truly appreciate what He has done for us, we would have no desire whatever to disrespect the day set aside to honor Him.

President Spencer W. Kimball asked, "When we love the Lord, why do we still break His laws? We implore you then, earnestly, to discontinue the purchase of things on the Sabbath day."[4] Elder Mark E. Petersen said, "One of the most glaring of our inconsistencies is our attitude toward the Sabbath day. It is a sacred day. It is holy, and we should not trifle with it."[5]

Elder Petersen also said:

> With this ... in mind, let us ask ourselves how important the Lord's atonement is to us. How dear to us is the Lord Jesus Christ? How deeply are we concerned about immortality? Is the resurrection of vital interest to us?

We can readily see that observance of the Sabbath is an indication of the depth of our conversion. Our observance or nonobservance of the Sabbath is an unerring measure of our attitude toward the Lord personally and toward His suffering in Gethsemane, His death on the cross, and His resurrection from the dead. It is a sign of whether we are Christians in very deed, or whether our conversion is so shallow that commemoration of His atoning sacrifice means little or nothing to us.

HOFFMAN 1889

Do we realize that most national holidays are observed more widely than is the Sabbath, so far as its divine purpose is concerned? Then have we put God in second or third place? And is that what we want to do? Is that where He belongs? … If we are to do none other thing on Sunday but to devote the day to holy purposes, what is our situation if we willfully choose to operate our businesses on the Sabbath, or if we patronize such Sunday businesses, or if we go to places of recreation on Sunday? …

I do not believe we will be saved if we constantly violate the Sabbath and fling our disobedience into the face of the very God we hope will save us… I bear you testimony that to properly observe the Lord's holy day is one of the most important things we can ever do. It is an essential step toward our eternal salvation.[6]

● **Matthew 12:8–12 Taught by the Lord during His mortal ministry.** (see also Mark 2:27–28; 3:2–4; Luke 6:5–10) He declared Himself to be "Lord even of the sabbath day" (v. 8) and then healed a man's withered hand as an example of doing good on the Sabbath day (vv. 9–12). Mark's account of these events includes the Lord's declaration that "The sabbath was made for man, and not man for the sabbath" (Mark 2:27). Thus it is not a day intended to punish us but to bless us. We get to rest. And by keeping this sacred and symbolic day holy we receive tremendous temporal and spiritual blessings. These will be discussed later in this chapter.

● **D&C 59:9–14 Taught again in our own dispensation.** This is the scripture we are studying in depth in this chapter, and greater detail follows below.

● **D&C 68:29 Especially important in the land of Zion.** They were standing on holy ground, and in order to be worthy to inherit it "the inhabitants of Zion [were commanded to] observe the Sabbath day to keep it holy." Their failure to do so was one of the reasons they were allowed to be driven out of Missouri.

● **D&C 77:12 Symbolic also of the seven periods of the earth's history.** As part of his vision of the last days, John observed seven angels sounding seven trumpets as they stood before God (Revelation 8:2). The Prophet Joseph Smith explained in this scripture, "We are to understand that as God made the world in six days, and on the seventh day he finished his work, and sanctified it, and also formed man out of the dust of the earth, even so, in the beginning of the seventh thousand years will the Lord God sanctify the earth, and complete the salvation of man … " Thus, just as the Sabbath day is symbolic of the creation of the earth, so too is the seventh period of the earth's history—the one in which the Lord will finish His work—symbolic of the end of the world, and "preparing of the way before the time of his coming."

- **Mark 16:9 Christ was resurrected on Sunday morning—the "Lord's day"** (see also Matthew 28:1; Mark 16:2; Luke 24:1; John 20:1, 19). Thus, Sunday became known among members of the Church as "the Lord's day" (Revelation 1:10; D&C 59:12).

"THE LIVING CHRIST" ©JOSEPH BRICKEY. USED BY PERMISSION

- **Acts 20:7 For Christians, Sunday became the new Sabbath.** The resurrection was the greatest miracle the world had ever seen since the creation—an even greater miracle than the creation itself. And thus, among members of the Church, the Lord's day (Sunday) became the new Sabbath day, on which to remember all the things that Christ did for us. Here we find Paul preaching "upon the first day of the week, when the disciples came together to break bread." Clearly, by this time, the Christians had adopted Sunday—"the Lord's day"—as their day for worship and partaking of the sacrament.

  Elder Bruce R. McConkie said: "Because Jesus came forth from the grave on the first day of the week, to commemorate that day and to keep in remembrance the glorious reality of the resurrection, the ancient Apostles, as guided by the Spirit, changed the Sabbath to Sunday. That this change had divine approval we know from latter-day revelation, in which Deity speaks of 'the Lord's day' as such and sets forth what should and should not be done on that day. (D&C 59:9–17)."[7]

- **1 Corinthians 16:2 Paul counseled the Corinthians to observe "the first day of the week."** He also counseled the Colossians to pay no attention to any criticism concerning the day of the week on which we worship (Colossians 2:16). It is likely that the Jews were critical of this practice since they continued to worship the Lord on their Sabbath—Saturday (Acts 13:42; Acts 18:4; Hebrews 4:4; etc.).

KEEPING THE SABBATH DAY HOLY

(D&C 59:9–24)

- **D&C 59:9 The Sabbath helps us stay unspotted from the world.** Just the mere fact that we are worshiping rather than recreating or working ensures that we will not be doing worldly things on the Lord's day. But there is more. When we "go to the house of prayer and offer up [our] sacraments upon [His] holy day" we are reminded of our dependence upon Christ for our salvation, we feel the need to repent, and we resolve to do better during the coming week. All of these things help us stay unspotted from the world.

There is another way to stay unspotted from the world. That is to practice the pure religion of charitable service toward others—which we should include among our Sunday activities.

President Howard W. Hunter said:

> James then very pointedly defines what he refers to as pure religion, as distinguished from forms of ritualistic worship and iron rules of practice as described by Paul. James said: "Pure religion and undefiled before God and the Father is this, To visit the fatherless and widows in their affliction, and to keep [oneself] unspotted from the world" (James 1:27). The wording is simple and unpretentious, yet the meaning is profound and has deep significance. The words "visit the fatherless and widows" are a reminder that we should have compassion for our neighbor, our fellowmen. This is the teaching of the Master in His frequent reference to love. The Lord said: "Thou shalt love thy neighbour as thyself" (Matt. 22:39). This is what James was expressing—a love for, and devotion to, God, by compassionate service to fellowmen.[8]

● **D&C 59:10 It is a day to rest from our labors.** The Lord rested from His labors after creating the earth for our habitation. We follow His example when we refrain from working, thus showing that our covenant relationship with Christ is more important to us than the wages or advantages we may gain by working on His holy day.

Elder Spencer W. Kimball said: "I wonder if money earned upon the Sabbath, when it is unnecessary Sabbath earning, might not also be unclean money. I realize that some people must work on the Sabbath; and when they do, if they are compelled, that is, of course, a different situation. But men and women who will deliberately use the Sabbath day to develop business propositions, to increase their holdings, to increase their income, I fear for them… There are people who work on the Sabbath, not through compulsion, but because the income is attractive, and others who work voluntarily to get the 'time and a half' that Sabbath work gives them… The Savior knew that the ox gets in the mire on the Sabbath, but He knew also that no ox deliberately goes into the mire every week."[9]

Sometimes it is true that we must do things on the Sabbath because of unusual circumstances. But the fact is that those who speak of having to pull the ox out of the mire on the Sabbath Day usually pushed him in on Saturday.

● **D&C 59:11 We must live our religion on every day of the week.** We should offer prayer, make sacrifices, make vows (covenants), and try to live in righteousness "on all days and at all times." Ours is not just a Sunday religion; it is a way of life—one that enters into our lives in everything we do on every day of the week.

● **D&C 59:10, 12 Sunday is a day to pay our devotions unto God.** What makes Sunday different from all other days is that we are commanded on that particular day to "pay thy devotions unto the Most High" (v. 10). We are to "offer thine oblations and thy sacraments unto the Most High, confessing thy sins unto thy brethren, and before the Lord" (v. 12). Oblations are offerings or sacrifices; thus, paying our tithes and offerings is an appropriate Sabbath activity. So, too, is the consecration of our talents on behalf of others. Sacraments are symbolic acts of worship; thus, partaking of the sacrament and other symbolic acts and covenants should be part of our Sundays also.

Together, offering our oblations and sacraments means that we should make offerings or sacrifices that show our devotion to Him. These may be material sacrifices like tithes and offerings, but they may also be spiritual sacrifices—giving up all that is ungodly. Elder M. Russell Ballard said: "This higher practice of the law of sacrifice reaches into the inner soul of a person… When we overcome our own selfish desires and put God first in our lives and covenant to serve Him regardless of the cost, we are then living the law of sacrifice."[10]

President John Taylor said to a congregation on a Sunday morning in June 1881: "I appreciate as a great privilege the opportunity we enjoy of worshiping God on the Sabbath day. And when we do meet to worship God, I like to see us worship Him with all our hearts. I think it altogether out of place on such occasions to hear people talk about secular things; these are times, above all others perhaps, when our feelings and affections should be drawn out towards God. If we sing praises to God, let us do it in the proper spirit; if we pray, let every soul be engaged in prayer, doing it with all our hearts, that through our union our spirits may be blended in one, that our prayers and our worship may be available with God, whose Spirit permeates all things, and is always present in the assemblies of good and faithful Saints."[11]

President John Taylor

- **D&C 59:13 And on the Lord's day we should do no other thing.** In other words, we may do all of the above-listed things on all other days of the week—including worship God—but on Sunday that is *all* we should do. We may, with righteousness, "let thy food be prepared with singleness of heart" and do other such necessary tasks. But otherwise we should be engaged in activities that worship our God and bless our families and fellow men.

Robert J. Matthews said: "The Sabbath has several purposes. It is a holy day specified in the scriptures as a day not only of rest but also of worship. The word *sabbath* is derived from the Hebrew *shabbath*, meaning 'to break off' or 'to desist,' and in this can be seen the idea of rest. But in the best sense, rest does not mean idleness; it signifies rather a change of emphasis. In plain terms, 'keeping the Sabbath day holy' means to cease or to rest from the secular labors of the week and to use the specified day in worshiping God and doing good to our fellow beings. It is a day for spiritual works and refreshment as compared to the secular accomplishments of other days."[12]

Bishop H. David Burton said: "Now, I know it's hard, particularly for our young people, to choose to observe the Sabbath day when athletic teams on which they so much want to participate regularly schedule games on Sunday. I too know it seems trivial to many who are in need of just a few items on the Sabbath to quickly stop at a convenience store to make a Sunday purchase. But I also know that remembering to keep the Sabbath day holy is one of the most important commandments we can observe in preparing us to be the recipients of the whisperings of the Spirit."[13]

President Spencer W. Kimball said: "No member of this Church can be justified in going to a store on Sunday. You won't have to if you prepare for the Sabbath on Saturday."[14]

● **Isaiah 58:13–14 We should not "do [our] pleasure" on the Sabbath day.** If we turn away from these things and "call the sabbath a delight, the holy of the LORD, honourable; and shalt honour him, not doing thine own ways, nor finding thine own pleasure, nor speaking thine own words" (v. 13), then the Lord "will cause thee to ride upon the high places of the earth, and feed thee with the heritage of Jacob thy father" (v. 14). Both of these phrases have symbolic reference to the blessings of the temple.

We live in a time when many people throughout the world have turned away from proper Sabbath worship to activities and places of amusement. Unfortunately, many Latter-day Saints do likewise. Elder Dallin H. Oaks said: "I am sorry when any Latter- day Saint does not understand the precious blessing that comes to those who keep the commandment to offer up their sacraments upon each Sabbath day. What is there in life—on the lakes or streams, in places of commercial recreation, or at home reading the Sunday paper—that can provide anything comparable to these blessings? No recreational pleasure can equal the cleansing renewal and the spiritual guidance and growth God has promised those who faithfully partake of the sacrament and honor Him each Sabbath day. I give thanks for the fulfillment of those promises in my life and affirm their availability to all."[15]

President Spencer W. Kimball said: " Innumerous times we have [asked] our people not to profane the Sabbath; and yet we see numerous cars lined up at merchandise stores on the Sabbath day, and places of amusement crowded, and we wonder… Today numerous of the people of this land spend the Sabbath working, devoting the day to the beaches, to entertainment, to shows, to their weekly purchases."[16]

Appropriate Sabbath Day Activities

● **D&C 59:10 A day to rest from our labors.**

Resting from our labors does not mean to sit idly around the house after going to Church. Rather, we should follow the Savior's example and "do well on the sabbath" (Matthew 12:12; Luke 13:10–17; John 5:1–19). The kinds of activities that would qualify as "doing well" might include those that:

— Honor God.
— Are spiritually uplifting.
— Nurture faith.
— Strengthen the family.
— Help or bless others.
— Are set apart from the daily activities of the world.

Elder Spencer W. Kimball said: "The Sabbath is a holy

day in which to do worthy and holy things. Abstinence from work and recreation is important but insufficient. The Sabbath calls for constructive thoughts and acts, and if one merely lounges about doing nothing on the Sabbath, he is breaking it. To observe it, one will be on his knees in prayer, preparing lessons, studying the gospel, meditating, visiting the ill and distressed, sleeping, reading wholesome material, and attending all the meetings of that day to which he is expected. [Failure] to do these proper things is a transgression on the omission side."[17]

● **D&C 59:14 A day of fasting and prayer.** These are personal acts of worship that are intended to strengthen us individually. And they are inseparably connected. Fasting is not complete without prayer. And prayer is made more effective through fasting. We should engage in both on the Lord's day, and especially on Fast Sundays. There is much in our own lives and in the lives of those around us that could benefit from our fasting and prayers. We should select certain of these needs each time we fast, devote our fasting and prayers to them during the day, and then close our fast with another prayer.

Elder Joseph B. Wirthlin said: "We observe that in the scriptures, fasting almost always is linked with prayer. Without prayer, fasting is not complete fasting; it's simply going hungry. If we want our fasting to be more than just going without eating, we must lift our hearts, our minds, and our voices in communion with our Heavenly Father. Fasting, coupled with mighty prayer, is powerful. It can fill our minds with the revelations of the Spirit. It can strengthen us against times of temptation."[18]

Elder Delbert L. Stapley said: "The Saints by fasting and praying can sanctify the soul and elevate the spirit to Christlike perfection, and thus the body would be brought into subjection to the spirit, promote communion with the Holy Ghost, and ensure spiritual strength and power to the individual. By observing fasting and prayer in its true spirit, the Latter-day Saints cannot be overpowered by Satan tempting them to evil."[19]

Blessings for Keeping the Sabbath Day Holy

● **D&C 59:15–17 A fruitful and abundant life.** If our Sabbath worship is done "with thanksgiving, with cheerful hearts and countenances, not with much laughter, for this is sin, but with a glad heart and a cheerful countenance" (v. 15), then the Lord promises us "the fulness of the earth" (v. 16)—all animals and plants in abundance "and the good things which come of the earth, whether for food or for raiment, or for houses, or for barns, or for orchards, or for gardens, or for vineyards" (v. 17). Thus, a clear connection exists between our Sabbath faithfulness and the bounties of the earth.

Elder James E. Faust said:

> Over a lifetime of observation, it is clear to me that the farmer who observes the Sabbath day seems to get more done on his farm than he would if he worked seven days. The mechanic will be able to turn out more and better products in six days than in seven. The doctor, the lawyer, the dentist, the scientist will accomplish more by trying to rest on the Sabbath than if he tries to utilize every day of the week for his professional work. I would counsel all students, if they can, to arrange their schedules so that they do not study on the Sabbath. If students and other seekers after truth will do this, their minds will be quickened and the infinite Spirit will lead them to the verities they wish to learn. This is

because God has hallowed His day and blessed it as a perpetual covenant of faithfulness (Ex. 31:16)… What is worthy or unworthy on the Sabbath day will have to be judged by each of us by trying to be honest with the Lord. On the Sabbath day we should do what we have to do and what we ought to do in an attitude of worshipfulness and then limit our other activities.[20]

- **Isaiah 56:2–5 Exaltation in God's kingdom.** Those who "keepeth the sabbath from polluting it, and keepeth his hand from doing any evil … and choose the things that please me, and take hold of my covenant; Even unto them will I give in mine house and within my walls a place and a name better than of sons and of daughters: I will give them an everlasting name, that shall not be cut off."

- **D&C 59:13–14 A fulness of joy and rejoicing.** When we engage in appropriate Sabbath activities, with a cheerful and willing attitude, then the Lord promises a fulness of joy in our lives. I think back upon our early married years when we were trying to teach our children that the Sabbath was a happy day even though they couldn't do all the things they wanted to do—things they did on other days. This was especially true of fast Sundays, which they referred to as "slow Sunday."

It is true that we could view the Sabbath as a day of "don'ts" rather than a day of "do's." But true joy does not come from temporary earthly pleasures. It comes for an eternity of blessings with those we love. And the Sabbath is an important part of preparing ourselves for that blessed future. President Brigham Young said: "[The laws of the Sabbath are] not imposed upon [us] as by a task-master, in the form of a rigid discipline; but they are bestowed upon [us] as a blessing, a favour, and a mercy, for his express benefit."[21]

President Gordon B. Hinckley said: "If you have any doubt about the wisdom, the divinity of observing the Sabbath Day, … stay home and gather your family about you, teach them the gospel, enjoy yourselves together on the Sabbath Day, come to your meetings, participate. You will know that the principle of the Sabbath is a true principle which brings with it great blessings… Now I do not want to be prudish. I do not want you to lock your children in the house and read the Bible all afternoon to them. Be wise. Be careful. But make that day a day when you can sit down with your families and talk about sacred and good things."[22]

The First Presidency said in 1980 when announcing the consolidated Sunday meeting schedule: "A greater responsibility will be placed upon the individual members and families for properly observing the Sabbath day. More time will be available for personal study of the scriptures and family-centered gospel study… It is expected that this new schedule of meetings and activities will result in greater spiritual growth for members of the Church."[23] I wonder sometimes if some of us haven't used this additional time instead for unholy and impure pursuits of entertainment and pleasure. When we do, we lose an opportunity for spiritual growth and forfeit the companionship of the Spirit of the Lord.[24]

Worshiping in Sunday Church Meetings

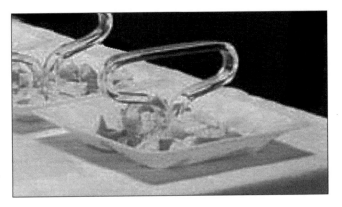

● **D&C 59:9 "Thou shalt go to the house of prayer ... upon my holy day."** Attending church is clearly appropriate on the Sabbath day. In fact, it is required. We are commanded to come together weekly to renew our covenants with the Lord. And while there, we are fed spiritually by our leaders, speakers, and teachers. Or at least, we ought to be. President Gordon B. Hinckley said: "Every sacrament meeting ought to be a spiritual feast" and "a time of spiritual refreshment."[25]

We have heard some people say that they do not come to Church because it bores them or is beneath their standards in some other way. These are selfish souls who see the Church as a vehicle for their personal intellectual fulfillment. President Spencer W. Kimball said: "We do not go to Sabbath meetings to be entertained or even solely to be instructed. We go to worship the Lord. It is an individual responsibility, and regardless of what is said from the pulpit, if one wishes to worship the Lord in spirit and truth, he may do so by attending his meetings, partaking of the sacrament, and contemplating the beauties of the gospel. If the service is a failure to you, you have failed. No one can worship for you."[26]

There are a number of things we can do to make sacrament meetings and other Sunday meetings more spiritually enriching by:

— Having an attitude of worship.
— Being on time.
— Studying scriptures and lesson materials before class.
— Participating actively.
— Listening carefully.
— Seeking to strengthen others.
— Not criticizing speakers or teachers.

President Brigham Young said: "When people assemble to worship they should leave their worldly cares where they belong; then their minds are in a proper condition to worship the Lord, to call upon Him in the name of Jesus, and to get His Holy Spirit, that they may hear and understand things as they are in eternity, and know how to comprehend the providences of our God. This is the time for their minds to be open, to behold the invisible things of God, that He reveals by His Spirit."[27]

Sometimes, people come away from the Sunday worship unfulfilled because that which has been spoken and taught has not been Christ-centered. When teachers or speakers spend their time putting forth the philosophies of men (including their own) it leaves the hearer feeling empty and unfulfilled.

Arthur R. Bassett said:

[Nephi said] "And we talk of Christ, we rejoice in Christ, we preach of Christ, we prophesy of Christ, and we write according to our prophecies, that our children may know to what source they may look for a remission of their sins" (2 Nephi 25:26). This was an oft- repeated pattern among the prophets. They realized that their total mission was to bring individuals to the Master in a way that would let them experience the warmth and vitality of His companionship. I have often wondered if we could truthfully say the same thing that Nephi said, concerning our homes and our wards today. How central to our lives is the Master? How often in our family home evenings, in our sacrament meetings, in our Sunday schools, in our Relief Societies, and in our priesthood meetings is He made the central topic of our discussions? If He has not become central to all that is said and done, then I fear we have missed the mark, and we should ask ourselves why.[28]

Music on the Sabbath Day

● **D&C 25:12 The Lord delights in music.** He particularly delights in "the song of the heart" and "the song of the righteous," which He receives as "a prayer unto me, and it shall be answered with a blessing upon their heads." Thus, our attitude toward music and singing on the Sabbath day is also our attitude toward worship of our God. I once attended a missionary farewell where the missionary himself got up and sang a popular song titled "Forever Young" which expressed the wish that he would never be changed. It was uncomfortable because the music was not sacred. And worse,

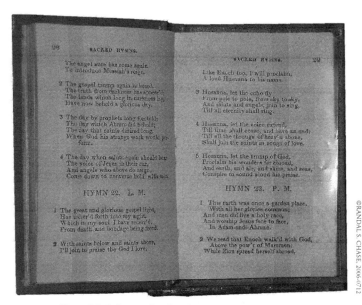

© RANDAL S. CHASE, 2006-1712

First LDS hymn book (1835) by Emma Smith

its message was inappropriate First LDS hymn book (1835) by Emma Smith for a young man embarking in the service of God. He turned out to be a fine missionary, but the Sunday service was wholly inappropriate.

Elder Boyd K. Packer said: "Music is of enormous importance in our worship services. I believe that those who choose, conduct, present, and accompany the music may influence the spirit of reverence in our meetings more than a speaker does. God bless them. Music can set an atmosphere of worship which invites that spirit of revelation, of testimony… An organist who has the sensitivity to quietly play prelude music from the hymnbook tempers our feelings and causes us to go over in our minds the lyrics which teach the peaceable things of the kingdom. If we will listen, they are teaching the gospel, for the hymns of the Restoration are, in fact, a course in doctrine!"[29]

CHAPTER 16 • *Keeping the Sabbath Day Holy* | 373

I've noticed that an increasing number of our members do not sing the congregational songs, which are an important part of our personal worship on Sundays. Other than partaking of the sacrament, we participate minimally in what goes on in a typical worship service. But when we sing we are actively worshiping. To sit and stare while others are singing the praises of God or His Christ or the Restoration, makes a profound statement about our apathy to these vital things in our lives. We need to sing.

Elder Dallin H. Oaks said: "The singing of hymns is one of the best ways to put ourselves in tune with the Spirit of the Lord. I wonder if we are making enough use of this heaven-sent resource in our meetings, in our classes, and in our homes… The singing of hymns is one of the best ways to learn the doctrine of the restored gospel… The scriptures contain many affirmations that hymn singing is a glorious way to worship … [and] sacred music has a unique capacity to communicate our feelings of love for the Lord. This kind of communication is a wonderful aid to our worship. Many have difficulty expressing worshipful feelings in words, but all can join in communicating such feelings through the inspired words of our hymns."[30]

Reverence in Church Meetings

President Gordon B. Hinckley told of an embarrassing incident he experienced as a missionary. They were meeting in a rented town hall with hard wood floors that amplified every movement of people or furniture. But "far worse was the noisy socializing of the members of the branch." The missionaries invited a family whom they had met while tracting to attend church with them. While the members engaged in noisy greetings with one another, this nonmember family "came into the room, … quietly moved toward some chairs, knelt for a moment, and closed their eyes in a word of prayer. They then sat in an attitude of reverence amidst all the commotion." They were surprised and disappointed at the lack of reverence in our worship services.[31]

Elder Boyd K. Packer said:

> Foyers are built into our chapels to allow for the greeting and chatter that are typical of people who love one another. However, when we step into the chapel, we must!—each of us must—watch ourselves lest we be guilty of intruding when someone is struggling to feel delicate spiritual communications…
>
> [We should be reverent in the chapel so we do not intrude] when someone is struggling to feel delicate spiritual communications. [Reverence] does not equate with absolute silence. We must be tolerant of little babies, even an occasional outburst from a toddler being ushered out to keep him from disturbing the peace. Unless the father is on the stand, he should do the ushering.[32]

Partaking of the Sacrament

● **D&C 59:9, 12 The Lord commands us to partake of the sacrament on the Sabbath day.**
Partaking of the sacrament is the most important thing we do on the Sabbath day. Only through this process of renewing our covenants can we continually ensure that we are cleansed of our sins and remain "unspotted from the world" (v. 9). We are not to do this at home but in a congregation of Saints in a "house of prayer … upon my holy day" (v. 9). And we should partake

of the sacrament with an attitude of repentance, "confessing thy sins unto thy brethren, and before the Lord" (v. 12).

President Gordon B. Hinckley said: "I am confident the Savior trusts us, and yet He asks that we renew our covenants with Him frequently and before one another by partaking of the sacrament, the emblems of His suffering in our behalf... I feel in my heart that if every member of the Church would resolve within himself or herself that they would partake of the sacrament every week, if possible, we would have greater spirituality and we would have fewer defaults, as it were, among our membership."[33]

Elder Joseph B. Wirthlin said: "Windows must be washed regularly to clean away dust and dirt... Just as earthly windows need consistent, thorough cleaning, so do the windows of our spirituality... By partaking of the sacrament worthily to renew our baptismal covenants, we clarify our view of life's eternal purpose and divine priorities. The sacrament prayers invite personal introspection, repentance, and rededication as we pledge our willingness to remember our Savior, Jesus the Christ."[34]

Karl R. Anderson said:

> Partaking of the sacrament should be a sacred experience for each of us. Perhaps on occasion we partake of the sacrament without sufficient thought or too hastily to feel its rich and deep significance. President David O. McKay once set an example for others to follow. Elder Paul H. Dunn shared the following experience with a small group of us in the School of the Prophets room in Kirtland, Ohio. He related sitting in a sacrament meeting with other General Authorities in the Salt Lake Temple. The bread was passed to President McKay first and then to others. Everyone waited for President McKay to eat. He just sat for some time observing the bread. He looked at it. He turned it side-ways. While contemplating what it represented, tears came to his eyes. Later in the meeting, he announced that he had indeed felt the presence of the Savior.[35]

Notes:

1. *History of the Church*, 1:196-201.

2. *History of the Church*, 1:199.

3. "Newel Knight's Journal," *Scraps of Biography—Tenth Book of the Faith Promoting Series*, (1883), 70; *History of the Church*, 1:199, Footnote.

4. *Ensign*, November 1975, 6.

5. In Conference Report, April 1975, 70; or *Ensign*, May 1975, 47.

6. In Conference Report, April 1975; or *Ensign*, May 1975, 49.

7. *Doctrinal New Testament Commentary*, 3 vols. [1965-1973], 1:841.

8. *That We Might Have Joy* [1994], 160.

9. In Conference Report, October 1953, 54-56.

10. "The Law of Sacrifice," *Ensign*, October 1998, 10.

11. In *Journal of Discourses*, 22:226.

12. *Ensign*, January 1978, 14-15.

13. In Conference Report, October 1998, 9; or *Ensign*, November 1998, 9.

14. Solemn Assembly address, Salt Lake Temple, December 13, 1975, Notes taken by and in possession of Randal S. Chase, Elders Quorum President, Crescent 9th Ward, Sandy, Utah.

15. *Ensign*, May 2002, 34.

16. "The Lord Expects His Saints to Follow the Commandments," *Ensign*, May 1977, 4.

17. *The Miracle of Forgiveness* [1969], 96-97.

18. "The Law of the Fast," *Ensign*, May 2001, 73.

19. In Conference Report, October 1951, 123.

20. "The Lord's Day," *Ensign*, November 1991, 34-35.

21. In *Journal of Discourses*, 6:278.

22. *Teachings of Gordon B. Hinckley* [1997], 559-560.

23. *Church News*, 2 February 1980, 3.

24. See Dallin H. Oaks, "The Blessing of Commandments," *Speeches of the Year, 1974*, 218.

25. *Teachings of Gordon B. Hinckley*, 563, 564.

26. "The Sabbath—A Delight," *Ensign*, January 1978, 4-5.

27. *Discourses of Brigham Young*, sel. John A. Widtsoe [1941], 167.

28. *Ensign*, July 1975, 24.

29. In Conference Report, October 1991, 29; or *Ensign*, November 1991, 22.

30. *Ensign*, November 1994, 10.

31. *Teachings of Gordon B. Hinckley*, 557.

32. In Conference Report, October 1991, 28; or *Ensign*, November 1991, 22.

33. *Teachings of Gordon B. Hinckley*, 561.

34. In Conference Report, October 1995, 103; or *Ensign*, November 1995, 77.

35. In Ed J. Allen, Richard J. Anderson, and Karl R. Pinegar, *Teachings and Commentaries on the Doctrine and Covenants* [2004], 195

About the Author

❧❦❧

Randal S. Chase spent his childhood years in Nephi, Utah, where his father was a dry land wheat farmer and a businessman. In 1959 their family moved to Salt Lake City and settled in the Holladay area. He served a full-time mission in the Central British (England Central) Mission, 1968–1970. He returned home and married Deborah Johnsen in 1971. They are the parents of six children—two daughters and four sons—and an ever-expanding number of grandchildren.

He was called to serve as a bishop at the age of 27 in the Sandy Crescent South Stake area of the Salt Lake Valley. He served six years in that capacity, and has since served as a high councilor, a Stake Executive Secretary and Clerk, and in many other stake and ward callings. Regardless of whatever other callings he has received over the years, one was nearly constant: He has taught Gospel Doctrine classes in every ward he has ever lived in as an adult—a total of 35 years.

Dr. Chase was a well-known media personality on Salt Lake City radio stations in the 1970s. He left on-air broadcasting in 1978 to develop and market a computer-based management, sales, and music programming system to radio and television stations in the United States, Canada, South America, and Australia. After the business was sold in 1984, he supported his family as a media and business consultant in the Salt Lake City area.

Having a great desire to teach young people of college age, he determined in the late 1980s to pursue his doctorate, and received his Ph.D. in Communication from the University of Utah in 1997. He has taught communication courses at that institution as well as at Salt Lake Community College and Dixie State College of Utah for 21 years. He is currently a full-time faculty member and Communication Department Chair at Dixie State College in St. George, Utah.

Concurrently with his academic career, brother Chase has served as a volunteer LDS Institute and Adult Education instructor in the CES system since 1974, both in Salt Lake City and St. George, where he currently teaches a weekly Adult Education class for three stakes in the Washington area. He has also conducted multiple Church History tours and seminars. During these years of gospel teaching, he has developed an extensive library of lesson plans and handouts which are the predecessors to these study guides.

Dr. Chase previously published a three-volume series of study guides on the Book of Mormon titled *Making Precious Things Plain*. Like those volumes, this three-volume series of study guides on Doctrine and Covenants and Church History is designed to assist teachers and students of Gospel Doctrine classes, as well as those who simply want to study on their own, our wonderful legacy of faith and revelation. If we keep these things close to our hearts, they will bless us forever, both individually and as a people.